D1256782

# The Hymnal 1982

*according to the use of*
## The Episcopal Church

*The Church Hymnal Corporation*
*800 Second Avenue, New York, New York 10017*

## Certificate

It was voted by both Houses of the General Convention, held in the year of our Lord one thousand nine hundred and eighty two:

That the *Hymnal*, as reported by the Standing Commission on Church Music, be authorized and approved for use in this Church.

That the work of the Commission be continued, with authority to perfect the details of its work and complete, for the benefit of The Church Pension Fund, pew and accompaniment editions of the revised *Hymnal*.

That the publication of the *Hymnal* be committed to the Trustees of The Church Pension Fund for the benefit of that Fund.

Attest:     Scott Field Bailey
           *Secretary of the House of Bishops*

           Charles R. Lawrence II
           *Secretary of the House of Deputies*

## Rubric from The Book of Common Prayer

Hymns referred to in the rubrics of this Book are to be understood as those authorized by this Church. The words of anthems are to be from Holy Scripture, or from this Book, or from texts congruent with them.

## Canon 24, Section 1

It shall be the duty of every Minister to see that music is used as an offering for the glory of God and as a help to the people in their worship in accordance with The Book of Common Prayer and as authorized by the rubrics or by the General Convention of this Church. To this end the Minister shall have final authority in the administration of matters pertaining to music. In fulfilling this responsibility the Minister shall seek assistance from persons skilled in music. Together they shall see that music is appropriate to the context in which it is used.

# The Hymnal 1982

# Contents

## Service Music

## Hymns

# Indexes

# Preface

In the past several decades, the renewal of the spiritual life of the Church has created a pressing need for new hymnody and liturgical music. This has served as a catalyst for a world-wide outburst of creative liturgical and musical activity of a magnitude perhaps unparalleled since the Reformation. *The Hymnal 1982*, the culmination of more than a decade of work by the Standing Commission on Church Music, incorporates many of the riches of this contemporary renaissance. This hymnal is a response to the challenge of the Church's mission to spread the Good News of Jesus Christ to a changed and changing world.

*The Hymnal 1982* is a revision of *The Hymnal 1940*, and as such stands on the foundation laid by The Joint Commission on Revision of the Hymnal. The precepts guiding that commission led to a comprehensive book of unusual appeal and excellence which served as a model for a number of hymnals produced since the middle of the twentieth century.

As an initial step in its revision process, the Standing Commission on Church Music developed a philosophical statement expressing the Commission's commitment to maintain and enhance the rich repertoire which constitutes the singing tradition of the people of God. This commitment led to the development of the following objectives:
— to prepare a body of texts which presents the Christian faith with clarity and integrity;
— to restore music which has lost some of its melodic, rhythmic, or harmonic vitality through prior revision;
— to reflect the nature of today's Church by including the works of contemporary artists and works representing many cultures;
— to strengthen ecumenical relationships through the inclusion of texts and tunes used by other Christian traditions;
— to create a hymnal embodying both practicality and esthetic excellence.

*The Hymnal 1982* retains the best of the past and sets forth many riches of our own time. The Commission looked for theological orthodoxy, poetic beauty, and integrity of meaning. At the same time the Commission was especially concerned that the hymnody affirm "the participation of all in the Body of Christ the Church, while recognizing our diverse natures as children of God." This work has resulted in the sensitive alteration of texts which "could be interpreted as either pejorative or discriminatory," while preserving the artistic quality and intent of the originals. Language deemed "obscure or so changed in the contemporary usage as to have a different meaning"* has been clarified. Texts and music which reflect the pluralistic nature of the Church have been included, affording the use of Native American, Afro-American, Hispanic, and Asian material. Study and research into historic hymnody have led to the inclusion of chant tunes in rhythmic forms, of early settings of chorales and Psalter tunes, and of tunes whose roots lie deep in the treasury of American folk hymnody.

Often, consistency of style and practice seemed a less important goal than a representation of the wonderful variety of materials that are available. The recent renaissance of hymn-writing imparts rich benefits to *The Hymnal 1982*. The Commission drew many new hymns from the wealth of available material and commissioned authors and composers to write hymns on themes for which nothing suitable could be found. Here we must record gratitude for the work of the late F. Bland Tucker, a poet and priest whose wisdom and skills enhanced the work of the commissions which produced both this book and *The Hymnal 1940*.

In designing *The Hymnal 1982*, the Commission sought to create a book which is comprehensive and musically practical. Most tunes which are used more than once appear in different keys or harmonizations. Further variety in the performance of hymns is facilitated by descants and alternative accompaniments. The use of instruments in addition to the organ is encouraged through the inclusion, where appropriate, of guitar chords and bell and percussion parts. Details on notation and performance appear in the general performance notes in the Accompaniment Edition and with some individual hymns.

The Commission gave serious thought to the evaluation of texts for theological and literary merit by consultants representing congregations across the country before reaching final decisions on the contents of the book. In addition, the testing of new tunes in liturgical settings over an extended period of time determined their appropriateness for congregational singing.

The Commission gratefully acknowledges the contributions of Carl P. Daw, Jr., Georgia M. Joyner, Marilyn J. Keiser, Anne K. Le Croy, J. Waring McCrady, James McGregor, Bruce Neswick, Charles P. Price, McNeil Robinson II, F. Bland Tucker†, and John E. Williams, Jr.

*The Hymnal 1982* is truly a book of and for the people, reflecting their involvement in its creation and responding to their desire for new songs with which to praise God. May God prosper this handiwork!

| | |
|---|---|
| Geoffrey Butcher | Marion J. Hatchett |
| Charles J. Child, Jr. | David J. Hurd, Jr. |
| Robert H. Cochrane | Roy F. Kehl |
| Elizabeth Morris Downie | James H. Litton |
| Carol Morey Foster | Richard T. Proulx |
| Raymond F. Glover | Arthur Rhea |
| Jerry D. Godwin | Walter C. Righter |
| Eric S. Greenwood | Russell Schulz-Widmar |
| William M. Hale | Frederic P. Williams |
| | Alec Wyton |

---

* Report of the Standing Commission on Church Music to the 1982 General Convention of the Episcopal Church.

† Deceased

# Service Music

# The Daily Office

## Daily Morning Prayer I
## Preces

*Officiant*

O Lord, o - pen thou our lips.

*People*

And our mouth shall show forth thy praise.

*Officiant and People*

Glory to the Father, and to the Son, and to the Holy Spi - rit:

as it was in the beginning, is now, and will be for ever. A - men.

*Except during Lent, may be added:*

Al - le - lu - ia.

## Daily Morning Prayer I
## The Invitatory: Venite

*Antiphons are sung with this setting.*

1. O come, let us sing un - to the Lord; let us heartily rejoice in the strength of

our sal - va - tion. 2. Let us come before his presence with thanks-giv-ing, and show ourselves glad in him with psalms. [Ant.] 3. For the Lord is a great God,

and a great King a-bove all gods. 4. In his hand are all the cor-ners

of the earth, and the strength of the hills is his al-so. 5. The sea is

his and he made it, and his hands pre-pared the dry land. [Ant.] 6. O come,

let us wor-ship and fall down and kneel before the Lord our Ma-ker.

7. For he is the Lord our God, and we are the people of his pasture

and the sheep of his hand. [Ant.] 8. O wor-ship the Lord in the

beau-ty of ho-li-ness; let the whole earth stand in awe of him.

9. For he cometh, for he com-eth to judge the earth, and with

righteousness to judge the world and the peo-ples with his truth. [Ant.]

*(Gloria Patri may be added)*

Glo-ry to the Fa-ther, and to the Son, and to the Ho-ly Spi-rit:

As it was in the be-gin-ning, is now, and will be for ev-er. A-men. [Ant.]

Setting: Plainsong, Tone 7; adapt. Bruce Ford (b. 1947)

*An antiphon may be sung before and after this setting.*

1. O come, let us sing unto the Lord; let us heartily rejoice in the strength of our sal - va - tion. 2. Let us come before his presence with thanks - giv - ing, and show ourselves glad in him with psalms. 3. For the Lord is a great God, and a great King a - bove all gods. 4. In his hand are all the corners of the earth, and the strength of the hills is his al - so. 5. The sea is his and he made it, and his hands prepared the dry land. 6. O come, let us worship and fall down and kneel before the Lord our Ma - ker. 7. For he is the Lord our God, and we are the people of his pasture and the sheep of his hand. 8. O worship the Lord in the beauty of ho - li - ness; let the whole earth stand in awe of him. 9. For he cometh, for he cometh to judge the earth, and with righteousness to judge the world and the peo - ples with his truth.

*(Gloria Patri may be added)*

Glory to the Father, and to the Son, and to the Ho - ly Spi - rit: As it was in the beginning, is now, and will be for ev - er. A - men.

Setting: Plainsong, Tone 2; adapt. The Standing Commission on Church Music, 1979, alt.

## The Invitatory: Venite

*Antiphons may be sung with these chants.*

1   O come, let us 'sing unto the 'Lord; *

    let us heartily rejoice in the 'strength of 'our sal 'vation.

2   Let us come before his 'presence with thanks 'giving, *

    and show ourselves 'glad in 'him with 'psalms.   [Ant.]

3     For the Lord is a'great'God, *
       and a great'King a'bove all'gods.

4     In his hand are all the'corners of the'earth, *
       and the strength of the'hills is'his'also.

†5    The sea is'his and he'made it, *
       and his hands pre'pared the'dry'land.   [Ant.]

6     O come, let us worship and'fall'down *
       and'kneel before the'Lord our'Maker.

7     For he is the'Lord our'God, *
       and we are the people of his'pasture
       and the'sheep of his'hand.   [Ant.]

8     O worship the Lord in the'beauty of'holiness; *
       let the'whole earth'stand in'awe of him.

9     For he cometh, for he cometh to'judge the'earth, *
       and with righteousness to judge the world
       and the'peoples'with his'truth.   [Ant.]

*(Gloria Patri may be added)*
Glory to the Father, and'to the'Son, *
       and'to the'Holy'Spirit:
As it was in the be'ginning, is'now, *
       and'will be for'ever. A'men.   [Ant.]

†*Second half of double chant.*

*When an antiphon is sung:*

1. O come, let us sing unto the Lord;

*When no antiphon is sung:*

1. O come, let us sing unto the Lord;

let us heartily rejoice in the strength of our sal-va-tion. 2. Let us come before his

presence with thanks-giv-ing, and show ourselves glad in him with psalms.[Ant.]

3. For the Lord is a great God, and a great King a-bove all gods.

4. In his hand are all the corners of the earth, and the strength of the hills is

his al-so. 5. The sea is his and he made it, and his hands prepared

the dry land. [Ant.] 6. O come, let us worship and fall down and kneel before the

Lord our Ma-ker. 7. For he is the Lord our God, and we are the people

of his pasture and the sheep of his hand. [Ant.] 8. Today if ye will hear

his voice, harden not your hearts as in the provocation, and as in the day

of temptation in the wil-der-ness; 9. When your fathers tempt-ed me, proved me,

and saw my works. 10. Forty years long was I grieved with this generation, and said,

It is a people that do err in their hearts, for they have not known my ways;

11. Unto whom I sware in my wrath, that they should not enter in-to my rest. [Ant.]

*(Gloria Patri may be added)*

Glory to the Father, and to the Son, and to the Ho - ly Spi - rit:

As it was in the beginning, is now, and will be for ev - er. A-men. [Ant.]

## The Invitatory: Psalm 95

**S 9**

George S. Talbot
(1875-1918)

**S 10**

Maurice Green
(1695-1755)

*Antiphons may be sung with these chants.*

1    O come, let us ꞌsing unto the ꞌLord; *

     let us heartily rejoice in the ꞌstrength of ꞌour salꞌvation.

2    Let us come before his ꞌpresence with thanksꞌgiving, *

     and show ourselves ꞌglad in ꞌhim with ꞌpsalms.   [Ant.]

3    For the Lord is a ꞌgreat ꞌGod, *

     and a great ꞌKing aꞌbove all ꞌgods.

4    In his hand are all the ꞌcorners of the ꞌearth, *

     and the strength of the ꞌhills is ꞌhis ꞌalso.

†5    The sea is ꞌhis and he ꞌmade it, *

     and his hands preꞌpared the ꞌdry ꞌland.   [Ant.]

6    O come, let us worship and ꞌfall ꞌdown *

     and ꞌkneel before the ꞌLord our ꞌMaker.

7    For he is the ꞌLord our ꞌGod, *

     and we are the people of his ꞌpasture

     and the ꞌsheep of his ꞌhand.   [Ant.]

*†Second half of double chant*

8   Today if ye will hear his voice, ⌐harden not your⌐hearts *

as in the provocation,

and as in the┐day of temp┐tation in the┐wilderness;

9   When your┐fathers┐tempted me, *

—┐proved me, and┐saw my┐works.  [Ant.]

10   Forty years long was I grieved with this gener┐ation, and┐said, *

It is a people that do err in their hearts,

for┐they have not┐known my┐ways;

11   Unto whom I┐sware in my┐wrath, *

that they should not┐enter┐into my┐rest.  [Ant.]

*(Gloria Patri may be added)*

Glory to the Father, and┐to the┐Son, *

and┐to the┐Holy┐Spirit:

As it was in the be┐ginning, is┐now, *

and┐will be for┐ever. A┐men.  [Ant.]

# Daily Morning Prayer I

## The Invitatory: Jubilate

**S 11**

*Antiphons are sung with this setting.*

1. O be joyful in the Lord all ye lands; serve the Lord with gladness

and come before his pres - ence with a song. [Ant.] 2. Be ye sure that the Lord he is God; it is he that hath made us and not

we our-selves; we are his people and the sheep of his pas - ture.[Ant.]

3. O go your way into his gates with thanksgiving and in - to

his courts with praise; be thankful unto him and speak good of his Name.[Ant.]

4. For the Lord is gracious; his mercy is ev - er - last - ing;

and his truth endureth from generation to gen - er - a - tion.[Ant.]

*(Gloria Patri may be added)*

Glo - ry to the Fa - ther, and to the Son, and to the Ho - ly Spi - rit:

As it was in the be - gin - ning, is now, and will be for ev - er. A - men. [Ant.]

Setting: Plainsong, Tone 7; adapt. Bruce Ford (b. 1947)

# Daily Morning Prayer I
## The Invitatory: Jubilate

**S 12** — Edward John Hopkins (1818-1901)

**S 13** — Henry Aldrich (1647-1710)

**S 14** — Thomas Kelway (1695-1749)

**S 15** — Christopher Gibbons (1615-1676)

*Antiphons may be sung with these chants.*

1 O be joyful in the ⌐Lord all ye⌐ lands, *
 serve the Lord with gladness
 and come before his ⌐presence ⌐with a ⌐song. [Ant.]

2 Be ye sure that the Lord he is God;
 it is he that hath made us and not ⌐we our ⌐selves; *
 we are his ⌐people and the ⌐sheep of his ⌐pasture. [Ant.]

3 O go your way into his gates with thanksgiving
 and into his ⌐courts with ⌐praise; *
 be thankful unto ⌐him and speak ⌐good of his ⌐Name. [Ant.]

4 For the Lord is gracious;
 his mercy is ⌐ever ⌐lasting; *
 and his truth endureth from gener ⌐ation to ⌐gener ⌐ation. [Ant.]

*(Gloria Patri may be added)*
Glory to the Father, and ⌐to the ⌐Son, *
 and ⌐to the ⌐Holy ⌐Spirit:
As it was in the be ⌐ginning, is ⌐now, *
 and ⌐will be for ⌐ever. A ⌐men. [Ant.]

## Christ our Passover    *Pascha nostrum*

Al - le - lu - ia,    al - le - lu - ia,    al - le - lu - ia.

1. Christ our Passover is sac - ri - ficed for us,    therefore let us keep the feast,

2. Not with old leaven, neither with the leaven of mal - ice and wick - ed - ness,

but with the unleaved bread of sin - cer - i - ty and truth. [Ant.] 3. Christ be - ing

raised from the dead di - eth no more;    death hath no more do - min - ion o - ver him.

4. For in that he died, he died un - to sin once;    but in that he liveth, he liv - eth un - to God.

5. Likewise reckon ye also yourselves to be dead in - deed un - to sin,

but alive unto God through Je - sus Christ our Lord. [Ant.] 6. Christ is ris-en

from the dead, and become the first fruits of them that slept. 7. For since by

man came death, by man came also the resur - rec-tion of the dead.

8. For as in Ad - am all die, even so in Christ shall all be made a - live. [Ant.]

*(Gloria Patri may be added)*

Glo - ry to the Fa - ther, and to the Son, and to the Ho - ly Spi - rit:

As it was in the be - gin-ning, is now, and will be for ev - er. A - men. [Ant.]

Setting: Plainsong, Tone 7; adapt. Bruce Ford (b. 1947)

## Christe our Passover  *Pascha nostrum*

1   Alleluia, 'alle'luia. *
    Alle'luia, 'alle'luia.

2   Christ our Passover is 'sacrificed for 'us, *
    therefore 'let us 'keep the 'feast,

3   Not with old leaven,
    neither with the leaven of 'malice and 'wickedness, *
    but with the unleavened 'bread of sin'cerity and 'truth.

4   Alleluia, 'alle'luia. *
    Alle'luia, 'alle'luia.

5   Christ being raised from the dead 'dieth no 'more; *
    death hath 'no more do'minion 'over him.

6   For in that he died, he died unto 'sin 'once; *
    but in that he liveth, he 'liveth 'unto 'God.

7   Likewise reckon ye also yourselves to be dead in'deed unto 'sin, *
    but alive unto God through 'Jesus 'Christ our 'Lord.

8   Alleluia, 'alle'luia. *
    Alle'luia, 'alle'luia.

9   Christt is ˈrisen from the ˈdead, *
    and become the ˈfirst fruits ofˈthem that ˈslept.

10  For since by ˈman came ˈdeath, *
    by man came also the resurˈrection ˈof the ˈdead.

11  For as in ˈAdam all ˈdie, *
    even so in Christ shall ˈall be ˈmade aˈlive.

12  Alleluia, ˈalleˈluia. *
    Alleˈluia, ˈalleˈluia.

    *(Gloria Patri may be added)*

    Glory to the Father, and ˈto the ˈSon, *
    and ˈto the ˈHoly ˈSpirit:

    As it was in the beˈginning, is ˈnow, *
    and ˈwill be for ˈever. Aˈmen.

    Alleluia, ˈalleˈluia. *
    Alleˈluia, ˈalleˈluia.

# Daily Morning Prayer I                                    S 21
## Salutation and The Lord's Prayer

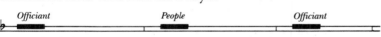

*Officiant*                    *People*              *Officiant*

The Lord be with you.   And with thy spirit.   Let us pray.

*Officiant and People*

Our Father, who art . . . . for ever and ever. A - men.

# S 22
## Suffrages A

*Cantor or Officiant*

V. O Lord, show thy mercy upon us;

*People*

R. And grant us thy salva - tion.

V. Endue thy ministers with right - eous - ness;

R. And make thy chosen people joy - ful.

V. Give peace, O Lord, in all the world;

R. For only in thee can we live in safe - ty.

V. Lord, keep this nation un - der thy care;

R. And guide us in the way of jus - tice and truth.

V. Let thy way be known up - on earth;

R. Thy saving health among all na - tions.

V. Let not the needy, O Lord, be forgot - ten;

R Nor the hope of the poor be ta - ken a - way.

V. Create in us clean hearts, O God;

R. And sustain us with thy Holy Spi - rit.

## Daily Morning Prayer I
## Suffrages B

**S 23**

*Cantor or Officiant*

V. O Lord, save thy people, and bless thine her - i - tage;

*People*

R. Govern them and lift them up for ev - er.

V. Day by day we mag - ni - fy thee;

R. And we worship thy Name ever, world with - out end.

V. Vouchsafe, O Lord, to keep us this day without sin;

R. O Lord, have mercy upon us, have mercy upon us.

V. O Lord, let thy mercy be upon us;

R. As our trust is in thee.

V. O Lord, in thee have I trust - ed;

R. Let me never be confound - ed.

# S 24

## Concluding Versicle and Response

*Cantor or Officiant*

Let us bless the Lord.

*People*

Thanks be to God.

# S 25

## Concluding Versicle and Response in Easter Season

*Cantor or Officiant*

Let us bless the Lord, al - le - lu - ia, al - le - lu - ia.

*People*

Thanks be to God, al - le - lu - ia, al - le - lu - ia.

## Daily Evening Prayer I
### Preces

*Officiant*

O God, make speed to save us.

*People*

O Lord, make haste to help us.

*Officiant and People*

Glory to the Father, and to the Son, and to the Holy Spi - rit:

as it was in the beginning, is now, and will be for ever. A - men.

*Except during Lent, may be added:*

Al - le - lu - ia.

## Daily Evening Prayer I
### O Gracious Light    *Phos hilaron*

1. O gra - cious Light, pure brightness of the everliving Father in hea - ven, O Jesus Christ, ho - ly and bless - ed! 2. Now as we come to the setting of the sun, and our eyes behold the ves - per light,

we sing thy praises, O God: Father, Son, and Ho - ly Spi - rit.

3. Thou art worthy at all times to be praised by happy voic - es, O Son of God,

O Giv - er of Life, and to be glo - ri - fied through all the worlds.

Setting: Victor Judson Schramm (1944-1984)

# S 28
Daily Evening Prayer I

## Salutation and The Lord's Prayer

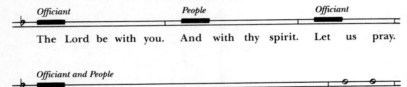

*Officiant*      *People*      *Officiant*

The Lord be with you. And with thy spirit. Let us pray.

*Officiant and People*

Our Father, who art . . . . for ever and ever. A - men.

*For Suffrages A, see S 22.*

# S 29
Daily Evening Prayer I

## Suffrages B, Tone I

*Cantor or Officiant*

That this evening may be holy, good, and peace - ful,

*People*

We en - treat thee, O Lord.

*(This response is sung after each of the following petitions)*

That thy holy angels may lead us in paths of peace and good-will,

That we may be pardoned and forgiven for our sins and of-fen-ses,

That there may be peace to thy Church and to the whole world,

That we may depart this life in thy faith and fear,

and not be condemned before the great judg-ment seat of Christ,

That we may be bound together by thy Holy Spirit in the communion of

[_____ and] all thy saints, entrusting one another and all our life to Christ,

Setting: Mason Martens (b. 1933)

## Daily Evening Prayer I
## Suffrages B, Tone II

S 30

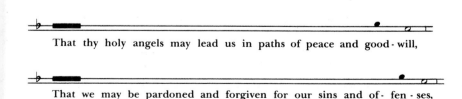

*Cantor or Officiant*

That this evening may be holy, good, and peace-ful,

*People*

We en-treat thee, O Lord.

*(This response is sung after each of the following petitions)*

That thy holy angels may lead us in paths of peace and good-will,

That we may be pardoned and forgiven for our sins and of-fen-ses,

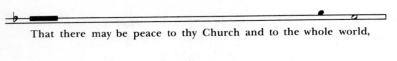

That there may be peace to thy Church and to the whole world,

That we may depart this life in thy faith and fear,

and not be condemned before the great judgment seat of Christ,

That we may be bound together by thy Holy Spirit in the communion of

[_____ and] all thy saints, entrusting one another and all our life to Christ,

Setting: From the Litany of the Saints; adapt. Mason Martens (b. 1933)

# S 31
## Concluding Versicle and Response

Daily Evening Prayer I

*Cantor or Officiant*

Let us bless the Lord.

*People*

Thanks be to God.

# S 32
## Concluding Versicle and Response in Easter Season

Daily Evening Prayer I

*Cantor or Officiant*

Let us bless the Lord, al - le - lu - ia, al - le - lu - ia.

*People*

Thanks be to God, al - le - lu - ia, al - le - lu - ia.

*Officiant*

Lord, o - pen our lips.

*People*

And our mouth shall pro - claim your praise.

*Officiant and People*

Glory to the Father, and to the Son, and to the Holy Spi - rit:

as it was in the beginning, is now, and will be for ever. A - men.

*Except in Lent, add:*

Al - le - lu - ia.

# Daily Morning Prayer II
## The Invitatory: Psalm 95   *Venite*

**S 34**

*Antiphons are sung with this setting.*

1. Come, let us sing to the Lord; let us shout for joy to the Rock of our

sal - va - tion. 2. Let us come before his presence with thanks-giv - ing and raise a loud shout to him with psalms. [Ant.] 3. For the Lord is a

great God, and a great King a-bove all gods. 4. In his hand are

the caverns of the earth, and the heights of the hills are his al-so.

5. The sea is his, for he made it, and his hands have mold-ed the dry land. [Ant.]

6. Come, let us bow down, and bend the knee, and kneel before the Lord

our Ma-ker. 7. For he is our God, and we are the people of his pasture

the sheep of his hand. Oh, that today you would heark-en to his voice! [Ant.]

*Venite ends here.*

*(Gloria Patri may be added)*

8. Hard - en    not your hearts, as your    forebears    did    in    the    wil - der - ness,

at    Meribah,    and    on    that    day    at    Mas - sah,    when    they    tempt - ed    me.

9. They    put    me    to    the    test,    though    they    had    seen    my    works. [Ant.]

10. For - ty    years    long    I    detested    that    genera - tion    and    said,

"This    people    are    wayward    in    their    hearts;    they    do    not    know    my    ways."

11. So    I    swore    in    my    wrath,    "They    shall    not    en - ter    in - to    my    rest." [Ant.]

*(Gloria Patri may be added)*

Glo - ry    to    the    Father,    and    to    the    Son,    and    to    the    Ho - ly    Spi - rit:

as    it    was    in    the    begin - ning,    is    now,    and    will    be    for    ev - er.    A - men. [Ant.]

Setting: Plainsong, Tone 4; adapt Bruce E. Ford (b. 1947)

## The Invitatory: Venite

1. Come, let us sing to the

Lord;_____ let us shout for joy to the Rock of our sal -

va - tion. _____ 2. Let us come be-fore his pres - ence with thanks-giv - ing,____

_____ and raise a loud shout to him with psalms. _____ 3. For the

Lord is a great God, _____ and a great King a - bove all

gods._____ 4. In his hand are the cav - erns of the earth, ____

_____ and the heights of the hills are his al · so. _____ 5. The

sea is his, for he made it, _____ and his hands have

mold · ed the dry land. ____ 6. Come, let us bow down, and bend the

knee, _____ and kneel be · fore the Lord our Ma · ker. ____ 7. For

he is our God, _____ and we are the peo · ple of his

pas · ture _____ and the sheep of his hand. ____

_____ Oh, that to · day you would heark · en to his voice! _____

Setting: Jack Noble White (b. 1938)

S 36 — George A. MacFarren (1813-1887)

S 37 — Stephen Elvey (1805-1860)

S 38 — Thomas Tertius Noble (1867-1953)

S 39 — Charles Villiers Stanford (1852-1924)

S 40 — George S. Talbot (1875-1918)

*Antiphons may be sung with these chants.*

1     Come, let us ' sing to the ' Lord; *

        let us shout for joy to the ' Rock of ' our sal ' vation.

2     Let us come before his ' presence with thanks ' giving *

        and raise a loud ' shout to ' him with ' psalms. [Ant.]

3    For the Lord is a'great'God, *

     and a great'King a'bove all'gods.

4    In his hand are the'caverns of the'earth, *

     and the heights of the'hills are'his'also.

†5    The sea is'his, for he'made it, *

     and his hands have'molded the'dry'land.   [Ant.]

6    Come, let us bow down, and'bend the'knee, *

     and'kneel before the'Lord our'Maker.

7    For he is our God,

     and we are the people of his pasture and the'sheep of his'hand. *

     Oh, that to'day you would'hearken to his'voice!   [Ant.]

*Venite ends here.*
*(Gloria Patri may be added)*


*Psalm 95 continues:*

8    Harden not your hearts,

     as your forebears'did in the'wilderness, *

     at Méribah, and on that day at'Massah,'when they'tempted me.

9    They'put me to the'test, *

     — 'though they had'seen my'works.   [Ant.]

10    Forty years long I detested that gener'ation and'said, *

     "This people are wayward in their hearts;

     'they do not'know my'ways."

11    So I'swore in my'wrath, *

     "They shall not'enter'into my'rest."   [Ant.]

*(Gloria Patri may be added)*

     Glory to the Father, and'to the'Son, *

     and'to the'Holy'Spirit:

     As it was in the be'ginning, is'now, *

     and'will be for'ever. A'men.   [Ant.]

†*Second half of double chant*

## The Invitatory: Jubilate

*Antiphons are sung with this setting.*

1. Be joy - ful in the Lord, all you lands; serve the Lord with gladness and come before his pres - ence with a song. [Ant.] 2. Know this: The Lord him - self is God; he himself has made us, and we are his; we are his people and the sheep of his pas - ture. [Ant.] 3. En - ter his gates with thanksgiving; go in - to his courts with praise; give thanks to him and call up - on his Name. [Ant.] 4. For the Lord is good; his mercy is ev - er - last - ing; and his faithfulness en - dures from age to age. [Ant.]

*(Gloria Patri may be added)*

Glo - ry to the Father, and to the Son, and to the Ho - ly Spi - rit:

As it was in the begin - ning, is now, and will be for ev - er. A - men. [Ant.]

Setting: Plainsong, Tone 4; adapt. Bruce E. Ford (b. 1947)

# Daily Morning Prayer II
## The Invitatory: Jubilate

S 42      Peter Hurford (b. 1930)

S 43      Richard Woodward (1744-1777)

S 44      James Nares (1715-1783)

S 45      Henry Walford Davies (1869-1941)

*Antiphons may be sung with these chants.*

1  Be joyful in the ʹLord, all youʹlands; *
    serve the Lord with gladness
    and come before hisʹpresenceʹwith aʹsong.  [Ant.]

2  Know this: The Lord himʹself isʹGod; *
    he himself has made us, and we are his;
    we are hisʹpeople and theʹsheep of hisʹpasture.  [Ant.]

3  Enter his gates with thanksgiving;
    go into hisʹcourts withʹpraise; *
    give thanks toʹhim andʹcall upon hisʹName.  [Ant.]

4  For the Lord is good;
    his mercy isʹeverʹlasting: *
    and his faithfulness enʹdures fromʹage toʹage.  [Ant.]

*(Gloria Patri may be added)*
Glory to the Father, andʹto theʹSon, *
    andʹto theʹHolyʹSpirit:
As it was in the beʹginning, isʹnow, *
    andʹwill be forʹever. Aʹmen.  [Ant.]

**Christ our Passover**  *Pascha nostrum*

1. Al - le - lu - ia. Christ our Passover has been sac - ri - ficed for

us; there - fore let us keep the feast, 2. Not with the old leaven,

the leaven of mal - ice and e - vil, but with the unleavened bread

of sincerity and truth. Al - le - lu - ia.

3. Christ be - ing raised from the dead will nev - er die a - gain;

death no longer has do - min - ion o - ver him. 4. The death that he died,

he died to sin, once for all; but the life he lives, he lives to God.

5. So al - so consider yourselves dead to sin, and a - live to God

in Jesus Christ our Lord. Al - le - lu - ia.

6. Christ has been raised from the dead, the first fruits of those who

have fal - len a - sleep. 7. For since by a man came death,

by a man has come also the resur - rec - tion of the dead.

8. For as in Ad - am all die, so al - so in Christ shall all

be made a - live. Al - le - lu - ia.

*(Gloria Patri may be added)*

Glo - ry to the Father, and to the Son, and to the Ho - ly

Spi - rit: As it was in the be - gin - ning, is now,

and will be for ever. A - men. Al - le - lu - ia.

Setting: Plainsong, Tone 1, Introit Form; adapt. Norman Mealy (b. 1923), alt.

## Christ our Passover  *Pascha nostrum*

**S 47**

William Henry Walter
(1825-1893)

**S 48**

Oxford Chant

**S 49**

John Hindle
(1761-1796)

**S 50**

Tonus Peregrinus; adapt. David Hurd
(b. 1950)

1   Alleluia, ˈalleˈluia. *
    Alleˈluia, ˈalleˈluia.

2   Christ our Passover has been ˈsacrificed for ˈus, *
    therefore ˈlet us ˈkeep the ˈfeast,

3   Not with the old leaven, the leaven of ˈmalice and ˈevil, *
    but with the unleavened ˈbread of sin ˈcerity and ˈtruth.

4   Alleluia, ˈalleˈluia. *
    Alleˈluia, ˈalleˈluia.

5   Christ being raised from the dead will ˈnever die aˈgain; *
    death no ˈlonger has doˈminion ˈover him.

6   The death that he died, he died to sin, ˈonce for ˈall; *
    but the life he ˈlives, he ˈlives to ˈGod.

7   So also consider yourselves'dead to'sin, *

     and alive to God in'Jesus'Christ our'Lord.

8   Alleluia,'alle'luia. *

     Alle'luia,'alle'luia.

9   Christ has been'raised from the'dead, *

     the first fruits of'those who have'fallen a'sleep.

10  For since by a'man came'death, *

     by a man has come also the resur'rection'of the'dead.

11  For as in'Adam all'die, *

     so also in Christ shall'all be'made a'live.

12  Alleluia,'alle'luia. *

     Alle'luia,'alle'luia.

*(Gloria Patri may be added)*

Glory to the Father, and'to the'Son, *

     and'to the'Holy'Spirit:

As it was in the be'ginning, is'now, *

     and'will be for'ever. A'men.

Alleluia,'alle'luia. *

     Alle'luia,'alle'luia.

# Daily Morning Prayer II
## Salutation and The Lord's Prayer

S 51

*Officiant*           *People*           *Officiant*

The Lord be with you.   And also with you.   Let us pray.

*Officiant and People*

Our  Father  in  heaven . . . ever.   A - men.

*or*

Our Father, who art in heaven . . . ever.   A - men.

## Suffrages A

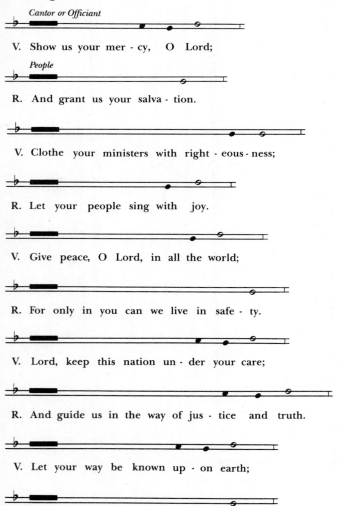

*Cantor or Officiant*

V. Show us your mer - cy,   O  Lord;

*People*

R. And grant us your salva - tion.

V. Clothe  your  ministers with  right - eous - ness;

R. Let  your  people  sing with   joy.

V. Give peace, O  Lord,  in  all  the  world;

R. For  only  in  you  can  we  live  in  safe - ty.

V. Lord,  keep  this  nation  un - der  your  care;

R. And  guide  us  in  the  way  of  jus - tice   and   truth.

V. Let  your  way  be  known  up - on  earth;

R. Your  saving  health  among  all  na - tions.

V. Let not the needy, O Lord, be forgot - ten;

R. Nor the hope of the poor be ta - ken a - way.

V. Create in us clean hearts, O God;

R. And sustain us with your Holy Spi - rit.

## Daily Morning Prayer II
## Suffrages B

S 53

*Cantor or Officiant*

V. Save your people, Lord, and bless your inher - i - tance;

*People*

R. Govern and uphold them, now and al - ways.

V. Day by day we bless you;

R. We praise your Name for ev - er.

V. Lord, keep us from all sin to - day;

R. Have mercy on us, Lord, have mer - cy.

V. Lord, show us your love and mer - cy;

R. For we put our trust in you.

V. In you, Lord, is our hope;

R. And we shall never hope in vain.

# S 54

## Concluding Versicle and Response

*Cantor or Officiant*

Let us bless the Lord.

*People*

Thanks be to God.

# S 55

## Concluding Versicle and Response in Easter Season

*Cantor or Officiant*

Let us bless the Lord, al - le - lu - ia, al - le - lu - ia.

*People*

Thanks be to God, al - le - lu - ia, al - le - lu - ia.

## An Order of Worship for the Evening
## Greeting: Tone I

S 56

*Officiant*                                   *People*

Light and peace, in Jesus Christ our Lord.      Thanks be to God.

*In Lent and in Easter Season, the Opening Acclamations S 78–S 83 are used instead.*

Setting: Ambrosian chant; adapt. Mason Martens (b. 1933)


## An Order of Worship for the Evening
## Greeting: Tone II

S 57

*Officiant*                                   *People*

Light and peace, in Je - sus Christ our Lord.      Thanks be to God.

*In Lent and in Easter Season, the Opening Acclamations S 78–S 83 are used instead.*


## Daily Evening Prayer II
## Preces

S 58

*Officiant*

O God, make speed to save us.

*People*

O Lord, make haste to help us.

*Officiant and People*

Glory to the Father, and to the Son, and to the Holy Spi - rit:

as it was in the beginning, is now, and will be for ever. A - men.

*Except in Lent, add:*

Al - le - lu - ia.

O Gracious Light     *Phos hilaron*

1. O gra-cious Light, pure bright-ness of the ev-er-liv-ing

Fa-ther in hea-ven, O Je-sus Christ, ho-ly and bless-ed!

2. Now as we come to the set-ting of the sun, and our

eyes be-hold the ves-per light, we sing your prais-es, O God:

Fa-ther, Son, and Ho-ly Spi-rit. 3. You are wor-thy at all times

to be praised by hap-py voic-es, O Son of God, O Giv-er

of life, and to be glo-ri-fied through all the worlds.

Setting: Mode 2 melody, centonized Bruce E. Ford (b. 1947) and James McGregor (b. 1930)

# Daily Evening Prayer II
## O Gracious Light *Phos hilaron*

1. O gra - cious Light, pure bright - ness of the ev - er - liv - ing Fa - ther in hea - ven, O Je - sus Christ, ho - ly and bless - ed! 2. Now as we come to the set - ting of the sun, and our eyes be - hold the ves - per light, we sing your prais - es, O God: Fa - ther, Son, and Ho - ly Spi - rit. 3. You are wor - thy at all times to be praised by hap - py voic - es, O Son of God, O Giv - er of life, and to be glo - ri - fied through all the worlds.

Setting: Ronald Arnatt (b. 1930)

# S 61

## O Gracious Light *Phos hilaron*

1. O gra-cious Light, pure bright-ness of the ev-er-liv-ing

Fa-ther in heaven, O Je-sus Christ, ho-ly and

bless-ed! 2. Now as we come to the set-ting of the

sun, and our eyes be-hold the ves-per light, we sing your

prais-es, O God: Fa-ther, Son, and Ho-ly Spi-rit.

3. You are wor-thy at all times to be praised by hap-py

voic-es, _____ O Son of God, O Giv-er of

life, and to be glo-ri-fied through all the worlds.

Setting: McNeil Robinson II (b. 1943)

# Daily Evening Prayer II
## Salutation and The Lord's Prayer

*Officiant*            *People*           *Officiant*

The Lord be with you.   And also with you.   Let us pray.

*Officiant and People*

Our   Father   in   heaven . . . ever.   A - men.
*or*
Our Father, who art in heaven . . . ever.   A - men.

*For Suffrages A, see S 52.*

# Daily Evening Prayer II
## Suffrages B, Tone I

*Cantor or Officiant*

That   this     evening may be holy, good, and peace - ful,

*People*

We   en - treat  you,  O   Lord.

*(This response is sung after each petition)*

That your    holy angels may lead us in paths of peace and good - will,

That we    may be pardoned and forgiven for our sins and of - fen - ses,

That there    may be peace to your Church and to the whole world,

That we may depart this life in your faith and fear,

and not be condemned before the great judg - ment seat of Christ,

That we may be bound together by your Holy Spirit in the communion of

[____ and] all your saints, entrusting one another and all our life to Christ,

Setting: Mason Martens (b. 1933)

# S 64
## Suffrages B, Tone II

Daily Evening Prayer II

*Cantor or Officiant*

That this evening may be holy, good, and peace-ful,

*People*

We en - treat you, O Lord.

*(This response is sung after each petition)*

That your holy angels may lead us in paths of peace and good - will,

That we may be pardoned and forgiven for our sins and of - fen - ses,

That there may be peace to your Church and to the whole world,

That we may depart this life in your faith and fear,

and not be condemned before the great judgment seat of Christ,

That we may be bound together by your Holy Spirit in the communion of

[____ and] all your saints, entrusting one another and all our life to Christ,

Setting: From the Litany of the Saints; adapt. Mason Martens (b. 1933)

## Daily Evening Prayer II
## Concluding Versicle and Response

**S 65**

*Cantor or Officiant*

Let us bless the Lord.

*People*

Thanks be to God.

## Daily Evening Prayer II
## Concluding Versicle and Response in Easter Season

**S 66**

*Cantor or Officiant*

Let us bless the Lord, al - le - lu - ia, al - le - lu - ia.

*People*

Thanks be to God, al - le - lu - ia, al - le - lu - ia.

# The Great Litany

*The Officiant at the Litany may be a lay cantor.*

**Officiant** / **People**

O God the Father, Creator of heaven and earth,    Have mer - cy up - on us.

**Officiant** / **People**

O God the Son, Redeemer of the world,    Have mer - cy up - on us.

**Officiant** / **People**

O God the Holy Ghost, Sanctifier of the faith - ful,    Have mer - cy up - on us.

**Officiant** / **People**

O holy, blessed, and glorious Trinity, one God,    Have mer - cy up - on us.

**Officiant**

Remember not, Lord Christ, our offenses, nor the offenses of our forefathers; neither reward us according to our sins. Spare us, good Lord, spare thy people, whom thou hast redeemed with thy most precious blood, and by thy mercy

**People**

preserve us for ev - er.    Spare us, good Lord.

**Officiant**

From all evil and wickedness; from sin; from the crafts and assaults of the devil; and from everlast - ing dam - na - tion,

**People**

Good Lord, de - liv - er us.

*(This same response is sung after the petitions that follow)*

We sinners do beseech thee to hear us, O Lord God; and that it may please thee to rule and govern thy holy Church Universal in the right way,

*People*

We beseech thee to hear us, good Lord.

*(This same response is sung after the petitions that follow)*

*Officiant*   Son of God, we beseech thee to hear us.
*People*   Son of God, we beseech thee to hear us.

*Officiant*                     *People*

O Lamb of God, that takest away the sins of the world, Have mer-cy up-on us.
O Lamb of God, that takest away the sins of the world, Have mer-cy up-on us.

*Officiant*                     *People*

O Lamb of God, that takest away the sins of the world, Grant us thy peace.

*Officiant*          *People*

O Christ, hear us.     O Christ, hear us.

*When the Litany is sung immediately before the Eucharist, the Litany concludes with the Kyries (which may be sung to any setting), and the Eucharist begins with the Salutation and the Collect of the day.*

*On all other occasions, the Litany continues as follows:*

*Officiant*   Lord, have mer-cy up-on us.
*People*   Christ, have mer-cy up-on us.     *or*
*Officiant*   Lord, have mer-cy up-on us.

Ky-ri-e e-lei-son.
Chri-ste e-lei-son.
Ky-ri-e e-lei-son.

*Officiant and People*

Our Father, who art in heaven . . . from evil. A-men.

*Officiant*                     *People*

V. O Lord, let thy mercy be showed up-on us. R. As we do put our trust in thee.

*The Officiant sings the concluding Collect.*

Setting: John Merbecke (1510?-1585?), alt.

# Proper Liturgies for Special Days

*For Palm Sunday, see Hymns 153-157*

## S 68                                            **The Great Vigil of Easter**

### Versicle and Response: "The Light of Christ"

The light of Christ.     Thanks be   to God.

*At the second and third pause, the Versicle and Response is sung successively a step higher.*

## S 69                                            **The Great Vigil of Easter**

### The Exsultet: Responses

... for ev-er and ev - er.     A - men.

The Lord be     with you.

And   al - so with you.

Let us give thanks to the Lord our God.

It is right to give him thanks and praise.

... for ev - er and ev - er. A - men.

## The Great Vigil of Easter
## Great Alleluia

S 70

*After the Epistle, this Alleluia is traditionally sung three times by the Celebrant or by a Cantor, at successively higher pitches (one whole tone each time), the Congregation repeating it each time.*

Al-le - - - lu - - ia.

# Holy Baptism

## S 71
### Opening Acclamation

*Celebrant*

Bless - ed be God: Father, Son, and Ho - ly Spi - rit.

*People*

And blessed be his kingdom, now and for ev - er. A - men.

Setting: Ambrosian chant; adapt. Mason Martens (b. 1933)

## S 72
### Opening Acclamation in Easter Season

*Celebrant*

Al - le - lu - ia. Christ is ris - en.

*People*

The Lord is risen indeed. Al - le - lu - ia.

Setting: Ambrosian chant; adapt. Mason Martens (b. 1933)

## S 73
### Opening Acclamation in Lent

*Celebrant*

Bless the Lord who forgives all our sins.

*People*

His mercy en - dures for ev - er.

Setting: Ambrosian chant; adapt. Mason Martens (b. 1933)

# Holy Baptism
## Versicles

*Celebrant*

There is one Body and one Spi - rit;

*People*

There is one hope in God's call to us;

*Celebrant*

One Lord, one Faith, one Bap - tism;

*People*

One God and Fa - ther of all.

Setting: Ambrosian chant; adapt. *Hymnal 1982*

# Holy Baptism
## Litany and Thanksgiving over the Water

**S 75**

*People's response*

Lord, hear our prayer.

*The Amen after the Collect is monotoned.*

*Celebrant* ... *People*

The Lord be with you. And al - so with you.

Let us give thanks to the Lord our God.

*People*

It is right to give him thanks and praise.

*Conclusion*

*Celebrant* ... *People*

A - men.

# The Holy Eucharist

## S 76
### Opening Acclamation

*Celebrant*

Bless-ed be God: Father, Son, and Ho - ly Spi - rit.

*People*

And blessed be his kingdom, now and for ev - er. A- men.

Setting: Ambrosian chant; adapt. Mason Martens (b. 1933)

## S 77
### Opening Acclamation

*Celebrant*

Bless - ed be God: Fa - ther, Son, and Ho - ly Spi - rit.

*People*

And bless - ed be his king-dom, now and for ev - er. A - men.

Setting: From *Missa orbis factor*; arr. David Hurd (b. 1950)

## The Holy Eucharist S 78
### Opening Acclamation for Easter Day through the Day of Pentecost

**Celebrant**

Al - le - lu - ia. Christ is ris - en.

**People**

The Lord is risen indeed. Al - le - lu - ia.

Setting: Ambrosian chant; adapt. Mason Martens (b. 1933)

## The Holy Eucharist S 79
### Opening Acclamation for Easter Day through the Day of Pentecost

**Celebrant**

Al - le - lu - ia. Christ is ris - en.

**People**

The Lord is ris - en in - deed. Al - le - lu - ia.

Setting: From *Missa orbis factor*; David Hurd (b. 1950)

## The Holy Eucharist I S 80
### Opening Acclamation in Lent

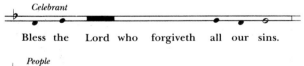

**Celebrant**

Bless the Lord who forgiveth all our sins.

**People**

His mercy endur - eth for ev - er.

Setting: Ambrosian chant; adapt. Mason Martens (b. 1933)

# S 81

## Opening Acclamation in Lent

*Celebrant*

Bless the Lord who for - giv - eth all our sins.

*People*

His mer - cy en - dur - eth for ev - er.

Setting: From *Missa orbis factor*; arr. David Hurd (b. 1950)


# S 82

## Opening Acclamation in Lent

*Celebrant*

Bless the Lord who forgives all our sins.

*People*

His mercy en - dures for ev - er.

Setting: Ambrosian chant; adapt. Mason Martens (b. 1933)


# S 83

## Opening Acclamation in Lent

*Celebrant*

Bless the Lord who for - gives all our sins.

*People*

His mer - cy en - dures for ev - er.

Setting: From *Missa orbis factor*; arr. David Hurd (b. 1950)

*For settings of* Gloria in excelsis, *see S 201–S 204 and S 272–S 281.*

# The Holy Eucharist
## Kyrie eleison

S 84

Setting: Plainsong, Mode 1; *Missa orbis factor*, Mass 11; arr. David Hurd (b. 1950)

## S 85
### Kyrie eleison

Cantor or Choir — Ky-ri-e e-le-i-son.  All — Ky-ri-e e-le-i-son.

Cantor or Choir — Chri-ste e-le-i-son.  All — Chri-ste e-le-i-son.

Cantor or Choir — Ky-ri-e e-le-i-son.  All — Ky-ri-e e-le-i-son.

Setting: Plainsong, Mode 3; Mass 16; adapt. Schola Antiqua, 1983
Melody rhythmic version © 1984, Schola Antiqua Inc. Used by permission.

## S 86
### Kyrie eleison

Ky-ri-e e-le-i-son. Ky-ri-e e-le-i-son. Ky-ri-e

e-le-i-son. Chri-ste e-le-i-son. Chri-ste e-

le-i-son. Chri-ste e-le-i-son. Ky-ri-e e-le-i-son.

Ky-ri-e e-le-i-son. Ky-ri-e e-le-i-son.

Setting: From *New Plainsong*; David Hurd (b. 1950)

# The Holy Eucharist
## Kyrie eleison

S 87

Ky - ri - e e - le - i - son. Ky - ri - e e - le - i - son. Ky - ri - e e - le - i - son. Chri - ste e - le - i - son. Chri - ste e - le - i - son. Chri - ste e - le - i - son. Ky - ri - e e - le - i - son. Ky - ri - e e - le - i - son. Ky - ri - e e - le - i - son.

Setting: From *Corpus Christi Mass*; Jackson Hill (b. 1941)

**Kyrie eleison**

Ky - ri - e        e - le - i - son.____

Ky - ri - e        e - le - i - son.____

Chri - ste        e - le - i - son.____

Chri - ste        e - le - i - son.____

Ky - ri - e        e - le - i - son.____        Ky - ri -

e        e - le - i - son.____

Setting: McNeil Robinson II (b. 1943)

# The Holy Eucharist
## Kyrie eleison

S 89

Setting: James McGregor (b. 1930), after *Verbum caro factum est*, Hans Leo Hassler (1564–1612)

## S 90
**Lord, have mercy upon us**   *Kyrie*                           The Holy Eucharist I

Lord, have mer - cy up - on us. Lord, have mer - cy up - on us. Lord, have mer - cy up - on us.

Christ, have mer - cy up - on us. Christ, have mer - cy up - on us.

Christ, have mer - cy up - on us. Lord, have mer - cy up - on us.

Lord, have mer - cy up - on us. Lord, have mer - cy up - on us.

Setting: John Merbecke (1510?–1585?)

## S 91
**Lord, have mercy upon us**   *Kyrie*                           The Holy Eucharist I

Lord, have mer - cy up - on us. Lord, have mer - cy up - on us. Lord, have mer - cy up - on us. Christ, have mer - cy up - on us. Christ, have mer - cy up - on us. Christ, have mer - cy up - on us. Lord, have mer - cy up - on us. Lord, have mer - cy up - on us. Lord, have mer - cy up - on us.

Setting: From *Missa de Sancta Maria Magdalena*, Healey Willan (1880-1968)

# The Holy Eucharist I
## Lord, have mercy upon us  *Kyrie*

Setting: From *Missa Marialis*; Mode 1; Mass 9, "Cum jubilo"; adapt. Charles Winfred Douglas (1867-1944)

# S 93

The Holy Eucharist I

## Lord, have mercy upon us *Kyrie*

Setting: Leo Sowerby (1895–1968)

## The Holy Eucharist II
## Lord, have mercy   *Kyrie*

Lord, have mer - cy.   Lord, have mer - cy.

Christ, have mer - cy.   Christ, have mer - cy.

Lord, have mer - cy.   Lord, have mer - cy.

Setting: Plainsong, Mode 4; Mass 18; adapt. Mason Martens (b. 1933)

## The Holy Eucharist II
## Lord, have mercy   *Kyrie*

Lord, have mer - cy.   Lord, have mer - cy.   Christ, have mer - cy.

Christ, have mer - cy.   Lord, have mer - cy.   Lord, have mer - cy.

Setting: From the Litany of the Saints; adapt. Richard Proulx (b. 1937)

# S 96

The Holy Eucharist II

**Lord, have mercy**    *Kyrie*

Lord,    have    mer - cy,   have    mer -    cy.

Lord,    have    mer - cy,   have    mer -    cy.

Setting: From *Deutsche Messe*; Franz Peter Schubert (1797-1828); arr. Richard Proulx (b. 1937)

## The Holy Eucharist II

### Lord, have mercy    *Kyrie*

S 97

Lord, have mer - cy.     Lord, have mer - cy.     Lord, have mer - cy.

Christ, have mer - cy.     Christ, have mer - cy.     Christ, have mer - cy.

Lord, have mer - cy.     Lord, have mer - cy.     Lord, have mer - cy. _____

Setting: Richard Felciano (b. 1930)

## S 98
### Lord, have mercy    *Kyrie*

Lord, have mer - cy.

Lord, have mer - cy.    Lord, have mer - cy.

Christ, have mer - cy.    Christ, have mer - cy.    Christ, have mer - cy.

Lord, have mer - cy.    Lord, have mer - cy.    Lord, have mer - cy.

Setting: William Mathias (b. 1934)

## S 99
### Holy God    *Trisagion*

Ho - ly God, Ho - ly and Might - y,

Ho - ly Im - mor - tal One, Have mer - cy up - on us.

Ho - ly God, Ho - ly and Might - y,

Ho - ly Im - mor - tal One, Have mer - cy up - on us.

Ho - ly God, Ho - ly and Might - y,

Ho - ly Im - mor - tal One, Have mer - cy up - on us.

Setting: Plainsong, Mode 1; adapt. Bruce E. Ford (b. 1947)

## The Holy Eucharist
## Holy God    *Trisagion*

S 100

Ho - ly God, Ho - ly and Might - y, Ho - ly Im -

mor - tal One, Have mer - cy up - on us. Ho - ly God,

Ho - ly and Might - y, Ho - ly Im - mor - tal One, Have mer - cy

up - on us. Ho - ly God, Ho - ly and Might - y,

Ho - ly Im - mor - tal One, Have mer - cy up - on us.

Setting: From *New Plainsong*; David Hurd (b. 1950)

## S 101
**Holy God**    *Trisagion*

Ho-ly God, Ho-ly and Might-y, Ho-ly Im-mor-tal One, Have mer-cy up-on us. Ho-ly God, Ho-ly and Might-y, Ho-ly Im-mor-tal One, Have mer-cy up-on us. Ho-ly God, Ho-ly and Might-y, Ho-ly Im-mor-tal One, Have mer-cy up-on us.

Setting: John Rutter (b. 1945)

## S 102
**Holy God**    *Trisagion*

Ho-ly God, Ho-ly and Might-y, Ho-ly Im-mor-tal One, Have mer-cy up-on us.

Setting: Ver. *Hymnal 1982,* after Alexander Archangelsky (1846-1924)

ac - cord - ing to the Scrip-tures, and a - scend - ed in - to hea - ven,

and sit - teth on the right hand of the Fa - ther; and he shall come

a - gain, with glo - ry, to judge both the quick and the dead; whose king-dom

shall have no end. And I be - lieve in the Ho - ly Ghost the Lord,

and Giv - er of Life, who pro - ceed - eth from the Fa - ther and the Son;

who with the Fa - ther and the Son to - geth - er is wor - shiped and glo - ri - fied;

who spake by the Pro - phets. And I be - lieve one ho - ly Cath - o - lic

and A - po - sto - lic Church; I ac - know - ledge one Bap - tism for the re-

mis - sion of sins; and I look for the re - sur - rec - tion of the dead,

and the life of the world to come. A - men.

Setting: Plainsong, Mode 4; Credo I; adapt. Charles Winfred Douglas (1867–1944), alt.

# The Holy Eucharist
## The Nicene Creed (Contemporary)

S 104

We be-lieve in one God, the Fa-ther, the Al-might-y, ma-ker of

hea-ven and earth, of all that is, seen and un-seen. We be-lieve

in one Lord, Je-sus Christ, the on-ly Son of God, e-ter-nal-ly

be-got-ten of the Fa-ther, God from God, Light from Light, true God

from true God, be-got-ten, not made, of one Be-ing with the Fa-ther.

Through him all things were made. For us and for our sal-va-tion

he came down from hea-ven: by the pow-er of the Ho-ly Spi-rit

he be-came in-car-nate from the Vir-gin Ma-ry, and was made man.

For our sake he was cru-ci-fied un-der Pon-tius Pi-late;

he suf-fered death and was bur-ied. On the third day he rose a-gain in ac - cord - ance with the Scrip-tures; he a - scend-ed in - to hea - ven

and is seat - ed at the right hand of the Fa - ther. He will come a -

gain in glo - ry to judge the liv - ing and the dead, and his king-dom

will have no end. We be - lieve in the Ho - ly Spi - rit, the Lord,

the Giv - er of life, who pro - ceeds from the Fa - ther and the Son.

With the Fa - ther and the Son he is wor-shiped and glo - ri - fied.

He has spo - ken through the Pro - phets. We be - lieve in one ho - ly

cath - o - lic and a - po - sto - lic Church. We ac - know-ledge one bap - tism

for the for - give-ness of sins. We look for the re - sur - rec - tion of the dead,

and the life of the world to come. A - men.

Setting: Plainsong, Mode 4; Credo I; adapt. Mason Martens (b. 1933)

rose a-gain in ac-cord-ance with the Scrip-tures; he a-scend-ed

in-to hea-ven and is seat-ed at the right hand of the Fa-ther.

He will come a-gain in glo-ry to judge the liv-ing and the

dead, and his king-dom will have no end. We be-lieve in the

Ho-ly Spi-rit, the Lord, the giv-er of life, who pro-ceeds from the

Fa-ther and the Son. With the Fa-ther and the Son he is wor-shiped and

glo-ri-fied. He has spo-ken through the Pro-phets. We be-lieve in

one ho-ly cath-o-lic and a-pos-to-lic Church.

We ac-know-ledge one bap-tism for the for-give-ness of sins.

We look for the re-sur-rec-tion of the dead,____

and the life of the world to come. A-men. A-men.____

Setting: Calvin Hampton (1938-1984)

# The Holy Eucharist
## The Prayers of the People: Form I

With all our heart and with all our mind, let us pray to the Lord, say-ing

"Lord, have mer - cy."

*Deacon or Cantor*

For . . ., let us pray to the Lord.

*People*

Lord, have mer - cy.

*(This response is sung after each petition.)*

*Deacon or Cantor concludes*

In the communion of [_____ and of all the] saints, let us commend

ourselves, and one an - o - ther, and all our life, to Christ our God.

*People*

To thee, O Lord our God.
   you,

*Silence*

*The Celebrant adds a concluding Collect which may be monotoned or sung to Collect Tone II found in the Musical Appendix to the Altar Edition of the Holy Eucharist.*

*The responses may be sung in harmony, as follows:*

Lord, have mer - cy.    To thee, O Lord our God.    A - men.
                            you,

## The Prayers of the People: Form III

*Deacon or Cantor*        *People*

Fa - ther, we pray for your holy Cath - o - lic Church; That we all may be one.

*Deacon or Cantor*

Grant that every member of the Church may truly and hum - bly serve you;

*People*

That your Name may be glorified by all peo - ple.

*Deacon or Cantor*

We pray for all bishops, priests, and dea - cons;

*People*

That they may be faithful ministers of your word and sac - ra - ments.

*Deacon or Cantor*

We pray for all who govern and hold authority in the nations of the world;

*People*

That there may be jus - tice and peace on earth.

*Deacon or Cantor*

Give us grace to do your will in all that we un - der - take;

*People*

That our works may find fa - vor in your sight.

*Deacon or Cantor*

Have com - passion on those who suffer from any grief or trou -ble;

*People*

That they may be deliv - ered from their dis - tress.

*Deacon or Cantor*

Give to the depart - ed e - ter - nal rest;

*People*

Let light perpetual shine up - on them.

*Deacon or Cantor*

We praise you for your saints who have entered in - to joy;

*People*

May we also come to share in your hea - ven - ly king -dom.

*Deacon or Cantor*

Let us pray for our own needs, and the needs of o - thers.

*Silence*

*The People may add their own petitions.*

*The Celebrant adds a concluding Collect which may be sung in monotone.*

Setting: Anaphoral chant; adapt. Bruce E. Ford (b. 1947)

## The Prayers of the People: Form IV

*Deacon or Cantor*

Let us pray for the Church and for the world.

Grant, Almighty God, that all who confess your Name may be united in your truth, live

together in your love, and reveal your glory / in the wórld. *Silence*

*Deacon or Cantor*     *People (unison or harmony)*

Lord, in your mer - cy     Hear our prayer.

Guide the people of this land, and of all the nations, in the ways of justice and peace; that we may honor one another and serve the / common góod.

*Silence*

Lord, in your mercy
*Hear our prayer.*

Give us all a reverence for the earth as your own creation, that we may use its resources rightly in the service of others and to your hon- / or and glóry.

*Silence*

Lord, in your mercy
*Hear our prayer.*

Bless all whose lives are closely linked with ours, and grant that we may serve Christ in them, and love one another as / he loves ús.

*Silence*

Lord, in your mercy
*Hear our prayer.*

Comfort and heal all those who suffer in body, mind, or spirit; give them courage and hope in their troubles, and bring them the joy of / your salvátion.

*Silence*

**Lord, in your mercy**
*Hear our prayer.*

We commend to your mercy all who have died, that your will for them may be fulfilled; and we pray that we may share with all your saints in your e- / ter-nal kíngdom.

*Silence*

**Lord, in your mercy**
*Hear our prayer.*

*The Celebrant adds a concluding Collect which may be monotoned or sung to Collect Tone II found in the Musical Appendix to the Altar Edition of the Holy Eucharist.*

*After the Collect*

A - men.

*The following alternative harmonizations may be sung:*

Hear our prayer.   Hear our prayer.   Hear our prayer.

Setting: David Hurd (b. 1950)

## The Prayers of the People: Form V

*Deacon or Cantor*

In peace, let us pray to the Lord,

saying, "Lord, have mer - cy." *or* "Ky - ri - e e - lei - son."

*Deacon or Cantor*

For . . . . , we pray to you, O Lord.

*People*

Lord, have mer - cy. *or* Ky - ri - e e - lei - son.
*(This response is sung after each petition)*

*Deacon or Cantor concludes*

Re - joic - ing    in the fellowship of [the ever-blessed Virgin Mary, (blessed N.) and] all

the saints,    let us commend ourselves, and one another, and all our life to Christ

*People*

our God.    To you, O Lord our God.

*Silence*

*The Celebrant adds a concluding Collect which may be monotoned or sung to Collect Tone I found in the Musical Appendix to the Altar Edition of the Holy Eucharist.*

*Alternatively, the Celebrant may conclude with the following Doxology.*

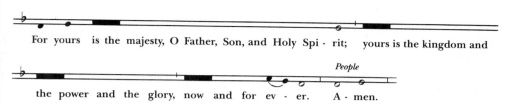

For yours is the majesty, O Father, Son, and Holy Spi - rit;  yours is the kingdom and

the power and the glory, now and for ev - er.  A - men.

Setting: Mason Martens (b. 1933)

## The Holy Eucharist I
## The Peace

# S 110

*Celebrant*

The peace of the Lord be al - ways with you.

*People*

And with thy spi - rit.

## The Holy Eucharist II
## The Peace

# S 111

*Celebrant*

The peace of the Lord be al - ways with you.

*People*

And al - so with you.

Setting: Ambrosian chant; adapt. Mason Martens (b. 1933)

# S 112

## Lift up your hearts  *Sursum corda*

*Celebrant* The Lord be with you. *People* And with thy spi - rit.

*Celebrant* Lift up your hearts. *People* We lift them up un - to the Lord.

*Celebrant* Let us give thanks un - to our Lord God.

*People* It is meet and right so to do.

# S 113

## Holy, holy, holy  *Sanctus*

Ho - ly, ho - ly, ho - ly, Lord God of Hosts:

Heaven and earth are full of thy glo - ry. Glo - ry be

to thee, O Lord Most High. Bless - ed is he that com - eth

in the name of the Lord. Ho - san - na in the high - est.

Setting: John Merbecke (1510?-1585?); adapt. *Hymnal 1982*

## The Holy Eucharist I
### Holy, holy, holy  *Sanctus*

S 114

Ho - ly, ho - ly, ho - ly, Lord God of Hosts: Hea - ven and earth are full____ of thy glo - ry. Glo - ry be to thee, O Lord Most High. Bless - ed ____ is he that com - eth ____ ____ in the name of the Lord. Ho - san - na in the high - est.

Setting: From *Missa de Sancta Maria Magdalena*, Healey Willan (1880-1968)

## The Holy Eucharist I
### Holy, holy, holy  *Sanctus*

S 115

Ho - ly, ho - ly, ho - ly, Lord God of Hosts: Hea - ven and earth are full of thy glo - ry. Glo - ry be to thee, O Lord Most High. Bless - ed is he that com - eth in the name of the Lord. Ho - san - a in the high - est.

Setting: From *Missa Marialis*; Plainsong, Mode 5; Mass 9; adapt. Charles Winfred Douglas (1867-1944) and Bruce E. Ford (b. 1947)

# S 116

**Holy, holy, holy** *Sanctus*

Ho - ly, ho - ly, ho - ly,

Lord God

of Hosts: Hea - ven and earth are full

of thy glo - ry. Glo - ry be to thee, O

Lord Most High. Bless - ed is he

that com - eth in the name of the Lord.

Ho - san - na in the high - est.

Setting: From *Missa de Angelis*; Mode 5; Mass 8; adapt. Charles Winfred Douglas (1867-1944)

# The Holy Eucharist I
## Holy, holy, holy *Sanctus*

S 117

Holy, holy, holy, Lord God of Hosts: Heaven and earth are full of thy glory. Glory be to thee, O Lord Most High. Bless-ed is he that com-eth in the name of the Lord. Ho-san-na in the high-est.

Setting: James McGregor (b. 1930), after *Verbum caro factum est*, Hans Leo Hassler (1564-1612)

# S 118

The Holy Eucharist I

**Conclusion of Eucharistic Prayer and Amen**

*Celebrant*  *People*

A - men.

# S 119

The Holy Eucharist

**The Lord's Prayer (Traditional)**

Our Fa - ther, who art in hea - ven, hal - low - ed

be thy Name, thy king - dom come, thy will be done,

on earth as it is in hea - ven. Give us this day our

dai - ly bread. and for - give us our tres - pas - ses,

as we for - give those who tres - pass a - gainst us. And lead

us not in - to temp - ta - tion, but de - liv - er us

from e - vil. For thine is the king - dom, and the power,

and the glo - ry, for ev - er and ev - er. A - men.

Setting: Plainsong; adapt. Charles Winfred Douglas (1867-1944)

## The Holy Eucharist II
## Lift up your hearts    *Sursum corda*

S 120

*Celebrant:* The Lord be with you.
*People:* And al-so with you.

*Celebrant:* Lift up your hearts.
*People:* We lift them to the Lord.

*Celebrant:* Let us give thanks to the Lord our God.

*People:* It is right to give him thanks and praise.

## The Holy Eucharist II
## Holy, holy, holy Lord    *Sanctus*

S 121

Ho - ly, ho - ly, ho - ly Lord,

God of power and might, heaven and earth are full of your glo - ry.

Ho - san - na in the high - est. Bless - ed is he who comes

in the name of the Lord. Ho - san - na in the high - est.

Setting: Plainsong, Te Deum Tone; adapt. James McGregor (b. 1930)

## S 122

**The Holy Eucharist II**

**Holy, holy, holy Lord** *Sanctus*

Ho - ly, ho - ly, ho - ly Lord, God of

power and might, heav - en and earth are full of your glo - ry.

Ho - san - na in the high - est. Bless - ed is he who comes

in the name of the Lord. Ho - san - na in the high - est.

Setting: Plainsong; Mass 18; adapt. Mason Martens (b. 1933)


## S 123

**The Holy Eucharist II**

**Holy, holy, holy Lord** *Sanctus*

Ho - ly, ho - ly, ho - ly Lord, God of power and might,

hea - ven and earth are full of your glory. Hosanna in the high - est.

Bless - ed is he who comes in the name of the Lord. Ho - san - na in the high - est.

Setting: Mozarabic chant, ca. 8th cent.; adapt. Howard E. Galley (b. 1929)

## The Holy Eucharist II
### Holy, holy, holy Lord  *Sanctus*

S 124

Ho - ly,  ho - ly,  ho - ly Lord,  God of pow-er and might,  heav-en and earth are full of your glo - ry.  Ho - san - na  in  the  high - est.  Bless - ed  is  he who comes in the name of the Lord.  Ho-san- na in the high - est.

Setting: From *New Plainsong*; David Hurd (b. 1950)

## The Holy Eucharist
### Holy, holy, holy Lord  *Sanctus*

S 125

Ho - ly,  ho - ly,  ho - ly Lord,  God  of pow - er  and  might,  heaven  and  earth  are  full  of your  glo - ry.  Ho - san - na  in  the  high - est.  Ho - san - na  in  the  high - est.  Blessed is  he  who  comes  in  the  name  of  the  Lord.  Ho - san - na  in  the  high-est.  Ho - san - na  in  the  high- est.

Setting: From *A Community Mass*; Richard Proulx (b. 1937)

**Holy, holy, holy Lord**     *Sanctus*

Setting: Richard Felciano (b. 1930)

**Holy, holy, holy Lord**     *Sanctus*

Setting: Calvin Hampton (1938-1984)

## The Holy Eucharist II
### Holy, holy, holy Lord *Sanctus*

**S 128**

Ho - ly, ho - ly, ho - ly Lord, God of power and might, heaven and earth are full of your glo - ry. Ho-san-na in the high - est. Bless - ed is he who comes in the name of the Lord. Ho-san-na in the high-est.

Setting: William Mathias (b. 1934)

## The Holy Eucharist II
### Holy, holy, holy Lord *Sanctus*

**S 129**

Ho - ly, ho - ly, ho - ly Lord, God of pow - er and might, hea - ven and earth are full of your glo - ry. Ho - san - na in the high - est. Bless - ed is he who comes in the name of the Lord. Ho - san - na in the high - est. _____

Setting: Robert Powell (b. 1932)

# S 130

### Holy, holy, holy Lord  *Sanctus*

Ho - ly, ho - ly, ho - ly Lord, God of power and might, _____ Ho - ly, ho - ly, ho - ly Lord,

God of power and might, _____ hea - ven and earth are full, _____ full of your glo - ry. Ho -

san - na in the high - est. Ho - san - na
in the high - est. Bless - ed is he who comes _____
_____ in the name of the Lord. _____ Ho - san - na
in the high - est. Ho - san - na in the high - est.

Setting: From *Deutsche Messe*, Franz Peter Schubert (1797-1828); arr. Richard Proulx (b. 1937)

# S 131
## Holy, holy, holy Lord  *Sanctus*

Ho - ly, ho - ly, ho - ly Lord, God of power and might,

heaven and earth are full of your glo - ry. Ho -

san - na in the high - est. Bless - ed is he who comes in the

name of the Lord. Ho - san - na in the high - est.

Setting: Gerald R. Near (b. 1942)

# S 132
The Holy Eucharist II
## Memorial Acclamation: Prayer A

Christ has died. Christ is ris - en. Christ will come a - gain.

Setting: Antiphon tone; adapt. Bruce Ford (b. 1947)

## The Holy Eucharist II
## Memorial Acclamation: Prayer A

## S 133

*Celebrant*

There - fore we pro - claim the mys - ter - y of faith:

*Celebrant and People*

Christ has died. Christ is ris - en. Christ will come a - gain.

Setting: Ambrosian chant; adapt. Mason Martens (b. 1933)

## The Holy Eucharist II
## Memorial Acclamation: Prayer A

## S 134

Christ has died. Christ is ris - en. Christ will come a - gain.

Setting: Plainsong, Te Deum tone; adapt. Richard Proulx (b. 1937)

## The Holy Eucharist II
## Memorial Acclamation: Prayer A

## S 135

Christ has died. Christ is ris - en. Christ will come a - gain.

Setting: Jackson Hill (b. 1941)

# S 136

The Holy Eucharist II

## Memorial Acclamation: Prayer B

*Celebrant*

There - fore, ac - cord - ing to his com - mand, O Fa - ther,

*Celebrant and People*

We re - mem - ber his death, We pro - claim his re - sur -

rec - tion, We a - wait his com - ing in glo - ry.

Setting: Ambrosian anaphora chant; adapt. Mason Martens (b. 1933)

# S 137

The Holy Eucharist II

## Memorial Acclamation: Prayer B

*Celebrant*

There - fore, ac - cord - ing to his com - mand, O Fa - ther,

*Celebrant and People*

We re - mem - ber his death, We pro - claim his re - sur -

rec - tion, We a - wait his com - ing in glo - ry.

Setting: Plainsong, Te Deum Tone; adapt. Mason Martens (b. 1933)

## The Holy Eucharist II
## Memorial Acclamation: Prayer B

# S 138

Therefore, according to his com-mand, O Fa-ther,

We re-mem-ber his death, We pro-claim his re-sur-

rec-tion, We a-wait his com-ing in glo-ry.

Setting: McNeil Robinson II (b. 1943)

## The Holy Eucharist II
## Memorial Acclamation: Prayer D

# S 139

...we praise you and we bless you.

We praise you, we bless you, we give

thanks to you, and we pray to you, Lord our God.

Setting: Plainsong, Te Deum Tone; adapt. Mason Martens (b. 1933)

# S 140

## Memorial Acclamation: Prayer D

We praise you, we bless you, we give thanks to you, and we pray to you, Lord our God.

Setting: Ambrosian chant; adapt. Richard Proulx (b. 1937)

# S 141

## Memorial Acclamation: Prayer D

Celebrant: ... we praise you and we bless you.

All: We praise you, we bless you, we give thanks to you, and we pray to you, Lord our God.

Setting: McNeil Robinson II (b. 1943)

# S 142

## Conclusion of Eucharistic Prayer and Amen

Celebrant ... People

A - men.

# The Holy Eucharist
## Amen

Setting: From *Missa de Angelis*; Plainsong, Mode 6; adapt. Mason Martens (b. 1933)

# The Holy Eucharist
## Amen

Setting: Henri Dumont (1610-1684); adapt. Mason Martens (b. 1933)

# The Holy Eucharist
## Amen

Setting: Henri Dumont (1610-1684); adapt. Mason Martens (b. 1933)

# The Holy Eucharist
## Amen

Setting: McNeil Robinson II (b. 1943)

A - men.  A - men.  A - men.

Setting: McNeil Robinson II (b. 1943)

**S 148**
The Lord's Prayer (Contemporary)

The Holy Eucharist II

*Celebrant*

As our Sa - vior Christ has taught us, we now pray,

*Celebrant and People*

Our Fa - ther in hea - ven, hal - lowed be your Name,

your king - dom come, your will be done, on earth as in hea - ven.

Give us to - day our dai - ly bread.

For - give us our sins as we for - give those who sin a - gainst us.

Save us from the time of tri - al, and de - liv - er us from e - vil.

For the king - dom, the power, and the glo - ry are yours,

now and for ev - er. A - men.

Setting: Ambrosian chant; adapt. Mason Martens (b. 1933)

Our Fa - ther in hea - ven, hal - lowed be your Name,

your king - dom come, your will be done, on earth as in

hea - ven. Give us to - day our dai - ly bread.

For - give us our sins as we for - give those who

sin a - gainst us. Save us from the time of trial,

and de - liv - er us from e - vil. For the king - dom the pow - er,

and the glo - ry are yours, now and for ev - er. A - men.

Setting: McNeil Robinson II (b. 1943)

**The Lord's Prayer (Contemporary)**

Setting: From *Intercession Mass*; David Hurd (b. 1950)

# The Holy Eucharist
## Fraction Anthem: Christ our Passover

*This setting is not used in Lent.*

Cantor

Al - le - lu - ia, al - le - lu - ia, al - le - lu - ia.

All

Al - le - lu - ia, al - le - lu - ia, al - le - lu - ia.

Cantor

Christ our Pass - o - ver is sac - ri - ficed for us; there-fore let us

All

keep the feast. Al - le - lu - ia, al - le - lu - ia, al - le - lu - ia.

Setting: From *Missa orbis factor*; Plainsong, Tonus Peregrinus; arr. David Hurd (b. 1950)

---

# The Holy Eucharist

## Fraction Anthem: Christ our Passover

*This setting is not used in Lent.*

Al - le - lu - ia. Christ our Pass - o - ver is sac - ri - ficed for us;

There - fore let us keep the feast. Al - le - lu - ia.

*This setting may be sung full by all, or by the choir, or as a versicle and response.*

Setting: Ambrosian chant; adapt. Mason Martens (b. 1933)

---

# The Holy Eucharist

## Fraction Anthem: Christ our Passover

Christ our Pass - o - ver is sac - ri - ficed for us;

There - fore let us keep the feast.

Setting: Ambrosian chant; adapt. Mason Martens (b. 1933)

## Fraction Anthem: Christ our Passover

(Al - le - lu - ia, al - le - lu - ia, al - le - lu - ia.)

Christ our Pass - o - ver is sac - ri - ficed for us;

there - fore let us keep the feast.

(Al - le - lu - ia, al - le - lu - ia, al - le - lu - ia.)

Setting: From *New Plainsong*; David Hurd (b. 1950)

## Fraction Anthem: Christ our Passover

*This setting is not used in Lent.*

Al - le - lu - ia, al - le -

lu - ia, al - le - lu - ia. Christ our Pass - o - ver is

sac - ri - ficed for us; there - fore let us keep the feast.

Al - le - lu - ia, al - le - lu - ia, al - le - lu - ia.

Setting: Gerald R. Near (b. 1942)

# The Holy Eucharist
## Fraction Anthem: Christ our Passover

# S 156

Christ our Pass - o - ver is sac - ri - ficed for us; there-fore let us keep the feast.

Setting: Gerald R. Near (b. 1942)

# The Holy Eucharist I
## Fraction Anthem: O Lamb of God    *Agnus Dei*

# S 157

O Lamb of God, that ta - kest a - way the sins of the world, have mer - cy up - on us.

O Lamb of God, that ta - kest a - way the sins of the world, have mer - cy up - on us.

O Lamb of God, that ta - kest a - way the sins of the world, grant us thy peace.

Setting: John Merbecke (1518?-1585?); adapt. *Hymnal 1982*

**Fraction Anthem: O Lamb of God** *Agnus Dei*

O Lamb of God, that ta - kest a -
way the sins of the world, have mer - cy up -
on us. O Lamb of God, that
ta - kest a - way the sins of the world, have
mer - cy up - on us. O Lamb of
God, that ta - kest a - way the sins of the
world, grant_____ us thy peace.

Setting: From *Missa de Sancta Maria Magdalena*, Healey Willan (1880-1968)

# The Holy Eucharist I
## Fraction Anthem: O Lamb of God   *Agnus Dei*

O　　Lamb　　of　God,　　　that　　ta - kest　a - way

the　sins　　　of　　　the　world,　have　　mer　-　cy

up - on　　us.　　O　　　Lamb　　of　　God,

that　ta - kest　a - way　the　sins　of　the　　world,　have

mer　-　cy　up - on　　us.　　O　　Lamb　　of

God,　　　that　　ta　-　kest　a - way　the　sins　　　of

the　world,　　grant　　　us　　　thy　　peace.

Setting: From *Missa Marialis*; Plainsong, Mode 5; Mass 9; adapt. Charles Winfred Douglas (1867-1944)

# S 160

**Fraction Anthem: Lamb of God** *Agnus Dei*

Lamb of God, you take a-way the sins of the world: have mer-cy on us. Lamb of God, you take a-way the sins of the world: have mer-cy on us. Lamb of God, you take a-way the sins of the world: grant us peace.

Setting: Anaphora chant; Mass 18; adapt. Mason Martens (b. 1933)

# S 161

**Fraction Anthem: Lamb of God** *Agnus Dei*

Lamb of God, you take a-way the sins of the world: have mer-cy on us. Lamb of God, you take a-way the sins of the world: have mer-cy on us. Lamb of God, you take a-way the sins of the world: grant us peace.

Setting: From *New Plainsong*; David Hurd (b. 1950)

## The Holy Eucharist II
### Fraction Anthem: Lamb of God *Agnus Dei*

S 162

Lamb of God, you take a-way the sins of the world: have mer-cy on us. Lamb of God, you take a-way the sins of the world: have mer-cy on us. Lamb of God, you take a-way the sins of the world: grant us peace.

Setting: Richard Felciano (b. 1930)

## The Holy Eucharist II
### Fraction Anthem: Lamb of God *Agnus Dei*

S 163

Lamb of God, you take a-way the sins of the world: have mer-cy on us. Lamb of God, you take a-way the sins of the world: have mer-cy on us. Lamb of God, you take a-way the sins of the world: grant us peace.

Setting: Robert Powell (b. 1932)

# S 164

## Fraction Anthem: Jesus, Lamb of God    *Agnus Dei*

Je - sus, Lamb of God: have mer - cy on us.

Je - sus, bear - er of our sins: have mer - cy on us.

Je - sus, re - deem - er, re - deem - er of the world:

give us your peace, give us your peace.

Setting: From *Deutsche Messe*; Franz Peter Schubert (1797-1828); arr. Richard Proulx (b. 1937)

# The Holy Eucharist
## Fraction Anthem: Jesus, Lamb of God   *Agnus Dei*

S 165

/ Je - sus, Lamb of   God:   have   mer - cy

on   us.   Je - sus, bear-er of our   sins:   have   mer - cy

on   us.   Je-sus, re-deem-er of the world:   give us your peace.

Setting: William Matthias (b. 1934)


# The Holy Eucharist
## Fraction Anthem: Jesus, Lamb of God   *Agnus Dei*

S 166

Je - sus, Lamb of   God:   have   mer - cy   on

us.   Je - sus, bear - er   of   our   sins:   have   mer - cy on   us.

Je - sus,   re - deem - er   of   the   world:   give   us   your   peace.

Setting: Gerald R. Near (b. 1942)

# S 167

## Fraction Anthem: The disciples knew the Lord Jesus

*This setting is not used in Lent.*

*Antiphon*
*Cantor; then All*

The dis-ci-ples knew the Lord Je-sus in the break-ing of the bread.

*Cantor*

1. The bread which we break, al-le-lu-ia,

is the com-mun-ion of the bo-dy of Christ. [Ant.]

*Cantor*

2. One bo-dy are we, al-le-lu-ia,

for though man-y we share one bread. [Ant.]

Setting: Mode 6 melody; adapt. Mason Martens (b. 1933)

# S 168

## Fraction Anthem: My flesh is food indeed

*Antiphon*
*Cantor; then All*

My flesh is food in-deed, and my blood is drink in-deed, says the Lord.

*Cantor*

Those who eat my flesh and drink my blood dwell in me and I in them. [Ant.]

Setting: Ambrosian chant; adapt. Mason Martens (b. 1933)

**Fraction Anthem: My flesh is food indeed**

S 169

*Cantor or Choir*

My flesh is food in - deed, and my blood is drink in -

deed, says the Lord. My Lord. Those who eat my

flesh and drink my blood dwell in me, and I in them. My

flesh is food in - deed, and my blood is drink in - deed, says the Lord.

Setting: Ray W. Urwin (b. 1950)

## The Holy Eucharist

**Fraction Anthem: Whoever eats this bread**

S 170

*Antiphon*
*Cantor; then All*

Who - ev - er eats this bread will live for ev - er.

*Cantor*

1. This is the true bread which comes down from hea - ven

and gives life to the world. [Ant.] 2. Who - ev - er

believes in me shall not hun - ger or thirst, for the bread

which I give for the life of the world is my flesh. [Ant.]

Setting: Mode 1 melody; adapt. Mason Martens (b. 1933)

# S 171

## Fraction Anthem: Be known to us

*This setting is not used in Lent.*

Be known to us, Lord Je - sus, in the break - ing of the bread.

1. The bread which we break, al - le - lu - ia,

is the com - mun - ion of the bo - dy of Christ. [Ant.]

2. One bo - dy are we, al - le - lu - ia,

for though man - y we share one bread. [Ant.]

Setting: Mode 6 melody; adapt. Mason Martens (b. 1933)

# S 172

## Fraction Anthem: Blessed are those who are called

Bless - ed are those who are called to the Sup - per of the Lamb.

Praise the Lord, all you nations; laud him, all you peo - ples.

For his loving - kindness toward us is great, and the

faithfulness of the Lord endures for ev - er. [Ant.]

Setting: Ambrosian chant; adapt. Mason Martens (b. 1933)

# The Holy Eucharist
## The Episcopal Blessing: Responses

*Bishop*

Our help is in the Name of the Lord;

*People*

The maker of heaven and earth.

*Bishop*

Blessed be the Name of the Lord;

*People*

From this time forth for ever - more.

*The Bishop sings the blessing.*

# The Holy Eucharist
## Dismissals

*Deacon*          *People*

Let us go forth in the name of Christ. Thanks be to God.

or

*Deacon*          *People*

Go in peace to love and serve the Lord. Thanks be to God.

or

*Deacon*

Let us go forth into the world, rejoicing in the pow - er of the Spi - rit.

*People*

Thanks be to God.

or

*Deacon*          *People*

Let us bless the Lord. Thanks be to God.

# S 175

## Dismissals in Easter Season

*Deacon*

Let us go forth in the name of Christ, al - le - lu - ia,

al - le - lu - ia.

*People*

Thanks be to God, al - le - lu - ia, al - le - lu - ia.

*or*

*Deacon*

Go in peace to love and serve the Lord, al - le - lu - ia,

al - le - lu - ia.

*People*

Thanks be to God, al - le - lu - ia, al - le - lu - ia.

*or*

*Deacon*

Let us go forth into the world, rejoicing in the power of the Spi - rit,

al - le - lu - ia, al - le - lu - ia.

*People*

Thanks be to God, al - le - lu - ia, al - le - lu - ia.

*or the following*

Deacon

Let us bless the Lord, al - le - lu - ia, al - le - lu - ia.

People

Thanks be to God, al - le - lu - ia, al - le - lu - ia.

# The Holy Eucharist
## Dismissals in Easter Season

S 176

Deacon

Let us go forth in the name of Christ, al - le - lu - ia, al - le - lu - ia.

People

Thanks be to God, al - le - lu - ia, al - le - lu - ia.

*or*

Deacon

Go in peace to love and serve the Lord, al - le - lu - ia, al - le - lu - ia.

People

Thanks be to God, al - le - lu - ia, al - le - lu - ia.

*or the following*

*Deacon*

Let us go forth into the world, rejoicing in the pow-er of the Spi-rit, al-le-lu-ia, al-le-lu-ia.

*People*

Thanks be to God, al-le-lu-ia, al-le-lu-ia.

*or*

*Deacon*

Let us bless the Lord, al-le-lu-ia, al-le-lu-ia.

*People*

Thanks be to God, al-le-lu-ia, al-le-lu-ia.

Setting: From *Missa orbis factor*; Plainsong, Tonus Peregrinus; adapt. David Hurd (b. 1950)

# Canticles

## Canticle 1
## A Song of Creation  *Benedicite, omnia opera Domini*

*This Canticle may be shortened by omitting section II or III.*

**I Invocation**

1. O all ye works of the Lord, bless ye the Lord; praise him and magnify him for ev - er. 2. O ye angels of the Lord, bless ye the Lord; praise him and magnify him for ev - er.

**II The Cosmic Order**

3. O ye heavens, bless ye the Lord; O ye waters that be above the firmament, bless ye the Lord; 4. O all ye powers of the Lord, bless ye the Lord; praise him and magnify him for ev - er.

5. O ye sun and moon, bless ye the Lord; O ye stars of heaven,

S 177

bless ye the Lord; 6. O ye showers and dew, bless ye the Lord;

praise him and magnify him for ev - er. 7. O ye winds of God,

bless ye the Lord; O ye fire and heat, bless ye the Lord;

8. O ye winter and summer, bless ye the Lord; praise him and magnify

him for ev - er. 9. O ye dews and frosts, bless ye the Lord;

O ye frost and cold, bless ye the Lord; 10. O ye ice and snow,

bless ye the Lord; praise him and magnify him for ev - er.

11. O ye nights and days, bless ye the Lord; O ye light and darkness,

bless ye the Lord; 12. O ye lightnings and clouds,

bless ye the Lord; praise him and magnify him for ev - er.

## III The Earth and its Creatures

13. O let the earth bless the Lord; O ye mountains and hills,

bless ye the Lord; 14. O all ye green things upon the earth,

bless ye the Lord; praise him and magnify him for ev - er.

15. O ye wells, bless ye the Lord; O ye seas and floods, bless ye the Lord;

16. O ye whales and all that move in the waters, bless ye the Lord;

praise him and magnify him for ev - er. 17. O all ye fowls of the air,

bless ye the Lord; O all ye beasts and cattle, bless ye the Lord;

18. O ye children of men, bless ye the Lord; praise him and magnify him for ev - er.

## IV The People of God

19. O ye people of God, bless ye the Lord; O ye priests of the Lord,

bless ye the Lord; 20. O ye servants of the Lord, bless ye the Lord;

praise him and magnify him for ev - er. 21. O ye spirits and souls of righteousness, bless ye the Lord; O ye holy and humble men of heart, bless ye the Lord. 22. Let us bless the Father, the Son, and the Ho - ly Spi - rit; praise him and magnify him for ev - er.

Setting: Plainsong, Tonus Peregrinus, verses 1-2, 19-22; Plainsong, Tone 1, verses 3-18;
    adapt. The Standing Commission on Church Music, 1979

## Canticle 1

### A Song of Creation    *Benedicite, omnia opera Domini*

S 178    Stephen Elvey (1805-1860)    S 179    John F. Burrows (19th. cent.)

*This canticle may be shortened by omitting section II or III. The entire Canticle, or section I with section II or III and section IV, may be sung to a double chant.*

**I    Invocation**

1    O all ye works of the Lord, ˈbless ye the ˈLord; *
    praise him and ˈmagnify ˈhim for ˈever.

2    O ye angels of the Lord, ˈbless ye the ˈLord; *
    praise him and ˈmagnify ˈhim for ˈever.

# S 178

John Robinson
(1682-1762)

# S 179

Jonathan Battishill
(1738-1801)

**II   The Cosmic Order**

3   O ye heavens, ⌐bless ye the⌐Lord; *

    O ye waters that be above the⌐firmament, ⌐bless ye the⌐Lord;

4   O all ye powers of the Lord, ⌐bless ye the⌐Lord; *

    praise him and⌐magnify⌐him for⌐ever.

5   O ye sun and moon, ⌐bless ye the⌐Lord; *

    O ye stars of⌐heaven, ⌐bless ye the⌐Lord;

6   O ye showers and dew, ⌐bless ye the⌐Lord; *

    praise him and⌐magnify⌐him for⌐ever.

7   O ye winds of God, ⌐bless ye the⌐Lord; *

    O ye fire and⌐heat, ⌐bless ye the⌐Lord;

8   O ye winter and summer, ⌐bless ye the⌐Lord; *

    praise him and⌐magnify⌐him for⌐ever.

9   O ye dews and frosts, ⌐bless ye the⌐Lord; *

    O ye frost and⌐cold, ⌐bless ye the⌐Lord;

10   O ye ice and snow, ⌐bless ye the⌐Lord; *

    praise him and⌐magnify⌐him for⌐ever.

11   O ye nights and days, ⌐bless ye the⌐Lord; *

    O ye light and⌐darkness, ⌐bless ye the⌐Lord;

12   O ye lightnings and clouds, ⌐bless ye the⌐Lord; *

    praise him and⌐magnify⌐him for⌐ever.

## S 178

James Turle
(1802-1882)

## S 179

Jonathan Battishill
(1738-1801)

**III   The Earth and its Creatures**

13   O let the earth ' bless the ' Lord; *

    O ye mountains and ' hills, ' bless ye the ' Lord;

14   O all ye green things upon the earth, ' bless ye the ' Lord; *

    praise him and ' magnify ' him for ' ever.

15   O ye wells, ' bless ye the ' Lord; *

    O ye seas and ' floods, ' bless ye the ' Lord;

16   O ye whales and all that move in the waters, ' bless ye the ' Lord; *

    praise him and ' magnify ' him for ' ever.

17   O all ye fowls of the air, ' bless ye the ' Lord; *

    O all ye beasts and ' cattle, ' bless ye the ' Lord;

18   O ye children of men, ' bless ye the ' Lord; *

    praise him and ' magnify ' him for ' ever.

S 178     Stephen Elvey (1805-1860)

S 179     John F. Burrows (19th cent.)

**IV    The People of God**

19   O ye people of God, 'bless ye the 'Lord; *

      O ye priests of the 'Lord, 'bless ye the 'Lord;

20   O ye servants of the Lord, 'bless ye the 'Lord; *

      praise him and 'magnify 'him for 'ever.

21   O ye spirits and souls of the righteous, 'bless ye the 'Lord; *

      O ye holy and humble men of 'heart, 'bless ye the 'Lord.

22   Let us bless the Father, the Son, and the 'Holy 'Spirit; *

      praise him and 'magnify 'him for 'ever.

# S 180

## A Song of Praise    *Benedictus es, Domine*

Canticle 2

*Antiphon*

Pro - claim the great-ness of the Lord our God: he is the Ho - ly One.

1. Bless - ed art thou, O Lord God of our fa - thers; praised and exalted above all for ev - er.

2. Blessed art thou for the Name of thy Maj - es - ty; praised and exalted above all for ev - er.

3. Blessed art thou in the temple of thy ho - li - ness; praised and exalted above all for ev - er.

4. Blessed art thou that beholdest the depths, and dwellest between the Cher - u - bim; praised and exalted above all for ev - er.

5. Blessed art thou on the glorious throne of thy king - dom; praised and exalted above all for ev - er.

6. Blessed art thou in the firmament of hea - ven, praised and exalted above all for ev - er.

7. Blessed art thou, O Father, Son, and Holy Spi - rit; praised and exalted above all for ev - er. [Ant.]

Setting: Plainsong, Tone 8; adapt. Bruce E. Ford (b. 1947)

# Canticle 2
## A Song of Praise    *Benedictus es, Domine*

S 181 — George A. MacFarren (1813-1887)

S 182 — John Jones (1757-1833)

S 183 — J. Soaper (1743-1794)

S 184 — John Goss (1800-1880)

1 Blessèd art thou, O Lord ˈGod of our ˈfathers; *
   praised and exalted aˈbove ˈall for ˈever.
2 Blessèd art thou for the ˈName of thy ˈMajesty; *
   praised and exalted aˈbove ˈall for ˈever.
3 Blessèd art thou in the ˈtemple of thy ˈholiness; *
   praised and exalted aˈbove ˈall for ˈever.
4 Blessèd art thou that beholdest the depths,
   and dwellest beˈtween the ˈCherubim; *
   praised and exalted aˈbove ˈall for ˈever.
5 Blessèd art thou on the glorious ˈthrone of thy ˈkingdom; *
   praised and exalted aˈbove ˈall for ˈever.
6 Blessèd art thou in the ˈfirmament of ˈheaven; *
   praised and exalted aˈbove ˈall for ˈever.
†7 Blessèd art thou, O Father, Son, and ˈHoly ˈSpirit; *
   praised and exalted aˈbove ˈall for ˈever.

† *Second half of double chant.*

# S 185

The Song of Mary    *Magnificat*

Antiphon

He that is might-y hath mag-ni-fied me:    and ho-ly    is his Name.

1. My    soul    doth    mag - ni - fy    the Lord,    and my    spi - rit

hath    rejoiced    in    God my Sav - ior.    2. For he    hath re - gard - ed

the    low - li-ness of    his hand-maid-en.    3. For be - hold from hence-forth

all gen - er - a - tions shall call me bless - ed.    4. For he    that    is

might - y    hath    mag - ni - fied    me,    and ho - ly    is his Name.

5. And his    mer - cy    is    on    them that fear him through-out all gen-er - a - tions.

6. He    hath    showed    strength with his    arm;    he hath scat - tered the

proud in the imagi - na - tion of their hearts. 7. He hath put

down the might - y from their seat, and hath ex - alt - ed the

hum - ble and meek. 8. He hath filled the hun - gry with good things,

and the rich he hath sent emp - ty a - way. 9. He re -

mem - ber - ing his mer - cy hath hol - pen his ser - vant Is - ra - el,

as he prom - ised to our forefathers, Abraham and his seed for ev - er. [Ant.]

*(Gloria Patri may be omitted)*

10. Glo - ry to the Fa - ther, and to the Son, and to the Ho - ly Spi - rit:

11. As it was in the be - gin - ning, is now, and will be for ev - er. A - men.

[Ant.]

Setting: Mode 8 antiphon; adapt. Bruce E. Ford (b. 1947).
      Plainsong, Tone 8 (Solemn); adapt. Charles Winfred Douglas (1867-1944), alt.

## The Song of Mary  *Magnificat*

### S 186

William Crotch
(1775-1847)

### S 187

Samuel Wesley
(1766-1837)

### S 188

Henry Walford Davies
(1869-1941)

### S 189

Benjamin Hutto
(b. 1947)

1   My soul doth ʹmagnify the ʹLord, *
   and my spirit hath reʹjoiced in ʹGod my ʹSavior.

2   For ʹhe hath reʹgarded *
   the ʹlowliness ʹof his ʹhandmaiden.

3   For beʹhold from ʹhenceforth *
   all generʹations shall ʹcall me ʹblessed.

4   For he that is mighty hath ʹmagnified ʹme, *
   and ʹholy ʹis his ʹName.

†5  And his mercy is on ʹthem that ʹfear him *
   throughout ʹall ʹgenerʹations.

6   He hath showed ʹstrength with his ʹarm; *
   he hath scattered the proud in the imagiʹnation ʹof their ʹhearts.

7   He hath put down the ʹmighty from their ʹseat, *
   and hath exʹalted the ʹhumble and ʹmeek.

8   He hath filled the ʹhungry with ʹgood things, *
   and the rich he hath ʹsent ʹempty aʹway.

9   He remembering his mercy hath holpen his ʹservant ʹIsrael, *
   as he promised to our forefathers, ʹ
   Abraham and his ʹseed for ʹever.

*(Gloria Patri may be omitted)*

Glory to the Father, and ʹto the ʹSon, *
   and ʹto the ʹHoly ʹSpirit:
As it was in the beʹginning, is ʹnow, *
   and ʹwill be for ʹever. Aʹmen.

---

† *Second half of double chant*

# S 190

## The Song of Zechariah  *Benedictus Dominus Deus*

*Antiphon*

Through the ten - der mer - cy of our God,

the day - spring from on high hath vis - it - ed us.

1. Bless - ed be the Lord God of Is - ra - el, for he hath visited and redeemed

his peo - ple; 2. And hath raised up a mighty sal - va - tion for us

in the house of his ser - vant Da - vid, 3. As he spake by the mouth of

his ho - ly pro - phets, which have been since the world be - gan: 4. That we should be

saved from our en - e - mies, and from the hand of all that hate us;

5. To perform the mercy prom - ised to our fore - fa - thers,

and to remember his ho - ly cov - e - nant; 6. To perform the oath which he

sware to our fore - fa - ther A - bra - ham, that he would give us,

7. That we being delivered out of the hand of our en - e - mies might serve him with - out fear, 8. In holiness and right - eous - ness be - fore him, all the days of our life. 9. And thou, child, shalt be called the pro - phet of the High - est, for thou shalt go before the face of the Lord to pre - pare his ways; 10. To give knowledge of salvation un - to his peo - ple for the remis - sion of their sins, 11. Through the tend - er mer - cy of our God, whereby the day spring from on high hath vis - it - ed us; 12. To give light to them that sit in darkness and in the shad - ow of death, and to guide our feet into the way of peace. [Ant.]

*(Gloria Patri may be omitted)*

13. Glo - ry to the Fa - ther, and to the Son, and to the Ho - ly Spi - rit: 14. As it was in the be - gin - ning, is now, and will be for ev - er. A - men.

[Ant.]

Setting: Plainsong, Tonus Peregrinus; adapt. Bruce E. Ford (b. 1947)

## The Song of Zechariah    *Benedictus Dominus Deus*

S 191 — Edward John Hopkins (1818-1901)

S 192 — Thomas Attwood (1765?-1838)

S 193 — George Mursell Garrett (1834-1897)

S 194 — Richard Lloyd (b. 1933)

S 195 — William Morley (1680-1731)

1   Blessèd be the Lord'God of'Israel, *
      for he hath'visited and re'deemed his'people;

2   And hath raised up a mighty sal'vation'for us *
      in the'house of his'servant'David,

3   As he spake by the mouth of his'holy'prophets, *
      which have'been since the'world be'gan:

4   That we should be'saved from our'enemies, *
      and from the'hand of'all that'hate us;

5   To perform the mercy'promised to our'forefathers, *
      and to re'member his'holy'covenant;

6   To perform the oath which he sware to our'forefather'Abraham, *
      that'he would'give'us,

7   That we being delivered out of the'hand of our'enemies *
      might'serve him with'out'fear,

8   In holiness and'righteousness be'fore him, *
      — 'all the'days of our'life.

9   And thou, child, shalt be called the'prophet of the'Highest, *
      for thou shalt go before the face of the'Lord to pre'pare his'ways;

10   To give knowledge of salvation'unto his'people *
      for the re'mission'of their'sins,

11   Through the tender'mercy of our'God, *
      whereby the dayspring from on'high hath'visited'us;

12   To give light to them that sit in darkness
      and in the'shadow of'death, *
      and to guide our'feet into the'way of'peace.

*(Gloria Patri may be omitted)*

Glory to the Father, and'to the'Son, *
      and'to the'Holy'Spirit:

As it was in the be'ginning, is'now, *
      and'will be for'ever. A'men.

# S 196

**The Song of Simeon**  *Nunc dimittis*

Canticle 5

Antiphon

Mine eyes have seen thy sal - va - tion, which thou hast pre - pared be - fore the face of all peo - ple.

1. Lord, now lettest thou thy ser - vant de - part in peace, ac - cord - ing to thy word;

2. For mine eyes have seen thy sal - va - tion, which thou hast prepared before the face of all peo - ple,

3. To be a light to light - en the Gen - tiles, and to be the glory of thy peo - ple Is - ra - el. [Ant.]

*(Gloria Patri may be omitted)*

4. Glo - ry to the Fa - ther, and to the Son, and to the Ho - ly Spi - rit:

5. As it was in the be - gin-ning, is now, and will be for ev- er. A - men.

[Ant.]

Setting: Mode 7 antiphon; adapt. Bruce E. Ford (b. 1947). Plainsong, Tone 7;
adapt. The Standing Commission on Church Music, 1979

# Canticle 5
## The Song of Simeon    *Nunc dimittis*

**S 197** — John Naylor (1838-1897)

**S 198** — Frederick A. Gore Ouseley (1825-1909)

**S 199** — John Blow (1649?-1708)

**S 200** — Michael Wise (1648?-1687)

1  Lord, now lettest thou thy servant de|part in |peace, *
   ac|cording |to thy |word;

2  for mine eyes have |seen thy sal|vation, *
   which thou hast prepared before the |face of |all |people,

3  To be a light to |lighten the |Gentiles, *
   and to be the |glory of thy |people |Israel.

   *(Gloria Patri may be omitted)*

   Glory to the Father, and |to the |Son, *
   and |to the |Holy |Spirit:

   As it was in the be|ginning, is |now, *
   and |will be for|ever. A|men.

# S 201

**Glory be to God** *Gloria in excelsis*

Canticle 6

1. Glo - ry be to God on high, and on earth peace, good will to - wards men. 2. We praise thee, we bless thee, we wor - ship thee, we glo - ri - fy thee, we give thanks to thee for thy great glo - ry, 3. O Lord God, heaven - ly King, God the Fa - ther Al - might - y. 4. O Lord, the on - ly - be - got - ten Son, Je - sus Christ; 5. O Lord God, Lamb of God, Son of the Fa - ther, that ta - kest a - way

the sins of the world, have mer - cy up - on us.

6. Thou that ta - kest a - way the sins of the world,

re - ceive our prayer. 7. Thou that sit - test at the right hand

of God the Fa - ther, have mer - cy up - on us.

8. For thou on - ly art ho - ly; thou on - ly art the Lord;

9. thou on - ly, O Christ, with the Ho - ly Ghost, art most

high in the glo - ry of God the Fa - ther. A - men.

Setting: John Merbecke (1510?-1585?); adapt. *Hymnal 1982*

# S 202

## Glory be to God    *Gloria in excelsis*

Canticle 6

1. Glo - ry be to God on high, and on earth peace,

good will towards men.  2. We praise thee,  we bless thee,

we wor - ship thee, we glo - ri - fy thee, we give

thanks to thee for thy great glo - ry, 3. O Lord God, heaven - ly

King, God ____ the Fa - ther Al - might - - - y. ____

4. O Lord, the on - ly be - got - ten Son, Je - sus Christ;

5. O Lord God, Lamb of God, Son of the Fa - ther, that

ta - kest a - way the sins of the world, have mer - cy up -

on us. 6. Thou that ta - kest a - way the sins of the

world, re - ceive our prayer. 7. Thou that sit - test at the

right hand of God the Fa - ther, have mer - cy up - on us.

8. For thou on - ly art ho - ly; thou on - ly art the Lord; 9. thou

on - ly, O Christ, with the Ho - ly Ghost, art most

high in the glo - ry of God the Fa - ther. ____

A - men.

Setting: From *Missa de Sancta Maria Magdalena,* Healey Willan (1880-1968)

# S 203

## Glory be to God　　*Gloria in excelsis*

1. Glo - ry be to God on high, and on earth peace, good will to - wards men.
2. We praise thee, we bless thee, we wor - ship thee, we glo - ri - fy thee, we give thanks to thee for thy great glo - ry,
3. O Lord God, hea - ven - ly King, God the Fa - ther Al - might - y.
4. O Lord, the on - ly be - got - ten Son, Je - sus Christ;
5. O Lord God, Lamb of God, Son of the Fa - ther, that ta - kest a - way the

sins of the world, have mer - cy up - on us.

6. Thou that ta - kest a - way the sins of the world,

re - ceive our prayer. 7. Thou that sit - test at the

right hand of God the Fa - ther, have mer - cy up - on us.

8. For thou on - ly art ho - ly; thou on - ly art the

Lord; thou on - ly, O Christ, with the Ho - ly

Ghost, art most high in the glo - ry of God the

Fa - ther. A - - men.

Setting: From *Missa Marialis*; Plainsong, Mode 8; Mass 9; adapt. Charles Winfred Douglas (1867-1944)

**Glory be to God**        *Gloria in excelsis*

1. Glory be to God on high, and on earth peace, good will towards men.

2. We praise thee, we bless thee, we wor-ship thee, we glorify thee, we give thanks

to thee for thy great glo - ry, 3. O Lord God, heaven - ly King,

God the Father Al - might - y. 4. O Lord, the only-begotten Son, Je - sus Christ;

O Lord God, Lamb of God, Son of the Fa - ther,

5. that takest away the sins of the world, have mercy up-on us.

6. Thou that takest away the sins of the world, re-ceive our prayer.

7. Thou that sittest at the right hand of God the Fa-ther, have mercy up-on us.

8. For thou on-ly art ho-ly; thou on-ly art the Lord; 9. Thou only, O Christ,

with the Ho-ly Ghost, art most high in the glory of God the Fa-ther. A - men.

Setting: *Old Scottish Chant*, from *Chants or Tunes for Particular Hymns*, 1763?, alt.

# S 205

## We Praise Thee  *Te Deum laudamus*

Canticle 7

1. We praise thee, O God; we acknowledge thee to be the Lord.

All the earth doth worship thee, the Father ev-er-last-ing.

2. To thee all Angels cry aloud, the Heavens and all the Powers there-in.

To thee Cherubim and Seraphim con - tin-ual-ly do cry:

3. Ho-ly, ho-ly, ho-ly, Lord God of Sa - ba-oth;

Heaven and earth are full of the majesty of thy glo - ry.

4. The glorious company of the apostles praise thee. The goodly

fellowship of the pro-phets praise thee. 5. The noble army of

martyrs praise thee. The holy Church throughout all the world

Setting: Plainsong, Tone 8; adapt. Alastair Cassels-Brown (b. 1927)

**We Praise Thee**   *Te Deum laudamus*

**S 206**
Stephen Elvey
(1805-1860)

**S 207**
T. Norris
(1741-1790)

*The entire canticle may be sung to one double chant.*

1   We praise thee, O God; we acknowledge ' thee to be the ' Lord. *

All the earth doth worship ' thee, the ' Father ever ' lasting.

2   To thee all ' Angels cry a ' loud, *

the Heavens and ' all the ' Powers there ' in.

3   To thee Cherubim and ' Sera ' phim *

con ' tinual ' ly do ' cry:

4   Holy, holy, holy, Lord ' God of ' Sabaoth; *

Heaven and earth are full of the ' majesty ' of thy ' glory.

5   The glorious company of the a ' postles ' praise thee. *

The goodly ' fellowship of the ' prophets ' praise thee.

6   The noble army of ' martyrs ' praise thee. *

The holy Church throughout all the ' world doth ac ' knowledge ' thee,

†7   The Father, of an ' infinite ' majesty, *

thine adorable, true, and only Son,

also the ' Holy ' Ghost the ' Comforter.

*†Second half of double chant.*

**S 206**
Richard Farrant
(1525?-1580)

## S 207

William Henry Havergal
(1793-1870)

8  Thou art the King of | glory, O | Christ. *
   Thou art the ever | lasting | Son of the | Father.

9  When thou tookest upon thee to de | liver | man, *
   thou didst humble thy | self to be | born of a | Virgin.

10 When thou hadst overcome the | sharpness of | death, *
   thou didst open the kingdom of | heaven to | all be | lievers.

11 Thou sittest at the right hand of God, in the | glory of the | Father. *
   We believe that thou shalt | come to | be our | judge.

## S 206

Stephen Elvey
(1805-1860)

## S 207

T. Norris
(1741-1790)

12 We therefore pray thee, | help thy | servants, *
   whom thou hast re | deemed with thy | precious | blood.

13 Make them to be | numbered with thy | saints, *
   in | glory | ever | lasting.

# S 208

**Canticle 8**

## The Song of Moses    *Cantemus Domino*

*Antiphon*

Al - le - lu - ia, al - le - lu - ia, al - le - lu - ia.

*Antiphon in Lent and at the Easter Vigil*

I will sing to the Lord for he has ris - en up in might.

*Antiphon in Easter Season*

I will sing to the Lord for he has ris - en up in might, al - le - lu - ia.

1. I will sing to the Lord, for he is lofty and up - lift - ed;
the horse and its rider has he hurled in - to the sea. 2. The Lord is my
strength and my re - fuge; the Lord has be - come my Sa - vior.
3. This is my God and I will praise him, the God of my people and I
will ex - alt him. 4. The Lord is a might - y war - rior;
Yah - weh is his Name. 5. The chariots of Pharaoh and his army has
he hurled in - to the sea; the finest of those who bear armor have been
drowned in the Red Sea. 6. The fathomless deep has o - ver - whelmed them;
they sank into the depths like a stone. 7. Your right hand, O Lord, is glor - ious

in might; your right hand, O Lord, has overthrown the en - e - my.

8. Who can be compared with you, O Lord, a - mong the gods? Who is like you,

glorious in holiness, awesome in renown, and worker of won - ders?

9. You stretched forth your right hand; the earth swal - lowed them up.

10. With your constant love you led the peo - ple you re - deemed;

with your might you brought them in safety to your ho - ly dwell - ing.

11. You will bring them in and plant them on the mount of your pos -

ses - sion, 12. The resting - place you have made for your - self, O Lord,

the sanctuary, O Lord, that your hand has es - tab - lished.

13. The Lord shall reign for ever and for ev - er. [Ant.]

*(Gloria Patri may be omitted)*

14. Glo - ry to the Fa - ther, and to the Son, and to the Ho - ly Spi - rit:

15. As it was in the be - gin - ning, is now, and will be for ev - er. A - men. [Ant.]

Setting: Mode 1 antiphons, adapt. Bruce E. Ford (b. 1947). Plainsong, tone 1, verses 1-3, 10-15; Plainsong, Tonus Peregrinus, verses 4-9; adapt. Norman Mealy (b. 1923)

S 209

James Turle
(1802 - 1882)

S 210

Richard Wayne Dirksen
(b. 1921)

S 211

Henry Edward Dibdin
(1813-1866)

S 212

Daniel Pinkham
(b. 1923)

1 I will sing to the Lord, for he is 'lofty and up'lifted; *
   the horse and its rider has he'hurled'into the'sea.

2 The Lord is my'strength and my'refuge; *
   the'Lord has be'come my'Savior.

3 This is my God and'I will'praise him, *
   the God of my'people and'I will ex'alt him.

4 The Lord is a'mighty'warrior; *
   — 'Yahweh'is his'Name.

5 The chariots of Pharaoh and his army has he'hurled into the'sea; *
   the finest of those who bear armor have been
       'drowned in the'Red'Sea.

6 The fathomless'deep has over'whelmed them; *
   they'sank into the'depths like a'stone.

7 Your right hand, O Lord, is'glorious in'might; *
   your right hand, O Lord, has'over'thrown the'enemy.

8 Who can be compared with you, O Lord, a'mong the'gods? *
   who is like you, glorious in holiness,
   awesome in re'nown, and'worker of'wonders?

9 You stretched forth your'right'hand; *
   the'earth'swallowed them'up.

10 With your constant love you led the'people you re'deemed; *
    with your might you brought them in
        'safety to your'holy'dwelling.

11 You will bring them'in and'plant them *
    on the'mount of'your pos'session,

12 The resting-place you have made for your'self, O'Lord, *
    the sanctuary, O'Lord, that your'hand has es'tablished.

†13 The'Lord shall'reign *
    for'ever'and for'ever.

   *(Gloria Patri may be omitted)*
   Glory to the Father, and'to the'Son, *
      and'to the'Holy'Spirit:
   As it was in the be'ginning, is'now, *
      and'will be for'ever. A'men.

†*Second half of double chant; for the triple chant, verse 13 and the Gloria Patri are sung to the entire chant*

# S 213

## The First Song of Isaiah     *Ecce, Deus*

**Canticle 9**

*Antiphon*

Sing the prais - es of the Lord, for he has done great things.

1. Sure - ly, it is God who saves me; I will trust in him and not

be a - fraid. 2. For the Lord is my stronghold and my sure de - fense,

and he will be my Sa - vior. 3. Therefore you shall draw water

with re - joic - ing from the springs of sal - va - tion.

4. And on that day you shall say, Give thanks to the Lord and call

up - on his Name; 5. Make his deeds known a - mong the peo - ples;

See that they remember that his Name is ex - alt - ed.

6. Sing the praises of the Lord, for he has done great things,

and this is known in all the world. 7. Cry aloud, inhabitants of

Zi - on, ring out your joy, for the great one in the

midst of you is the Holy One of Is - ra - el. [Ant.]

*(Gloria Patri may be omitted)*

Glory to the Fa - ther, and to the Son, and to the Ho - ly Spi - rit:

As it was in the be - gin - ning, is now, and will be for ev - er. A - men.

[Ant.]

Setting: Plainsong, Tone 3; adapt. Bruce E. Ford (b. 1947)

# The First Song of Isaiah    *Ecce, Deus*    Canticle 9

S 214    Ray Francis Brown
(1897–1965)

S 215    Robert Bremner
(1720–1789)

S 216    David Hurd
(b. 1950)

1    Surely, it is'God who'saves me; *
     I will trust in'him and'not be a'fraid.

2    For the Lord is my stronghold and my'sure de'fense, *
     and'he will'be my'Savior.

3    Therefore you shall draw'water with re'joicing *
     —'from the'springs of sal'vation.

4    And on that'day you shall'say, *
     Give thanks to the'Lord and'call upon his'Name;

†5    Make his deeds known a'mong the'peoples; *
     see that they re'member that his'Name is ex'alted.

6    Sing the praises of the Lord, for'he has done'great things, *
     and this is'known in'all the'world.

7    Cry aloud, inhabitants of Zion,'ring out your'joy, *
     for the great one in the midst of you is the'Holy'One of'Israel.

     *(Gloria Patri may be omitted)*

     Glory to the Father, and'to the'Son, *
     and'to the'Holy'Spirit: *
     As it was in the be'ginning, is'now, *
     and'will be for'ever. A'men.

†*Second half of double chant*

# Canticle 10
## The Second Song of Isaiah    *Quaerite Dominum*

S 217

1. Seek the Lord while he wills to be found; call upon him when he draws near.

2. Let the wicked for-sake their ways and the e-vil ones their thoughts;

3. And let them turn to the Lord, and he will have com-pas-sion, and to our God, for he will rich-ly par-don. 4. For my thoughts are not your thoughts,

nor your ways my ways, says the Lord. 5. For as the heavens are higher than the earth,

so are my ways higher than your ways, and my thoughts than your thoughts.

6. For as rain and snow fall from the hea-vens and return not again, but wa-ter the earth,

7. Bringing forth life and giv-ing growth, seed for sowing and bread for eat-ing,

8. So is my word that goes forth from my mouth; it will not return to me emp-ty;

9. But it will accomplish that which I have pur-posed, and prosper in that for which

*(Gloria Patri may be omitted)*

I sent it. 10. Glory to the Father, and to the Son, and to the Ho-ly Spi-rit:

11. As it was in the beginning, is now, and will be for ev-er. A-men.

Setting: Plainsong, Tone 2; adapt. The Standing Commission on Church Music, 1979, alt.

# The Second Song of Isaiah *Quaerite Dominum*

## S 218
John Goss
(1800-1880)

## S 219
Richard Clark
(1786-1856)

## S 220
Ned Rorem
(b. 1923)

## S 221
Henry Purcell (1659-1695)
arr. James Turle (1802-1882)

| 1 | Seek the Lord while he'wills to be'found; * |
|---|---|
|   | call up'on him when'he draws'near. |
| 2 | Let the wicked for'sake their'ways * |
|   | and the'evil'ones their'thoughts; |
| 3 | And let them turn to the Lord, and he will'have com'passion, * |
|   | and to our God, for'he will'richly'pardon. |
| 4 | For my thoughts'are not'your thoughts, * |
|   | nor your ways'my ways,'says the'Lord. |
| 5 | For as the heavens are'higher than the'earth, * |
|   | so are my ways higher than your ways, |
|   | and'my'thoughts than'your thoughts. |
| 6 | For as rain and snow'fall from the'heavens * |
|   | and return not a'gain, but'water the'earth, |
| †7 | Bringing forth life and'giving'growth, * |
|   | seed for'sowing and'bread for'eating, |
| 8 | So is my word that goes'forth from my'mouth; * |
|   | it will'not re'turn to me'empty; |
| 9 | But it will accomplish that which'I have'purposed, * |
|   | and prosper in'that for'which I'sent it. |

*(Gloria Patri may be omitted)*

Glory to the Father, and'to the'Son, *
and'to the'Holy'Spirit:
As it was in the be'ginning, is'now, *
and'will be for'ever. A'men.

† *Second half of double chant*

# Canticle 10

## The Second Song of Isaiah   *Quaerite Dominum*

S 222

1. Seek the Lord while he wills to be found;   call upon him when he draws near.

2. Let the wicked for - sake their ways   and the evil ones their thoughts;

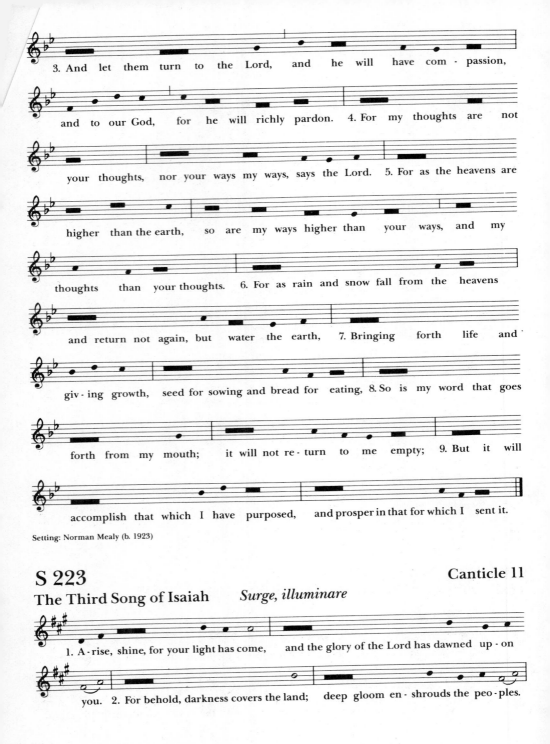

3. And let them turn to the Lord, and he will have com-passion,

and to our God, for he will richly pardon. 4. For my thoughts are not

your thoughts, nor your ways my ways, says the Lord. 5. For as the heavens are

higher than the earth, so are my ways higher than your ways, and my

thoughts than your thoughts. 6. For as rain and snow fall from the heavens

and return not again, but water the earth, 7. Bringing forth life and

giv-ing growth, seed for sowing and bread for eating, 8. So is my word that goes

forth from my mouth; it will not re-turn to me empty; 9. But it will

accomplish that which I have purposed, and prosper in that for which I sent it.

Setting: Norman Mealy (b. 1923)

# S 223
Canticle 11

## The Third Song of Isaiah *Surge, illuminare*

1. A-rise, shine, for your light has come, and the glory of the Lord has dawned up-on

you. 2. For behold, darkness covers the land; deep gloom en-shrouds the peo-ples.

3. But over you the Lord will rise, and his glory will ap-pear up-on you. 4. Nations will

stream to your light, and kings to the brightness of your dawn - ing. 5. Your gates will

always be o - pen; by day or night they will nev-er be shut. 6. They will call you,

The City of the Lord, The Zion of the Holy One of Is - ra - el. 7. Violence will

no more be heard in your land, ruin or destruction with - in your bor - ders.

8. You will call your walls, Sal - va - tion, and all your por - tals, Praise. 9. The sun will no

more be your light by day; by night you will not need the bright-ness of the moon.

10. The Lord will be your everlasting light, and your God will be your glo - ry.

11. Glory to the Father, and to the Son, and to the Ho - ly Spi - rit:

12. As it was in the beginning, is now, and will be for ev - er. A - men.

Setting: Plainsong, Tone 5, adapt. The Standing Commission on Church Music, 1979, alt.

# The Third Song of Isaiah *Surge, illuminare*

**S 224**

Cambridge Chant

**S 225**

Herbert S. Oakeley
(1830-1903)

**S 226**

W. H. Longhurst
(1819-1904)

**S 227**

J. Marcus Ritchie
(b. 1946)

1   Arise, shine, for your'light has'come, *
    and the glory of the'Lord has'dawned up'on you.

2   For behold, darkness'covers the'land; *
    deep'gloom en'shrouds the'peoples.

3   But over you the'Lord will'rise, *
    and his'glory will ap'pear up'on you.

4   Nations will'stream to your'light, *
    and kings to the'brightness'of your'dawning.

5   Your gates will'always be'open; *
    by day or'night they will'never be'shut.

6   They will call you, The'City of the'Lord, *
    The Zion of the'Holy'One of'Israel.

7   Violence will no more be'heard in your'land, *
    ruin or de'struction with'in your'borders.

8   You will call your'walls, Sal'vation, *
    and'all your'portals,'Praise.

9   The sun will no more be your'light by'day; *
    by night you will not'need the'brightness of the'moon.

10   The Lord will be your ever'lasting'light, *
    and your'God will'be your'glory.

*(Gloria Patri may be omitted)*

  Glory to the Father, and'to the'Son, *
    and'to the'Holy'Spirit:

  As it was in the be'ginning, is'now, *
    and'will be for'ever. A'men.

*Gloria Patri must be used with chant S 225.*

# S 228

**A Song of Creation** *Benedicite, omnia opera Domini*

Canticle 12

*One or more sections of this Canticle may be used. Whatever the selection, it begins with the Invocation and concludes with the Doxology.*

**Invocation**

1. Glo - rify the Lord, all you works of the Lord, praise him and highly

exalt him for ev - er. 2. In the firmament of his pow - er,

glo - ri - fy the Lord, praise him and highly exalt him for ev - er.

**I The Cosmic Order**

3. Glo - ri - fy the Lord, you angels and all pow - ers of the Lord,

O heavens and all waters a - bove the hea - vens. 4. Sun and moon and

stars of the sky, glo - ri - fy the Lord, praise him and highly exalt him for ev-

er. 5. Glo - ri - fy the Lord, every shower of rain and fall of dew,

all winds and fire and heat. 6. Winter and summer, glo - ri - fy the Lord, praise him and highly exalt him for ev - er. 7. Glo - ri - fy the Lord,

O chill and cold, drops of dew and flakes of snow. 8. Frost and cold,

ice and sleet, glo - ri - fy the Lord, praise him and highly exalt him

for ev - er. 9. Glo - ri - fy the Lord, O nights and days,

O shining light and en - fold - ing dark. 10. Storm clouds and thunderbolts,

glo - ri - fy the Lord, praise him and highly exalt him for ev - er.

## II The Earth and its Creatures

11. Let the earth glori - fy the Lord, praise him and highly ex - alt him for ev - er.

12. Glorify the Lord, O mountains and hills, and all that grows up - on the earth,

praise him and highly ex - alt him for ev - er. 13. Glorify the Lord, O springs

of water, seas, and streams, O whales and all that move in the wa - ters.

14. All birds of the air, glori-fy the Lord, praise him and highly ex-alt him for ev-er. 15. Glorify the Lord, O beasts of the wild, and all you flocks and herds. 16. O men and women everywhere, glori-fy the Lord, praise him and highly ex-alt him for ev-er.

**III The People of God**

17. Let the people of God glo-ri-fy the Lord, praise him and highly ex-alt him for ev-er. 18. Glorify the Lord, O priests and ser-vants of the Lord, praise him and highly ex-alt him for ev-er. 19. Glorify the Lord, O spirits and souls of the right-eous, praise him and highly ex-alt him for ev-er. 20. You that are holy and humble of heart, glo-ri-fy the Lord, praise him and highly ex-alt him for ev-er.

**Doxology**

21. Let us glorify the Lord: Father, Son, and Ho - ly Spi - rit;
praise him and highly exalt him for ev - er. 22. In the firmament of his
pow - er, glo - ri - fy the Lord, praise him and highly exalt him for ev - er.

Setting: Plainsong, Tonus Peregrinus, verses 1-2, 21-22; Plainsong, Tone 1, verses 3-10; Plainsong, Tone 4; verses 11-16; Plainsong, Tone 8, verses 17-20; adapt. The Standing Commission on Church Music, 1979, alt.

## Canticle 12
## A Song of Creation   *Benedicite, omnia opera Domini*

S 229    R. Goodson (1655-1719)

S 230    Edwin George Monk (1819-1909)

*One or more sections of this Canticle may be used. Whatever the selection, it begins with the Introduction and concludes with the Doxology. The entire Canticle, or the Introduction with one or more sections and the Doxology, may be sung to one double chant.*

### Invocation

1   Glorify the Lord, all you ' works of the ' Lord, *
    praise him and ' highly ex ' alt him for ' ever.

2   In the firmament of his power, ' glorify the ' Lord, *
    praise him and ' highly ex ' alt him for ' ever.

S 229 — William Crotch (1775-1847)

S 230 — Thomas Attwood (1765?-1838)

I  The Cosmic Order

3  Glorify the Lord, you angels and all⌐powers of the⌐Lord, *
  O heavens and all⌐waters a⌐bove the⌐heavens.

4  Sun and moon and stars of the sky,⌐glorify the⌐Lord, *
  praise him and⌐highly ex⌐alt him for⌐ever.

5  Glorify the Lord, every shower of rain and⌐fall of⌐dew, *
  all⌐winds and⌐fire and⌐heat.

6  Winter and summer,⌐glorify the⌐Lord, *
  praise him and⌐highly ex⌐alt him for⌐ever.

7  Glorify the Lord, O⌐chill and⌐cold, *
  drops of⌐dew and⌐flakes of⌐snow.

8  Frost and cold, ice and sleet,⌐glorify the⌐Lord, *
  praise him and⌐highly ex⌐alt him for⌐ever.

9  Glorify the Lord, O⌐nights and⌐days, *
  O shining⌐light and en⌐folding⌐dark.

10  Storm clouds and thunderbolts,⌐glorify the⌐Lord, *
  praise him and⌐highly ex⌐alt him for⌐ever.

# S 229

William Boyce
(1711-1779)

# S 230

John Goss
(1800-1880)

II  The Earth and its Creatures

11  Let the earth ˈglorify the ˈLord, *
      praise him and ˈhighly exˈalt him for ˈever.

12  Glorify the Lord, O mountains and hills,
      and all that ˈgrows upon the ˈearth, *
      praise him and ˈhighly exˈalt him for ˈever.

13  Glorify the Lord, O springs of water, ˈseas, and ˈstreams, *
      O whales and ˈall that ˈmove in the ˈwaters.

14  All birds of the air, ˈglorify the ˈLord, *
      praise him and ˈhighly exˈalt him for ˈever.

15  Glorify the Lord, O ˈbeasts of the ˈwild, *
      and ˈall you ˈflocks and ˈherds.

16  O men and women everywhere, ˈglorify the ˈLord, *
      praise him and ˈhighly exˈalt him for ˈever.

# S 229

William Crotch
(1775-1847)

# S 230

Thomas Attwood
(1765?-1838)

## III   The People of God

17   Let the people of God⎜glorify the⎜Lord, *
      praise him and⎜highly ex⎜alt him for⎜ever.

18   Glorify the Lord, O priests and⎜servants of the⎜Lord, *
      praise him and⎜highly ex⎜alt him for⎜ever.

19   Glorify the Lord, O spirits and⎜souls of the⎜righteous, *
      praise him and⎜highly ex⎜alt him for⎜ever.

20   You that are holy and humble of heart,⎜glorify the⎜Lord, *
      praise him and⎜highly ex⎜alt him for⎜ever.

# S 229

R. Goodson
(1655-1719)

# S 230

Edwin George Monk
(1819-1909)

## Doxology

21   Let us glorify the Lord: Father, Son, and⎜Holy⎜Spirit; *
      praise him and⎜highly ex⎜alt him for⎜ever.

22   In the firmament of his power,⎜glorify the⎜Lord, *
      praise him and⎜highly ex⎜alt him for⎜ever.

# Canticle 13
## A Song of Praise
*Benedictus es, Domine*

**S 231**

1. Glo-ry to you, Lord God of our fa-thers; you are worthy of praise; glo-ry to you. 2. Glory to you for the radiance of your ho-ly Name; we will praise you and highly ex-alt you for ev-er. 3. Glory to you in the splendor of your tem-ple; on the throne of your majesty, glo-ry to you. 4. Glory to you, seated between the Cher-u-bim; we will praise you and highly ex-alt you for ev-er. 5. Glory to you, beholding the depths; in the high vault of heaven, glo-ry to you. 6. Glory to you, Father, Son, and Holy Spi-rit; we will praise you and highly exalt you for ev-er.

Setting: Plainsong; Tone 8; adapt. The Standing Commission on Church Music, 1979, alt.

# A Song of Praise   *Benedictus es, Domine*

**S 232**   R. Tomlinson (19th cent.)   **S 233**   The Imperial Tune (ca. 1630)

**S 234**   Thomas Attwood (1765?-1838)

**S 235**   David Koehring (b. 1940)

1  Glory to you, Lord⸍God of our⸍fathers; *
    you are worthy of⸍präise;⸍glory to⸍you.

2  Glory to you for the radiance of your⸍holy⸍Name; *
    we will praise you and⸍highly ex⸍alt you for⸍ever.

3  Glory to you in the⸍splendor of your⸍temple; *
    on the throne of your⸍majesty,⸍glory to⸍you.

4  Glory to you, seated be⸍tween the⸍Cherubim; *
    we will praise you and⸍highly ex⸍alt you for⸍ever.

5  Glory to you, be⸍holding the⸍depths; *
    in the high vault of⸍heaven,⸍glory to⸍you.

6  Glory to you, Father, Son, and⸍Holy⸍Spirit; *
    we will praise you and⸍highly ex⸍alt you for⸍ever.

# Canticle 13
## A Song of Praise
*Benedictus es, Domine*

S 236

1. Glory to you, Lord God of our fathers; you are worthy of praise; glory to you.
2. Glory to you for the radiance of your holy Name; we will praise you and highly exalt you for ever.
3. Glory to you in the splendor of your temple; on the throne of your majesty, glory to you.
4. Glory to you, seated between the Cherubim; we will praise you and highly exalt you for ever.

*Descant*

5. Glory to you, _____ be -

5. Glory to you, _____ be - hold - ing the

hold - ing the depths; in the high vault of

depths; _____ in the high vault of hea·ven, glo - ry to

hea - ven, 6. Glo - ry to you, _____

you. _____ 6. Glo - ry to you, _____ Fa - ther,

\_\_\_ Fa - ther, Son, and Ho - ly Spi - rit; we will

Son, and Ho - ly Spi - rit; \_\_\_\_\_ we will praise you and

high - ly ex - alt you. Glo - ry to you! \_\_\_\_\_

high - ly ex - alt you for ev - er. _____

Setting: John Rutter (b. 1945)

# Canticle 14

## A Song of Penitence

*Kyrie Pantokrator*

S 237

*Antiphon*

Your mer - ci - ful prom - ise is be - yond all mea - sure;

it sur - pas - ses all that our minds can fath - om.

1. O Lord and Ruler of the hosts of hea - ven, God of Abraham,

Isaac, and Jacob, and of all their right - eous off - spring:

2. You made the heavens and the earth, with all their vast ar - ray.

3. All things quake with fear at your pres - ence; they tremble be -

cause of your power. 4. But your merciful promise is be -

yond all mea - sure; it surpasses all that our minds can fath - om.

5. O Lord, you are full of com - pas - sion, long-suffering,

and abound - ing in mer - cy. 6. You hold back your hand;

you do not pun - ish as we de - serve. 7. In your great goodness, Lord,

you have promised forgiveness to sin - ners, that they may repent

of their sin and be saved. 8. And now, O Lord, I bend the knee

of my heart, and make my appeal, sure of your gra - cious good - ness.

9. I have sinned, O Lord, I have sinned, and I know my wickedness

on - ly too well. 10. Therefore I make this prayer to you:

Forgive me, Lord, for - give me. 11. Do not let me per - ish

in my sin, nor condemn me to the depths of the earth.

12. For you, O Lord, are the God of those who re - pent,

and in me you will show forth your good - ness. 13. Unworthy as I am,

you will save me, in accordance with your great mer - cy,

and I will praise you without ceasing all the days of my life.

14. For all the powers of heaven sing your prais - es,

and yours is the glory to ages of a - ges. A - men.

Setting: Mode 3 antiphon, adapt. Bruce E. Ford (b. 1947). Plainsong, Tone 3, verses 1-4, 12-14; Plainsong, Irregular Tone, verses 5-11; adapt. The Standing Commission on Church Music, 1979

# A Song of Penitence  *Kyrie Pantokrator*

**S 238** Verses 1-11

Matthew Camidge
(1758-1844)

Verses 12-14

**S 239**

*Allison's Psalms*, 1599;
arr. Luke Flintoff (1678-1727)

**S 240**

Ned Rorem
(b. 1923)

**S 241**

Samuel Wesley
(1766-1837)

1  O Lord and Ruler of  the ' hosts of ' heaven, *
    God of Abraham, Isaac, and Jacob,
    and of ' all their ' righteous ' offspring:

2  You made the ' heavens and the ' earth, *
    with ' all their ' vast ar ' ray.

3  All things quake with ' fear at your ' presence; *
    they ' tremble be ' cause of your ' power.

4  But your merciful promise is be ' yond all ' measure; *
    it surpasses ' all that our ' minds can ' fathom.

5  O Lord, you are ' full of com ' passion, *
    long- ' suffering, and a ' bounding in ' mercy.

6  You hold ' back your ' hand; *
    you do not ' punish as ' we de ' serve.

7  In your great goodness, Lord, you have promised for ' giveness to ' sinners, *
    that they may re ' pent of their ' sin and be ' saved.

8  And now, O Lord, I bend the ' knee of my ' heart, *
    and make my appeal, ' sure of your ' gracious ' goodness.

9  I have sinned, O ' Lord, I have ' sinned, *
    and I know my ' wickedness ' only too ' well.

10  Therefore I ' make this ' prayer to you: *
    For ' give me, ' Lord, for ' give me.

†11  Do not let me ' perish in my ' sin, *
    nor condemn me to the ' depths ' of the ' earth.

12  For you, O Lord, are the God of ' those who re ' pent, *
    and in me ' you will show ' forth your ' goodness.

13  Unworthy as I am, you will save me,
    in accordance with your ' great ' mercy, *
    and I will praise you without ' ceasing all the ' days of my ' life.

†14  For all the powers of heaven ' sing your ' praises, *
    and yours is the glory to ' ages of ' ages. A ' men.

†*Second half of double chant if the Camidge tunes, S 238, are used together.*

# S 242

## Canticle 15

## The Song of Mary   *Magnificat*

*Antiphon*

The  Al - might - y  has  done  great  things  for  me,

and  ho - ly  is  his  Name.

1. My  soul proclaims the greatness of the Lord, my  spirit  rejoices

in  God  my  Sa - vior;  for  he  has  looked  with  favor  on  his

low - ly  ser - vant.  2. From  this  day  all  generations will

call  me  bless - ed:  the  Almighty  has  done  great  things  for  me,

and ho - ly  is  his  Name.  3. He  has mercy on those who fear him

in  every gen - er - a - tion.  4. He  has shown the strength of  his  arm, he has scattered the proud in their con - ceit. 5. He has cast down

the might - y from their thrones, and has lifted up the low - ly.

6. He has filled the hun-gry with good things, and the rich he has sent a - way

emp - ty. 7. He has come to the help of his ser - vant Is - ra - el,

for he has remembered his promise of mer - cy, 8. The promise he

made to our fa - thers, to Abraham and his children for ev - er. [Ant.]

*(Gloria Patri may be omitted)*

9. Glo - ry to the Fa - ther, and to the Son, and to the Ho - ly Spi - rit:

10. As it was in the be - gin-ning, is now, and will be for ev - er. A - men.

[Ant.]

Setting: Plainsong, *Tonus Peregrinus*; adapt. Bruce E. Ford (b. 1947)

## The Song of Mary   *Magnificat*

**S 243**

William Henry Havergal
(1793-1870)

**S 244**

George Mursell Garrett
(1834-1897)

**S 245**

Benjamin Hutto
(b. 1947)

**S 246**

W. Lawes (1596-1662);
arr. Joseph Corfe (1790 1820)

1 My soul proclaims the greatness of the Lord,
   my spirit rejoices in'God my'Savior; *
     for he has looked with'favor on his'lowly'servant.

2 From this day all generations will'call me'blessed: *
     the Almighty has done great things for me,
     and'holy'is his'Name.

3 He has mercy on'those who'fear him *
     in'every'gener'ation.

4 He has shown the'strength of his'arm, *
     he has scattered the'proud in'their con'ceit.

5 He has cast down the'mighty from their'thrones, *
     and has'lifted'up the'lowly.

6 He has filled the'hungry with'good things, *
     and the'rich he has'sent away'empty.

7 He has come to the help of his'servant'Israel, *
     for he has re'membered his'promise of'mercy,

8 The promise he'made to our'fathers, *
     to'Abraham and his'children for'ever.

*(Gloria Patri may be omitted)*

Glory to the Father, and'to the'Son, *
     and'to the'Holy'Spirit:
As it was in the be'ginning, is'now, *
     and'will be for'ever. A'men.

# S 247

Canticle 15

## The Song of Mary     *Magnificat*

Antiphon
Unison or harmony

1. My soul pro - claims the great - ness

1. My soul pro -

of the Lord, my spi - rit re - joic - es in

claims the great - ness of the Lord, my

God my Sa - vior; for he has looked

spi - rit re - joic - es in God;

with fa - vor on his low - ly ser - vant.

2 From this day all generations will     call    me    blessed:
3 He has mercy on                   those   who   fear him
4 He has shown the .   .   .   .   . strength of his    arm,
5 He has cast down the mighty        from    their    thrones,
6 He has filled the hungry with      good     _____    things,
7 He has come to the help of his .   .   . ser - vant    Israel,
8 The promise he made                to     our    fathers,
9 Glory to the Father, and            to     the    Son,
10 As it was in the be -   .   .   .   . ginning,    is    now,

2 the Almighty has done great things for me, and holy    is    his Name.
3 in                                   every   gen - er - ation. [Ant.]
4 he has scattered the .   .   .   .   . proud in their   con - ceit.
5 and has                         lifted   up    the   lowly. [Ant.]
6 and the rich he has             sent    a - way empty.
7 for he has remembered his .   .   .   . prom - ise    of   mercy,
8 to Abraham and his             chil - dren   for   ever. [Ant.]
9 and                           to the   Ho - ly   Spirit.
10 and will be for .   .   .   .   .   . ev - er.    A - men. [Ant.]

*The Antiphon may be sung in unison, with the counter-melody played by an instrument, or it may be sung in three parts.*

Setting: *Cathedral of the Isles*, Betty Carr Pulkingham (b. 1928)

# S 248

**The Song of Zechariah**  *Benedictus Dominus Deus*

Antiphon

In the ten - der com - pas - sion of our God

the dawn from on high shall break up - on us.

1. Bless - ed be the Lord, the God of Is - ra - el; he has come

to his peo - ple and set them free. 2. He has raised up for us

a mighty sa - vior, born of the house of his ser - vant Da - vid.

3. Through his holy prophets he promised of old, that he would save us

from our en - e - mies, from the hands of all who hate us.

4. He prom - ised to show mercy to our fa - thers and to remember his

ho - ly cov - e - nant. 5. This was the oath he swore to our father

A - bra - ham, to set us free from the hands of our en - e - mies,

6. Free to worship him with-out fear, holy and righteous in his sight all the

days of our life. 7. You, my child, shall be called the prophet of the Most High,

for you will go before the Lord to pre - pare his way, 8. To give

his people knowledge of sal - va - tion by the for - give - ness of their sins.

9. In the tender compassion of our God the dawn from on high shall

break up - on us, 10. To shine on those who dwell in darkness and the

shadow of death, and to guide our feet in - to the way of peace. [Ant.]

*(Gloria Patri may be omitted)*

11. Glo - ry to the Father, and to the Son, and to the Ho - ly Spi - rit:

12. As it was in the beginning, is now, and will be for ev - er. A - men. [Ant.]

Setting: Plainsong, Tone 8; adapt. Bruce E. Ford (b. 1947)

# Canticle 16

The Song of Zechariah    *Benedictus Dominus Deus*

**S 249**

Thomas Attwood Walmisley
(1814-1856)

**S 250**

John Fenstermaker, Jr.
(b. 1942)

**S 251**

Samuel Sebastian Wesley
(1810-1876)

**S 252**

Anon.

1 Blessèd be the Lord, the ' God of ' Israel; *
   he has come to his ' people and ' set them ' free.

2 He has raised up for us a ' mighty ' savior, *
   born of the ' house of his ' servant ' David.

3 Through his holy prophets he promised of old,
   that he would ' save us from our ' enemies, *
   from the ' hands of ' all who ' hate us.

4 He promised to show ' mercy to our ' fathers *
   and to re ' member his ' holy ' covenant.

5 This was the oath he swore to our ' father ' Abraham, *
   to set us ' free from the ' hands of our ' enemies,

6 Free to worship him with ' out ' fear, *
   holy and righteous in his ' sight all the ' days of our ' life.

7 You, my child, shall be called the prophet of the ' Most ' High, *
   for you will go before the ' Lord to pre ' pare his ' way,

8 To give his people ' knowledge of sal ' vation *
   by the for ' giveness ' of their ' sins.

9 In the tender com ' passion of our ' God *
   the dawn from on ' high shall ' break up ' on us,

10 To shine on those who dwell in darkness and the
   ' shadow of ' death, *
   and to guide our ' feet into the ' way of ' peace.

*(Gloria Patri may be omitted)*

Glory to the Father, and ' to the ' Son, *
   and ' to the ' Holy ' Spirit:

As it was in the be ' ginning, is ' now, *
   and ' will be for ' ever. A ' men.

# S 253

Canticle 17

## The Song of Simeon   *Nunc dimittis*

1. Lord, you now have set your ser‑vant free to go in peace as

you have prom‑ised; 2. For these eyes of mine have seen the Sa‑vior,

whom you have prepared for all the world to see: 3. A Light to en‑

lighten the na‑tions, and the glory of your peo‑ple Is‑ra‑el.

(Gloria Patri may be omitted)

4. Glo‑ry to the Father, and to the Son, and to the Ho‑ly Spi‑rit:

5. As it was in the begin‑ning, is now, and will be for ev‑er. A‑men.

Setting: Plainsong, Irregular Tone; adapt. The Standing Commission on Church Music, 1979

# Canticle 17
## The Song of Simeon   *Nunc Dimittis*

Setting: Plainsong, Tone 4; adapt. Bruce E. Ford (b. 1947)

# The Song of Simeon   *Nunc dimittis*

**S 255** — Thomas Purcell (d. 1682?)

**S 256** — William Richard Bexfield (1824-1853)

**S 257** — Henry G. Ley (1887-1962)

**S 258** — Thomas Dupuis (1733-1796)

**S 259** — Charles Fisk (1925-1983)

1 Lord, you now have set your⎮servant⎮free *
   to go in⎮peace as⎮you have⎮promised;

2 For these eyes of mine have⎮seen the⎮Savior, *
   whom you have prepared for⎮all the⎮world to⎮see:

†3 A Light to en⎮lighten the⎮nations, *
   and the⎮glory of your⎮people⎮Israel.

   *(Gloria Patri may be omitted)*

   Glory to the Father, and⎮to the⎮Son, *
   and⎮to the⎮Holy⎮Spirit:

   As it was in the be⎮ginning, is⎮now, *
   and⎮will be for⎮ever. A⎮men.

†*Second half of double chant*

# Canticle 17

## The Song of Simeon  *Nunc dimittis*

# S 260

1. Lord, you now have set your ser-vant

free to go in peace as you have prom-ised; 2. For these

eyes of mine have seen the Sa - vior, whom you have pre-pared for all the

world to see: 3. A Light to en - light - en the na - tions, and the

glo - ry of your peo - ple Is - ra - el. 4. Glo - ry to the

Fa - ther, and to the Son, and to the Ho - ly Spi - rit: 5. As it

was in the be - gin - ning, is now, and will be for ev - er. A - men.

Setting: Ronald Arnatt (b. 1930)

# S 261

## A Song to the Lamb     *Dignus es*

Canticle 18

1. Splen-dor and hon-or and king-ly power are yours by right, O Lord our God.

2. For you created everything that is, and by your will they were created and

have their be-ing; 3. And yours by right, O Lamb that was slain,

for with your blood you have re-deemed for God, 4. From every family,

language, people, and na-tion, a kingdom of priests to serve our God.

5. And so, to him who sits up-on the throne, and to Christ the Lamb,

6. Be worship and praise, dominion and splen-dor, for ever and for ev-er-more.[Ant.]

*When the Antiphon is not sung, this setting of the first two verses is used.*

1. Splen-dor and honor and kingly power are yours by right, O Lord our God,

2. For you created everything that is, and by your

will they were created and have their be-ing;

Setting: Plainsong, Tone 8; adapt. Bruce E. Ford (b. 1947)

# Canticle 18
## A Song to the Lamb     *Dignus es*

S 262 — C. Hylton Stewart (1884-1932)

S 263 — E. Stanley Roper (1878-1953)

S 264 — Richard Woodward (1744-1777)

S 265 — Daniel Pinkham (b. 1923)

1    Splendor and honor and ꞌkingly ꞌpower *
        are yours by ꞌright, O ꞌLord our ꞌGod,

2    For you created ꞌeverything that ꞌis, *
        and by your will they were creꞌated and ꞌhave their ꞌbeing;

3    And yours by right, O ꞌLamb that was ꞌslain, *
        for with your ꞌblood you have reꞌdeemed for ꞌGod,

4    From every family, language, ꞌpeople, and ꞌnation, *
        a kingdom of ꞌpriests to ꞌserve our ꞌGod.

5    And so, to him who sits up ꞌon the ꞌthrone, *
        — ꞌand to ꞌChrist the ꞌLamb,

6    Be worship and praise, doꞌminion and ꞌsplendor, *
        for ꞌever and for ꞌever ꞌmore.

# S 266

## A Song to the Lamb   *Dignus es*

**Canticle 18**

Splen-dor and hon-or and king-ly power are yours by right,___ O Lord our God.

1. Splen-dor and hon-or and king-ly power are yours by right___ O Lord our God,

2. For you cre-a-ted ev-ery-thing that is, and by your will they were cre-a-ted and have their be-ing. [Ant.]

3. And yours by right, O Lamb that was slain, for with your blood you have re-deemed for God,

4. From ev-ery fam-ily, lan-guage, peo-ple, and na-tion, a king-dom of priests to serve our God. [Ant.]

5. And so, to him who sits up-on the throne, and to Christ the Lamb, 6. Be wor-ship and praise, do-min-ion and splen-dor, for ev-er and for ev-er-more. [Ant.]

Setting: Calvin Hampton (1938-1984)

# Canticle 19

## The Song of the Redeemed   *Magna et mirabilia*

S 267

Antiphon

All na-tions will draw near and fall down be-fore you, be-cause your just and ho-ly works have been re-vealed.

1. O ru-ler of the universe, Lord God, great deeds are they that you have done, surpassing human un-der-stand-ing.

2. Your ways are ways of right-eous-ness and truth, O King of all the a-ges.

3. Who can fail to do you homage, Lord, and sing the prais-es of your Name? for you only are the Ho-ly One. 4. All nations will draw near and fall down be-fore you, because your just and holy works have been re-vealed. [Ant.]

*(Gloria Patri may be omitted)*

5. Glory to the Fa-ther, and to the Son, and to the Ho-ly Spi-rit:

6. As it was in the be-gin-ning, is now, and will be for ev-er. A-men. [Ant.]

Setting: Plainsong, Tone 1; adapt. Bruce E. Ford (b. 1947)

# The Song of the Redeemed    *Magna et mirabilia*

S 268    Thomas Purcell (d. 1682?)

S 269    John Goss (1800-1880)

S 270    Henry Smart (1813-1879)

S 271    Maurice Greene (1695-1755)

1  O ruler of the universe, Lord God,
   great deeds are they that'you have'done, *
      surpassing'human'under'standing.

2  Your ways are ways of'righteousness and'truth, *
      O'King of'all the'ages.

3  Who can fail to do you homage, Lord,
   and sing the'praises of your'Name? *
      for you'only'are the'Holy One.

4  All nations will draw near and fall'down be'fore you, *
      because your just and holy'works have'been re'vealed.

*(Gloria Patri may be omitted)*

Glory to the Father, and'to the'Son, *
   and'to the'Holy'Spirit:
As it was in the be'ginning, is'now, *
   and'will be for'ever. A'men.

# Canticle 20
## Glory to God *Gloria in excelsis*

S 272

1. Glo - ry to God in the highest, and peace to his peo - ple on earth.

2. Lord God, hea - ven - ly King, almighty God and Fa - ther,

we worship you, we give you thanks, we praise you for your glo - ry.

3. Lord Jesus Christ, only Son of the Fa - ther, Lord God, Lamb of God,

4. you take away the sin of the world: have mer - cy on us;

5. you are seated at the right hand of the Fa - ther: re - ceive our prayer.

6. For you alone are the Ho - ly One, you alone are the Lord,

7. you alone are the Most High, Jesus Christ, with the Ho - ly Spi - rit,

in the glory of God the Fa - ther. A - men.

Setting: Mozarabic chant (15th cent.); adapt. David Warren Steel (b. 1947), alt.

Glory to God        *Gloria in excelsis*

Setting: Plainsong, Mode 7; Mass 13 (12th cent.); adapt. Mason Martens (b. 1933)

# Canticle 20
## Glory to God  *Gloria in excelsis*

S 274

Glo-ry to God in the high-est, and peace to his peo-ple on earth.

Lord God, hea-ven-ly King, al-might-y God and Fa-ther, we

wor-ship you, we give you thanks, we praise you for your glo-ry.

Lord Je-sus Christ, on-ly Son of the Fa-ther, Lord God, Lamb

of God, you take a-way the sin of the world: have mer-cy on us;

you are seat-ed at the right hand of the Fa-ther: re-ceive our prayer.

For you a-lone are the Ho-ly One, you a-lone are the Lord, you a-

lone are the Most High, Je-sus Christ, with the Ho-ly Spi-rit,

in the glo-ry of God the Fa - ther. A - men.

Setting: Plainsong, Mode 4; Mass 15; adapt. Schola Antiqua, 1983
Melody rhythmic version © 1984, Schola Antiqua Inc. Used by permission.

## Glory to God   *Gloria in excelsis*

S 275   verses 1-2; 5-6          verses 3-4

J. Harrison
(1808-1871)

S 276

Edward Hodges
(1796-1867)

1  Glory to 'God in the 'highest, *
   and 'peace to his 'people on 'earth.

2  Lord God, heavenly King,
   almighty 'God and 'Father, *
     we worship you, we give you thanks,
     we 'praise you 'for your 'glory.

3  Lord Jesus Christ, only 'Son of the 'Father, *
   Lord 'Göd, 'Lamb of 'God,

4  you take away the sin of the world; have 'mercy 'on us; *
   you are seated at the right hand of the 'Father; re 'ceive our 'prayer.

5  For you a 'lone are the 'Holy One, *
   you a 'lone 'are the 'Lord,

6  you alone are the 'Möst 'High, *
   Jesus Christ, with the Holy Spirit,
   in the glory of 'God the 'Father. A 'men.

# Canticle 20
## Glory to God    *Gloria in excelsis*

S 277

1. Glo-ry to God in the high-est, and peace to his peo-ple on earth.

2. Lord God, hea-ven-ly King, al-might-y God and Fa-ther, we wor-ship you,

we give you thanks, we praise you for your glo-ry. 3. Lord Je-sus Christ,

on-ly Son of the Fa-ther, Lord God, Lamb of God,

4. you take a-way the sin of the world: have mer-cy on us;

5. you are seat-ed at the right hand of the Fa-ther: re-ceive our prayer.

6. For you a-lone are the Ho-ly One, you a-lone are the Lord,

7. You a-lone are the Most High, Je-sus Christ, with the Ho-ly Spi-rit,

in the glo-ry of God the Fa-ther. A-men.

Setting: From *New Plainsong*; David Hurd (b. 1950)

# S 278

## Glory to God  *Gloria in excelsis*

Canticle 20

1. Glo-ry to God in the high-est, and peace to his peo-ple on earth. 2. Lord God, heaven-ly King, al-might-y God and Fa-ther, we wor-ship you, we give you thanks, we praise you for your glo-ry. 3. Lord Je-sus Christ, on-ly Son of the Fa-ther, Lord God, Lamb of God, 4. you take a-way the sin of the world: have mer-cy on us; 5. you are seat-ed at the right hand of the Fa-ther: re-ceive our prayer. 6. For you a-lone are the Ho-ly One, you a-lone are the Lord, 7. you a-lone are the Most High, Je-sus Christ, with the Ho-ly Spi-rit, in the glo-ry of God the Fa-ther. A - - men.

Setting: William Mathias (b. 1934)

# Canticle 20
## Glory to God
*Gloria in excelsis*

S 279

1. Glo - ry to God in the high - est, __ and peace to his peo - ple on earth. 2. Lord God, hea - ven - ly King, al - might - y God and Fa - ther, we wor - ship you, we give you thanks, we praise you for your glo - ry. 3. Lord Je - sus Christ, on - ly Son of the Fa - ther, Lord God, Lamb of God, 4. you take a - way the sin of the world: have mer - cy on us; 5. you are seat - ed at the right hand of the Fa - ther: __ re - ceive our prayer. 6. For you a - lone are the Ho - ly One, you a - lone are the Lord, 7. you a - lone are the Most High, Je - sus Christ, with the Ho - ly Spi - rit, in the glo - ry of God the Fa - ther. A - - men.

Setting: Gerald R. Near (b. 1942)

# S 280

## Glory to God    *Gloria in excelsis*

1. Glo-ry to God in the high-est, and peace to his peo-ple on earth. 2. Lord God, heaven-ly King, al-might-y God and Fa-ther, we wor-ship you, we give you thanks, we praise you for your glo-ry. 3. Lord Je-sus Christ, on-ly Son of the Fa-ther, Lord God, Lamb of God, 4. you take a-way the sin of the world: have mer-cy on us; 5. you are seat-ed at the right hand of the Fa-ther: re-ceive our prayer. 6. For you a-lone are the Ho-ly One, you a-lone are the Lord, 7. you a-lone are the Most High, Je-sus Christ, with the Ho-ly Spi-rit, in the glo-ry of God the Fa-ther. A-men.

Setting: Robert Powell (b. 1932)

# Canticle 20
## Glory to God    *Gloria in excelsis*

Setting: Richard Felciano (b. 1930)

# S 282

## You are God  *Te Deum laudamus*

Canticle 21

Setting: Plainsong, Te Deum Tone (Solemn); adapt. Bruce E. Ford (b. 1947)

# You Are God   *Te Deum laudamus*

**S 283**

Arr. after Martin Luther
(1483-1546)

**S 284**

Thomas Attwood
(1765?-1838)

**S 285**

Benjamin Hutto
(b. 1947)

**S 286** Verses 1-8; 13-14

Jonathan Battishill
(1738-1801)

Verses 9-12

S 287  Verses 1-2; 13-14    Richard Wayne Dirksen
(b. 1921)

Verses 3-12

1  You are 'God: we 'praise you; *
   You are the 'Lörd: 'we ac'claim you;

2  You are the e 'ternal 'Father: *
   All cre 'ation 'worships 'you.

3  To you all angels, all the 'powers of 'heaven, *
   Cherubim and Seraphim, 'sing in 'endless 'praise:

4  Holy, holy, holy Lord, God of 'power and 'might, *
   heaven and 'earth are 'full of your 'glory.

5  The glorious company of a 'postles 'praise you. *
   The noble 'fellowship of 'prophets 'praise you.

6  The white-robed army of 'martyrs 'praise you. *
   Throughout the world the 'holy 'Church ac'claims you;

7  Father, of 'majesty un 'bounded, *
   your true and only Son, 'worthy 'of all 'worship,

8  And the 'Holy 'Spirit, *
   — 'advo 'cate and 'guide.

9  You, Christ, are the 'king of 'glory, *
   the e 'ternal 'Son of the 'Father.

10 When you became man to 'set us 'free *
   you did not 'shun the 'Virgin's 'womb.

11 You overcame the 'sting of 'death *
   and opened the kingdom of 'heaven to 'all be'lievers.

12 You are seated at God's right 'hand in 'glory. *
   We believe that you will 'come and 'be our 'judge.

13 Come then, Lord, and 'help your 'people, *
   bought with the 'price of 'your own 'blood,

14 And bring us 'with your 'saints *
   to 'glory 'ever 'lasting.

# S 288

## Canticle 21

**You are God**   *Te Deum laudamus*

1. You are God: we praise you; You are the Lord: we ac-

claim you; 2. You are the eternal Father: All creation

worships you. 3. To you all angels, all the powers of hea-

ven, Cherubim and Seraphim, sing in endless praise:

4. Ho - ly, ho - ly, ho - ly Lord, God of power and might, heaven and

earth are full of your glo - ry. 5. The glo - rious com-pany of

a - pos - tles praise you. The no - ble fel - low-ship of pro - phets

praise you. The white-robed ar - my of mar - tyrs praise you.

6. Through-out the world the ho - ly Church ac - claims you; Fa - ther, of

ma - jes - ty un - bound - ed, your true and on - ly Son, wor - thy

of all wor - ship, and the Ho - ly Spi - rit, ad - vo - cate

and guide. 7. You, Christ, are the king of glo - ry, the e - ter - nal Son

of the Fa - ther. 8. When you be - came man to set us free

you did not shun the Vir - gin's womb. 9. You o - ver - came the sting

*This pitch for unison singing and for men's voices in harmony; for singing in harmony by mixed voices, a whole tone or minor third higher.*

Setting: Slavonic chant; adapt. and harm. Mason Martens (b. 1933)

# Hymns

# Hymns

## Morning

1 Fa - ther, we praise thee, now the night is
2 Mon - arch of all things, fit us for thy
3 All ho - ly Fa - ther, Son, and e - qual

o - ver, ac - tive and watch - ful, stand we all be -
man - sions; ban - ish our weak - ness, health and whole-ness
Spi - rit, Trin - i - ty bless - ed, send us thy sal -

fore thee; sing - ing we of - fer prayer and med - i -
send - ing; bring us to hea - ven, where thy saints u -
va - tion; thine is the glo - ry, gleam - ing and re -

ta - tion: thus we a - dore thee.
nit - ed joy with - out end - ing.
sound - ing through all cre - a - tion.

Words: Latin, 10th cent.; tr. Percy Dearmer (1867-1936)
Music: *Christe sanctorum,* melody from *Antiphoner,* 1681

11 11. 11 5

1 Fa - ther, we praise thee, now the night is o - ver, ac - tive and
2 Mon - arch of all things, fit us for thy man - sions; ban - ish our
3 All ho - ly Fa - ther, Son, and e - qual Spi - rit, Trin - i - ty

watch - ful, stand we all be - fore thee; sing - ing we of - fer
weak - ness, health and whole - ness send - ing; bring us to hea - ven,
bless - ed, send us thy sal - va - tion; thine is the glo - ry,

prayer and med - i - ta - tion: thus we a - dore thee.
where thy saints u - nit - ed joy with - out end - ing.
gleam - ing and re - sound - ing through all cre - a - tion.

Words: Latin, 10th cent.; tr. Percy Dearmer (1867-1936)
Music: *Nocte surgentes*, plainsong, Mode 3, Nevers MS., 13th cent.;
ver. Schola Antiqua, 1983

11 11. 11 5

Music: Melody rhythmic version © 1984, Schola Antiqua Inc. Used by permission.

3

**Morning**

1 Now that the day - light fills the sky, we
2 Our hearts and lips may he re - strain; keep
3 From e - vil may he guard our eyes, our
4 that we, when this new day is gone, and
5 To God the Fa - ther, heaven - ly Light, to

1 lift our hearts to God on high, that he, in all we
2 us from caus - ing o - thers pain, that we may see and
3 ears from emp - ty praise and lies; from self - ish - ness our
4 night in turn is draw - ing on, with con - science free from
5 Christ, re - vealed in earth - ly night, to God the Ho - ly

1 do or say, would keep us free from harm this day:
2 serve his Son, and grow in love for ev - ery - one.
3 hearts re - lease, that we may serve, and know his peace;
4 sin and blame, may praise and bless his ho - ly Name.
5 Ghost we raise our e - qual and un - ceas - ing praise.

Words: Latin, 6th cent.; st. 1, tr. John Mason Neale (1818-1866); sts. 2-4, tr. Peter Scagnelli (b. 1949).
St. 5, Charles Coffin (1676-1749); tr. John Chandler (1806-1876)
Music: *Herr Jesu Christ*, melody from *Cantionale Germanicum*, 1628

LM

## Morning

4

1 Now that the day - light fills the sky, we lift our
2 Our hearts and lips may he re - strain; keep us from
3 From e - vil may he guard our eyes, our ears from
4 that we, when this new day is gone, and night in
5 To God the Fa - ther, heaven - ly Light, to Christ, re -

1 hearts to God on high, that he, in all we
2 caus - ing o - thers pain, that we may see and
3 emp - ty praise and lies; from self - ish - ness our
4 turn is draw - ing on, with con - science free from
5 vealed in earth - ly night, to God the Ho - ly

1 do or say, would keep us free from harm this day:
2 serve his Son, and grow in love for ev - ery - one.
3 hearts re - lease, that we may serve, and know his peace;
4 sin and blame, may praise and bless his ho - ly Name.
5 Ghost we raise our e - qual and un - ceas - ing praise.

Words: Latin, 6th cent.; st. 1, tr. John Mason Neale (1818-1866); sts. 2-4, tr. Peter Scagnelli (b. 1949).
St. 5, Charles Coffin (1676-1749); tr. John Chandler (1806-1876)
Music: *Verbum supernum prodiens*, plainsong, Mode 2, Nevers MS., 13th cent.

LM

1. O splen-dor of God's glo - ry bright, O thou that
2. O thou true Sun of heaven-ly love, pour down thy
3. With prayer the Fa - ther we im - plore: O Fa - ther,
4. to guide what - e'er we no - bly do, with love all
5. All laud to God the Fa - ther be; all praise, e -

1. bring - est light from light, O Light of Light, light's
2. ra - diance from a - bove: the Spi - rit's sanc - ti -
3. glo - rious ev - er - more, we plead with thee for
4. en - vy to sub - due, to give us grace our
5. ter - nal Son, to thee; all glo - ry to the

1. liv - ing spring, O Day, all days il - lu - mi - ning,
2. fy - ing beam up - on our earth - ly sen - ses stream.
3. grace and power to con - quer in temp - ta - tion's hour,
4. wrongs to bear, to make ill for - tune turn to fair.
5. Spi - rit raise in e - qual and un - end - ing praise.

Words: Ambrose of Milan (340-397); tr. Robert Seymour Bridges (1844-1930), alt.
Music: *Splendor paternae gloriae*, plainsong, Mode 1, Worcester MS., 13th cent.

LM

## 6

1. Christ, whose glo - ry fills the skies, Christ, the true, the
2. Dark and cheer - less is the morn un - ac - com - pan -
3. Vis - it then this soul of mine! Pierce the gloom of

on - ly Light, Sun of Right - eous - ness, a - rise!
ied by thee; joy - less is the day's re - turn,
sin and grief! Fill me, ra - dian - cy di - vine;

Tri - umph o'er the shades of night: Day - spring from on
till thy mer - cy's beams I see, till they in - ward
scat - ter all my un - be - lief; more and more thy -

high, be near; Day-star, in my heart ap - pear.
light im - part, glad my eyes, and warm my heart.
self dis - play, shin-ing to the per - fect day.

Words: Charles Wesley (1707-1788)
Music: *Christ Whose Glory*, Malcolm Williamson (b. 1931)

77. 77. 77

## Morning

7

1 Christ, whose glo - ry fills the skies, Christ the true, the on - ly Light,
2 Dark and cheer-less is the morn un - ac - com - pan - ied by thee;
3 Vis - it then this soul of mine! Pierce the gloom of sin and grief!

Sun of Right-eous - ness, a - rise! Tri-umph o'er the shades of night:
joy - less is the day's re - turn, till thy mer - cy's beams I see,
Fill me, ra - dian - cy di - vine; scat - ter all my un - be - lief;

Day - spring from on high, be near; Day-star, in my heart ap - pear.
till they in - ward light im - part, glad my eyes, and warm my heart.
more and more thy - self dis - play, shin-ing to the per - fect day.

Words: Charles Wesley (1707-1788)
Music: *Ratisbon*, melody from *Geystliche gesangk Buchleyn*, 1524; adapt. att. William Henry Havergal
(1793-1870); harm. William Henry Havergal (1793-1870), alt.

77. 77. 77

*Unison or harmony*

1 Morn-ing has bro - ken like the first morn - ing,
2 Sweet the rain's new fall sun - lit from hea - ven,
3 Mine is the sun - light! Mine is the morn - ing

black-bird has spo - ken like the first bird._____
like the first dew - fall on the first grass._____
born of the one light E - den saw play!_____

Praise for the sing - ing! Praise for the morn - ing!
Praise for the sweet - ness of the wet gar - den,
Praise with e - la - tion, praise ev - ery morn - ing,

Praise for them, spring - ing fresh from the Word!_____
sprung in com - plete - ness where his feet pass._____
God's re - cre - a - tion, of the new day!_____

Words: Eleanor Farjeon (1881-1965), alt.
Music: *Bunessan*, Gaelic melody; harm. Alec Wyton (b. 1921)

55. 54. D

| | | | | | | | |
|---|---|---|---|---|---|---|---|
| *1 Not | here for high and | ho - ly | things we | ren - der thanks to |
| *2 the | roy - al robes of | au - tumn moors the | gold - en gates of |
| *3 of | faith and hope and | love un - dimmed, un - | dy - ing still through |
| 4 A - | wake, a - wake to | love and work! The | lark is in the |
| 5 Come, | let thy voice be | one with theirs, shout | with their shout of |
| 6 to | give and give, and | give a - gain, what | God hath giv - en |

| | | | | | |
|---|---|---|---|---|---|
| 1 thee, | but | for the | com - mon | things of | earth, the |
| 2 spring, | the | vel - vet | of soft | sum - mer | nights, the |
| 3 death, | the | re - sur - rec - tion | of the | world, what |
| 4 sky, | the | fields are | wet with | dia - mond | dew, the |
| 5 praise; | see | how the | gi - ant | sun soars | up, great |
| 6 thee; | to | spend thy - self nor | count the | cost; to |

| | | | | | |
|---|---|---|---|---|---|
| 1 pur - ple | pa - gean - try | of | dawn - ing | and of |
| 2 sil - ver | glis - ter - ing | of | all the | mil - lion |
| 3 time there | comes the | breath | of | dawn that | rus - tles |
| 4 worlds a - | wake to | cry | their | bless - ings | on the |
| 5 lord of | years and | days! | So | let the | love of |
| 6 serve right | glo - rious - ly | the | God who | gave all |

| | | | | | |
|---|---|---|---|---|---|
| 1 dy - ing | days, the | splen - dor | of the | sea, |
| 2 mil - lion | stars, the | si - lent | song they | sing, |
| 3 through the | trees, and | that clear | voice that | saith: |
| 4 Lord of | life, as | he goes | meek - ly | by. |
| 5 Je - sus | come and | set thy | soul a - | blaze, |
| 6 worlds that | are, and | all that | are to | be. |

Words: Geoffrey Anketel Studdert-Kennedy (1883-1929)
Music: *Morning Song*, melody att. Elkanah Kelsay Dare (1782-1826)

86. 86. 86

1 New ev - ery morn - ing is the love
2 New mer - cies, each re - turn - ing day,
*3 If on our dai - ly course our mind
*4 Old friends, old scenes, will love - lier be,
*5 The tri - vial round, the com - mon task,
6 On - ly, O Lord, in thy dear love,

1 our wak - ening and up - ris - ing prove;
2 a - round us hov - er while we pray;
3 be set to hal - low all we find,
4 as more of heaven in each we see;
5 will fur - nish us for per - fect rest a - bove;
6 fit us for per - fect rest a - bove;

1 through sleep and dark - ness safe - ly brought,
2 new per - ils past, new sins for - given,
3 new trea - sures still, of count - less price,
4 some soft - ening gleam of love and prayer
5 room to den - y our - selves; a road
6 and help us, this and ev - ery day,

1 re - stored to life and power and thought.
2 new thoughts of God, new hopes of heaven.
3 God will pro - vide for sac - ri - fice.
4 shall dawn on ev - ery cross and care.
5 to bring us dai - ly near - er God.
6 to live more near - ly as we pray.

Words: John Keble (1792-1866)
Music: *Kedron*, melody att. Elkanah Kelsay Dare (1782-1826)

LM

# Morning

## 11

1 A - wake, my soul, and with the sun thy
2 Lord, I my vows to thee re - new; dis -
3 Di - rect, con - trol, sug - gest, this day, all
*4 Praise God, from whom all bless - ings flow; praise

dai - ly stage of du - ty run; shake off dull sloth, and
perse my sins as morn-ing dew; guard my first springs of
I de - sign, or do, or say; that all my powers, with
him, all crea - tures here be - low; praise him a - bove, ye

joy - ful rise to pay thy morn - ing sac - ri - fice:
thought and will, and with thy - self my spi - rit fill.
all their might, in thy sole glo - ry may u - nite.
heaven - ly host: praise Fa - ther, Son, and Ho - ly Ghost.

Words: Thomas Ken (1637-1711), alt.
Music: *Morning Hymn*, melody François Hippolyte Barthélémon (1741-1808);
    harm. *The Church Hymnal for the Church Year*, 1917

LM

**12**  **Noonday**

1 The gold-en sun lights up the sky, im-part-ing
2 At the third hour you took your cross, you stum-bled,
3 At the third hour your faith-ful band was clothed with
4 O God, cre-a-tion's rul-ing force, O Je-sus,

vi-gor to the day. A-mid our cus-tom-ar-y
Lord, be-neath its weight. Now help us bear our dai-ly
power on Pen-te-cost. Be-stow your Spi-rit on us
cru-ci-fied for us, O Spi-rit, love's life-giv-ing

round, we of-fer you our prayer and praise.
load, and strive to fol-low where you lead.
now, and give us strength to do your will.
ray, we praise and bless you ev-er-y hour.

Words: Charles P. Price (b. 1920)
Music: *Danby*, English melody; adapt. Ralph Vaughan Williams (1872-1958)                    LM

**13**  **Noonday**

1 The gold-en sun lights up the sky,
2 At the third hour you took your cross,
3 At the third hour your faith-ful band
4 O God, cre-a-tion's rul-ing force,

im-part-ing vi-gor to the day.
you stum-bled, Lord, be-neath its weight.
was clothed with power on Pen-te-cost.
O Je-sus, cru-ci-fied for us,

A - mid our cus - tom - ar - y round,
Now help us bear our dai - ly load
Be - stow your Spi - rit on us now,
O Spi - rit, love's life - giv - ing ray,

we of - fer you our prayer and praise.
and strive to fol - low where you lead.
and give us strength to do your will.
we praise and bless you ev - ery hour.

Words: Charles P. Price (b. 1920)
Music: *Verbum supernum prodiens*, plainsong, Mode 8, Einsiedeln MS., 13th cent.

LM

## Noonday

**14**

1 O God, cre - a - tion's se - cret force,  your - self un -
2 Grant us, when this short life is past,  the glo - rious
*3 Al - might - y Fa - ther, hear our cry  through Je - sus

moved, all mo - tion's source,  you, from the morn till eve - ning's
eve - ning that shall last;  that, by a ho - ly death at -
Christ, our Lord Most High,  whom with the Spi - rit we a -

ray, through all its chan - ges guide the day:
tained, e - ter - nal glo - ry may be gained.
dore for ev - er and for ev - er - more.

Words: Ambrose of Milan (340-397); tr. John Mason Neale (1818-1866), alt.
    St. 3, James Waring McCrady (b. 1938)
Music: *O Heiland, reiss*, melody from *Rheinfelsisches Deutsches Catholisches Gesangbuch*, 1666

LM

## 15                                             Noonday

1 O God, creation's secret force, yourself un-
2 Grant us, when this short life is past, the glorious
*3 Almighty Father, hear our cry through Jesus

moved, all motion's source, you, from the morn till
evening that shall last; that, by a holy
Christ, our Lord Most High, whom with the Spirit

evening's ray, through all its changes guide the day:
death attained, eternal glory may be gained.
we adore for ever and for evermore.

Words: Ambrose of Milan (340-397); tr. John Mason Neale (1818-1866), alt.
    St. 3, James Waring McCrady (b. 1938)
Music: *Te lucis ante terminum*, plainsong, Mode 8, *Antiphonale Sarisburiense*, Vol. II           LM


## 16                                             Noonday

Now let us sing our praise to God
For at this hour to all the world
So dazzling is its holy light,
All glory be to you, Lord Christ,

with fervent heart and ready mind:
the grace of true salvation came:
it puts the noonday sun in shade.
who, conquering death, reign gloriously

each day the sun at ze-nith calls
the Lamb of God re-stored our peace
Then let us all with joy em-brace
with God, Cre-a-tor of all things

the faith-ful to their noon-day prayers.
by vir-tue of his sav-ing cross.
the flam-ing splen-dor of such grace.
and with the Spi-rit, Com-fort-er.

Words: Latin; ver. *Hymnal 1982*. St. 4, Anne K. LeCroy (b. 1930)
Music: *Dicamus laudes Domino*, plainsong, Mode 5, Nevers MS., 13th cent.

LM

## Noonday 17

1 Now let us sing our praise to God with fer-vent
2 For at this hour to all the world the grace of
3 So daz-zling is its ho-ly light, it puts the
4 All glo-ry be to you, Lord Christ, who, con-quering

heart and rea-dy mind: each day the sun at
true sal-va-tion came: the Lamb of God re-
noon-day sun in shade. Then let us all with
death, reign glo-rious-ly with God, Cre-a-tor

ze-nith calls the faith-ful to their noon-day prayers.
stored our peace by vir-tue of his sav-ing cross.
joy em-brace the flam-ing splen-dor of such grace.
of all things and with the Spi-rit, Com-fort-er.

Words: Latin; ver. *Hymnal 1982*. St. 4, Anne K. LeCroy (b. 1930)
Music: *Solemnis haec festivitas*, melody from *Graduale*, 1685

LM

# 18

1 As now the sun shines down at noon, your light, O
2-4 *(Insert stanzas appropriate to the day)*
5 O God, cre - a - tion's rul - ing force, O Je - sus,

Lord, burns in our hearts; as - sist us to en - dure that
cru - ci - fied for us, O Spi - rit, bring - ing truth and

light, and through your judg - ment find your grace.
love, we praise and bless you ev - ery hour.

### Monday and Thursday

2 The sun stood still for Joshua
while he contended, Lord, for you;
so may we struggle faithfully
and seek our victory in your peace.

3 At noon you hung upon the cross
betrayed, forsaken, all alone;
help us to share your pain and grief,
and, sharing, know life's victory won.

4 At noon you came to Jacob's well,
athirst and spent, you asked for aid;
to us, like her who saw your need,
your living water give to drink.

### Tuesday and Saturday

2 Elijah taunted Baal at noon;
he knew you, Lord, would answer him;
may we, too, trust your sovereign power
when we must act in day's hard light.

3 On Golgotha the sky turned dark;
all shadows of the morn and eve
converged to shield frail human eyes
from all the woe you bore for us.

4 At noontime Paul beheld your light,
so bright it cancelled out the sun;
you blinded and converted him:
O turn us now to see your face.

2 By noon's bright light, destruction stalks;
ten thousand perish at our side;
held by your unrelenting grace,
let us cling always to your love.

3 The dark midday could not conceal
your cry of awful agony;
teach us to hear its echoes still
in every human misery.

4 In noonday vision Peter saw
that all you made was pure and clean;
grant us that same revealing light
that we may see your world is good.

Words: Charles P. Price (b. 1920) and Carl P. Daw, Jr. (b. 1944)
Music: *Jesu dulcis memoria*, plainsong, Mode 2

LM

# Noonday

# 19

1 Now Ho - ly Spi - rit, ev - er One
2 Let mouth and tongue, mind, sense, and strength
*3 Al - might - y Fa - ther, hear our cry

with God the Fa - ther and the Son,
God's might - y ac - tions tell at length;
through Je - sus Christ, our Lord Most High,

pour forth in - to our hearts, we pray,
let love in flames of liv - ing fire
whom with in the Spi - rit we a - dore

the full - ness of your grace to - day.
the hearts of all the world in - spire.
for ev - er and for ev - er - more.

Words: Ambrose of Milan (340-397); ver. *Hymnal 1982*. St. 3, James Waring McCrady (b. 1938)
Music: *Nunc Sancte nobis Spiritus*, plainsong, Mode 5, Verona MS., 12th cent.

LM

## 20

1 Now Holy Spirit, ever One with God the
2 Let mouth and tongue, mind, sense, and strength God's might-y
*3 Al-might-y Father, hear our cry through Jesus

Fa-ther and the Son, pour forth in-to our
ac-tions tell at length; let love in flames of
Christ, our Lord Most High, whom with the Spi-rit

hearts, we pray, the full-ness of your grace to-day.
liv-ing fire the hearts of all the world in-spire.
we a-dore for ev-er and for ev-er-more.

Words: Ambrose of Milan (340-397); ver. Hymnal 1982. St. 5, James Waring McCrady (b. 1938)
Music: *Wareham*, melody William Knapp (1698-1768), alt.; harm *Hymns Ancient and Modern*, 1875,
after James Turle (1802-1882)

LM

## 21

1 O God of truth, O Lord of might, you or-der time and
2 Quench now on earth the flames of strife; from pas-sion's heat pre-
*3 Al-might-y Fa-ther, hear our cry through Je-sus Christ, our

change a - right, you send the ear - ly morn - ing
serve our life; and while you keep our bo - dy
Lord Most High, whom with the Spi - rit we a -

ray, and light the glow of per - fect day:
whole, pour heal - ing peace up - on our soul.
dore for ev - er and for ev - er - more.

Words: Ambrose of Milan (340-397); tr. John Mason Neale (1818-1866), alt.
    St. 3, James Waring McCrady (b. 1938)
Music: *Song 34*, melody and bass Orlando Gibbons (1583-1625); harm. *The English Hymnal*, 1906, alt.

LM

## Noonday

22

1 O God of truth, O Lord of might, you or - der
2 Quench now on earth the flames of strife; from pas - sion's
*3 Al - might - y Fa - ther, hear our cry through Je - sus

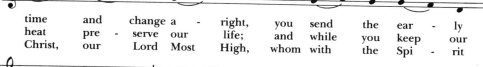

time and change a - right, you send the ear - ly
heat pre - serve our life; and while you keep our
Christ, our Lord Most High, whom with the Spi - rit

morn - ing ray, and light the glow of per - fect day:
bo - dy whole, pour heal - ing peace up - on our soul.
we a - dore for ev - er and for ev - er - more.

Words: Ambrose of Milan (340-397); tr. John Mason Neale (1818-1866), alt.
    St. 3, James Waring McCrady (b. 1938)
Music: *Rector potens, verax Deus*, plainsong, Mode 1, *Klosterneuburger Hymnar*, 1336

LM

23

Noonday

1 The fleet - ing day is near - ly gone;
2 At prayer time, near the Tem - ple gate,
3 With "It is fi - nished" on your lips,
4 O God, cre - a - tion's rul - ing force,

we har - vest what the morn - ing sowed.
A - pos - tles made a lame man walk.
at that ninth hour you died for us.
O Je - sus, cru - ci - fied for us,

Now grant us un - di - mi - nished strength
They gave him heal - ing in your Name;
In - spire us by your dy - ing breath
O Spi - rit, bring - ing power and health,

to stand and do what still re - mains.
now give us grace to walk your way.
to live for you and do your will.
we praise and bless you ev - ery hour.

Words: Charles P. Price (b. 1920)
Music: *Du meiner Seelen*, from *Cantica Spiritualia*, 1847

LM

1 The day thou gav - est, Lord, is end - ed, the dark - ness
2 We thank thee that thy Church, un - sleep-ing while earth rolls
3 As o'er each con - ti - nent and is - land the dawn leads
4 So be it, Lord; thy throne shall nev - er, like earth's proud

falls at thy be - hest; to thee our morn - ing hymns a -
on - ward in - to light, through all the world her watch is
on an - oth - er day, the voice of prayer is nev - er
em - pires, pass a - way; thy king - dom stands, and grows for

scend - ed, thy praise shall sanc - ti - fy our rest.
keep - ing and rests not now by day or night.
si - lent, nor dies the strain of praise a - way.
ev - er, till all thy crea - tures own thy sway.

*This hymn may be used in the morning by omitting stanza 1.*

Words: John Ellerton (1826-1893)
Music: *St. Clement*, Clement Cottevill Scholefield (1839-1904)     98. 98

# 25

1 O gra - cious Light, Lord Je - sus Christ, in
2 Now sun - set comes, but light shines forth, the
3 Wor - thy are you of end - less praise, O

you the Fa - ther's glo - ry shone. Im - mor - tal, ho - ly,
lamps are lit to pierce the night. Praise Fa - ther, Son, and
Son of God, Life - giv - ing Lord; where - fore you are through

blest is he, and blest are you, his ho - ly Son.
Spi - rit: God who dwells in the e - ter - nal light.
all the earth and in the high - est heaven a - dored.

*This hymn may be sung unaccompanied as a four-part canon at a distance of one measure.*

Words: Greek, 3rd cent.; tr. F. Bland Tucker (1895-1984); para. of *O Gracious Light*
Music: *The Eighth Tune*, Thomas Tallis (1505?-1585)

LM

# 26

1 O gra - cious Light, Lord Je - sus Christ, in you the
2 Now sun - set comes, but light shines forth, the lamps are
3 Wor - thy are you of end - less praise, O Son of

Fa - ther's glo - ry shone. Im - mor - tal, ho - ly,
lit to pierce the night. Praise Fa - ther, Son, and
God, Life - giv - ing Lord; where - fore you are through

| blest | is | he, | and | blest | are | you, | his | ho - ly | Son. |
| Spi - rit: | God | who | dwells | in | the | e - ter - nal | light. |
| all | the | earth | and | in | the | high - est | heaven | a - dored. |

*This melody may be sung in rhythmic form:* ♪ ♩ ♪ ♩

Words: Greek, 3rd cent.; tr. F. Bland Tucker (1895-1984); para. of *O Gracious Light*
Music: *Conditor alme siderum*, plainsong, Mode 4

LM

## Evening

**27**

| 1 | O | | blest | Cre | - a - tor, | source | of | light, |
| 2 | You | | joined | the | morn and | eve | - ning | ray; |
| 3 | Lest | | we, | be - set | by | doubt | and | strife, |
| 4 | E | - ter - nal | Fa - ther, | help | us | rise |
| 5 | De | - fend | us, | Fa - ther, | through | the | night, |

| 1 | you | gave | the | day | with | splen - dor | bright. |
| 2 | you | found | it | good | and | called | it | 'day.' |
| 3 | for - get | your | bless - ed | gift | of | life, |
| 4 | and | strive | to | gain | the | heaven - ly | prize; |
| 5 | and | with | your | Son, | and | Spi - rit | bright |

| 1 | when | on | the | new | and | liv - ing | earth |
| 2 | But | now | the | threat - ening | dark - ness | nears |
| 3 | and | an - guished | and | in | mind dis - tressed, |
| 4 | for | you | a - lone | can | make us | strong |
| 5 | the | Tri - ni - ty | whom | we | a - dore |

| 1 | you | brought | all | things | to | glo - rious | birth. |
| 2 | we | pray | you, | Fa - ther, | calm | our | fears. |
| 3 | be | crushed | by | guilt, | by | sin | op - pressed. |
| 4 | to | turn | from | sin | and | cease | from | wrong. |
| 5 | be | with | us | now | and | ev - er - more. |

Words: Latin, 6th cent.; tr. Anne K. LeCroy (b. 1930), alt.
Music: *Lucis creator optime*, plainsong, Mode 8, Verona MS., 11th cent.

LM

28

# Evening

1 O blest Cre - a - tor, source of light, you gave the
2 You joined the morn and eve - ning ray; you found it
3 Lest we, be - set by doubt and strife, for - get your
4 E - ter - nal Fa - ther, help us rise and strive to
*5 De - fend us, Fa - ther, through the night, and with your

1 day with splen - dor bright, when on the new and
2 good and called it 'day.' But now the threat - ening
3 bless - ed gift of life, and an - guished and in
4 gain the heaven - ly prize; for you a - lone can
5 Son, and Spi - rit bright the Tri - ni - ty whom

1 liv - ing earth you brought all things to glo - rious birth.
2 dark - ness nears we pray you, Fa - ther, calm our fears.
3 mind dis - tressed, be crushed by guilt, by sin op - pressed.
4 make us strong to turn from sin and cease from wrong.
5 we a - dore be with us now and ev - er - more.

Words: Latin, 6th cent.; tr. Anne K. LeCroy (b. 1930), alt.
Music: *Bromley*, Franz Joseph Haydn (1732-1809), alt.

LM

# Evening

29

1 O Trin-i-ty of bless-ed light, O U-ni-
2 To thee our morn-ing song of praise, to thee our
3 To God the Fa-ther, heaven-ly Light, to Christ re-

ty of prince-ly might, the fier-y sun now
eve-ning prayer we raise; O grant us withy thy
vealed in earth-ly night, to God the Ho-ly

goes his way; shed thou with-in our hearts thy ray.
saints on high to praise thee through e-ter-ni-ty.
Ghost we raise our e-qual and un-ceas-ing praise.

Words: Latin, 6th cent.; tr. John Mason Neale (1818-1866). St. 3, Charles Coffin (1676-1749);
tr. John Chandler (1806-1876)
Music: *Bromley*, Franz Joseph Haydn (1732-1809), alt.

LM

1 O Trin - i - ty of bless - ed light,
2 To thee our morn-ing song of praise,
3 To God the Fa - ther, heaven - ly Light,

O U - ni - ty of prince - ly might,
to thee our eve - ning prayer we raise;
to Christ re - vealed in earth - ly night,

the fier - y sun now goes his way;
O grant us with thy saints on high
to God the Ho - ly Ghost we raise

shed thou with - in our hearts thy ray.
to praise thee through e - ter - ni - ty.
our e - qual and un - ceas - ing praise.

Words: Latin, 6th cent.; tr. John Mason Neale (1818-1866). St. 3, Charles Coffin (1676-1749);
        tr. John Chandler (1806-1876)
Music: *O lux beata Trinitas*, plainsong, Mode 8

LM

1 Most Ho - ly God, the Lord of heaven, who in the
2 for you the daz - zling star shines forth which in its
3 The day de - parts, the eve - ning stars se - rene - ly
4 You, Ho - ly One, Cre - a - tor, Lord, you in the
5 Like sun and day, shine in our hearts; like moon and

1 high arched sky has placed the sun that flames up from the
2 gleam - ing path de - clares the won - ders of your glo - rious
3 light the dark - ening sky; the moon with cool re - flect - ed
4 pri - mal world once set the bound-aries of the day and
5 night, give lov - ing peace. Free us from bonds of blind - ing

1 east and brings the splen - dors of the dawn:
2 power, and beck - ons us to wor - ship you.
3 glow will bring the si - lenc - es of night.
4 night and or - dered sea - sons in their round.
5 sin and guide us on our path to you.

Words: Latin; tr. Ann K. LeCroy (b. 1930)
Music: *Dunedin,* Vernon Griffiths (b. 1894)

LM

## Evening

**32**

1 Most Ho - ly God, the Lord of heaven, who in the
2 for you the daz - zling star shines forth which in its
3 The day de - parts, the eve - ning stars se - rene - ly
4 You, Ho - ly One, Cre - a - tor, Lord, you in the
5 Like sun and day, shine in our hearts; like moon and

1 high - arched sky has placed the sun that flames up
2 gleam - ing path de - clares the won - ders of your
3 light the dark - ening sky; the moon with cool re -
4 pri - mal world once set the bound - aries of the
5 night, give lov - ing peace. Free us from bonds of

1 from the east and brings the splen - dors of the dawn:
2 glo - rious power, and beck - ons us to wor - ship you.
3 flect - ed glow will bring the si - lenc - es of night.
4 day and night and or - dered sea - sons in their round.
5 blind - ing sin and guide us on our path to you.

Words: Latin; tr. Anne K. LeCroy (b. 1930)
Music: *Immense caeli Conditor,* plainsong, Mode 1; ver. Schola Antiqua, 1983
Music: Melody rhythmic version © 1984, Schola Antiqua Inc. Used by permission.

LM

## 33

1 Christ, might - y Sa - vior, Light of all cre - a - tion, you make the
2 Now comes the day's end as the sun is set-ting: mir-ror of
3 There - fore we come now eve - ning rites to of - fer, joy - ful - ly
4 Give heed, we pray you, to our sup - pli - ca - tion: that you may
5 Though bo - dies slum-ber, hearts shall keep their vi - gil, for ev - er

1 day - time ra - diant with the sun - light and to the night give
2 day - break, pledge of re - sur - rec - tion; while in the hea - vens
3 chant - ing ho - ly hymns to praise you, with all cre - a - tion
4 grant us par - don for of - fens - es, strength for our weak hearts,
5 rest - ing in the peace of Je - sus, in light or dark - ness

1 glit - ter - ing a - dorn - ment, stars in the hea - vens.
2 choirs of stars ap - pear - ing hal - low the night-fall.
3 join - ing hearts and voic - es sing - ing your glo - ry.
4 rest for ach - ing bo - dies, sooth - ing the wear - y.
5 wor - ship-ing our Sa - vior now and for ev - er.

Words: Mozarabic, 10th cent.; tr. Alan G. McDougall (1895-1964); rev. Anne K. LeCroy (b. 1930)
Music: *Christe, Lux mundi*, plainsong, Mode 7, Freiburg MS., 14th cent.

11. 11. 11. 5

1 Christ, might - y Sa - vior, Light of all cre - a - tion, you make the
2 Now comes the day's end as the sun is set - ting: mir - ror of
3 There - fore we come now eve - ning rites to of - fer, joy - ful - ly
4 Give heed, we pray you, to our sup - pli - ca - tion: that you may
5 Though bo - dies slum - ber, hearts shall keep their vi - gil, for ev - er

1 day - time ra - diant with the sun - light and to the night give
2 day - break, pledge of re - sur - rec - tion; while in the hea - vens
3 chant - ing ho - ly hymns to praise you, with all cre - a - tion
4 grant us par - don for of - fens - es, strength for our weak hearts,
5 rest - ing in the peace of Je - sus, in light or dark - ness

Words: Mozarabic, 10th cent.; tr. Alan G. McDougall (1895-1964); rev. Anne K. LeCroy (b. 1930)
Music: *Innisfree Farm*, Richard Wayne Dirksen (b. 1921)

11. 11. 11. 5

## Evening

35

Words: Mozarabic, 10th cent.; tr. Alan G. McDougall; (1895-1964) rev. Anne K. LeCroy (b. 1930)
Music: *Mighty Savior*, David Hurd (b. 1950)

11. 11. 11. 5

1 O glad-some Light, O grace of God the Fa-ther's face,
2 Now, ere day fad - eth quite, we see the eve-ning light,
3 To thee of right be - longs all praise of ho - ly songs,

thee - ter - nal splen-dor wear - ing; ce - les - tial, ho - ly, blest,
our wont - ed hymn out - pour - ing; Fa - ther of might un - known,
O Son of God, Life - giv - er; thee, there-fore, O Most High,

our Sa - vior Je - sus Christ, joy - ful in thine ap-pear - ing.
thee, his in - car - nate Son, and Ho - ly Spirit a - dor - ing.
the world doth glo - ri - fy, and shall ex - alt for ev - er.

Words: Greek, 3rd cent.; tr. Robert Seymour Bridges (1844-1930); para. of *O Gracious Light*
Music: *Le Cantique de Siméon*, melody Louis Bourgeois (1510?-1561?);
harm. Claude Goudimel (1514-1572)

667. 667

## 37

1 O bright-ness of the im-mor-tal Fa-ther's face, most ho - ly,
2 the sun is sink - ing now, and one by one the lamps of
3 Worth - y art thou at all times to re - ceive our hal - lowed

heaven - ly, blest, Lord Je - sus Christ, in whom his
eve - ning shine; we hymn thee - ter - nal Fa - ther,
prais - es, Lord. O Son of God, be thou, in

| | | | | | | | | |
|---|---|---|---|---|---|---|---|---|
| truth | and | grace | are | | vi | - si - | bly | ex - pressed: |
| and | the | Son, | and | | Ho | - ly | Ghost | di - vine. |
| whom | we | live, | through | | all | the | world | a - dored. |

Words: Greek, 3rd cent.; tr. Edward W. Eddis (1825-1905); para. of *O Gracious Light*
Music: *Evening Hymn*, Gerald Near (b. 1942)

10 6. 10 6

## Compline

38

| | | | | | | | | |
|---|---|---|---|---|---|---|---|---|
| 1 Je | - sus, | Re | - deem | - er | of | the | world, |
| 2 The | whole | cre | - a - | tion's | ar - | chi - | tect, |
| 3 You | broke | the | chains | of | death | and | hell: |
| 4 Lord, | while | we | live | for | this | short | time |
| *5 All | glo - | ry | be | to | you, | Lord | Christ, |

| | | | | | | | | |
|---|---|---|---|---|---|---|---|---|
| 1 Word | of | the | Fa - | ther | throned | on | high, |
| 2 you | set | the | bounds | of | night | and | day; |
| 3 Lord, | free | us | from | our | an - | cient | foe |
| 4 as | mor - | tals | clothed | in | earth - | bound | frame, |
| 5 who, | con - | quering | death, | reign | glo - | rious - | ly |

| | | | | | | | | |
|---|---|---|---|---|---|---|---|---|
| 1 light | from | the | light | in - | vi - | si - | ble, |
| 2 give | to | our | wea - | ried | bo - | dies | rest |
| 3 and | let | him | nev - | er | lead | a - | stray |
| 4 re - | fresh | us | now | with | rest - | ful | sleep |
| 5 with | God, | Cre - | a - | tor | of | all | things |

| | | | | | | | | |
|---|---|---|---|---|---|---|---|---|
| 1 and | watch - | ful | guard - | ian | o - | ver | all: |
| 2 in | night's | en - | fold - | ing | qui - | et - | ness. |
| 3 those | you | have | ran - | somed | by | your | blood. |
| 4 that | wak - | ing | we | may | watch | with | you. |
| 5 and | with | the | Spi - | rit, | Com - | fort - | er. |

Words: Latin, 10th cent.; ver *Hymnal 1982*. St. 5, Anne K. LeCroy (b. 1930)
Music: *Jesu, nostra redemptio*, plainsong, Mode 8, Worcester MS., 13th cent.

LM

1 Je - sus, Re - deem - er of the world, Word of the
2 The whole cre - a - tion's ar - chi - tect, you set the
3 You broke the chains of death and hell: Lord, free us
4 Lord, while we live for this short time as mor - tals
*5 All glo - ry be to you, Lord Christ, who, con - quering

1 Fa - ther throned on high, light from the light in - vi - si -
2 bounds of night and day, give to our wea - ried bo - dies
3 from our an - cient foe and let him nev - er lead a -
4 clothed in earth - bound frame, re - fresh us now with rest - ful
5 death, reign glo - rious - ly with God, Cre - a - tor of all

1 ble, and watch - ful guard - ian o - ver all:
2 rest in night's en - fold - ing qui - et - ness.
3 stray those you have ran - somed by your blood.
4 sleep that wak - ing we may watch with you.
5 things and with the Spi - rit, Com - fort - er.

Words: Latin, 10th cent.; ver. *Hymnal 1982*. St. 5, Anne K. LeCroy (b. 1930)
Music: *Wilderness*, Reginald Sparshatt Thatcher (1888-1957)

LM

1 O Christ, you are both light and day, you drive a -
2 We pray you, O most ho - ly Lord, to be our
3 Al - though our eyes in sleep be closed, let hearts in
4 De - fend - er of us all, look down; re - pel our
*5 O Christ, Re - deem - er of the world, O God, our

1 way the sha - dowed night; as Day - star you pre -
2 guard - ian while we sleep; be - stow on us who
3 con - stant vi - gil watch; with your right hand you
4 dread, ma - li - cious foe; di - rect your faith - ful
5 Ma - ker and our end, O Spi - rit, bond of

1 cede the dawn, the Her - ald of the light to come.
2 rest in you the bless - ing of a qui - et night.
3 will pro - tect those who be - lieve and trust in you.
4 house - hold Lord, whom you have pur - chased with your blood.
5 peace and love, to you be thanks and end - less praise.

Words: Latin, 6th cent.; ver. *Hymnal 1982.* St. 5, Charles P. Price (b. 1920)
Music: *Christe, qui Lux es et dies,* plainsong, Mode 2, *Mailander Hymnen,* 15th cent.

LM

# Compline

## 41

1 O Christ, you are both light and day,
2 We pray you, O most ho - ly Lord,
3 Al - though our eyes in sleep be closed,
4 De - fend - er of us all, look down;
*5 O Christ, Re - deem - er of the world,

1 you drive a - way the sha - dowed night;
2 to be our guard - ian while we sleep;
3 let hearts in con - stant vi - gil watch;
4 re - pel our dread, ma - li - cious foe;
5 O God, our Ma - ker and our end,

1 as Day - star you pre - cede the dawn,
2 be - stow on us who rest in you
3 with your right hand you will pro - tect
4 di - rect your faith - ful house - hold, Lord,
5 O Spi - rit, bond of peace and love,

1 the Her - ald of the light to come.
2 the bless - ing of a qui - et night.
3 those who be - lieve and trust in you.
4 whom you have pur - chased with your blood.
5 to you be thanks and end - less praise.

Words: Latin, 6th cent.; ver. *Hymnal 1982.* St. 5, Charles P. Price (b 1920)
Music: *Compline,* David Hurd (b. 1950)

LM

1 Now the day is o - ver, night is draw - ing nigh,
2 Je - sus, give the wear - y calm and sweet re - pose;
3 Grant to lit - tle child - ren vis - ions bright of thee;
4 Com - fort ev - ery suf - ferer watch - ing late in pain;
5 Through the long night watch - es may thine an - gels spread

1 sha - dows of the eve - ning steal a - cross the sky.
2 with thy tend - erest bless - ing may our eye - lids close.
3 guard the sail - ors toss - ing on the deep, blue sea.
4 those who plan some e - vil from their sin re - strain.
5 their white wings a - bove me, watch - ing round my bed.

1 eve - ning steal a - cross the sky.
2 bless - ing may our eye - lids close.
3 toss - ing on the deep, blue sea.
4 e - vil from their sin re - strain.
5 bove me, watch - ing round my bed.

6 When the morning wakens,
   then may I arise
Pure, and fresh, and sinless
   in thy holy eyes.

Words: Sabine Baring-Gould (1834-1924), alt.
Music: *Merrial*, Joseph Barnby (1838-1896)

65.65

43

Compline

1 All praise to thee, my God, this night, for
2 For - give me, Lord, for thy dear Son, the
3 O may my soul on thee re - pose, and
4 Praise God, from whom all bless - ings flow; praise

all    the   bless-ings    of    the    light: keep    me,    O    keep    me,
ill    that    I    this    day    have   done; that    with    the    world,   my -
with    sweet sleep mine    eye-lids   close; sleep    that    shall    me    more
him,    all    crea-tures   here    be-low; praise    him   a-bove,    ye

King    of    kings,    be-neath thine   own    al-might-y    wings.
self,    and    thee,    I,    ere    I    sleep,   at    peace  may    be.
vi-gorous make    to    serve   my    God   when    I    a-wake.
heaven-ly   host: praise   Fa-ther,   Son,   and    Ho-ly    Ghost.

*This hymn may be sung unaccompanied as a four-part canon at the distance of one measure.*
Words: Thomas Ken (1637-1711)
Music: *The Eighth Tune,* Thomas Tallis (1505?-1585)

LM

## Compline 44

1 To   you   be-fore   the   close   of   day,   Cre-a-tor
2 Save   us   from   trou-bled,   rest-less   sleep,   from   all   ill
3 A   health-y   life   we   ask   of   you,   the   fire   of
4 Al-might-y   Fa-ther,   hear   our   cry   through   Je-sus

of   all   things, we   pray   that   in   your   con-stant
dreams   your   child-ren keep;   so   calm   our   minds   that
love   in   us   re-new,   and   when   the   dawn   new
Christ,   our   Lord Most High,   whom with   the   Spi-rit

clem-en-cy   our   guard   and   keep-er   you   would   be.
fears   may   cease   and   rest-ed   bo-dies   wake   in   peace.
light   will   bring   your   praise and   glo-ry   we   shall   sing.
we   a-dore   for   ev-er   and   for   ev-er-more.

Words: Latin, 6th cent.; ver. *Hymnal 1982.* St. 4, James Waring McCrady (b. 1938)
Music: *Te lucis ante terminum,* plainsong, Mode 8, *Antiphonale Sarisburiense,* Vol. II

LM

1 To you be - fore the close of day, Cre - a - tor
2 Save us from trou - bled, rest - less sleep, from all ill
3 A health - y life we ask of you, the fire of
4 Al - might - y Fa - ther, hear our cry through Je - sus

of all things, we pray that in your con - stant
dreams your child - ren keep; so calm our minds that
love in us re - new, and when the dawn new
Christ, our Lord Most High, whom with the Spi - rit

clem - en - cy our guard and keep - er you would be.
fears may cease and rest - ed bo - dies wake in peace.
light will bring your praise and glo - ry we shall sing.
we a - dore for ev - er and for ev - er - more.

Words: Latin, 6th cent.; ver. *Hymnal 1982*. St. 4, James Waring McCrady (b. 1938)
Music: *Te lucis ante terminum*, plainsong, Mode 8

LM

# Compline

1 The du-teous day now clos-eth, each flower and tree re-
2 Now all the heaven-ly splen-dor breaks forth in star-light
3 Though long our mor-tal blind-ness has missed God's lov-ing-

pos - eth, shade creeps o'er wild and wood: let
ten - der from myr-iad world's un - known; and
kind - ness and plunged us in - to strife; yet

us, as night is fall - ing, on God our Ma - ker
we, this mar - vel see - ing, for - get our sel - fish
when life's day is o - ver, shall death's fair night dis -

call - - ing, give thanks to him, the Giv - er good.
be - - ing for joy of beau - ty not our own.
cov - - er the fields of ev - er - last - ing life.

Words: Paul Gerhardt (1607-1676); tr. Robert Seymour Bridges (1844-1930) and others
Music: *O Welt, ich muss dich lassen*, melody att. Heinrich Isaac (1450?-1517);
     harm. Johann Sebastian Bach (1685-1750)

776. 778

## 47

Sunday

1 On this day, the first of days, God the Fa-ther's Name we praise,
2 On this day the e-ter-nal Son o-ver death his tri-umph won;
3 Ma-ker, who didst fa-shion me im-age of thy-self to be,
4 Ho-ly Je-sus, may I be dead and bur-ied here with thee;
5 Thou, who dost all gifts im-part, shine, blest Spi-rit, in my heart;

1 who, cre-a-tion's Lord and spring, did the world from dark-ness bring.
2 on this day the Spi-rit came with his gifts of liv-ing flame.
3 fill me with thy love di-vine, let my ev-ery thought be thine.
4 and, by love in-flamed, a-rise un-to thee a sac-ri-fice.
5 best of gifts, thy-self be-stow; make me burn thy love to know.

6 God, the blessed Three in One
  dwell within my heart alone;
  thou dost give thyself to me:
  help me give myself to thee.

Words: Latin; tr. Henry Williams Baker (1821-1877), alt.
Music: *Gott sei Dank*, melody from *Geistreiches Gesangbuch*, 1704;
    adapt. and harm. William Henry Havergal (1793-1870), alt.

77. 77

## 48

Sunday

1 O day of ra-diant glad - ness, O day of joy and
2 This day at the cre-a - - tion, the light first had its
3 This day, God's peo-ple meet - ing, his Ho - ly Scrip-ture
4 That light our hope sus - tain - ing, we walk the pil-grim

light, O balm of care and sad - - ness, most
birth; this day for our sal - va - - tion Christ
hear; his liv - ing pres - ence greet - - ing, through
way, at length our rest at - tain - - ing, our

beau - ti - ful, most bright; this day the high and
rose from depths of earth; this day our Lord vic -
Bread and Wine made near. We jour - ney on, be -
end - less Sab - bath day. We sing to thee our

low - ly, through a - ges joined in tune, sing,
to - rious the Spi - rit sent from heaven, and
liev - ing, re - newed with heaven - ly might, from
prais - es, O Fa - ther, Spi - rit, Son; the

"Ho - ly, ho - ly, ho - ly," to the great God Tri - une.
thus this day most glo - rious a tri - ple light was given.
grace more grace re - ceiv - ing on this blest day of light.
Church her voice up - rais - es to thee, blest Three in One.

Words: Sts. 1-2, Christopher Wordsworth (1807-1885), alt.; st. 3, Charles P. Price (b. 1920);
st. 4, *Hymnal 1982*
Music: *Es flog ein kleins Waldvögelein*, German folk song;
harm. George Ratcliffe Woodward (1848-1934)

76. 76. D

1 Come, let us with our Lord a - rise, our Lord who made both
2 This is the day the Lord hath made that all may see his
3 Then let us ren - der him his own, with sol - emn prayer ap -

earth and skies, who died to save the world he made
love dis - played, may feel his re - sur - rec - tion's power
proach the throne, with meek - ness hear the gos - pel word,

and rose tri - um - phant from the dead; he rose, the
and rise a - gain to fall no more, in per - fect
with thanks his dy - ing love re - cord; our joy - ful

prince of life and peace, and stamped the day for ev - er his.
right - eous - ness re - newed and filled with all the life of God.
hearts and voic - es raise and fill his courts with songs of praise.

Words: Charles Wesley (1707-1788)
Music: *Meadville*, Walter Pelz (b. 1926); adapt. W. Thomas Jones (b. 1956)

88. 88. 88

*Unison or harmony*

1 This is the day the Lord hath made, he calls the hours his own;
2 To - day he rose and left the dead, and Sa - tan's em - pire fell;
3 Ho - san - na to the a - noint - ed King, to Da - vid's ho - ly Son!
4 Blest be the Lord, who comes to us with mes - sag - es of grace!
5 Ho - san - na in the high - est strains the Church on earth can raise;

1 let heaven re-joice, let earth be glad, and praise sur-round the throne.
2 to-day the saints his tri-umphs spread, and all his won-ders tell.
3 Make haste to help us, Lord, and bring sal-va-tion from thy throne.
4 Who comes, in God his Fa-ther's name, to save our sin-ful race.
5 the high-est heavens in which he reigns shall give him no-bler praise.

Words: Isaac Watts (1674-1748), alt.
Music: *London New*, melody from *The Psalms of David in Prose and Meeter*, 1635, alt.
harm. John Playford (1623-1686)

CM

## Sunday

**51**

1 We the Lord's peo-ple, heart and voice u-nit-ing, praise him who
2 This is the Lord's house, home of all his peo-ple, school for the
3 This is the Lord's day, day of God's own mak-ing, day of cre-
4 In the Lord's ser-vice bread and wine are of-fered, that Christ may

called us out of sin and dark-ness in-to his own light,
faith-ful, ref-uge for the sin-ner, rest for the pil-grim,
a-tion, day of re-sur-rec-tion, day of the Spi-rit,
take them, bless them, break, and give them to all his peo-ple,

that he might a-noint us a roy-al priest-hood.
ha-ven for the wea-ry; all find a wel-come.
sign of hea-ven's ban-quet, day for re-joic-ing.
his own life im-part-ing, food ev-er-last-ing.

Words: John E. Bowers (b. 1923), alt.
Music: *Decatur Place*, Richard Wayne Dirksen (b. 1921)

11. 11. 11. 5

52

1 This day at thy cre - at - ing word
2 This day the Lord for sin - ners slain
3 This day the Ho - ly Spi - rit came
4 All praise to God the Fa - ther be,

first o'er the earth the light was poured;
in might vic - to - rious rose a - gain;
with fier - y tongues of clo - ven flame;
all praise, e - ter - nal Son, to thee,

O Lord, this day up - on us shine
O Je - sus, may we lift - ed be
O Spi - rit, fill our hearts this day
whom, with the Spi - rit, we a - dore

and fill our souls with light di - vine.
from death of sin to life in thee!
with grace to hear and grace to pray.
for ev - er and for ev - er - more.

Words: William Walsham How (1823-1897), alt.
Music: *Rushford*, Henry G. Ley (1887-1962)

LM

53

1 Once he came in bless - ing, all our ills re - dress - ing;
2 Still he comes with - in us, still his voice would win us
3 Thus, if thou canst name him, not a-shamed to claim him,
4 One who thus en - dur - eth bright re - ward se - cur - eth.

came in like-ness low - ly, Son of God most ho - ly;
from the sins that hurt us, would to Truth con - vert us:
but wilt trust him bold - ly nor dost love him cold - ly,
Come, then, O Lord Je - sus, from our sins re - lease us;

bore the cross to save us, hope and free - dom gave us.
not in tor - ment hold us, but in love en - fold us.
he will then re - ceive thee, heal thee, and for - give thee.
let us here con - fess thee till in heaven we bless thee.

Words: Jan Roh (1485?-1547); tr. Catherine Winkworth (1827-1878), alt.
Music: *Gottes Sohn ist kommen*, melody Michael Weisse (d. 1534)

66. 66. 66

## Advent

### 54

1 Sa - vior of the na - tions, come! Vir - gin's
2 Won - drous birth! Oh, won - drous child of the
3 Thus on earth the Word ap - pears, grac - ing
4 Come, O Fa - ther's sav - ing Son, who o'er

Son, make here your home. Mar - vel now, both
Vir - gin un - de - filed! Might - y God and
his cre - a - ted spheres; hence to death and
sin the vic - tory won. Bound - less shall your

heaven and earth, that the Lord chose such a birth.
Ma - ry's son, ea - ger now his race to run!
hell de - scends, then the heaven - ly throne a - scends.
king - dom be; grant that we its glo - ries see.

Words: Martin Luther (1483-1546) after Ambrose of Milan (340-397);
    tr. William M. Reynolds (1812-1876) and James Waring McCrady (b. 1938)
Music: *Nun komm, der Heiden Heiland*, melody from *Erfurt Enchiridia*, 1524

77. 77

Advent

1 Redeemer of the nations, come; reveal yourself in virgin birth, the birth which ages all adore, a wondrous birth, befitting God.
2 From human will you do not spring, but from the Spirit of our God; O Word of God, come; take our flesh and grow as child in Mary's womb.
3 You came forth from the eternal God, and you returned to that same source. You suffered death and harrowed hell, and reigned once more from God's high throne.
4 With God the Father you are one, and one with us in human flesh. Oh, fill our weak and dying frame with godly strength which never fails.
5 Your cradle shines with glory's light, its splendor pierces all our gloom. Our faith reflects those radiant beams; no night shall overcome it now.
6 All praise, O unbegotten God, all praise to you, eternal Word, all praise, life-giving Spirit, praise, all glory to our God Triune.

Words: Att. Ambrose of Milan (340-397); tr. Charles P. Price (b. 1920)
Music: *Veni Redemptor gentium*, plainsong, Mode 1, Einsiedeln MS., 12th cent.

LM

1 (Dec. 23) O come, O come, Em-man-u-el, and ran-som
2 (Dec. 17) O come, thou Wis-dom from on high, who or-derest
3 (Dec. 18) O come, O come, thou Lord of might, who to thy
4 (Dec. 19) O come, thou Branch of Jes-se's tree, free them from
5 (Dec. 20) O come, thou Key of Da-vid, come, and o-pen
6 (Dec. 21) O come, thou Day-spring from on high, and cheer us
7 (Dec. 22) O come, De-sire of na-tions, bind in one the
8 (Dec. 23) O come, O come, Em-man-u-el, and ran-som

1 cap-tive Is-ra-el, that mourns in lone-ly ex-ile
2 all things might-i-ly; to us the path of know-ledge
3 tribes on Si-nai's height in an-cient times didst give the
4 Sa-tan's ty-ran-ny that trust thy might-y power to
5 wide our heaven-ly home; make safe the way that leads on
6 by thy draw-ing nigh; dis-perse the gloom-y clouds of
7 hearts of all man-kind; bid thou our sad di-vi-sions
8 cap-tive Is-ra-el, that mourns in lone-ly ex-ile

1 here un-til the Son of God ap-pear.
2 show, and teach us in her ways to go.
3 law, in cloud, and ma-jes-ty, and awe.
4 save, and give them vic-tory o'er the grave.
5 high, and close the path to mis-er-y. Re-joice! Re-joice!
6 night, and death's dark shad-ow put to flight.
7 cease, and be thy-self our King of Peace.
8 here un-til the Son of God ap-pear.

Em-man-u-el shall come to thee, O Is-ra-el!

*The stanzas may be used as antiphons with "The Song of Mary" on the dates given.*

Words: Latin, ca. 9th cent.; ver. *Hymnal 1940*, alt.
Music: *Veni, veni, Emmanuel*, plainsong, Mode 1, *Processionale*, 15th cent.;
    adapt. Thomas Helmore (1811-1890)

LM with Refrain

1 Lo! he comes, with clouds de - scend - ing, once for
2 Ev - ery eye shall now be - hold him, robed in
3 Those dear to - kens of his pas - sion still his
4 Yea, a - men! let all a - dore thee, high on

our sal - va - tion slain; thou - sand thou - sand
dread - ful ma - jes - ty; those who set at
daz - zling bo - dy bears, cause of end - less
thine e - ter - nal throne; Sa - vior, take the

saints at - tend - ing swell the tri - umph of his
nought and sold him, pierced, and nailed him to the
ex - ul - ta - tion to his ran - somed wor - ship -
power and glo - ry; claim the king - dom for thine

train: Al - le - lu - ia! Al - le - lu - ia!
tree, deep - ly wail - ing, deep - ly wail - ing,
ers; with what rap - ture, with what rap - ture,
own: Al - le - lu - ia! Al - le - lu - ia!

Al - le - lu - ia! Christ the Lord re - turns to reign.
deep - ly wail - ing, shall the true Mes - si - ah see.
with what rap - ture gaze we on those glo - rious scars!
Al - le - lu - ia! Thou shalt reign, and thou a - lone.

Words: Charles Wesley (1707-1788)
Music: *Helmsley*, melody Augustine Arne (1710-1778)

87. 87 12 7

Words: Charles Wesley (1707-1788)
Music: *St. Thomas*, melody att. John Francis Wade (1711-1786);
harm. att. Vincent Francis Novello (1781-1861)

87. 87

Words: Latin, ca. 6th cent.; tr. *Hymns Ancient and Modern*, 1861, alt.
Music: *Merton*, William Henry Monk (1823-1889); desc. Alan Gray (1855-1935)

87. 87

1 Cre - a - tor of the stars of night,
2 In sor - row of that the an - cient curse
3 When this old world drew on toward night,
4 At your great Name, O Je - sus, now
5 Come in your ho - ly might, we pray,
*6 To God the Fa - ther, God the Son,

1 your peo - ple's ev - er - last - ing light,
2 should doom to death a u - ni - verse,
3 you came; but not in splen - dor bright,
4 all knees must bend, all hearts must bow:
5 re - deem us for e - ter - nal day;
6 and God the Spi - rit, Three in One,

1 O Christ, Re - deem - er of us all,
2 you came, O Sa - vior, to set free
3 not as a mon - arch, but the child
4 all things on earth with one ac - cord,
5 de - fend us while we dwell be - low
6 praise, hon - or, might, and glo - ry be

1 we pray you hear us when we call.
2 your own in glo - rious li - ber - ty.
3 of Ma - ry, blame - less mo - ther mild.
4 like those in heaven, shall call you Lord.
5 from all as - saults of our dread foe.
6 from age to age e - ter - nal - ly.

Words: Latin, 9th cent.; ver. *Hymnal 1940*, alt.
Music: *Conditor alme siderum*, plainsong, Mode 4

LM

1 "Sleep-ers, wake!" A voice a - stounds us, the shout of ram - part - guards sur - rounds us: "A - wake, Je - ru - sa - lem, a - rise!" Mid - night's peace their cry has bro - ken, their ur - gent sum-mons clear - ly spo -

2 Zi - on hears the watch - man sing - ing; her heart with joy - ful hope is spring - ing, she wakes and hur - ries through the night. Forth he comes, her Bride - groom glo - rious in strength of grace, in truth vic - to -

3 Lamb of God, the heavens a - dore you; let saints and an - gels sing be - fore you, as harps and cym - bals swell the sound. Twelve great pearls, the ci - ty's por - tals: through them we stream to join the im - mor -

ken:     "The    time   has   come,   O    maid - ens  wise!
rious:    her    star    is   risen,  her    light  grows bright.
tals     as     we   with    joy   your   throne  sur - round.

Rise   up,    and  give   us   light;   the   Bride - groom is   in
Now  come,  most wor - thy  Lord,   God's   Son,   In - car - nate
No   eye   has known the  sight,   no   ear   heard such  de -

sight.  Al - le - lu - ia!    Your  lamps  pre - pare  and
Word,  Al - le - lu - ia!    We  fol - low  all   and
light:  Al - le - lu - ia!   There - fore  we  sing  to

has - ten  there, that   you   the  wed - ding  feast  may share."
heed  your  call   to   come  in - to   the  ban - quet hall.
greet  our  King;  for   ev - er  let  our   prais - es  ring.

Words: Philipp Nicolai (1556-1608); tr. Carl P. Daw, Jr. (b. 1944)
Music: *Wachet auf*, melody Hans Sachs (1494-1576); adapt. Philipp Nicolai (1556-1608);
arr. and harm. Johann Sebastian Bach (1685-1750)

Irr.

1 "Sleep-ers, wake!" A voice a-stounds us, the shout of ram-part-
2 Zi-on hears the watch-man sing - ing; her heart with joy-ful
3 Lamb of God, the heavens a-dore you; let saints and an-gels

guards sur-rounds us: "A-wake, Je-ru-sa-lem, a-rise!"
hope is spring-ing, she wakes and hur-ries through the night.
sing be-fore you, as harps and cym-bals swell the sound.

Mid-night's peace their cry has bro-ken, their ur-gent sum-mons
Forth he comes, her Bride-groom glo - rious in strength of grace, in
Twelve great pearls, the ci-ty's por-tals: through them we stream to

clear-ly spo-ken: "The time has come, O maid-ens wise!
truth vic-to-rious: her star is risen, her light grows bright.
join the im-mor-tals as we with joy your throne sur-round.

Rise up, and give us light; the Bride-groom is in sight.
Now come, most wor-thy Lord, God's Son, In-car-nate Word,
No eye has known the sight, no ear heard such de-light:

Al-le-lu-ia! Your lamps pre-pare and has-ten there,
Al-le-lu-ia! We fol-low all and heed your call
Al-le-lu-ia! There-fore we sing to greet our King;

| | | | | | | | |
|---|---|---|---|---|---|---|---|
| that | you | the | wed - ding | feast | may | share." |
| to | come | in - to | the | ban - quet | hall. |
| for | ev - er | let | our | prais - es | ring. |

Words: Philipp Nicolai (1556-1608); tr. Carl P. Daw, Jr. (b. 1944)
Music: *Wachet auf*, melody Hans Sachs (1494-1576); adapt. Philipp Nicolai (1556-1608)       Irr.

## Advent                                                                       63

| | | | | | | | | |
|---|---|---|---|---|---|---|---|---|
| 1 | O | heaven - ly | Word, | e - | ter - nal | Light, |
| 2 | pour | light | up - on | us | from | a - bove, |
| 3 | and | when, | as | judge, | thou | draw - est | nigh |
| 4 | O | let | us | not, | for | e - vil | past, |
| *5 | To | God | the | Fa - ther, | God | the | Son, |

| | | | | | | | |
|---|---|---|---|---|---|---|---|
| 1 | be - got - ten | of | the | Fa - ther's | might, |
| 2 | and | fire | our | hearts | with | ar - dent | love, |
| 3 | the | se - crets | of | our | hearts | to | try, |
| 4 | be | driv - en | from | thy | face | at | last, |
| 5 | and | God | the | Spi - rit, | ev - er | One, |

| | | | | | | | |
|---|---|---|---|---|---|---|---|
| 1 | who | in | these | lat - ter | days | wast | born |
| 2 | that, | as | we | hear | thy | truth | to - day, |
| 3 | to | rec - om - pense | each | hid - den | sin |
| 4 | but | with | thy | saints | for | ev - er - more |
| 5 | praise, | hon - or, | might, | and | glo - ry | be |

| | | | | | | | |
|---|---|---|---|---|---|---|---|
| 1 | for | bless - ing | to | a | world | for - lorn; |
| 2 | all | wrong | de - sires | may | burn | a - way; |
| 3 | and | bid | the | saints | their | reign | be - gin; |
| 4 | be - hold | thee, | love | thee, | and | a - dore. |
| 5 | from | age | to | age | e - ter - nal - ly. |

Words: Latin, ca. 7th cent.; tr. *Hymnal 1982*
Music: *Verbum supernum prodiens*, plainsong, Mode 2, Nevers MS., 13th cent.                LM

1 O heaven-ly Word, e-ter-nal Light, be-got-ten
2 pour light up-on us from a-bove, and fire our
3 and when, as judge, thou draw-est nigh the se-crets
4 O let us not, for e-vil past, be driv-en
*5 To God the Fa-ther, God the Son, and God the

1 of the Fa-ther's might, who in these lat-ter days wast
2 hearts with ar-dent love, that, as we hear thy truth to-
3 of our hearts to try, to rec-om-pense each hid-den
4 from thy face at last, but with thy saints for ev-er-
5 Spi-rit, ev-er One, praise, hon-or, might, and glo-ry

1 born for bless-ing to a world for-lorn;
2 day, all wrong de-sires may burn a-way;
3 sin and bid the saints their reign be-gin;
4 more be-hold thee, love thee, and a-dore.
5 be from age to age e-ter-nal-ly.

Words: Latin, ca. 7th cent.; tr. *Hymnal 1982*
Music: *O Heiland, reiss*, melody from *Rheinfelsisches Deutsches Catholisches Gesangbuch*, 1666

1 Pre-pare the way, O Zi-on, your Christ is draw-ing near!
2 He brings God's rule, O Zi-on; he comes from heaven a-bove.
3 Fling wide your gates, O Zi-on; your Sa-vior's rule em-brace.

Let ev-ery hill and val-ley a lev-el way ap-pear.
His rule is peace and free-dom, and jus-tice, truth, and love.
His tid-ings of sal-va-tion pro-claim in ev-ery place.

Greet One who comes in glo - ry, fore - told in sa - cred sto - ry.
Lift high your praise re - sound-ing, for grace and joy a - bound - ing.
All lands will bow be - fore him, their voic - es will a - dore him.

*Refrain*

Oh, blest is Christ that came in God's most ho - ly name.

Words: Frans Mikael Franzen (1772-1847); tr. composite; adapt. Charles P. Price (b. 1920)
Music: *Bereden väg för Herran,* melody from *Then Swenska Psalmboken,* 1697

76. 76. 77 with Refrain

## Advent

# 66

1 Come, thou long - ex - pect-ed Je - sus, born to set thy peo - ple free;
2 Is - rael's strength and con - so - la - tion, hope of all the earth thou art:
3 Born thy peo - ple to de - liv - er, born a child, and yet a king,
4 By thine own e - ter - nal Spi - rit rule in all our hearts a - lone;

from our fears and sins re - lease us, let us find our rest in thee.
dear de - sire of ev - ery na - tion, joy of ev - ery long - ing heart.
born to reign in us for ev - er, now thy gra-cious king - dom bring.
by thine all - suf - fi-cient mer - it raise us to thy glo - rious throne.

Words: Charles Wesley (1707-1788)
Music: *Stuttgart,* melody from *Psalmodia Sacra, oder Andächtige und Schöne Gesange,* 1715;
adapt. and harm. William Henry Havergal (1793-1870), alt.

87. 87

1 Com - fort, com - fort ye my peo - ple,    speak ye peace, thus
2 Hark, the voice of one that cri - eth    in the des - ert
3 Make ye straight what long was crook - ed,    make the rough - er

saith our God;    com - fort those who sit in dark - ness
far and near,    call - ing us to new re - pent - ance
pla - ces plain;    let your hearts be true and hum - ble,

mourn - ing 'neath their sor - rows' load.    Speak ye to Je -
since the king - dom now is here.    Oh, that warn - ing
as be - fits his ho - ly reign.    For the glo - ry

ru - sa - lem    of the peace that waits for them;
cry o - bey!    Now pre - pare for God a way;
of the Lord    now o'er earth is shed a - broad;

tell her that her sins I cov - er,
let the val - leys rise to meet him
and all flesh shall see the to - ken

and her war - fare now is o - ver.
and the hills bow down to greet him.
that the word is nev - er bro - ken.

Words: Johann G. Olearius (1611-1684); tr. Catherine Winkworth (1827-1878), alt.
Music: *Psalm 42*, melody Claude Goudimel (1514-1572)          87. 87. 77. 88

1 Re - joice! re - joice, be - liev - ers, and let your lights ap - pear!
2 See that your lamps are burn - ing, re - ple - nish them with oil;
3 Our hope and ex - pec - ta - tion, O Je - sus, now ap - pear;

The eve - ning is ad - vanc - ing, and dark - er night is near.
look now for your sal - va - tion, the end of sin and toil.
a - rise, thou Sun so longed for, a - bove this dark - ened sphere!

The Bride-groom is a - ris - ing, and soon he will draw nigh;
The mar - riage - feast is wait - ing, the gates wide o - pen stand;
With hearts and hands up - lift - ed, we plead, O Lord, to see

up, watch in ex - pec - ta - tion! at mid - night comes the cry.
rise up, ye heirs of glo - ry, the Bride-groom is at hand!
the day of earth's re - demp - tion, and ev - er be with thee!

Words: Laurentius Laurenti (1660-1722); tr. Sarah B. Findlater (1823-1907), alt.
Music: *Llangloffan*, melody from *Hymnau a Thonau er Gwasanaeth yr Eglwys yng Nghymru*, 1865

76. 76 D

1 What is the cry - ing at Jor - dan? Who
2 Who then shall stir in this dark - ness, pre -
3 Lord, give us grace to a - wake us, to
4 Now comes the day of sal - va - tion, in

hears, O God, the___ pro - phe - cy? Dark is the
pare for joy in the win - ter night? Mor - tal in
see the branch that be - gins to bloom; in great hu -
joy and ter - ror the Word is born! God gives him -

sea - son, dark our hearts and shut___ to mys - ter - y.
dark - ness we lie down, blind - heart - ed see - ing no light.
mil - i - ty is hid all heaven in a lit - tle room.
self in - to our lives; O let___ sal - va - tion dawn!

Words: Carol Christopher Drake (b. 1933), alt.
Music: *St. Mark's, Berkeley,* Irish melody from *Danta De: Hymns to God, Ancient and Modern*

88. 86

1 Her - ald, sound the note of judg - ment, warn - ing us of right and
2 Her - ald, sound the note of glad - ness; tell the news that Christ is
3 Her - ald, sound the note of par - don— those re - pent - ing are for -
4 Her - ald, sound the note of tri - umph; Christ has come to share our

wrong, turn - ing us from sin and sad - ness
here; make a path - way through the des - ert
given; God re - ceives his way - ward chil - dren,
life, bring - ing God's own love and pow - er,

till once more we sing the song.
for the one who brings God near.
and to them new life is given.
grant-ing vic-tory in our strife.

*Refrain*

Sound the trum - pet!
Tell the mes - sage! Christ, the Sa - vior King, has come!

Words: Moir A. J. Waters (1906-1980), alt.
Music: *Herald, Sound,* Robert Powell (b. 1932)

87. 87 with Refrain

## Advent

# 71

1 Hark! the glad sound! the Sa - vior comes, the Sa - vior
2 He comes, the pris - on̲ers to re - lease in Sa - tan's
3 He comes, the bro - ken heart to bind, the bleed - ing
4 Our glad ho - san - nas, Prince of Peace, thy wel - come

prom - ised long: let ev - ery heart pre -
bond - age held; the gates of brass be -
soul to cure; and with the trea - sures
shall pro - claim; and heaven's e - ter - nal

pare a throne, and ev - ery voice a song.
fore him burst, the i - ron fet - ters yield.
of his grace to en - rich the hum - ble poor.
arch - es ring with thy be - lov - ed Name.

Words: Philip Doddridge (1702-1751)
Music: *Bristol,* from *The Whole Booke of Psalmes,* 1621

CM

*Descant*

4 Our glad ho - san - nas, Prince of Peace, thy wel - come

1 Hark! the glad sound! the Sa - vior comes, the Sa - vior
2 He comes, the pris - oners to re - lease in Sa - tan's
3 He comes, the bro - ken heart to bind, the bleed - ing
4 Our glad ho - san - nas, Prince of Peace, thy wel - come

shall pro - claim; and heaven's e - ter - nal

prom - ised long; let ev - ery heart pre -
bond - age held; the gates of brass be -
soul to cure; and with the trea - sures
shall pro - claim; and heaven's e - ter - nal

arch - es ring with thy be - lov - ed Name.

pare a throne, and ev - ery voice a song.
fore him burst, the i - ron fet - ters yield.
of his grace to en - rich the hum - ble poor.
arch - es ring with thy be - lov - ed Name.

Words: Philip Doddridge (1702-1751)
Music: *Richmond*, melody Thomas Haweis (1734-1820); adapt. Samuel Webbe (1740-1816);
harm. *Hymns Ancient and Modern, Revised,* 1950; desc. Craig Sellar Lang (1891-1971)

CM

# Advent

Words: Greek; tr. John Brownlie (1859-1925), alt.
Music: *St. Stephen*, William Jones (1726-1800), alt.

CM

*Descant*

3 Blest be the King whose com - ing is in the name of

1 Blest be the King whose com - ing is in the name of
2 Blest be the King whose com - ing is in the name of
3 Blest be the King whose com - ing is in the name of
4 Blest be the King whose com - ing is in the name of

God! He on - ly to the hum - ble re - veals the face of

God! For him let doors be o - pened, no hearts a - gainst him
God! By those who tru - ly lis - ten his voice is tru - ly
God! He on - ly to the hum - ble re - veals the face of
God! He of - fers to the bur - dened the rest and grace they

God. All power is his, all glo - ry! All

barred! Not robed in roy - al splen - dor, in
heard; pi - ty the proud and haugh - ty, who
God. All power is his, all glo - ry! All
need. Gen - tle is he and hum - ble! And

things    are    in    his    hand,    all    a - ges    and    all

power and    pomp,    comes    he;    but    clad    as    are    the
have not    learned    to    heed    the    Christ who    is    the
things are    in    his    hand,    all    a - ges    and    all
light his    yoke    shall    be,    for    he    would    have us

peo - ples,    till    time    it - self    shall    end!

poor - est,    such    his    hu - mil - i - ty!
Prom - ise,    who    has    a - tone - ment    made.
peo - ples,    till    time    it - self    shall    end!
bear    it    so    he    can    make    us    free!

Words: Frederico J. Pagura (b. 1923); tr. F. Pratt Green (b. 1903), alt.
Music: *Valet will ich dir geben,* melody Melchior Teschner (1584-1635) alt.;
    harm. and desc. Ronald Arnatt (b. 1930)

76. 76 D

1 There's a voice in the wil - der - ness cry - ing, a___
2 O___ Zi - on, that bring - est good tid - ings, get thee
3 but the word of our God___ en - dur - eth, the___

call from the ways un - trod: Pre - pare in the des - ert a
up to the heights and sing! Pro - claim to a des - o - late
arm of the Lord is strong; he stands in the midst___ of

high - way, a high - way for our God! The___
peo - ple the com - ing of their King. Like the
na - tions, and he will right the wrong. He shall

val - leys shall be ex - alt - ed, the
flowers of the field they___ per - ish, like
feed his___ flock like a shep - herd, the

lof - ty hills brought low; make straight all the crook - ed
grass our works de - cay, the power and___ pomp of
lambs he'll gent - ly hold; to pas - tures of peace he'll

pla - ces where the Lord our___ God___ may go!
na - tions shall___ pass like a dream_ a - way;
lead them, and___ bring them_ safe to his fold.

Words: James Lewis Milligan (1876-1961), alt.
Music: *Ascension*, Henry Hugh Bancroft (b. 1904)

Irr.

# Advent

1 On Jor - dan's bank the Bap - tist's cry an -
2 Then cleansed be ev - ery breast from sin; make
3 For thou art our sal - va - tion, Lord, our
4 To heal the sick stretch out thine hand, and
5 All praise, e - ter - nal Son, to thee, whose

1 noun - ces that the Lord is nigh; a - wake and heark - en,
2 straight the way for God with - in, and let each heart pre -
3 ref - uge, and our great re - ward; with - out thy grace we
4 bid the fall - en sin - ner stand; shine forth, and let thy
5 ad - vent doth thy peo - ple free; whom with the Fa - ther

1 for he brings glad tid - ings of the King of kings.
2 pare a home where such a might - y guest may come.
3 waste a - way like flowers that with - er and de - cay.
4 light re - store earth's own true love - li - ness once more.
5 we a - dore and Ho - ly Spi - rit ev - er - more.

Words: Charles Coffin (1676-1749); tr. Charles Winfred Douglas (1867-1944),
after John Chandler (1806-1876); alt.
Music: *Winchester New*, melody from *Musicalishes Hand-Buch*, 1690;
harm. William Henry Monk (1823-1889), alt.

LM

# 77

Christmas

1 From east to west, from shore to shore, let
2 Be - hold, the world's cre - a - tor wears the
3 For this how won - drous - ly he wrought! A
4 And while the an - gels in the sky sang
5 All glo - ry for this bless - ed morn to

1 ev - ery heart a - wake and sing the ho - ly child whom
2 form and fa - shion of a slave; our ve - ry flesh our
3 maid in low - ly hu - man place be - came, in ways be -
4 praise a - bove the si - lent field, to shep - herds poor the
5 God the Fa - ther ev - er be; all praise to thee, O

1 Ma - ry bore, the Christ, the ev - er - last - ing King.
2 Ma - ker shares, his fal - len crea - tures all to save.
3 yond all thought, the cho - sen ves - sel of his grace.
4 Lord Most High, the one great Shep - herd, was re - vealed.
5 Vir - gin - born, all praise, O Ho - ly Ghost, to thee.

Words: Caelius Sedulius (5th cent.); tr. John Ellerton (1826-1893), alt.
Music: *Vom Himmel kam der Engel Schar*, melody source unknown

LM

# 78

Christmas

*Unison or harmony*

1 O lit - tle town of Beth - le - hem, how still we see thee lie!
2 For Christ is born of Ma - ry; and gath - ered all a - bove,
3 How si - lent - ly, how si - lent - ly, the won - drous gift is given!
*4 Where child-ren pure and hap - py pray to the bless - ed Child,
5 O ho - ly Child of Beth - le - hem, de - scend to us, we pray;

1 A - bove thy deep and dream-less sleep the si - lent stars go by;
2 while mor-tals sleep, the an - gels keep their watch of won-dering love.
3 So God im-parts to hu - man hearts the bless-ings of his heaven.
4 where mis - er - y cries out to thee, Son of the mo - ther mild;
5 cast out our sin and en - ter in, be born in us to - day.

1 yet in thy dark streets shin - eth the ev - er - last - ing Light;
2 O morn-ing stars, to - geth - er pro - claim the ho - ly birth!
3 No ear may hear his com - ing, but in this world of sin,
4 where char - i - ty stands watch - ing and faith holds wide the door,
5 We hear the Christ-mas an - gels the great glad tid - ings tell;

1 the hopes and fears of all the years are met in thee to - night.
2 and prais - es sing to God the King, and peace to men on earth.
3 where meek souls will re - ceive him, still the dear Christ en - ters in.
4 the dark night wakes, the glo - ry breaks, and Christ-mas comes once more.
5 O come to us, a - bide with us, our Lord Em - man - u - el!

Words: Philips Brooks (1835-1893)
Music: *Forest Green*, English melody; adapt. and harm. Ralph Vaughan Williams (1872-1958)

CMD

79

1 O lit - tle town of Beth - le - hem, how still we see thee lie!
2 For Christ is born of Ma - ry; and gath - ered all a - bove,
3 How si - lent - ly, how si - lent - ly, the won - drous gift is given!
*4 Where child - ren pure and hap - py pray to the bless - ed Child,
5 O ho - ly Child of Beth - le - hem, de - scend to us, we pray;

1 A - bove thy deep and dream-less sleep the si - lent stars go by;
2 while mor-tals sleep, the an - gels keep their watch of won-dering love.
3 So God im-parts to hu - man hearts the bless-ings of his heaven.
4 where mis-er - y cries out to thee, Son of the mo - ther mild;
5 cast out our sin and en - ter in, be born in us to - day.

1 yet in thy dark streets shin - eth the ev - er - last - ing Light;
2 O morn-ing stars, to - geth - er pro - claim the ho - ly birth!
3 No ear may hear his com - ing, but in this world of sin,
4 where char - i - ty stands watch - ing and faith holds wide the door,
5 We hear the Christ-mas an - gels the great glad tid - ings tell;

1 the hopes and fears of all the years are met in thee to - night.
2 and prais - es sing to God the King, and peace to men on earth.
3 where meek souls will re - ceive him, still the dear Christ en - ters in.
4 the dark night wakes, the glo - ry breaks, and Christ - mas comes once more.
5 O come to us, a - bide with us, our Lord Em - man - u - el!

Words: Phillips Brooks (1835-1893)
Music: *St. Louis*, Lewis H. Redner (1831-1908)

CMD

## Christmas

# 80

1 From heaven a - bove to earth I come to bring good
2 to you this night is born a child of Ma - ry,
3 This is the Christ, God's Son most high, who hears your
4 The bless - ing which the Fa - ther planned the Son holds

news to ev - ery - one! Glad tid - ings of great
cho - sen vir - gin mild; this new - born child of
sad and bit - ter cry; he will him - self your
in his in - fant hand, that in his king - dom,

joy I bring to all the world, and glad - ly sing:
low - ly birth shall be the joy of all the earth.
Sa - vior be and from all sin will set you free.
bright and fair, you may with us his glo - ry share.

Words: Martin Luther (1483-1546); tr. *Lutheran Book of Worship*, 1978
Music: *Vom Himmel hoch*, melody from *Geistliche lieder auffs new gebessert und gemehrt*, 1539

LM

81                                                        Christmas

1 Lo, how a Rose e'er bloom-ing   from ten - der    stem    hath sprung!
2 I - sa - iah 'twas fore - told it,   the Rose I    have    in mind,
*3 O Flower, whose fra-grance ten - der   with sweet-ness   fills   the air,

Of Jes - se's lin - eage com - ing   as seers of   old   have sung.
with Ma - ry we be - hold it,   the Vir - gin   Mo - ther kind.
dis - pel in glo-rious splen - dor   the dark-ness   ev - ery-where;

It   came,   a   blos - som bright,      a - mid   the
To   show God's love   a - right,      she   bore   to
true man, yet   ve - ry   God,      from   sin   and

cold   of   win - ter,   when   half spent   was   the night.
us   a   Sa - vior,   when   half spent   was   the night.
death now save   us,   and   share our   ev - ery   load.

**Words:** St. 1-2, German, 15th cent.; tr. Theodore Baker (1851-1934). st. 3, Friedrich Layritz (1808-1859);
tr. Harriet Reynolds Krauth Spaeth (1845-1925); ver. *Hymnal 1940*
**Music:** *Es ist ein Ros*, melody from *Alte Catholische Geistliche Kirchengesäng*, 1599;
harm. Michael Praetorius (1571-1621)

76. 76. 676

# Christmas

82

*This hymn may be performed in equal note values:* ♩ ♩ ♩ ♩

Words: Marcus Aurelius Clemens Prudentius (348-410?); tr. John Mason Neale (1818-1866)
and Henry Williams Baker (1821-1877), alt.
Music: *Divinum mysterium,* Sanctus trope, 11th cent.; adapt. *Piae Cantiones,* 1582

87. 87. 87 with Refrain

dore him, O come, let us a - dore him, Christ, the Lord.

6    Yea, Lord, we greet thee,
     born this happy morning;
     Jesus, to thee be glory given;
     Word of the Father,
     now in flesh appearing;

*Refrain*

Words: John Francis Wade (1711-1786); tr. Frederick Oakeley (1802-1880) and others
Music: *Adeste fideles*, present form of melody att. John Francis Wade (1711-1786);
       harm. *The English Hymnal*, 1906                                                Irr.

# Christmas                                                                    84

1 Love came down at Christ - mas, love all love - ly, love di - vine;
2 Wor-ship we the God - head, love in - car - nate, love di - vine;
3 Love shall be our to - ken; love be yours and love be mine,

love   was born at   Christ - mas:   star   and an - gels   gave the sign.
wor - ship we our   Je - sus,   but where-with for   sa - cred sign?
love   to God and   neigh - bor,   love   for plea   and   gift and sign.

Words: Christina Rossetti (1830-1894), alt.
Music: *Gartan*, melody from *Petrie Collection of Irish Melodies, Part II*, 1902;
       harm. David Evans (1874-1948)

67. 67

```
1 O  Sa - vior      of    our    fall - en      race,
2 O  Je - sus,      ve -  ry     Light  of      Light,
3 Re - mem - ber,   Lord  of     life   and     grace,
4 To - day,  as     year  by     year   its     light
5 For from   the    Fa -  ther's throne you      came,
6 O  Christ, Re -   deem - er    vir -  gin -    born,
```

```
1 O        Bright - ness  of     the    Fa -   ther's   face,
2 our      con -   stant   star   in     sin's  deep     night;
3 how      once,   to      save   our    fall - en       race,
4 bathes   all     the     world  in     ra -   diance   bright,
5 his      ban -   ished   chil - dren   to     re -     claim;
6 let      songs   of      praise your   Name   a -      dorn,
```

```
1 O        Son     who    shared the    Fa -   ther's   might
2 now      hear    the    prayers your   peo -  ple      pray
3 you      put     our    hu -   man    ves -  ture     on
4 one      pre -   cious  truth  out -  shines the      sun:
5 and      earth   and    sea    and    sky    re -     vere
6 whom     with    the    Fa -   ther   we     a -      dore
```

```
1 be - fore   the    world  knew   day   or      night,
2 through-out  the    world  this   ho -  ly      day.
3 and  came    to     us     as     Ma -  ry's    son.
4 sal - va -   tion   comes  from   you   a -     lone.
5 the  love    of     him    who    sent  you     here.
6 and  Ho -    ly     Spi -  rit    ev -  er -    more.
```

Words: Latin, ca. 6th cent.; tr. Gilbert E. Doan (b. 1930)
Music: *Christe, Redemptor omnium*, plainsong, Mode 1

LM

1. O Sa - vior of our fall - en race,_____
2. O Je - sus, ve - ry Light of Light,_____
3. Re - mem - ber, Lord of life and grace,_____
4. To - day, as year by year its light_____
5. For from the Fa - ther's throne you came,_____
6. O Christ, Re - deem - er vir - gin - born,_____

1. O Bright - ness of the Fa - ther's face,
2. our con - stant star in sin's deep night;
3. how once, to save our fall - en race,
4. bathes all the world in ra - diance bright,
5. his ban - ished chil - dren to re - claim;
6. let songs of praise your Name a - dorn,

1. O Son who shared the Fa - ther's might be - fore the world knew
2. now hear the prayers your peo - ple pray through - out the world this
3. you put our hu - man ves - ture on and came to us as
4. one pre - cious truth out - shines the sun: sal - va - tion comes from
5. and earth and sea and sky re - vere the love of him who
6. whom with the Fa - ther we a - dore and Ho - ly Spi - rit

*(After stanza 6)*

1. day or night,
2. ho - ly day.
3. Ma - ry's son.
4. you a - lone.
5. sent you here.
6. ev - er - more. Al - le - lu - ia!

Words: Latin, ca. 6th cent.; tr. Gilbert E. Doan (b. 1930)
Music: *Gonfalon Royal*, Percy Carter Buck (1871-1947)

LM

1 Hark! the her - ald an - gels sing glo - ry to the new-born King!
2 Christ, by high - est heaven a - dored; Christ, the ev - er - last - ing Lord;
3 Mild he lays his glo - ry by, born that we no more may die,

Peace on earth and mer - cy mild, God and sin - ners rec - on - ciled!
late in time be - hold him come, off - spring of the Vir-gin's womb.
born to raise us from the earth, born to give us sec - ond birth.

Joy - ful, all ye na - tions, rise, join the tri - umph of the skies;
Veiled in flesh the God-head see; hail the in-car-nate De - i - ty.
Risen with heal-ing in his wings, light and life to all he brings,

with the an-gel - ic host pro - claim Christ is born in Beth - le - hem!
Pleased as man with us to dwell; Je - sus, our Em - man - u - el!
hail, the Sun of Right-eous-ness! hail, the heaven-born Prince of Peace!

Hark! the her-ald an-gels sing glo-ry to the new-born King!

Words: Charles Wesley (1707-1788), alt.
Music: *Mendelssohn*, Felix Mendelssohn (1809-1847); adapt. William
H. Cummings (1831-1915)

77. 77. D with Refrain

## Christmas

88

1 Sing, O sing, this bless-ed morn, un-to us a child is born,
2 God from God, and Light from Light, comes with mer-cies in-fi-nite,
3 God with us, Em-man-u-el, deigns for ev-er now to dwell;
4 God comes down that we may rise, lift-ed by him to the skies;
5 O re-new us, Lord, we pray, with thy Spi-rit day by day,

1 un-to us a son is given, God him-self comes down from heaven.
2 from high heaven he comes to earth, one with us in hu-man birth.
3 he on Ad-am's fall-en race sheds the full-ness of his grace.
4 Christ is born for us that we born a-gain in him may be.
5 that we ev-er one may be with the Fa-ther and with thee.

*Refrain*

Sing, O sing, this bless-ed morn, Je-sus Christ to-day is born.

Words: Christopher Wordsworth (1807-1885), alt.
Music: *England's Lane*, English melody; adapt. and harm. Geoffrey Turton Shaw (1879-1943)

77. 77. 77

1 It came up - on the mid - night clear, that
2 Still through the clov - en skies they come with
3 Yet with the woes of sin and strife the
4 For lo! the days are haste - ning on, by

glo - rious song of old, from an - gels bend - ing
peace - ful wings un - furled, and still their heaven - ly
world has suf - fered long; be - neath the heaven - ly
pro - phets seen of old, when with the ev - er -

near the earth to touch their harps of gold:
mu - sic floats o'er all the wea - ry world;
hymn have rolled two thou - sand years of wrong;
cir - cling years shall come the time fore - told,

"Peace on the earth, good will to men, from
a - bove its sad and low - ly plains they
and war - ring hu - man - kind hears not the
when peace shall o - ver all the earth its

heaven's all - gra - cious King." The world in sol - emn
bend on hov - ering wing, and ev - er o'er its
tid - ings which they bring; O hush the noise and
an - cient splen - dors fling, and all the world give

still - ness lay to hear the an - gels sing.
Ba - bel - sounds the bless - ed an - gels sing.
cease your strife and hear the an - gels sing!
back the song which now the an - gels sing.

Words: Edmund H. Sears (1810-1876), alt.
Music: *Carol*, Richard Storrs Willis (1819-1900)

CMD

1 It came up-on the mid-night clear, that glo-rious song of old,
2 Still through the clov-en skies they come with peace-ful wings un-furled,
3 Yet with the woes of sin and strife the world has suf-fered long;
4 For lo! the days are haste-ning on, by pro-phets seen of old,

from an-gels bend-ing near the earth to touch their harps of gold:
and still their heaven-ly mu-sic floats o'er all the wea-ry world;
be-neath the heaven-ly hymn have rolled two thou-sand years of wrong;
when with the ev-er-cir-cling years shall come the time fore-told,

"Peace on the earth, good will to men, from heaven's all-gra-cious King."
a-bove its sad and low-ly plains they bend on hov-ering wing,
and war-ring hu-man-kind hears not the tid-ings which they bring;
when peace shall o-ver all the earth its an-cient splen-dors fling,

The world in sol-emn still-ness lay to hear the an-gels sing.
and ev-er o'er its Ba-bel-sounds the bless-ed an-gels sing.
O hush the noise and cease your strife and hear the an-gels sing!
and all the world give back the song which now the an-gels sing.

Words: Edmund H. Sears (1810-1876), alt.
Music: *Noel*, English melody; adapt. Arthur Seymour Sullivan (1842-1900)

CMD

# Christmas

Break forth, O beau-teous heaven-ly light, and ush - er in the morn - ing; O shep - herds, greet that glo - rious sight, our Lord a crib a - dorn - ing. This child, this lit - tle help - less boy, shall be our con - fi - dence and joy, the power of Sa - tan break - ing, our peace e - ter - nal mak - ing.

Words: Johann Rist (1607-1667); ver. *Hymnal 1982*
Music: *Ermuntre dich*, melody Johann Schop (d. 1665?), alt.;
   harm. Johann Sebastian Bach (1685-1750)

87. 87. 88. 77

1 On this day          earth shall ring
2 His the doom,        ours the mirth;
3 God's bright star,   o'er his head,
4 On this day          an - gels sing;

with the song         chil - dren sing        to the Lord,      Christ our King,
when he came          down to earth          Beth - le - hem    saw his birth;
Wise Men three        to him led;            kneel they low     by his bed,
with their song       earth shall ring,      prais - ing Christ, hea - ven's King,

born on earth to      save us;               him the Fa - ther  gave us.
ox and ass be - side  him                    from the cold would hide him.
lay their gifts be - fore him,               praise him and a - dore him.
born on earth to      save us;               peace and love he  gave us.

Id - e - o - o - o,          Id - e - o - o - o,

Id - e - o          glo - ri - a          in ex - cel - sis De - o!

*"Ideo gloria in excelsis Deo!" is Latin for "Therefore, glory to God in the highest!"*

Words: *Piae Cantiones*, 1582; tr. Jane M. Joseph (1894-1929)
Music: *Personent hodie*, melody from *Piae Cantiones*, 1582

666. 66 with Refrain

1 An - gels, from the realms of glo - ry, wing your flight o'er
2 Shep - herds in the field a - bid - ing, watch - ing o'er your
3 Sa - ges, leave your con - tem - pla - tions; bright - er vi - sions
4 Saints be - fore the al - tar bend - ing, watch - ing long in

all the earth; ye, who sang cre - a - tion's sto - ry,
flocks by night, God with you is now re - sid - ing;
beam a - far; seek the great De - sire of na - tions;
hope and fear, sud - den - ly the Lord, de - scend - ing,

*Refrain*

now pro - claim Mes - si - ah's birth:
yon - der shines the in - fant Light:
ye have seen his na - tal star: come and wor - ship,
in his tem - ple shall ap - pear:

come and wor - ship, wor - ship Christ, the new - born King.

Words: James Montgomery (1771-1854), alt.
Music: *Regent Square*, Henry Thomas Smart (1813-1879)

87. 87. 87

*Descant*

2 "Fear not," said he, for might - y dread had seized their trou - bled mind;
6 "All glo - ry be to God on high and on the earth be peace;

1 While shep-herds watched their flocks by night, all seat - ed on the ground,
2 "Fear not," said he, for might - y dread had seized their trou-bled mind;
3 "To you, in Da - vid's town, this day is born of Da - vid's line
4 "The heaven - ly Babe you there shall find to hu - man view dis - played,
5 Thus spake the ser - aph, and forth-with ap-peared a shin-ing throng

2 "Glad tid - ings of great joy I bring to you and all man-kind."
6 good will hence-forth from heaven to men be - gin and nev - er cease."

1 the an - gel of the Lord came down, and glo - ry shone a - round.
2 "Glad tid - ings of great joy I bring to you and all man-kind.
3 the Sa - vior, who is Christ the Lord; and this shall be the sign:
4 all mean - ly wrapped in swath-ing bands, and in a man - ger laid."
5 of an - gels prais - ing God, who thus ad - dressed their joy - ful song:

6 "All glory be to God on high
    and on the earth be peace;
  good will henceforth from heaven to men
    begin and never cease."

**Words:** Nahum Tate (1625-1715)
**Music:** *Winchester Old,* melody from *The Whole Booke of Psalmes,* 1592; harm. *Hymns Ancient and Modern,* 1922; desc. Craig Sellar Lang (1891-1971)

CM

# Christmas

95

Stanzas 1, 3, and 5 in unison

1 While shep-herds watched their flocks by night, all
2 "Fear not," said he, for might-y dread had
3 "To you, in Da-vid's town, this day is
4 "The heaven-ly Babe you there shall find to
5 Thus spake the ser-aph, and forth-with ap -

1 seat-ed on the ground, the an-gel of the
2 seized their trou-bled mind; "Glad tid-ings of great
3 born of Da-vid's line the Sa-vior, who is
4 hu-man view dis-played, all mean-ly wrapped in
5 peared a shin-ing throng of an-gels prais-ing

1 Lord came down, and glo-ry shone a-round.
2 joy I bring to you and all man-kind.
3 Christ the Lord; and this shall be the sign:
4 swath-ing bands, and in a man-ger laid."
5 God, who thus ad-dressed their joy-ful song:

6 "All glory be to God on high
and on the earth be peace;
good will henceforth from heaven to men
begin and never cease."

Words: Nahum Tate (1625-1715)
Music: *Hampton*, McNeil Robinson II (b. 1943)

CM

96 Christnmas

1 An - gels we have heard on high, sing - ing sweet - ly through the night,
2 Shep-herds, why this ju - bi - lee? Why these songs of hap - py cheer?
3 Come to Beth - le - hem and see him whose birth the an - gels sing;
4 See him in a man - ger laid whom the an - gels praise a - bove;

and the moun-tains in re - ply ech - o - ing their brave de - light.
What great bright-ness did you see? What glad tid - ings did you hear?
come, a - dore on bend - ed knee Christ, the Lord, the new - born King.
Ma - ry, Jo - seph, lend your aid, while we raise our hearts in love.

*Refrain*

Glo - - - - - - - ri - a

in ex - cel - sis De - o. Glo - - - - -

- - - - ri-a    in ex-cel-sis   De -   o.

Words: French carol; tr. James Chadwick (1813-1882), alt.
Music: *Gloria*, French carol; arr. Edward Shippen Barnes (1887-1958)

77. 77 with Refrain

## Christmas

# 97

1 Dost thou in a man-ger lie, who hast all cre - a - ted,
2 "For the world a love su - preme brought me to this sta - ble;
3 Christ we praise with voic - es bold, laud and hon - or rais - ing;

stretch-ing in - fant hands on high, Sa - vior, long a - wait - ed?
all cre - a - tion to re - deem I a - lone am a - ble.
for these mer - cies man - i - fold join the hosts in prais - ing:

If a mon-arch, where thy state? Where thy court on thee to wait?
By this low - ly birth of mine, sin - ner, rich - es shall be thine,
Fa - ther, glo - ry be to thee for the won - drous char - i - ty

Scep - ter, crown, and sphere? Here no re - gal pomp we see,
match-less gifts and free; will - ing - ly this yoke I take,
of thy Son, our Lord. Bet - ter wit - ness to thy worth,

nought but need and pen - u - ry: why thus cra - dled here?
and this sac - ri - fice I make, heap-ing joys for thee."
pur - er praise than ours on earth, an - gels' songs af - ford.

Words: Jean Mauburn (1460-1503); tr. Elizabeth Rundle Charles (1828-1896) and others
Music: *Dies est laetitiae*, melody from *Piae Cantiones*, 1582

76. 76. 775. 775

1 Un - to us a boy is born! The King of all cre -
2 Cra - dled in a stall was he with sleep - y cows and
3 He - rod then with fear was filled; "A prince," he said, "in
4 Now may Ma - ry's son, who came so long a - go to
*5 Un - to us a boy is born! The King of all cre -

1 a - tion, came he to a world for - lorn, the
2 ass - es; but the ve - ry beasts could see that
3 Jew - ry!" All the lit - tle boys he killed at
4 love us, lead us all with hearts a - flame un -
5 a - tion, came he to a world for - lorn, the

1 Lord of ev - ery na - - - tion.
2 he all men sur - pass - - - es.
3 Beth-le-hem in his fu - - - ry.
4 to the joys a - bove - us.
5 Lord of ev - ery na - - - tion.

Words: Latin carol, 15th cent.; tr. Percy Dearmer (1867-1936), alt.
Music: *Puer nobis nascitur*, melody from *Piae Cantiones*, 1582

77. 77

*Refrain*

Go tell it on the moun - tain, o - ver the hills and

ev - ery - where; go tell it on the moun - tain, that
Je - sus Christ is born!

1 While shep - herds kept their
2 The shep - herds feared and
3 Down in a low - ly

1 watch - ing o'er si - lent flocks by night, be -
2 trem - bled when lo! a - bove the earth rang
3 man - ger the hum - ble Christ was born, and

*Repeat Refrain*

1 hold, through-out the hea - vens there shone a ho - ly light.
2 out the an - gel cho - rus that hailed our Sa - vior's birth.
3 God sent us sal - va - tion that bless - ed Christ - mas morn.

Words: Afro-American spiritual, 19th cent.; adapt. John W. Work (b. 1901)
Music: *Go Tell It on the Mountain*, Afro-American spiritual, 19th cent.;
    arr. Horace Clarence Boyer (b. 1935)

76. 76 with Refrain

1 Joy   to   the  world!  the  Lord   is      come:  let   earth  re -
2 Joy   to   the  world!  the  Sa - vior   reigns;  let   us    our
*3 No   more  let  sins  and   sor - rows   grow,  nor  thorns  in -
4 He   rules  the  world  with  truth and   grace,  and  makes  the

ceive her King;  let  ev - ery   heart  pre - pare  him   room,  and
songs em - ploy,  while fields and  floods,  rocks, hills  and   plains,  re -
fest  the ground; he   comes to   make  his   bless - ings  flow   far
na - tions prove  the  glo - ries   of    his   right - eous - ness,  and

heaven and  na - ture   sing,            and  heaven and  na - ture
peat  the sound - ing   joy,            re -  peat  the sound - ing
as    the curse is    found,           far   as    the curse is
won - ders of   his   love,            and  won - ders of   his

1 and      heaven and  na - ture   sing,            and
2 re -    peat  the sound - ing   joy,            re -
3 far      as    the curse is    found,           far
4 and     won - ders of   his   love,            and

sing, and heaven, and heaven and na-ture sing.
joy, re - peat, re - peat the sound-ing joy.
found, far as, far as the curse is found.
love, and won - ders, won - ders of his love.

heaven and na-ture sing,
peat the sound-ing joy,
as the curse is found,
won - ders of his love,

Words: Isaac Watts (1674-1748), alt.
Music: *Antioch*, George Frideric Handel (1685-1759); adapt. and arr. Lowell Mason (1792-1872)

CM with Repeat

## Christmas

# 101

1 A - way in a man - ger, no crib for his bed,
2 The cat - tle are low - ing, the ba - by a - wakes,
*3 Be near me, Lord Je - sus; I ask thee to stay

the lit - tle Lord Je - sus laid down his sweet head.
but lit - tle Lord Je - sus no cry - ing he makes.
close by me for ev - er, and love me I pray.

The stars in the bright sky looked down where he lay,
I love thee, Lord Je - sus! Look down from the sky,
Bless all the dear chil - dren in thy ten - der care,

the lit - tle Lord Je - sus a - sleep on the hay.
and stay by my side un - til morn - ing is nigh.
and fit us for hea - ven to live with thee there.

Words: Traditional carol
Music: *Cradle Song*, melody William James Kirkpatrick (1838-1921)

11 11. 11 11

1 Once in roy - al Da - vid's ci - ty stood a
2 He came down to earth from hea - ven, who is
*3 We, like Ma - ry, rest con - found - ed that a
4 For he is our life - long pat - tern; dai - ly,
*5 And our eyes at last shall see him, through his
6 Not in that poor low - ly sta - ble, with the

1 low - ly cat - tle shed, where a mo - ther laid her
2 God and Lord of all, and his shel - ter was a
3 sta - ble should dis - play hea - ven's Word, the world's cre -
4 when on earth he grew, he was tempt - ed, scorned, re -
5 own re - deem - ing love; for that child who seemed so
6 ox - en stand - ing round, we shall see him; but in

1 ba - by in a man - ger for his bed: Ma - ry
2 sta - ble, and his cra - dle was a stall; with the
3 a - tor, cra - dled there on Christ - mas Day, yet this
4 ject - ed, tears and smiles like us he knew. Thus he
5 help - less is our Lord in heaven a - bove; and he
6 hea - ven, where his saints his throne sur - round: Christ, re -

1 was that mo-ther mild,___ Je-sus Christ her lit-tle child.___
2 poor, the scorned, the low-ly, lived on earth our Sa-vior ho-ly.
3 child, our Lord and bro-ther, brought us love for one an-oth-er.
4 feels for all our sad-ness, and he shares in all our glad-ness.
5 leads his chil-dren on___ to the place where he is gone.___
6 vealed to faith-ful eye,___ set at God's right hand on high.___

Words: Sts. 1-2 and 4-6, Cecil Frances Alexander (1818-1895), alt.;
st. 3, James Waring McCrady (b. 1938)
Music: *Irby*, melody Henry John Gauntlett (1805-1876); harm. Arthur Henry Mann (1850-1929)

87. 87. 77

## Christmas

## 103

1 A child is born in Beth-le-hem, Al-le-lu-ia! there-
2 The babe with-in a man-ger poor, Al-le-lu-ia! will
3 Up-on this joy-ful ho-ly night, Al-le-lu-ia! we
4 We praise you, Ho-ly Trin-i-ty, Al-le-lu-ia! a-

fore re-joice Je-ru-sa-lem, Al-le-lu-
rule the world for ev-er-more, Al-le-lu-
bless your Name, O Lord of Light, Al-le-lu-
dor-ing you e-ter-nal-ly. Al-le-lu-

*Refrain*

ia, al-le-lu-ia!
ia, al-le-lu-ia!
ia, al-le-lu-ia! Come, join the an-gel throng in songs of
ia, al-le-lu-ia!

joy, in one ac-cord a-dor-ing Christ the Lord.

Words: Latin, 14th cent.; tr. Ruth Fox Hume (1922-1980), alt.
Music: *Puer natus in Bethlehem*, plainsong, Mode 1,
*Benedictine Processional*, 14th cent.

88 with Alleluias and Refrain

1 A sta - ble lamp is light - ed Whose
2 (This) child through Da - vid's ci - ty Shall
3 (Yet) he shall be for - sak - en, And
4 (But) now, as at the end - ing, The

glow shall wake the sky; The stars shall bend their voic - es,
ride in tri - umph by; The palm shall strew its branch - es,
yield - ed up to die; The sky shall groan and dark - en,
low is lift - ed high; The stars shall bend their voic - es,

And ev - ery stone shall cry.____ And ev - ery stone shall cry,
And ev - ery stone shall cry.____ And ev - ery stone shall cry;
And ev - ery stone shall cry.____ And ev - ery stone shall cry,
And ev - ery stone shall cry.____ And ev - ery stone shall cry,

And straw like gold shall shine; A barn shall har - bor hea - ven,
Though hea - vy, dull, and dumb, And lie with - in the road - way
For ston - y hearts of men: God's blood up - on the spear - head,
In prais - es of the Child By whose de - scent a - mong us

1-3

A stall be - come a shrine.____
To pave his king - dom come.____
God's love re - fused a - gain.____
The worlds are rec - on - ciled.____

2 This
3 Yet
4 But

Final Ending

Words: © Richard Wilbur (b. 1921)
Music: *Andújar*, David Hurd (b. 1950)

76. 76. 66. 76

1 God rest you mer - ry, gen - tle-men, let noth-ing you dis - may;
2 From God our heaven - ly Fa - ther a bless - ed an - gel came
3 "Fear not, then," said the an - gel, "Let noth-ing you af - fright;
4 Now to the Lord sing prais - es, all you with - in this place,

re - mem-ber Christ our Sa - vior was born on Christ-mas Day,
and un - to cer - tain shep - herds brought tid - ings of the same:
this day is born a Sa - vior of a pure vir - gin bright,
and with true love and char - i - ty each o - ther now em - brace;

to save us all from Sa - tan's power when we were gone a - stray.
how that in Beth - le - hem was born the Son of God by name.
to free all those who trust in him from Sa - tan's power and might."
this ho - ly tide of Christ - mas doth bring re - deem-ing grace.

*Refrain*

O tid - ings of com - fort and joy, com-fort and

joy; O tid - ings of com - fort and joy!

Words: London carol, 18th cent.
Music: *God Rest You Merry*, melody from *Little Book of Christmas Carols*, ca. 1850     76. 76. 86 with Refrain

1 Chris - tians, a - wake, sa - lute the hap - py morn
2 Then to the watch - ful shep - herds it was told,
*3 He spoke, and straight - way the ce - les - tial choir
*4 In Beth - le - hem the hap - py shep - herds sought
5 Let us, like these good shep - herds, then em - ploy

1 where - on the Sa - vior of the world was born;
2 who heard the an - gel - ic her - ald's voice: "Be - hold,
3 in hymns of joy, un - known be - fore, con - spire;
4 to see the won - der God for us had wrought,
5 our grate - ful voic - es to pro - claim the joy;

1 rise to a - dore the mys - ter - y of love,
2 I bring good tid - ings of a Sa - vior's birth
3 the prais - es of re - deem - ing love they sang,
4 and found, with Jo - seph and the bless - ed maid,
5 trace we the Babe, who hath re - trieved our loss,

1 which hosts of an - gels chant - ed from a - bove;
2 to you and all the na - tions on the earth:
3 and heaven's whole orb with al - le - lu - ias rang;
4 her Son, the Sa - vior, in a man - ger laid;
5 from his poor man - ger to his bit - ter cross;

1 with them the joy - ful tid - ings first be - gun of
2 this day hath God ful - filled his prom - ised word, this
3 God's high - est glo - ry was their an - them still, peace
4 a - mazed, the won - drous sto - ry they pro - claim, the
5 tread - ing his steps, as - sist - ed by his grace, till

1 God In - car - nate and the Vir - gin's Son.
2 day is born a Sa - vior, Christ the Lord."
3 on the earth, and un - to men good will.
4 ear - liest her - alds of the Sa - vior's name.
5 our first heaven - ly state a - gain takes place.

6 Then may we hope, the angelic thrones among,
   to sing, redeemed, a glad triumphal song;
   he that was born upon this joyful day
   around us all his glory shall display;
   saved by his love, incessant we shall sing
   eternal praise to heaven's almighty King.

Words: John Byrom (1692-1763), alt.
Music: *Yorkshire*, John Wainwright (1723-1768)

10 10. 10 10. 10 10

1 Good Chris-tian friends, re - joice    with heart and soul and    voice;
2 Good Chris-tian friends, re - joice    with heart and soul and    voice;
3 Good Chris-tian friends, re - joice    with heart and soul and    voice;

give   ye heed   to    what we say:    Je - sus Christ is    born    to - day;
now   ye hear   of    end - less bliss;    Je - sus Christ was   born    for this!
now   ye need not   fear   the grave:    Je - sus Christ was   born    to save!

ox    and ass   be - fore him bow, and    he    is   in     the    man - ger now.
He   hath o - pened hea - ven's door, and    we   are blest   for    ev - er-more.
Calls you one and   calls you all    to    gain his ev -   er - last - ing hall.

Christ   is   born    to -    day!       Christ   is   born    to -    day!
Christ was born   for     this!       Christ was born   for     this!
Christ was born   to      save!       Christ was born   to      save!

Words: John Mason Neale (1818-1866), alt.
Music: *In dulci jubilo*, German carol, 14th cent.; harm. Charles Winfred Douglas (1867-1944)      66. 77. 78. 55

# Christmas

108

Words: Howard Chandler Robbins (1876-1952)
Music: *Was frag' ich nach der Welt*, melody Ahasuerus Fritsch (1629-1701);
harm. Johann Sebastian Bach (1685-1750)

67. 67. 66. 66

109

Christmas

1 on a cold win-ter's night___ that was___ so deep.
2 and___ so it con-tin-ued both day___ and night.
3 and to fol-low the star___ wher-ev-er it went.
4 right___ o-ver the place___ where Je-sus lay.
5 their___ gold,___ and myrrh,___ and frank-in-cense.

*Refrain*

No-well, No-well, No-well, No-well,

born is the King of Is-ra-el.

6 Then let us all with one accord
   sing praises to our heavenly Lord;
   that hath made heaven and earth of nought,
   and with his blood our life hath bought.

*Refrain*

Words: English carol, 18th cent.
Music: *The First Nowell*, English carol, 17th cent.; harm. John Stainer (1840-1901)                    Irr. with Refrain

*Alternative Refrain*
Descant (others unison)

No - well, No - well, No - well, No - well,

born is the King of Is - ra - el.

Music: *The First Nowell*, English carol, 17th cent.; desc. Healey Willan (1880-1968)

# 110

1 The snow lay on the ground, the stars shone bright,
2 'Twas Ma - ry, daugh - ter pure of ho - ly Anne,
3 Saint Jo - seph, too, was by to tend the child;
4 And thus that man - ger poor be - came a throne;

when Christ our Lord was born on Christ - mas night. Ve -
that brought in - to this world the God made man. She
to guard him, and pro - tect his mo - ther mild; the
for he whom Ma - ry bore was God the Son. O

ni - te a - do - re - mus Do - mi - num. Ve -
laid him in a stall at Beth - le - hem; the
an - gels hov - ered round, and sang this song, Ve -
come, then, let us join the heaven - ly host; to

*Refrain*

ni - te a - do - re - mus Do - mi - num.
ass and ox - en shared the roof with them.
ni - te a - do - re - mus Do - mi - num.
praise the Fa - ther, Son, and Ho - ly Ghost.
Ve -

ni - te a - do - re - mus Do - mi - num. Ve -

ni - te a - do - re - mus Do - mi - num.

Words: Source unknown, 19th cent.
Music: *Venite adoremus*, melody adapt. Charles Winfred Douglas (1867-1944)

Irr. with Refrain

1 Si - lent night, ho - ly night, all is calm,
2 Si - lent night, ho - ly night, shep - herds quake
3 Si - lent night, ho - ly night, Son of God,

all is bright round yon vir - gin mo - ther and child.
at the sight, glo - ries stream from hea - ven a - far,
love's pure light ra - diant beams from thy ho - ly face,

Ho - ly in - fant, so ten - der and mild, sleep in hea - ven - ly
heaven - ly hosts__ sing al - le - lu - ia; Christ, the Sa - vior, is
with the dawn of re - deem - ing grace, Je - sus, Lord, at thy

peace.
born!
birth.

Sleep in hea - ven - ly peace.
Christ, the Sa - vior, is born!
Je - sus, Lord, at thy birth.

Words: Joseph Mohr (1792-1848); tr. John Freeman Young (1820-1885)
Music: *Stille Nacht*, melody Franz Xaver Gruber (1787-1863); harm. Carl H. Reinecke (1824-1910)

Irr.

# 112

**Christmas**

1 In the bleak mid - win - ter, frost - y wind made moan,
2 Our God, heaven can - not hold him, nor____ earth sus - tain;
3 An - gels and arch - an - gels may have gath - ered there,
4 What____ can I give him, poor____ as I am?

earth stood hard as i - ron, wa - ter like a stone;
heaven and earth shall flee a-way when he comes to reign:
cher - u - bim and ser - a-phim throng - ed the air;
If I were a shep - herd, I would bring a lamb;

snow had fall - en, snow on snow, snow____ on____ snow,
in the bleak mid - win - ter a sta - ble - place suf - ficed
but his mo - ther on - ly, in her maid - en bliss,
if I were a wise____ man, I would do my part;

in the bleak mid - win - ter, long a - go.
the Lord____ God in - car - nate, Je - sus Christ.
wor - shiped the be - lov - ed with a kiss.
yet what I can I give him give my heart.

Words: Christina Rossetti (1830-1894)
Music: *Cranham*, Gustav Theodore Holst (1874-1934)

Irr.

*Introduction/Interlude*

1 Duér-
2 No

1 Oh,
2 You

1 me - te, Ni - ño lin - do, en los bra - zos del a -
2 te - mas al rey He - ro - des que na - da te ha de ha -

1 sleep now, ho - ly ba - by, with your head a - gainst my
2 need not fear___ King He - rod, he will bring no harm to

1 mor mien - tras___ que duer-me y des - can - sa la
2 cer; en los___ bra - zos de tu ma - dre y ahí

1 breast;___ mean - while the pangs of my sor - row are
2 you; so rest in the arms of your mo - ther who

*Refrain*

1 pe - na de mi do - lor.
2 na - die te ha de o - fen - der.

A la ru, a la

1 soothed and put___ to rest.
2 sings you a___ la ru.

mè, a la ru, a la mè, a la ru, a la

mè, a la ru, a la ru, a la mè.

Words: Hispanic folk song; tr. John Donald Robb (b. 1892), alt.
Music: *A la ru,* Hispanic folk melody; arr. John Donald Robb (b. 1892)

Irr. with Refrain

| | | | | | | | | |
|---|---|---|---|---|---|---|---|---|
| 1 'Twas | in | the moon of | win - ter - time, when | all | the birds had |
| 2 (With - in | a | lodge of) | bro - ken bark the | ten - der babe was |
| 3 (The | ear - liest moon of) | win - ter - time is | not so round and |
| 4 (O | chil-dren of the) | for - est free, the | an - gel song is |

| | | | | | | | | |
|---|---|---|---|---|---|---|---|---|
| fled, | that | God | the | Lord | of | all | the | earth | sent |
| found, | a | rag - ged | robe | of | rab - bit | skin | en - |
| fair | as | was | the | ring | of | glo - ry | on | the |
| true; | the | ho - ly | child | of | earth | and | heaven | is |

| | | | | | | | | |
|---|---|---|---|---|---|---|---|---|
| an - gel - choirs in - stead; | be - fore | their | light | the |
| wrapped his | beau - ty | round; | but | as | the | hunt - er |
| help - less | in - fant | there. | The | chiefs from far | be - |
| born | to - day | for | you. | Come | kneel be - fore | the |

| | | | | | | | | |
|---|---|---|---|---|---|---|---|---|
| stars | grew dim, | and | won - dering hunt - ers | heard | the | hymn: |
| braves | drew nigh, | the | an - gel - song rang | loud | and | high: |
| fore | him knelt | with | gifts of fox | and | bea - ver - pelt. |
| ra - diant boy, | who | brings you beau - ty, | peace, | and | joy. |

Je - sus your King is born, Je - sus is

*(Fine)* *Optional Interlude*

1-3

born, in ex - cel-sis glo-ri - a.

2 With - in a lodge of
3 The ear - liest moon of
4 O chil-dren of the

*Final Ending*

**Words:** Jesse Edgar Middleton (1872-1960), alt.
**Music:** *Une jeune pucelle*, French folk melody, 16th cent.

86. 86. 88 with Refrain

*Unison or harmony*

1 What child is this, who, laid to rest, on
2 Why lies he in such mean es - tate, where
3 So bring him in - cense, gold, and myrrh, come,

Ma - ry's lap is sleep - ing? Whom an - gels greet with
ox and ass are feed - ing? Good Chris - tian, fear: for
peas - ant, king, to own him; the King of kings sal -

an - thems sweet, while shep - herds watch are keep - ing?
sin - ners here the si - lent Word is plead - ing.
va - tion brings, let lov - ing hearts en - throne him.

*Refrain*

This, this is Christ the King, whom shep - herds

guard and an - gels sing; haste, haste to

bring him laud, the babe, the son of Ma - ry.

Words: William Chatterton Dix (1837-1898)
Music: *Greensleeves*, English melody; harm. *Christmas Carols New and Old*, 1871

87. 87 with Refrain

## 116

Epiphany

1 "I come," the great Re - deem-er cries, "To do thy will, O Lord!"
2 "Thus it be - comes us to ful - fill all right-eous-ness," he said.
3 Hark, a glad voice! The Fa - ther speaks from heaven's ex-alt - ed height:
4 The Sa - vior Je - sus, well - be - loved! His Name we will pro - fess,
5 No more we'll count our - selves our own but his in bonds of love.

1 At Jor-dan's stream, be - hold! He seals the sure pro-phet - ic word.
2 Then, faith-ful to the Lord's com-mands, through Jor-dan's flood was led.
3 "This is my Son, my well - be - loved in whom I take de - light."
4 like him de - sir - ous to ful - fill God's will in right-eous - ness.
5 Oh, may such bonds for ev - er draw our souls to things a - bove!

Words: *Christian Hymnbook*, 1865, alt.
Music: *This Endris Nyght*, English melody; harm. Ralph Vaughan Williams (1872-1958)

CM

## 117

Epiphany

1 Bright - est and best of the stars of the morn - ing,
2 Cold on his cra - dle the dew - drops are shin - ing,
3 Shall we then yield him, in cost - ly de - vo - tion,
4 Vain - ly we of - fer each am - ple o - bla - tion,
5 Bright - est and best of the stars of the morn - ing,

1 dawn on our dark - ness, and lend us thine aid;
2 low lies his head with the beasts of the stall;
3 o - dors of E - dom, and of - ferings di - vine,
4 vain - ly with gifts would his fa - vor se - cure,
5 dawn on our dark - ness, and lend us thine aid;

1 star of the east, the hor - i - zon a - dorn - ing,
2 an - gels a - dore him in slum - ber re - clin - ing,
3 gems of the moun - tain, and pearls of the o - cean,
4 rich - er by far is the heart's a - dor - a - tion,
5 star of the east, the hor - i - zon a - dorn - ing,

1 guide where our in - fant Re - deem - er is laid.
2 Ma - ker and Mon - arch and Sa - vior of all.
3 myrrh from the for - est, and gold from the mine?
4 dear - er to God are the prayers of the poor.
5 guide where our in - fant Re - deem - er is laid.

Words: Reginal Heber (1783-1826), alt.
Music: *Morning Star*, James Proctor Harding (1850-1911)

11 10. 11 10

*Unison*

1 Bright - est and best of the stars of the morn - ing,
2 Cold on his cra - dle the dew - drops are shin - ing,
3 Shall we then yield him, in cost - ly de - vo - tion,
4 Vain - ly we of - fer each am - ple o - bla - tion,
5 Bright - est and best of the stars of the morn - ing,

1 dawn on our dark - ness, and lend us thine aid;
2 low lies his head with the beasts of the stall;
3 o - dors of E - dom, and of - ferings di - vine,
4 vain - ly with gifts would his fa - vor se - cure,
5 dawn on our dark - ness, and lend us thine aid;

1 star of the east, the hor - i - zon a - dorn - ing.
2 an - gels a - dore him in slum - ber re - clin - ing,
3 gems of the moun - tain, and pearls of the o - cean,
4 rich - er by far is the heart's a - dor - a - tion,
5 star of the east, the hor - i - zon a - dorn - ing,

1 guide where our in - fant Re - deem - er is laid.
2 Ma - ker and Mon - arch and Sa - vior of all.
3 myrrh from the for - est, and gold from the mine?
4 dear - er to God are the prayers of the poor.
5 guide where our in - fant Re - deem - er is laid.

*Refrain*

Bright - est and best of the stars of the morn - ing,

dawn on our dark - ness, and lend us thine aid;

star of the east, the hor - i - zon a - dorn - ing,

guide where our in - fant Re - deem - er is laid.

Words: Reginald Heber (1783-1826), alt.
Music: *Star in the East*, from *The Southern Harmony*, 1835

11 10. 11 10 with Refrain

*Harmony (the melody is in the tenor)*

1 Bright - est and best of the stars of the morn - ing,
2 Cold on his cra - dle the dew - drops are shin - ing,
3 Shall we then yield him, in cost - ly de - vo - tion,
4 Vain - ly we of - fer each am - ple o - bla - tion,
5 Bright - est and best of the stars of the morn - ing,

1 dawn on our dark - ness, and lend us thine aid;
2 low lies his head with the beasts of the stall;
3 o - dors of E - dom, and of - ferings di - vine,
4 vain - ly with gifts would his fa - vor se - cure,
5 dawn on our dark - ness, and lend us thine aid;

1 star of the east, the hor - i - zon a - dorn - ing,
2 an - gels a - dore him in slum - ber re - clin - ing,
3 gems of the moun - tain, and pearls of the o - cean,
4 rich - er by far is the heart's a - dor - a - tion,
5 star of the east, the hor - i - zon a - dorn - ing,

1 guide where our in - fant Re - deem - er is laid.
2 Ma - ker and Mon - arch and Sa - vior of all.
3 myrrh from the for - est, and gold from the mine?
4 dear - er to God are the prayers of the poor.
5 guide where our in - fant Re - deem - er is laid.

Words: Reginald Heber (1783-1826), alt.
Music: *Star in the East*, from *The Southern Harmony*, 1835

11 10. 11 10 with Refrain

1 As with glad-ness men of old did the guid-ing star be-hold;
2 As with joy-ful steps they sped to that low-ly man-ger-bed;
3 As they of-fered gifts most rare at that man-ger rude and bare;
4 Ho-ly Je-sus! ev-ery day keep us in the nar-row way;
5 In the heaven-ly coun-try bright, need they no cre-a-ted light;

1 as with joy they hailed its light, lead-ing on-ward, beam-ing bright;
2 there to bend the knee be-fore him whom heaven and earth a-dore;
3 so may we with ho-ly joy, pure and free from sin's al-loy,
4 and, when earth-ly things are past, bring our ran-somed souls at last
5 thou its light, its joy, its crown, thou its sun which goes not down:

1 so, most gra-cious Lord, may we ev-er-more be led to thee.
2 so may we with will-ing feet ev-er seek the mer-cy-seat.
3 all our cost-liest trea-sures bring, Christ! to thee, our heaven-ly King.
4 where they need no star to guide, where no clouds thy glo-ry hide.
5 there for ev-er may we sing al-le-lu-ias to our King.

Music: William Chatterton Dix (1837-1898)
Music: *Dix*, melody Conrad Kocher (1786-1872); arr. William Henry Monk (1823-1889);
    harm. *The English Hymnal*, 1906

77. 77. 77

1 The sin - less one to Jor - dan came,
2 Up - ris - ing from the wa - ters there,
3 A - bove him see the heaven - ly Dove,
4 How blest that mis - sion then be - gun
5 O Christ, may we bap - tized from sin,
6 On you may all your peo - ple feed,

1 and in the riv - er shared our stain;
2 the Fa - ther's voice did then de - clare
3 the sign of God the Fa - ther's love,
4 to heal and save a race un - done!
5 go forth with you a world to win:
6 and know you are the Bread in - deed,

1 God's right - eous - ness he thus ful - filled,
2 that Christ, the Son of God, had come
3 now by the Ho - ly Spi - rit shed
4 Straight to the wil - der - ness he goes
5 grant us the Ho - ly Spi - rit's power
6 who gives e - ter - nal life to those

1 and chose the path his Fa - ther willed.
2 to lead his scat - tered peo - ple home.
3 up - on the Son's a - noint - ed head.
4 to wres - tle with his peo - ple's foes.
5 to shield us in temp - ta - tion's hour.
6 that with you died, and with you rose.

Words: George B. Timms (b. 1910), alt.
Music: *Solemnis haec festivitas*, melody from *Graduale*, 1685

LM

1 Christ, when for us you were bap - tized, God's Spi - rit on you came,
2 God called you his be - lov - ed Son, called you his ser - vant true,
3 Straight-way and stead-fast un - til death you then o - beyed his call
4 Bap - tize us with your Spi - rit, Lord, your cross on us be signed,

as peace-ful as a dove and yet as ur - gent as a flame.
sent you his king-dom to pro-claim, his ho - ly will to do.
free - ly as Son of Man to serve and give your life for all.
that, like-wise in God's ser - vice we may per - fect free - dom find.

Words: F. Bland Tucker (1895-1984), rev.
Music: *Caithness*, melody from *The Psalmes of David in Prose and Meeter*, 1635;
     harm. *The English Hymnal*, 1906

CM

1 Al - le - lu - ia, song of glad-ness, voice of joy that can-not die;
2 Al - le - lu - ia thou re-sound-est, true Je - ru - sa - lem and free;
3 Al - le - lu - ia though we cher - ish and would chant for ev - er-more
4 There-fore in our hymns we pray thee, grant us, bless-ed Trin - i - ty,

al - le - lu - ia is the an - them ev - er raised by choirs on high;
al - le - lu - ia, joy - ful mo - ther, all thy chil-dren sing with thee;
al - le - lu - ia in our sing - ing, let us for a while give o'er,
at the last to keep thine Eas - ter with thy faith-ful saints on high;

in the house of God a-bid-ing thus they sing e - - ter-nal-ly.
but by Bab-y-lon's sad wa-ters mourn-ing ex - iles now are we.
as our Sa-vior in his fast-ing plea-sures of the world for-bore.
there to thee for ev-er sing-ing al-le-lu - ia joy-ful-ly.

Words: Latin, 11th cent.; tr. John Mason Neale (1818-1866), alt.
Music: *Urbs beata Jerusalem*, plainsong, Mode 2, Nevers MS., 13th cent.

87. 87. 87

## Epiphany

# 123

1 Al - le - lu - ia, song of glad-ness, voice of joy that
2 Al - le - lu - ia thou re - sound-est, true Je - ru - sa -
3 Al - le - lu - ia though we cher-ish and would chant for
4 There-fore in our hymns we pray thee, grant us, bless - ed

can - not die; al - le - lu - ia is the an - them
lem and free; al - le - lu - ia, joy - ful mo - ther,
ev - er - more al - le - lu - ia in our sing - ing,
Trin - i - ty, at the last to keep thine Eas - ter,

ev - er raised by choirs on high; in the house of
all thy chil - dren sing with thee; but by Bab - y -
let us for a while give o'er, as our Sa - vior
with thy faith - ful saints on high; there to thee for

God a - bid - ing thus they sing e - ter - nal - ly.
lon's sad wa - ters mourn-ing ex - iles now are we.
in his fast - ing plea - sures of the world for - bore.
ev - er sing - ing al - le - lu - ia joy - ful - ly.

Words: Latin, 11th cent.; tr. John Mason Neale (1818-1866), alt.
Music: *Tibi, Christe, splendor Patris*, plainsong, Mode 2, Moissac MS., 12th cent.;
ver. Schola Antiqua, 1983

87. 87. 87

Music: Melody rhythmic version © 1984, Schola Antiqua Inc. Used by permission.

*Unison or harmony*

1 What star is this, with beams so bright, more beau - teous
2 True spake the pro - phet from a - far who told the
3 The guid - ing star a - bove is bright; with - in them
4 O Je - sus, while the star of grace im - pels us
5 To God the Fa - ther, heaven - ly Light, to Christ, re -

1 than the noon - day light? It shines to her - ald
2 rise of Ja - cob's star; and east - ern sa - ges
3 shines a clear - er light, and leads them on with
4 on to seek thy face, let not our sloth - ful
5 vealed in earth - ly night, to God the Ho - ly

1 forth the King, and Gen - tiles to his crib to bring.
2 with a - maze up - on the won - drous to - ken gaze.
3 power be - nign to seek the Giv - er of the sign.
4 hearts re - fuse the guid - ance of thy light to use.
5 Ghost we raise our e - qual and un - ceas - ing praise.

Words: Charles Coffin (1676-1749); tr. *Hymns Ancient and Modern*, 1861, after John Chandler (1807-1876), alt.
Music: *Puer nobis*, melody from Trier MS., 15th cent.; adapt. Michael Praetorius (1571-1621);
    harm. *Cowley Carol Book*, 1902

LM

## 125

1 The peo-ple who in dark-ness walked have seen a glo-rious light;
2 To hail thy ris-ing, Sun of life, the ga-thering na-tions come,
3 To us the prom-ised Child is born, to us the Son is given;
4 His name shall be the Prince of Peace for ev - er-more a - dored,
5 His power in-creas-ing still shall spread, his reign no end shall know;

1 on them broke forth the heaven-ly dawn who dwelt in death and night.
2 joy - ous as when the reap-ers bear their har-vest trea-sures home.
3 him shall the tribes of earth o-bey, and all the hosts of heaven.
4 the Won-der - ful, the Coun-sel-lor, the might-y God and Lord.
5 jus - tice shall guard his throne a-bove, and peace a-bound be - low.

Words: John Morison (1749-1798), alt.; para. of Isaiah 9:2-7
Music: *Perry*, Leo Sowerby (1895-1968)

CM

## 126

1 The peo - ple who in dark-ness walked have seen a glo-rious light;
2 To hail thy ris - ing, Sun of life, the ga-thering na - tions come,
3 To us the prom-ised Child is born, to us the Son is given;
4 His name shall be the Prince of Peace for ev - er-more a - dored,
5 His power in - creas-ing still shall spread, his reign no end shall know;

1 on them broke forth the heaven-ly dawn who dwelt in death and night.
2 joy - ous as when the reap-ers bear their har-vest trea-sures home.
3 him shall the tribes of earth o - bey, and all the hosts of heaven.
4 the Won-der - ful, the Coun-sel - lor, the might-y God and Lord.
5 jus - tice shall guard his throne a - bove, and peace a - bound be - low.

Words: John Morison (1749-1798), alt.; para. of Isaiah 9:2-7
Music: *Dundee*, melody *The CL Psalmes of David*, 1615; harm. Thomas Ravenscroft (1592?-1635?), alt.

CM

1 Earth has man-y a no - ble ci - ty; Beth-lehem, thou dost all ex - cel:
2 Fair - er than the sun at morn-ing was the star that told his birth,
3 East-ern sa - ges at his cra - dle make ob - la - tions rich and rare;
4 Sa - cred gifts of mys - tic mean-ing: in - cense doth their God dis-close,
5 Je - sus, whom the Gen-tiles wor-shiped at thy glad e - piph - a - ny,

1 out of thee the Lord from hea - ven came to rule his Is - ra - el.
2 to the world its God an - nounc-ing seen in flesh - ly form on earth.
3 see them give, in deep de - vo - tion, gold and frank - in - cense and myrrh.
4 gold the King of kings pro - claim-eth, myrrh his sep - ul - cher fore-shows.
5 un - to thee, with God the Fa - ther and the Spi - rit, glo - ry be.

Words: Marcus Aurelius Clemens Prudentius (348-410?); tr. *Hymns Ancient and Modern*, 1861, alt.
Music: *Stuttgart*, melody from *Psalmodia Sacra, oder Andächtige and Schöne Gesänge*, 1715;
    adapt. William Henry Havergal (1793-1870); harm. K. D. Smith (b. 1928)

87. 87

1 We three kings of O - ri - ent are, bear - ing
2 Born a King on Beth - le - hem's plain, gold I
3 Frank - in - cense to of - fer have I: in - cense
4 Myrrh is mine; its bit - ter per - fume breathes a
5 Glo - rious now be - hold him a - rise, King and

1 gifts we tra - verse a - far, field and foun - tain,
2 bring to crown him a - gain, King for ev - er,
3 owns a De - i - ty nigh; prayer and prais - ing,
4 life of gath - er - ing gloom; sor - row-ing, sigh - ing,
5 God and Sac - ri - fice; heaven sings al - le -

1 moor and moun - tain, fol - low - ing yon - der star.
2 ceas - ing nev - er o - ver us all to reign.
3 glad - ly rais - ing, wor - ship him, God Most High.
4 bleed - ing, dy - ing, sealed in the stone - cold tomb.
5 lu - ia: al - le - lu - ia the earth re - plies.

*Refrain*

O_____ star of won - der, star of night,

star with roy - al beau - ty bright; west - ward lead - ing,

still pro - ceed - ing, guide us to thy per - fect light!

*Interlude*

*The stanzas may be sung by three soloists: 1 and 5 by the ensemble; 2-4 by individuals; and the refrain by all.*

Words: John Henry Hopkins, Jr. (1820-1891), alt.
Music: *Three Kings of Orient*, John Henry Hopkins, Jr. (1820-1891)

88. 446 with Refrain

1 Christ up - on the moun-tain peak stands a - lone in
2 Trem-bling at his feet we saw Mo - ses and E -
3 Swift the cloud of glo - ry came. God pro - claim-ing
4 This is God's be - lov - ed Son! Law and pro - phets

glo - ry blaz - ing; let us, if we dare to speak,
li - jah speak - ing. All the pro - phets and the Law
in its thun - der Je - sus as his Son by name!
fade be - fore him; first and last and on - ly One,

with the saints and an - gels praise him. Al - le - lu - ia!
shout through them their joy - ful greet - ing. Al - le - lu - ia!
Na - tions cry a - loud in won - der! Al - le - lu - ia!
let cre - a - tion now a - dore him! Al - le - lu - ia!

Words: Brian A. Wren (b. 1936)
Music: *Mowsley*, Cyril Vincent Taylor (b. 1907)

78. 78 with Alleluia

1 Christ up - on the moun-tain peak stands a - lone in glo - ry
2 Trem-bling at his feet we saw Mo - ses and E - li - jah
3 Swift the cloud of glo - ry came. God pro-claim-ing in its
4 This is God's be - lov - ed Son! Law and pro - phets fade be -

| | | | | | | | |
|---|---|---|---|---|---|---|---|
| blaz - ing; | let | us, | if | we | dare | to | speak, |
| speak - ing. | All | the | pro - phets | and | the | Law | |
| thun - der | Je - sus | as | his | Son | by | name! | |
| fore | him; | first | and | last | and | on - ly | One, |

| | | | | | |
|---|---|---|---|---|---|
| with | the | saints and | an - gels | praise him. | Al - le - lu - ia! |
| shout | through | them their | joy - ful | greet - ing. | Al - le - lu - ia! |
| Na - tions | cry | a - loud | in | won - der! | Al - le - lu - ia! |
| let | cre - | a - tion now | a - dore | him! | Al - le - lu - ia! |

Words: Brian A. Wren (b. 1936)  
Music: *Shillingford*, Peter Cutts (b. 1937)

78. 78 with Alleluia

## Epiphany

# 131

| | | | | | | | |
|---|---|---|---|---|---|---|---|
| 1 When | Christ's | ap - pear - ing | was | made | known, | King |
| 2 The | east - ern | sa - ges | saw | from | far | and |
| 3 With - in | the | Jor - dan's | sa - cred | flood | the |
| 4 Oh, | what | a | mir - a - cle | di - vine, | when |
| 5 All | glo - ry, | Je - sus, | be | to | thee | for |

| | | | | | | | |
|---|---|---|---|---|---|---|---|
| 1 He - rod | trem - bled | for | his | throne; | but | he who of - fers |
| 2 fol - lowed | on | his | guid - ing | star; | by | light their way to |
| 3 heaven - ly | Lamb | in | meek - ness | stood, | that | he, to whom no |
| 4 wa - ter | red - dened | in - to | wine! | He | spoke the word, and |
| 5 this | thy | glad | e - piph - a - ny: | whom | with the Fa - ther |

| | | | | | | | |
|---|---|---|---|---|---|---|---|
| 1 heaven - ly | birth | sought | not | the | king - doms | of | this earth. |
| 2 Light | they | trod, | and | by | their | gifts con - fessed | their God. |
| 3 sin | was known, | might | cleanse | his | peo - ple | from | their own. |
| 4 forth | it | flowed | in | streams | that | na - ture ne'er | be - stowed. |
| 5 we | a - dore | and | Ho - ly | Ghost | for | ev - | er - more. |

Words: Caelius Sedulius (5th cent.); st. 1, tr. *The Hymn Book of the Anglican Church of Canada and the United Church of Canada*, 1971; sts. 2-5, tr. John Mason Neale (1818-1866), alt.  
Music: *Vom Himmel kam der Engel Schar*, melody source unknown

LM

1 When Christ's ap - pear - ing was made known, King He - rod
2 The east - ern sa - ges saw from far and fol - lowed
3 With - in the Jor - dan's sa - cred flood the heaven - ly
4 Oh, what a mir - a - cle di - vine, when wa - ter
5 All glo - ry, Je - sus, be to thee for this thy

1 trem - bled for his throne; but he who of - fers
2 on his guid - ing star; by light their way to
3 Lamb in meek - ness stood, that he, to whom no
4 red - dened in - to wine! He spoke the word, and
5 glad e - piph - a - ny: whom with the Fa - ther

1 heaven - ly birth sought not the king - doms of this earth.
2 Light they trod, and by their gifts con - fessed their God.
3 sin was known, might cleanse his peo - ple from their own.
4 forth it flowed in streams that na - ture ne'er be - stowed.
5 we a - dore and Ho - ly Ghost for ev - er - more.

Words: Caelius Sedulius (5th cent.); st. 1, tr. *The Hymn Book of the Anglican Church of Canada
     and the United Church of Canada*, 1971; sts. 2-5, tr. John Mason Neale (1818-1866), alt.
Music: *Erhalt uns, Herr*, melody from *Geistliche Lieder*, 1543                    LM

1 O Light of Light, Love giv - en birth; Je - sus, Re -
2 Two pro - phets, who had faith to see, with your e -
3 May all who seek to praise a - right through pur - er

deem - er of the earth: more bright than day your face did
lect found com - pa - ny; the heavens a - bove your glo - ry
lives show forth your light. To you, the King of glo - ry,

show, your rai - ment whit - er than the snow.
named, your Fa - ther's voice his son pro - claimed.
now all

*Final Ending*

faith - ful hearts a - dor - ing bow.

Words: Latin, 10th cent.; tr. Laurence Housman (1865-1959), alt.
Music: *Elmhurst,* Cary Ratcliff (b. 1953)

LM

## Epiphany 134

1 O light of Light, Love giv - en birth;
2 Two pro - phets, who had faith to see,
3 May all who seek to praise a - right

Je - sus, Re - deem - er of the earth:
with your e - lect found com - pa - ny;
through pur - er lives show forth your light.

more bright than day your face did show,
the heavens a - bove your glo - ry named,
To you, the King of glo - ry, now

your rai - ment whit - er than the snow.
your Fa - ther's voice his Son pro - claimed.
all faith - ful hearts a - dor - ing bow.

Words: Latin, 10th cent.; tr. Laurence Housman (1865-1959), alt.
Music: *Jesu dulcis memoria,* plainsong, Mode 2

LM

1 Songs of thank-ful - ness and praise, Je - sus, Lord, to thee we raise,
2 Man - i - fest at Jor - dan's stream, Pro-phet, Priest, and King su-preme;
3 Man - i - fest in mak - ing whole pal - sied limbs and faint-ing soul;
4 Man - i - fest on moun - tain height, shin-ing in re - splen-dent light,

man - i - fest-ed by the star to the sa - ges from a - far;
and at Ca - na, wed - ding-guest, in thy God-head man - i - fest;
man - i - fest in val - iant fight, quell-ing all the dev-il's might;
where dis - ci - ples filled with awe thy trans - fi - gured glo - ry saw.

branch of roy - al Da - vid's stem in thy birth at Beth - le - hem;
man - i - fest in power di - vine, chang-ing wa - ter in - to wine;
man - i - fest in gra - cious will, ev - er bring-ing good from ill;
When from there thou led - dest them stead - fast to Je - ru - sa - lem,

an - thems be to thee ad - dressed, God in man made man - i - fest.
an - thems be to thee ad - dressed, God in man made man - i - fest.
an - thems be to thee ad - dressed, God in man made man - i - fest.
cross and Eas - ter Day at - test God in man made man - i - fest.

Words: Sts. 1-3, Christopher Wordsworth (1807-1885); st. 4, F. Bland Tucker (1895-1984)
Music: *Salzburg*, melody Jakob Hintze (1622-1702); harm. Johann Sebastian Bach (1685-1750)

77. 77. D

1 O won - drous type! O vi - sion fair
2 With Mo - ses and E - li - jah nigh
3 With shin - ing face and bright ar - ray,
4 And faith - ful hearts are raised on high
5 O Fa - ther, with the e - ter - nal Son,

of glo - ry that the Church may share,
the in - car - nate Lord holds con - verse high;
Christ deigns to man - i - fest to - day
by this great vi - sion's mys - ter - y;
and Ho - ly Spi - rit, ev - er One,

which Christ up - on the moun - tain shows,
and from the cloud, the Ho - ly One
what glo - ry shall be theirs a - bove
for which in joy - ful strains we raise
vouch - safe to bring us by thy grace

where bright - er than the sun he glows!
bears re - cord to the on - ly Son.
who joy in God with per - fect love.
the voice of prayer, the hymn of praise.
to see thy glo - ry face to face.

Words: Latin, 15th cent.; tr. *Hymns Ancient and Modern*, 1861, after John Mason Neale (1818-1866), alt.
Music: *Aeterne Rex altissime*, plainsong, Mode 1, *Zisterzienser Hymnar*, 14th cent.                    LM

# 137

Epiphany

**Descant**

4 And faith - ful hearts are raised on high by this great

1 O won - drous type! O vi - sion fair of glo - ry
2 With Mo - ses and E - li - jah nigh the in - car - nate
3 With shin - ing face and bright ar - ray, Christ deigns to
4 And faith - ful hearts are raised on high by this great
5 O Fa - ther, with the e - ter - nal Son, and Ho - ly

vi - sion's mys - ter - y; for which in joy - ful

1 that the Church may share, which Christ up - on the
2 Lord holds con - verse high; and from the cloud, the
3 man - i - fest to - day what glo - ry shall be
4 vi - sion's mys - ter - y; for which in joy - ful
5 Spi - rit, ev - er One, vouch - safe to bring us

strains we raise the voice of prayer, the hymn of praise.

1 moun - tain shows, where bright -er than the sun he glows!
2 Ho - ly One bears re - cord to the on - ly Son.
3 theirs a - bove who joy in God with per - fect love.
4 strains we raise the voice of prayer, the hymn of praise.
5 by thy grace to see thy glo - ry face to face.

Words: Latin, 15th cent.; tr. *Hymns Ancient and Modern*, 1861, after John Mason Neale (1818-1866), alt.
Music: *Wareham*, melody William Knapp (1698-1768), alt.; harm. *Hymns Ancient and Modern*, 1875, after James Turle (1802-1882); desc. Sydney Hugo Nicholson (1875-1947)

LM

## Epiphany

**138**

1 All praise to you, O Lord, who by your might-y power did
2 You speak, and it is done; o - be - dient to your word, the
3 Oh, may this grace be ours: in you al - ways to live and
4 So, led from strength to strength, grant us, O Lord, to see the

man - i - fest your glo - ry forth in Ca - na's mar-riage hour.
wa - ter red - dening in - to wine pro - claims the pres-ent Lord.
drink of those re - fresh - ing streams which you a - lone can give.
mar - riage sup - per of the Lamb, the great e - piph - a - ny.

Words: Hyde W. Beadon (1812-1891), alt.
Music: *Carlisle*, Charles Lockhart (1745-1815)

SM

1 When Jesus went to Jordan's stream his Father's will obeying,
and was baptized by John, there came a voice from heaven saying,
"This is my dear beloved Son upon whom rests my favor."
And till God's will is fully done he will not bend or waver,
for he is Christ the Savior.

2 The Holy Spirit then was shown, a dove on him descending;
the Triune God is thus made known in Christ as love unending.
He taught, he healed, he raised the dead, yet, in his great endeavor
but death could hold him never.
to save us, his own blood was shed;
He rose, and lives for ever.

3 He came by water and by blood to heal our lost condition;
he cleanses, reconciles to God, and gives the Great Commission.
Then let us not heed worldly lies nor rest upon our merit,
but trust in Christ who will baptize with water and the Spirit
that we may life inherit.

Words: Martin Luther (1483-1546); para. F. Bland Tucker (1895-1984), rev.
Music: *Christ unser Herr zum Jordan kam*, melody from *Geystliche gesangk Buchleyn*, 1524

87. 87. 87. 877

1 Wilt thou for-give that sin, where I be - gun,
2 Wilt thou for-give that sin, by which I won
3 I have a sin of fear that when I've spun

which is my sin, though it were done be - fore?
o - thers to sin, and made my sin their door?
my last thread, I shall per - ish on the shore;

Wilt thou for - give those sins through which I run,
Wilt thou for - give that sin which I did shun
swear by thy - self, that at my death thy Son

and do run still, though still I do de - plore?
a year or two, but wal - lowed in a score?
shall shine as he shines now, and here - to - fore.

When thou hast done, thou hast not done, for I have more.
When thou hast done, thou hast not done, for I have more.
And hav-ing done that, thou hast done, I fear no more.

Words: John Donne (1573-1631)
Music: *Donne*, melody John Hilton (1599-1657), alt.

10 10. 10 10. 84

# 141

Lent

1 Wilt thou for-give that sin, where I be - gun,
2 Wilt thou for-give that sin, by which I won
3 I have a sin of fear that when I've spun

which is my sin, though it were done be - fore?
o - thers to sin, and made my sin their door?
my last thread, I shall per - ish on the shore;

Wilt thou for-give those sins through which I run,
Wilt thou for-give that sin which I did shun
swear by thy-self, that at my death thy Son

and do run still, though still I do de-plore?
a year or two, but wal - lowed in a score?
shall shine as he shines now, and here - to-fore.

When thou hast done, thou hast not done, for I have more.
When thou hast done, thou hast not done, for I have more.
And hav-ing done that, thou hast done, I fear no more.

Words: John Donne (1573-1631)
Music: *So giebst du nun*, melody from *Geist und Lehr-reiches Kirchen und Haus Buch*, 1694; harm. Johann Sebastian Bach (1685-1750)

10 10. 10 10. 84

## Lent

## 142

1 Lord, who through-out these for - ty days for us didst fast and pray,
2 As thou with Sa - tan didst con-tend and didst the vic - to-ry win,
3 As thou didst hun - ger bear and thirst, so teach us, gra-cious Lord,
4 And through these days of pen - i - tence, and through thy Pas-sion - tide,
5 A - bide with us, that so, this life of suf - fering o - ver - past,

1 teach us with thee to mourn our sins, and close by thee to stay.
2 O give us strength in thee to fight, in thee to con-quer sin.
3 to die to self, and chief - ly live by thy most ho - ly word.
4 yea, ev - er - more, in life and death, Je - sus! with us a - bide.
5 an Eas-ter of un - end - ing joy we may at - tain at last!

Words: Claudia Frances Hernaman (1838-1898)
Music: *St. Flavian*, melody from *Day's Psalter*, 1562; adapt. and harm. Richard Redhead (1820-1901)

CM

1 The glo - ry of these for - ty days we
2 A - lone and fast - ing Mo - ses saw the
3 So Dan - iel trained his mys - tic sight, de -
4 Then grant us, Lord, like them to be full
*5 O Fa - ther, Son, and Spi - rit blest, to

1 cel - e - brate with songs of praise; for Christ, through whom all
2 lov - ing God who gave the law; and to E - li - jah,
3 liv - ered from the li - ons' might; and John, the Bride - groom's
4 oft in fast and prayer with thee; our spi - rits strength-en
5 thee be ev - ery prayer ad-dressed, who art in three - fold

1 things were made, him - self has fast - ed and has prayed.
2 fast - ing, came the steeds and char - i - ots of flame.
3 friend, be - came the her - ald of Mes - si - ah's name.
4 with thy grace, and give us joy to see thy face.
5 Name a - dored, from age to age, the on - ly Lord.

Words: Latin, 6th cent.; tr. Maurice F. Bell (1862-1947), alt.
Music: *Erhalt uns, Herr,* melody from *Geistliche Lieder,* 1543

LM

1 Lord Je - sus, Sun of Right - eous - ness, shine
2 Give guid - ance to our wan - dering ways, for -
3 Lord, grant that we in pen - i - tence may
4 Now near - er draws the day of days when
5 The u - ni - verse your glo - ry shows, blest

1 in our hearts, we pray; dis - pel the gloom that
2 give us, Lord, our sin; re - store us by your
3 of - fer you our praise, and through your sav - ing
4 par - a - dise shall bloom, when we shall be at
5 Fa - ther, Spi - rit, Son; we shall ac - claim your

1 shades our minds and be to us as day.
2 lov - ing care to peace and joy with - in.
3 sac - ri - fice re - ceive your gift of grace.
4 one with you, Lord, ris - en from the tomb.
5 ma - jes - ty, e - ter - nal Three in One.

Words: Latin; tr. Anne K. LeCroy (b. 1930)
Music: *Cornhill*, Harold Darke (1888-1976), alt.                    CM

1 Now quit your care and anx-ious fear and wor - ry; for
2 To bow the head in sack-cloth and in ash - es, or
3 For is not this the fast that I have cho - sen? (The
4 For right - eous - ness and peace will show their fa - ces to
5 Then shall your light break forth as doth the morn - ing; your

1 schemes are vain and fret - ting brings no gain. Lent calls to
2 rend the soul, such grief is not Lent's goal; but to be
3 pro - phet spoke) To shat - ter ev - ery yoke, of wick - ed -
4 those who feed the hun - gry in their need, and wrongs re -
5 health shall spring, the friends you make shall bring God's glo - ry

1 prayer, to trust and ded - i - ca - tion; God brings new beau - ty
2 led to where God's glo - ry flash - es, his beau - ty to come
3 ness the griev - ous bands to loos - en, op - pres - sion put to
4 dress, who build the old waste pla - ces, and in the dark-ness
5 bright, your way through life a - dorn - ing; and love shall be the

Unison          Harmony

1 nigh; re - ply, re - ply, re - ply with love to love most high;
2 near. Make clear, make clear, make clear where truth and light ap - pear;
3 flight, to fight, to fight, to fight till ev - ery wrong's set right.
4 shine. Di - vine, di - vine, di - vine it is when all com - bine!
5 prize. A - rise, a - rise, a - rise! and make a par - a - dise!

Unison          Harmony

1 re - ply, re - ply, re - ply with love to love most high.
2 Make clear, make clear, make clear where truth and light ap - pear.
3 to fight, to fight, to fight till ev - ery wrong's set right.
4 Di - vine, di - vine, di - vine it is when all com - bine!
5 A - rise, a - rise, a - rise! and make a par - a - dise!

Words: Percy Dearmer (1867-1936), alt.
Music: *Quittez, Pasteurs*, French carol; harm. Martin Fallas Shaw (1875-1958)          Irr.

1 Now let us all with one ac - cord,
2 The cov - e - nant, so long re - vealed
3 Your love, O Lord, our sin - ful race
4 Re - mem - ber, Lord, though frail we be,
5 There - fore, we pray you, Lord, for - give;

1 in com - pa - ny with a - ges past,
2 to those of faith in for - mer time,
3 has not re - turned, but fal - si - fied;
4 in your own im - age were we made;
5 so when our wan - derings here shall cease,

1 keep vi - gil with our heaven - ly Lord
2 Christ by his own ex - am - ple sealed,
3 au - thor of mer - cy, turn your face
4 help us, lest in anx - i - e - ty,
5 we may with you for ev - er live,

1 in his temp - ta - tion and his fast.
2 the Lord of love, in love sub - lime.
3 and grant re - pent - ance for our pride.
4 we cause your Name to be be - trayed.
5 in love and u - ni - ty and peace.

Words: Att. Gregory the Great (540-604); tr. *Praise the Lord*, 1972, alt.
Music: *Ex more docti mystico*, plainsong, Mode 2, Verona MS., 12th cent.

LM

1 Now let us all with one ac - cord, in
2 The cov - e - nant, so long re - vealed to
3 Your love, O Lord, our sin - ful race has
4 Re - mem - ber, Lord, though frail we be, in
5 There - fore, we pray you, Lord, for - give; so

1 com - pa - ny with a - ges past, keep vi - gil with our
2 those of faith in for - mer time, Christ by his own ex -
3 not re - turned, but fal - si - fied; au - thor of mer - cy,
4 your own im - age were we made; help us, lest in anx -
5 when our wan - derings here shall cease, we may with you for

1 heaven-ly Lord in his temp - ta - tion and his fast.
2 am - ple sealed, the Lord of love, in love sub - lime.
3 turn your face and grant re - pent - ance for our pride.
4 i - e - ty, we cause your Name to be be - trayed.
5 ev - er live, in love and u - ni - ty and peace.

Words: Att. Gregory the Great (540-604); tr. *Praise the Lord*, 1972, alt.
Music: *Bourbon*, melody att. Freeman Lewis (1780-1859)

LM

## Lent

# 148

1 Cre - a - tor of the earth and skies, to whom the
2 We have not known you: to the skies our mon - u -
3 We have not loved you: far and wide the wreck-age
4 For this, our fool - ish con - fi - dence, our pride of
5 Teach us to know and love you, Lord, and hum - bly

1 words of life be - long, grant us your truth to make us
2 ments of fol - ly soar, and all our self - wrought mis - er -
3 of our ha - tred spreads, and e - vils wrought by hu - man
4 know-ledge and our sin, we come to you in pen - i -
5 fol - low in your way. Speak to our souls the quick - ening

1 wise; grant us your power to make us strong.
2 ies have made us trust our - selves the more.
3 pride re - coil on un - re - pent - ant heads.
4 tence; in us the work of grace be - gin.
5 word, and turn our dark - ness in - to day.

Words: David W. Hughes (1911-1967), alt.
Music: *Uffingham*, melody Jeremiah Clarke (1670-1707), alt.

LM

# 149

Lent

*Unison or harmony*

1 E - ter - nal Lord of love, be - hold your Church
2 So dai - ly dy - ing to the way of self,
3 If dead in you, so in you we a - rise,

walk - ing once more the pil - grim way of Lent,
so dai - ly liv - ing to your way of love,
you the first - born of all the faith - ful dead;

led by your cloud by day, by night your fire,
we walk the road, Lord Je - sus, that you trod,
and as through ston - y ground the green shoots break,

moved by your love and toward your pres - ence bent:
know - ing our - selves bap - tized in - to your death:
glo - rious in spring - time dress of leaf and flower,

far off yet here— the goal of all de - sire.
so we are dead and live with you in God.
so in the Fa - ther's glo - ry shall we wake.

Words: Thomas H. Cain (b. 1931)
Music: *Old 124th*, melody *Pseaumes octante trois de David*, 1551;
harm. Charles Winfred Douglas (1867-1944)

10 10. 10 10 10

## Lent

# 150

1 For - ty days and for - ty nights thou wast fast - ing in the wild;
2 Should not we thy sor - row share and from world - ly joys ab - stain,
3 Then if Sa - tan on us press, Je - sus, Sa - vior, hear our call!
4 So shall we have peace di - vine: ho - lier glad-ness ours shall be;
5 Keep, O keep us, Sa - vior dear, ev - er con - stant by thy side;

1 for - ty days and for - ty nights tempt - ed, and yet un - de - filed.
2 fast - ing with un - ceas - ing prayer, strong with thee to suf - fer pain?
3 Vic - tor in the wil - der - ness, grant we may not faint nor fall!
4 round us, too, shall an - gels shine, such as min - is - tered to thee.
5 that with thee we may ap - pear at the e - ter - nal Eas - ter - tide.

Words: George Hunt Smyttan (1822-1870), alt.
Music: *Aus der Tiefe rufe ich*, melody att. Martin Herbst (1654-1681), alt.;
harm. William Henry Monk (1823-1889)

77. 77

1 From deep-est woe I cry to thee; Lord, hear me, I im-
2 Thou grant-est par-don through thy love; thy grace a-lone a-
3 And thus my hope is in the Lord, and not in my own

plore thee! Bend down thy gra-cious ear to me;
vail - eth. Our works could ne'er our guilt re-move;
mer - it; I rest up-on his faith-ful word

I lay my sins be - fore thee.
yea, e'en the best life fail - eth.
to them of con - trite spi - rit.

If thou re - mem - berest ev - ery sin,
For none may boast them - selves of aught,
That he is mer - ci - ful and just,

if nought but just re - ward we win,
but must con - fess thy grace hath wrought
here is my com - fort and my trust;

could we a - bide thy pres - ence?
what - e'er in them is wor - thy.
his help I wait with pa - tience.

Words: Martin Luther (1483-1546); tr. Catherine Winkworth (1827-1878), alt.; based on Psalm 130
Music: *Aus tiefer Not*, melody att. Martin Luther (1483-1546)

87. 87. 887

1 Kind Ma-ker of the world, O hear the fer-vent
2 Each heart is man-i-fest to thee; thou know-est
3 Spare us, O Lord, who now con-fess our sins and
4 Give us the dis-ci-pline that springs from ab-sti-
5 Grant, O thou bless-ed Trin-i-ty; grant, O un-

1 prayer, with man-y a tear poured forth by all the
2 our in-fir-mi-ty; now we re-pent, and
3 all our wick-ed-ness, and, for the glo-ry
4 nence in out-ward things with in-ward fast-ing,
5 chang-ing U-ni-ty; that this our fast of

1 pen-i-tent who keep this ho-ly fast of Lent!
2 seek thy face; grant un-to us thy par-doning grace.
3 of thy Name, our weak-ened souls to health re-claim.
4 so that we in heart and soul may dwell with thee.
5 for-ty days may work our pro-fit and thy praise!

Words: Att. Gregory the Great (540-604); ver. *Hymnal 1940*, alt.
Music: *A la venue de Noël*, melody from *Fleurs des noëls*, 1535

LM

## Opening Anthem

*Cantor or Celebrant*

Blessed is the King who comes in the name of the Lord:

*People*

Peace in heaven and glory in the high - est.

## Blessing over the Branches

*Celebrant*

The Lord be with you.

*People*

And al - so with you.

*Celebrant*

Let us give thanks to the Lord our God.

*People*

It is right to give him thanks and praise.

*Celebrant*

. . . ev - - er.

*People*

A - men.

*Cantor or Celebrant*

Blessed is he who comes in the name of the Lord.

*People*

Ho - san - na in the high - est.

## At the Procession

*Deacon*

Let us go forth in peace.

*People*

In the name of Christ. A - men.

*The stanzas may be sung by choir alone or alternately by contrasted groups; all sing the refrain.*

Words: Theodulph of Orleans (d. 821); tr. John Mason Neale (1818-1866), alt.
Music: *Valet will ich dir geben*, melody Melchior Teschner (1584-1635), alt.;
    harm. Wiliam Henry Monk (1823-1889)

76. 76. D

*Refrain (sung by all)*

All glo - ry, laud, and hon - or to thee, Re-deem-er, King!

to whom the lips of chil - dren made sweet ho - san - nas ring.

*Cantor or choir*

1 Thou art the King of Is - ra - el, thou Da - vid's roy - al Son,
2 The com - pa - ny of an - gels is prais - ing thee on high;
3 The peo - ple of the He - brews with palms be - fore thee went;
4 To thee be - fore thy pas - sion they sang their hymns of praise;
5 Thou didst ac - cept their prais - es; ac - cept the prayers we bring,

*Repeat Refrain*

1 who in the Lord's Name com - est, the King and Bless - ed One.
2 and we with all cre - a - tion in cho - rus make re - ply.
3 our praise and prayers and an - thems be - fore thee we pre - sent.
4 to thee, now high ex - alt - ed, our mel - o - dy we raise.
5 who in all good de - light est, thou good and gra - cious King.

Words: Theodulph of Orleans (d. 821); tr. John Mason Neale (1818-1866), alt.
Music: *Gloria, laus, et honor*, plainsong, Mode 1, Einsiedeln MS. and St. Gall MS., 10th cent.;
    ver. Schola Antiqua, 1983
Music: Melody rhythmic version © 1984, Schola Antiqua Inc. Used by permission.

76. 76 with Refrain

1 Ride on! ride on in ma - jes - ty! Hark! all the
2 Ride on! ride on in ma - jes - ty! In low - ly
3 Ride on! ride on in ma - jes - ty! The an - gel
4 Ride on! ride on in ma - jes - ty! Thy last and
5 Ride on! ride on in ma - jes - ty! In low - ly

| | | | | | | | | | |
|---|---|---|---|---|---|---|---|---|---|
| 1 | tribes | ho - san - na | | cry; | thy | hum - ble | beast | pur - sues | his |
| 2 | pomp | ride on | to | die; | O | Christ, thy | tri - umphs now | be - |
| 3 | ar - mies of | the | sky | look down with | sad and | won - dering |
| 4 | fierc - est strife | is | nigh; | the | Fa - ther | on | his | sap - phire |
| 5 | pomp | ride on | to | die; | bow thy | meek | head | to | mor - tal |

| | | | | | | | | |
|---|---|---|---|---|---|---|---|---|
| 1 | road | with | palms | and | scat - tered | gar - ments | strowed. |
| 2 | gin | o'er | cap - tive | death and | con - quered | sin. |
| 3 | eyes | to | see | the ap - proach - ing | sac - ri - | fice. |
| 4 | throne | ex - pects | his | own | a - noint - ed | Son. |
| 5 | pain, | then | take, | O | God, thy | power, and | reign. |

Words: Henry Hart Milman (1791-1868), alt.
Music: *The King's Majesty*, Graham George (b. 1912)

LM

## The Liturgy of the Palms: Processional

**157**

*Antiphon (at the beginning)*

Ho - san - na in the high - est. Bless - ed is he who comes

in the name of the Lord. Ho - san - na in the high - est.

*(The phrase "Hosanna in the highest" may be repeated as a Refrain after each verse.)*

O - pen for me the gates of righteousness; I will enter them; I will

offer thanks to the Lord. [R] "This is the gate of the Lord; he who is righteous may en - ter." [R] I will give thanks to you, for you answered me

and have become my sal- va- tion. [R] The same stone which the builders rejected

has become the chief cor -ner-stone. [R] This is the Lord's doing, and it is

marve - lous in our eyes. [R] On this day the Lord has acted; we will

rejoice and be glad in it. [R] Ho -san - na, Lord, hosanna! Lord, send us

now suc-cess. [R] Bless-ed is he who comes in the name of the Lord; we bless you

from the house of the Lord. [R] God is the Lord; he has shined upon us;

form a procession with branches up to the horns of the al - tar. [R]

"You are my God, and I will thank you; you are my God, and I will ex-alt you." [R]

Give thanks to the Lord, for he is good; his mercy endures for ev-er. [R]

*Antiphon (at the end)*

Ho - san - na in the high - est. Bless - ed is he who comes

in the name of the Lord. Ho - san - na in the high-est.

Words: Psalm 118:19-29
Music: Ancient Gallican chant; adapt. Howard E. Galley (b. 1929)

1 Ah, ho-ly Je-sus, how hast thou of-fend-ed, that man to
2 Who was the guilt-y? Who brought this up-on thee? A-las, my
3 Lo, the Good Shep-herd for the sheep is of-fered; the slave hath
4 For me, kind Je-sus, was thy in-car-na-tion, thy mor-tal
5 There-fore, kind Je-sus, since I can-not pay thee, I do a-

1 judge thee hath in hate pre-tend-ed? By foes de-rid-ed,
2 trea-son, Je-sus, hath un-done thee. 'Twas I, Lord Je-sus,
3 sin-ned, and the Son hath suf-fered; for our a-tone-ment,
4 sor-row, and thy life's ob-la-tion; thy death of an-guish
5 dore thee, and will ev-er pray thee, think on thy pi-ty

1 by thine own re-ject-ed, O most af-flict-ed.
2 I it was de-nied thee: I cru-ci-fied thee.
3 while we noth-ing heed-ed, God in-ter-ced-ed.
4 and thy bit-ter pas-sion, for my sal-va-tion.
5 and thy love un-swerv-ing, not my de-serv-ing.

Words: Johann Heermann (1585-1647); tr. Robert Seymour Bridges (1844-1930)
Music: *Herzliebster Jesu*, Johann Cruger (1598-1662), alt.

11 11. 11 5

1 At the cross her vig - il keep - ing, stood the mourn - ful
2 With what pain and des - o - la - tion, with what grief and
3 Him she saw for our sal - va - tion mocked with cru - el
4 Who, on Christ's dear mo - ther gaz - ing, pierced by an - guish
5 Je - sus, may her deep de - vo - tion stir in me the

1 mo - ther weep - ing, where he hung, the dy - ing Lord:
2 res - ig - na - tion, Mar - y watched her dy - ing son.
3 ac - cla - ma - tion, scourged, and crowned with thorns en - twined;
4 so a - maz - ing, born of wo - man, would not weep?
5 same e - mo - tion, Fount of love, Re - deem - er kind;

1 there she wait - ed in her an - guish, see - ing Christ in
2 Deep the woe of her af - flic - tion, when she saw the
3 saw him then from judg - ment tak - en, and in death by
4 Who, on Christ's dear mo - ther think - ing, such a cup of
5 that my heart fresh ar - dor gain - ing, and a pur - er

1 tor - ment lan - guish, in her heart the pierc - ing sword.
2 cru - ci - fi - xion of the sole - be - got - ten one.
3 all for - sak - en, till his spi - rit he re - signed.
4 sor - row drink - ing, would not share her sor - rows deep?
5 love at - tain - ing, may with thee ac - cept - ance find.

Words: Latin, 13th cent.; ver. *Hymnal 1982*
Music: *Stabat Mater dolorosa*, melody from *Maintzisch Gesangbuch*, 1661

1 Cross of Je - sus, cross of sor - row, where the
2 Here the King of all the a - ges, throned in
3 O mys - ter - ious con - de - scend - ing! O a -
4 Cross of Je - sus, cross of sor - row, where the

blood of Christ was shed, per - fect Man on
light ere worlds could be, robed in mor - tal
ban - don - ment sub - lime! Ve - ry God him -
blood of Christ was shed, per - fect Man on

thee did suf - fer, per - fect God on thee has bled!
flesh is dy - ing, cru - ci - fied by sin for me.
self is bear - ing all the suf - fer - ings of time!
thee did suf - fer, per - fect God on thee has bled!

Words: William J. Sparrow-Simpson (1860-1952)
Music: *Cross of Jesus*, John Stainer (1840-1901)

87. 87

1 The flam - ing ban - ners of our King
2 A Ro - man sol - dier drew a spear
3 The crowd would have been sat - is - fied
4 With what strange light the rough trunk shone,
5 The best are shamed be - fore that wood;

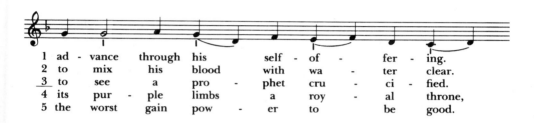

1 ad - vance through his self - of - fer - ing.
2 to mix his blood with wa - ter clear.
3 to see a pro - phet cru - ci - fied.
4 its pur - ple limbs a roy - al throne,
5 the worst gain pow - er to be good.

1 He lived to rob death of its sting;
2 That blood re - tains its liv - ing power;
3 They stum - bled on a mys - ter - y:
4 its load a roy - al trea - sur - y:
5 O grant, most bless - ed Trin - i - ty,

1 he died e - ter - nal life to bring.
2 the wa - ter cleans - es to this hour.
3 Mes - si - ah reign - ing from a tree.
4 the ran - som of a world set free.
5 that all may share the vic - to - ry.

Words: Venantius Honorius Fortunatus (540?-600?); para. John Webster Grant (b. 1919)
Music: *Vexilla Regis prodeunt*, plainsong, Mode 1, Rome MS., 12th cent.;
    ver. Schola Antiqua, 1983
Music: Melody rhythmic version © 1984, Schola Antiqua Inc. Used by permission.

LM

1 The roy - al ban - ners for - ward go, the cross shines
2 Ful - filled is all that Da - vid told in true pro -
3 O tree of beau - ty, tree most fair, or - dained those
4 Blest tree, whose cho - sen branch - es bore the wealth that
5 O cross, our one re - li - ance, hail! Still may thy
6 To thee, e - ter - nal Three in One, let hom - age

forth in mys - tic glow where he through whom our flesh
phet ic song of old; how God the na - tions' King
ho - ly limbs to bear gone is thy shame, each crim -
did the world re - store, the price which none but he
power with us a - vail to save us sin - ners from
meet by all be done; as by the cross thou dost

was made, in that same flesh our ran - som paid.
should be, for God is reign - ing from the tree.
soned bough pro - claims the King of glo - ry now.
could pay to spoil the spoil - er of his prey.
our sin, God's right - eous - ness for all to win.
re - store so rule and guide us ev - er - more.

Words: Venantius Honorius Fortunatus (540?-600?); ver. *Hymnal 1982*
Music: *Vexilla Regis prodeunt*, plainsong, Mode 1, Rome MS., 12th cent.      LM

1 Sun - set to sun - rise chang - es now, for
2 E'en though the sun with - holds its light, lo!
3 Here in o'er - whelm - ing fi - nal strife the

God doth make his world a - new; on the Re - deem - er's
a more heaven - ly lamp shines here, and from the cross on
Lord of life hath vic - to - ry, and sin is slain, and

thorn-crowned brow the won-ders of that dawn we view.
Cal - vary's height gleams of e - ter - ni - ty ap - pear.
death brings life, and earth in - her - its hea - ven's key.

Words: Clement of Alexandria (170?-220?); para. Howard Chandler Robbins (1876-1952), alt.
Music: *Kedron*, melody att. Elkanah Kelsay Dare (1782-1826)                           LM

## Holy Week                                                                    **164**

1 A - lone thou go - est forth, O Lord, in
2 Our sins, not thine, thou bear - est, Lord; make
3 This is earth's dark - est hour, but thou dost
4 Grant us with thee to suf - fer pain that,

sac - ri - fice to die; is this thy sor - row
us thy sor - row feel, till through our pit - y
light and life re - store; then let all praise be
as we share this hour, thy cross may bring us

nought to us who pass un - heed - ing by?
and our shame love an - swers love's ap - peal.
giv - en thee who liv - est ev - er - more.
to thy joy and re - sur - rec - tion power.

Words: Peter Abelard (1079-1142); tr. F. Bland Tucker (1895-1984)
Music: *Bangor*, from *A Compleat Melody or Harmony of Zion*, 1734          CM

# 165

1 Sing, my tongue, the glo - rious bat - tle; of the might - y
2 Thir - ty years a - mong us dwell - ing, his ap - point - ed
3 He en - dures the nails, the spit - ting, vin - e - gar, and
4 Faith - ful cross! a - bove all o - ther, one and on - ly
5 Bend thy boughs, O tree of glo - ry! Thy re - lax - ing
*6 Praise and hon - or to the Fa - ther, praise and hon - or

1 con - flict sing; tell the tri - umph of the vic - tim,
2 time ful - filled, born for this, he meets his pas - sion,
3 spear, and reed; from that ho - ly bo - dy bro - ken
4 no - ble tree! None in fo - liage, none in blos - som,
5 sin - ews bend; for a - while the an - cient ri - gor
6 to the Son, praise and hon - or to the Spi - rit,

1 to his cross thy tri - bute bring. Je - sus Christ, the
2 this the Sa - vior free - ly willed: on the cross the
3 blood and wa - ter forth pro - ceed: earth, and stars, and
4 none in fruit thy peer may be: sweet - est wood and
5 that thy birth be - stowed, sus - pend; and the King of
6 ev - er Three and ev - er One: one in might and

1 world's Re - deem - er from that cross now reigns as King.
2 Lamb is lift - ed, where his pre - cious blood is spilled.
3 sky, and o - cean, by that flood from stain are freed.
4 sweet - est i - ron! sweet - est weight is hung on thee.
5 heaven - ly beau - ty gent - ly on thine arms ex - tend.
6 one in glo - ry while e - ter - nal a - ges run.

Words: Venantius Honorius Fortunatus (540?-600?); ver. *Hymnal 1982*, after John Mason Neale (1818-1866)
Music: *Pange lingua*, plainsong, Mode 1, St. Gall MS., 10th cent.; ver. Schola Antiqua, 1983    87. 87. 87

1 Sing, my tongue, the glo-rious bat - tle; of the might - y con - flict
2 Thir - ty years a - mong us dwell - ing, his ap - point - ed time ful -
3 He en - dures the nails, the spit - ting, vin - e - gar, and spear, and
4 Faith - ful cross! a - bove all o - ther, one and on - ly no - ble
5 Bend thy boughs, O tree of glo - ry! Thy re - lax - ing sin - ews
*6 Praise and hon - or to the Fa - ther, praise and hon - or to the

1 sing; tell the tri - umph of the vic - tim, to his
2 filled, born for this, he meets his pas - sion, this the
3 reed; from that ho - ly bo - dy bro - ken blood and
4 tree! None in fo - liage, none in blos - som, none in
5 bend; for a - while the an - cient ri - gor that thy
6 Son, praise and hon - or to the Spi - rit, ev - er

1 cross thy tri - bute bring. Je - sus Christ, the world's Re -
2 Sa - vior free - ly willed: on the cross the Lamb is
3 wa - ter forth pro - ceed: earth, and stars, and sky, and
4 fruit thy peer may be: sweet - est wood and sweet - est
5 birth be - stowed, sus - pend; and the King of heaven - ly
6 Three and ev - er One: one in might and one in

1 deem - er from that cross now reigns as King.
2 lift - ed, where his pre - cious blood is spilled.
3 o - cean, by that flood from stain are freed.
4 i - ron! sweet - est weight is hung on thee.
5 beau - ty gent - ly on thine arms ex - tend.
6 glo - ry while e - ter - nal a - ges run.

Words: Venantius Honorius Fortunatus (540?-600?); ver. *Hymnal 1982*, after John Mason Neale (1818-1866)
Music: *Pange lingua*, plainsong, Mode 3, *Zisterzienser Hymnar*, 14th cent.                    87. 87. 87

## 167

1 There is a green hill far a - way, out - side a ci - ty wall,
2 We may not know, we can - not tell, what pains he had to bear,
*3 He died that we might be for - given, he died to make us good,
*4 There was no o - ther good e - nough to pay the price of sin,
5 O dear - ly, dear - ly has he loved! And we must love him too,

1 where our dear Lord was cru - ci - fied who died to save us all.
2 but we be - lieve it was for us he hung and suf - fered there.
3 that we might go at last to heaven, saved by his pre - cious blood.
4 he on - ly could un - lock the gate of heaven and let us in.
5 and trust in his re - deem - ing blood, and try his works to do.

Words: Cecil Frances Alexander (1818-1895), alt.
Music: *Horsley*, William Horsley (1774-1858)

CM

## 168

1 O sa - cred head, sore wound - ed, de - filed and put to scorn;
2 Thy beau - ty, long - de - sir - ed, hath va - nished from our sight;
3 In thy most bit - ter pas - sion my heart to share doth cry,
*4 What lan - guage shall I bor - row to thank thee, dear - est friend,
*5 My days are few, O fail not, with thine im - mor - tal power,

1 O king-ly head, sur - round - ed with mock - ing crown of thorn:
2 thy power is all ex - pir - ed, and quenched the light of light.
3 with thee for my sal - va - tion up - on the cross to die.
4 for this thy dy - ing sor - row, thy pi - ty with - out end?
5 to hold me that I quail not in death's most fear - ful hour;

1 what sor - row mars thy gran - deur? Can death thy bloom de - flower?
2 Ah me! for whom thou di - est, hide not so far thy grace:
3 Ah, keep my heart thus mov - ed to stand thy cross be - neath,
4 Oh, make me thine for ev - er! and should I faint - ing be,
5 that I may fight be - friend - ed, and see in my last strife

1 O coun - te - nance whose splen - dor the hosts of heaven a - dore!
2 show me, O Love most high - est, the bright-ness of thy face.
3 to mourn thee, well - be - lov - ed, yet thank thee for thy death.
4 Lord, let me nev - er, nev - er, out - live my love for thee.
5 to me thine arms ex - tend - ed up - on the cross of life.

Words: Paul Gerhardt (1607-1676); sts. 1-3 and 5, tr. Robert Seymour Bridges (1844-1930);
     st. 4, tr. James Waddell Alexander (1804-1859), alt.
Music: *Herzlich tut mich verlangen [Passion Chorale]*, Hans Leo Hassler (1564-1612);
     adapt. and harm. Johann Sebastian Bach (1685-1750)

76. 76. D

1 O sa - cred head, sore wound-ed, de - filed and put to scorn;
2 Thy beau - ty, long - de - sir - ed, hath va - nished from our sight;
3 In thy most bit - ter pas - sion my heart to share doth cry,
*4 What lan - guage shall I bor - row to thank thee, dear - est friend,
*5 My days are few, O fail not, with thine im - mor - tal power,

1 O king - ly head, sur-round - ed with mock - ing crown of thorn:
2 thy power is all ex - pir - ed, and quenched the light of light.
3 with thee for my sal - va - tion up - on the cross to die.
4 for this thy dy - ing sor - row, thy pi - ty with - out end?
5 to hold me that I quail not in death's most fear - ful hour;

1 what sor - row mars thy gran - deur? Can death thy bloom de - flower?
2 Ah me! for whom thou di - est, hide not so far thy grace:
3 Ah, keep my heart thus mov - ed to stand thy cross be - neath,
4 Oh, make me thine for - ev - er! and should I faint - ing be,
5 that I may fight be - friend - ed, and see in my last strife

1 O coun - te - nance whose splen - dor the hosts of heaven a - dore!
2 show me, O Love most high - est, the bright-ness of thy face.
3 to mourn thee, well - be - lov - ed, yet thank thee for thy death.
4 Lord, let me nev - er, nev - er, out - live my love for thee.
5 to me thine arms ex - tend - ed up - on the cross of life.

Words: Paul Gerhardt (1607-1676); sts. 1-3 and 5, tr. Robert Seymour Bridges (1844-1930);
st. 4, tr. James Waddell Alexander (1804-1859), alt.
Music: *Herzlich tut mich verlangen*, Hans Leo Hassler (1564-1612)

76. 76. D

1 To mock your reign, O dear-est Lord, they made a crown of thorns;
2 In mock ac-claim, O gra-cious Lord, they snatched a pur-ple cloak,
3 A scep-tered reed, O pa-tient Lord, they thrust in-to your hand,

set you with taunts a-long that road from which no one re-turns.
your pas-sion turned, for all they cared, in-to a sol-dier's joke.
and act-ed out their grim cha-rade to its ap-point-ed end.

*

They did not know, as we do now, that glo-rious is your crown;
They did not know, as we do now, that though we mer-it blame
They did not know, as we do now, though em-pires rise and fall,

that thorns would flower up-on your brow, your sor-rows heal our own.
you will your robe of mer-cy throw a-round our na-ked shame.
your King-dom shall not cease to grow till love em-bra-ces all.

*The bracketed notes are to be treated as triplet groups.

Words: F. Pratt Green (b. 1903), alt.
Music: *The Third Tune,* Thomas Tallis (1505?-1585); ed. John Wilson (b. 1905)      CMD
Words: Copyright © 1973 by Hope Publishing Company. All Rights Reserved. Used by Permission.

1 Go to dark Gethsemane, ye that feel the tempter's power;
your Redeemer's conflict see, watch with him one bitter hour;
turn not from his griefs away, learn of Jesus Christ to pray.

2 Follow to the judgment hall; view the Lord of life arraigned;
O the wormwood and the gall! O the pangs his soul sustained!
Shun not suffering, shame, or loss; learn of him to bear the cross.

3 Calvary's mournful mountain climb; there, adoring at his feet,
mark the miracle of time, God's own sacrifice complete;
"It is finished!" hear him cry; learn of Jesus Christ to die.

Words: James Montgomery (1771-1854)
Music: *Petra*, Richard Redhead (1820-1901)

77. 77. 77

Words: Afro-American spiritual
Music: *Were You There*, Afro-American spiritual; harm. Charles Winfred Douglas (1867-1944)

Irr.

1 O sor - row deep! Who would not weep
2 The Pas - chal Lamb, like I - saac's ram,
3 Blest shall they be e - ter - nal - ly
4 O Je - sus blest, my help and rest,

with heart - felt pain and sigh - ing!
in blood was of - fered for us,
who pon - der in their weep - ing
with tears I pray thee, hear me:

*slightly slower*

God the Fa - ther's on - ly Son he
pour - ing out his life that of Life
that the glo - rious Prince of death,
now, and e - ven un - to

in the tomb is ly - ing.
might to life re - store us.
should in death be sleep - ing.
dear - est Lord, be near me.

Words: St. 1, Friedrich von Spee (1591-1635); tr. Charles Winfred Douglas (1867-1944).
Sts. 2-3, James Waring McCrady (b. 1938). St. 4, Johann Rist (1607-1667);
tr. Charles Winfred Douglas (1867-1944)
Music: *O Traurigkeit,* melody and bass *Himlischer Lieder,* 1641, alt.; harm. *Hymnal 1982*

447. 76

1  At the Lamb's high feast we sing praise to our vic-to-rious King,
2  Where the Pas-chal blood is poured, death's dark an-gel sheathes his sword;
3  Might-y vic-tim from on high, hell's fierce powers be-neath thee lie;
4  Eas-ter tri-umph, Eas-ter joy, these a-lone do sin de-stroy.

who hath washed us in the tide flow-ing from his pierc-ed side;
Is-rael's hosts tri-um-phant go through the wave that drowns the foe.
thou hast con-quered in the fight, thou hast brought us life and light:
From sin's power do thou set free soul's new-born, O Lord, in thee.

praise we him, whose love di-vine gives his sa-cred Blood for wine,
Praise we Christ, whose blood was shed, Pas-chal vic-tim, Pas-chal bread;
now no more can death ap-pall, now no more the grave en-thrall;
Hymns of glo-ry, songs of praise, Fa-ther, un-to thee we raise:

gives his Bo-dy for the feast, Christ the vic-tim, Christ the priest.
with sin-cer-i-ty and love eat we man-na from a-bove.
thou hast o-pened par-a-dise, and in thee thy saints shall rise.
ris-en Lord, all praise to thee with the Spi-rit ev-er be.

Words: Latin, 1632; tr. Robert Campbell (1814-1868), alt.
Music: *Salzburg*, melody Jakob Hintze (1622-1702); harm. Johann Sebastian Bach (1685-1750)

77. 77. D

*Refrain*

Hail thee, fes - ti - val day! blest day that art hal-lowed for -
ev - er, day where-on Christ a - rose, break - ing the
king - dom of death.

*First time only* | 2
death.

1 Lo, the fair beau - ty of earth, from the death of the
3 Dai - ly the love - li - ness grows, a - dorned with the
5 God the Cre - a - tor, the Lord, who___ rul - est the
7 Spi - rit of life and of power, now___ flow in us,

win - ter a - ris - ing! Ev - ery good
glo - ry of blos - som; hea - ven her
earth and the hea - vens, guard us from
fount of our be - ing, light that dost

*Repeat Refrain*

gift of the year now with its Mas - ter re - turns:
gates un - bars, fling - ing her in - crease of light:
harm with - out, cleanse us from e - vil with - in:
light - en___ all, life that in all dost a - bide:

2 He who was nailed to the cross is___ Lord and the
4 Rise from the grave now, O Lord, who art au - thor of
6 Je - sus the health of the world, en - light - en our
8 Praise to the Giv - er of good! Thou___ Love who art

| | | | | | | |
|---|---|---|---|---|---|---|
| ru | - ler of | na | - ture; | all things cre - a - ted on |
| life | and cre - | a | - tion. | Tread - ing the path-way of |
| minds, | thou Re - deem | - er, | Son of | the Fa - ther su - |
| au | - thor of | con | - cord, | pour out thy balm on our |

*Repeat Refrain*

| | | | | | | |
|---|---|---|---|---|---|---|
| earth | sing | to | the | glo - ry | of | God: |
| death, | life | thou | be - stow | - est | on | all: |
| preme, | on - ly - | be - got | - ten | of | God: |
| souls, | or - der | our | ways | in | thy | peace: |

*The refrain may be sung once by choir alone and repeated by all. The stanzas may be sung by choir alone, alternately by contrasted groups, or by all.*

Words: Venantius Honorius Fortunatus (540?-600?); tr. *The English Hymnal*, 1906, alt.
Music: *Salve festa dies*, Ralph Vaughan Williams (1872-1958)

79. 77 with Refrain

# Easter

# 176

| | | | | | | | |
|---|---|---|---|---|---|---|---|
| 1 | O - ver the | cha - os | of the emp - ty | wa - ters | hov-ered the |
| 2 | By the same | Spi - rit, | we, re - gen - er - at - ed | in - to the |
| 3 | By the same | Spi - rit | we are called to | wor - ship | God our Cre - |

| | | | | | | |
|---|---|---|---|---|---|---|
| Spi - rit, | bring-ing forth cre - a - tion; | so from the | emp - ty |
| bo - dy | of our ris - en | Sa - vior, | seek through the | pow - er |
| a - tor, | Sa - vior, Sanc - ti - fi - er, | of whom the | glo - ry, |

| | | | | |
|---|---|---|---|---|
| tomb the Sec - ond | Ad - am | is - sued tri - um - phant.___ |
| of the new cre - | a - tion | life ev - er - last - ing.___ |
| in both earth and | hea - ven, | is man - i - fest - ed.___ |

Words: Sts. 1-2, *A Monastic Breviary*, 1976; st. 3, *Hymnal 1982*
Music: *West Park*, Robert Roth (b. 1928)

11 11. 11 5

1 O - ver the cha - os  of the emp - ty wa - ters  hov - ered the
2 By  the same Spi - rit  we, re - gen - er - at - ed  in - to the
3 By  the same Spi - rit  we are called to wor - ship  God our Cre -

Spi - rit,  bring-ing forth cre - a - tion;  so  from the emp - ty
bo - dy  of our ris - en Sa - vior,  seek through the pow - er
a - tor,  Sa - vior, Sanc - ti - fi - er,  of  whom the glo - ry,

tomb the Sec - ond Ad - am  is - sued tri - um - phant.____
of the new cre - a - tion  life ev - er - last - ing.____
in both earth and hea - ven,  is man - i - fest - ed.____

Words: Sts. 1-2, *A Monastic Breviary*, 1976; st. 3, *Hymnal 1982*
Music: *Bickford*, Hank Beebe (b. 1926)

11 11. 11 5

*Descant*

Al - le - lu - ia,  al - le -

*Refrain*

Al - le - lu - ia, al - le - lu - ia! Give thanks to the

The descant may be sung after stanzas 3 and 4.

Words: Donald Fishel (b. 1950)
Music: *Alleluia No. 1*, Donald Fishel (b. 1950); arr. Betty Pulkingham (b. 1928),
   Charles Mallory (b. 1950) and George Mims (b. 1938)
Music: Arrangement copyright © 1979, Celebration.

887. 85

1 "Wel - come, hap - py morn-ing!" age to age shall say:
*2 Earth her joy con - fess - es, cloth-ing her for spring,
*3 Months in due suc - ces - sion, days of length-ening light,
4 Ma - ker and Re - deem-er, life and health of all,
5 Thou, of life the au - thor, death didst un - der - go,

1 hell to - day is van - quished, heaven is won to - day!
2 all fresh gifts re - turned with her re - turn - ing King:
3 hours and pass - ing mo - ments praise thee in their flight.
4 thou from heaven be - hold - ing hu - man na - ture's fall,
5 tread the path of dark - ness, sav - ing strength to show;

1 Lo! the dead is liv - ing, God for ev - er - more!
2 bloom in ev - ery mea - dow, leaves on ev - ery bough,
3 Bright-ness of the morn - ing, sky and fields and sea,
4 of the Fa - ther's God - head true and on - ly Son,
5 come then, true and faith - ful, now ful - fill thy word,

1 Him their true Cre - a - tor, all his works a - dore!
2 speak his sor - row end - ed, hail his tri - umph now.
3 Van - quish - er of dark - ness, bring their praise to thee.
4 man - kind to de - liv - er, man - hood didst put on.
5 'tis thine own third morn - ing! rise, O bur - ied Lord!

*Refrain*

"Wel - come, hap - py morn - ing!" age to age shall say.

6 Loose the souls long prisoned, bound with Satan's chain;
   all that now is fallen raise to life again;
   show thy face in brightness, bid the nations see;
   bring again our daylight: day returns with thee!

*Refrain*

Words: Venantius Honorius Fortunatus (540?-600?); tr. John Ellerton (1826-1893), alt.
Music: *Fortunatus*, Arthur Seymour Sullivan (1842-1900)

11 11. 11 11. 11

1 He is ris - en, he is ris - en! Tell it out with
2 Come, ye sad and fear - ful - heart - ed, with glad smile and
*3 Come, with high and ho - ly hymn - ing, hail our Lord's tri -
4 He is ris - en, he is ris - en! He hath o - pened

joy - ful voice: he has burst his three days' pris - on;
ra - diant brow! Death's long sha - dows have de - part - ed;
um - phant day; not one dark - some cloud is dim - ming
hea - ven's gate: we are free from sin's dark pris - on,

let the whole wide earth re - joice: death is con - quered,
Je - sus' woes are o - ver now, and the pas - sion
yon - der glo - rious morn - ing ray, break - ing o'er the
ris - en to a ho - lier state; and a bright - er

we are free, Christ has won the vic - to - ry.
that he bore— sin and pain can vex no more.
pur - ple east, sym - bol of our Eas - ter feast.
Eas - ter beam on our long - ing eyes shall stream.

Words: Cecil Frances Alexander (1818-1895), alt.
Music: *Unser Herrscher*, Joachim Neander (1650-1680)

87. 87. 77

*Descant*

4 Soon shall each rap - tured tongue his

1 A - wake and sing the song of
2 Sing of his dy - ing love, his
3 You pil - grims on the road to
4 Soon shall each rap - tured tongue his

end - less praise pro - claim, and sing in sweet-er

Mo - ses and the Lamb; wake ev - ery heart and
re - sur - rec - tion power; sing how he in - ter -
Zi - on's ci - ty, sing, re - joic - ing in the
end - less praise pro - claim, and sing in sweet-er

notes the song of Mo - ses and the Lamb.

ev - ery tongue to praise the Sa - vior's name.
cedes a - bove for those whose sins he bore.
Lamb of God, to Christ th'e - ter - nal King.
notes the song of Mo - ses and the Lamb.

Words: William Hammond (1719-1783), alt.
Music: *St. Ethelwald*, William Henry Monk (1823-1889)

SM

1 Christ is a - live! Let Chris - tians sing. His cross stands
2 Christ is a - live! No long - er bound to dis - tant
3 Not throned a - bove, re - mote - ly high, un - touched, un -
4 In ev - ery in - sult, rift, and war where co - lor,
5 Christ is a - live! His Spi - rit burns through this and

1 emp - ty to the sky. Let streets and homes with
2 years in Pal - es - tine, he comes to claim the
3 moved by hu - man pains, but dai - ly, in the
4 scorn or wealth di - vide, he suf - fers still, yet
5 ev - ery fu - ture age, till all cre - a - tion

1 prais - es ring. His love in death shall nev - er die.
2 here and now and con - quer ev - ery place and time.
3 midst of life, our Sa - vior with the Fa - ther reigns.
4 loves the more, and lives, though ev - er cru - ci - fied.
5 lives and learns his joy, his jus - tice, love, and praise.

Words: Brian A. Wren (b. 1936), rev.
Music: *Truro*, melody from *Psalmodia Evangelica, Part II*, 1789; harm. Lowell Mason (1792-1872), alt.

LM

1. Chris-tians, to the Pas-chal vic-tim of-fer your thank-ful prais-es!

2. A lamb the sheep re-deem-eth: Christ, who on-ly is sin-less,

rec-on-cil-eth sin-ners to the Fa-ther.

3. Death and life have con-tend-ed in that com-bat stu-pen-dous:

the Prince of life, who died, reigns im-mor-tal.

4. Speak, Ma-ry, de-clar-ing what thou saw-est, way-far-ing:

5. "The tomb of Christ, who is liv-ing, the glo-ry of

Je-sus' re-sur-rec-tion; 6. bright an-gels at-test-ing,

the shroud and nap-kin rest-ing. 7. Yea, Christ my hope is a-ris - en; to Gal - i - lee he will go be - fore you."

*All*

8. Christ in - deed from death is ris - en, our new life ob - tain - ing;

have mer - cy, vic - tor King, ev - er reign - ing!

A - - men. Al - le - lu - ia!

Words: Wigbert [Wipo of Burgundy] (d. 1050?); tr. *The Antiphoner and Grail*, 1880, alt.
Music: *Victimae Paschali laudes*, plainsong, Mode 1; melody att. Wigbert [Wipo of Burgundy] (d. 1050?)    Irr.

# 184

Easter

1 Christ the Lord is risen a - gain! Christ has bro - ken ev - ery chain!
2 He who gave for us his life, who for us en - dured the strife,
3 He who bore all pain and loss com - fort - less up - on the cross

Now through all the world it rings that the Lamb is King of kings.
takes our sin and guilt a - way that with an - gels we may say:
is ex - alt - ed now to save, wrest - ing vic - to - ry from the grave.

*Refrain*

Al - le - lu - ia!
Al - le - lu - ia! Al - le - lu - ia, al - le - lu - ia,
Al - le - lu - ia!

al - le - lu - ia! Christ, our Pas - chal lamb in - deed,

Christ, to - day your peo - ple feed. Al - le - lu - ia!

Words: Michael Weisse (1480-1534); tr. Catherine Winkworth (1827-1878), alt.
Music: *Christ ist erstanden*, melody from *Geistliche Lieder*, 1533

77. 77. 4 with Refrain

## Easter

185

1 Christ Je - sus lay in death's strong bands    for our of - fens - es giv - en;
2 It was a strange and dread - ful strife    when life and death con - tend - ed;
3 So let us keep the fes - ti - val    to which the Lord in - vites us;
4 Then let us feast this ho - ly day    on the true bread of hea - ven;

but now at God's right hand he stands    and brings us life from hea - ven;
the vic - to - ry re - mained with life,    the reign of death was end - ed;
Christ is him - self the joy of all,    the sun that warms and lights us;
the word of grace hath purged a - way    the old and wick - ed lea - ven;

there - fore let us joy - ful be,    and sing to God right thank - ful - ly
stripped of power, no more he reigns,    an emp - ty form a - lone re - mains;
by his grace he doth im - part    e - ter - nal sun - shine to the heart;
Christ a - lone our souls will feed,    he is our meat and drink in - deed;

loud songs of al - le - lu - ia!    Al - le - lu - ia!
his sting is lost for ev - er!    Al - le - lu - ia!
the night of sin is end - ed!    Al - le - lu - ia!
faith lives up - on no o - ther!    Al - le - lu - ia!

Words: Martin Luther (1483-1546); tr. Richard Massie (1800-1887), alt.
Music: *Christ lag in Todesbanden*, melody from *Geystliche gesangk Buchleyn*, 1524

87. 87. 78. 74

# 186

1 Christ Je - sus lay in death's strong bands for
2 It was a strange and dread - ful strife when
3 So let us keep the fes - ti - val to
4 Then let us feast this ho - ly day on

our of - fens - es giv - en; but now at God's right
life and death con - tend - ed; the vic - to - ry re -
which the Lord in - vites us; Christ is him - self the
the true bread of hea - ven; the word of grace hath

hand he stands and brings us life from hea - ven;
mained with life, the reign of death was end - ed;
joy of all, the sun that warms and lights us;
purged a - way the old and wick - ed lea - ven;

there - fore let us joy - ful be, and sing to
stripped of power, no more he reigns, an emp - ty
by his grace he doth im - part e - ter - nal
Christ a - lone our souls will feed, he is our

God right thank-ful - ly loud songs of al - le -
form a - lone re - mains; his sting is lost for
sun - shine to the heart; the night of sin is
meat and drink in - deed; faith lives up - on no

lu - ia! Al - le - lu - ia!
ev - er! Al - le - lu - ia!
end - ed! Al - le - lu - ia!
o - ther! Al - le - lu - ia!

Words: Martin Luther (1483-1546); tr. Richard Massie (1800-1887), alt.
Music: *Christ lag in Todesbanden*, melody from *Geystliche gesangk Buchleyn*, 1524;
adapt. and harm. Johann Sebastian Bach (1685-1750)

87. 87. 78. 74

## Easter

## 187

1 Through the Red Sea brought at last, Al - le - lu - ia!
2 Like the cloud that o - ver - head, Al - le - lu - ia!
3 In that cloud and in that sea, Al - le - lu - ia!

E - gypt's chains be - hind we cast, Al - le - lu - ia! deep and wide
through the bil - lows Is - rael led, Al - le - lu - ia! by his tomb
bur - ied and bap - tized were we, Al - le - lu - ia! Earth - ly night

flows the tide sev-ering us from bond-age past, Al - le - lu - ia!
Christ makes room, souls re - stor - ing from the dead, Al - le - lu - ia!
brought us light which is ours e - ter - nal - ly, Al - le - lu - ia!

Words: Ronald A. Knox (1888-1957)
Music: *Straf mich nicht*, melody from *Hundert Arien*, 1694

76. 76. 676

## 188

Easter

1 Love's re - deem - ing work is done, fought the fight, the bat - tle won.
2 Lives a - gain our glo - rious King; where, O death, is now thy sting?
3 Soar we now where Christ has led, fol-lowing our ex - alt - ed Head;

Death in vain for - bids him rise; Christ has o - pened par - a - dise.
Once he died our souls to save, where thy vic - to - ry, O grave?
made like him, like him we rise, ours the cross, the grave, the skies.

Words: Charles Wesley (1707-1788), alt.
Music: *Savannah*, from *Harmonia Sacra*, ca. 1760

77. 77

## 189

Easter

1 Love's re - deem - ing work is done, fought the fight, the
2 Lives a - gain our glo - rious King; where, O death, is
3 Soar we now where Christ has led, fol - lowing our ex -

bat - tle won. Death in vain for - bids him rise;
now thy sting? Once he died our souls to save,
alt - ed Head; made like him, like him we rise,

Christ has o - pened par - a - dise. Al - le - lu - ia,
where thy vic - to - ry, O grave? Al - le - lu - ia,
ours the cross, the grave, the skies. Al - le - lu - ia,

al - le - lu - ia!
al - le - lu - ia!
al - le - lu - (ia!)

*Final Ending*

ia!

Words: Charles Wesley (1707-1788), alt.
Music: *Resurrexit*, Robert Sherlaw Johnson (b. 1932)

77. 77 with Alleluias

## Easter

# 190

1 Lift your voice re - joic - ing, Ma - ry, Christ has
2 Raise your wea - ry eye - lids, Ma - ry, see him
3 Life is yours for ev - er, Ma - ry, for your

ris - en from the tomb; on the cross a suf - fering
liv - ing ev - er - more; see his coun - te - nance, how
light is come once more and the strength of death is

vic - tim, now as vic - tor he is come. Whom your
gra - cious, see the wounds for you he bore. All the
bro - ken; now your songs of joy out - pour. End - ed

tears in death were mourn - ing, wel - come with your smiles re -
glo - ry of the morn - ing pales be - fore those wounds re -
now the night of sor - row, love has brought the bless - ed

turn - ing. Let your al - le - lu - ias rise!
deem - ing. Let your al - le - lu - ias rise!
mor - row. Let your al - le - lu - ias rise!

Words: Latin; tr. Elizabeth Rundle Charles (1828-1896), alt.
Music: *Fisk of Gloucester*, Thomas Foster (b. 1938)

87. 87. 887

1 Al - le -lu - ia, al - le - lu - ia! Hearts and voic - es heaven-ward raise:
2 Now the i - ron bars are bro - ken, Christ from death to life is born,
3 Christ is ris - en, Christ, the first-fruits of the ho - ly har - vest -field,
4 Christ is ris - en, we are ris - en! Shed up - on us heaven - ly grace,
5 Al - le -lu - ia, al - le - lu - ia! Glo - ry be to God on high;

1 sing to God a hymn of glad - ness, sing to God a hymn of praise.
2 glo - rious life, and life im - mor - tal, on his res - ur - rec - tion morn.
3 which will all its full a - bun-dance at his sec - ond com - ing yield:
4 rain and dew and gleams of glo - ry from the bright-ness of thy face,
5 Al - le - lu - ia! to the Sa - vior who has won the vic - to - ry;

1 He, who on the cross a vic - tim, for the world's sal - va - tion bled,
2 Christ has tri - umphed, and we con - quer by his might - y en - ter-prise:
3 then the gold - en ears of har - vest will their heads be - fore him wave,
4 that, with hearts in hea - ven dwell-ing, we on earth may fruit-ful be,
5 Al - le - lu - ia! to the Spi - rit, fount of love and sanc - ti - ty:

1 Je - sus Christ, the King of glo - ry, now is ris - en from the dead.
2 we with him to life e - ter - nal by his re - sur - rec - tion rise.
3 ri -pened by his glo - rious sun -shine from the fur -rows of the grave.
4 and by an - gel hands be gath -ered, and be ev - er, Lord, with thee.
5 Al - le - lu - ia, al - le - lu - ia! to the Tri -une Ma - jes - ty.

Words: Christopher Wordsworth (1807-1885), alt.
Music: *Lux eoi*, Arthur Seymour Sullivan (1842-1900)

87. 87. D

*Unison or harmony*

1 This joy - ful Eas - ter - tide, a - way with sin and
2 Death's flood hath lost its chill, since Je - sus crossed the
3 My flesh in hope shall rest, and for a sea - son

sor - row! My Love, the Cru - ci - fied, hath
riv - er: Lord of all life, from ill my
slum - ber, till trump from east to west shall

sprung to life this mor - row.
pass - ing life de - liv - er, Had Christ, that once was
wake the dead in num - ber.

*Refrain*

slain, ne'er burst his three-day pris - on, our faith had been in vain; but now is Christ a - ris - en, a - ris - en, a - ris - en, a - ris - - - en.

Words: George R. Woodward (1848-1934), alt.
Music: *Vruechten*, melody from *Psalmen*, 1685; harm. Charles Wood (1866-1926)

67. 67 with Refrain

## Easter

# 193

1 That Eas - ter day with joy was bright, the sun shone out with fair - er light, when, to their long - ing eyes re - stored, the a - pos - tles saw their ris - en Lord.

2 His ris - en flesh with ra - diance glowed; his wound - ed hands and feet he showed; those scars their sol - emn wit - ness gave that Christ was ris - en from the grave.

3 O Je - sus, King of gen - tle - ness, do thou thy - self our hearts pos - sess that we may give thee all our days the will - ing tri - bute of our praise.

4 O Lord of all, with us a - bide in this our joy - ful Eas - ter - tide; from ev - ery wea - pon death can wield thine own re - deemed for ev - er shield.

5 All praise, O ris - en Lord, we give to thee, who, dead, a - gain dost live; to God the Fa - ther e - qual praise, and God the Ho - ly Ghost, we raise.

Words: Latin, 5th cent.; ver. *Hymnal 1940*
Music: *Puer nobis*, melody from Trier MS., 15th cent.; adapt. Michael Praetorius (1571-1621)

LM

1 Je - sus lives! thy ter - rors now can no long - er, death, ap -
2 Je - sus lives! for us he died; then, a - lone to Je - sus
3 Je - sus lives! our hearts know well nought from us his love shall
4 Je - sus lives! to him the throne o - ver all the world is

pall us; Je - sus lives! by this we know thou, O
liv - ing, pure in heart may we a - bide, glo - ry
sev - er; life, nor death, nor powers of hell tear us
giv - en: may we go where he has gone, rest and

grave, canst not en - thrall us. Al - le - lu - ia!
to our Sa - vior giv - ing. Al - le - lu - ia!
from his keep - ing ev - er. Al - le - lu - ia!
reign with him in hea - ven. Al - le - lu - ia!

Words: Christian Furchtegott Gellert (1715-1769); tr. Frances Elizabeth Cox (1812-1897), alt.
Music: *St. Albinus*, Henry John Gauntlett (1805-1876)

78. 78 with Alleluia

1 Je - sus lives! thy ter - rors now can no long - er,
2 Je - sus lives! for us he died; then, a - lone to
3 Je - sus lives! our hearts know well nought from us his
4 Je - sus lives! to him the throne o - ver all the

death, ap - pall us; Je - sus lives! by this we know
Je - sus liv - ing, pure in heart may we a - bide,
love shall sev - er; life, nor death, nor powers of hell
world is giv - en: may we go where he has gone,

thou, O grave, canst not en - thrall us. Al - le - lu - ia!
glo - ry to our Sa - vior giv - ing. Al - le - lu - ia!
tear us from his keep - ing ev - er. Al - le - lu - ia!
rest and reign with him in hea - ven. Al - le - lu - ia!

Words: Christian Furchtegott Gellert (1715-1769); tr. Frances Elizabeth Cox (1812-1897), alt.
Music: *Mowsley*, Cyril Vincent Taylor (b. 1907)

78. 78 with Alleluia

Music: Copyright © 1985 by Hope Publishing Company. All Rights Reserved. Used by Permission.

1 Look there! the Christ, our Bro-ther, comes re-
2 Good Je - sus Christ in - side his pain looked
3 Good Je - sus Christ, our Bro - ther, died in
4 Look there! the Christ, our Bro - ther, comes re -

splen-dent from the gal-lows tree____ and what he brings in
down Gol - go - tha's ston-y slope____ and let the blood flow
dark - est hurt up - on the tree____ to of - fer us the
splen-dent from the gal-lows tree____ and what he brings in

his hurt hands is life on life for you and me.____
from his flesh to fill the springs of liv-ing hope.____
worlds of light that live in-side the Trin - i - ty.____
his hurt hands is life on life for you and me.____

Refrain

Joy! (joy) joy! (joy) joy to the heart and all in this good day's dawn-

- ing! Joy! (joy) joy! (joy) joy to the heart and

all in this good day's dawn - ing!

Words: John Bennett (b. 1920), alt.
Music: *Petrus*, William Albright (b. 1944)

LM with Refrain

1 Look there! the Christ, our Bro - ther,
2 Good Je - sus Christ in - side his
3 Good Je - sus Christ, our Bro - ther,
4 Look there! the Christ, our Bro - ther,

comes re - splen-dent from the gal - lows tree and what he
pain looked down Gol - go - tha's ston - y slope and let the
died in dark - est hurt up - on the tree to of - fer
comes re - splen-dent from the gal - lows tree and what he

brings in his hurt hands is life on life for you and
blood flow from his flesh to fill the springs of liv - ing
us the worlds of light that live in - side the Trin - i -
brings in his hurt hands is life on life for you and

*Refrain*

me. Joy! joy!_____ joy to the
hope.
ty.
me.

heart and all in this good day's dawn - ing!

Words: John Bennett (b. 1920), alt.
Music: *Grand Prairie*, Peter Cutts (b. 1937)

LM with Refrain

1 Thou hal - lowed cho - sen morn of praise, that best and great - est
2 Come, let us taste the vine's new fruit, for heaven - ly joy pre -

shin - est: fair Eas - ter, queen of all the days, of
par - ing; to - day the branch - es with the root in

sea - sons, best, di - vin - est! Christ rose from death; and
re - sur - rec - tion shar - ing: whom as true God our

we a - dore for ev - er and for ev - er - more.
hymns a - dore for ev - er and for ev - er - more.

Words: John of Damascus (8th cent.); tr. John Mason Neale (1818-1866), alt.
Music: *Mach's mit mir, Gott*, melody from *Das ander Theil des andern newen Operis Geistlicher
Deutscher Lieder*, 1605; adapt., att., and harm. Johann Hermann Schein (1586-1630)

87. 87. 88

1 Come, ye faith - ful, raise the strain of tri - um - phant glad - ness!
2 'Tis the spring of souls to - day: Christ hath burst his pris - on,
3 Now the queen of sea - sons, bright with the day of splen - dor,
4 Nei - ther might the gates of death, nor the tomb's dark por - tal,

God hath brought his Is - ra - el in - to joy from sad - ness:
and from three days' sleep in death as a sun hath ris - en;
with the roy - al feast of feasts, comes its joy to ren - der;
nor the watch - ers, nor the seal hold thee as a mor - tal:

loosed from Pha - roah's bit - ter yoke Ja - cob's sons and daugh - ters,
all the win - ter of our sins, long and dark, is fly - ing
comes to glad Je - ru - sa - lem, who with true af - fec - tion
but to - day a - midst thine own thou didst stand, be - stow - ing

led them with un - mois - tened foot through the Red Sea wa - ters.
from his light, to whom we give laud and praise un - dy - ing.
wel - comes in un - wea - ried strains Je - sus' re - sur - rec - tion.
that thy peace which ev - er - more pass - eth hu - man know - ing.

Words: John of Damascus (8th cent.); tr. John Mason Neale (1818-1866), alt.
Music: *St. Kevin*, Arthur Seymour Sullivan (1842-1900)

76. 76. D

# 200

**Easter**

1 Come, ye faith-ful, raise the strain of tri-um-phant glad-ness!
2 'Tis the spring of souls to-day: Christ hath burst his pris-on,
3 Now the queen of sea-sons, bright with the day of splen-dor,
4 Nei-ther might the gates of death, nor the tomb's dark por-tal,

God hath brought his Is-ra-el in-to joy from sad-ness:
and from three days' sleep in death as a sun hath ris-en;
with the roy-al feast of feasts, comes its joy to ren-der;
nor the watch-ers, nor the seal hold thee as a mor-tal:

loosed from Pha-roah's bit-ter yoke Ja-cob's sons and daugh-ters,
all the win-ter of our sins, long and dark, is fly-ing
comes to glad Je-ru-sa-lem, who with true af-fec-tion
but to-day a-midst thine own thou didst stand, be-stow-ing

led them with un-mois-tened foot through the Red Sea wa-ters.
from his light, to whom we give laud and praise un-dy-ing.
wel-comes in un-wea-ried strains Je-sus' re-sur-rec-tion.
that thy peace which ev-er-more pass-eth hu-man know-ing.

Words: John of Damascus (8th cent.); tr. John Mason Neale (1818-1866), alt.
Music: *Gaudeamus pariter*, melody from *Medieval [German or] Bohemian Carol Melody*, 1544

76. 76. D

# 201

**Easter**

1 On earth has dawned this day of days, where-on the
2 At ear-ly morn, with spi-ces rare, the wo-men
3 "Whom seek ye here?" the an-gel said; "The Lord is
4 So let our songs to hea-ven wing, the vault with

| faith - ful give God | praise! For Christ is | ris - en from the | tomb, |
| three as - sem-bled | there, all to a - | noint fair Ma - ry's | Son, |
| ris - en from the | dead; see where he | lay; let joy be - | gin, |
| al - le - lu - ias | ring, in praise of | Christ, our ris - en | Lord; |

| and light and | joy have con-quered | doom. Al - le - lu - | ia! |
| who o - ver | death had vic - to,ry | won. Al - le - lu - | ia! |
| the tomb is | emp - ty: en - ter | in!" Al - le - lu - | ia! |
| new life to | all he doth af - | ford. Al - le - lu - | ia! |

Words: Nikolaus Hermann (1480?-1561); tr. Charles Sanford Terry (1864-1936), alt.
Music: *Erschienen ist der herrlich Tag*, melody Nickolaus Hermann (1480?-1561)

LM with Alleluia

## Easter

# 202

| 1 The Lamb's high | ban - quet | called to | share, ar - rayed | in |
| 2 Pro - tect - ed | in the | Pas - chal | night from the | de - |
| 3 Now Christ our | Pass - o - | ver is | slain, the | Lamb of |
| 4 O all - suf - | fi - cient | Sac - ri - fice, be - | neath thee |
| 5 All praise be | thine, O | ris - en | Lord, from death | to |

| 1 gar - ments | white and | fair, | the Red Sea | past, we |
| 2 stroy - ing | an - gel's | might, | in tri - umph | went the |
| 3 God with - out | a | stain; | his flesh, the | true un - |
| 4 hell de - | feat - ed | lies; | thy cap - tive | peo - ple |
| 5 end - less | life re - | stored; | all praise to | God the |

| 1 now would sing | to Je - sus | our tri - um - phant | King. |
| 2 ran - somed free | from Pha - roah's | cru - el ty - ran - | ny. |
| 3 lea - vened bread, | is free - ly | of - fered in our | stead. |
| 4 are set free, | and end - less | life re - stored in | thee. |
| 5 Fa - ther be | and Ho - ly | Ghost e - ter - nal - | ly. |

Words: Latin, 7th-8th cent.; tr. John Mason Neale (1818-1866) and others
Music: *Ad cenam Agni providi*, plainsong, Mode 8, Paris MS., 12th cent.; ver. A. Gregory Murray (b. 1905)

LM

*Antiphon (at the beginning)*

Al - le - lu - ia, al - le - lu - ia!

Al - le - lu - ia, al - le - lu - ia!

1 O sons and daugh-ters, let us sing! The King of heaven, the
2 That Eas - ter morn, at break of day, the faith - ful wo - men
3 An an - gel clad in white they see, who sat and spake un -
4 That night the a - pos - tles met in fear; a - midst them came their
5 On this most ho - ly day of days, to God your hearts and

1 glo - rious King, o'er death and hell rose tri - umph - ing.
2 went their way to seek the tomb where Je - sus lay.
3 to the three, "Your Lord doth go to Gal - i - lee."
4 Lord most dear, and said, "My peace be on all here."
5 voic - es raise, in laud and ju - bi - lee and praise.

1 Al - le - lu - ia, al - le - lu - ia!
2 Al - le - lu - ia, al - le - lu - ia!
3 Al - le - lu - ia, al - le - lu - ia!
4 Al - le - lu - ia, al - le - lu - ia!
5 Al - le - lu - ia, al - le - lu - ia! [Ant.]

Antiphon (at the end)

Al - le - lu - ia, al - le - lu - ia!

Al - le - lu - ia, al - le - lu - ia!

Words: Att. Jean Tisserand (15th cent.); tr. John Mason Neale (1818-1866)
Music: *O filii et filiae*, melody from *Airs sur les hymnes sacrez, odes et noëls*, 1623; harm.
    *Hymnal 1982*

888 with Alleluias

## Easter

## 204

1. Now the green blade ris - eth from the bur - ied grain,
2. In the grave they laid him, Love whom hate had slain,
3. Forth he came at Eas - ter, like the ris - en grain,
4. When our hearts are win - try, griev - ing, or in pain,

wheat that in dark earth man - y days has lain;
think - ing that nev - er he would wake a - gain,
he that for three days in the grave had lain,
thy touch can call us back to life a - gain,

love lives a - gain, that with the dead has been:
laid in the earth like grain that sleeps un - seen:
quick from the dead my ris - en Lord is seen:
fields of our hearts that dead and bare have been:

*Refrain*

Love is come a - gain like wheat that spring-eth green.

Words: John Macleod Campbell Crum (1872-1958), alt.
Music: *Noël nouvelet*, medieval French carol

11 10. 10 11

1 Good Chris-tians all, re - joice and sing! Now is the
*2 The Lord of life is risen to - day! Sing songs of
3 Praise we in songs of vic - to - ry that love, that
4 Your Name we bless, O ris - en Lord, and sing to -
5 To God the Fa - ther, God the Son, to God the

1 tri - umph of our King! To all the world glad news we bring:
2 praise a - long his way; let all the earth re - joice and say:
3 life which can - not die, and sing with hearts up - lift - ed high:
4 day with one ac - cord the life laid down, the life re - stored:
5 Spi - rit, al - ways One, we sing for life in us be - gun:

Al - le - lu - ia, al - le - lu - ia, al - le - lu - ia!

Al - le - lu - ia, al - le - lu - ia, al - le - lu - ia!

Al - le - lu - ia, al - le - lu - ia, al - le - lu - ia!

Words: Cyril A. Alington (1872-1955), alt. St. 5, Norman Mealy (b. 1923)
Music: *Gelobt sei Gott*, Melchior Vulpius (1560?-1616)

888 with Alleluias

*Antiphon (at the beginning)*

Al - le - lu - ia, al - le - lu - ia, al - le - lu - ia!

1 O sons and daugh - ters, let us sing!
2 That night the a - pos - tles met in fear;
3 When Thom - as first the tid - ings heard,
4 "My pierc - ed side, O Thom - as, see;
5 No long - er Thom - as then de - nied,
6 How blest are they who have not seen,

1 The King of heaven, the glo - rious King,
2 a - midst them came their Lord most dear,
3 how they had seen the ris - en Lord,
4 my hands, my feet, I show to thee;
5 he saw the feet, the hands, the side;
6 and yet whose faith has con - stant been,

1 o'er death and hell rose tri - umph - ing. Al - le - lu - ia!
2 and said, "My peace be on all here." Al - le - lu - ia!
3 he doubt - ed the dis - ci - ples' word. Al - le - lu - ia!
4 not faith - less, but be - liev - ing be." Al - le - lu - ia!
5 "Thou art my Lord and God," he cried. Al - le - lu - ia!
6 for they e - ter - nal life shall win. Al - le - lu ia! [Ant.]

*Antiphon (at the end)*

Al - le - lu - ia, al - le - lu - ia, al - le - lu - ia!

*This hymn is for the Second Sunday of Easter and St. Thomas' Day.*

Words: Att. Jean Tisserand (15th cent.); tr. John Mason Neale (1818-1866)
Music: *O filii et filiae,* melody from *Airs sur les hymnes sacrez, odes et noëls,* 1623

888 with Alleluias

1 Je - sus Christ is risen to - day, Al - le - lu - ia!
2 Hymns of praise then let us sing, Al - le - lu - ia!
3 But the pains which he en - dured, Al - le - lu - ia!
4 Sing we to our God a - bove, Al - le - lu - ia!

our tri - um - phant ho - ly day, Al - le - lu - ia!
un - to Christ, our heaven - ly King, Al - le - lu - ia!
our sal - va - tion have pro - cured, Al - le - lu - ia!
praise e - ter - nal as his love, Al - le - lu - ia!

who did once up - on the cross, Al - le - lu - ia!
who en - dured the cross and grave, Al - le - lu - ia!
now a - bove the sky he's King, Al - le - lu - ia!
praise him, all ye heaven - ly host, Al - le - lu - ia!

suf - fer      to      re - deem our loss.      Al    -    le - lu  -  ia!
sin - ners    to      re - deem and save.      Al    -    le - lu  -  ia!
where the    an - gels    ev - er  sing.        Al    -    le - lu  -  ia!
Fa - ther,    Son, and    Ho -ly  Ghost.       Al    -    le - lu  -  ia!

Words: Latin, 14th cent.; tr. *Lyra Davidica*, 1708, alt. St. 4, Charles Wesley (1707-1788)
Music: *Easter Hymn*, from *Lyra Davidica*, 1708; adapt. *The Compleat Psalmodist*, 1749, alt.;
       desc. *Hymns Ancient and Modern, Revised*, 1950

77. 77 with Alleluias

*Antiphon (at the beginning)*

Al - le - lu - ia, al - le - lu - ia, al - le - lu - ia!

Ped.

1 The strife is o'er, the bat - tle done, the vic - to -
2 The powers of death have done their worst, but Christ their
*3 The three sad days are quick - ly sped, he ris - es
4 He closed the yawn - ing gates of hell, the bars from
5 Lord! by the stripes which wound - ed thee, from death's dread

1 ry of life is won; the song of tri - umph
2 le - gions hath dis - persed: let shout of ho - ly
3 glo - rious from the dead: all glo - ry to our
4 heaven's high por - tals fell; let hymns of praise his
5 sting thy serv - ants free, that we may live and

1 has be - gun. Al - le - lu - ia!
2 joy out - burst. Al - le - lu - ia!
3 ris - en Head! Al - le - lu - ia!
4 tri - umphs tell! Al - le - lu - ia!
5 sing to thee. Al - le - lu - ia! [Ant.]

Antiphon (at the end)

Al - le - lu - ia, al - le - lu - ia, al - le - lu - ia!

Ped.

Words: Latin, 1695; tr. Francis Pott (1832-1909), alt.
Music: *Victory*, Giovanni Pierluigi da Palestrina (1525-1594); adapt. and arr.
William Henry Monk (1823-1889)

888 with Alleluias

## Easter

## 209

1 We walk by faith, and not by sight; no
2 We may not touch his hands and side, nor
3 Help then, O Lord, our un - be - lief; and
4 that, when our life of faith is done, in

gra - cious words we hear from him who spoke as
fol - low where he trod; but in his prom - ise
may our faith a - bound, to call on you when
realms of clear - er light we may be - hold you

none e'er spoke; but we be - lieve him near.
we re - joice; and cry, "My Lord and God!"
you are near, and seek where you are found:
as you are, with full and end - less sight.

Words: Henry Alford (1810-1871), alt.
Music: *St. Botolph*, Gordon Slater (1896-1979)

CM

Descant

3 Now let the heavens be joy - ful, let earth her song be - gin,

1 The day of re - sur - rec - tion! Earth, tell it out a - broad;
2 Our hearts be pure from e - vil, that we may see a - right
3 Now let the heavens be joy - ful, let earth her song be - gin,

the round world keep high tri - umph, and all that is there - in;

the Pass - o - ver of glad - ness, the Pass - o - ver of God.
the Lord in rays e - ter - nal of re - sur - rec - tion light;
the round world keep high tri - umph, and all that is there - in;

let all things seen and un - seen their notes to - geth - er blend,

From death to life e - ter - nal, from earth un - to the sky,
and, lis - tening to his ac - cents, may hear so calm and plain
let all things seen and un - seen their notes to - geth - er blend,

for Christ the Lord is ris - en, our joy that hath no end.

our Christ hath brought us o - ver with hymns of vic - to - ry.
his own "All hail!" and, hear - ing, may raise the vic - tor strain.
for Christ the Lord is ris - en, our joy that hath no end.

Words: John of Damascus (8th cent.); tr. John Mason Neale (1818-1866), alt.
Music: *Ellacombe*, from *Gesangbuch . . . der Herzogl. Wirtembergischen katholischen Hofkapelle*, 1784, alt.;
  adapt. *Katholisches Gesangbuch*, 1863; harm. William Henry Monk (1823-1889);
  desc. Cyril Winn (1884-1973)

76. 76. D

## Easter

# 211

1 The whole bright world re - joic - es now, Hi - lar - i - ter,
2 Then shout be - neath the rac - ing skies, Hi - lar - i - ter,
3 And all you liv - ing things make praise, Hi - lar - i - ter,
4 To Fa - ther, Son, and Ho - ly Ghost— Hi - lar - i - ter,

— hi - lar - i - ter! — The birds do sing on ev - ery bough, —
— hi - lar - i - ter! — To him who rose that we might rise, —
— hi - lar - i - ter! — He guid - eth you on all your ways, —
— hi - lar - i - ter! — Our God most high, our joy and boast. —

— Al - le - lu - ia, — al - le - lu - ia! —
— Al - le - lu - ia, — al - le - lu - ia! —
— Al - le - lu - ia, — al - le - lu - ia! —
— Al - le - lu - ia, — al - le - lu - ia! —

*"Hilariter" is Latin for "joyfully" and is pronounced "hi-lair-i-tair" in this hymn.*

Words: Friedrich von Spee (1591-1635); tr. Percy Dearmer (1867-1936)
Music: *Hilariter*, Richard Wayne Dirksen (b. 1921)

LM

## 212

1 A - wake, a - rise, lift up your voice, let
2 Oh, with what glad - ness and sur - prise the
3 those hands of lib - eral love in - deed in
4 His en - e - mies had sealed the stone as
5 O Dead a - rise! O Friend - less stand by

1 Eas - ter mu - sic swell; re - joice in Christ, a -
2 saints their Sa - vior greet; nor will they trust their
3 in - fi - nite de - gree, those feet still free to
4 Pi - late gave them leave, lest dead and friend - less
5 ser - a - phim a - dored! O Sol - i - tude a -

1 gain re - joice and on his prais - es dwell.
2 ears and eyes but by his hands and feet,
3 move and bleed for mil - lions and for me.
4 and a - lone he should their skill de - ceive.
5 gain com - mand your host from heaven re - stored!

Words: Christopher Smart (1722-1771), alt.
Music: *Richmond,* melody Thomas Haweis (1734-1820); adapt. Samuel Webbe (1740-1816)                    CM

*Unison or harmony*

1 Come a - way to the skies, my be - lov - ed, a - rise and re -
2 Now with sing - ing and praise, let us spend all the days, by our
3 For the glo - ry we were first cre - a - ted to share, both the
4 We with thanks do ap - prove the de - sign of that love which hath
*5 Hal - le - lu - jah we sing, to our Fa - ther and King, and his

1 joice in the day thou wast born;_____ on this fes - ti - val day,
2 hea - ven - ly Fa - ther be - stowed,_____ while his grace we re - ceive
3 na - ture and king - dom di - vine!_____ Now cre - a - ted a - gain
4 joined us to Je - sus'__ Name;_____ so u - ni - ted in heart,
5 rap - tu - rous prais - es, re - peat:_____ to the Lamb that was slain,

1 come ex - ult - ing a - way, and with sing - ing to Zi - on re - turn.__
2 from his boun - ty, and live to the hon - or and glo - ry of God.__
3 that our lives may re - main, through-out time and e - ter - ni - ty thine.__
4 let us nev - er - more part, till we meet at the feast of the Lamb.__
5 hal - le - lu - jah a - gain, sing, all hea - ven, and fall at his feet.__

Words: Anon., *The Southern Harmony*, 1835, alt.
Music: *Middlebury*, melody from *The Southern Harmony;* harm. Jack W. Burnam (b. 1946)     669. 669

1 Hail the day that sees him rise, Al - le - lu - ia!
2 There the glo - rious tri - umph waits; Al - le - lu - ia!
*3 See! he lifts his hands a - bove; Al - le - lu - ia!
4 Lord be - yond our mor - tal sight, Al - le - lu - ia!

glo - rious to his na - tive skies; Al - le - lu - ia!
lift your heads, e - ter - nal gates! Al - le - lu - ia!
See! he shows the prints of love: Al - le - lu - ia!
raise our hearts to reach thy height, Al - le - lu - ia!

Christ, a - while to mor - tals given, Al - le - lu - ia!
Wide un - fold the ra - diant scene; Al - le - lu - ia!
Hark! his gra - cious lips be - stow, Al - le - lu - ia!
there thy face un - cloud - ed see, Al - le - lu - ia!

en - ters now the high - est heaven! Al - le - lu - ia!
take the King of glo - ry in! Al - le - lu - ia!
bless - ings on his Church be - low. Al - le - lu - ia!
find our heaven of heavens in thee. Al - le - lu - ia!

Words: Charles Wesley (1707-1788), alt.
Music: *Llanfair*, Robert Williams (1781-1821)

77. 77 with Alleluias

1 See the Con - queror mounts in tri - umph; see the King in
2 He who on the cross did suf - fer, he who from the
3 Thou hast raised our hu - man na - ture on the clouds to

roy - al state, rid - ing on the clouds, his
grave a - rose, he has van - quished sin and
God's right hand: there we sit in heaven - ly

char - iot, to his heaven - ly pal - ace gate!
Sa - tan; he by death has spoiled his foes.
pla - ces, there with thee in glo - ry stand.

Hark! the choirs of an - gel voic - es joy - ful
While he lifts his hands in bless - ing, he is
Je - sus reigns, a - dored by an - gels; Man with

al - le - lu - ias sing, and the por - tals
part - ed from his friends; while their ea - ger
God is on the throne; might - y Lord, in

high are lift - ed to re - ceive their heaven - ly King.
eyes be - hold him, he up - on the clouds a - scends.
thine as - cen - sion, we by faith be - hold our own.

Words: Christopher Wordsworth (1807-1885), alt.
Music: *In Babilone*, melody from *Oude en Nieuwe Hollantse Boerenlities en Contradanseu*, 1710

87. 87. D

*Refrain*

Hail thee, fes - ti - val day! blest day that art hal-lowed for

ev - er, day when the Christ a - scends, high in the

hea - vens to reign. *(First time only)* reign. *2*

1 He who was nailed to the cross is Lord and the
3 God the Cre - a - tor, the Lord who rul - est the
5 Spi - rit of life and of power, now flow in us,

ru - ler of na - ture; all things cre -
earth and the hea - vens, guard us from
fount of our be - ing, light that dost

*Repeat Refrain*

a - ted on earth sing to the glo - ry of God:
harm with - out, cleanse us from e - vil with - in:
light - en___ all, life that in all dost a - bide:

2 Dai - ly the love - li - ness grows, a - dorned with the
4 Je - sus the health of the world, en - light - en our
6 Praise to the Giv - er of good! Thou Love who art

| glo | - | ry | of | blos | - | som; | hea - ven her gates un - |
| minds, | | thou | Re - | deem | - | er, | Son of the Fa - ther su - |
| au | - | thor | of | con | - | cord, | pour out thy balm on our |

*Repeat Refrain*

| bars, | fling - ing her | in | - | crease | of | light: |
| preme, | on - ly - be - | got | - | ten | of | God: |
| souls, | or - der our | ways | in | thy | | peace: |

*The refrain may be sung once by choir alone and repeated by all. The stanzas may be sung alternately
by contrasted groups, or by all.*

Words: Venantius Honorius Fortunatus (540?-600?); tr. *The English Hymnal,* 1906, alt.
Music: *Salve festa dies,* Ralph Vaughan Williams (1872-1958)
79. 77 with Refrain

## Ascension                                         217

| 1 A | hymn | of | glo - ry | let | us | sing, | new | hymns through - |
| 2 You | are | a | pre - sent | joy, | O | Lord; | you | will be |
| 3 O | ris - en | Christ, a - | scend - ed | Lord, | all | | praise to |

| out | the | world shall | ring; | by | a | new | way | none |
| ev - | er | our | re - ward; | and | great | the | light | in |
| you | let | earth | ac - cord, | who | are, | while | end - | less |

| ev - er | trod | Christ takes his | place— | the throne of | God! |
| you | we | see | to | guide us | to | e - ter - ni - ty. |
| a - | ges | run, | with | Fa - ther | and | with Spi - rit, One. |

Words: The Venerable Bede (673-735); sts. 1-2, tr. Elizabeth Rundle Charles (1828-1896), alt.; st. 3,
    tr. Benjamin Webb (1819-1885), alt.
Music: *Jam lucis orto sidere,* plainsong, Mode 1, *Mailander Hymnen,* 15th cent.
LM

*Fanfare*

1 A hymn of glo - ry let us sing, new
2 You are a pre - sent joy, O Lord; you
3 O ris - en Christ, a - scend-ed Lord, all

hymns through-out the world shall ring; by a new way none
will be ev - er our re - ward; and great the light in
praise to you let earth ac - cord, who are, while end - less

ev - er trod Christ takes his place— the throne of God!
you we see to guide us to e - ter - ni - ty. Al -
a - ges run, with Fa - ther and with Spi - rit, One.

- le - lu - ia, al - le - lu - ia, al - le -

lu - ia, al - le - lu - ia, al - le - lu - ia!

*The fanfare may be used as introduction, interlude or conclusion.*

Words: The Venerble Bede (673-735); sts. 1-2, tr. Elizabeth Rundle Charles (1828-1896), alt.; st. 3,
    tr. Benjamin Webb (1819-1885), alt.
Music: *Deo gracias*, English ballad melody, Trinity College MS., 15th cent.

LM with Alleluias

*Unison or harmony*

1 The Lord a-scend-eth up on high, the Lord hath tri-umphed
2 The heavens with joy re-ceive their Lord, by saints, by an-gel
3 Our great High Priest hath gone be-fore, up-on his Church his

glo-rious-ly, in power and might ex-cel - ling;
hosts a-dored; O day of ex-ul-ta - tion!
grace to pour; and still his love he giv - eth.

the grave and hell are cap-tive led. Lo! he re-
O earth, a-dore thy glo-rious King! His ris-ing,
O may our hearts to him a-scend; may all with-

turns, our glo-rious Head, to his e-ter-nal dwell-ing.
his as-cen-sion sing with grate-ful a-dor-a-tion!
in us up-ward tend to him who ev-er liv-eth!

Words: Arthur T. Russell (1806-1874), alt.
Music: *Ach Herr, du allerhöchster Gott*, Michael Praetorius (1571-1621)

887. 887

1 O Lord Most High, e - ter - nal King,
2 A - scend - ing to the Fa - ther's throne
3 Be thou our joy, O Might - y Lord,
4 O ris - en Christ, a - scend - ed Lord,

by thee re - deemed thy praise we sing.
thou claim'st the king - dom as thine own;
as thou wilt be our great re - ward;
all praise to thee let earth ac - cord,

The bonds of death are burst by thee,
and an - gels won - der when they see
let all our glo - ry be in thee
who art, while end - less a - ges run,

and grace has won the vic - to - ry.
how changed is our hu - man - i - ty.
both now and through e - ter - ni - ty.
with Fa - ther and with Spi - rit, One.

Words: Medieval Latin; sts. 1-3, tr. F. Bland Tucker (1895-1984); st. 4, tr. Benjamin Webb (1819-1885)
Music: *Aeterne Rex altissime*, plainsong, Mode 1, *Zisterzienser Hymnar*, 14th cent.                    LM

1 O Lord Most High, e - ter - nal King,_____ by
2 A - scend - ing to the Fa - ther's throne_____ thou
3 Be thou our joy, O might - y Lord,_____ as
4 O ris - en Christ, a - scend - ed Lord,_____ all

thee re - deemed thy praise we sing. The bonds of
claim'st the king - dom as thine own; and an - gels
thou wilt be our great re - ward; let all our
praise to thee let earth ac - cord, who art, while

death are burst by thee, and grace has won the
won - der when they see how changed is our hu -
glo - ry be in thee both now and through e -
end - less a - ges run, with Fa - ther and with

*After stanza 4*

vic - to - ry.
man - i - ty.
ter - ni - ty.
Spi - rit, One. Al - le - lu - ia!

Words: Medieval Latin; sts. 1-3, tr. F. Bland Tucker (1895-1984); st. 4, tr. Benjamin Webb (1819-1885)
Music: *Gonfalon Royal*, Percy Carter Buck (1871-1947)　　　　　　　　　　　　　　　　　　LM

1 Re - joice, the Lord of life a - scends
2 No more his mor - tal form we see;
3 He reigns, but with a love that shares
4 He reigns in heaven un - til the hour

in tri - umph from earth's bat - tle - field:
he reigns in - vis - i - ble but near:
the trou - bles of our earth - ly life;
when he, who once was cru - ci - fied,

his strife with hu - man ha - tred ends,
for in the midst of two or three
he takes up - on his heart the cares,
shall come in all love's glo - rious power

as sin and death their con - quests yield.
he makes his glo - rious pres - ence clear.
the pain, and shame of hu - man strife.
to rule the world for which he died.

Words: Albert F. Bayly (1901-1984)
Music: *Parker*, Horatio Parker (1864-1919)

LM

1 Hail this joy - ful day's re - turn, hail the
2 Like to clo - ven tongues of flame on the
3 Lord, to you your peo - ple bend; un - to
4 You who did our fore - bears guide, with their

Pen - te - cos - tal morn, morn when our a -
twelve the Spi - rit came— tongues, that earth may
us your Spi - rit send; bless - ings of this
chil - dren still a - bide; grant us par - don,

scend - ed Lord on his Church his Spi - rit poured!
hear their call, fire, that love may burn in all.
sa - cred day grant us, dear - est Lord, we pray.
grant us peace, till our earth - ly wan - derings cease.

Words: Att. Hilary of Poitiers (4th cent.); tr. Robert Campbell (1814-1868), alt.
Music: *Beata nobis gaudia*, plainsong, Mode 1, *Zisterzienser Hymnar*, 14th cent.

77. 77

1 Hail this joy - ful day's re - turn, hail the Pen - te -
2 Like to clo - ven tongues of flame on the twelve the
3 Lord, to you your peo - ple bend; un - to us your
4 You who did our fore - bears guide, with their chil - dren

cos - tal morn, morn when our a - scend - ed Lord
Spi - rit came— tongues, that earth may hear their call,
Spi - rit send; bless - ings of this sa - cred day
still a - bide; grant us par - don, grant us peace,

on his Church his Spi - rit poured! Al - le - lu - ia!
fire, that love may burn in all. Al - le - lu - ia!
grant us, dear - est Lord, we pray. Al - le - lu - ia!
till our earth - ly wan - derings cease. Al - le - lu - ia!

Words: Att. Hilary of Poitiers (4th cent.); tr. Robert Campbell (1824-1868), alt.
Music: *Sonne der Gerechtigkeit*, melody from *Bohemian Brethren, Kirchengeseng*, 1566

77. 77 with Alleluia

*Refrain*

Hail thee, fes - ti - val day! blest day that art hal-lowed for

ev - er, day when the Ho - ly Ghost shone in the

*First time only* 2

world with God's grace. grace.

1 Lo, in the like - ness of fire, on those who a -
3 Hark! for in myr - i - ad tongues Christ's own, his___

wait his ap - pear - ing, he whom the
cho - sen a - pos - tles, preach to the

*Repeat Refrain*

Lord fore - told sud - den - ly, swift - ly de - scends:
ends of the earth Christ and his won - der - ful works:

2 Forth from the Fa - ther he comes with sev - en - fold___
4 Praise to the Spi - rit of Life, all praise to the

mys - ti - cal of - fering, pour-ing on all hu - man
fount of our be - ing, light that dost light - en___

*Repeat Refrain*

souls in - fi - nite rich - es of God:
all, life that in all dost a - bide:

*The refrain may be sung once by choir alone and repeated by all. The stanzas may be sung by choir alone, alternately by contrasted groups, or by all.*

Words: Venantius Honorius Fortunatus (540?-600?); tr. *English Hymnal*, 1906, alt.
Music: *Salve festa dies*, Ralph Vaughan Williams (1872-1958)

Irr.

1. Come, thou Ho - ly Spi - rit bright; come with thy ce - les - tial light;

pour on us thy love di - vine. Come, pro - tec - tor of the poor;

come, thou source of bless - ings sure; come with - in our hearts to shine.

2. Thou, of com - fort - ers the best, thou, the soul's most wel - come guest,

of our peace thou art the sign. In our la - bor, be our aid;

in our sum - mer, cool - ing shade. Ev - ery bit - ter tear re - fine.

3. Bright-er than the noon - day sun, fill our lives which Christ has won;

fill our hearts and make them thine. Where thou art not, we have nought:

all our word and deed and thought twist - ed from thy true de - sign.

4. Bend the stub - born heart and will; melt the fro - zen, warm the chill;

rule us by thy judg-ment's line. Cleanse us with thy heal - ing power;

what is bar - ren bring to flower; to thy love our sins con - sign.

5. To thy peo - ple who a - dore and con - fess thee ev - er - more,

thy blest sev_en -fold gift as - sign. Grant us thy sal - va - tion, Lord,

bound-less mer - cy our re - ward, joys which earth and heaven en - twine.

Words: Latin, 12th cent.; tr. Charles P. Price (b. 1920)
Music: *Veni Sancte Spiritus*, plainsong, Mode 1, *Dublin Troper*, ca. 1360

777. 777

# 227

5 twine.

Words: Latin, 12th cent.; tr. Charles P. Price (b. 1920)
Music: *Arbor Street*, William Albright (b. 1944)

777. 777

1 Ho - ly Spi - rit, font of light, fo - cus of God's glo - ry bright,
2 Source of strength and sure re - lief, com - fort - er in time of grief,
3 En - ter each as - pir - ing heart, oc - cu - py its in - most part
4 With your soft, re - fresh - ing rains break our drought, re - move our stains;
5 As your prom - ise we be - lieve, make us rea - dy to re - ceive

1 shed on us a shin - ing ray. Fa - ther of the fa - ther - less,
2 en - ter in and be our guest. On our jour - ney grant us aid,
3 with your daz - zling pu - ri - ty. All that gives to us our worth,
4 bind up all our in - ju - ries. Shake with rush - ing wind our will;
5 gifts from your un - bound - ed store. Grant en - a - bling en - er - gy,

1 giv - er of gifts lim - it - less, come and touch our hearts to - day.
2 fresh - ening breeze and cool - ing shade, in our la - bor in - ward rest.
3 all that ben - e - fits the earth, you bring to ma - tu - ri - ty.
4 melt with fire our i - cy chill; bring to light our per - ju - ries.
5 cour - age in ad - ver - si - ty, joys that last for ev - er - more.

Words: Latin, 12th cent.; tr. John Webster Grant (b. 1919), alt.
Music: *Webbe*, melody from *An Essay on the Church Plain Chant*, 1782; adapt. att. Samuel Webbe
(1740-1816), alt.; harm. *Hymns Ancient and Modern*, 1916

77. 77. 77

1 Spi - rit of mer - cy, truth, and love, O shed thine
2 In ev - ery clime, by ev - ery tongue, be God's a -
3 Un - fail - ing Com - fort, heaven - ly Guide, still o'er thy

in - fluence from a - bove; and still from age to
maz - ing glo - ry sung: let all the lis - tening
ho - ly Church pre - side; O shed thine in - fluence

age con - vey the won - ders of this sa - cred day.
earth be taught the deeds our great Re - deem - er wrought.
from a - bove, Spi - rit of mer - cy, truth, and love.

Words: Anon., *Psalms, Hymns, and Anthems*, 1774, alt.
Music: *Cornish*, M. Lee Suitor (b. 1942)

LM

1 A might - y sound from hea - ven at Pen - te - cost there came,
2 In Sa - lem's street was gath - ered a crowd from man - y a land,
3 Then come, all Chris - tian peo - ple, keep fes - ti - val to - day,

and filled the place of meet - ing with rush-ing wind and flame:
and all in their own tongues did the Gos-pel un - der - stand:
for God the Ho - ly Spi - rit dwells with the Church al - way:

what   Christ had prom-ised    now  oc - curred as    each  A - pos - tle
for     by   the   tri - umph    of   the  Son  the    curse  of  Bab - el
and   grieve him not,  O     Chris-tian soul,  his    grace with - in  shall

spoke the word be - neath the Spi - rit's   thun  -  der, and    to  the
was un - done when God did send the  Spi  -  rit; so     to  the
make you whole in   bo - dy, mind, and  spi  -  rit, un - til  you

ears  of     all  who heard pro - claimed sal - va - tion's  won     -     der.
bless - ed  Three in One be  hon - or, praise, and  mer     -     it.
reach the  prom-ised goal, a   king - dom to  in - her    -     it.

Words: George B. Timms (b. 1910), alt.
Music: *Song of the Holy Spirit*, Dutch melody; harm. Alec Wyton (b. 1921)         76. 76. 887. 87

1 By all your saints still striv - ing, for all your saints at rest,
2 *(Insert the stanza appropriate to the day)*
3 Then let us praise the Fa - ther and wor - ship God the Son

your ho - ly Name, O Je - sus, for ev - er - more be blessed.
and sing to God the Spi - rit, e - ter - nal Three in One,

You rose, our King vic - to - rious, that they might wear the crown
till all the ran - somed num - ber who stand be - fore the throne

and ev - er shine. in splen - dor re - flect - ed from your throne.
a - scribe all power and glo - ry and praise to God a - lone.

*Saints' Days.*

Words: Horatio Bolton Nelson (1823-1913); ver. *Hymnal 1982*
Music: *King's Lynn*, English melody; adapt. Ralph Vaughan Williams (1872-1958)

76. 76. D

Saint Andrew *November 30*

All praise, O Lord, for Andrew,
    the first to follow you;
he witnessed to his brother,
    "This is Messiah true."
You called him from his fishing
    upon Lake Galilee;
he rose to meet your challenge,
    "Leave all and follow me."

Saint Thomas *December 21*

All praise, O Lord, for Thomas
    whose short-lived doubtings prove
your perfect two-fold nature,
    the depth of your true love.
To all who live with questions
    a steadfast faith afford;
and grant us grace to know you,
    made flesh, yet God and Lord.

## Saint Stephen *December 26*

All praise, O Lord, for Stephen
    who, martyred, saw you stand
to help in time of torment,
    to plead at God's right hand.
Like you, our suffering Savior,
    his enemies he blessed,
with "Lord, receive my spirit,"
    his faith, in death, confessed.

## Saint John *December 27*

For John, your loved disciple,
    exiled to Patmos' shore,
and for his faithful record,
    we praise you evermore;
praise for the mystic vision
    his words to us unfold.
Instill in us his longing,
    your glory to behold.

## The Holy Innocents *December 28*

Praise for your infant martyrs,
    whom your mysterious love
called early from life's conflicts
    to share your peace above.
O Rachel, cease your weeping;
    they're free from pain and cares.
Lord, grant us crowns as brilliant
    and lives as pure as theirs.

## Confession of Saint Peter *January 18*

We praise you, Lord, for Peter,
    so eager and so bold:
thrice falling, yet repentent,
    thrice charged to feed your fold.
Lord, make your pastors faithful
    to guard your flock from harm
and hold them when they waver
    with your almighty arm.

## Conversion of Saint Paul *January 25*

Praise for the light from heaven
    and for the voice of awe,
praise for the glorious vision
    the persecutor saw.
O Lord, for Paul's conversion,
    we bless your Name today.
Come shine within our darkness
    and guide us in the Way.

## Saint Matthias *February 24*

For one in place of Judas,
    the apostles sought God's choice:
the lot fell to Matthias
    for whom we now rejoice.
May we like true apostles
    your holy Church defend,
and not betray our calling
    but serve you to the end.

## Saint Joseph *March 19*

All praise, O God, for Joseph,
    the guardian of your Son,
who saved him from King Herod
    when safety there was none.
He taught the trade of builder,
    when they to Nazareth came,
and Joseph's love made "Father"
    to be, for Christ, God's Name.

## Saint Mark *April 25*

For Mark, O Lord, we praise you,
    the weak by grace made strong:
his witness in his Gospel
    becomes victorious song.
May we, in all our weakness,
    receive your power divine,
and all, as faithful branches
    grow strong in you, the Vine.

## Saint Philip and Saint James *May 1*

We praise you, Lord, for Philip,
    blest guide to Greek and Jew,
and for young James the faithful,
    who heard and followed you.
O grant us grace to know you,
    the victor in the strife,
that we with all your servants
    may wear the crown of life.

## Saint Barnabas *June 11*

For Barnabas we praise you,
    who kept your law of love
and, leaving earthly treasures,
    sought riches from above.
O Christ, our Lord and Savior,
    let gifts of grace descend,
that your true consolation
    may through the world extend.

1 By      all your saints still      striv - ing, for      all your saints at      rest,
2 *(Insert the stanza appropriate to the day)*
3 Then    let    us  praise the      Fa - ther and      wor-ship God the      Son

your      ho - ly  Name, O      Je - sus for      ev - er - more be      blessed.
and      sing  to  God   the      Spi - rit,  e - ter - nal      Three in      One,

You      rose, our King  vic - to - rious, that      they might wear the      crown
till      all   the  ran - somed      num - ber  who  stand be - fore the      throne

and      ev - er shine in      splen - dor re - flect - ed      from your      throne.
a - scribe all power and      glo - ry and      praise to      God   a - lone.

*Saints' Days.*

Words: Horatio Bolton Nelson (1823-1913); ver. *Hymnal 1982*
Music: *Nyland,* Finnish folk melody; adapt. David Evans (1874-1948)

76. 76. D

### The Nativity of Saint John the Baptist *June 24*

All praise for John the Baptist,
    forerunner of the Word,
our true Elijah, making
    a highway for the Lord.
The last and greatest prophet,
    he saw the dawning ray
of light that grows in splendor
    until the perfect day.

## Saint Peter and Saint Paul *June 29*

We praise you for Saint Peter;
  we praise you for Saint Paul.
They taught both Jew and Gentile
  that Christ is all in all.
To cross and sword they yielded
  and saw the kingdom come:
O God, your two apostles,
  won life through martyrdom.

## Saint Mary Magdalene *July 22*

All praise for Mary Magdalene,
  whose wholeness was restored
by you, her faithful Master,
  her Savior and her Lord.
On Easter morning early,
  a word from you sufficed:
her faith was first to see you,
  her Lord, the risen Christ.

## Saint James *July 25*

O Lord, for James, we praise you,
  who fell to Herod's sword.
He drank the cup of suffering
  and thus fulfilled your word.
Lord, curb our vain impatience
  for glory and for fame,
equip us for such sufferings
  as glorify your Name.

## Saint Mary the Virgin *August 15*

We sing with joy of Mary
  whose heart with awe was stirred
when, youthful and unready,
  she heard the angel's word;
yet she her voice upraises,
  God's glory to proclaim,
as once for our salvation
  your mother she became.

## Saint Bartholomew *August 24*

Praise for your blest apostle
  surnamed Bartholomew;
we know not his achievements
  but know that he was true,
for he at the ascension
  was an apostle still.
May we discern your presence
  and seek, like him, your will.

## Saint Matthew *September 21*

We praise you, Lord, for Matthew,
  whose gospel words declare
that, worldly gain forsaking,
  your path of life we share.
From all unrighteous mammon,
  O raise our eyes anew,
that we, whate'er our station
  may rise and follow you.

## Saint Luke *October 18*

For Luke, beloved physician,
  all praise, whose Gospel shows
the healer of the nations,
  the one who shares our woes.
Your wine and oil, O Savior,
  upon our spirits pour,
and with true balm of Gilead
  anoint us evermore.

## Saint James of Jerusalem *October 23*

Praise for the Lord's own brother,
  James of Jerusalem;
he saw the risen Savior
  and placed his faith in him.
Presiding at the council
  that set the Gentiles free,
he welcomed them as kindred
  on equal terms to be.

## Saint Simon and Saint Jude *October 28*

Praise, Lord, for your apostles,
  Saint Simon and Saint Jude.
One love, one hope, impelled them
  to tread the way, renewed.
May we with zeal as earnest
  the faith of Christ maintain,
be bound in love together,
  and life eternal gain.

## All Saints' Day *November 1*

Apostles, prophets, martyrs,
  and all the noble throng
who wear the spotless raiment
  and raise the ceaseless song:
for them and those whose witness
  is only known to you—
by walking in their footsteps
  we give you praise anew.

1 The eternal gifts of Christ the King, the apostles'
2 The princes of the Church are they, triumphant
3 Theirs is the steadfast faith of saints, the hope that
4 In them the Father's glory shone, in them the

glorious deeds we sing, and all, with hearts of
leaders in the fray, in heaven's hall a
never yields nor faints; the perfect love of
Spirit's will was done, the Son himself ex-

gladness, raise due hymns of thankful love and praise.
victor band, true lights that lighten every land.
Christ they know: these lay the prince of this world low.
ults in them; joy fills the new Jerusalem.

*Apostles.*

Words: Ambrose of Milan (340-397); ver. *Hymnal 1940*, alt.
Music: *Jesu, nostra redemptio*, plainsong, Mode 8, Worcester MS., 13th cent.; ver. A. Gregory Murray (b. 1905)     LM

1 The eternal gifts of Christ the King, the apostles'
2 The princes of the Church are they, triumphant
3 Theirs is the steadfast faith of saints, the hope that
4 In them the Father's glory shone, in them the

glorious deeds we sing, and all, with hearts of gladness, raise due
leaders in the fray, in heaven's hall a victor band, true
never yields nor faints; the perfect love of Christ they know: these
Spirit's will was done, the Son himself exults in them; joy

hymns     of     thank-ful     love and praise.
lights     that     light-en     ev-ery land.
lay     the     prince of     this world low.
fills     the     new Je-ru-sa-lem.     Al - le - lu - ia!

*Apostles.*

Words: Ambrose of Milan (340-397); ver. *Hymnal 1940*, alt.
Music: *Gonfalon Royal*, Percy Carter Buck (1871-1947)

LM

## Holy Days and Various Occasions

**235**

1 Come sing, ye choirs ex - ult - ant, those mes - sen - gers of God,
2 In one har - mo - nious wit - ness the cho - sen four com - bine,
3 Four-square on this foun - da - tion the Church of Christ re - mains,

through whom the liv - ing Gos - pels came sound-ing all a - broad!
while each his own com - mis - sion ful - fills in ev - ery line;
a house to stand un - shak - en by floods or winds or rains.

Whose voice pro-claimed sal - va - tion that poured up-on the night,
as, in the pro - phet's vi - sion from out the am - ber flame
How blest this ha - bi - ta - tion of gos - pel li - ber - ty,

and drove a - way the sha - dows, and filled the world with light.
in mys - tic form and im - age four liv - ing crea-tures came.
where with a ho - ly peo - ple God dwells in U - ni - ty.

*Evangelists.*

Words: Latin, 12th cent.; tr. Jackson Mason (1833-1889), alt.
Music: *Ach Gott, vom Himmelreiche*, melody Michael Praetorius (1571-1621)

76. 76. D

1 King of the mar - tyrs' no - ble band,
2 hear us as now we cel - e - brate
3 Dy - ing, through thee they o - ver - came;
4 Glo - ry to God the Fa - ther be;

crown of the true of ev - ery land,
faith un - de - terred by cru - el hate;
liv - ing, were faith - ful to thy Name.
glo - ry to Christ, who set us free;

strength of the pil - grim on the way,
hear and for - give us, sin - ners who
Turn our re - bel - lious hearts, and thus
and to the Spi - rit, liv - ing flame,

bea - con by night and cloud by day:
are bur - dened by the wrong we do.
win a like vic - to - ry in us.
glo - ry un - ceas - ing we pro - claim.

*Martyrs.*

Words: Latin; tr. John Webster Grant (b. 1919), alt.
Music: *Jesu, nostra redemptio*, plainsong, Mode 8, Worcester MS., 13th cent.                    LM

1 Let us now our voic - es raise, wake the day with glad - ness;
2 Nev - er flinched they from the flame, from the tor - ment nev - er;
3 Up and fol - low, Chris - tians all: press through toil and sor - row;

God him - self to joy and praise turns our hu - man sad - ness;
vain the ty - rant's sharp - est aim, vain each fierce en - deav - or:
turn from fear, and heed the call to a glo - rious mor - row!

joy that mar-tyrs won their crown o - pened hea - ven's por - tal,
for by faith they saw the land decked in all its glo - ry,
Who will ven-ture on the strife; who will first be - gin it?

when they laid the mor - tal down for the life im - mor - tal.
where tri - um - phant now they stand with the vic - tor's sto - ry.
Who will grasp the land of Life? Chris - tians, up and win it!

*Martyrs.*

Words: Joseph the Hymnographer (9th cent.); tr. John Mason Neale (1818-1866), alt.
Music: *Gaudeamus pariter,* melody from *Medieval [German or] Bohemian Carol Melody,* 1544          76. 76. D

## Holy Days and Various Occasions                                    **238**

1 Bless - ed feasts of bless - ed mar - tyrs, ho - ly wo - men,
2 Faith pre - vail - ing, hope un - fail - ing, lov - ing Christ with
3 There - fore, ye that reign in glo - ry, fel - low - heirs with

ho - ly men, with af - fec - tion's re - col - lec - tions
sin - gle heart, thus they, glo - rious and vic - to - rious,
Christ on high, join to ours your sup - pli - ca - tion

greet we your re - turn a - gain. Wor - thy deeds they
brave - ly bore the mar - tyr's part, by con - tempt of
when be - fore him we draw nigh, pray - ing that, this

wrought, and won - ders, wor - thy of the Name they bore; we, with
ev - ery an - guish, by un - yield - ing bat - tle done; vic - tors
life com - plet - ed, all its fleet - ing mo - ments past, by his

meet - est praise and sweet - est, hon - or them for ev - er - more.
at the last, they tri - umph, with the host of an - gels one.
grace we may be wor - thy of e - ter - nal bliss at last.

*Martyrs.*

Words: Latin, 12th cent.; tr. John Mason Neale (1818-1866), alt.
Music: *Holy Manna,* melody from *The Southern Harmony,* 1835          87. 87. D

*Unison or harmony*

1 Bless-ed feasts of bless-ed mar-tyrs, ho-ly wo-men, ho-ly men, with af-fec-tion's re-col-lec-tions greet we your re-turn a-gain. Wor-thy deeds they wrought, and won-ders, wor-thy of the Name they bore; we, with meet-est

2 Faith pre-vail-ing, hope un-fail-ing, lov-ing Christ with sin-gle heart, thus they, glo-rious and vic-to-rious, brave-ly bore the mar-tyr's part, by con-tempt of ev-ery an-guish, by un-yield-ing bat-tle done; vic-tors at the

3 There-fore, ye that reign in glo-ry, fel-low-heirs with Christ on high, join to ours your sup-pli-ca-tion when be-fore him we draw nigh, pray-ing that, this life com-plet-ed, all its fleet-ing mo-ments past, by his grace we

praise and sweet - est, hon - or them for ev - er - more.
last, they tri - umph, with the host of an - gels one.
may be wor - thy of e - ter - nal bliss at last.

*Martyrs.*

Words: Latin, 12th cent.; tr. John Mason Neale (1818-1866), alt.
Music: *Alta Trinità beata,* melody from *Laudi Spirituali,* 14th cent.; adapt. and
harm. Charles Burney (1726-1814)

87. 87. D

## Holy Days and Various Occasions

# 240

*Optional Introduction/Interlude*

1 Heark-en to the an - them glo - rious of the mar - tyrs
2 Liv - ing, they pro - claimed sal - va - tion, heaven - en - dowed with
3 Christ, for cru - el trai - tors plead - ing, tri - umphed in his
4 Take from him what ye will give him, of his full - ness

robed in white; they, like Christ, in death vic - to - rious
grace and power; and they died in im - i - ta - tion
part - ing breath o'er all mir - a - cles pre - ced - ing
grace for grace; strive to think him, speak him, live him,

dwell for ev - er in the light.
of their Sa - vior's fi - nal hour.
his in - es - ti - ma - ble death.
till you find him face to face.

*Martyrs. The C♯ applies to the final stanza only.*

Words: Christopher Smart (1722-1771), alt.
Music: *Faciem ejus videtis,* David Thompson Childs (b. 1938)

87. 87

Take from him what ye will give him, of his

1 Heark - en to the an - them glo - rious of the
2 Liv - ing, they pro - claimed sal - va - tion, heaven - en -
3 Christ, for cru - el trai - tors plead - ing, tri - umphed
4 Take from him what ye will give him, of his

full - ness grace for grace; strive to think him,

mar - tyrs robed in white; they, like Christ, in
dowed with grace and power; and they died in
in his part - ing breath o'er all mir - a -
full - ness grace for grace; strive to think him,

speak him, live him, till you find him face to face.

death vic - to - rious dwell for ev - er in the light.
im - i - ta - tion of their Sa - vior's fi - nal hour.
cles pre - ced - ing his in - es - ti - ma - ble death.
speak him, live him, till you find him face to face.

*Martyrs.*

**Words:** Christopher Smart (1722-1771), alt.
**Music:** *Laus Deo*, Richard Redhead (1820-1901); desc. Percy William Whitlock (1903-1946)                    87. 87

1 How oft, O Lord, thy face hath shone on doubt-ing souls whose
2 He loved thee well, and firm - ly said, "Come, let us go, and
3 His breth-ren's word he would not take, but craved to touch those
4 He saw thee risen; at once he rose to full be - lief's un -
5 O Sa - vior, make thy pres - ence known to all who doubt thy

1 wills were true! Thou Christ of Pe - ter and of John,
2 die with him"; yet when thine Eas - ter - news was spread,
3 hands of thine; when thou didst thine ap - pear - ance make,
4 cloud - ed height; and still through his con - fes - sion flows
5 Word and thee; and teach us in that Word a - lone

1 thou art the Christ of Thom - as too.
2 mid all its light his faith was dim.
3 he saw, and hailed his Lord Di - vine.
4 to Chris - tian souls thy life and light.
5 to find the truth that sets us free.

*Saint Thomas (December 21).*

**Words:** *William Bright (1824-1901), alt.*
**Music:** *Jacob,* Jane Manton Marshall (b. 1924)      LM

1 When Ste-phen, full of power and grace, went forth through-out the
2 When Ste-phen preached a - gainst the laws and by those laws was
3 When Ste-phen, young and doomed to die, fell crushed be - neath the
4 Let me, O Lord, thy cause de - fend, a knight with - out a

land, he bore no shield be - fore his face, no
tried, he had no friend to plead his cause, no
stones, he had no curse nor venge - ful cry for
sword; no shield I ask, no faith - ful friend, no

wea - pon in his hand; but on - ly in his
spokes - man at his side; but on - ly in his
those who broke his bones; but on - ly in his
ven - geance, no re - ward; but on - ly in my

heart a flame and on his lips a sword where -
heart a flame and on his eyes a light where -
heart a flame and on his lips a prayer that
heart a flame and in my soul a dream, so

with he smote and o - ver - came the foe - men of the Lord.
with God's day - break to pro - claim and rend the veils of night.
God, in sweet for - give - ness' name, should un - der - stand and spare.
that the stones of earth - ly shame a jew - eled crown may seem.

*Saint Stephen (December 26).*

Words: Jan Struther (1901-1953), alt.
Music: *Salvation*, melody from *Kentucky Harmony*, 1816

CMD

1 Come, pure hearts, in joy-ful mea-sure sing of those who
2 See the riv-ers four that glad-den, with their streams, the
3 O that we, thy truth con-fess-ing, and thy ho-ly

spread the trea-sure in the ho-ly Gos-pels shrined;
bet-ter E-den plant-ed by our Lord most dear;
word pos-sess-ing, Je-sus may thy love a-dore;

bless-ed tid-ings of sal-va-tion, peace on earth their
Christ the foun-tain, these the wa-ters; drink, O Zi-on's
un-to thee our voic-es rais-ing, thee with all thy

proc-la-ma-tion, love from God to lost man-kind.
son and daugh-ters, drink, and find sal-va-tion here.
ran-somed prais-ing, ev-er and for ev-er-more.

*Evangelists.*

Words: Latin, 12th cent.; tr. *Hymns Ancient and Modern*, 1861, after Robert Campbell (1814-1868), alt.
Music: *Alles ist an Gottes Segen*, melody att. Johann Balthasar König (1691-1758), alt.;
  harm. Johan Löhner (1645-1705), after chorale version by Johann Sebastian Bach (1685-1750)    887. 887

1 Praise God for John, e - van - ge - list, who bore the Spi - rit's
2 Your great I AM's Saint John re - cords, signs of your grace di -
3 O Word made flesh, your deeds and words re - fresh our hearts like

sword, whose words re - flect, like ea - gles' wings, the
vine: "I am the way, the truth, the life; the
dew. Our thanks we raise that all John wrote bears

glo - ry of our Lord. Your bright - ness, O e -
light; the liv - ing vine; your soul's true bread; thirst -
wit - ness, Lord, to you. We praise you that John's

ter - nal Word, A - pos - tle John un - furled, the
quench - ing stream. All these I am, and more: the
voice still lives your glo - ry to pro - claim where -

full - ness of your grace and truth for us and all the world.
faith - ful shep - herd of the flock, the sheep-fold's on - ly door."
by your Spi - rit gives us life, the faith to bear your Name.

*Saint John (December 27).*

Words: F. Samuel Janzow (b. 1913)
Music: *Noel*, English melody; adapt. Arthur Seymour Sullivan (1842-1900)     CMD

## Holy Days and Various Occasions                  246

1  In      Beth - le - hem   a        new - born boy   was     hailed  with songs of
2  (The)   sol - diers sought the    child   in     vain: not    yet     was   he    to
3  (Still)  rage    the fires of      hate   to - day,  and     in - no - cents the
4  (Lord)  Je - sus, through our    night  of     loss shines  out     the   won - der
5  (May)   that    great love  our   lives  con - trol  and     con - quer hate  in

1  praise and   joy.   Then    warn - ing came  of      dan - ger   near: King
2  share   our   pain.  But     down   the   a - ges    rings   the    cry    of
3  price   must  pay,   while   ach - ing hearts in      ev - ery   land   cry
4  of      your  cross, the     love   that can - not    cease   to     bear   our
5  ev - ery soul, till,   pledged to build and     not    des - troy,  we

                                                                    |1-4            |Final Ending

1  He - rod's troops would   soon  ap - pear._____   2  The
2  those   who  saw   their   chil - dren  die._____   3  Still
3  out    "We  can - not    un - der - stand!"_____   4  Lord
4  hu - man an - guish    ev - ery - where._____   5  May
5  share   your pain  and    find   your  joy._____         _____

*Holy Innocents (December 28).*

Words: Rosamond E. Herklots (b. 1905)
Music: *In Bethlehem*, Wilbur Held (b. 1914)     LM

Lul - ly, lul - lay, thou lit - tle tin - y child, bye - bye, lul -
ly lul - lay.

1 O sis - ters, too, how may we do
2 He - rod the King, in his ra - ging
3 That woe is me, poor child for thee!

for to pre - serve this day this poor young - ling for
charg - ed he hath this day his men of might, in
And ev - ery morn and day, for thy part - ing nor

*Repeat Burden after verse 3*

whom we sing bye - bye, lul - ly lul - lay?
his own sight, all young chil - dren to slay.
say nor sing bye - bye, lul - ly lul - lay.

*Holy Innocents (January 28).*

**Words:** Coventry carol, 15th cent.
**Music:** *Coventry Carol,* melody from *Pageant of the Shearmen and Tailors,* 15th cent.;
     harm. Martin Fallas Shaw (1875-1958)

44. 6 D with Refrain

1 To the Name of our sal - va - tion laud and hon - or
2 Je - sus is the Name we trea - sure; Name be - yond what
3 'Tis the Name that who - so preach - eth speaks like mu - sic
4 There-fore we, in love a - dor - ing, this most bless - ed

let us pay, which for man - y a gen - er - a - tion
words can tell; Name of glad - ness, Name of plea - sure,
to the ear; who in prayer this Name be - seech - eth
Name re - vere, ho - ly Je - sus, thee im - plor - ing

hid in God's fore - know-ledge lay; but with ho - ly
ear and heart de - light - ing well; Name of sweet-ness,
sweet - est com - fort find - eth near; who its per - fect
so to write it in us here that here - af - ter,

ex - ul - ta - tion we may sing a - loud to - day.
pass - ing mea - sure, sav - ing us from sin and hell.
wis - dom reach - eth, heaven - ly joy pos - ess - eth here.
heaven-ward soar - ing, we may sing with an - gels there.

*Holy Name; New Year (January 1).*

Words: Latin, 15th cent.; tr. *Hymns Ancient and Modern,* 1861
Music: *Oriel,* Caspar Ett (1788-1847)

87. 87. 87

1 To the Name of our sal-va-tion laud and hon-or let us pay, which for man-y a gen-er-a-tion hid in God's fore-know-ledge lay; but with ho-ly ex-ul-ta-tion we may sing a-loud to-day.

2 Je-sus is the Name we trea-sure; Name be-yond what words can tell; Name of glad-ness, Name of plea-sure, ear and heart de-light-ing well; Name of sweet-ness, pass-ing mea-sure, sav-ing us from sin and hell.

3 'Tis the Name that who-so preach-eth speaks like mu-sic to the ear; who in prayer this Name be-seech-eth sweet-est com-fort find-eth near; who its per-fect wis-dom reach-eth, heaven-ly joy pos-sess-eth here.

4 There-fore we, in love a-dor-ing, this most bless-ed Name re-vere, ho-ly Je-sus, thee im-plor-ing so to write it in us here that here-af-ter, heaven-ward soar-ing, we may sing with an-gels there.

*Holy Name; New Year (January 1).*

**Words**: Latin, 15th cent.; tr. *Hymns Ancient and Modern*, 1861
**Music**: *Grafton*, melody from *Chants ordinaires de l'Office Divin*, 1881;
    harm. *Songs of Praise*, 1925

87. 87. 87

1 Now greet the swift - ly chang - ing year with
2 For Je - sus came to wage sin's war; this
3 His love a - bun - dant far ex - ceeds the
4 With such a Lord to lead our way in
5 "All glo - ry be to God on high and

1 joy and pen - i - tence sin - cere; re - joice, re - joice, with
2 Name of names for us he bore; re - joice, re - joice, with
3 vol - ume of a whole year's needs; re - joice, re - joice, with
4 haz - ard and pros - per - i - ty, what need we fear in
5 peace on earth," the an - gels cry; re - joice, re - joice, with

1 thanks em - brace an - oth - er year of grace.
2 thanks em - brace an - oth - er year of grace.
3 thanks em - brace an - oth - er year of grace.
4 earth or space in this new year of grace?
5 thanks em - brace an - oth - er year of grace.

*Holy Name; New Year (January 1). The melody may be sung in canon at a distance of one measure.*

Words: Slovak, 17th cent.; tr. Jaroslav J. Vajda (b. 1919), alt.
Music: *Sixth Night*, Alfred V. Fedak (b. 1953)

88. 86

*Unison or harmony*

1 O    God, whom nei - ther time nor space    can lim - it, hold, or bind,
2 An - oth - er    year its course has run;    thy lov - ing care re - new:
3 In    doubt or    dan - ger, all    our days,    be near    to guard us    still;
4 O    help us    here on earth to    live    from self - ish pas - sions free;

look down from heaven, thy dwell-ing - place,    with love    for hu - man-kind.
for - give the    ill    that we    have done,    the good    we failed to    do.
let    all our thoughts and all    our    ways    be gov - erned by    thy will.
to    us    at last in mer - cy    give    e - ter - nal life with thee.

*Holy Name; New Year (January 1). This hymn may be used at other times by omitting stanza 2.*

Words: Horace Smith (1836-1922) and others
Music: *London New,* melody from *The Psalmes of David in Prose and Meeter,* 1635, alt.;
        harm. John Playford (1623-1686)
                                                                        CM

1 Je - sus! Name of won-drous love!    Name all    o - ther names    a - bove!
2 Je - sus! Name de-creed of old,    to    the maid-en mo - ther    told,
3 Je - sus! Name of pric-less worth    to    the fall-en of    the    earth,
4 Je - sus! Name of mer - cy mild,    giv - en    to the ho - ly    child
5 Je - sus! on - ly Name that's given,    un - der all the might - y    heaven,

1 Un - to which must ev - ery knee    bow in    deep hu - mil - i - ty.
2 kneel - ing in her low - ly cell,    by the    an - gel Ga - bri - el.
3 for the prom - ise that it gave,    "Je - sus    shall his peo - ple save."
4 when the cup of hu - man woe    first he    tast - ed here be - low.
5 where - by those to sin en - slaved,    burst their    fet - ters and are saved.

6 Jesus! Name of wondrous love!
Human Name of God above;
pleading only this we flee,
helpless, O our God, to thee.

*Holy Name; New Year (January 1).*

Words: William Walsham How (1823-1897), alt.
Music: *Louez Dieu*, from *Les cent cinquante Pseaumes de David*, 1564

77. 77

## Holy Days and Various Occasions      253

1 Give us the wings of faith to rise with - in the veil, and
2 We ask them whence their vic - tory came; they, with u - ni - ted
3 They marked the foot - steps that he trod, his zeal in - spired their
4 Our glo - rious Lead - er claims our praise for his own pat - tern

see the saints a - bove, how great their joys, how
breath, as - cribe their con - quest to the Lamb, their
quest, and fol - lowing their in - car - nate God, they
given; while the long cloud of wit - ness - es show

*Optional Interlude Between Stanzas*    ‖*Ending*

bright their glo - ries be.      (be.)
tri - umph to his death.      (death.)
reached the prom - ised rest.      (rest.)
the same path to (heaven.)      heaven.

*Saints' Days; All Saints' Days (November 1).*

Words: Isaac Watts (1674-1748), alt.
Music: *San Rocco*, Derek Williams (b. 1945)

CM

1 You         are      the    Christ, O   Lord, the
2 Oh!     Pe - ter   was   most blest with

Son   of  God most  high!   For   ev - er    be   a - dored that
bless - ed - ness un - priced, who,  taught  of    God,  con - fessed the

Name  in   earth  and  sky,   in    which, though mor - tal
God - head  in   the  Christ!  For   of   your  Church, Lord,

strength may  fail,   the   saints of God at   last pre - vail!____
you  made known  this   saint a true foun - da - tion-stone.____

*Confession of Saint Peter (January 18). This hymn may be sung as a two- or four-part canon with entrances alternating between treble and male voices.*

Words: William Walsham How (1823-1897), alt.
Music: *Wyngate Canon*, Richard Wayne Dirksen (b. 1921)

66. 66. 88

1 We sing the glo-rious con-quest be-fore Da-mas-cus' gate,
when Saul, the church-'s spoil-er came spread-ing fear and hate.
God's light shone down from hea - ven and broke a-cross the path.
His pres-ence pierced and blind-ed the zeal-ot in his wrath.

2 O Voice that spoke with - in him; O strong, re-prov-ing Word;
O Love that sought and held him a pris-oner of his Lord;
help us to know your king - ship that we, in ev-ery hour,
in all that may con - front us, will trust your hid-den power.

3 Your grace, by ways mys - te - rious, our sin-ful wrath can bind,
and in those least ex - pect-ed true ser-vants you can find.
In us you seek dis - ci - ples to share your cross and crown
and give you fi - nal ser-vice in glo-ry at your throne.

*Conversion of Saint Paul (January 25).*

Words: John Ellerton (1826-1893), alt.

Music: *Munich*, melody from *Neu-vermehrtes und zu Ubung Christl. Gottseligkeit eingerichtetes*
    *Meiningisches Gesangbuch*, 1693; adapt. and harm. Felix Mendelssohn (1809-1847)     76. 76. D

1 A light from hea - ven shone a - round, and in that
2 It was the bless - ed Son come down to save him
3 Saint Paul was changed by God's free love. The scales fell
4 Re - new us with your love, O Lord. Your new cre -

light a voice was heard. Then Saul fell blind - ed
from his fear - ful ways and free him from the
from this eyes, he saw the love of God, the
a - tion let us be; re - deemed for ev - er

to the ground and cried a - loud, "Who are you, Lord?"
bonds of sin, a sin - ner saved by Je - sus' grace.
cos - mos move in time with grace, be - yond the law.
and re - stored, with Paul's new vi - sion, let us see.

*Conversion of Saint Paul (January 25).*

Words: Gracia Grindal (b. 1943), alt.
Music: *Cornish,* M. Lee Suitor (b. 1942)

LM

1 O Zi - on, o - pen wide thy gates, let
2 A - ware of hid - den de - i - ty, the
3 The a - ged Si - meon sees at last his
4 But si - lent knelt the mo - ther blest of
5 All glo - ry to the Fa - ther be, all

1 sym - bols dis - ap - pear; a priest and vic - tim,
2 low - ly Vir - gin brings her new - born babe, with
3 Lord, so long de - sired, and An - na wel - comes
4 the yet si - lent Word, and pon - dering all things
5 glo - ry to the Son, all glo - ry, Ho - ly

1 both in one, the Truth him - self, is here.
2 two young doves, her hum - ble of - fer - ings.
3 Is - rael's hope, with ho - ly rap - ture fired.
4 in her heart, with speech - less praise a - dored.
5 Ghost, to thee, while end - less a - ges run.

*The Presentation (February 2).*

Words: Jean Baptiste de Santeüil (1630-1697); tr. Edward Caswall (1814-1878), alt.
Music: *Edmonton*, from *Harmonia Sacra*, ca. 1760                     CM

258

Holy Days and Various Occasions

par - ent's eye that watched thy slum-bering in - fan - cy.
meek and mild,_____ bless - ed was she in her Child.

*The Presentation (February 2); The Annunciation (March 25).*

Words: Reginald Heber (1783-1826)
Music: *Psalm 86*, Claude Goudimel (1514-1572), alt.

88. 77. D

## Holy Days and Various Occasions 259

1 Hail to the Lord who comes, comes to his tem - ple gate;
2 but, borne up - on the throne of Ma - ry's gen - tle breast,
3 There Jo - seph at her side in rev - erent won - der stands;
4 O Light of all the earth, thy chil-dren wait for thee!

not with his an - gel host, not in his king - ly state;
watched by her du - teous love, in her fond arms at rest,
and, filled with ho - ly joy, old Si - meon in his hands
Come to thy tem - ples here, that we, from sin set free,

no shouts pro-claim him nigh, no crowds his com - ing wait;
thus to his Fa - ther's house he comes, the heaven - ly guest.
takes up the prom-ised child, the glo - ry of all lands.
be - fore thy Fa - ther's face may all pre - sent - ed be!

*The Presentation (February 2).*

Words: John Ellerton (1826-1893), alt.
Music: *Old 120th,* melody from *The Whole Booke of Psalmes,* 1570; harm. Thomas Ravenscroft (1592?-1635?),
    after Richard Allison (16th cent.); adapt. Ralph Vaughan Williams (1872-1958)

66. 66. 66

1 Come now, and praise the hum-ble saint of Da-vid's house and line,
2 The Ar-chi-tect's high mir-a-cles he saw, and what was done,
3 For him there was no glo-ry here, no crown or mar-tyr's fame;
4 But now with-in the Fa-ther's grace where saints and an-gels throng,

the car-pen-ter whose life ful-filled our gra-cious God's de-sign.
the Vir-gin's spouse, the guard-ian of great Da-vid's great-er Son.
for him there was the pa-tient life of faith and hum-ble name.
be-side his spouse, be-fore the Son, he joins the heaven-ly song.

*Saint Joseph (March 19).*

Words: George W. Williams (b. 1922)
Music: *Tallis' Ordinal*, Thomas Tallis (1505?-1585)      CM
Words: Copyright © 1979 by Hymn Society of America. All rights reserved. Used by permission.

1 By the Cre-a-tor, Jo-seph was ap-point-ed
2 Christ in whose pres-ence hosts of hell must trem-ble,
3 To God e-ter-nal be all praise and glo-ry,

spouse of the Vir-gin guard-ian of the In-car-nate;
Ru-ler of all things, Lord of earth and hea-ven,
who to Saint Jo-seph gave su-per-nal hon-or;

Music: Melody rhythmic version © 1984, Schola Antiqua Inc. Used by permission.

he     by    his    car  -  ing    min - is - tered   to    Je  -  sus,
Mon - arch  of   mon  -  archs,    to    his   earth - ly    fa  -  ther
grant  that  we    al  -  so      may   like   him   be   faith  -  ful

source              of    sal  -  va  -  tion.
free      -         ly    was      sub  -  ject.
in                  our    o   -   be  -  dience.

*Saint Joseph (March 19).*

Words: Hieronimo Casanate (d. 1700); tr. *Hymnal 1982*
Music: *Caelitum Joseph*, plainsong, Mode 1, Worcester MS., 13th cent; ver. Schola Antiqua, 1983          11 11. 11 5

## Holy Days and Various Occasions          262

1  By    the   Cre - a - tor,   Jo - seph was   ap - point - ed    spouse  of  the
2  Christ in  whose pres - ence hosts  of  hell must trem - ble,   Ru - ler   of
3  To   God  e - ter - nal     be   all praise and glo - ry,     who   to Saint

Vir - gin,    guard-ian  of  the In-car - nate;   he   by   his  car - ing
all  things,  Lord   of  earth and  hea - ven,   Mon - arch of mon - archs,
Jo - seph    gave  su - per - nal  hon - or;    grant that we   al - so

min - is - tered to   Je - sus,   source  of   sal - va - tion._____
to   his earth-ly   fa - ther   free - ly  was sub - ject._____
may  like him  be  faith - ful   in   our  o - be - dience._____

*Saint Joseph (March 19).*

Words: Hieronimo Casanate (d. 1700); tr. *Hymnal 1982*
Music: *Bickford*, Hank Beebe (b. 1926)          11 11. 11 5

1 The Word whom earth and sea and sky
2 To Ma - ry the Arch - an - gel came
3 Blest in the mes - sage Ga - briel brought,
4 Lord Je - sus, Vir - gin - born, to thee

a - dore and laud and mag - ni - fy,
and God's new mes - sage did pro - claim,
blest in the work the Spi - rit wrought,
e - ter - nal praise and glo - ry be,

whose might they show, whose praise they tell,
"Hail, Ma - ry, you shall bear a son
most blest to bring to hu - man birth
whom with the Fa - ther we a - dore

in Ma - ry's bo - dy deigned to dwell.
who shall be called the Ho - ly One."
the long - de - sired of all the earth.
and Ho - ly Spi - rit ev - er - more.

*The Annunciation (March 25).*

Words: Latin, 7th-8th cent.; sts. 1 and 3-4, tr. *Hymns Ancient and Modern*, 1861,
      after John Mason Neale (1818-1866); st. 2, tr. Anne K. LeCroy (b. 1930)
Music: *Quem terra, pontus, aethera*, plainsong, Mode 2, *Mailander Hymnen*, 15th cent.        LM

1 The Word whom earth and sea and sky a - dore and laud and
2 To Ma - ry the Arch - an - gel came and God's new mes - sage
3 Blest in the mes - sage Ga - briel brought, blest in the work the
4 Lord Je - sus, Vir - gin - born, to thee e - ter - nal praise and

mag - ni - fy, whose might they show, whose praise they
did pro - claim, "Hail, Ma - ry, you shall bear a
Spi - rit wrought, most blest to bring to hu - man
glo - ry be, whom with the Fa - ther we a -

tell, in Ma - ry's bo - dy deigned to dwell.
son who shall be called the Ho - ly One."
birth the long - de - sired of all the earth.
dore and Ho - ly Spi - rit ev - er - more.

*The Annunciation (March 25).*

Words: Latin, 7th-8th cent.; sts. 1 and 3-4, tr. *Hymns Ancient and Modern,* 1861,
after John Mason Neale (1818-1866); st. 2, tr. Anne K. LeCroy (b. 1930)
Music: *Song 34,* melody and bass Orlando Gibbons (1583-1625); harm. *The English Hymnal,* 1906, alt.                    LM

1 The an-gel Ga-bri-el from hea - ven came,
2 "For know a bless-ed Mo-ther thou shalt be,
3 Then gen-tle Ma-ry meek-ly bowed her head,
4 Of her, Em-man-u-el, the Christ, was born

his wings as drift-ed snow, his eyes as flame;
all gen-er-a-tions laud and hon - or thee,
"To me be as it pleas-eth God," she said,
in Beth-le-hem, all on a Christ - mas morn,

"All hail," said he, "thou low-ly maid-en Ma - ry,
thy Son shall be Em-man-u-el, by seers fore-told,
"my soul shall laud and mag-ni-fy his ho-ly Name."
and Chris-tian folk through-out the world will ev-er say—

most high-ly fa-vored la - dy," Glo - ri - a!
most high-ly fa-vored la - dy," Glo - ri - a!
Most high-ly fa-vored la - dy, Glo - ri - a!
"Most high-ly fa-vored la - dy," Glo - ri - a!

*The Annunciation (March 25).*

Words: Basque carol; para. Sabine Baring-Gould (1834-1924)
Music: *Gabriel's Message*, Basque carol; harm. Edgar Pettman (1865-1943)

♩.=66
10 10. 12 10

Burden

No - va, no - va. A - ve fit ex E - va.

1 Ga - bri - el of high de - gree, he was sent___
2 He met a maid - en in that place; there he knelt___
3 When___ the maid - en heard his song, she was filled___
4 Said___ the an - gel, "Have no fear; by con - cep -
5 "There___ are yet but six months gone since E - liz - a -
6 Said___ the maid - en, "Ver - i - ly, I am your___

1 from the Trin - i - ty, to Naz - a - reth in
2 down be - fore her face and said, "Hail Ma - ry,
3 with con - fu - sion strong and feared that she had
4 tion with - out com - pare the Sa - vior Je - sus
5 beth con - ceiv - ed John, to be the her - ald
6 ser - vant right tru - ly, the hand - maid of the

Repeat Burden

1 Gal - i - lee. No - va, no - va.
2 full of grace." No - va, no - va.
3 done a wrong. No - va, no - va.
4 shall you bear." No - va, no - va.
5 of God's Son." No - va, no - va.
6 Lord now see." No - va, no - va.

*The Annunciation (March 25). The following burden and final line may be used with each stanza:*
*"Tidings! Tidings! Promise of salvation!" and "Tidings! Tidings!".*

Words: Hunterian MS. 83, 15th cent.; adapt. Carl P. Daw, Jr. (b. 1944)
Music: *Nova, nova*, melody Hunterian MS., 15th cent.

Irr. with Refrain

1 Praise we the Lord this day, this day so long fore - told, whose
2 The pro - phet gave the sign for faith - ful folk to read: a
3 Ask not how this should be, but wor - ship and a - dore, like
4 She meek - ly bowed her head to hear the gra - cious word, Ma -
5 Most blest shall be her name in all the Church on earth, through

1 prom - ise shone with cheer-ing ray on wait - ing saints of old.
2 vir - gin born of Da - vid's line shall bear the prom-ised seed.
3 her whom hea - ven's Ma - jes - ty came down to sha - dow o'er.
4 ry, the pure and low - ly maid, the fa - vored of the Lord.
5 whom that won - drous mer - cy came, the in - car - nate Sa - vior's birth.

*The Annunciation (March 25).*

Words: Anon., *Hymns for the Festivals and Saints' Days of the Church of England*, 1846, alt.
Music: *St. George*, Henry John Gauntlett (1805-1876)

SM

*Introduction/Interlude*

*Descant*

4 "Mag - ni - fi - cat

1 Ye who claim the faith of Je - sus, sing the
2 Bless - ed were the cho - sen peo - ple out of
3 There-fore let all faith - ful peo - ple sing the
4 "Mag - ni - fy, my soul, God's great - ness; in my

| an | - | | i - ma | me - | a |
|---|---|---|---|---|---|

| won | - | ders that were | done | when the | love | of | God the |
| whom | | the Lord did | come; | bless - ed | was | the | land of |
| hon | - | or of her | name; | let the | Church, in | | her fore - |
| Sa | - | vior I re - | joice; | all the | a - ges | | call me |

| Do | - | mi | - | num. | | Mag | - |

| Fa | - ther | o - ver | sin | the | vic - to̧ry | won, | when he |
| prom | - ise | fa - shioned for | his | earth - ly | home; | | but more |
| shad | - owed, | part in | her | thanks - giv - ing | claim; | | what Christ's |
| bless | - ed, | in his | praise | I | lift my | voice; | he has |

| ni | - fi | - cat, | mag | - ni | - fi | - cat." |

| made the | Vir - gin | Ma - ry | mo - ther | of | his on - ly | Son. |
| bless - ed | far the | mo - ther, she | who bore | | him in her | womb. |
| mo - ther | sang in | glad - ness | let Christ's peo - | | ple sing the | same: |
| cast down | all the | might - y, | and the | low | - ly are his | choice." |

**Conclusion**

*The Annunciation (March 25); The Visitation (May 31).*

Words: Sts. 1-3, Vincent Stucky Stratton Coles (1845-1929), alt; st. 4, F. Bland
    Tucker (1895-1984)
Music: *Julion*, David Hurd (b. 1950)

87. 87. 87

1 Ye who claim the faith of Je - sus, sing the won - ders that were done
when the love of God the Fa - ther o - ver sin the
vic - tory won, when he made the Vir - gin Ma - ry
mo - ther of his on - ly Son. Hail Ma - ry, full of grace.

2 Bless - ed were the cho - sen peo - ple out of whom the Lord did come;
bless - ed was the land of prom - ise fa - shioned for his
earth - ly home; but more bless - ed far the mo - ther,
she who bore him in her womb. Hail Ma - ry, full of grace.

3 There - fore let all faith - ful peo - ple sing the hon - or of her name;
let the Church, in her fore - shad - owed, part in her thanks -
giv - ing claim; what Christ's mo - ther sang in glad - ness
let Christ's peo - ple sing the same. Hail Ma - ry, full of grace.

4 "Mag - ni - fy, my soul, God's great - ness; in my Sa - vior I re - joice;
all the a - ges call me bless - ed, in his praise I
lift my voice; he has cast down all the might - y,
and the low - ly are his choice." Hail Ma - ry, full of grace.

*The Annunciation (March 25); The Visitation (May 31).*

Words: Sts. 1-3, Vincent Stucky Stratton Coles (1845-1929), alt; st. 4, F. Bland
         Tucker (1845-1894)
Music: *Den des Vaters Sinn geboren*, melody from *Hundert Arien*, 1694;
         harm. Conrad Kocher (1786-1872)                           87. 87. 87

1 Ga - briel's mes - sage does a - way Sa - tan's curse and
2 He that comes de - spised shall reign; he that can - not
3 Weak - ness shall the strong con - found; by the hands, in
4 Art by art shall be as - sailed; to the cross shall

Sa - tan's sway, out of dark - ness brings our Day:
die, be slain; death by death its death shall gain:
grave clothes wound, Ad - am's chains shall be un - bound:
Life be nailed; from the grave shall hope be hailed:

*Refrain*

so, be - hold, all the gates of heaven un - fold.

*The Annunciation (March 25).*

Words: *Piae Cantiones*, 1582; tr. John Mason Neale (1818-1866)
Music: *Angelus emittitur*, melody from *Piae Cantiones*, 1582;
    harm. Richard Runciman Terry (1865-1938)

777 with Refrain

```
1 The    great   fore - run -      ner     of        the     morn,
2 With   heaven-ly      mes -      sage    Ga -      briel   came,
*3 John, still   un - born,        yet     gave      a -     right
4 His    might - y      deeds      ex - alt         his     fame
*5 To    God     the    Fa -       ther,   God       the     Son,
```

```
1 the            her - ald   of    the     Word,   is      born;
2 that           John  should be   that    her -   ald's   name,
3 his            wit - ness  to    the     com -   ing     light;
4 to             great - er  than  a       pro -   phet's  name;
5 and            God   the   Spi - rit,    Three   in      One,
```

```
1 and            faith - ful      hearts  shall   nev -   er      fail
2 and            with   pro - phet - ic   ut -    terance told
3 and            Christ, the      Sun     of      all     the     earth,
4 of             wo -   man       born    shall   nev -   er      be
5 praise,        hon -  or,       might,  and     glo -   ry      be
```

```
1 with   thanks  and        praise  his     light   to      hail.
2 his    ac - tions          great   and     man -   i -     fold.
3 ful - filled   that        wit -   ness    at      his     birth.
4 a      great - er          pro -   phet    than    was     he.
5 from   age     to          age     e -     ter -   nal -   ly.
```

*The Nativity of Saint John the Baptist (June 24).*

Words: The Venerable Bede (673-735); tr. John Mason Neale (1818-1866), alt.
Music: *Ut queant laxis*, plainsong, Mode 2, Theoretikerquellen MS., 12th cent.      LM

*Unison or harmony*

1 The great fore - run - ner of the morn, the
2 With heaven - ly mes - sage Ga - briel came, that
*3 John, still un - born, yet gave a - right his
4 His might - y deeds ex - alt his fame to
*5 To God the Fa - ther, God the Son, and

1 her - ald of the Word, is born; and faith - ful hearts shall
2 John should be that her - ald's name, and with pro - phet - ic
3 wit - ness to the com - ing light; and Christ, the Sun of
4 great - er than a pro - phet's name; of wo - man born shall
5 God the Spi - rit, Three in One, praise, hon - or, might, and

1 nev - er fail with thanks and praise his light to hail.
2 ut - terance told his ac - tions great and man - i - fold.
3 all the earth, ful - filled that wit - ness at his birth.
4 nev - er be a great - er pro - phet than was he.
5 glo - ry be from age to age e - ter - nal - ly.

*The Nativity of Saint John the Baptist (June 24).*

Words: The Venerable Bede (673-735); tr. John Mason Neale (1818-1866), alt.
Music: *The Truth From Above*, English melody; harm. Ralph Vaughan Williams (1872-1958)

LM

1 Two stal - wart trees both root - ed in faith and ho - ly love,
2 One on a cross is mar - tyred, one by the sword is slain;
3 The words of Paul as - sure us of Christ's re - deem - ing word;
*4 All glo - ry to the Fa - ther, all glo - ry to the Son,

by hope of God u - nit - ed they reach to heaven a - bove.
both tri - umph in their dy - ing, both glo - rious saint - hood gain.
the works of Pe - ter show us how we may serve the Lord.
who with the Ho - ly Spi - rit, now reign, blest Three in One.

*Saint Peter and Saint Paul (June 29).*

Words: Latin; tr. Anne K. LeCroy (b. 1930)
Music: *Ave caeli janua*, plainsong, Mode 4, Moissac MS., 12th cent.

76. 76

1 Two stal - wart trees both root - ed in faith and ho - ly love,
2 One on a cross is mar - tyred, one by the sword is slain;
3 The words of Paul as - sure us of Christ's re - deem-ing word;
*4 All glo - ry to the Fa - ther, all glo - ry to the Son,

by hope of God u - nit - ed they reach to heaven a - bove.
both tri - umph in their dy - ing, both glo - rious saint - hood gain.
the works of Pe - ter show us how we may serve the Lord.
who with the Ho - ly Spi - rit, now reign, blest Three in One.

*Saint Peter and Saint Paul (June 29).*

Words: Latin; tr. Anne K. LeCroy (b. 1930)
Music: *De eersten zijn de laatsten*, Frederik August Mehrtens (b. 1922)

76. 76

1 Hark! the sound of ho - ly voic - es, chant - ing at the crys - tal sea,
2 Pa - tri - arch, and ho - ly pro - phet, who pre - pared the way for Christ,
3 March - ing with thy cross, their ban - ner, they have tri - umphed fol - low - ing
4 Now they reign in heaven - ly glo - ry, now they walk in gold - en light,

Al - le - lu - ia, al - le - lu - ia, al - le - lu - ia! Lord, to thee!
king, a - pos - tle, saint, con - fes - sor, mar - tyr and e - van - gel - ist,
thee, the Cap - tain of sal - va - tion, thee, their Sa - vior and their King.
now they drink, as from a riv - er, ho - ly bliss and in - fi - nite;

Mul - ti - tude which none can num - ber like the stars in glo - ry stands,
saint - ly maid - en, god - ly ma - tron, wid - ows who have watched to prayer,
Glad - ly, Lord, with thee they suf - fered; glad - ly, Lord, with thee they died;
love and peace they taste for ev - er, and all truth and know - ledge see

clothed in white ap - par - el, hold - ing palms of vic - to - ry in their hands.
joined in ho - ly con - cert, sing - ing to the Lord of all, are there.
and by death to life im - mor - tal they were born and glo - ri - fied.
in the be - a - tif - ic vi - sion of the bless - ed Trin - i - ty.

*Saints' Days; All Saints' Days (November 1).*

**Words:** Christopher Wordsworth (1807-1885)
**Music:** *Moultrie*, Gerard Francis Cobb (1838-1904)

87. 87. D

1 For  thy blest  saints,  a  no - ble throng,  who  fell by
2 For  James who  left  his  fa - ther's side,  not  lin - gering
3 he  stood with  thee  be - side the  dead;  he  climbed the
4 he  knelt be - neath  the  ol - ive shade;  he  drank thy
5 Lord,  may  we  learn  to  drink thy  cup,  and  meek and

1 fire  and  sword,  or  ear - ly  died  or
2 by  the  sea:  he  heard what  could  not
3 mount  with  thee,  and  saw  the  glo - ry
4 cup  of  pain;  and  slain  by  He - rod's
5 firm  be  found,  when  thou  shalt  come  to

1 flour - ished  long,  we  praise thy  Name,  O  Lord.
2 be  de - nied,  thy  sum - mons,  "Fol - low  me";
3 round  thy  head,  one  of  thy  cho - sen  three;
4 flash - ing  blade,  he  saw  thy  face  a - gain.
5 take  us  up  where  thine  e - lect  are  crowned.

*Saint James (July 25).*

Words: Cecil Frances Alexander (1818-1895), alt.
Music: *Dunlap's Creek*, melody Freeman Lewis (1780-1859)

CM

1 Sing of Ma - ry, pure and low - ly, vir - gin - mo - ther un - de - filed; sing of God's own Son most ho - ly, who be - came her lit - tle child. Fair - est child of fair - est mo - ther, God the Lord who came to earth, Word made flesh, our ve - ry bro - ther, takes our na - ture by his birth.

2 Sing of Je - sus, son of Ma - ry, in the home at Naz - a - reth, toil and la - bor can - not wea - ry love en - dur - ing un - to death. Con - stant was the love he gave her, though he went forth from her side, forth to preach, and heal, and suf - fer, till on Cal - va - ry he died.

3 Glo - ry be to God the Fa - ther; glo - ry be to God the Son; glo - ry be to God the Spi - rit; glo - ry to the Three in One. From the heart of bless - ed Ma - ry, from all saints the song a - scends, and the Church the strain re - ech - oes un - to earth's re - mot - est ends.

*Saint Mary the Virgin (August 15).*

Words: Roland Ford Palmer (b. 1891)
Music: *Raquel*, Skinner Chavez-Mélo (b. 1944)

87. 87. D

1 Sing we of the bless-ed Mo-ther who re-ceived the an-gel's
2 Sing we, too, of Ma-ry's sor-rows, of the sword that pierced her
3 Sing a-gain the joys of Ma-ry when she saw the ris-en
4 Sing the chief-est joy of Ma-ry when on earth her work was

word, and o-be-dient to the sum-mons bore in
through, when be-neath the cross of Je-sus she his
Lord, and in prayer with Christ's a-pos-tles, wait-ed
done, and the Lord of all cre-a-tion brought her

love the in-fant Lord; sing we of the joys of
weight of suf-fering knew, looked up-on her Son and
on his prom-ised word; from on high the blaz-ing
to his heaven-ly home; where, raised high with saints and

Ma-ry at whose breast the child was fed who is
Sa-vior reign-ing from the aw-ful tree, saw the
glo-ry of the Spi-rit's pres-ence came, heaven-ly
an-gels, in Je-ru-sa-lem a-bove, she be-

Son of God e - ter - nal and the ev - er - last - ing Bread.
price of our re - demp-tion paid to set the sin - ner free.
breath of God's own be - ing, man - i - fest in wind and flame.
holds her Son and Sa - vior reign-ing as the Lord of love.

*Saint Mary the Virgin (August 15).*

Words: George B. Timms (b. 1910), alt.
Music: *Rustington*, Charles Hubert Hastings Parry (1848-1918)

87. 87. D

# Holy Days and Various Occasions

1 For thy dear saints, O Lord, who strove in thee to live, who
2 They all in life and death, with thee their Lord in view, learned
3 Thine earth - ly mem-bers fit to join thy saints a - bove, in
4 Je - sus, thy Name we bless, and hum - bly pray that we may

fol - lowed thee, o - beyed, a - dored, our grate-ful hymn re - ceive.
from thy Ho - ly Spi - rit's breath to suf - fer and to do.
one com - mun - ion ev - er knit, one fel - low - ship of love.
fol - low them in ho - li - ness, who live and died for thee.

*Saints' Days; All Saints' Day (November 1).*

Words: Richard Mant (1776-1848), alt.
Music: *St. George*, Henry John Gauntlett (1805-1876)

SM

1 God of saints, to whom the num-ber of the star-ry
2 In the roll of your a-pos-tles stands the name Bar-
3 All his faith and prayer and pa-tience, all his toil-ing
4 There are named the bless-ed faith-ful of the new Je-

host is known: man-y saints by earth for-
thol-o-mew, for this faith-ful saint we
and his strife, all are veiled from us, but
ru-sa-lem. When Christ comes a-gain in

got-ten live for ev-er round your throne.
of-fer, year by year, our thanks to you.
writ-ten in the Lamb's great book of life.
glo-ry, num-ber us, we pray, with them.

*Saint Bartholomew (August 24).*

Words: John Ellerton (1826-1893), alt.
Music: *Halton Holgate*, William Boyce (1711-1779)

87. 87

1 He sat to watch o'er cus - toms paid, a man of scorned and hard-ening trade, a - like the sym - bol and the tool of for - eign mas - ter's hat - ed rule.

2 But grace with - in his heart had stirred, there need - ed but the time - ly word; it came, true Lord of souls, from thee, that roy - al sum - mons, "Fol - low me."

3 E - nough, when thou wast pass - ing by, to hear thy voice, to meet thine eye; he rose, re - spon - sive to the call, and left his task, his gains, his all.

4 O wise ex - change! with these to part, and lay up trea - sures in the heart; let them of Mat - thew's wealth par - take, who yield up all for Je - sus' sake.

*Saint Matthew (September 21).*

Words: William Bright (1824-1901), alt.
Music: *Breslau*, melody from *Lochamer Gesangbuch*, 1450?, alt. harm. after Felix Mendelssohn (1809-1847)      LM

1 Christ, the fair glo - ry of the ho - ly an - gels,
2 Send thine arch - an - gel Mi - chael to our suc - cor;
3 Send thine arch - an - gel Ga - bri - el, the might - y;
4 Send from the hea - vens Ra - phael thine arch - an - gel,
5 May the blest mo - ther of our God and Sa - vior,
6 Fa - ther Al - might - y, Son, and Ho - ly Spi - rit,

1 ma - ker of all things, ru - ler of all
2 peace - ma - ker bless - ed, may he ban - ish
3 her - ald of hea - ven, may he, from us
4 health - bring - er bless - ed, aid - ing ev - ery
5 may the ce - les - tial com - pa - ny of
6 God ev - er bless - ed, hear our thank - ful

1 na - tions, grant of thy mer - cy un - to us thy
2 from us striv - ing and ha - tred, so that for the
3 mor - tals, drive ev - ery e - vil, watch - ing o'er the
4 suf - ferer, that, in thy ser - vice, he may wise - ly
5 an - gels, may the as - sem - bly of the saints in
6 prais - es; thine is the glo - ry which from all cre -

1 ser - vants steps up to hea - ven.
2 peace - ful all things may pros - per.
3 tem - ples where thou art wor - shiped.
4 guide us, heal - ing and bless - ing.
5 hea - ven, help us to praise thee.
6 a - tion ev - er a - scend - eth.

*Saint Michael and All Angels (September 29).*

*Words: Rabanus Maurus (776-856); ver. Hymnal 1940, alt.*
Music: *Caelites plaudant,* melody from *Antiphoner,* 1728

11 11. 11 5

1 Christ, the fair glo - ry of the ho - ly an - gels,
2 Send thine arch - an - gel Mi - chael to our suc - cor;
3 Send thine arch - an - gel Ga - bri - el, the might - y;
4 Send from the hea - vens Ra - pha̧el thine arch - an - gel,
5 May the blest mo - ther of our God and Sa - vior,
6 Fa - ther Al - might - y, Son, and Ho - ly Spi - rit,

1 ma - ker of all things, ru - ler of all
2 peace - ma - ker bless - ed, may he ban - ish
3 her - ald of hea - ven, may he, from us
4 health - bring - er bless - ed, aid - ing ev - ery
5 may the ce - les - tial com - pa - ny of
6 God ev - er bless - ed, hear our thank - ful

1 na - tions, grant of thy mer - cy un - to us thy
2 from us striv - ing and ha - tred, so that for the
3 mor - tals, drive ev - ery e - vil, watch - ing o'er the
4 suf - ferer, that, in thy ser - vice, he may wise - ly
5 an - gels, may the as - sem - bly of the saints in
6 prais - es; thine is the glo - ry which from all cre -

1 ser - vants steps up to hea - ven.
2 peace - ful all things may pros - per.
3 tem - ples where thou art wor - shiped.
4 guide us, heal - ing and bless - ing.
5 hea - ven help us to praise thee.
6 a - tion ev - er a - scend - eth.

*Saint Michael and All Angels (September 29).*

Words: Rabanus Maurus (776-856); ver. *Hymnal 1940*, alt.
Music: *Caelitum Joseph*, plainsong, Mode 1, Worcester MS. 13th cent.; ver. Schola Antiqua, 1983    11 11. 11 5
Music: Melody rhythmic version © 1984, Schola Antiqua Inc. Used by permission.

1 O    ye  im - mor - tal   throng   of   an - gels round the
2 Ye   saw   the heaven-born child   in   hu - man flesh ar -
3 Ye   in   the  wil - der - ness   be - held  the Tempt-er
4 In   dark  Geth - sem - a - ne  the  night  be - fore  he
5 Ye   thronged to Cal - va - ry  and  pressed with sad  de -

1 throne,   join   with   our   earth - bound   song   to
2 rayed,    so    in - no - cent  and   mild   while
3 spoiled,  un - masked in   ev - ery   dress,   in
4 died,    ye   saw   his   ag - o - ny,   ye
5 sire    that   awe - ful  sight  to   see—  the

1 make   the  Sa - vior  known.   On   earth  ye  knew  his
2 in   the  man - ger  laid.  "Glo - ry   to   God  and
3 ev - ery  com - bat  foiled.  With  great  de - light  ye
4 heard  the  plaint  he  cried.  When  hope  was  dim,  and
5 Lord  of   life  ex - pire.  E'en  an - gel  eyes  slow

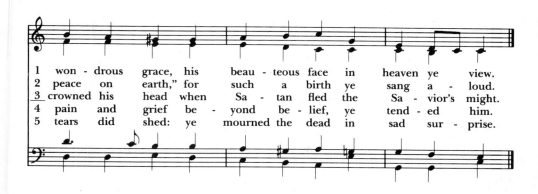

| | | | | | | | | | | |
|---|---|---|---|---|---|---|---|---|---|---|
| 1 | won - drous | grace, his | beau - teous face | in | heaven ye | view. |
| 2 | peace on | earth," for | such a | birth | ye | sang a - loud. |
| 3 | crowned his | head when | Sa - tan | fled | the | Sa - vior's might. |
| 4 | pain and | grief be - yond | be - lief, | ye | tend - ed | him. |
| 5 | tears did | shed: ye | mourned the dead | in | sad sur - prise. |

6 Around his sacred tomb  
   a willing watch ye kept;  
till out from death's vast room,  
   up from the grave, he leapt.  
     Ye rolled the stone,  
       and all adored  
       your rising Lord  
     with joy unknown.

7 When all arrayed in light  
   the shining conqueror rode,  
ye hailed his wondrous flight  
   up to the throne of God.  
     And waved around  
       your golden wings,  
       and struck your strings  
     of sweetest sound.

8 The joyous notes pursue  
   and louder anthems raise;  
while mortals sing with you  
   their own Redeemer's praise.  
     With equal flame  
       and equal art,  
       do thou my heart  
     extol his Name.

*Saint Michael and All Angels (September 29).*

Words: Sts. 1-3 and 5-8, Philip Doddridge (1702-1751), alt.; st. 4, Charles P. Price (b. 1920)
Music: *Croft's 136th,* melody and bass William Croft (1678-1727);
    harm. *Hymns Ancient and Modern, Revised,* 1950

66. 66. 44. 44

1 What thanks and praise to thee we owe, e-ter-nal
2 O hap-py saint! his sa-cred page, so rich in
3 His-to-rian of the Sa-vior's life, the great a-
4 So grant us, Lord, like him to live, be-loved on

God and Word di-vine, for Luke, thy saint, through
words of truth and love, pours on the Church from
pos-tle's cho-sen friend, through wea-ry years of
earth, ap-proved by thee, till thou at last the

whom we know so man-y gra-cious words of thine.
age to age the heal-ing unc-tion from a-bove.
toil and strife was still found faith-ful to the end.
sum-mons give, and we, with him, thy face shall see.

*Saint Luke (October 18).*

Words: William Dalrymple Maclagan (1826-1910), alt.
Music: *Deus tuorum militum,* melody from *Antiphoner,* 1753; adapt. *The English Hymnal,* 1906, alt.

LM

1 Who are these like stars ap-pear-ing, these, be-fore God's
2 Who are these of daz-zling bright-ness, these in God's own
3 These are they who have con-tend-ed for their Sa-vior's
4 These are they whose hearts were riv-en, sore with woe and
5 These, like priests, have watched and wait-ed, of-fering up to

1 throne who stand? Each a gold - en crown is wear - ing;
2 truth ar - rayed, clad in robes of pur - est white - ness,
3 hon - or long, wres - tling on till life was end - ed,
4 an - guish tried, who in prayer full oft have striv - en
5 Christ their will, soul and bo - dy con - se - crat - ed,

1 who are all this glo - rious band? Al - le - lu - ia!
2 robes whose lus - ter ne'er shall fade, ne'er be touched by
3 fol - lowing not the sin - ful throng; these, who well the
4 with the God they glo - ri - fied; now, their pain - ful
5 day and night they serve him still. Now in God's most

1 hark, they sing, prais - ing loud their heaven - ly King.
2 time's rude hand? Whence comes all this glo - rious band?
3 fight sus - tained, tri - umph by the Lamb have gained.
4 con - flict o'er, God has bid them weep no more.
5 ho - ly place, blest they stand be - fore his face.

*All Saints' Day (November 1).*

Words: Theobald Heinrich Schenck (1656-1727); tr. Frances Elizabeth Cox (1812-1897), alt.
Music: *Zeuch mich, zeuch mich*, melody from *Geistreiches Gesang-buch*, 1698;
    harm. William Henry Monk (1823-1889), alt.

87. 87. 77

1 For all the saints, who from their la - bors rest, who
2 Thou wast their rock, their for - tress, and their might:__
3 O may thy sol - diers, faith - ful, true, and bold,__
4 O blest com - mun - ion, fel - low - ship di - vine!__

thee__ by faith be - fore the world con - fessed, thy
thou, Lord, their Cap - tain in the well - fought fight;__
fight as the saints who no - bly fought of old, and
We feeb - ly strug - gle, they in glo - ry shine; yet

Name, O__ Je - sus, be for ev - er blessed.
thou, in the dark - ness drear, the one true Light.
win, with__ them, the vic - tor's crown of gold.
all are__ one in thee, for all are thine.

Al - le - lu - ia, al - le - lu - ia!

*5 And when the strife is fierce, the war-fare long, steals on the ear the
*6 The gold - en eve - ning bright-ens in the west; soon, soon to faith-ful

dis-tant tri-umph song, and hearts are _____ brave a-gain, and arms are
war-riors com-eth rest; _____ sweet is the calm of par-a-dise the

strong.
blest. Al - le-lu - ia. al - le-lu - ia!

*7 But lo! there breaks a yet more glo-rious day; the
*8 From earth's wide bounds, from o-cean's far-thest coast, through

saints tri-umph-ant rise in bright ar - ray; the
gates of pearl streams in the count-less host, _____

King of_____ glo - ry pass - es on his way.
sing - ing to Fa - ther, Son, and Ho - ly Ghost,

Al - le-lu - ia, al - le-lu - ia!

*All Saints' Day (November 1).*

Words: William Walsham How (1823-1897)
Music: *Sine Nomine*, Ralph Vaughan Williams (1872-1958)

10 10 10 with Alleluias

1 Praise to God, im - mor - tal praise, for the love that crowns our days;
2 All the plen - ty sum - mer pours; au - tumn's rich o'er - flow - ing stores;
3 As thy pros-pering hand hath blessed, may we give thee of our best;

boun - teous source of ev - ery joy, let thy praise our tongues em - ploy:
flocks that whit - en all the plain; yel - low sheaves of ri - pened grain:
and by deeds of kind - ly love for thy mer - cies grate - ful prove;

all to thee, our God, we owe, source whence all our bless-ings flow.
Lord, for these our souls shall raise grate - ful vows and sol - emn praise.
sing - ing thus through all our days praise to God, im - mor - tal praise.

*Thanksgiving Day.*

Words: Anna Laetitia Barbauld (1743-1825)
Music: *Dix*, melody Conrad Kocher (1786-1872); arr. William Henry Monk (1823-1889);
    harm. *The English Hymnal*, 1906

77. 77. 77

**289**        Holy Days and Various Occasions

1 Our Fa - ther, by whose ser - vants our house was built of
2 The change - ful years un - rest - ing their si - lent course have
3 They reap not where they la - bored; we reap what they have

old,        whose    hand hath   crowned her    chil -  dren  with
sped,        new    com-rades   ev - er     bring - ing  in
sown:      our    har - vest   may  be    gar -  nered by

bless-ings  man - i - fold,         for     thine un - fail - ing
com-rades'  steps  to   tread:       and    some are long  for -
a - ges  yet  un - known.    The    days of old  have

mer -  cies  far - strewn a - long our   way,         with
got -  ten,  long  spent their hopes and  fears;      safe
dowered  us  with   gifts be - yond all  praise:    our

all who passed be - fore   us, we  praise thy  Name to - day.
rest they  in   thy   keep - ing, who chan-gest  not  with  years.
Fa-ther, make us   faith - ful to  serve the  com - ing  days.

*On the Anniversary of the Dedication of a Church.*

Words: George Wallace Briggs (1875-1959)
Music: *Wolvercote*, William Harold Ferguson (1874-1950)

76. 76. D

1 Come, ye thank-ful    peo - ple, come,    raise the song of    har - vest-home:
2 All    the world is    God's own field,    fruit un - to his    praise to yield;
3 For    the Lord our    God shall come,    and shall take his    har - vest home;
4 E - ven so, Lord, quick - ly come    to    thy fi - nal    har - vest-home;

all    is safe - ly    gath - ered in,    ere the win - ter    storms be - gin;
wheat and tares to - geth - er sown,    un - to joy or    sor - row grown:
from his field shall    in    that day    all of - fens - es    purge a - way;
gath - er thou thy    peo - ple in,    free from sor - row,    free from sin;

*Descant*

4 there,    for ev - er    pur - i - fied,    in    thy pres - ence

1 God,    our Ma - ker,    doth pro - vide    for    our wants to
2 first    the blade, and    then the    ear,    then    the full    corn
3 give    his an - gels    charge at    last    in    the fire    the
4 there,    for ev - er    pur - i - fied,    in    thy pres - ence

to a-bide; come, with all thine an-gels

be sup-plied; come to God's own tem-ple,
shall ap-pear: grant, O har-vest Lord, that
tares to cast, but the fruit-ful ears to
to a-bide; come, with all thine an-gels

come, raise the glo-rious har-vest-home.

come, raise the song of har-vest-home.
we whole-some grain and pure may be.
store in his gar-ner ev-er-more.
come, raise the glo-rious har-vest-home.

*Thanksgiving Day.*

Words: Henry Alford (1810-1871), alt.
Music: *St. George's, Windsor,* George Job Elvey (1816-1893); desc. Craig Sellar Lang (1891-1971)

77. 77. D

1 We plow the fields, and scat - ter the good seed on the land,
2 He on - ly is the Ma - ker of all things near and far;
3 We thank thee, then, O Fa - ther, for all things bright and good,

but it is fed and wa - tered by God's al - might - y hand;
he paints the way-side flow - er, he lights the eve - ning star;
the seed - time and the har - vest, our life, our health, our food:

he sends the snow in win - ter, the warmth to swell the grain,
the winds and waves o - bey him, by him the birds are fed;
the gifts we have to of - fer are what thy love im - parts,

the breez-es and the sun - shine, and soft re-fresh-ing rain.
much more to us, his chil - dren, he gives our dai - ly bread.
but chief-ly thou de - sir - est our hum - ble thank-ful hearts.

All good gifts a - round us are sent from heaven a - bove;

then thank the Lord, O thank the Lord for all his love.

*Thanksgiving Day.*

Words: Matthias Claudius (1740-1815); tr. Jane Montgomery Campbell (1817-1878), alt.
Music: *Wir pflugen*, Johann Abraham Peter Schulz (1747-1800)       76. 76. D with Refrain

1 O      Je - sus, crowned with all   re - nown, since   thou the   earth hast
2 Lord,   in their change, let  frost and heat, and   winds and  dews be
3 that    we may feed the   poor a - right, and,   gath - ering round thy

trod,     thou    reign - est and   by    thee come down   hence -
given;    all    fos - tering power, all   in - fluence sweet,   breathe
throne,   here,   in   the  ho - ly   an - gel's sight,   re -

forth the   gifts    of    God.    Thine    is   the   health and
from the   boun - teous heaven.  At - tem - per   fair  with
pay thee   of    thine   own:    That    we   may   praise thee

thine the  wealth that    in    our   halls a - bound,   and
gen - tle  air   the    sun - shine and the  rain,    that
all  our   days, and    with   the   Fa - ther's Name,   and

thine the  beau - ty    and the joy  with   which the  years are  crowned.
kind - ly  earth with   time - ly birth may   yield her  fruits a - gain:
with the  Ho - ly    Spi - rit's gifts, the   Sa - vior's love pro - claim.

*Rogation Days.*

Words: Edward White Benson (1829-1896), alt.
Music: *Kingsfold*, English melody; adapt. Ralph Vaughan Williams (1872-1958)             CMD

1 I sing a song of the saints of God,
  pa - tient and brave and true, who toiled and fought and
  lived and died for the Lord they loved and knew. And
  one was a doc - tor, and one was a queen, and one was a shep -
  herd - ess on the green: they were all of them saints of
  God— and I mean, God help - ing, to be one too.

2 They loved their Lord so dear, so dear, and
  his love made them strong; and they fol - lowed the right, for
  Je - sus' sake, the whole of their good lives long. And
  one was a sold - ier, and one was a priest, and one was slain
  by a fierce wild beast: and there's not an - y rea - son—
  no, not the least, why I should-n't be one too.

3 They lived not on - ly in a - ges past, there are
  hund - reds of thou - sands still, the world is bright with the
  joy - ous saints who love to do Je - sus' will. You can
  meet them in school, or in lanes, or at sea, in church, or in trains,
  or in shops, or at tea, for the saints of God are just
  folk like me, and I mean to be one too.

*Saints' Days; All Saints' Day (November 1).*

Words: Lesbia Scott (b. 1898), alt.
Music: *Grand Isle,* John Henry Hopkins (1861-1945)

Irr.

## 294

Holy Baptism

1 Bap - tized in wa - ter, sealed by the Spi - rit,
2 Bap - tized in wa - ter, sealed by the Spi - rit,
3 Bap - tized in wa - ter, sealed by the Spi - rit,

cleansed by the blood of Christ our King:
dead in the tomb with Christ our King:
marked with the sign of Christ our King:

heirs of sal - va - tion, trust - ing his prom - ise,
one with his ris - ing, freed and for - giv - en,
born of one Fa - ther, we are his chil - dren,

faith - ful - ly now God's praise we sing.
thank - ful - ly now God's praise we sing.
joy - ful - ly now God's praise we sing.

Words: Michael Saward (b. 1932), alt.
Music: *Point Loma*, David Charles Walker (b. 1938)

558. 558

## 295

Holy Baptism

1 Sing praise to our Cre - a - tor, O you of Ad - am's race—
2 To Je - sus Christ give glo - ry, God's co - e - ter - nal Son;
3 And praise the Ho - ly Spi - rit poured forth up - on the earth;

God's chil-dren by a - dop - tion, bap - tized in - to his grace.
as mem-bers of his Bo - dy we live in him as one.
who sanc - ti - fies and guides us, made strong in our re - birth.

Words: Mark Evans (b. 1916), alt.
Music: *Christus, der ist mein Leben*, melody Melchior Vulpius (1560?-1616);
  harm. after Melchior Vulpius (1560?-1616)

76. 76

## Holy Baptism

1 We know that Christ is raised and dies no more.____
2 We share by wa - ter in his sav - ing death.____
3 The Fa - ther's splen - dor clothes the Son with life.____
4 A new cre - a - tion comes to life and grows____

Em - braced by death he broke its fear - ful hold;____
Re - born we share with him an Eas - ter life____
The Spi - rit's pow - er shakes the Church of God.____
as Christ's new bo - dy takes on flesh and blood.____

1-3

and our de - spair he turned to blaz - ing joy.____
as liv - ing mem-bers of a liv - ing Christ.____
Bap-tized we live with God the Three in One.____ Al - le -
The u - ni - verse re - stored and whole will sing:____

Final Ending

lu - ia! ___ Al - le - lu - ia! A - men.

Words: John Brownlow Geyer (b. 1932), alt.
Music: *Engelberg*, Charles Villiers Stanford (1852-1924)

10 10 10 with Alleluia

1 De - scend, O Spi - rit, purg - ing flame, brand
2 For - bid us not this sec - ond birth; grant

us this day with Je - sus' Name! Con - firm our faith, con -
un - to us the great - er worth! En - list us in your

sume our doubt; sign us as Christ's, with - in, with - out.
ser - vice, Lord; bap - tize all na - tions with your Word.

Words: Scott Francis Brenner (b. 1903), alt.
Music: *Erhalt uns, Herr*, melody from *Geistliche Lieder*, 1543                             LM

# Holy Baptism

1 All who be - lieve and are bap - tized shall see the Lord's sal -
2 With one ac - cord, O God, we pray: grant us thy Ho - ly

va - tion; bap-tized in - to the death of Christ, each is a
Spi - rit; help us in our in - fir - mi - ty through Je - sus'

new cre - a - tion. Through Christ's re-demp-tion we shall stand a-mong the
blood and mer - it. Grant us to grow in grace each day that as is

glo - rious heaven - ly band of ev - ery tribe and na - tion.
prom - ised here we may e - ter - nal life in - her - it.

Words: Thomas Hansen Kingo (1634-1703); tr. George Alfred Taylor Rygh (1860-1942), alt.
Music: *Es ist das Heil*, Hans Leo Hassler (1564-1612), alt.

87. 87. 887

1 Spirit of God, unleashed on earth
2 You came in power; the Church was born;
3 With burning words of victory won

with rush of wind and roar of flame!
O Holy Spirit, come again!
inspire our hearts grown cold with fear,

With tongues of fire saints spread good news;
From living waters raise new saints;
revive in us baptismal grace,

earth, kindling, blazed her loud acclaim.
let new tongues hail the risen Lord.
and fan our smoldering lives to flame.

Words: John W. Arthur (1922-1980), alt.
Music: *Lledrod,* melody from *Llyfr Tonau Cynnulleidfaol,* 1859; harm. *Hymnal 1940*

LM

1 Glo - ry, love, and praise, and hon - or for our food now be - stowed ren - der we the Do - nor. Boun - teous God, we now con - fess thee: God, who thus bless - est us, right it is to bless thee.

2 Thank-ful for our ev - ery bless - ing, let us sing Christ the Spring, nev - er, nev - er ceas - ing. Source of all our gifts and gra - ces, Christ we own; Christ a - lone calls for all our prais - es.

3 He dis - pels our sin and sad - ness, life im - parts, cheers our hearts, fills with food and glad - ness. Who him - self for all hath giv - en, us he feeds, us he leads to a feast in hea - ven.

Words: Charles Wesley (1707-1788), alt.
Music: *Benifold*, Francis B. Westbrook (1903-1975)

8. 33. 6. D

**301**

Bread of the world, in mer-cy bro-ken, Wine of the soul, in mer-cy shed, by whom the words of life were spo-ken, and in whose death our sins are dead: look on the heart by sor-row bro-ken, look on the tears by sin-ners shed; and be thy feast to us the to-ken that by thy grace our souls are fed.

Words: Reginald Heber (1783-1826)
Music: *Rendez à Dieu*, melody att. Louis Bourgeois (1510?-1561?)

98. 98. D

**302**

Holy Eucharist

1 Fa - ther, we thank thee who hast plant - ed thy ho - ly Name with -
2 Watch o'er thy Church, O Lord, in mer - cy, save it from e - vil,

in our hearts. Know-ledge and faith and life im-mor - tal Je - sus thy
guard it still, per - fect it in thy love, u - nite it, cleansed and con-

Son to us im-parts. Thou, Lord, didst make all for thy plea - sure,
formed un - to thy will. As grain, once scat - tered on the hill - sides,

didst give us food for all our days, giv - ing in Christ the
was in this bro - ken bread made one, so from all lands thy

Bread e - ter - nal; thine is the power, be thine the praise.
Church be gath - ered in - to thy king - dom by thy Son.

Words: Greek, ca. 110; tr. F. Bland Tucker (1895-1984), rev.
Music: *Rendez à Dieu*, melody and harm. att. Louis Bourgeois (1510?-1561?)

98. 98. D

**303**

Holy Eucharist

1 Fa - ther, we thank thee
2 Thou, Lord, didst make all
3 Watch o'er thy Church, O
4 As grain, once scat - tered

who hast plant - ed thy ho - ly
for thy plea - sure, didst give us
Lord, in mer - cy, save it from
on the hill - sides, was in this

Name with - in our hearts. Know-ledge and
food for all our days, giv - ing in
e - vil, guard it still, per - fect it
bro - ken bread made one, so from all

faith and life im - mor - tal Je - sus thy
Christ the Bread e - ter - nal; thine is the
in thy love, u - nite it, cleansed and con -
lands thy Church be gath - ered in - to thy

Son to us im - parts.
power, be thine the praise.
formed un - to thy will.
king - dom by thy Son.

Words: Greek, ca. 110; tr. F. Bland Tucker (1895-1984), rev.
Music: *Albright*, William Albright (b. 1944)

98. 98

# Holy Eucharist

*Unison or harmony*

1 I come with joy to meet my Lord, for -
2 I come with Chris - tians far and near to
3 As Christ breaks bread and bids us share, each
4 And thus with joy we meet our Lord. His
5 To - geth - er met, to - geth - er bound, we'll

1 giv - en, loved, and free, in awe and won - der
2 find, as all are fed, the new com - mu - ni -
3 proud di - vi - sion ends. That love that made us
4 pres - ence, al - ways near, is in such friend - ship
5 go our dif - ferent ways, and as his peo - ple

1 to re - call his life laid down for me.
2 ty of love in Christ's com - mun - ion bread.
3 makes us one, and stran - gers now are friends.
4 bet - ter known: we see and praise him here.
5 in the world we'll live and speak his praise.

Words: Brian A. Wren (b. 1936), alt.
Music: *Land of Rest,* American folk melody; adapt. and harm. Annabel Morris Buchanan (1889-1983)

CM

Descant

3 One bo-dy we, one Bo-dy who par-take, one

1 Come, ris-en Lord, and deign to be our guest; nay,
2 We meet, as in that up-per room they met; thou
3 One bo-dy we, one Bo-dy who par-take, one
4 One with each o - ther, Lord, for one in thee, who

Ped.

Church u - nit - ed in com-mun-ion blest; one Name we

let us be thy guests; the feast is thine;
at the ta - ble, bless - ing, yet dost stand:
Church u - nit - ed in com - mun - ion blest;
art one Sa - vior and one liv - ing Head;

bear,_____ one Bread of life we break, with all thy

thy - self at thine own board make man - i - fest in
"This is my Bo - dy"; so thou giv - est yet: faith
one Name we bear, one Bread of life we break, with
then o - pen thou our eyes, that we may see; be

saints on earth and saints at rest.

thine own Sac - ra - ment of Bread and Wine.
still re - ceives the cup as from thy hand.
all thy saints on earth and saints at rest.
known to us in break-ing of the Bread.

Words: George Wallace Briggs (1875-1959), alt.
Music: *Rosedale*, Leo Sowerby (1895-1968)

10 10. 10 10

## Holy Eucharist

**306**

1 Come, ris - en Lord, and deign to be our guest;
2 We meet, as in that up - per room they met;
3 One bo - dy we, one Bo - dy who par - take,
4 One with each o - ther, Lord, for one in thee,

nay, let us be thy guests; the feast is thine;
thou at the ta - ble, bless - ing, yet dost stand:
one Church u - nit - ed in com - mun - ion blest;
who art one Sa - vior and one liv - ing Head;

thy - self at thine own board make man - i - fest
"This is my Bo - dy"; so thou giv - est yet:
one Name we bear, one Bread of life we break,
then o - pen thou our eyes, that we may see;

in thine own Sac - ra - ment of Bread and Wine.
faith still re - ceives the cup as from thy hand.
with all thy saints on earth and saints at rest.
be known to us in break - ing of the Bread.

Words: George Wallace Briggs (1875-1959), alt.
Music: *Sursum Corda*, Alfred Morton Smith (1879-1971)

10 10. 10 10

1 Lord, en - throned in heaven - ly splen - dor, first - be -
*2 Here our hum - blest hom - age pay we, here in
*3 Though the low - liest form doth veil thee as of
4 Pas - chal Lamb, thine of - fering, fi - nished once for
5 Life - im - part - ing heaven - ly Man - na, smit - ten

1 got - ten from the dead. Thou a - lone, our strong de -
2 lov - ing rev - erence bow; here for faith's dis - cern - ment
3 old in Beth - le - hem, here as there thine an - gels
4 all when thou was slain, in its full - ness un - di -
5 Rock with stream - ing side, heaven and earth with loud ho -

Al - le -

1 fend - er, lift - est up thy peo - ple's head.
2 pray we, lest we fail to know thee now.
3 hail thee, branch and flower of Jes - se's stem.
4 min - ished shall for ev - er - more re - main.
5 san - na wor - ship thee, the Lamb who died.

lu - ia!     Al - le - lu - ia!     Al - le -

Al - le - lu - ia!     Al - le - lu - ia!

lu - ia!

Al - le - lu - ia!

| 1 | Je - | sus, | true | and | liv - | ing |
| 2 | Thou | art | here, | we | ask | not |
| 3 | We | in | wor - ship | join | with |  |
| 4 | Cleans - ing | us | from | ev - | ery |  |
| 5 | Risen, | a - scend - ed, | glo - | ri - |  |  |

| 1 | bread! | Je - sus, | true | and | liv - ing | bread! |
| 2 | how. | Thou | are | here, | we | ask | not | how. |
| 3 | them. | We | in | wor - ship | join | with | them. |
| 4 | stain. | Cleans - ing | us | from | ev - ery | stain. |
| 5 | fied! | Risen, | a - scend - ed, | glo - ri - | fied! |

Words: George Hugh Bourne (1840-1925), alt.
Music: *Bryn Calfaria*, melody William Owen (1813-1893); harm. *Christian Hymns*, 1977      87. 87. 12 77

*Unison or harmony*

1 O Food to pil - grims giv - en, O Bread of
2 O stream of love past tell - ing, O pur - est
3 O Je - sus, by thee bid - den, we here a -

life from hea - ven, O Man - na from on high!
foun - tain, well - ing from out the Sa - vior's side!
dore thee, hid - den in forms of bread and wine.

We hun - ger; Lord, sup - ply us, nor thy de -
We faint with thirst; re - vive us, of thine a -
Grant when the veil is riv - en, we may be -

lights de - ny us, whose hearts to thee draw nigh.
bun - dance give us, and all we need pro - vide.
hold, in hea - ven, thy coun - te - nance di - vine.

Words: Latin, 1661; tr. John Athelstan Laurie Riley (1858-1945), alt.
Music: *Psalm 6*, from *Les cent cinquante Pseaumes de David*, 1564, alt.

776. D

1 O Food to pil - grims giv - en, O Bread of life from
2 O stream of love past tell - ing, O pur - est foun - tain,
3 O Je - sus, by thee bid - den, we here a - dore thee,

hea - ven, O Man - na from on high! We
well - ing from out the Sa - vior's side! We
hid - den in forms of bread and wine. Grant

hun - ger; Lord, sup - ply us, nor thy de - lights de -
faint with thirst; re - vive us, of thine a - bun - dance
when the veil is riv - en, we may be - hold, in

ny us, whose hearts to thee draw nigh.
give us, and all we need pro - vide.
hea - ven, thy coun - te - nance di - vine.

Words: Latin, 1661; tr. John Athelstan Laurie Riley (1858-1945), alt.
Music: *O Welt, ich muss dich lassen*, present form of melody att. Heinrich Isaac (1450?-1517), alt.;
    harm. Johann Sebastian Bach (1685-1750)

776 D

1 O sav - ing Vic - tim, o - pening wide the
2 All praise and thanks to thee a - scend for

gate of heaven to us be - low, our foes press on from
ev - er - more, blest One in Three; O grant us life that

ev - ery side, thine aid sup - ply, thy strength be - stow.
shall not end in our true na - tive land with thee.

Words: Att. Thomas Aquinas (1225?-1274); tr. Edward Caswall (1814-1878), alt.
Music: *Herr Jesu Christ,* melody from *Cantionale Germanicum,* 1628; adapt. and harm.
    Johann Sebastian Bach (1685-1750)

LM

1 O sav - ing Vic - tim, o - pening wide
2 All praise and thanks to thee a - scend

the gate of heaven to us be - low,
for ev - er - more, blest One in Three;

our foes press on from ev - ery side,
O grant us life that shall not end

thine aid sup - ply, thy strength be - stow.
in our true na - tive land with thee.

Words: Att. Thomas Aquinas (1225?-1274); tr. Edward Caswall (1814-1878), alt.
Music: *Verbum supernum prodiens*, plainsong, Mode 2, Nevers MS., 13th cent.

LM

## Holy Eucharist                                312

1 Strength - en for ser - vice, Lord, the hands that ho - ly
2 Lord, may the tongues which "Ho - ly" sang keep free from
3 The feet that tread thy hal - lowed courts from light do

things have tak - en; let ears that now have
all de - ceiv - ing; the eyes which saw thy
thou not ban - ish; the bo - dies by thy

heard thy songs to clam - or nev - er wak - en.
love be bright, thy bless - ed hope per - ceiv - ing.
Bo - dy fed with thy new life re - ple - nish.

Words: Syriac Liturgy of Malabar; tr. Charles William Humphreys (1840-1921);
      alt. Percy Dearmer (1867-1936)
Music: *Malabar*, David McKinley Williams (1887-1978)

87. 87

1 Let thy Blood in mer-cy poured, let thy gra-cious
2 Thou didst die that I might live; bless-ed Lord, thou
3 By the thorns that crowned thy brow, by the spear-wound
4 Wilt thou own the gift I bring? All my pen-i-

Bo-dy bro-ken, be to me, O gra-cious Lord,
cam'st to save me; all that love of God could give
and the nail-ing, by the pain and death, I now
tence I give thee; thou art my ex-alt-ed King,

*Refrain*

of thy bound-less love the to-ken.
Je-sus by his sor-rows gave me.
claim, O Christ, thy love un-fail-ing. Thou didst give thy-
of thy match-less love for-give me.

self for me, now I give my-self to thee.

Words: John Brownlie (1859-1925)
Music: *Jesus, meine Zuversicht*, melody Johann Cruger (1598-1662);
harm. after *The Chorale Book for England*, 1863

78. 78. 77

1 Hum - bly I a - dore thee, Ver - i - ty un - seen,
2 Taste and touch and vi - sion to dis - cern thee fail;
3 O me - mo - rial won - drous of the Lord's own death;
4 Je - sus, whom now hid - den, I by faith be - hold,

who thy glo - ry hid - est 'neath these sha - dows mean;
faith, that comes by hear - ing, pierc - es through the veil.
liv - ing Bread that giv - est all thy crea - tures breath,
what my soul doth long for, that thy word fore - told:

lo, to thee sur - ren - dered, my whole heart is bowed,
I be - lieve what - e'er the Son of God hath told;
grant my spi - rit ev - er by thy life may live,
face to face thy splen - dor, I at last shall see,

tranced as it be - holds thee, shrined with - in the cloud.
what the Truth hath spo - ken, that for truth I hold.
to my taste thy sweet - ness nev - er - fail - ing give.
in the glo - rious vi - sion, bless - ed Lord, of thee.

Words: Att. Thomas Aquinas (1225?-1274); sts. 1-3, tr. *Hymnal 1940;* st. 4, tr. *Hymnal 1982*
Music: *Adoro devote,* French church melody, Mode 5, *Processionale,* 1697

11 11. 11 11

**315**

Holy Eucharist

*Unison or harmony*

1 Thou, who at thy first Eu - cha - rist didst pray
2 For all thy Church, O Lord, we in - ter - cede;
3 So, Lord, at length when sac - ra - ments shall cease,

that all thy Church might be for ev - er one,
make thou our sad di - vi - sions soon to cease;
may we be one with all thy Church a - bove,

grant us at ev - ery Eu - cha - rist to say
draw us the near - er each to each, we plead,
one with thy saints in one un - bro - ken peace,

with long - ing heart and soul, "Thy will be done."
by draw - ing all to thee, O Prince of Peace;
one with thy saints in one un - bound - ed love;

| | | | | | | | | | |
|---|---|---|---|---|---|---|---|---|---|
| O | may | we | all | one | bread, | one | bo - | dy | be, |
| thus | may | we | all | one | bread, | one | bo - | dy | be, |
| more | bless - ed | | still, | in | peace | and | love | to | be |

| | | | | | | | | |
|---|---|---|---|---|---|---|---|---|
| through this | blest | sac - ra - ment | of | u - ni - ty. |
| through this | blest | sac - ra - ment | of | u - ni - ty. |
| one | with | the | Trin - i - ty | in | U - ni - ty. |

Words: William Harry Turton (1856-1938)
Music: *Song 1*, melody and bass Orlando Gibbons (1583-1625);
  harm. Ralph Vaughan Williams (1872-1958), alt.

10 10. 10 10. 10 10

## 316

Holy Eucharist

1 This is the hour of ban - quet and of song;
2 Too soon we rise; we go our sev - eral ways;
3 Feast af - ter feast thus comes and pass - es by,

this is the heaven - ly ta - ble spread for me;
the feast, though not the love, is past and gone,
yet, pass - ing, points to the glad feast a - bove,

here let me feast, and feast - ing, still pro - long the
the Bread and Wine con - sumed: yet all our days thou
giv - ing us fore - taste of the fes - tal joy, the

brief, bright hour of fel - low - ship with thee.
still art here with us— our Shield and Sun.
Lamb's great mar - riage feast of bliss and love.

Words: Horatius Bonar (1808-1889), alt.
Music: *Canticum refectionis*, David McKinley Williams (1887-1978)

10 10. 10 10

## 317

Holy Eucharist

1 This is the hour of ban - quet and of song;
2 Too soon we rise; we go our sev - eral ways;
3 Feast af - ter feast thus comes and pass - es by,

this is the heaven - ly ta - ble spread for me;
the feast, though not the love, is past and gone,
yet, pass - ing, points to the glad feast a - bove,

here     let     me     feast, and   feast - ing,     still     pro - long
the     Bread   and     Wine con - sumed: yet     all     our     days
giv - ing     us     fore - taste   of     the     fes - tal     joy,

the     brief, bright     hour   of   fel - low - ship     with     thee.
thou     still     art     here with   us — our     Shield   and     Sun.
the     Lamb's great     mar - riage feast   of     bliss     and     love.

Words: Horatius Bonar (1808-1889), alt.
Music: *Morestead*, Sidney Watson (b. 1903)

10 10. 10 10

## Holy Eucharist      318

1 Here,   O     my     Lord,     I     see     thee face   to     face;
2 Here would   I     feed     up - on     the     Bread   of     God;
3 I     have     no     help     but     thine; nor   do     I     need
4 Mine     is     the     sin,     but     thine   the   right - eous - ness;

here   would     I     touch   and   han - dle   things   un - seen;
here   drink   with     thee     the     roy - al     Wine   of     heaven;
an - oth - er     arm     save   thine   to     lean   up - on;
mine   is     the     guilt,   but     thine   the     cleans - ing   Blood.

here   grasp   with     firm - er     hand   e - ter - nal     grace,
here   would   I     lay     a - side   each   earth - ly     load,
it     is     e - nough,     my     Lord,   e - nough   in - deed;
Here   is     my     robe,     my     ref - uge,   and     my     peace;

and     all     my     wea - ri - ness   up - on     thee     lean.
here   taste   a - fresh   the     calm   of     sin   for - given.
my   strength   is     in     thy     might, thy   might   a - lone.
thy   Blood,   thy     right - eous - ness,   O     Lord,   my     God.

Words: Horatius Bonar (1808-1889)
Music: *Nyack*, Warren Swenson (b. 1937)

10 10. 10 10

1 You, Lord, we praise in songs of cel - e - bra - tion for this
2 You, Lord, in our stead to the grave de - scend - ed when by

feast of our sal - va - tion. Here at your
sin our life was end - ed. No great - er

ta - ble ev - ery life you nour - ish; by your grace we
love than this to you could bind us; dai - ly still your

all may flour - ish. Ky - ri - e e - le - i - son.
mer - cies find us. Ky - ri - e e - le - i - son.

In the light of your In - car - na - tion, all cre -
Bind our hearts as one we im - plore you, who a -

a - tion knows the love of God, and in
dore you and con - fess your Name. Thus may

you finds re - lease that we all might
we ev - er be yours in peace and

live in peace. Ky - ri - e e - le - i - son. _____
u - ni - ty. Ky - ri - e e - le - i - son. _____

Words: Russell Schulz-Widmar (b. 1944), based on German folk hymn and Martin Luther (1483-1546)
Music: *Gott sei gelobet*, melody from *Miltenberger Processionale*, 15th cent. adapt. *Geistliche Gesangbüchlein*, 1524    Irr.

# Holy Eucharist

320

1 Zi - on, praise thy Sa - vior, sing - ing hymns with ex - ul -
Hon - or Christ, thy voice up - rais - ing, who sur - pass - eth

ta - tion ring - ing, praise thy King and Shep - herd true.
all thy prais - ing; nev - er canst thou reach his due.

2 Let the Bread, life - giv - ing, liv - ing, be our
as of old the Lord pro - vid - ed when the

theme of glad thanks - giv - ing, now in truth be - fore thee set;
twelve, di - vine - ly guid - ed, at the ho - ly ta - ble met.

3 What he did, at sup - per seat - ed, Christ or - dained to
4 Full and clear sing out thy prais - ing, gra - cious hymns of

be re - peat - ed, his me - mo - rial ne'er to cease;
joy up - rais - ing in thy heart and soul to - day;

his com - mand for guid - ance tak - ing, bread and wine we
for to - day the new ob - la - tion of the new King's

hal - low, mak - ing thus our sac - ri - fice of peace.
rev - e - la - tion bids us feast in glad ar - ray.

\*5 Ve - ry Bread, good Shep-herd, tend     us,     Je - sus, of thy love
\*6 thou, who all     things canst and     know - est,     who on earth such food

be - friend us,     Lord, re - fresh us and     de - fend us,     thine e -
be - stow - est,     grant us, with thy saints, though low - est,     where the

ter - nal good-ness send us     in the     land     of life to     see:
heaven-ly feast thou show - est,     fel - low - heirs     and guests to     be.

*When stanzas 5 and 6 are omitted, stanzas 1 through 4 may be sung to the tune of stanza 1,*
*or the tunes of stanzas 1 and 2 may be repeated for stanzes 3 and 4.*

Words: Att. Thomas Aquinas (1225?-1274); tr. *Hymnal 1940;* rev. *Hymnal 1982*
Music: *Lauda Sion Salvatorem,* plainsong, Mode 7, 12th cent.                    887. 887

## 321                                                Holy Eucharist

1 My     God,     thy     ta - ble     now is     spread,     thy     cup     with
2 O     let     thy     ta - ble     hon - ored     be,     and     fur - nished
3 Drawn     by     thy     quick-ening grace, O     Lord,     in     count - less
4 Nor     let     thy     spread-ing     Gos - pel     rest     till     through the

love     doth     o - ver - flow;     be     all     thy     chil - dren
well     with     joy - ful guests;     and     may     each     soul     sal -
num - bers     let     them come     and     gath - er     from     their
world     thy     truth     has     run,     till     with     this     Bread     shall

thith - er led, and let them thy sweet mer - cies know.
a - tion see, that here its sa - cred pledg - es tastes.
Fa - ther's board the Bread that lives be - yond the tomb.
all be blessed who see the light or feel the sun.

Words: Sts. 1-3, Philip Doddridge (1702-1751), alt.; st. 4, Isaac Watts (1674-1748), alt.
Music: *Rockingham*, melody from *Second Supplement to Psalmody in Miniature*, ca. 1780;
adapt. Edward Miller (1731-1807); harm. Samuel Webbe (1740-1816)

LM

## Holy Eucharist

**322**

1 When Je - sus died to save us, a word, an act he
2 (He) was the Word that spake it, he took the bread and

gave us; and still that word is spo - ken,
brake it, and what that Word did make it,

and still the bread is bro - ken. 2 He
I do be - lieve and (take it.) take it.

Words: St. 1, F. Bland Tucker (1895-1984); st. 2, att. John Donne (1573-1631)
Music: *Tucker*, David Hurd (b. 1950)

77. 77

1 Bread of heaven, on thee we feed, for thy Flesh is
2 Vine of heaven, thy Blood sup-plies this blest cup of

meat in-deed; ev - er may our souls be fed
sac - ri - fice; Lord, thy wounds our heal - ing give,

with this true and liv - ing Bread; day by day with
to thy cross we look and live: Je - sus, may we

strength sup-plied, through the life of him who died.
ev - er be graft - ed, root - ed, built in thee.

Words: Josiah Conder (1789-1855), alt.
Music: *Jesu, Jesu, du mein Hirt*, melody Paul Heinlein (1626-1686); harm. *The English Hymnal*, 1906     77. 77. 77

# Holy Eucharist

324

1 Let all mor-tal flesh keep si-lence, and with fear and trem-bling stand; pon-der noth-ing earth-ly mind-ed, for with bless-ing in his hand Christ our God to earth de-scend-eth, our full hom-age to de-mand.

2 King of kings, yet born of Ma-ry, as of old on earth he stood, Lord of lords in hu-man ves-ture, in the Bo-dy and the Blood he will give to all the faith-ful his own self for heaven-ly food.

3 Rank on rank the host of hea-ven spreads its van-guard on the way, as the Light of Light de-scend-eth from the realms of end-less day, that the powers of hell may va-nish as the dark-ness clears a-way.

4 At his feet the six-winged ser-aph; cher-u-bim with sleep-less eye, veil their fa-ces to the Pres-ence, as with cease-less voice they cry, "Al-le-lu-ia, al-le-lu-ia! Al-le-lu-ia, Lord Most High!"

Words: Liturgy of St. James; para. Gerard Moultrie (1829-1885)
Music: *Picardy*, French carol, 17th cent.; melody from *Chansons populaires des Provinces de France*, 1860    87. 87. 87

Words: Afro-American spiritual
Music: *Let Us Break Bread*, Afro-American spiritual

10 10 with Refrain

# Holy Eucharist

1 From glo - ry to glo - ry ad - vanc - ing, we
2 Thanks - giv - ing, and glo - ry and wor - ship, and

praise thee, O Lord; thy Name with the Fa - ther and
bless - ing and love, one heart and one song have the

Spi - rit be ev - er a - dored. From strength un - to
saints up - on earth and a - bove. O Lord, ev - er -

strength we go for - ward on Zi - on's high -
more to thy ser - vants thy pres - ence be

way, to ap - pear be - fore God in the
nigh; ev - er fit us by ser - vice on

ci - ty of in - fi - nite day.
earth for thy ser - vice on high.

*The small notes in the vocal part are recommended for stanza 2.*

Words: Liturgy of St. James; tr. Charles William Humphreys (1840-1921)
Music: *St. Keverne*, Craig Sellar Lang (1891-1971)

14 14. 14 15

1 Draw nigh and take the Bo - dy of the Lord,
2 Saved by that Bo - dy and that ho - ly Blood,
3 Sal - va - tion's giv - er, Christ, the on - ly Son,
4 Of - fered was he for great - est and for least,
5 Ap - proach ye then with faith - ful hearts sin - cere,

1 and drink the ho - ly Blood for you out - poured.
2 with souls re - freshed, we ren - der thanks to God.
3 by his dear cross and blood the vic - tory won.
4 him - self the Vic - tim, and him - self the Priest.
5 and take the pledg - es of sal - va - tion here.

6 He that his saints in this world rules and shields
to all believers life eternal yields;

7 with heavenly bread he makes the hungry whole,
gives living waters to the thirsting soul.

8 Alpha-Omega, unto whom shall bow
all nations at the doom, is with us now.

Words: *Bangor Antiphoner*, ca. 690; tr. John Mason Neale (1818-1866), alt.
Music: *Palmer Church*, David Ashley White (b. 1944)

10. 10

# Holy Eucharist

1. Draw nigh and take the Bo - dy of the Lord,
2. Saved by that Bo - dy and that ho - ly Blood,
3. Sal - va - tion's giv - er, Christ, the on - ly Son,
4. Of - fered was he for great - est and for least,
5. Ap - proach ye then with faith - ful hearts sin - cere,

1. and drink the ho - ly Blood for you out - poured.
2. with souls re - freshed, we ren - der thanks to God.
3. by his dear cross and blood the vic - tory won.
4. him - self the Vic - tim, and him - self the Priest.
5. and take the pledg - es of sal - va - tion here.

6 He that his saints in this world rules and shields
to all believers life eternal yields;

7 with heavenly bread he makes the hungry whole,
gives living waters to the thirsting soul.

8 Alpha-Omega, unto whom shall bow
all nations at the doom, is with us now.

Words: *Bangor Antiphoner*, ca. 690; tr. John Mason Neale (1818-1866), alt.
Music: *Song 46*, melody and bass Orlando Gibbons (1583-1625); harm. *The English Hymnal*, 1906

10. 10

1 Now, my tongue, the mys-tery tell - ing of the glo - rious
2 Given for us, and con - de - scend - ing to be born for
3 That last night at sup - per ly - ing mid the twelve, his
4 Word made flesh, the bread he tak - eth, by his word his
*5 There - fore we, be - fore him bend - ing, this great Sac - ra -
*6 Glo - ry let us give and bless - ing to the Fa - ther

1 Bo - dy sing, and the Blood, all price ex - cell - ing,
2 us be - low, he with us in con - verse blend - ing
3 cho - sen band, Je - sus, with the Law com - ply - ing,
4 Flesh to be; wine his sa - cred Blood he mak - eth,
5 ment re - vere; types and sha - dows have their end - ing,
6 and the Son, hon - or, thanks, and praise ad - dress - ing,

1 which the Gen - tiles' Lord and King, once on earth a -
2 dwelt, the seed of truth to sow, till he closed with
3 keeps the feast its rites de - mand; then, more pre - cious
4 though the sens - es fail to see; faith a - lone the
5 for the new - er rite is here; faith, our out - ward
6 while e - ter - nal a - ges run; ev - er too his

1 mong us dwell - ing, shed for this world's ran - som - ing.
2 won - drous end - ing his most pa - tient life of woe.
3 food sup - ply - ing, gives him - self with his own hand.
4 true heart wak - eth to be - hold the mys - ter - y.
5 sense be - friend - ing, makes our in - ward vi - sion clear.
6 love con - fess - ing who from both with both is One.

Words: Att. Thomas Aquinas (1225?-1274); ver. *Hymnal 1940*, rev.
Music: *Pange lingua*, plainsong, Mode 3, *Zisterzienser Hymnar*, 14th cent.                    87. 87. 87

5 There-fore we, be - fore him bend - ing,
6 Glo - ry let us give and bless - ing

this great Sac - ra - ment re - vere;
to the Fa - ther and the Son,

types and sha - dows have their end - - ing,
hon - or, thanks, and praise ad - dress - ing,

for the new - er rite is here;
while e - ter - nal a - ges run;

faith, our out - ward sense be - friend - ing,
ev - er too his love con - fess - - ing

makes our in - ward vi - sion clear.
who from both with both is One.

*These are stanzas from the hymns found at 329 and 331.*

Words: Att. Thomas Aquinas (1225?-1274); ver. *Hymnal 1940*
Music: *Tantum ergo Sacramentum*, plainsong, Mode 5, *Zisterzienser Hymnar*, 14th cent.

87. 87. 87

1 Now, my tongue, the mys - tery tell - ing of the glo - rious
2 Given for us, and con - de - scend-ing to be born for
3 That last night at sup - per ly - ing mid the twelve,his
4 Word made flesh, the bread he tak - eth, by his word his
*5 There- fore we, be - fore him bend -ing, this great Sac - ra -

1 Bo - dy sing, and the Blood, all price ex - cell - ing,
2 us be - low, he with us in con - verse blend-ing
3 cho - sen band, Je - sus, with the Law com - ply - ing,
4 Flesh to be; wine his sa - cred Blood he mak - eth,
5 ment re - vere; types and sha - dows have their end - ing,

1 which the Gen-tiles' Lord and King, once on earth a -
2 dwelt the seed of truth to sow, till he closed with
3 keeps the feast its rites de - mand; then, more pre - cious
4 though the sens - es fail to see; faith a - lone the
5 for the new - er rite is here; faith, our out - ward

| | | | | | | |
|1 | mong | us | dwell-ing, | shed | for | this | world's ran - som - ing. |
|2 | won - drous | end - ing | his | most | pa - tient | life | of | woe. |
|3 | food | sup - ply - ing, | gives | him - self | with | his | own | hand. |
|4 | true | heart wak - eth | to | be - hold | the | mys - te - ry. |
|5 | sense | be - friend - ing, | makes | our | in - ward | vi - sion | clear. |

*6 Glory let us give and blessing
   to the Father and the Son,
   honor, thanks, and praise addressing,
   while eternal ages run;
   ever too his love confessing
   who from both with both is One.

Words: Att. Thomas Aquinas (1225?-1274); ver. *Hymnal 1940*, rev.
Music: *Grafton*, melody from *Chants ordinaires de l'Office Divin*, 1881; harm. *Songs of Praise*, 1925          87. 87. 87

## Holy Eucharist                                                    332

| | | | | |
|1 | O | God, | un - seen yet | ev - er | near, | thy pres - ence may we | feel; |
|2 | Here | may | thy faith - ful | peo - ple | know | the bless - ings of thy love, |
|3 | We | come, | o - be - dient | to thy | word, | to feast | on heaven-ly food: |
|4 | Thus | may | we all | thy word o - bey, | for we, | O God, are thine; |

| | | | |
| and | thus | in-spired with ho - ly | fear, | be - fore | thine al - tar kneel. |
| the | streams | that through the des - ert | flow, | the man - na from a - bove. |
| our | meat | the Bo - dy of the | Lord, | our drink his pre-cious Blood. |
| and | go | re - joic - ing on our | way, | re - newed with strength di-vine. |

Words: Edward Osler (1798-1863)
Music: *St. Flavian*, from *Day's Psalter*, 1562                              CM

Now the silence Now the peace Now the emp - ty

hands up - lift - ed Now the kneel - ing Now the plea

Now the Fa - ther's arms in wel - come Now the hear - ing

Now the power Now the ves - sel brimmed for pour - ing

Now the Bo - dy Now the Blood Now the joy - ful

cel - e - bra - tion Now the wed - ding Now the songs

Now the heart for - giv - en leap - ing Now the Spi - rit's

vis - i - ta - tion Now the Son's e - piph - a - ny

Now the Fa - ther's bless - ing Now Now Now

Words: Jaroslav J. Vajda (b. 1919)
Music: *Now*, Carl Flentge Schalk (b. 1929)

Irr.

1 Praise the Lord, rise up re-joic-ing, wor - ship, thanks, de-
2 Scat-tered flock, one shep-herd shar-ing, lost and lone - ly,
3 Sins for-giv-en, wrong for-giv-ing, we go forth a-

vo - tion voic-ing; glo - ry be to God on high!
one voice hear-ing, ears at - ten - tive to your word;
lert and liv-ing in your Spi - rit, strong and free.

Christ, your cross and pas - sion shar-ing, by this Eu-cha-
by your Blood new life re-ceiv-ing, in your Bo - dy,
Part - ners in your new cre - a - tion, seek-ing peace in

rist de - clar - ing yours the fi - nal vic - to - ry.
firm be - liev - ing, we are yours, and you the Lord.
ev - ery na - tion, may we faith - ful fol - lowers be.

Words: Howard Charles Adie Gaunt (b. 1902), alt.
Music: *Alles ist an Gottes Segen*, melody att. Johann Balthasar König (1691-1758), alt.;
   harm. Johann Löhner (1645-1705), after chorale ver. Johann Sebastian Bach (1685-1750)

887. 887

# 335

Words: © 1970, 1975, Celebration.

up,      and   I   will    raise      them     up      on      the

up,      and   I   will    raise      them     up      on      the

1-4                  Final Ending

last          day. _____      5 Yes,     day.

last          day. _____      2 The
                                            3 Un-    day.
                                            4 __
                                            5 Yes,

*The descant may be sung after stanzas 4 and 5.*

Words: Suzanne Toolan (b. 1927); adapt. of John 6
Music: *I Am the Bread of Life,* Suzanne Toolan (b. 1927); arr. Betty Pulkingham (b. 1928)        Irr. with Refrain

# 336

Holy Eucharist

1 Come with us, O blessed Jesus, with us ever-
*2 Come with us, O mighty Savior, God from God, and
*3 Come with us, O King of glory, by angelic

more to be; and though leaving now thine
Light from Light; thou art God, thy glory
voices praised; in our hearts as in thy

altar, let us nevermore leave thee.
veiling, so that we may bear the sight.
heaven, be enraptured anthems raised.

Be thou one with us for ever, in our life thy
Now we go to seek and serve thee, through our work as
Let the mighty chorus ever sing its glad ex-

love di - vine our own flesh and blood has
through our prayer; grant us light to see and
ul - tant songs; let its hymn be heard for

tak - en, and to us thou giv - est thine.
know thee, in thy peo - ple ev - ery - where.
ev - er— peace for which cre - a - - - tion longs.

Words: John Henry Hopkins, Jr. (1820-1891) and Charles P. Price (b. 1920)
Music: *Werde munter,* Johann Schop (d. 1665?); arr. and harm.
      Johann Sebastian Bach (1685-1750)

87. 87. 76. 86

1 And now, O Father, mind - ful of the love that
2 Look Fa - ther, look on his a - noint - ed face, and
*3 And then for those, our dear - est and our best, by
*4 And so we come; O draw us to thy feet, most

bought us, once for all, on Cal - vary's tree, and hav - ing with us
on - ly look on us as found in him; look not on our mis -
this pre - vail - ing pres-ence we ap - peal; O fold them clos - er
pa - tient Sa - vior, who canst love us still! And by this food, so

him that pleads a - bove, we here pre - sent, we here spread
us - ings of thy grace, our prayer so lan - guid, and our
to thy mer - cy's breast! O do thine ut - most for their
awe - some and so sweet, de - liv - er us from ev - ery

forth to thee, that on - ly of - fering per - fect in thine
faith so dim: for lo! be - tween our sins and their re -
soul's true weal! From taint - ing mis - chief keep them pure and
touch of ill: in thine own ser - vice make us glad and

eyes, the one true, pure, im - mor - tal sac - ri - fice.
ward, we set the pas - sion of thy Son our Lord.
clear, and crown thy gifts with strength to per - se - vere.
free, and grant us nev - er - more to part from thee.

Words: William Bright (1824-1901), alt.
Music: *Unde et memores*, William Henry Monk (1823-1889)

10 10. 10 10. 10 10

## Holy Eucharist

### 338

*Unison or harmony*

1 Where-fore, O Fa - ther, we thy hum-ble ser - vants here bring be -
2 See now thy chil - dren, ma-king in - ter - ces - sion through him our

fore thee Christ thy well - be - lov - ed, All - per - fect Of - fering,
Sa - vior, Son of God in - car - nate, for all thy peo - ple,

sac - ri - fice im - mor - tal, spot - less ob - la - tion.
liv - ing and de - part - ed, plead - ing be - fore thee.

Words: William Henry Hammond Jervois (1852-1905)
Music: *Lobet den Herren*, melody Johann Cruger (1598-1662); harm. Friedrich Layriz (1808-1859)

11 11. 11 5

1 Deck thy- self, my soul, with glad - ness, leave the gloom-y haunts of sad - ness, come in - to the day-light's splen - dor, there with joy thy prais - es ren - der un - to him whose grace un - bound - ed hath this

2 Sun, who all my life dost bright - en; Light, who dost my soul en - light - en; Joy, the best that an - y know - eth; Fount, whence all my be - ing flow - eth: at thy feet I cry, my Ma - ker, let me

3 Je - sus, Bread of life, I pray thee, let me glad - ly here o - bey thee; nev - er to my hurt in - vit - ed, be thy love with love re - quit - ed; from this ban - quet let me mea - sure, Lord, how

won-drous ban-quet found - ed;   high o'er   all the heavens he
be   a   fit par - ta - ker   of this   bless-ed food from
vast and deep its trea - sure;   through the   gifts thou here dost

reign - eth,   yet   to   dwell with thee he   deign - eth.
hea - ven,   for   our   good, thy glo - ry,   giv - en.
give   me,   as   thy   guest in heaven re - ceive   me.

Words: Johann Franck (1618-1677); tr. Catherine Winkworth (1827-1878), alt.
Music: *Schmücke dich,* melody Johann Cruger (1598-1662); harm. *The English Hymnal,* 1906

LMD

1 For the bread which you have bro - ken, for the
2 By this pledge, Lord, that you love us, by your
3 As our bless - ed ones a - dore you, seat - ed
4 In your ser - vice, Lord, de - fend us; in our

wine which you have poured, for the words which you have
gift of peace re - stored, by your call to heaven a -
at our Fa - ther's board, may the Church still wait - ing
hearts keep watch and ward, in the world to which you

spo - ken, now we give you thanks, O Lord.
bove us, hal - low all our lives, O Lord.
for you keep love's tie un - bro - ken, Lord.
send us let your king - dom come, O Lord.

Words: Louis F. Benson (1855-1930), alt.
Music: *Beng-Li*, I-to Loh (b. 1936)

87. 87

1 For the bread which you have bro - ken, for the
2 By this pledge, Lord, that you love us, by your
3 As our bless - ed ones a - dore you, seat - ed
4 In your ser - vice, Lord, de - fend us; in our

wine which you have poured, for the words which you have
gift of peace re - stored, by your call to heaven a -
at our Fa - ther's board, may the Church still wait - ing
hearts keep watch and ward, in the world to which you

spo - ken, now we give you thanks, O Lord.
bove us, hal - low all our lives, O Lord.
for you keep love's tie un - bro - ken, Lord.
send us let your king - dom come, O Lord.

Words: Louis F. Benson (1855-1930), alt.
Music: *Omni die*, melody from *Gross Catolisch Gesangbuch*, 1631;
harm. William Smith Rockstro (1823-1895)

87. 87

## Holy Eucharist

342

1 O Bread of life, for sin - ners bro - ken,
2 For all we seek your grace sus - tain - ing;
3 Now may your life to us de - scend - ing

of God's own love his dear - est tok - en,
your love shines though your strength is wan - ing,
en - ter our lives, all veils thus rend - ing,

we hear the words so gen - tly spo - ken,
thus by your death our life ob - tain - ing.
Em - man - u - el, our joy un - end - ing.

"Do this for me in my re - mem - brance."
"Come un - to me, you hea - vy la - den."
"I am with you, this day and ev - er."

Words: Timothy T'ing Fang Lew (1892-1947); tr. Frank W. Price (1895-1974), alt.
Music: *Sheng En*, melody Su Yin-Lan (20th cent.)

99. 99

1 Shep-herd of souls, re-fresh and bless thy cho-sen
2 We would not live by bread a - lone, but by thy
3 Be known to us in break - ing bread, and do not
4 Lord, sup with us in love di - vine, thy Bo-dy

pil - grim flock with man - na in the
word of grace, in strength of which we
then de - part; Sa - vior, a - bide with
and thy Blood, that liv - ing bread, that

wil - der - ness, with wa - ter from the rock.
trav - el on to our a - bid - ing - place.
us, and spread thy ta - ble in our heart.
heaven - ly wine, be our im - mor - tal food.

Words: James Montgomery (1771-1854), alt.
Music: *St. Agnes*, melody John Bacchus Dykes (1823-1876); harm. Richard Proulx (b. 1937),
    after John Bacchus Dykes (1823-1876)

                                                                        CM

1 Lord, dis - miss us with thy bless - ing; fill our hearts with
2 Thanks we give and a - dor - a - tion for thy Gos - pel's
3 so that when thy love shall call us, Sa - vior, from the

joy and peace; let us each, thy love pos - sess - ing,
joy - ful sound: may the fruits of thy sal - va - tion
world a - way, fear of death shall not ap - pall us,

tri - umph in re - deem - ing grace: O re - fresh us,
in our hearts and lives a - bound: ev - er faith - ful,
glad thy sum - mons to o - bey. May we ev - er,

O re - fresh us, trav - eling through this wil - der - ness.
ev - er faith - ful to thy truth may we be found;
may we ev - er reign with thee in end - less day.

Words: Att. John Fawcett (1739/40-1817)
Music: *Sicilian Mariners*, Sicilian melody; first published
   *The European Magazine and London Review*, 1792, alt.

87. 87. 87

1 Sa - vior, a - gain to thy dear Name we raise
with one ac - cord our part - ing hymn of praise;
guard thou the lips from sin, the hearts from shame,
that in this house have called up - on thy Name.

*2 Grant us thy peace up - on our home-ward way;
with thee be - gan, with thee shall end the day:
from harm and dan - ger keep thy chil - dren free,
for dark and light are both a - like to thee.

3 Grant us thy peace through - out our earth - ly life;
peace to thy Church from er - ror and from strife;
peace to our land, the fruit of truth and love;
peace in each heart, thy Spi - rit from a - bove:

4 thy peace in life, the balm of ev - ery pain;
thy peace in death, the hope to rise a - gain;
then, when thy voice shall bid our con - flict cease,
call us, O Lord, to thine e - ter - nal peace.

Words: John Ellerton (1826-1893), alt.
Music: *Ellers*, Edward John Hopkins (1818-1901)

10 10. 10 10

# Holy Eucharist

1 Com - plet - ed, Lord, the Ho - ly Mys - ter - ies,
2 Here we have tast - ed in - fi - nite de - lights,
3 Through God's good grace these Mys - ter - ies are ours,

as far as lies with - in our mor - tal power!
be - held a - far that life which soon shall be;
or - dained by thee, the ev - er - last - ing Son;

Thy death re - mem - bered, feed - ing thus on thee,
oh, count us wor - thy, Christ, thy joys to share
blest by the Spi - rit, breath and flame of life,

we here have know the re - sur - rec - tion hour.
for ev - er in e - ter - ni - ty with thee.
to whom be praise while end - less a - ges run.

Words: Liturgy of St. Basil; tr. Cyril E. Pocknee (1906-1980)
Music: *Song 4*, Orlando Gibbons (1583-1625), alt.

10 10. 10 10

## 347

1 Go forth for God; go_____ to the world in peace;
2 Go forth for God; go_____ to the world in love;
3 Go forth for God; go_____ to the world in strength;
4 Go forth for God; go_____ to the world in joy;

be of good cour - age, armed with heaven - ly grace,
strength - en the faint, give cour - age to the weak;
hold fast the good, be ur - gent for the right;
to serve God's peo - ple ev - er - y day and hour,

in God's good Spi - rit dai - - - ly to in - crease,
help the af - flict - ed; rich - - ly from a - bove
ren - der to no one e - - vil; Christ at length
and serv - ing Christ, our ev - - ery gift em - ploy,

till in his king - dom we_____ be - hold his face.
his love sup - plies the grace_____ and power we seek.
shall o - ver - come all dark - ness with his light.
re - joic - ing in the Ho - ly Spi - rit's power.

Words: John Raphael Peacey (1896-1971) and *English Praise*, 1975, alt.
Music: *Litton*, Erik Routley (1917-1982)     10 10. 10 10
Words: Copyright © 1985 by Hope Publishing Company. All Rights Reserved. Used by Permission.

# Confirmation

348

1 Lord, we have come at your own in - vi - ta - tion,
2 Here, at your ta - ble, con - firm our in - ten - tion
3 When, at your ta - ble, each time of re - turn - ing,
4 So, in the world where each du - ty as - signed us

cho - sen by you, to be coun - ted as friends:
ev - er to cher - ish the gifts you pro - vide;
vows are re - newed, and our cour - age re - stored:
gives us the chance to cre - ate or des - troy,

yours is the strength that sus - tains our vo - ca - tion,
teach us to serve with - out pride or pre - ten - sion,
may we in - creas - ing - ly glo - ry in learn - ing
help us to make those de - ci - sions that bind us,

ours a com - mit - ment we know nev - er ends.
led by your Spi - rit, de - fend - er and guide.
all that it means to ac - cept you as Lord.
Lord, to your - self, in o - be - dience and joy.

Words: F. Pratt Green (b. 1903), rev.
Music: *O quanta qualia*, melody from *Antiphoner*, 1681

10 10. 10 10

1 Ho - ly  Spi - rit,  Lord  of  love,  who de - scend -ed
2 When the  sa - cred  vow  is  made,  when the hands are

from  a - bove,  gifts  of  bless - ing  to  be - stow
on  them laid,  come  in  this  most  sol - emn  hour

on  your  wait - ing  Church be - low,  once a - gain  in
with  your strength-en-ing  gift  of  power.  Give them light,  your

love  draw  near  to  your ser -vants  gath - ered here;  from their
truth  to  see;  give them life, your  own  to  be;  dai - ly

bright bap - tis - mal day you have led them on their way.
power to con-quer sin; pa - tient faith, the crown to win.

Words: William Dalrymple Maclagen (1826-1910), alt.
Music: *Aberystwyth*, Joseph Parry (1841-1903)

77. 77. D

## Marriage                                                350

1 O God of love, _____ to thee we bow, _____
2 What-ev - er comes _____ to be their share _____
3 E - ter - nal love, _____ with them a - bide; _____

____ and pray for these be-fore thee now, that close-ly knit in
____ of quick-ening joy or bur-dening care, in power to do and
____ through change and chance be thou their guide, let noth-ing in this

ho - ly vow, they may in thee be one.
grace to bear, may they in thee be one.
life di - vide those whom thou mak - est one.

Words: William Vaughan Jenkins (1868-1920), alt.
Music: *St. Mary Magdalene*, Gerre Hancock (b. 1934)

888. 6

1 May the grace of Christ our Sa - vior, and the
2 Thus may they a - bide in un - ion with each

Fa - ther's bound - less love, with the Ho - ly
o - ther and the Lord, and pos - sess, in

Spi - rit's fa - vor, rest up - on them from a - bove.
sweet com - mun - ion, joys which earth can - not af - ford.

Words: John Newton (1725-1807), alt.
Music: *Halton Holgate*, William Boyce (1711-1779)

87. 87

1 O God, to those who here pro - fess their vows of life - long love,
2 Christ, grant that nei - ther grief nor place nor life nor death may part
3 Spi - rit of God, whom we a - dore: pre - serve, pro - tect, de - fend,

grant joy and peace; their mar-riage bless with glad-ness from a - bove.
those who, en - joy - ing your sweet grace, in you are one in heart.
in - crease, re - kin - dle, and re - store their love till life shall end.

Words: Sts. 1 and 3, Charles P. Price (b. 1920); st. 2, Charles Wesley (1707-1788), alt.
Music: *Caithness,* melody from *The Psalmes of David in Prose and Meeter,* 1635;
　　harm. *The English Hymnal,* 1906

CM

## Marriage

# 353

1 Your love, O God, has called us here, for all love
2 O gra - cious God, you con - se - crate all that is
3 O God of love, in - spire our life, re - veal your

finds its source in you, the per - fect love that
love - ly, good, and true. Bless those who in your
will in all we do; join ev - ery hus - band,

casts out fear, the love that Christ makes ev - er new.
pres - ence wait and ev - ery day their love re - new.
ev - ery wife in mu - tual love and love for you.

Words: Russell Schulz-Widmar (b. 1944)
Music: *Wareham,* melody William Knapp (1698-1768); harm. *Hymns Ancient and Modern,* 1875,
　　after James Turle (1802-1882)

LM

1. In - to par - a - dise may the an - gels lead you.

At your com - ing may the mar-tyrs re - ceive you,

and bring you in - to the ho - ly ci - ty Je - ru - sa - lem.

2. May the choirs of an - gels wel - come you,

and with Laz - a - rus who once was poor

may you have peace ev - er - last - ing.

Words: Latin; tr. *The Book of Common Prayer*, 1979, and Theodore Marier (b. 1912)
Music: *In paradisum*, plainsong, Mode 7 and Mode 8; *Graduale Romanum*, 1974

Irr.

Give rest, O Christ, to your ser-vant(s) with your

saints, where sor - row and pain are no more, nei - ther

*Fine*

sigh - ing, but life ev - er - last - ing.

You on - ly are im - mor - tal, the cre - a - tor

and ma - ker of man - kind; and we are mor - tal,

Al - le - lu - ia, al - le - lu - ia, al - le - lu - ia.

Words: Eastern Orthodox Memorial Service; tr. *The Book of Common Prayer*, 1979
Music: *Kontakion [Kievan chant]*, from Eastern Orthodox Memorial Service; ed. Walter Parratt (1841-1924), alt.     Irr.

## Burial                                                            356

1 May choirs of an - gels lead you to Par - a - dise on high,
2 And at your com-ing thith - er may you be brought by them
3 As an - gels gave poor Laz - arus from all his ills re - lease,

where dwell the white-robed mar - tyrs who now no more can die.
in - to the ho - ly ci - ty, God's true Je - ru - sa - lem.
so may they give you wel - come to ev - er - last - ing peace.

Words: Latin; tr. F. Bland Tucker (1895-1984)
Music: *Christus, der ist mein Leben*, melody Melchior Vulpius (1560?-1616);
    harm. after Melchior Vulpius (1560?-1616)                      76. 76

# 357

Burial

1 Je - sus, Son of Ma - ry, fount of life a - lone,
2 Think, O Lord, in mer - cy on the souls of those
3 Of - ten were they wound - ed in the dead - ly strife;
4 Rest e - ter - nal grant them, af - ter wea - ry fight;

now we hail thee pres - ent on thine al - tar throne.
who, in faith gone from us, now in death re - pose.
heal them, Good Phy - si - cian, with the balm of life.
shed on them the ra - diance of thy heaven - ly light.

Hum - bly we a - dore thee, Lord of end - less might,
Here mid stress and con - flict toils can nev - er cease;
Ev - ery taint of e - vil, frail - ty and de - cay,
Lead them on - ward, up - ward, to the ho - ly place,

in the mys - tic sym - bols veiled from earth - ly sight.
there, the war - fare end - ed, bid them rest in peace.
good and gra - cious Sa - vior, cleanse and purge a - way.
where thy saints made per - fect gaze up - on thy face.

Words: Edmund Stuart Palmer (1856-1931)
Music: *Adoro devote*, French church melody, Mode 5, *Processionale*, 1697

11 11. 11 11

# Burial

**358**

1 Christ the Vic - to - ri - ous, give to your ser - vants
2 On - ly Im - mor - tal One, Might - y Cre - a - tor!
3 God - spo - ken pro - phe - cy, word at cre - a - tion:
4 Christ the Vic - to - ri - ous, give to your ser - vants

rest with your saints in the re - gions of light.
We are your crea - tures and chil - dren of earth.
"You came from dust and to dust shall re - turn."
rest with your saints in the re - gions of light.

Grief and pain end - ed, and sigh - ing no long - er,
From earth you formed us, both glo - rious and mor - tal,
Yet at the grave shall we raise up our glad song,
Grief and pain end - ed, and sigh - ing no long - er,

there may they find ev - er - last - ing life.
and to the earth shall we all re - turn.
"Al - le - lu - ia, al - le - lu - ia!"
there may they find ev - er - last - ing life.

Words: Carl P. Daw, Jr. (b. 1944)
Music: *Russia*, Alexis Lvov (1799-1870)

11 10. 11 9

1 God of the pro - phets, bless the pro - phets' heirs! E - li - jah's
2 A - noint them pro - phets! Teach them thine in - tent: to hu - man
3 A - noint them priests! help them to in - ter - cede with all thy
*4 A - noint them kings! Yea, king - ly kings, O Lord! A - noint them
5 Make them a - pos - tles, her - alds of thy cross; forth may they

1 man - tle o'er E - li - sha cast: each age for thine own sol - emn
2 need their quick-ened hearts a - wake; fill them with power, their lips make
3 roy - al priest-hood born of grace; through them thy Church pre - sents in
4 with the Spi - rit of thy Son: theirs not a mon - arch's crown or
5 go to tell all realms thy grace: in - spired of thee, may they count

1 task pre - pares, make each one strong - er, no - bler than the last.
2 el - o - quent for right-eous - ness that shall all e - vil break.
3 word and deed Christ's one true sac - ri - fice with thank - ful praise.
4 ty - rant's sword; theirs by the love of Christ a king - dom won.
5 all but loss, and stand at last with joy be - fore thy face.

Words: St. 1-2 and 4-5, Denis Wortman (1835-1922), alt.; st. 3, Carl P. Daw, Jr. (b. 1944)
Music: *Toulon*, melody from *Pseaumes octante trois de David*, 1551, abridged;
   harm. Charles Winfred Douglas (1867-1944)

10 10. 10 10

1 On - ly - be - got - ten, Word of God e -
2 This is thy tem - ple; here thy pres - ence -
3 Here in our sick - ness heal - ing grace a -
*4 Hal - lowed this dwell - ing where the Lord a -
5 Lord, we be - seech thee, as we throng thy
6 God in three Per - sons, Fa - ther ev - er -

1 ter - nal, Lord of cre - a - tion, mer - ci - ful and
2 cham - ber; here may thy ser - vants, at the mys - tic
3 bound - eth, light in our blind - ness, in our toil re -
4 bid - eth, this is none o - ther than the gate of
5 tem - ple, by thy past bless - ings, by thy pres - ent
6 last - ing, Son co - e - ter - nal, ev - er-bless - ed

1 might - y, hear now thy ser - vants when their joy - ful
2 ban - quet, hum - bly a - dor - ing, take thy Bo - dy
3 fresh - ment: sin is for - giv - en, hope o'er fear pre -
4 hea - ven; strang - ers and pil - grims, seek - ing homes e -
5 boun - ty, fa - vor thy chil - dren, and with ten - der
6 Spi - rit, thine be the glo - ry, praise, and a - dor -

1 voic - es rise to thy pres - ence.
2 bro - ken, drink of thy chal - ice.
3 vail - eth, joy o - ver sor - row.
4 ter - nal, pass through its por - tals.
5 mer - cy, hear our pe - ti - tions.
6 a - tion, now and for ev - er.

Words: Latin, ca. 9th cent.; tr. Maxwell Julius Blacker (1822-1888)
Music: *Rouen*, melody from *Vesperale*, 1746

11 11. 11 5

1 On - ly - be - got - ten, Word of God e - ter - nal,
2 This is thy tem - ple; here thy pres - ence - cham - ber;
3 Here in our sick - ness heal - ing grace a - bound - eth,
*4 Hal - lowed this dwell - ing where the Lord a - bid - eth,
5 Lord, we be - seech thee, as we throng thy tem - ple,
6 God in three Per - sons, Fa - ther ev - er - last - ing,

1 Lord of cre - a - tion, mer - ci - ful and might - y,
2 here may thy ser - vants, at the mys - tic ban - quet,
3 light in our blind - ness, in our toil re - fresh - ment:
4 this is none o - ther than the gate of hea - ven;
5 by thy past bless - ings, by thy pres - ent boun - ty,
6 Son co - e - ter - nal, ev - er - bless - ed Spi - rit,

1 hear now thy ser - vants when their joy - ful voic - es
2 hum - bly a - dor - ing, take thy Bo - dy bro - ken,
3 sin is for - giv - en, hope o'er fear pre - vail - eth,
4 strang - ers and pil - grims, seek - ing homes e - ter - nal,
5 fa - vor thy chil - dren, and with ten - der mer - cy
6 thine be the glo - ry, praise, and a - dor - a - tion,

1 rise to thy pres - ence.
2 drink of thy chal - ice.
3 joy o - ver sor - row.
4 pass through its por - tals.
5 hear our pe - ti - tions.
6 now and for ev - er.

Words: Latin, ca. 9th cent.; tr. Maxwell Julius Blacker (1822-1888)
Music: *Caelitum Joseph*, plainsong, Mode 1, Worcester MS., 13th cent.; ver. Schola Antiqua, 1983     11 11. 11 5
Music: Melody rhythmic version © 1984, Schola Antiqua Inc. Used by Permission.

1 Ho - ly, ho - ly ho - ly! Lord___ God Al - might - y!
*2 Ho - ly, ho - ly, ho - ly! All the saints a - dore thee,
3 Ho - ly, ho - ly, ho - ly! Though the dark-ness hide thee,
4 Ho - ly, ho - ly, ho - ly! Lord___ God Al - might - y!

Ear - ly in the morn - ing our song shall rise to thee:
cast - ing down their gold-en crowns a - round the glass - y sea;
though the sin - ful hu - man eye thy glo - ry may not see,
All thy works shall praise thy Name, in earth, and sky, and sea;

Ho - ly, ho - ly, ho - ly! Mer - ci - ful and might - y,
cher - u - bim and ser - a - phim fall - ing down be - fore thee,
on - ly thou art ho - ly; there is none be - side thee,
Ho - ly, ho - ly, ho - ly! Mer - ci - ful and might - y,

God in three Per - sons, bless - ed Trin - i - ty.
which wert, and art, and ev - er - more shalt be.
per - fect in power, in love, and pu - ri - ty.
God in three Per - sons, bless - ed Trin - i - ty.

Words: Reginald Heber (1783-1826), alt.
Music: *Nicaea,* John Bacchus Dykes (1823-1876)

11 12. 12 10

1 An - cient of Days, who sit - test throned in glo - ry,
2 O ho - ly Fa - ther, who hast led thy chil - dren
5 O Tri - une God, with heart and voice a - dor - ing,

to thee all knees are bent, all voic - es pray;
in all the a - ges with the fire and cloud,
praise we the good - ness that doth crown our days;

thy love has blessed the wide world's won - drous sto - ry
through seas dry - shod, through wea - ry wastes be - wil - dering
pray we that thou wilt hear us, still im - plor - ing

with light and life since E - den's dawn - ing day.
to thee in rev - erent love our hearts are bowed.
thy love and fa - vor, kept to us al - ways.

3 O ho - ly Je - sus, Lord of our sal - va - tion,
4 O Ho - ly Ghost, the Lord and the Life - giv - er,

ped.

call - ing the least, the last, the lost to thee,
thine is the quick - ening power that gives in - crease:

sum - mon - ing all to share thy new cre - a - tion,
from thee have flowed, as from a might - y riv - er,

thou, Lord, by death hast won life's vic - to - ry.
our faith and hope, our fel - low-ship and peace.

Words: William Croswell Doane (1832-1913), alt.
Music: *Coburn*, Alec Wyton (b. 1921)

11 10. 11 10

1 O God, we praise thee, and con - fess that thou the on - ly Lord
2 To thee all an - gels cry a - loud; to thee the powers on high,
3 O ho - ly, ho - ly, ho - ly Lord, whom heaven-ly hosts o - bey,
4 The apos-tles' glo - rious com - pa - ny, and pro - phets crowned with light,
5 The ho - ly Church in faith ac - claims thy Son who for us died,

1 and ev - er - last - ing Fa - ther art, by all the earth a - dored.
2 both cher - u - bim and ser - a - phim, con - tin - ual - ly do cry:
3 the world is with the glo - ry filled of thy ma - jes - tic sway!
4 with all the mar - tyrs' no - ble host, thy con-stant praise re - cite.
5 al - so the Ho - ly Com - fort - er, our ad - vo - cate and guide.

*6 Thou art the King of glory, Christ,
    the everlasting Son;
humbly thou cam'st to set us free,
    nor Virgin womb didst shun.

*7 When thou hadst overcome death's sting
    and opened heaven's door,
thou didst ascend to God's right hand
    in glory evermore.

*8 When thou shalt come to be our judge,
    bring us whom thou hast bought
to dwell on high with all thy saints
    in joy surpassing thought.

*The G♯ may be reserved for the final stanza.*

Words: Para. of *Te Deum;* sts. 1-5, *A Supplement to the New Version of the Psalms of David,* 1698, alt.;
    sts. 6-8, ver. *Hymnal 1982*
Music: *Manchester,* melody and bass Thomas Ravenscroft (1592?-1635?); harm. *Hymnal 1982*

CM

# The Holy Trinity

1 Come, thou al-might-y King, help us thy Name to sing, help us to praise. Fa-ther whose love un-known all things cre-at-ed own, build in our hearts thy throne, An-cient of Days.

2 Come, thou in-car-nate Word, by heaven and earth a-dored; our prayer at-tend: come, and thy peo-ple bless; come, give thy word suc-cess; stab-lish thy right-eous-ness, Sa-vior and friend.

3 Come, ho-ly Com-fort-er, thy sa-cred wit-ness bear in this glad hour: thou, who al-might-y art, now rule in ev-ery heart, and ne'er from us de-part, Spi-rit of power.

4 To Thee, great One in Three, the high-est prais-es be, hence ev-er-more; thy sov-ereign ma-jes-ty may we in glo-ry see, and to e-ter-ni-ty love and a-dore.

Words: Anon., ca. 1757, alt.
Music: *Moscow* Felice de Giardini (1716-1796); harm. *The New Hymnal*, 1916, based on *Hymns Ancient and Modern*, 1875, and Lowell Mason (1792-1872)

664. 6664

1 Ho - ly God we praise thy Name, Lord of all, we bow be - fore thee;
2 Hark, the loud ce - les - tial hymn an - gel choirs a - bove are rais-ing;
3 Lo, the a - po - sto - lic train join, thy sa - cred Name to hal-low;
4 Ho - ly Fa - ther, ho - ly Son, Ho - ly Spi - rit, Three we name thee,
*5 Christ, thou art our glor-ious King, Son of God en-throned in splen-dor;

all on earth thy scep - ter claim, all in heaven a - bove a - dore thee;
cher - u - bim and ser - a - phim, in un - ceas - ing cho-rus prais-ing,
pro - phets swell the loud re - frain, and the white robed mar-tyrs fol - low;
while in es - sence on - ly One, un - di - vid - ed God we claim thee;
but de - liv - er - ence to bring thou all hon - ors didst sur - ren - der,

in - fi - nite thy vast do - main, ev - er - last - ing is thy reign.
fill the heavens with sweet ac - cord: ho - ly, ho - ly, ho - ly Lord!
and, from morn till set of sun, through the Church the song goes on.
then, a - dor - ing, bend the knee and con - fess the mys - ter - y.
and wast of a vir - gin born hum - bly on that bless - ed morn.

*6 Thou didst take the sting from death,
    Son of God, as Savior given;
on the cross thy dying breath
    opened wide the realm of heaven.
In the glory of that land
thou art set at God's right hand.

*7 As our judge thou wilt appear.
    Savior, who hast died to win us.
help thy servants, drawing near.
    Lord, renew our hearts within us.
Grant that with thy saints we may
dwell in everlasting day.

Words: Para. of *Te Deum*, Sts. 1-4, Ignaz Franz (1719-1790); tr. Clarence Walworth (1820-1900).
    Sts. 5-7, F. Bland Tucker (1895-1984)
Music: *Grosser Gott* melody from *Katholisches Gesangbuch*, 1686; alt. *Cantate*, 1851;
    harm. Charles Winfred Douglas (1867-1944), after Conrad Kocher (1786-1872)
                                         78. 78. 77

1 Round the Lord in glo - ry seat-ed cher - u - bim and ser - a - phim
2 Heaven is still with glo - ry ring-ing, earth takes up the an - gels' cry,
3 "Lord, thy glo - ry fills the hea-ven, earth is with thy full - ness stored;

filled his tem-ple, and re - peat-ed each to each the al-ter - nate hymn:
"Ho - ly, ho - ly, ho - ly," sing-ing, "Lord of hosts, the Lord Most High."
un - to thee be glo - ry giv - en, ho - ly, ho - ly, ho - ly, Lord."

"Lord, thy glo - ry fills the hea-ven, earth is with thy full - ness stored;
With his ser - aph train be - fore him, with his ho - ly Church be - low,
Thus thy glo - rious Name con - fess-ing, with thine an - gel hosts we cry

un - to thee be glo - ry giv - en, ho - ly, ho - ly, ho - ly Lord."
thus u - nite we to a - dore him, bid we thus our an - them flow:
"Ho - ly, ho - ly, ho - ly," bless-ing thee, the Lord of hosts Most High.

Words: Richard Mant (1776-1848)
Music: *Rustington*, Charles Hubert Hastings Parry (1848-1918)

87. 87. D

great Je - ho-vah, form our hearts _____ and make them thine.

heaven - ly Fa - ther, through the Sa - vior hear and bless.
dear Re-deem - er, in our hearts thy peace pro - claim.
Source of com - fort, cheer us with the Sa - vior's love.
Great Je - ho - vah, form our hearts and make them thine.

Words: Alexander Viets Griswold (1766-1843), alt.
Music: *Regent Square*, Henry Thomas Smart (1813-1879); desc. Craig Sellar Lang (1891-1971)

87. 87. 87

## The Holy Trinity

# 369

1 How won-drous great, how glo - rious bright must our Cre - a - tor be,
2 Our soar-ing spi - rits up - ward rise to reach the burn-ing throne
3 Our rea - son stretch-es all its wings, and climbs a - bove the skies;
4 While all the heaven-ly powers con - spire e - ter - nal praise to sing,

who dwells a - midst the daz - zling light of vast e - ter - ni - ty.
and long to see the bless - ed Three in the Al - might - y One.
but still how far be-neath thy feet our ground-ling know-ledge lies!
let faith in hum-ble notes a - dore the great mys - te - rious King.

Words: Isaac Watts (1674-1748), alt; st. 3, alt. Caryl Micklem (b. 1925)
Music: *Shorney*, Alec Wyton (b. 1921)

CM

1. I bind un-to my-self to-day the strong Name
of the Trin-i-ty, by in-vo-ca-tion
of the same, the Three in One, and One in Three.

2. I bind this day to me for ev-er, by power of
* 3. I bind un-to my-self the power_ of the great
* 4. I bind un-to my-self to-day___ the vir-tues
* 5. I bind un-to my-self to-day___ the power of

faith, Christ's In-car-na-tion; his bap-tism in the
love of cher-u-bim;___ the sweet "Well done" in
of the star-lit heaven_ the glo-rious sun's life-
God to hold and lead,___ his eye to watch, his

Jor-dan riv-er; his death on cross for my sal-va-tion;
judg-ment hour;_ the ser-vice of the ser-a-phim;___
giv-ing ray,___ the white-ness of the moon at even,___
might to stay,___ his ear to heark-en, to my need;___

his burst-ing from the spic-èd tomb; his rid-ing
con-fess-ors' faith, a-pos-tles' word, the pa-triarchs'
the flash-ing of the light-ning free, the whirl-ing
the wis-dom of my God to teach, his hand to

up      the   heaven - ly   way;   his   com  -  ing   at    the
prayers, the    pro - phet's scrolls; all   good   deeds  done  un -
wind's  tem - pes - tuous  shocks, the   sta  -  ble   earth,  the
guide,   his   shield  to   ward;  the   word   of    God    to

day   of    doom:   I    bind  un - to   my - self   to - day.
to   the   Lord,   and   pu - ri - ty   of   vir - gin  souls.
deep salt  sea,    a - round the  old   e - ter - nal  rocks.
give  me   speech,  his  heaven - ly  host   to   be   my  guard

* 6. Christ  be   with    me,  Christ with - in   me,  Christ be - hind  me,
   Christ be - neath   me,  Christ  a - bove  me,  Christ in  qui - et,

Christ  be - fore    me,   Christ  be - side   me,  Christ  to
Christ  in   dan  -  ger,  Christ  in   hearts  of   all    that

win   me,  Christ  to   com - fort   and   re - store   me,
love  me,  Christ  in   mouth  of    friend and  stran  -  ger.

7. I bind un - to my - self the Name, the strong Name
of the Trin - i - ty, by in - vo - ca - tion
of the same, the Three in One, and One in Three.
Of whom all na - ture hath cre - a - tion, e - ter - nal
Fa - ther, Spi - rit, Word: praise to the Lord of
my sal - va - tion, sal - va - tion is of Christ the Lord.

Words: Att. Patrick (372-466); tr. Cecil Frances Alexander (1818-1895)
Music: *St. Patrick's Breastplate*, Irish melody; adapt. Charles Villiers Stanford (1852-1924).

LMD

1 Thou, whose al - might - y word / cha - os and dark - ness heard, / and took their flight; / hear us, we / hum - bly pray, / and, where the / Gos - pel day / sheds not its / glo - rious ray, / let there be / light!

2 Thou who didst come to bring / on thy re - deem - ing wing / heal - ing and sight, / heal to the / sick in mind, / sight to the / in - ly blind, / now to all / hu - man-kind, / let there be / light!

3 Spi - rit of truth and love, / life - giv - ing, ho - ly Dove, / speed forth thy flight! / Move on the / wa - ters' face / bear - ing the / gifts of grace, / and, in earth's dark - est place, / let there be / light!

4 Ho - ly and bless - ed Three, / glo - ri - ous Trin - i - ty, / wis - dom, love, might; / bound-less as / o - cean's tide, / roll - ing in / full - est pride, through the world far and wide, / let there be / light!

Words: John Marriott (1780-1825), alt.
Music: *Moscow*, Felice de Giardini (1716-1796); harm. *The New Hymnal*, 1916,
  based on *Hymns Ancient and Modern*, 1875, and Lowell Mason (1792-1872)

664. 6664

1 Praise to the liv - ing God! All prais - ed be his Name
2 Form - less, all love - ly forms de - clare his love - li - ness;
3 His Spr - rit flow - eth free, high surg - ing where it will:
4 E - ter - nal life hath he im - plant - ed in the soul;

who was, and is, and is to be, for ay the same.
ho - ly, no ho - li - ness of earth can his ex - press.
in pro-phet's word he spoke of old; he speak - eth still.
his love shall be our strength and stay while a - ges roll.

The one e - ter - nal God ere aught that now ap - pears:
Lo, he is Lord of all. Cre - a - tion speaks his praise,
Es - tab-lished is his law, and change-less it shall stand,
Praise to the liv - ing God! All prais - ed be his Name

the first, the last, be - yond all thought his time - less years!
and ev - ery-where a - bove, be - low, his will o - beys.
deep writ up - on the hu - man heart, on sea, on land.
who was, and is, and is to be, for ay the same.

Words: Medieval Jewish liturgy; tr. Max Landsberg (1845-1928) and Newton M. Mann (1836-1926)
Music: *Leoni*, Hebrew melody; harm. *Hymns Ancient and Modern*, 1875, alt.

66. 84. D

# Praise to God     373

1 Praise the Lord! ye heavens a - dore him; praise him an - gels in the height;
2 Praise the Lord! for he is glo - rious; nev - er shall his prom - ise fail;

sun and moon, re - joice be - fore him; praise him, all ye stars of light.
God hath made his saints vic - to - rious; sin and death shall not pre - vail.

Praise the Lord! for he hath spo - ken; worlds his might - y voice o - beyed;
Praise the God of our sal - va - tion! Hosts on high, his power pro - claim;

laws which nev - er shall be bro - ken for their guid-ance he hath made.
heaven and earth, and all cre - a - tion, laud and mag - ni - fy his Name.

Words: Anon. *Foundling Hospital Psalms and Hymns*, 1797; para. of Psalm 148
Music: *Daniel's Tune*, David N. Johnson (b. 1922)

87. 87. D

# Praise to God     374

1 Come, let us join our cheer - ful songs with an - gels round the throne;
2 "Wor - thy the Lamb that died," they cry, "to be ex - alt - ed thus";
3 Je - sus is wor - thy to re - ceive hon - or and power di - vine;
4 The whole cre - a - tion joins in one to bless the sa - cred Name

ten thou-sand thou - sand are their tongues, but all their joys are one.
"Wor - thy the Lamb," our lips re - ply, "for he was slain for us."
may bless-ings, more than we can give, be, Lord, for ev - er thine.
of him that sits up - on the throne, and to a - dore the Lamb.

Words: Isaac Watts (1674-1748); para. of *A Song of the Lamb*
Music: *Nun danket all und bringet Ehr*, melody att. Johann Cruger (1598-1662), alt.

CM

# 375

Praise to God

1 Give praise and glo-ry un-to God, the Fa-ther of all bless-ing;
2 The host of hea-ven prais-eth thee, O Lord of all do-min-ions;
3 What God hath wrought to show his power he ev-er-more sus-tain-eth;

his might-y won-ders tell a-broad, his gra-cious-ness con-
and mor-tals then, on land and sea, be-neath thy sha-dowing
he watch-es o'er us ev-ery hour, his mer-cy nev-er

fess-ing. With balm my in-most heart he fills, his
pin-ions, ex-ult in thy cre-a-tive might that
wan-eth. Through all his king-dom's wide do-main, his

com-fort all my an-guish stills. To God be praise and glo-ry.
do-eth all things well and right. To God be praise and glo-ry.
right-eous-ness and jus-tice reign. To God be praise and glo-ry.

Words: Johann Jacob Schütz (1640-1690); tr. Arthur William Farlander (1898-1952)
and Charles Winfred Douglas (1867-1944), alt.
Music: *Du Lebensbrot, Herr Jesu Christ,* Peter Sohren (1630?-1692?);
adapt. Johann Anastasius Freylinghausen (1670-1739), alt.

87. 87. 887

# Praise to God

1 Joy-ful, joy-ful, we a-dore thee, God of glo-ry, Lord of love;
2 All thy works with joy sur-round thee, earth and heaven re-flect thy rays,
3 Thou art giv-ing and for-giv-ing, ev-er bless-ing, ev-er blest,

hearts un-fold like flowers be-fore thee, prais-ing thee, their sun a-bove.
stars and an-gels sing a-round thee, cen-ter of un-bro-ken praise.
well-spring of the joy of liv-ing, o-cean-depth of hap-py rest!

Melt the clouds of sin and sad-ness; drive the dark of doubt a-way;
field and for-est, vale and moun-tain, bloom-ing mea-dow, flash-ing sea,
Thou our Fa-ther, Christ our Bro-ther: all who live in love are thine;

giv - er of im-mor-tal glad-ness, fill us with the light of day.
chant - ing bird and flow-ing foun-tain, call us to re-joice in thee.
teach __ us how to love each o-ther, lift us to the joy di-vine.

Words: Henry Van Dyke (1852-1933)
Music: *Hymn to Joy,* Ludwig van Beethoven (1770-1827); adapt. Edward Hodges (1796-1867), alt.

87. 87. D

# 377

Praise to God

*Unison or harmony*

1 All peo-ple that on earth do dwell, sing to the Lord with
2 Know that the Lord is God in - deed; with - out our aid he
3 O en - ter then his gates with praise, ap - proach with joy his
4 For why? the Lord our God is good, his mer - cy is for
*5 To Fa - ther, Son, and Ho - ly Ghost, the God whom heaven and

1 cheer - ful voice: him serve with mirth, his praise forth
2 did us make: we are his folk, he doth us
3 courts un - to; praise, laud, and bless his Name al -
4 ev - er sure; his truth at all times firm - ly
5 earth a - dore, from men and from the an - gel

1 tell, come ye be - fore him and re - - joice.
2 feed, and for his sheep he doth us take.
3 ways, for it is seem - ly so to do.
4 stood, and shall from age to age en - - dure.
5 host be praise and glo - ry ev - er - - more.

Words: William Kethe (d. 1608?); para. of Psalm 100
Music: *Old 100th*, melody from *Pseaumes octante trois de David*, 1551, alt.;
     harm. after Louis Bourgeois (1510?-1561?)

LM

# Praise to God

Words: William Kethe (d. 1608?); para. of Psalm 100
Music: *Old 100th*, melody from *Pseaumes octante trois de David*, 1551, alt.;
fauxbourdon and harm. by John Dowland (1563-1626), alt.

LM

# 379

Praise to God

1 God is Love, let heaven a - dore him; God is Love, let
2 God is Love; and love en - folds us, all the world in
3 God is Love; and though with blind-ness sin af - flicts all

earth re - joice; let cre - a - tion sing be - fore him
one em - brace: with un - fail - ing grasp God holds us,
hu - man life, God's e - ter - nal lov - ing - kind-ness

and ex - alt him with one voice. God who laid the earth's foun-
ev - ery child of ev - ery race. And when hu - man hearts are
guides us through our earth - ly strife. Sin and death and hell shall

da - tion, God who spread the heavens a - bove, God who breathes through
break-ing un - der sor - row's i - ron rod, then we find that
nev - er o'er us fi - nal tri - umph gain; God is Love, so

all cre - a - tion: God is Love, e - ter - nal Love.
self - same ach - ing deep with - in the heart of God.
Love for ev - er o'er the u - ni - verse must reign.

Words: Timothy Rees (1874-1939), alt.
Music: *Abbot's Leigh*, Cyril Vincent Taylor (b. 1907)

87. 87. D

## Praise to God

## 380

1 From all that dwell be - low the skies let
2 E - ter - nal are thy mer - cies, Lord, and
*3 Praise God, from whom all bless - ings flow; praise

the Cre - a - tor's praise a - rise! Let the Re - deem - er's
truth e - ter - nal is thy word: thy praise shall sound from
him, all crea - tures here be - low; praise him a - bove, ye

Name be sung through ev - ery land, by ev - ery tongue!
shore to shore till suns shall rise and set no more.
heaven - ly host: praise Fa - ther, Son, and Ho - ly Ghost.

Words: Isaac Watts (1674-1748), para. of Psalm 117. St. 3, Thomas Ken (1637-1711)
Music: *Old 100th*, melody from *Pseaumes octante trois de David*, 1551, alt.;
  harm. after Louis Bourgeois (1510?-1561?)

LM

# 381

Praise to God

1 Thy strong word did cleave the dark-ness; at thy speak-ing
2 Lo, on those who dwelt in dark-ness, dark as night and
3 Thy strong word be-speaks us right-eous; bright with thine own
4 God the Fa-ther, Light-Cre-a-tor, to thee laud and

it was done; for cre-a-ted light we thank thee,
deep as death, broke the light of thy sal-va-tion,
ho-li-ness, glo-rious now, we press toward glo-ry,
hon-or be; to thee, Light of Light be-got-ten,

while thine or-dered sea-sons run: Al-le-lu-ia, al-le-
breathed thine own life-giv-ing breath: Al-le-lu-ia, al-le-
and our lives our hopes con-fess: Al-le-lu-ia, al-le-
praise be sung e-ter-nal-ly; Ho-ly Spi-rit, Light-Re-

lu-ia! Praise to thee who light dost send! Al-le-lu-ia,
lu-ia! Praise to thee who light dost send! Al-le-lu-ia,
lu-ia! Praise to thee who light dost send! Al-le-lu-ia,
veal-er, glo-ry, glo-ry be to thee; mor-tals, an-gels,

al-le-lu-ia! Al-le-lu-ia with-out end!
al-le-lu-ia! Al-le-lu-ia with-out end!
al-le-lu-ia! Al-le-lu-ia with-out end!
now and ev-er praise the Ho-ly Tri-ni-ty.

*The Alleluias in stanzas 1-3 may be sung antiphonally.*

**Words:** Martin H. Franzman (1907-1976)
**Music:** *Ton-y-Botel,* Thomas John Williams (1869-1944)

87. 87. D

# Praise to God

**382**

*Tenor or soprano ad libitum*

1 King of glo - ry, King of peace, I will love thee;
2 Where - fore with my ut - most art, I will sing thee;
3 Seven whole days, not one in seven, I will praise thee;

3 Seven whole days, not one in seven, I will praise thee;

and that love may nev - er cease, I will move thee.
and the cream of all my heart, I will bring thee.
in my heart, though not in heaven, I can raise thee.

in my heart, though not in heaven, I can raise thee.

Thou hast grant - ed my re - quest, thou hast heard me;
Though my sins a - gainst me cried, thou didst clear me;
Small it is in this poor sort to en - roll thee;

Small it is in this poor sort to en - roll thee;

thou didst note my work - ing breast, thou hast spared me.
and a - lone, when they re - plied, thou didst hear me.
e'en e - ter - ni - ty's too short to ex - tol thee.

e'en e - ter - ni - ty's too short to ex - tol thee.

Words: George Herbert (1593-1633)
Music: *General Seminary*, David Charles Walker (b. 1938)

74. 74. D

1 Fair - est Lord Je - sus, Ru - ler of all na - ture, O thou of
2 Fair are the mea - dows, fair - er still the wood - lands, robed in the
3 Fair is the sun - shine, fair - er still the moon - light, and all the

God and man the Son; thee will I cher - ish,
bloom - ing garb of spring: Je - sus is fair - er,
twink - ling, star - ry host: Je - sus shines bright - er,

thee will I hon - or, thou, my soul's glo - ry, joy, and crown.
Je - sus is pur - er, who makes the woe - ful heart to sing.
Je - sus shines pur - er, than all the an - gels heaven can boast.

Words: German composite; tr. pub. New York, 1850, alt.
Music: *St. Elizabeth*, melody from *Schlesische Volkslieder*, 1842; harm. Thomas Tertius Noble (1867-1953)    568. 558

1 Fair - est Lord Je - sus, Ru - ler of all na - ture, ____
2 Fair are the mea - dows, fair - er still the wood - lands, ____
3 Fair is the sun - shine, fair - er still the moon - light, and

O thou of God and man the Son; thee will I cher-ish,
robed in the bloom-ing garb of spring: Je-sus is fair-er,
all the__ twink-ling, star-ry host: Je-sus shines bright-er,

thee will I hon-or,__ thou, my soul's glo-ry, joy, and crown.
Je-sus is pur-er, who makes the__ woe-ful heart to sing.
Je-sus shines pur-er, than all the__ an-gels heaven can boast.

Words: German composite; tr. pub. New York, 1850, alt.
Music: *Schönster Herr Jesu,* melody from *Münster Gesangbuch,* 1677; harm. *The English Hymnal,* 1906          568. 558

## Praise to God                                                        385

1 Man - y and great, O God, are thy works, ma - ker of
2 Grant un - to us com - mun - ion with thee, thou star - a -

earth and sky; thy hands have set the hea - vens with stars;
bid - ing one; come un - to us and dwell with__ us;

thy fin - gers spread the moun-tains and plains. Lo, at thy
with thee are found the gifts of__ life. Bless us with

word the wa - ters were formed; deep seas o - bey thy voice.
life that has no__ end, e - ter-nal life with thee.

Words: American folk hymn; rev. Philip Frazier (1892-1964), alt.
Music: *Dakota Indian Chant [Lacquiparle],* Native American melody          96. 99. 96

Praise to God

1 We sing of God, the might-y source of all things; the stu-
*2 Tell them I AM, the Lord God said, to Mo-ses while on
3 Glo-rious the sun in mid ca-reer; glo-rious the as-sem-bled
4 Glo-rious, most glo-rious, is the crown of him that brought sal-

pen-dous force on which all strength de - pends; from
earth in dread and smit-ten to the heart, at
fires ap-pear; glo - rious the com-et's train: glo-
va-tion down by meek-ness, Ma-ry's son; seers

whose right arm, be - neath whose eyes, all pe - ri-od, power, and
once, a - bove, be - neath, a - round, all na - ture with-out
rious the trum-pet and a - larm; glo - rious the al-might-y
that stu-pen-dous truth be-lieved, and now the match-less

en - ter - prise com - men - ces, reigns, and ends.
voice or sound re - plied, O Lord, thou art.
stretched-out arm; glo - rious the en-rap - tured main:
deed's a - chieved, de - ter - mined, dared, and done.

Words: Christopher Smart (1722-1771), alt.
Music: *Cornwall*, Samuel Sebastian Wesley (1810-1876)

886. 886

1 We sing of God, the might - y source of all things;
*2 Tell them I AM, the Lord God said, to Mo - ses
3 Glo - rious the sun in mid ca - reer; glo - rious the as -
4 Glo - rious, most glo - rious, is the crown of him that

the stu - pen - dous force on which all strength de - pends;
while on earth in dread and smit - ten to the heart,
sem - bled fires ap - pear; glo - rious the com - et's train:
brought sal - va - tion down by meek - ness, Ma - ry's son;

from whose right arm, be - neath whose eyes, all pe - ri_od,
at once, a - bove, be - neath, a - round, all na - ture
glo - rious the trum - pet and a - larm; glo - rious the al -
seers that stu - pen - dous truth be - lieved, and now the

power, and en - ter - prise com - men - ces, reigns, and ends.
with - out voice or sound re - plied, O Lord, thou art.
might - y stretched-out arm; glo - rious the en-rap - tured main:
match - less deed's a - chieved, de - ter - mined, dared, and done.

Words: Christopher Smart (1722-1771), alt.
Music: *Magdalen College*, William Hayes (1706-1777)

886. 886

# 388

Praise to God

1 O wor - ship the King, all glo - rious a - bove!
2 O tell of his might! O sing of his grace!
3 The earth, with its store of won - ders un - told,
4 Thy boun - ti - ful care, what tongue can re - cite?
5 Frail chil - dren of dust, and fee - ble as frail,

1 O grate - ful - ly sing his power and his love!
2 Whose robe is the light, whose can - o - py space.
3 Al - might - y, thy power hath found - ed of old,
4 It breathes in the air; it shines in the light;
5 in thee do we trust, nor find thee to fail;

1 Our shield and de - fend - er, the An - cient of Days,
2 His char - iots of wrath the deep thun - der - clouds form,
3 hath stab - lished it fast by a change - less de - cree,
4 it streams from the hills, it de - scends to the plain,
5 thy mer - cies, how ten - der! how firm to the end!

1 pa - vil - ioned in splen-dor, and gird - ed with praise.
2 and dark is his path on the wings of the storm.
3 and round it hath cast, like a man - tle, the sea.
4 and sweet - ly dis - tills in the dew and the rain.
5 Our Ma - ker, De - fend - er, Re - deem - er, and Friend!

Words: Robert Grant (1779-1838)
Music: *Hanover*, att. William Croft (1678-1727)

10 10. 11 11

## Praise to God 389

1 Let us, with a glad-some mind, praise the Lord, for he is kind:
2 Let us blaze his Name a - broad, for of gods he is the God:
3 He with all - com - mand-ing might filled the new - made world with light:
4 He the gold - en - tress - ed sun caused all day his course to run:
5 The horn-ed moon to shine by night, mid her span - gled sis - ters bright:

*Refrain*

for his mer-cies ay en - dure, ev - er faith-ful, ev - er sure.

6  All things living he doth feed,
   his full hand supplies their need:

   *Refrain*

7  Let us, with a gladsome mind,
   praise the Lord, for he is kind:

   *Refrain*

Words: John Milton (1608-1674); para. Psalm 136
Music: *Monkland*, melody from *Freylinghausen*, 1704; adapt. John Antes (1740-1811);
    arr. John Bernard Wilkes (1785-1869)

77. 77

Descant
4 Praise to the Lord! O let all that is in me a-

1 Praise to the Lord, the Al-might-y, the King of cre-
2 Praise to the Lord; o-ver all things he glo-rious-ly
3 Praise to the Lord, who doth pros-per thy way and de-
4 Praise to the Lord! O let all that is in me a-

dore him! All that hath life and breath come now with

a-tion; O my soul, praise him, for he is thy
reign-eth: borne as on ea-gle-wings, safe-ly his
fend thee; sure-ly his good-ness and mer-cy shall
dore him! All that hath life and breath come now with

prais-es be-fore him! Let the a-men sound _ from his

health and sal-va-tion: join the great throng, psal-ter-y,
saints he sus-tain-eth. Hast thou not seen how all thou
ev-er at-tend thee; pon-der a-new what the Al-
prais-es be-fore him! Let the a-men sound from his

peo - ple a - gain; glad - ly for ev - er a - dore him.

or - gan, and song, sound-ing in glad ad - o - ra - - tion.
need - est hath been grant - ed in what he or - dain - - eth?
might - y can do, who with his love doth be - friend thee.
peo - ple a - gain; glad - ly for ev - er a - dore him.

Words: Joachim Neander (1650-1680); tr. *Hymnal 1940*, alt.
Music: *Lobe den Herren*, melody from *Erneuerten Gesangbuch*, 1665;
    harm. *The Chorale Book for England*, 1863; desc. Craig Sellar Lang (1891-1971)

14 14. 478

## 391

Praise to God

1 Be - fore the Lord's e - ter - nal throne, ye
2 His sov - ereign power with - out our aid formed
3 We are his peo - ple, we his care, our
4 We'll crowd thy gates with thank - ful songs, high
5 Wide as the world is thy com - mand, vast

1 na - tions, bow with sa - cred joy; know that the Lord is
2 us of clay and gave us breath; and when like wan-dering
3 souls, and all our mor - tal frame: what last - ing hon - ors
4 as the heaven our voic - es raise; and earth, with her ten
5 as e - ter - ni - ty thy love; firm as a rock thy

1 God a - lone; he can cre - ate, and he des - troy.
2 sheep we strayed, he saved us from the power of death.
3 shall we rear, al - might - y Ma - ker, to thy Name?
4 thou - sand tongues, shall fill thy courts with sound - ing praise.
5 truth must stand, when roll - ing years shall cease to move.

Words: Isaac Watts (1674-1748), alt.; para. of Psalm 100
Music: *Winchester New*, melody from *Musicalisches Hand-Buch*, 1690;
    harm. William Henry Monk (1823-1889)

LM

## 392

Praise to God

1 Come, we that love the Lord, and let our joys be known; join
2 Let those re - fuse to sing that nev - er knew our God; but
3 The heirs of grace have found glo - ry be - gun be - low; ce -
4 Then let our song a - bound and let our tears be dry; we're

in a song with sweet ac - cord and thus sur - round the throne.
chil - dren of the heaven-ly King may speak their joys a - broad.
les - tial fruits on earth - ly ground from faith and hope may grow.
march - ing through Em - man - uel's ground to fair - er worlds on high.

*Refrain*

Ho - san - na, ho - san - na! Re - joice, give thanks and sing.

Words: Isaac Watts (1674-1748), alt.
Music: *Vineyard Haven*, Richard Wayne Dirksen (b. 1921)

SM with Refrain

## Praise to God — 393

1 Praise our great and gra - cious Lord, call up - on his ho - ly Name;
2 God has given the cloud by day, given the mov - ing fire by night;

rais - ing hymns in glad ac - cord, all his might - y acts pro-claim:
guides his Is - rael on their way from the dark - ness in - to light.

how he leads his cho - sen un - to Ca - naan's prom - ised land,
God it is who grants us sure re - treat and ref - uge nigh;

how the word we have heard firm and change-less still shall stand.
light of dawn leads us on: 'tis the Day - spring from on high.

Words: Harriet Auber (1773-1862), alt.
Music: *Maoz Zur*, Hebrew melody; adapt. Eric Werner (b. 1901)

77. 77. 67. 67

1 Cre - at - ing God, your fin - gers trace the bold de -
2 Sus - tain - ing God, your hands up - hold earth's mys - te-ries
3 Re - deem - ing God, your arms em - brace all now de -
4 In - dwell - ing God, your gos - pel claims one fam - i-ly

signs of farth - est space; let sun and moon and stars and
known or yet un - told; let wa - ter's fra - gile blend with
spised for creed or race; let peace, de - scend-ing like a
with a bil - lion names; let ev - ery life be touched by

light and what lies hid - den praise your might.
air, en - a - bling life, pro - claim your care.
dove, make known on earth your heal - ing love.
grace un - til we praise you face to face.

Words: Jeffery Rowthorn (b. 1934), alt.
Music: *Wilderness*, Reginald Sparshatt Thatcher (1888-1957)  LM

*Introduction/Interlude*

1 Cre - at - ing God, your fin - gers trace the bold de - signs of
2 Sus - tain - ing God, your hands up - hold earth's mys-teries known or
3 Re - deem - ing God, your arms em - brace all now de - spised for
4 In - dwell - ing God, your gos - pel claims one fam - i-ly with a

| | | | | | | |
|---|---|---|---|---|---|---|
| farth-est space; | let | sun and | moon and | stars and | light | and |
| yet un - told; | let | wa - ter's | fra - gile | blen with | air, | en - |
| creed or race; | let | peace, de - | scend-ing | like a | dove, | make |
| bil - lion names; | let | ev - ery | life | be touched by | grace | un - |

| | | | | | |
|---|---|---|---|---|---|
| what lies | hid - | den | praise | your | might. |
| a - bling | life, | pro - | claim | your | care. |
| known on | earth | your | heal - | ing | love. |
| til we | praise | you | face | to | face. |

Words: Jeffery Rowthorn (b. 1934), alt.
Music: *King*, David Hurd (b. 1950)

LM

## Praise to God  396

| | | | | | | | | |
|---|---|---|---|---|---|---|---|---|
| 1 Now | thank we all our | God, | with | heart, and hands, and | voic - es, |
| 2 O | may this boun-teous | God | through | all our life | be | near | us! |
| 3 All | praise and thanks to | God | the | Fa - ther now | be | giv - en, |

| | | | | | | |
|---|---|---|---|---|---|---|
| who | won-drous things hath done, | in | whom his world re - | joic - es; |
| with | ev - er - joy - ful | hearts | and | bless - ed peace to | cheer | us; |
| the | Son, and him who | reigns | with | them in high - est | hea - ven, |

| | | | | | | |
|---|---|---|---|---|---|---|
| who | from our mo - ther's | arms | hath | blessed us | on our | way |
| and | keep us in his | grace, | and | guide us | when per - | plexed, |
| e - | ter - nal, Tri - une | God, | whom | earth and heaven a - | dore; |

| | | | | | |
|---|---|---|---|---|---|
| with | count-less gifts of | love, | and | still is ours to - | day. |
| and | free us from all | ills | in | this world and the | next. |
| for | thus it was, is | now, | and | shall be, ev - er - | more. |

Words: Martin Rinckart (1586-1649); tr. Catherine Winkworth (1827-1878), alt.
Music: *Nun danket alle Gott*, melody Johann Cruger (1598-1662)

67. 67. 66. 66

# 397

1 Now thank we all our God, with heart, and hands, and voic - es,
2 O may this boun - teous God through all our life be near us!
3 All praise and thanks to God the Fa - ther now be giv - en,

who won-drous things hath done, in whom his world re - joic - es;
with ev - er - joy - ful hearts and bless - ed peace to cheer us;
the Son, and him who reigns with them in high-est hea - ven,

who from our mo - ther's arms hath blessed us on our way
and keep us in his grace, and guide us when per - plexed,
e - ter - nal, Tri - une God, whom earth and heaven a - dore;

with count-less gifts of love, and still is ours to - day.
and free us from all ills in this world and the next.
for thus it was, is now, and shall be, ev - er - more.

Words: Martin Rinckart (1586-1649); tr. Catherine Winkworth (1827-1878), alt.
Music: *Nun danket alle Gott*, melody Johann Cruger (1598-1662);
  harm. William Henry Monk (1823-1889), after Felix Mendelssohn (1809-1847)          67. 67. 66. 66

1 I sing the al-might-y power of God, that made the moun-tains rise,
2 I sing the good-ness of the Lord, that filled the earth with food;
3 There's not a plant or flower be - low, but makes thy glo - ries known;

that spread the flow-ing seas a - broad and built the lof - ty skies.
he formed the crea-tures with his Word, and then pro-nounced them good.
and clouds a - rise, and tem - pests blow, by or - der from thy throne;

I sing the wis - dom that or - dained the sun to rule the day;
Lord, how thy won - ders are dis - played, wher - e'er I turn my eye,
while all that bor - rows life from thee is ev - er in thy care,

the moon shines full at his com-mand, and all the stars o - bey.
if I sur - vey the ground I tread, or gaze up - on the sky!
and ev - ery - where that I - could be, thou, God, art pres-ent there.

Words: Isaac Watts (1674-1748), alt.
Music: *Forest Green*, English melody; adapt. and harm. Ralph Vaughan Williams (1872-1958)   CMD

# Praise to God

*Descant*

3 Your heaven-ly Fa - ther praise ac - claim his

1 To God with glad - ness sing, your Rock and Sa - vior
2 He cra - dles in his hand the heights and depths of
3 Your heaven - ly Fa - ther praise, ac - claim his on - ly

on - ly Son, your voic - es raise to him who

bless; in - to his tem - ple bring your songs of
earth; he made the sea and land, he brought the
Son, your voice in hom - age raise to him who

makes all one, O Dove on

thank - - ful - - ness! O God of might, to
world to birth! O God Most High, we
makes all one! O Dove of peace, on

us de - scend joy_____ in - crease!

you we sing, en - throned as King on hea - ven's height!
are your sheep; on us you keep your shep - herd's eye!
us de - scend that strife may end and joy in - crease!

Words: James Quinn (b. 1919), alt.; para. of Psalm 95 (Venite)
Music: *Camano*, Richard Proulx (b. 1937)

66. 66. 44. 44

1 All crea-tures of our God and King, lift up your voic-es, let us
*2 Great rush-ing winds and breez-es soft, you clouds that ride the heavens a-
*3 Swift flow-ing wa-ter, pure and clear, make mu-sic for your Lord to
4 Dear mo-ther earth, you day by day un-fold your bless-ings on our
5 All you with mer-cy in your heart, for-giv-ing o-thers, take your
*6 And e-ven you, most gen-tle death, wait-ing to hush our fi-nal
7 Let all things their cre-a-tor bless, and wor-ship him in hum-ble-

1 sing: Al-le-lu-ia, al-le-lu-ia! Bright burn-ing
2 loft, O___ praise him, Al-le-lu-ia! Fair ris-ing
3 hear, Al-le-lu-ia, al-le-lu-ia! Fire, so in-
4 way, O___ praise him, Al-le-lu-ia! All flowers and
5 part, O___ sing now: Al-le-lu-ia! All you that
6 breath, O___ praise him, Al-le-lu-ia! You lead back
7 ness, O___ praise him, Al-le-lu-ia! Praise God the

1 sun with gold-en beams, pale sil-ver moon that gen-tly gleams,
2 morn, with praise re-joice, stars night-ly shin-ing, find a voice,
3 tense and fierce-ly bright, you give to us both warmth and light,
4 fruits that in you grow, let them his glo-ry al-so show:
5 pain and sor-row bear, praise God, and cast on him your care:
6 home the child of God, for Christ our Lord that way has trod:
7 Fa-ther, praise the Son, and praise the Spi-rit, Three in One:

*Refrain*

O praise him, O praise him, Al-le-lu-ia,

al-le-lu-ia, al-le-lu-ia!

*The refrain may be sung antiphonally, by phrase; all join in the final Alleluia.*

Words: Francis of Assisi (1182-1226); tr. William H. Draper (1855-1933), alt.
Music: *Lasst uns erfreuen,* melody from *Auserlesene Catholische Geistliche Kirchengeseng,* 1623;
adapt. Ralph Vaughan Williams (1872-1958)

88. 44. 88 with Refrain

# 401

Praise to God

1 The God of A-braham praise, who reigns en-throned a - bove;
2 He by him-self hath sworn: we on his oath de - pend;
3 There dwells the Lord, our King, the Lord, our Right-eous - ness,
4 The God who reigns on high the great arch-an - gels sing,
5 The whole tri-um-phant host give thanks to God on high;

1 An - cient of ev-er-last-ing days, and God of love;
2 we shall, on ea-gle-wings up-borne, to heaven a - scend:
3 tri - um-phant o'er the world and sin, the Prince of Peace;
4 and "Ho-ly, ho-ly, ho-ly," cry, "Al-might-y King!
5 "Hail, Fa-ther, Son, and Ho-ly Ghost" they ev-er cry;

1 the Lord, the great I AM, by earth and heaven con - fessed:
2 we shall be-hold his face, we shall his power a - dore,
3 on Zi-on's sa-cred height his king-dom he main - tains,
4 Who was, and is, the same, and ev-er-more shall be:
5 hail, A-braham's Lord di - vine! With heaven our songs we raise;

1 we bow and bless the sa - cred Name for ev - er blest.
2 and sing the won - ders of his grace for ev - er - more.
3 and, glo - rious with his saints in light, for ev - er reigns.
4 e - ter - nal Fa - ther, great I AM, we wor - ship thee."
5 all might and ma - jes - ty are thine, and end - less praise.

Words: Thomas Olivers (1725-1799), alt.
Music: *Leoni*, Hebrew melody; harm. *Hymns Ancient and Modern*, 1875, alt.

66. 84. D

## Praise to God

**402**

Antiphon

Let all the world in ev - ery cor - ner sing, my God and King! King!

1 The heavens are not too high, his praise may thith - er fly; the
2 The Church with psalms must shout, no door can keep them out; but,

earth is not too low, his prais - es there may grow.
a - bove all, the heart must bear the lon - gest part.

Repeat Antiphon

Words: George Herbert (1593-1633)
Music: *Augustine*, Erik Routley (1917-1982)

66. 66 with Refrain

# 403

Praise to God

Let all the world in ev-ery cor-ner sing, my God and King! Let all the world in ev-ery cor-ner sing, my God and King!

1 The heavens are not too high, his praise may thith-er fly; the earth is not too low, his prais-es there may grow.

2 The Church with psalms must shout, no door can keep them out; but, a-bove all, the heart must bear the long-est part.

Let all the world in ev-ery cor-ner sing, my God and King! King! A - - men.

Words: George Herbert (1593-1633)
Music: *MacDougall*, Calvin Hampton (1938-1984)

66. 66 with Refrain

1 We will ex - tol you, ev - er - bless - ed Lord; your ho - ly
2 Age shall to age pass on the end - less song, tell - ing the
3 You, Lord, are gra - cious, mer - ci - ful to all, close to your

Name for ev - er be a - dored; each day we live our
won - ders which to you be - long, your might - y acts with
chil - dren when on you they call; and slow to an - ger,

psalm to you we raise; you, God and King, are wor - thy of all
joy and fear re - late; praise we your glo - ry while on you we
mer - ci - ful and kind, in your com - pas - sion we your bless-ings

praise, great and un - search - a - ble in all your ways.
wait, glad in the know - ledge of your love so great.
find. We love you with our heart and strength and mind.

*The first stanza may be repeated at the end.*

Words: J. Nichol Grieve, alt.; para. of Psalm 145
Music: *Old 124th,* melody from *Pseaumes octante trois de David,* 1551;
  harm. Charles Winfred Douglas (1867-1944)

10 10. 10 10 10

**405**

*Descant*

All things bright and beau - ti - ful, crea-tures great and small,

*Refrain*

All things bright and beau - ti - ful, all crea-tures great and small,

all things wise and won - der - ful, God made them all.

all things wise and won - der - ful, the Lord God made them all.

1 Each lit - tle flower that o - pens, each lit - tle bird that sings,
2 The pur - ple - head - ed moun-tain, the riv - er run - ning by,
3 The cold wind in the win - ter, the pleas-ant sum - mer sun,
4 He gave us eyes to see them, and lips that we might tell

*Repeat Refrain*

he made their glow-ing col - ors, he made their ti - ny wings.
the sun - set, and the morn - ing that bright - ens up the sky.
the ripe fruits in the gar - den, he made them ev - ery one.
how great is God Al - might - y, who has made all things well.

Words: Cecil Frances Alexander (1818-1895)
Music: *Royal Oak,* melody from *The Dancing Master,* 1686;
    adapt. Martin Fallas Shaw (1875-1958); desc. Richard Proulx (b. 1937)

76. 76 with Refrain

# Praise to God

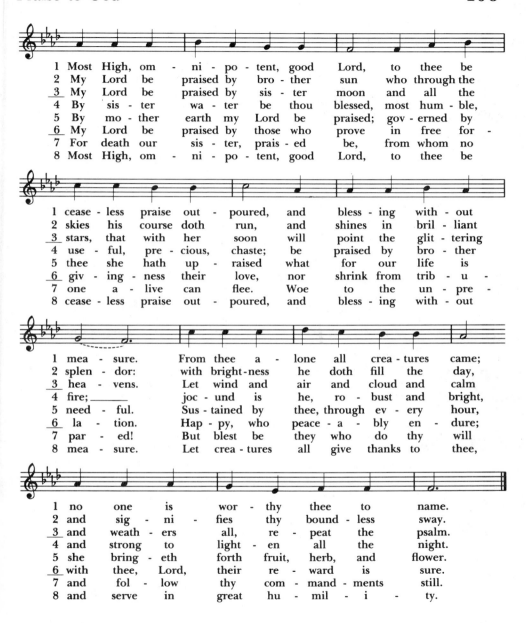

1 Most High, om - ni - po - tent, good Lord, to thee be
2 My Lord be praised by bro - ther sun who through the
3 My Lord be praised by sis - ter moon and all the
4 By sis - ter wa - ter be thou blessed, most hum - ble,
5 By mo - ther earth my Lord be praised; gov - erned by
6 My Lord be praised by those who prove in free for -
7 For death our sis - ter, prais - ed be, from whom no
8 Most High, om - ni - po - tent, good Lord, to thee be

1 cease - less praise out - poured, and bless - ing with - out
2 skies his course doth run, and shines in bril - liant
3 stars, that with her soon will point the glit - tering
4 use - ful, pre - cious, chaste; be praised by bro - ther
5 thee she hath up - raised what for our life is
6 giv - ing - ness their love, nor shrink from trib - u -
7 one a - live can flee. Woe to the un - pre -
8 cease - less praise out - poured, and bless - ing with - out

1 mea - sure. From thee a - lone all crea - tures came;
2 splen - dor: with bright-ness he doth fill the day,
3 hea - vens. Let wind and air and cloud and calm
4 fire; joc - und is he, ro - bust and bright,
5 need - ful. Sus - tained by thee, through ev - ery hour,
6 la - tion. Hap - py, who peace - a - bly en - dure;
7 par - ed! But blest be they who do thy will
8 mea - sure. Let crea - tures all give thanks to thee,

1 no one is wor - thy thee to name.
2 and sig - ni - fies thy bound - less sway.
3 and weath - ers all, re - peat the psalm.
4 and strong to light - en all the night.
5 she bring - eth forth fruit, herb, and flower.
6 with thee, Lord, their re - ward is sure.
7 and fol - low thy com - mand - ments still.
8 and serve in great hu - mil - i - ty.

*This hymn may be sung by alternating groups, with all singing the first and final stanzas.*

**Words:** Francis of Assisi (1182-1226); tr. Howard Chandler Robbins (1876-1952), alt.
**Music:** *Assisi*, Alfred Morton Smith (1879-1971)

887. 88

# 407
Praise to God

*Introduction*

1 Most High, om - ni - po - tent, good Lord, to thee be
2 (My Lord be) praised by bro - ther sun who through the
3 (My Lord be) praised be sis - ter moon and all the
4 (By sis - ter) wa - ter be thou blessed, most hum - ble,
5 (By mo - ther) earth my Lord be praised; gov - erned by
6 (My Lord be) praised by those who prove in free for -
7 (For death our) sis - ter, prais - ed be, from whom no
8 (Most High, om) - ni - po - tent, good Lord, to thee be

1 cease-less praise out - poured, and bless - ing with - out mea - sure.
2 skies his course doth run, and shines in bril - liant splen - dor:
3 stars, that with her soon will point the glit - tering hea - vens.
4 use - ful, pre - cious, chaste; be praised by bro - ther fire;____
5 thee she hath up - raised what for our life is need - ful.
6 giv - ing-ness their love, nor shrink from trib - u - la - tion.
7 one a - live can flee. Woe to the un - pre - par - ed!
8 cease-less praise out - poured, and bless - ing with - out mea - sure.

1 From thee a - lone all crea - tures came; no one is
2 with bright-ness he doth fill the day, and sig - ni -
3 Let wind and air and cloud and calm and weath-ers
4 joc - und is he, ro - bust and bright, and strong to
5 Sus - tained by thee, through ev - ery hour, she bring-eth
6 Hap - py, who peace - a - bly en - dure; with thee, Lord,
7 But blest be they who do thy will and fol - low
8 Let crea - tures all give thanks to thee, and serve in

| | | | | | |
|---|---|---|---|---|---|
| 1 | wor - thy | thee | to | name. | 2 My Lord be |
| 2 | fies | thy bound - less | | sway. | 3 My Lord be |
| 3 | all, | re - peat | the | psalm. | 4 By sis - ter |
| 4 | light - en | all | the | night. | 5 By mo - ther |
| 5 | forth fruit, | herb, | and | flower. | 6 My Lord be |
| 6 | their | re - ward | is | sure. | 7 For death our |
| 7 | thy | com - mand - ments | | still. | 8 Most High, om - |
| 8 | great | hu - mil - i | - | (ty.) | |

ty.

*This hymn may be sung by alternating groups, with all singing the first and final stanzas.*

Words: Francis of Assisi (1182-1226); tr. Howard Chandler Robbins (1876-1952), alt.
Music: *Lukkason*, Calvin Hampton (1938-1984)

887. 88

## Praise to God 408

| | | | | | |
|---|---|---|---|---|---|
| 1 Sing | praise to God | who | reigns a - bove, the | God of all | cre - |
| 2 What | God's al - might - y | | power hath made, his | gra - cious mer - cy | |
| 3 Let | all who name Christ's | ho - ly Name give | God all praise and | | |

| | | | | |
|---|---|---|---|---|
| a - tion, the | God of power, the | God of love, the | God of |
| keep - eth; by | morn-ing glow or | eve-ning shade his | watch-ful |
| glo - ry; let | all who know his | power pro-claim a - | loud the |

| | | | | |
|---|---|---|---|---|
| our sal - va - tion; with | heal-ing balm my | soul he fills, and |
| eye ne'er sleep - eth. With - | in the king - dom | of his might, lo! |
| won - drous sto - ry! Cast | each false i - dol | from its throne, the |

| | | | | |
|---|---|---|---|---|
| ev - ery faith-less | mur-mur stills: to | God all praise and | glo - ry. |
| all is just and | all is right: to | God all praise and | glo - ry. |
| Lord is God, and | he a - lone: to | God all praise and | glo - ry. |

Words: Johann Jacob Schütz (1640-1690); tr. Frances Elizabeth Cox (1812-1897), alt.
Music: *Mit Freuden zart*, melody from "Une pastourelle gentille," 1529;
adapt. *Pseaumes cinquante de David*, 1547, and *Kirchengeseng darinnen die Heubtartickel*
*des Christlichen Glaubens gefasset*, 1566

87. 87. 887

# 409

Praise to God

The un-wea - ried sun from day to day
whilst all the stars that round her burn,
In rea - son's ear they all re - joice,

does his Cre - a - tor's power dis - play;
and all the plan - ets in their turn,
and ut - ter forth a glo - rious voice;

and pub - lish - es to ev - ery land
con - firm the ti - dings, as they roll
for ev - er sing - ing as they shine,

the work of an al - might - y hand.
and spread the truth from pole to pole.
"The hand that made us is di - vine."

Words: Joseph Addison (1672-1719); para. of Psalm 19:1-6
Music: *Creation*, Franz Joseph Haydn (1732-1809);
   adapt. *Dulcimer, or New York Collection of Sacred Music*, 1850, alt.

LMD

# 410

Praise to God

*Unison or harmony*

1 Praise, my soul, the King of hea - ven; to his feet thy tri - bute bring;
2 Praise him for his grace and fa - vor to his peo - ple in dis - tress;
3 Fa - ther - like he tends and spares us; well our fee - ble frame he knows;
4 An - gels, help us to a - dore him; ye be - hold him face to face;

ran - somed, healed, re - stored, for - giv - en, ev - er - more his prais - es sing:
praise him still the same as ev - er, slow to chide, and swift to bless:
in his hand he gen - tly bears us, res - cues us from all our foes.
sun and moon, bow down be - fore him, dwell - ers all in time and space.

Al - le - lu - ia, al - le - lu - ia! Praise the ev - er - last - ing King.
Al - le - lu - ia, al - le - lu - ia! Glo - rious in his faith - ful - ness.
Al - le - lu - ia, al - le - lu - ia! Wide - ly yet his mer - cy flows.
Al - le - lu - ia, al - le - lu - ia! Praise with us the God of grace.

Words: Henry Francis Lyte (1793-1847), alt.
Music: *Lauda anima*, John Goss (1800-1880)

87. 87. 87

*Descant for use with unison singing*

4 An - gels, help us to a - dore him; ye be - hold him face to face;

sun and moon, bow down be - fore him, dwell - ers all in time and space.

Al - le - lu - ia,  al - le - lu - ia!  Praise____with us the God of  grace.

Music: *Lauda anima*, desc. Craig Sellar Lang (1891-1971)

## Praise to God

**411**

1 O    bless the Lord, my    soul!    His    grace to    thee pro - claim!
2 O    bless the Lord, my    soul!    His    mer - cies    bear in    mind!
3 He   will not al - ways    chide;    he    will with    pa - tience    wait;
4 He   par - dons all    thy    sins,    pro - longs thy    fee - ble    breath;
5 He   clothes thee with his    love,    up - holds thee    with his    truth;

1 And   all that is with - in    me join to    bless his    ho - ly    Name!
2 For - get not all his    ben - e - fits! The    Lord to    thee    is    kind.
3 his   wrath is ev - er    slow to    rise and    rea - dy    to a - bate.
4 he    heal-eth thine in - fir - mi - ties and    ran - soms thee from    death.
5 and   like the ea - gle    he re - news the    vi - gor of thy    youth.

6    Then bless his holy Name,
        whose grace hath made thee whole,
    whose loving-kindness crowns thy days:
        O bless the Lord, my soul!

Words: James Montgomery (1771-1854); para. of Psalm 103:1-5
Music: *St. Thomas (Williams)*, melody Aaron Williams (1731-1776); harm. Lowell Mason (1792-1872)    SM

# 412

1 Earth and all stars, loud rush-ing plan-ets, sing to the
2 Hail, wind, and rain, loud blow-ing snow-storms, sing to the
3 Trum-pet and pipes, loud clash-ing cym-bals, sing to the
4 En-gines and steel, loud pound-ing ham-mers, sing to the
5 Class-rooms and labs loud boil-ing test-tubes, sing to the
6 Know-ledge and truth, loud sound-ing wis-dom, sing to the

1 Lord_____ a new song! O vic-to-ry,
2 Lord_____ a new song! Flow-ers and trees,
3 Lord_____ a new song! Harp, lute, and lyre,
4 Lord_____ a new song! Lime-stone and beams,
5 Lord_____ a new song! Ath-lete and band,
6 Lord_____ a new song! Daugh-ter and son,

1 loud shout-ing ar-my, sing to the Lord_____ a new song!
2 loud rus-tling dry leaves, sing to the Lord_____ a new song!
3 loud hum-ming cel-los, sing to the Lord_____ a new song!
4 loud build-ing work-ers, sing to the Lord_____ a new song!
5 loud cheer-ing peo-ple, sing to the Lord_____ a new song!
6 loud pray-ing mem-bers, sing to the Lord_____ a new song!

*Refrain*

He has done mar - vel-ous things.

I, too, will praise him with a new song!

Words: Herbert F. Brokering (b. 1926)
Music: *Earth and All Stars*, David N. Johnson (b. 1922)

45. 7. D with Refrain

# Praise to God

1 New songs of cel - e - bra - tion ren - der to him who
2 Joy - ful - ly, heart - i - ly re - sound - ing, let ev - ery
3 Riv - ers and seas and tor - rents roar - ing, hon - or the

has great won - ders done; awed by his love his
in - stru - ment and voice peal out the praise of
Lord with wild ac - claim; moun - tains and stones look

foes sur - ren - der and fall be - fore the Might - y One.
grace a - bound - ing, call - ing the whole world to re - joice.
up a - dor - ing and find a voice to praise his Name.

He has made known his great sal - va - tion which
Trum - pets and or - gans set in mo - tion such
Right - eous, com - mand - ing, ev - er glo - rious, prais -

all his friends with joy con - fess; he has re - vealed to
sounds as make the hea - vens ring: all things that live in
es be his that nev - er cease; just is our God, whose

ev - ery na - tion his ev - er - last - ing right - eous - ness.
earth and o - cean, make mu - sic for your might - y King.
truth vic - to - rious es - tab - lish - es the world in peace.

Words: Erik Routley (1917-1982); para. of Psalm 98
Music: *Rendez à Dieu*, melody att. Louis Bourgeois (1510?-1561?)

98. 98. D

# 414

Praise to God

*Descant*

6 All thy works, O Lord, shall bless thee; thee shall all thy

1 God, my King, thy might con - fess - ing, ev - er will I
2 Hon - or great our God be - fit - teth; who his ma - jes -
3 They shall talk of all thy glo - ry, on thy might and
4 Nor shall fail from mem-ory's trea - sure works by love and
5 Full of kind - ness and com - pas - sion, slow to an - ger,

saints a - dore: King su - preme shall they con - fess thee,

1 bless thy Name; day by day thy throne ad - dress - ing,
2 ty can reach? Age to age his works trans - mit - teth,
3 great - ness dwell, speak of thy dread acts the sto - ry,
4 mer - cy wrought, works of love sur - pass - ing mea - sure,
5 vast in love, God is good to all cre - a - tion;

| | | | | | | |
|---|---|---|---|---|---|---|
| and | pro - | claim | thy | sov - | ereign | power. |

1 still will I thy praise pro - claim.
2 age to age his power shall teach.
3 and thy deeds of won - der tell.
4 works of mer - cy pass - ing thought.
5 all his works his good - ness prove.

6  All thy works, O Lord, shall bless thee:
   thee shall all thy saints adore:
   King supreme shall they confess thee,
   and proclaim thy sovereign power.

Words: Richard Mant (1776-1848); para. of Psalm 145:1-12
Music: *Stuttgart*, melody from *Psalmodia Sacra, oder Andächtige und Schöne Gesänge*, 1715;
    adapt. and harm. William Henry Havergal (1793-1870); desc. John Wilson (b. 1905)        87. 87

## Praise to God                                                          415

1 When all thy mer - cies, O my God, my ris - ing soul sur - veys,
2 O how shall words with e - qual warmth the grat - i - tude de - clare,
3 Ten thou-sand thou-sand pre-cious gifts my dai - ly thanks em-ploy;
4 When na - ture fails, and day and night di - vide thy works no more,
5 Through all e - ter - ni - ty, to thee a joy - ful song I'll raise;

1 trans - port - ed with the view, I'm lost in won - der, love, and praise.
2 that glows with - in my fer - vent heart? But thou canst read it there.
3 nor is the least a cheer-ful heart that tastes those gifts with joy.
4 my ev - er grate-ful heart, O Lord, thy mer - cy shall a - dore.
5 but oh, e - ter - ni - ty's too short to ut - ter all thy praise!

Words: Joseph Addison (1672-1719), alt.
Music: *Durham*, melody and bass Thomas Ravenscroft (1592?-1635?)                          CM

1 For the beau - ty of the earth, for the beau - ty of the skies,
2 For the beau - ty of each hour of the day and of the night,
3 For the joy of ear and eye, for the heart and mind's de - light,
4 For the joy of hu-man love, bro-ther, sis - ter, par - ent, child,
5 For the Church which ev - er - more lift-eth ho - ly hands a - bove,

1 for the love which from our birth o - ver and a - round us lies,
2 hill and vale, and tree and flower, sun and moon, and stars of light,
3 for the mys - tic har - mo - ny link-ing sense to sound and sight,
4 friends on earth, and friends a - bove, for all gen - tle thoughts and mild,
5 of - fering up on ev - ery shore thy pure sac - ri - fice of love,

*Refrain*

Christ our God, to thee we raise this our hymn of grate-ful praise.

6    For each perfect gift of thine
        to the world so freely given,
    faith and hope and love divine,
        peace on earth and joy in heaven

    **Refrain**

Words: Folliot Sandford Pierpoint (1835-1917), alt.
Music: *Lucerna Laudoniae*, David Evans (1874-1948)

77. 77 with Refrain

# Praise to God

**Antiphon**

This is the feast of vic-to-ry for our God.

Al-le-lu - ia, al-le-lu-ia, al-le-lu - ia!

1 Wor - thy is Christ, the Lamb who was slain,_____ whose
2 Pow - er, rich - es, wis - dom, and strength,___ and
3 Sing___ with all the peo - ple of God,_____ and
4 Bless - ing, hon - or, glo - ry, and might be to
5 For___ the Lamb_____ who was slain has be -

1 blood set us free_____ to be peo - ple of God. [Ant.]
2 hon - or,___ bless - ing, and glo - ry are his. [Ant.]
3 join in the hymn of all cre - a - - - tion. [Ant.]
4 God and the Lamb for ev - er. A - - - men. [Ant.]
5 gun his___ reign.___ Al - le - lu - - - ia! [Ant.]

**Final Antiphon**

This is the feast of vic-to-ry for our God.

Al-le-lu - ia, al-le-lu-ia, al-le-lu - ia!

Words: Revelation 5:12-13; adapt. John W. Arthur (1922-1980)
Music: *Festival Canticle*, Richard Hillert (b. 1923)

Irr. with Refrain

*Antiphon*

This is the feast of vic-to-ry for our God. Al - le -
lu - ia, al - - - le - lu - ia!

1. Wor - thy is Christ, the Lamb who was slain, whose
blood set us free to be peo - ple of God. [Ant.]

2. Pow - er, rich - es, wis-dom and strength, and
hon - or, bless-ing, and glo - ry are his. [Ant.]

3. Sing with all the peo - ple of God, and
join in the hymn of all cre - a - tion. [Ant.]

4. Bless - ing, hon - or, glo - ry, and might be to
God and the Lamb for ev - er. A - men. [Ant.]

5. For the Lamb who was slain has be - gun his
reign. Al - le - lu - ia! [Ant.]

*Final Antiphon*

This is the feast of vic - to - ry for our God. Al - le -
lu - ia, al - le - lu - ia!

Words: Revelation 5:12-13; adapt. John W. Arthur (1922-1980)
Music: *Raymond*, Peter R. Hallock (b. 1923)

Irr. with Refrain

## 419

Praise to God

1 Lord of all be - ing, throned a - far, thy glo - ry flames from sun and star; cen - ter and soul of ev - ery sphere, yet to each lov - ing heart how near!

2 Sun of our life, thy quick - ening ray sheds on our path the glow of day; star of our hope, thy soft - ened light cheers the long watch - es of the night.

3 Lord of all life, be - low, a - bove, whose light is truth, whose warmth is love, be - fore thy ev - er - blaz - ing throne we ask no lus - ter of our own.

4 Grant us thy truth to make us free, and kin - dling hearts that burn for thee, till all thy liv - ing al - tars claim one ho - ly light, one heaven - ly flame.

Words: Oliver Wendell Holmes (1809-1894)

Music: *Mendon*, melody from *Methodist Harmonist*, 1821; adapt. Lowell Mason (1792-1872)

LM

## 420

Praise to God

1 When in our mu - sic God is glo - ri - fied, _____

2 How of - ten, mak - ing mu - sic, we have found _____

3 So has the Church, in lit - ur - gy and song, _____

4 And did not Je - sus sing a psalm that night, _____

5 Let ev - ery in - stru-ment be tuned for praise! _____

1 and a - dor - a - tion leaves no room for pride,____
2 a new di - men - sion in the world of sound,____
3 in faith and love, through cen - tu - ries of wrong,____
4 when ut - most e - vil strove a - gainst the Light?____
5 Let all re - joice who have a voice to raise!____

1 it is as though the whole cre - a - tion cried____
2 as wor - ship moved us to a more pro - found____
3 borne wit - ness to the truth in ev - ery tongue,____
4 Then let us sing, for whom he won the fight,____
5 And may God give us faith to sing al - ways____

1-4 | Final Ending

____ Al - le - lu - ia! ____ Al - le - lu - ia! A - men.

Words: F. Pratt Green (b. 1903)
Music: *Engelberg*, Charles Villiers Stanford (1852-1924)

10 10 10 with Alleluia

## Praise to God

# 421

1 All glo - ry be to God on high, and peace on earth from
2 O Lamb of God, Lord Je - sus Christ, whom God the Fa - ther
3 You on - ly are the Ho - ly One, who came for our sal -

hea - ven, and God's good will un - fail - ing - ly be
gave us, who for the world was sac - ri - ficed up -
va - tion, and on - ly you are God's true Son, who

to all peo - ple giv - en. We bless, we wor - ship you, we raise for
on the cross to save us; and, as you sit at God's right hand and
was be - fore cre - a - tion. You, on - ly, Christ, as Lord we own and,

your great glo - ry thanks and praise, O God, Al - might - y Fa - ther.
we for judg - ment there must stand, have mer - cy, Lord, up - on us.
with the Spi - rit, you a - lone share in the Fa - ther's glo - ry.

Words: Nikolaus Decius (1490?-1541); tr. F. Bland Tucker (1895-1984), rev.;
para. of *Gloria in excelsis*
Music: *Allein Gott in der Höh*, melody att. Nikolaus Decius (1490?-1541);

87. 87. 887

# 422

1 Not far be - yond the sea, nor high a - bove the heavens, but
2 Root - ed and ground - ed in thy love, with saints on earth and
3 Help us to press on toward that mark, and, though our vi - sion

ve - ry high thy voice, O God, is heard. For
saints a - bove we join in full ac - cord: to
now is dark, to live by what we see. So,

each new step of faith we take thou hast more truth and
know the breadth, length, depth, and height, the cru - ci - fied and
when we see thee face to face, thy truth and light our

light to break forth from thy Ho - ly Word.
ris - en might of Christ, the in - car - nate Word.
dwell - ing - place for ev - er - more shall be.

Words: George B. Caird (b. 1917), alt.
Music: *Cornwall*, Samuel Sebastian Wesley (1810-1876)

886. 886

# Praise to God

1 Im - mor - tal, in - vis - i - ble, God on - ly wise,
2 Un - rest - ing, un - hast - ing, and si - lent as light,
3 To all life thou giv - est, to both great and small;
4 Thou reign - est in glo - ry, thou rul - est in light,

in light in - ac - ces - si - ble hid from our eyes,
nor want - ing, nor wast - ing, thou rul - est in might;
in all life thou liv - est, the true life of all;
thine an - gels a - dore thee, all veil - ing their sight;

most bless - ed, most glo - rious, the An - cient of Days,
thy jus - tice like moun-tains high soar - ing a - bove
we blos - som and flour - ish, like leaves on the tree,
all laud we would ren - der: O help us to see

al - might - y, vic - tor - ious, thy great Name we praise.
thy clouds, which are foun - tains of good - ness and love.
then with - er and per - ish; but nought chan - geth thee.
'tis on - ly the splen - dor of light hid - eth thee.

Words: Walter Chalmers Smith (1824-1908), alt.
Music: *St. Denio*, Welsh hymn, from *Caniadau y Cyssegr*, 1839; adapt. John Roberts (1822-1877);
   harm. *The English Hymnal*, 1906, alt.                    11 11. 11 11

Praise to God

1 For the fruit of all cre - a - tion, thanks be to
2 In the just re - ward of la - bor, God's will be
3 For the har - vests of the Spi - rit, thanks be to

God. For his gifts to ev - ery na - tion,
done. In the help we give our neigh - bor,
God. For the good we all in - her - it,

thanks be to God. For the plow - ing, sow - ing, reap - ing,
God's will be done. In our world-wide task of car - ing
thanks be to God. For the won - ders that as - tound us,

si - lent growth while we are sleep - ing, fu - ture needs in
for the hun - gry and de - spair - ing, in the har - vests
for the truths that still con-found us, most of all that

earth's safe - keep - ing, thanks be to God.
we are shar - ing, God's will be done.
love has found us, thanks be to God.

Words: F. Pratt Green (b. 1903), alt.
Music: *East Acklam*, Francis Jackson (b. 1917)
84. 84. 888. 4
Words: Copyright © 1972 by Hope Publishing Company. All Rights Reserved. Used by Permission.

425

Praise to God

1 Sing now with joy un - to the Lord, for
2 God is our strength, he is our song, he
3 He on - ly is the might - y Lord. He

he has tri - umphed glo - rious - ly! The horse, the rid - er,
saved us from our en - e - my. All praise and thanks to
on - ly can des - troy the foe. He on - ly is to

and the sword he cast in - to the rag - ing sea.
him be - long who came to set his peo - ple free.
be a - dored for he a - lone can strength be - stow.

Words: Anon., ca. 1976, alt.; based on Exodus 15:1-2
Music: *Adon Olam,* Eliezer Gerovitch (1844-1914)

LM

## Praise to God

# 426

1 Songs of praise the an - gels sang, heaven with al - le - lu - ias rang,
2 Songs of praise a - woke the morn when the Prince of Peace was born;
3 Heaven and earth must pass a - way; songs of praise shall crown that day;
4 And shall Chris - tians fail to sing till on earth Christ come as King?
5 Saints be - low, with heart and voice, still in songs of praise re - joice,

1 when cre - a - tion was be - gun, when God spoke and it was done.
2 songs of praise a - rose when he cap - tive led cap - tiv - i - ty.
3 God will make new heavens and earth; songs of praise shall hail their birth.
4 No; the Church de - lights to raise psalms and hymns and songs of praise.
5 learn - ing here, by faith and love, songs of praise to sing a - bove.

6 Borne upon their latest breath,
   songs of praise shall conquer death;
   then, amidst eternal joy,
   songs of praise their powers employ.

Words: James Montgomery (1771-1854), alt.
Music: *Northampton,* Charles John King (1859-1934)

77. 77

**427**

1 When morn-ing gilds the skies, my heart, a - wak - ing, cries,
2 When mirth for mu - sic longs, this is my song of songs:
3 No love - lier an - ti - phon in all high heaven is known
4 Ye na - tions of man - kind, in this your con - cord find:
5 Sing, suns and stars of space, sing, ye that see his face,

1 may Je - sus Christ be praised! When eve - ning sha - dows fall,
2 may Je - sus Christ be praised! God's ho - ly house of prayer
3 than, Je - sus Christ be praised! There to the e - ter - nal Word
4 may Je - sus Christ be praised! Let all the earth a - round
5 sing, Je - sus Christ be praised! God's whole cre - a - tion o'er,

1 this rings my cur - few call, may Je - sus Christ be praised!
2 hath none that can com - pare with: Je - sus Christ be praised!
3 the e - ter - nal psalm is heard: may Je - sus Christ be praised!
4 ring joy - ous with the sound: may Je - sus Christ be praised!
5 both now and ev - er - more shall Je - sus Christ be praised!

Words: German, ca. 1800; tr. Robert Seymour Bridges (1844-1930), alt.
Music: *Laudes Domini*, Joseph Barnby (1838-1896)

666. 666

1 O all ye works of God, now come to thank him
2 O sun and moon and stars of heaven, your end - less
3 O heat and cold, O night and day, O storms and
4 O earth and sea, O all that live in wa - ter
5 O let his peo - ple bless the Lord like right - eous

1 and a - dore; O an - gels, sing and
2 praise out - pour; O chang - ing sea - sons,
3 thun - der's roar, O fields and for - ests,
4 or on shore, O men and wo - men,
5 souls of yore; let those of ho - ly,

1 bless the Lord and praise him ev - er - more.
2 bless the Lord and praise him ev - er - more.
3 bless the Lord and praise him ev - er - more.
4 bless the Lord and praise him ev - er - more.
5 hum - ble heart come praise him ev - er - more.

Words: F. Bland Tucker (1895-1984), rev.; para. of *A Song of Creation*
Music: *Irish*, melody from *Hymns and Sacred Poems*, 1749; harm. *The English Hymnal*, 1906

CM

1 I'll praise my Ma - ker while I've breath; and when my voice is lost in
2 How hap - py they whose hopes re - ly on Is - rael's God, who made the
3 The Lord pours eye - sight on the blind; the Lord sup - ports the faint-ing
4 I'll praise him while he lends me breath; and when my voice is lost in

death, praise shall em - ploy my no - bler powers. My
sky and earth and seas with all their train; whose
mind and sends the la - boring con - science peace. He
death, praise shall em - ploy my no - bler powers. My

days of praise shall ne'er be past while life and thought and be - ing
truth for ev - er stands se - cure, who saves the op-pressed, and feeds the
helps the strang - er in dis - tress, the wid - owed and the fa - ther -
days of praise shall ne'er be past while life and thought and be - ing

last, or im - mor - tal - i - ty en - dures.
poor. And none shall find his prom - ise vain.
less, and grants the pris - oner sweet re - lease.
last, or im - mor - tal - i - ty en - dures.

Words: Isaac Watts (1674-1748); alt. by John Wesley (1703-1791), alt.; para. of Psalm 146
Music: *Old 113th*, melody from *Strassburger Kirchenamt*, 1525        88. 88. 88

1 Come, O come, our voic - es raise, sound - ing
2 Sound the trum - pet, touch the lute, let no
3 Come ye all be - fore his face, in this
4 Let, in praise of God, the sound run a
5 So this huge wide orb we see shall one
6 Thus our song shall o - ver - climb all the

| | | | | | | | |
|---|---|---|---|---|---|---|---|
| 1 | God | Al - might - - - y's praise; | hith - er | bring | in |
| 2 | tongue nor | string | be mute, | nor a | voice - less |
| 3 | cho - rus | take | your place; | and a - mid | the |
| 4 | nev - er - | end - - ing round, | that our | songs | of |
| 5 | choir, one | tem - - ple be; | where in | such | a |
| 6 | bounds of | space | and time; | come, then, come, | our |

1 one con - sent heart, and voice, and in - stru - ment. Al - le - lu - ia!
2 crea - ture found, that hath nei - ther note nor sound. Al - le - lu - ia!
3 mor - tal throng, be you mas - ters of the song. Al - le - lu - ia!
4 praise may be ev - er - last - ing, as is he. Al - le - lu - ia!
5 praise - ful tone we will sing what he hath done. Al - le - lu - ia!
6 voic - es raise, sound - ing God Al - might - y's praise. Al - le - lu - ia!

Words: George Wither (1588-1667), alt.
Music: *Sonne der Gerechtigkeit*, melody from *Bohemian Brethren, Kirchengeseng*, 1566　　　77. 77 with Alleluia

## Praise to God 　　　　431

1 The stars de - clare his glo - ry; the vault of hea - ven springs
2 The dawn re - turns in splen - dor, the hea - vens burn and blaze,
3 So shine the Lord's com - mand - ments to make the sim - ple wise;
4 So or - der too this life of mine, di - rect it all my days;

mute wit - ness of the Mas - ter's hand in all cre - at - ed things, and
the ris - ing sun re - news the race that mea - sures all our days, and
more swe tha hon - ey to the taste, more rich than an - y prize, a
the med - i - ta - tions of my heart be in - no - cen and praise, my

through the si - lenc - es of space their sound - less mu - sic sings. ____
writes in fire a - cross the skies God's ma - jes - ty and praise. ____
law of love with - in our hearts, a light be - fore our eyes. ____
rock, and my re - deem - ing Lord, in all my words and ways. ____

Words: Timothy Dudley-Smith (b. 1926); para. of Psalm 19
Music: *Aldine*, Richard Proulx (b. 1937)　　　　　76. 86. 86

# 432

Praise to God

1 O praise ye the Lord! Praise him in the height;
2 O praise ye the Lord! Praise him up-on earth,
*3 O praise ye the Lord! All things that give sound;
4 O praise ye the Lord! Thanks-giv-ing and song

re - joice in his word, ye an-gels of light;
in tune-ful ac - cord, all ye of new birth;
each ju-bi-lant chord re-ech-o a - round;
to him be out-poured all a-ges a - long!

ye hea-vens, a - dore him by whom ye were made,
praise him who hath brought you his grace from a - bove,
loud or-gans, his glo - ry forth tell in deep tone,
For love in cre - a - tion, for hea-ven re - stored,

and wor-ship be - fore him, in bright-ness ar - rayed.
praise him who hath taught you to sing of his love.
and sweet harp, the sto - ry of what he hath done.
for grace of sal - va - tion, O praise ye the Lord!

Words: Henry Williams Baker (1821-1877), alt.; based on Psalms 148 and 150
Music: *Laudate Dominum*, Charles Hubert Hastings Parry (1848-1918)

10 10. 11 11

1 We gath-er to-geth-er to ask the Lord's bless-ing;
2 Be-side us to guide us, our God with us join-ing,
3 We all do ex-tol thee, thou lead-er tri-um-phant,

he chas-tens and has-tens his will to make known;
or-dain-ing, main-tain-ing his king-dom di-vine;
and pray that thou still our de-fend-er wilt be.

the wick-ed op-press-ing now cease from dis-tress-ing:
so from the be-gin-ning the fight we were win-ning:
Let thy con-gre-ga-tion es-cape trib-u-la-tion:

sing prais-es to his Name; he for-gets not his own.
thou, Lord, wast at our side: all glo-ry be thine!
thy Name be ev-er praised! O Lord, make us free!

Words: Anon. 1625; tr. Theodore Baker (1851-1934)
Music: *Kremser*, from *Nederlandtsch Gedenckclank*, 1626; arr. Eduard Kremser (1838-1914)     12 11. 12 11

*Unison or harmony*

1 Na - ture with o - pen vol - ume stands to spread her
2 But in the grace that res - cued man his bright - est
3 Here his whole Name ap - pears com - plete; nor wit can
4 Oh, the sweet won - ders of that cross where Christ my
5 I would for ev - er speak his Name in sounds to

1 Ma - ker's praise a - broad and ev - ery la - bor of his
2 form of glo - ry shines; here, on the cross, 'tis fair - est
3 guess, nor rea - son prove which of the let - ters best is
4 Sa - vior loved and died! Her no - blest life my spi - rit
5 mor - tal ears un - known, with an - gels join to praise the

1 hands shows some - thing wor - thy of a God.
2 drawn in pre - cious blood and crim - son lines.
3 writ, the power, the wis - dom, or the love.
4 draws from his dear wounds and bleed - ing side.
5 Lamb and wor - ship at his Fa - ther's throne!

*The G♯ in the final chord should be reserved for stanza 5.*

Words: Isaac Watts (1674-1748)
Music: *Eltham*, melody Nathaniel Gawthorn (18th cent.); harm. Samuel Sebastian Wesley (1810-1876)                LM

1 At the Name of Je - sus ev - ery knee shall bow,
2 Hum-bled for a sea - son, to re - ceive a Name
3 bore it up tri - um - phant, with its hu - man light,
4 Name him, Chris - tians, name him, with love strong as death,
*5 In your hearts en - throne him; there let him sub - due
*6 Chris-tians, this Lord Je - sus shall re - turn a - gain,

1 ev - ery tongue con - fess him King of glo - ry now;
2 from the lips of sin - ners, un - to whom he came,
3 through all ranks of crea - tures, to the cen - tral height,
4 name with awe and won - der and with bat - ed breath;
5 all that is not ho - ly, all that is not true;
6 with his Fa - ther's glo - ry o'er the earth to reign;

1 'tis the Fa - ther's plea - sure we should call him Lord,
2 faith - ful - ly he bore it spot - less to the last,
3 to the throne of God - head, to the Fa - ther's breast;
4 he is God the Sa - vior, he is Christ the Lord,
5 crown him as your Cap - tain in temp - ta - tion's hour;
6 for all wreaths of em - pire meet up - on his brow,

1 who from the be - gin - ning was the might - y Word.
2 brought it back vic - to - rious, when from death he passed;
3 filled it with the glo - ry of that per - fect rest.
4 ev - er to be wor - shiped, trust - ed, and a - dored.
5 let his will en - fold you in its light and power.
6 and our hearts con - fess him King of glo - ry now.

Words: Caroline Maria Noel (1817-1877), alt.
Music: *King's Weston*, Ralph Vaughan Williams (1872-1958)

65. 65. D

1 Lift up your heads, ye might-y gates; be-hold the
2 O blest the land, the ci-ty blest, where Christ the
3 Fling wide the por-tals of your heart; make it a
*4 Re-deem-er come! I o-pen wide my heart to
5 So come, my Sov-ereign; en-ter in! Let new and

1 King of glo-ry waits! The King of kings is
2 ru-ler is con-fessed! O hap-py hearts and
3 tem-ple, set a-part from earth-ly use for
4 thee: here, Lord, a-bide! Let me thy in-ner
5 no-bler life be-gin; thy Ho-ly Spi-rit

1 draw-ing near; the Sa-vior of the world is here.
2 hap-py homes to whom this King of tri-umph comes!
3 heaven's em-ploy, a-dorned with prayer and love and joy.
4 pres-ence feel: thy grace and love in me re-veal.
5 guide us on, un-til the glo-rious crown be won.

Words: Georg Weissel (1590-1635); tr. Catherine Winkworth (1827-1878)
Music: *Truro*, melody from *Psalmodia Evangelica, Part II*, 1789; harm. Lowell Mason (1792-1872), alt.          LM

# Jesus Christ our Lord

**437**

1 Tell out, my soul, the great-ness of the Lord!
2 Tell out, my soul, the great-ness of his Name!
3 Tell out, my soul, the great-ness of his might!
4 Tell out, my soul, the glo-ries of his word!

Un - num - bered bless - ings give my spi - rit voice;
Make known his might, the deeds his arm has done;
Powers and do - min - ions lay their glo - ry by.
Firm is his prom - ise, and his mer - cy sure.

ten - der to me the prom - ise of his word;
his mer - cy sure, from age to age the same;
Proud hearts and stub - born wills are put to flight,
Tell out, my soul, the great - ness of the Lord

in God my Sa - vior shall my heart re - joice.
his ho - ly Name— the Lord, the Might - y One.
the hun - gry fed, the hum - ble lift - ed high.
to chil-dren's chil - dren and for ev - er - more!

Words: Timothy Dudley-Smith (b. 1926); based on *The Song of Mary*
Music: *Birmingham*, from *Repository of Sacred Music, Part II*, 1813; harm. *Songs of Praise*, 1925

10 10. 10 10

**438**

Jesus Christ our Lord

1 Tell out, my soul, the great-ness of the Lord!
2 Tell out, my soul, the great-ness of his Name!
3 Tell out, my soul, the great-ness of his might!
4 Tell out, my soul, the glo-ries of his word!

Un-num-bered bless-ings give my spi-rit voice;
Make known his might, the deeds his arm has done;
Powers and do-min-ions lay their glo-ry by.
Firm is his prom-ise, and his mer-cy sure.

ten-der to me the prom-ise of his word;
his mer-cy sure, from age to age the same;
Proud hearts and stub-born wills are put to flight,
Tell out, my soul, the great-ness of the Lord

in God my Sa-vior shall my heart re-joice.
his ho-ly Name— the Lord, the Might-y One.
the hun-gry fed, the hum-ble lift-ed high.
to chil-dren's chil-dren and for ev-er-more!

Words: Timothy Dudley-Smith (b. 1926); based on *The Song of Mary*
Music: *Woodlands*, Walter Greatorex (1877-1949)

10 10. 10 10

**439**

Jesus Christ our Lord

*Unison*

1 What won-drous love is this, O my soul, O my soul! What
2 To God and to the Lamb, I will sing, I will sing, to
3 And when from death I'm free, I'll sing on, I'll sing on, and

won-drous love is this, O my soul! What won-drous love is this that
God and to the Lamb, I will sing. To God and to the Lamb who
when from death I'm free, I'll sing on. And when from death I'm free I'll

caused the Lord of bliss to lay a - side his crown for my
is the great I AM, while mil - lions join the theme, I will
sing and joy - ful be, and through e - ter - ni - ty I'll sing

soul, for my soul, to lay a - side his crown for my soul.
sing, I will sing, while mil - lions join the theme I will sing.
on, I'll sing on, and through e - ter - ni - ty I'll sing on.

*Harmony (the melody is in the tenor)*

1 What won - drous love is this, O my soul, O my soul! What
2 To God and to the Lamb, I will sing, I will sing, to
3 And when from death I'm free, I'll sing on, I'll sing on, and

won - drous love is this, O my soul! What won - drous love is this that
God and to the Lamb, I will sing. To God and to the Lamb who
when from death I'm free, I'll sing on. And when from death I'm free I'll

caused the Lord of bliss to lay a - side his crown for my
is the great I AM, while mil - lions join the theme, I will
sing and joy - ful be, and through e - ter - ni - ty I'll sing

soul, for my soul, to lay a - side his crown for my soul.
sing, I will sing, while mil - lions join the theme I will sing.
on, I'll sing on, and through e - ter - ni - ty I'll sing on.

Words: American folk hymn, ca. 1835
Music: *Wondrous Love*, from *The Southern Harmony*, 1835

12 9. 12. 12 9

# 440

1 Bless-ed Je-sus, at thy word we are gath-ered all to hear thee; let our hearts and souls be stirred now to seek and love and fear thee; by thy teach-ings pure and ho-ly, drawn from earth to love thee sole-ly.

2 All our know-ledge, sense, and sight lie in deep-est dark-ness shroud-ed, till thy Spi-rit breaks our night with the beams of truth un-cloud-ed; thou a-lone to God canst win us; thou must work all good with-in us.

3 Gra-cious Lord, thy-self im-part! Light of Light, from God pro-ceed-ing, o-pen thou our ears and heart, help us by thy Spi-rit's plead-ing. Hear the cry thy Church up-rais-es; hear, and bless our prayers and prais-es.

Words: Tobias Clausnitzer (1619-1684); tr. Catherine Winkworth (1827-1878), alt.
Music: *Liebster Jesu*, melody Johann Rudolph Ahle (1625-1673); alt. *Das grosse Cantional oder Kirchen-Gesangbuch*, 1687; harm. George Herbert Palmer (1846-1926)

78. 78. 88

1 In the cross of Christ I glo - ry,
  tower - ing o'er the wrecks of time;
  all the light of sa - cred sto - ry
  gath - ers round its head sub - lime.

2 When the woes of life o'er - take me,
  hopes de - ceive, and fears an - noy,
  nev - er shall the cross for - sake me:
  lo, it glows with peace and joy.

3 When the sun of bliss is beam - ing
  light and love up - on my way,
  from the cross the ra - diance stream - ing
  adds new lus - ter to the day.

4 Bane and bless - ing, pain and plea - sure,
  by the cross are sanc - ti - fied;
  peace is there that knows no mea - sure,
  joys that through all time a - bide.

*5 In the cross of Christ I glo - ry,
  tower - ing o'er the wrecks of time;
  all the light of sa - cred sto - ry
  gath - ers round its head sub - lime.

Words: John Bowring (1792-1872)
Music: *Rathbun*, Ithamar Conkey (1815-1867)

87. 87

## 442

```
1 In    the    cross    of    Christ  I      glo - ry,    tower - ing  o'er  the
2 When  the    woes     of    life    o'er - take me,    hopes de - ceive, and
3 When  the    sun      of    bliss   is     beam - ing  light  and   love  up -
4 Bane  and    bless - ing,   pain    and    plea - sure, by    the    cross  are
*5 In   the    cross    of    Christ  I      glo - ry,    tower - ing  o'er  the
```

```
1 wrecks  of    time;      all    the    light   of    sa -  cred
2 fears   an -  noy,       nev - er    shall   the   cross  for -
3 on      my    way,       from   the    cross   the   ra -  diance
4 sanc -  ti -  fied;      peace  is     there   that  knows no
5 wrecks  of    time;      all    the    light   of    sa -  cred
```

```
1 sto - ry    gath - ers   round  its    head   sub - lime.
2 sake  me:   lo,    it     glows  with   peace  and   joy.
3 stream - ing  adds  new   lus -  ter    to     the   day.
4 mea - sure,  joys   that  through all   time   a -   bide.
5 sto - ry    gath - ers   round  its    head   sub - lime.
```

Words: John Bowring (1792-1872)
Music: *Tomter*, Bruce Neswick (b. 1956)

87. 87

## 443

```
1 From God  Christ's de - i - ty  came forth,  his   man - hood from hu -
2 He joined with  guests at wed - ding feast,  yet   in    the   wil - der -
3 The dis - so - lute  he  did  not  scorn,    nor   turn  from those who
4 He  did  not  dis - re - gard the  sick;  to  sim - ple ones his
5 Who then,  my   Lord, com - pares to  you?  The  Watch - er  slept, the
```

1 man - i - ty; his priest-hood from Mel - chi - ze - dek, his
2 ness did fast; he taught with - in the tem - ple's gates; his
3 were in sin; he for the right - eous did re - joice but
4 word was given; and he de - scend - ed to the earth and
5 Great was small, the Pure bap - tized, the Life who died, the

1 roy - al - ty from Da - vid's tree: praised be his One - ness.
2 peo - ple saw him die at last: praised be his teach - ing.
3 bade the fall - en to come in: praised be his mer - cy.
4 his work done, went up to heaven: praised by his com - ing.
5 King a - based to hon - or all: praised be your glo - ry.

Words: Ephrem of Edessa (4th cent.); tr. J. Howard Rhys (b. 1917);
adapt. and alt. F. Bland Tucker (1895-1984)
Music: *Salem Harbor*, Ronald Arnatt (b. 1930)

88. 88. 5

## Jesus Christ our Lord

# 444

1 Blessed be the God of Is - rael, who comes to set us free;
2 He from the house of Da - vid a child of grace has given;
3 On pris - on - ers of dark - ness the sun be - gins to rise,

he vis - its and re - deems us, he grants us lib - er - ty.
a Sa - vior comes a - mong us to raise us up to heaven.
the dawn-ing of for - give - ness up - on the sin - ner's eyes.

The pro - phets spoke of mer - cy, of free-dom and re - lease;
Be - fore him goes his her - ald, fore - run - ner in the way,
He guides the feet of pil - grims a - long the paths of peace.

God shall ful - fill his prom - ise and bring his peo - ple peace.____
the pro - phet of sal - va - tion, the har - bin - ger of Day.____
O bless our God and Sa - vior with songs that nev - er cease.____

Words: Michael A. Perry (b. 1942), alt.; para. of *The Song of Zechariah*
Music: *Thornbury*, Basil Harwood (1859-1949)

76. 76. D

1 Praise to the Ho - liest in the height, and in the
2 O lov - ing wis - dom of our God! When all was
3 O wis - est love! that flesh and blood, which did in
4 and that the high - est gift of grace should flesh and
5 Praise to the Ho - liest in the height, and in the

1 depth be praise; in all his words most
2 sin and shame, a sec - ond Ad - am
3 Ad - am fail, should strive a - fresh a -
4 blood re - fine: God's pres - ence and his
5 depth be praise; in all his words most

1 won - der - ful, most sure in all his ways!
2 to the fight and to the res - cue came.
3 gainst the foe, should strive, and should pre - vail;
4 ve - ry self, and es - sence all - di - vine.
5 won - der - ful, most sure in all his ways!

Words: John Henry Newman (1801-1890), alt.
Music: *Gerontius,* John Bacchus Dykes (1823-1876)

CM

# Jesus Christ our Lord

446

1 Praise to the Ho - liest in the height, and in the
2 O lov - ing wis - dom of our God! When all was
3 O wis - est love! that flesh and blood, which did in
4 and that the high - est gift of grace should flesh and
5 Praise to the Ho - liest in the height, and in the

1 depth be praise; in all his words most
2 sin and shame, a sec - ond Ad - am
3 Ad - am fail, should strive a - fresh a -
4 blood re - fine: God's pres - ence and his
5 depth be praise; in all his words most

1 won - der - ful, most sure in all his ways!
2 to the fight and to the res - cue came.
3 gainst the foe, should strive, and should pre - vail;
4 ve - ry self, and es - sence all - di - vine.
5 won - der - ful most sure in all his ways!

Words: John Henry Newman (1801-1890), alt.
Music: *Newman*, Richard Runciman Terry (1865-1938)

CM

# 447

1 The Christ who died but rose a-gain tri-um-phant from the grave,
2 What now can sep-a-rate us from the love of Christ our Lord?
3 The trou-bles that are ours to bear are trials we can-not flee;
4 Thus noth-ing in the heights or depths, no power earth can af-ford,

now pleads our cause at God's right hand all - pow-er-ful to save.
Can per - se - cu - tion, na - ked-ness, or per - il, or the sword?
yet he who loved us from the first en - sures our vic - to - ry.
will sep - a - rate us from the love of Je - sus Christ our Lord.

Words: Granton Douglas Hay (b. 1943), alt.; based on *Paraphrases*, 1781; para. of Romans 8:34-39
Music: *St. Magnus*, melody from *Divine Companion*, 1707; harm. William Henry Monk (1823-1889),
after John Pyke Hullah (19th cent.)

CM

# 448

1 O love, how deep, how broad, how high, how pass - ing
2 For us bap - tized, for us he bore his ho - ly
3 For us he prayed; for us he taught; for us his
4 For us to wick - ed hands be - trayed, scourged, mocked, in
5 For us he rose from death a - gain; for us he
6 All glo - ry to our Lord and God for love so

1 thought and fan - ta - sy, that God, the Son of
2 fast and hun - gered sore; for us temp - ta - tions
3 dai - ly works he wrought: by words and signs and
4 pur - ple robe ar - rayed, he bore the shame - ful
5 went on high to reign; for us he sent his
6 deep, so high, so broad; the Trin - i - ty whom

1 God, should take our mor - tal form for mor - tals' sake.
2 sharp he knew; for us the tempt - er o - ver - threw.
3 ac - tions, thus still seek - ing not him - self, but us.
4 cross and death; for us gave up his dy - ing breath.
5 Spi - rit here to guide, to strength - en, and to cheer.
6 we a - dore for ev - er and for ev - er - more.

Words: Latin, 15th cent.; tr. Benjamin Webb (1819-1885), alt.
Music: *Deus tuorum militum*, from *Antiphoner*, 1753; adapt. *The English Hymnal*, 1906, alt.                    LM

## Jesus Christ our Lord                                                              449

1 O love, how deep, how broad, how high, how pass - ing
2 For us bap - tized, for us he bore his ho - ly
3 For us he prayed; for us he taught; for us his
4 For us to wick - ed hands be - trayed, scourged, mocked, in
5 For us he rose from death a - gain; for us he
6 All glo - ry to our Lord and God for love so

1 thought and fan - ta - sy, that God, the Son of
2 fast and hun - gered sore; for us temp - ta - tions
3 dai - ly works he wrought: by words and signs and
4 pur - ple robe ar - rayed, he bore the shame - ful
5 went on high to reign; for us he sent his
6 deep, so high, so broad; the Trin - i - ty whom

1 God, should take our mor - tal form for mor - tals' sake.
2 sharp he knew; for us the tempt - er o - ver - threw.
3 ac - tions, thus still seek - ing not him - self, but us.
4 cross and death; for us gave up his dy - ing breath.
5 Spi - rit here to guide, to strength - en, and to cheer.
6 we a - dore for ev - er and for ev - er - more.

Words: Latin, 15th cent.; tr. Benjamin Webb (1819-1885), alt.
Music: *Deo gracias*, English ballad melody, Trinity College MS., 15th cent.                    LM

6 O ev - ery kin - dred, ev - ery tribe, on this ter - res-trial

1 All hail the power of Je - sus' Name! Let an - gels pros-trate
2 Crown him ye mar - tyrs of our God, who from his al - tar
3 Hail him, the Heir of Da - vid's line, whom Da - vid Lord did
*4 Ye heirs of Is - rael's cho - sen race, ye ran - somed of the
*5 Sin - ners, whose love can ne'er for - get the worm-wood and the

ball, to him a - scribe, and

1 fall; bring forth the roy - al di - a - dem, and
2 call: praise him whose way of pain ye trod, and
3 call, the God in - car - nate, Man di - vine, and
4 fall, hail him who saves you by his grace, and
5 gall, go, spread your tro - phies at his feet, and

crown him Lord of all! to him a -

1 crown him Lord of all! bring forth the roy - al
2 crown him Lord of all! praise him whose way of
3 crown him Lord of all! the God in - car - nate,
4 crown him Lord of all! hail him who saves you
5 crown him Lord of all! go, spread your tro - phies

scribe, and crown him Lord of all!

1 di - a - dem, and crown him Lord of all!
2 pain ye trod, and crown him Lord of all!
3 Man di - vine, and crown him Lord of all!
4 by his grace, and crown him Lord of all!
5 at his feet, and crown him Lord of all!

6 Let every kindred, every tribe,
on this terrestrial ball,
to him all majesty ascribe,
and crown him Lord of all!

Words: Edward Perronet (1726-1792), alt.
Music: *Coronation*, Oliver Holden (1765-1844), alt.; desc. Michael E. Young (b. 1939)

86. 86. 86

1 All hail the power of Je - sus' Name! Let an - gels
2 Crown him, ye mar - tyrs of our God, who from his
3 Hail him, the Heir of Da - vid's line, whom Da - vid
*4 Ye heirs of Is - rael's cho - sen race, ye ran - somed
*5 Sin - ners, whose love can ne'er for - get the worm - wood

1 pros - trate fall; bring forth the roy - al di - a - dem,
2 al - tar call: praise him whose way of pain ye trod,
3 Lord did call, the God in - car - nate, Man di - vine,
4 of the fall, hail him who saves you by his grace,
5 and the gall, go, spread your tro - phies at his feet,

*Refrain*

and crown him, crown him, crown him, crown him Lord of all!

6 Let every kindred, every tribe,
on this terrestrial ball,
to him all majesty ascribe,

*Refrain*

Words: Edward Perronet (1726-1792), alt.
Music: *Miles Lane*, William Shrubsole (1760-1806)

868 with Refrain

# Jesus Christ our Lord

## 452

1 Glo - rious the day when Christ was born to wear the
2 Glo - rious the day when Christ a - rose, the sur - est
3 Glo - rious the days of gos - pel grace when Christ re -
4 Glo - rious the day when Christ ful - fills what self re -

crown that Cea - sars scorn, whose life and death that
friend of all his foes; who for the sake of
stores the fal - len race, when doubt - ers kneel and
jects yet fee - bly wills; when that strong Light puts

love re - veal which mor - tals need and need to feel.
those he grieves tran - scends the world he nev - er leaves.
wa - verers stand, and faith a - chieves what rea - son planned.
out the sun and all is end - ed, all be - gun.

*Refrain*

Al - le - lu - ia! Al - le - lu - ia! Al - le - lu - ia!

Words: F. Pratt Green (b. 1903), rev.
Music: *Frohlockt mit Freud'*, Heinrich Schütz (1585-1672), alt.

LM with Refrain

1 As Jacob with travel was weary one day,
2 The ladder is long, it is strong and well-made,
3 Come, let us ascend! All may climb it who will,
4 And when we arrive at the haven of rest,

at night on a stone for a pillow he lay;
has stood hundreds of years and is not yet decayed;
for the angels of Jacob are guarding it still;
we shall hear the glad words, "Come to me all the blest,

he saw in a vision a ladder so high,
many millions have climbed it and reached Zion's hill,
and remember, each step that by faith we pass o'er,
here are regions of light, here are mansions of bliss."

that its foot was on earth and its top in the sky:
many millions by faith now are climbing it still;
many prophets and martyrs have trod it before:
Who would not want to climb such a ladder as this:

**Refrain**

Alleluia to Jesus, who died on the tree

and has raised up a ladder of mercy for me,

and has raised up a ladder of mercy for me.

Words: English carol, ca. 18th cent.
Music: *Jacob's Ladder*, English folk melody

Irr. with Refrain

# Jesus Christ our Lord

## 454

1 Je - sus came, a - dored by an - gels, came with peace from
2 Je - sus comes a - gain in mer - cy, when our hearts are
3 Je - sus comes to hearts re - joic - ing, bring - ing news of
4 Je - sus comes on clouds tri - um - phant, when the heavens shall

realms on high; Je - sus came for our re - demp - tion,
bowed with care: Je - sus comes a - gain in an - swer
sins for - given: Je - sus comes in sounds of glad - ness,
pass a - way; Je - sus comes a - gain in glo - ry;

low - ly came on earth to die: Al - le - lu - ia,
to our ear - nest heart - felt prayer; Al - le - lu - ia,
lead - ing souls re - deemed to heaven; Al - le - lu - ia,
let us then our hom - age pay; Al - le - lu - ia,

al - le - lu - ia! came in deep hu - mil - i - ty.
al - le - lu - ia! comes to save us from de - spair.
al - le - lu - ia! now the gate of death is riven.
al - le - lu - ia! till the dawn of end - less day.

Words: Godfrey Thring (1823-1903), alt.
Music: *Lowry*, Gerald Near (b. 1942)

87. 87. 87

## 455

**Jesus Christ our Lord**

1 O Love of God, how strong and true, e - ter - nal
2 O wide - em - brac - ing, won - drous Love, we read thee
3 We read thee best in him who came to bear for
4 We read thy power to bless and save e'en in the

and yet ev - er new; un - com - pre - hend - ed and un -
in the sky a - bove; we read thee in the earth be -
us the cross of shame, sent by the Fa - ther from on
dark - ness of the grave; still more in re - sur - rec - tion

bought, be - yond all know - ledge and all thought.
low, in seas that swell and streams that flow.
high, our life to live, our death to die.
light we read the full - ness of thy might.

Words: Horatius Bonar (1808-1889)
Music: *Dunedin,* Vernon Griffiths (b. 1894)

LM

## 456

**Jesus Christ our Lord**

1 O Love of God, how strong and true, e - ter - nal
2 (O wide - em - brac - ing, won - drous) Love, we read thee
3 (We read thee best in him who) came to bear for
4 (We read thy power to bless and) save e'en in the

and yet ev - er new; un - com - pre - hend - ed and un -
in the sky a - bove; we read thee in the earth be -
us the cross of shame, sent by the Fa - ther from on
dark - ness of the grave; still more in re - sur - rec - tion

| | | | | | | |
|---|---|---|---|---|---|---|
| bought, | be - yond | all | know - ledge | and | all |
| low, | in seas | that | swell | and streams | that |
| high, | our life | to | live, | our death | to |
| light | we read | the | full - ness | of | thy |

[1-3] / Final Ending

| | |
|---|---|
| thought. | 2 O wide-em-brac-ing, won-drous |
| flow. | 3 We read thee best in him who |
| die. | 4 We read thy power to bless and |
| might. | |

Words: Horatius Bonar (1808-1899)
Music: *de Tar*, Calvin Hampton (1938-1984)

LM

## Jesus Christ our Lord

# 457

1 Thou art the Way, to thee a - lone from sin and death we flee;
2 Thou art the Truth, thy word a - lone true wis - dom can im - part;
3 Thou art the Life, the rend - ing tomb pro - claims thy con - quering arm;
4 Thou art the Way, the Truth, the Life: grant us that way to know,

and all who would the Fa - ther seek, must seek him, Lord, by thee.
thou on - ly canst in - form the mind and pu - ri - fy the heart.
and those who put their trust in thee nor death nor hell shall harm.
that truth to keep, that life to win, whose joys e - ter - nal flow.

Words: George Washington Doane (1799-1859), alt.
Music: *St. James*, Raphael Courteville (d. 1735)

CM

458        Jesus Christ our Lord

*6  In life no house, no home
    my Lord on earth might have;
    in death no friendly tomb
    but what a stranger gave.
       What may I say?
         Heaven was his home;
         but mine the tomb
      wherein he lay.

7  Here might I stay and sing,
    no story so divine:
    never was love, dear King,
    never was grief like thine.
       This is my friend,
         in whose sweet praise
         I all my days
      could gladly spend.

Words: Samuel Crossman (1624-1683), alt.
Music: *Love Unknown*, John Ireland (1879-1962)

66. 66. 44. 44

# Jesus Christ our Lord

**459**

1 And have the bright im - men - si - ties re - ceived our ris - en Lord, where light-years frame the Plei - a - des and point O - ri - on's sword? Do flam - ing suns his foot - steps trace through cor - ri - dors sub - lime, the Lord of in - ter - stel - lar space and Con - quer - or of time?

2 The heaven that hides him from our sight knows nei - ther near nor far; an al - tar can - dle sheds its light as sure - ly as a star: and where his lov - ing peo - ple meet to share the gift di - vine, there stands he with un - hur - ry - ing feet; there heaven - ly splen - dors shine.

Words: Howard Chandler Robbins (1876-1952)
Music: *Halifax*, George Frideric Handel (1685-1759); adapt. David Hurd (b. 1950)

CMD

1 songs of peace - ful Zi - on thun - der like a
2 cloud from sight re - ceived him, when the for - ty
3 ces - sor, friend of sin - ners, earth's Re - deem - er,
4 in the veil hast en - tered, robed in flesh, our
5 songs of ho - ly Zi - on thun - der like a

1 might - y flood; Je - sus out of ev - ery
2 days were o'er, shall our hearts for - get his
3 plead for me, where the songs of all the
4 great High Priest: thou on earth both Priest and
5 might - y flood; Je - sus out of ev - ery

1 na - tion hath re - deemed us by his blood.
2 prom - ise, "I am with you ev - er - more"?
3 sin - less sweep a - cross the crys - tal sea.
4 Vic - tim in the eu - cha - ris - tic feast.
5 na - tion hath re - deemed us by his blood.

Words: William Chatterton Dix (1837-1898)
Music: *Hyfrydol,* Rowland Hugh Prichard (1811-1887)

87. 87. D

1 Al - le - lu - ia! sing to Je - sus! his the scep - ter, his the throne;
*2 Al - le - lu - ia! not as or - phans are we left in sor - row now;
3 Al - le - lu - ia! Bread of Hea - ven, thou on earth our food, our stay!
4 Al - le - lu - ia! King e - ter - nal, thee the Lord of lords we own:
*5 Al - le - lu - ia! sing to Je - sus! his the scep - ter, his the throne;

1 Al - le - lu - ia! his the tri - umph, his the vic - to - ry a - lone;
2 Al - le - lu - ia! he is near us, faith be - lieves, nor ques - tions how:
3 Al - le - lu - ia! here the sin - ful flee to thee from day to day:
4 Al - le - lu - ia! born of Ma - ry, earth thy foot - stool, heaven thy throne:
5 Al - le - lu - ia! his the tri - umph, his the vic - to - ry a - lone;

1 Hark! the songs of peace - ful Zi - on thun - der like a might - y flood;
2 though the cloud from sight re - ceived him, when the for - ty days were o'er,
3 In - ter - ces - sor, friend of sin - ners, earth's Re - deem - er, plead for me,
4 thou with - in the veil hast en - tered, robed in flesh, our great High Priest:
5 Hark! the songs of ho - ly Zi - on thun - der like a might - y flood;

1 Je - sus out of ev - ery na - tion hath re-deemed us by his blood.
2 shall our hearts for - get his prom - ise, "I am with you ev - er - more"?
3 where the songs of all the sin - less sweep a - cross the crys-tal sea.
4 thou on earth both Priest and Vic - tim in the eu - cha - ris - tic feast.
5 Je - sus out of ev - ery na - tion hath re-deemed us by his blood.

Words: William Chatterton Dix (1837-1898)
Music: *Alleluia*, Samuel Sebastian Wesley (1810-1876)

87. 87. D

## Jesus Christ our Lord

# 462

1 The Lord will come and not be slow, his foot - steps can - not err;
2 Truth from the earth, like to a flower, shall bud and blos - som show;
3 Rise, God, judge thou the earth in might, this wick - ed earth re - dress;
4 The na - tions all whom thou hast made shall come, and all shall frame
5 For great thou art, and won-ders great by thy strong hand are done:

1 be - fore him right-eous - ness shall go, his roy - al har - bin - ger.
2 and jus - tice, from her heaven - ly bower, look down on us be - low.
3 for thou art he who shalt by right the na - tions all pos - sess.
4 to bow them low be - fore thee, Lord, and glo - ri - fy thy Name.
5 thou in thy ev - er - last - ing seat re - main - est God a - lone.

Words: John Milton (1608-1674), alt.
Music: *York*, melody from *The CL Psalmes of David*, 1615; adapt. *The Whole Booke of Psalmes*, 1621;
   harm. John Milton, Sr. (1563?-1647)

CM

1. He is the Way. Fol-low him through the Land of Un-like -

ness; you will see rare beasts ___ and have u - nique ___ ad -

ven - tures. 2. He is the Truth. Seek him in the

King - dom of An - xi - e - ty: you will come to a great

ci - ty that has ex - pec - ted your re - turn for years.

3. He is the Life. Love him in the World of the Flesh: and

at your mar - riage all its oc - ca - sions shall dance for joy.

Words: W. H. Auden (1907-1973)
Music: *Hall*, David Hurd (b. 1950)

Irr.

1. He is the Way. Fol-low him through the Land of Un-like-ness;

you will see rare beasts and have u-nique ad - ven - tures.

2. He is the Truth. Seek him in the King-dom of Anx-i - e - ty:

you will come to a great ci - ty that has ex -

pect - ed your re - turn for years. 3. He is the

Life. Love him in the World of the Flesh: and at your

mar - riage all its oc - ca - sions shall dance for joy.

Words: W. H. Auden (1907-1973)
Music: *New Dance*, Richard Wetzel (b. 1935)

Irr.

*Unison or harmony*

1 E - ter - nal light, shine in my heart; e - ter - nal
2 E - ter - nal life, raise me from death; e - ter - nal
3 un - til by your most cost - ly grace, in - vit - ed

hope, lift up my eyes; e - ter - nal power, be
bright-ness, help me see; e - ter - nal Spi - rit,
by your ho - ly word, at last I come be -

my sup - port; e - ter - nal wis - dom, make me wise.
give me breath; e - ter - nal Sa - vior, come to me:
fore your face to know you, my e - ter - nal God.

Words: Christopher Idle (b. 1938); from a prayer of Alcuin (735?-804)
Music: *Ach bleib bei uns*, melody Samuel Scheidt (1587-1654); harm. Seth Calvisius (1556-1615)     LM

1 E - ter - nal light, shine in my heart; e - ter - nal
2 E - ter - nal life, raise me from death; e - ter - nal
3 un - til by your most cost - ly grace, in - vit - ed

hope,     lift     up    my    eyes;     e - ter - nal   power,   be
bright - ness,   help   me    see;     e - ter - nal   Spi -    rit,
by      your    ho - ly   word,    at    last   I    come   be -

my   sup - port;     e - ter - nal   wis - dom,   make me   wise.
give   me   breath;     e - ter - nal   Sa -    vior,   come   to    me:
fore   your   face     to   know you,   my     e - ter - nal   God.

Words: Christopher Idle (b. 1938); from a prayer by Alcuin (735?-804)
Music: *Jacob*, Jane Manton Marshall (b. 1924)

LM

## Jesus Christ our Lord

**467**

1 Sing, my soul, his won-drous love,   who, from yon bright throne a - bove,
2 Heaven and earth by him were made;   all   is   by   his   scep - ter swayed;
3 God, the mer - ci - ful and good, bought us with the   Sa - vior's blood,
4 Sing, my soul, a - dore his Name! Let   his   glo - ry   be    thy theme:

ev - er watch-ful o'er our race,   still   to   us   ex - tends his grace.
what are we that he should show   so   much love to    us   be - low?
and, to make sal - va - tion sure, guides us by his   Spi - rit pure.
praise him till he calls thee home; trust his love for    all   to come.

Words: Anon., 1800, alt.
Music: *St. Bees*, John Bacchus Dykes (1823-1876)

77. 77

# 468

Jesus Christ our Lord

1 It was poor lit - tle Je - sus, yes, yes; \_\_\_ he was
2 It was poor lit - tle Je - sus, yes, yes; \_\_\_ \_\_\_
3 It was poor lit - tle Je - sus, yes, yes; \_\_\_ they\_\_\_
4 It was poor lit - tle Je - sus, yes, yes; \_\_\_ he's\_\_\_

born on \_\_\_ Christ - mas, yes, yes; \_\_\_ and \_\_
child of \_\_\_ Ma - ry, yes, yes; \_\_\_ \_\_\_
nailed him to the cross, Lord, yes, yes; \_\_\_ they\_\_\_
ris - en from \_\_ dark - ness, yes, yes; \_\_\_ he's \_\_

laid\_\_ in a man - ger, yes, yes; \_\_\_
did - n't have a cra - dle, yes, yes; \_\_\_
hung him with a rob - ber, yes, yes; \_\_\_
'scend - ed in - to glo - ry, yes, yes; \_\_\_

was - n't that a pi - ty and a shame, Lord, Lord,
was - n't that a pi - ty and a shame, Lord, Lord,
was - n't that a pi - ty and a shame, Lord, Lord,
no\_\_ more a pi - ty and a shame, Lord, Lord,

was - n't that a pi - ty and a shame? _____
was - n't that a pi - ty and a shame? _____
was - n't that a pi - ty and a shame? _____
no\_\_ more a pi - ty and a shame. _____

Words: Afro-American spiritual
Music: *Poor Little Jesus*, Afro-American spiritual; melody from *Songs and Games of American Children, 1884-1911*

Irr. with Refrain

# Jesus Christ our Lord

1 There's a wide-ness in God's mer - cy like the wide-ness
2 There is no place where earth's sor - rows are more felt than
3 For the love of God is broad - er than the mea - sure

of the sea; there's a kind - ness in his jus -
up in heaven; there is no place where earth's fail -
of the mind; and the heart of the E - ter -

tice, which is more than lib - er - ty. There is wel - come
ings have such kind - ly judg - ment given. There is plen - ti -
nal is most won - der - ful - ly kind. If our love were

for the sin - ner, and more grac - es for the good; there is mer - cy
ful re - demp-tion in the blood that has been shed; there is joy for
but more faith - ful, we should take him at his word; and our life would

with the Sa - vior; there is heal - ing in his blood.
all the mem-bers in the sor - rows of the Head.
be thanks - giv - ing for the good-ness of the Lord.

Words: Frederick William Faber (1814-1863), alt.
Music: *St. Helena*, Calvin Hampton (1938-1984)

87. 87. D

1 There's a wide-ness in God's mer - cy like the wide-ness of the sea;
2 There is no place where earth's sor - rows are more felt than up in heaven;
3 For the love of God is broad - er than the mea-sure of the mind;

there's a kind-ness in his jus-tice, which is more than lib - er - ty.
there is no place where earth's fail-ings have such kind - ly judg-ment given.
and the heart of the E - ter-nal is most won - der - ful - ly kind.

There is wel - come for the sin - ner, and more gra - ces for the good;
There is plen - ti - ful re - demp-tion in the blood that has been shed;
If our love were but more faith-ful, we should take him at his word;

there is mer - cy with the Sa - vior; there is heal - ing in his blood.
there is joy for all the mem-bers in the sor - rows of the Head.
and our life would be thanks-giv - ing for the good-ness of the Lord.

Words: Frederick William Faber (1814-1863), alt.
Music: *Beecher*, John Zundel (1815-1882), alt.

87. 87. D

1 We sing the praise of him who died, of
2 In-scribed up-on the cross we see in
3 The cross: it takes our guilt a-way, and
4 It makes the cow-ard spi-rit brave, and
5 The balm of life, the cure of woe, the

1 him who died up-on the cross; the sin-ner's hope let
2 shin-ing let-ters, God is love: he bears our sins up-
3 holds the faint-ing spi-rit up; it cheers with hope the
4 nerves the fee-ble arm for fight; it takes its ter-ror
5 mea-sure and the pledge of love, the sin-ner's ref-uge

1 sin de-ride; for this we count the world but loss.
2 on the tree: he brings us mer-cy from a-bove.
3 gloom-y day, and sweet-ens ev-ery bit-ter cup.
4 from the grave, and gilds the bed of death with light.
5 here be-low, the an-gel's theme in heaven a-bove.

Words: Thomas Kelly (1769-1855), alt.
Music: *Breslau*, melody from *Lochamer Gesangbuch*, ca. 1450; harm. Felix Mendelssohn (1809-1847)     LM

1 Hope of the world, thou Christ of great com - pas - sion,
2 Hope of the world, God's gift from high - est hea - ven,
3 Hope of the world, a - foot on dust - y high - ways,
4 Hope of the world, who by thy cross didst save us
5 Hope of the world, O Christ, o'er death vic - to - rious,

1 speak to our fear - ful hearts by con - flict rent.
2 bring - ing to hun - gry souls the bread of life,
3 show - ing to wan - dering souls the path of light,
4 from death and dark de - spair, from sin and guilt,
5 who by this sign didst con - quer grief and pain,

1 Save us, thy peo - ple, from con - sum - ing pas - sion,
2 still let thy Spi - rit un - to us be giv - en
3 walk thou be - side us lest the tempt - ing by - ways
4 we rend - er back the love thy mer - cy gave us;
5 we would be faith - ful to thy gos - pel glo - rious;

1 who by our own false hopes and aims are spent.
2 to heal earth's wounds and end her bit - ter strife.
3 lure us a - way from thee to end - less night.
4 take thou our lives, and use them as thou wilt.
5 thou art our Lord! Thou dost for ev - er reign!

Words: Georgia Harkness (1891-1974)
Music: *Donne secours*, melody from *Trente quatre pseaumes de David*, 1551        11 10. 11 10

# Jesus Christ our Lord

473

Words: George William Kitchin (1827-1912); alt. Michael Robert Newbolt (1874-1956)
Music: *Crucifer*, Sydney Hugo Nicholson (1875-1947); desc. Richard Proulx (b. 1937)

10 10 with Refrain

1 When I sur - vey the won - drous cross where the young
2 For - bid it, Lord, that I should boast, save in the
3 See, from his head, his hands, his feet, sor - row and
4 Were the whole realm of na - ture mine, that were an

Prince of Glo - ry died, my rich - est gain I
cross of Christ, my God: all the vain things that
love flow min - gled down! Did e'er such love and
of - fering far too small; love so a - maz - ing,

count but loss, and pour con - tempt on all my pride.
charm me most, I sac - ri - fice them to his blood.
sor - row meet, or thorns com - pose so rich a crown?
so di - vine, de - mands my soul, my life, my all.

Words: Isaac Watts (1674-1748)
Music: *Rockingham*, from *Second Supplement to Psalmody in Miniature*, ca. 1780; harm. Edward Miller (1731-1807)   LM

1 God him - self is with us; let us all a - dore him,
2 Glad - ly, Lord, we of - fer thine to be for ev - er,
3 Thou per - vad - est all things; let thy rad - iant beau - ty
4 Come, a - bide with - in me; let my soul, like Ma - ry,

and with awe ap - pear be - fore him. God is here with -
soul and life and each en - deav - or. Help us to sur -
light mine eyes to see my du - ty. As the ten - der
be thine earth - ly sanc - tu - ar - y. Come, in - dwell - ing

in us; souls in si - lence fear him, hum - bly, fer - vent -
rend - er earth's de - ceit - ful trea - sures, pride of life, and
flow - ers ea - ger - ly un - fold them, to the sun - light
Spi - rit, with trans - fi - guring splen - dor; love and hon - or

ly draw near him. Now his own who have known
sin - ful plea - sures: thou a - lone shalt be known
calm - ly hold them, so let me qui - et - ly
will I ren - der. Where I go here be - low,

God, in wor - ship low - ly, yield their spi - rits whol - ly.
Lord of all our be - ing, life's true way de - cree - ing.
in thy rays im - bue me; let thy light shine through me.
let me bow be - fore thee, know thee, and a - dore thee.

Words: Gerhardt Tersteegen (1697-1769); tr. *Hymnal 1940*, alt.;
    st. 3, tr. Henry Sloane Coffin (1877-1954)
Music: *Tysk*, from *Psalm und Choralbuch*, 1719

668. 668. 666

**476**

1 Can we by search-ing find out God or for - mu - late his ways?
2 Al - though his be - ing is too bright for hu - man eyes to scan,
3 Our boast-ful - ness is turned to shame, our prof - it counts as loss,
4 There God breaks in up - on our search, makes birth and death his own;

Can num - bers mea - sure what he is or words con - tain his praise?
his mean-ing lights our sha-dowed world through Christ, the Son of Man.
when earth - ly val - ues stand be - side the man - ger and the cross.
he speaks to us in hu - man terms to make his glo - ry known.

Words: Elizabeth Cosnett (b. 1936), alt.
Music: *Epworth*, melody att. Charles Wesley (1757-1834), alt.;
     harm. Martin Fallas Shaw (1875-1958), alt.

CM

**477**

Descant

5 Let ev - ery tongue con-fess with one ac - cord

1 All praise to thee, for thou, O King di - vine,
2 Thou cam'st to us in low - li - ness of thought;
3 Let this mind be in us which was in thee,
4 Where-fore, by God's e - ter - nal pur - pose, thou
5 Let ev - ery tongue con-fess with one ac - cord

Je - sus Christ is Lord;

| | | | | | | | | | |
|---|---|---|---|---|---|---|---|---|---|
| 1 | didst | yield | the | glo - ry | that | of | right | was | thine,_____ |
| 2 | by | thee | the | out - cast | and | the | poor | were | sought;_____ |
| 3 | who | wast | a | ser - vant | that | we | might | be | free,_____ |
| 4 | art | high | ex - | alt - ed | o'er | all | crea - | tures | now,_____ |
| 5 | in | heaven | and | earth | that Je - | sus | Christ | is | Lord;_____ |

and God the Fa - ther be by all a - dored.

| | | | | | | | | | |
|---|---|---|---|---|---|---|---|---|---|
| 1 | that | in | our | dark - ened | hearts | thy | grace might | shine._____ |
| 2 | and | by | thy | death was | God's | sal - | va - tion | wrought.____ |
| 3 | hum - bling | thy - | self | to | death | on | Cal - va - | ry._____ |
| 4 | and | given | the | Name | to | which | all | knees shall | bow._____ |
| 5 | and | God | the | Fa - ther | be | by | all | a - dored._____ |

Al - le - lu - ia! A - men.

Al - le - lu - ia! A - men.

Words: F. Bland Tucker (1895-1984)
Music: *Engelberg*, Charles Villiers Stanford (1852-1924); desc. Richard Proulx (b. 1937)     10 10 10 with Alleluia

1 Je - sus, our might - y Lord, our strength in sad - ness,____
2 Good shep-herd of your sheep, your own de - fend - ing,____
3 Glo - rious their life who sing, with glad thanks - giv - ing,____

the Fa - ther's con - quering Word, true source of glad - ness;____
in love your chil - dren keep to life un - end - ing.____
true hymns to Christ the King in all their liv - ing:____

your Name we glo - ri - fy, O Je - sus, throned on high;
You are your-self the Way: lead us then day by day
all who con - fess his Name, come then with hearts a - flame;

you gave your - self to die for our sal - va - tion.
in your own steps, we pray, O Lord most ho - ly.
the God of peace ac - claim as Lord and Sa - vior.

Words: Clement of Alexandria (170?-220?); para. F. Bland Tucker (1895-1984), rev.
Music: *Monk's Gate*, Sussex folk melody; adapt. Ralph Vaughan Williams (1872-1958)          11 11. 12 11

1 Glo - ry be to Je - sus, who in bit - ter pains
2 Grace and life e - ter - nal in that blood I find,
3 Blest through end - less a - ges be the pre - cious stream
4 Oft as earth ex - ult - ing wafts its praise on high,
5 Lift ye then your voic - es; swell the might - y flood;

1 poured for me the life - blood from his sa - cred veins!
2 blest be his com - pas - sion in - fi - nite - ly kind!
3 which from sin and sor - row doth the world re - deem!
4 an - gel hosts, re - joic - ing, make their glad re - ply.
5 loud - er still and loud - er praise the pre - cious blood.

Words: Italian, 18th cent.; tr. Edward Caswall (1814-1878), alt.
Music: *Wem in Leidenstagen*, Friedrich Filitz (1804-1860)

65. 65

## Jesus Christ our Lord

480

1 When Je - sus left his Fa-ther's throne, he chose an hum - ble birth;
2 Sweet were his words and kind his look, when mo-thers round him pressed;
3 When Je - sus in - to Zi - on rode, the chil - dren sang a - round;

like us, un - hon - ored and un-known, he came to dwell on earth.
their in-fants in his arms he took, and on his bos - om blessed.
for joy they plucked the palms and strowed their gar - ments on the ground.

Like him may we be found be - low in wis-dom's path of peace;
Safe from the world's al - lur - ing harms, be - neath his watch-ful eye,
Ho - san - na our glad voic - es raise, ho - san - na to our King!

like him in grace and know-ledge grow as years and strength in - crease.
thus in the cir - cle of his arms may we for ev - er lie.
Should we for - get our Sa - vior's praise, the stones them-selves would sing.

Words: James Montgomery (1771-1854)
Music: *Kingsfold*, English folk melody; adapt. Ralph Vaughan Williams (1872-1958)

CMD

1 Re - joice, the Lord is King! Your Lord and King a - dore! Mor -
2 The Lord the Sa - vior reigns, the God of truth and love: when
3 His king-dom can - not fail; he rules o'er earth and heaven; the
4 Re - joice in glo - rious hope! Our Lord the Judge shall come, and

*Refrain*

tals, give thanks and sing, and tri - umph ev - er - more.
he had purged our stains, he took his seat a - bove. Lift
keys of death and hell to Christ the Lord are given.
take his ser - vants up to their e - ter - nal home.

1-3

up your heart! lift up your voice! Re - joice! a - gain I say, re -

*Final Ending*

joice! up your heart! lift up your voice! Re - joice! a -

gain I say, re - joice!

Words: Charles Wesley (1707-1788), alt.
Music: *Gopsal*, George Frideric Handel (1685-1759); arr. John Wilson (b. 1905)

66. 66 with Refrain

1 Lord of all hope - ful - ness, Lord of all joy,
2 Lord of all ea - ger - ness, Lord of all faith,
3 Lord of all kind - li - ness, Lord of all grace,
4 Lord of all gen - tle - ness, Lord of all calm,

whose trust, ev - er child - like, no cares could des - troy,
whose strong hands were skilled at the plane and the lathe,
your hands swift to wel - come, your arms to em - brace,
whose voice is con - tent - ment, whose pres - ence is balm,

be there at our wak - ing, and give us, we pray,
be there at our la - bors, and give us, we pray,
be there at our hom - ing, and give us, we pray,
be there at our sleep - ing, and give us, we pray,

your bliss in our hearts, Lord, at the break of the day.
your strength in our hearts, Lord, at the noon of the day.
your love in our hearts, Lord, at the eve of the day.
your peace in our hearts, Lord, at the end of the day.

Words: Jan Struther (1901-1953)
Music: *Slane,* Irish ballad melody; adapt. *The Church Hymnary,* 1927

10 11. 11 12

## Jesus Christ our Lord  483

1 The head that once was crowned with thorns is crowned with glo - ry now;
2 The high - est place that heaven af - fords is his, is his by right,
3 the joy of all who dwell a - bove, the joy of all be - low,
4 To them the cross with all its shame, with all its grace is given;
5 They suf - fer with their Lord be - low, they reign with him a - bove,

1 a roy - al di - a - dem a - dorns the might - y vic - tor's brow.
2 the King of kings, and Lord of lords, and heaven's e - ter - nal Light;
3 to whom he man - i - fests his love and grants his Name to know.
4 their name, an ev - er - last - ing name; their joy, the joy of heaven.
5 their prof - it and their joy to know the mys - ter - y of his love.

6 The cross he bore is life and health,
   though shame and death to him:
   his people's hope, his people's wealth,
   their everlasting theme.

Words: Thomas Kelly (1769-1855)
Music: *St. Magnus,* melody *Divine Companion,* 1707; harm. William Henry Monk (1823-1889),
   after John Pyke Hullah (19th cent.)

CM

1 Praise the Lord through ev - ery na - tion; his ho - ly
2 Je - sus, Lord, our Cap - tain glo - rious, o'er sin, and

arm hath wrought sal - va - tion; ex - alt him on his
death, and hell vic - to - rious, wis - dom and might to

Fa - ther's throne. Praise your King, ye Chris - tian le -
thee be - long: we con - fess, pro - claim, a - dore

gions, who now pre - pares in heaven - ly re -
thee; we bow the knee, we fall be - fore

gions un - fail - ing man - sions for his own: with
thee; thy love hence - forth shall be our song. The

voice and min - strel - sy ex - tol his ma - jes -
cross mean-while we bear, the crown ere-long to

ty: Al - le - lu - ia! His praise shall sound all
wear: Al - le - lu - ia! Thy reign ex - tend world

na - ture round, and hymns on ev - ery tongue a - bound.
with - out end; let praise from all to thee a - scend.

Words: Rhijnvis Feith (1753-1824); para. James Montgomery (1771-1854), alt.
Music: *Wachet auf*, melody Hans Sachs (1494-1576); adapt. Philipp Nicolai (1556-1608);
    arr. and harm. Johann Sebastian Bach (1685-1750)

Irr.

1 Praise the Lord through ev-ery na - tion;
2 Je - sus, Lord, our Cap-tain glo - rious,

his ho-ly arm hath wrought sal-va - tion; ex-alt him
o'er sin, and death, and hell vic-to - rious, wis-dom and

on his Fa-ther's throne. Praise your King, ye Chris-tian
might to thee be - long: we con-fess, pro-claim, a -

le - gions, who now pre-pares in heaven-ly re - gions
dore thee; we bow the knee, we fall be-fore thee;

un - fail - ing man - sions for his own:
thy love hence - forth shall be our song.

with voice and min-strel-sy ex - tol his ma-jes-ty:
The cross mean-while we bear, the crown ere-long to wear:

Al - le - lu - ia! His praise shall sound all na-ture round,
Al - le - lu - ia! Thy reign ex-tend world with-out end;

and hymns on ev - ery tongue a - bound.
let praise from all to thee a - scend.

Words: Rhijnvis Feith (1753-1824); para. James Montgomery (1771-1854), alt.
Music: *Wachet auf*, melody Hans Sachs (1494-1576); adapt. Philipp Nicolai (1556-1608)

Irr.

# Jesus Christ our Lord

486

1 Ho - san - na to the liv - ing Lord! Ho -
2 Ho - san - na Lord! thine an - gels cry; Ho -
3 O Sa - vior, with pro - tect - ing care a -
4 But, chief - est, in our cleans - ed breast, E -
5 So in the last and dread - ful day, when

1 san - na to the in - car - nate Word! To Christ, Cre - a - tor
2 san - na Lord! thy saints re - ply; a - bove, be - neath us,
3 bide in this thy house of prayer, where we as - sem - bled
4 ter - nal! bid thy Spi - rit rest; and make our se - cret
5 earth and heaven shall melt a - way, thy flock, re - deemed from

1 Sa - vior, King, let earth, let heaven, ho - san - na sing!
2 and a - round, both dead and liv - ing swell the sound:
3 in thy Name, in faith, thy part - ing prom - ise claim.
4 soul to be a tem - ple pure and wor - thy thee.
5 sin - ful stain, shall swell the sound of praise a - gain.

*Refrain*

Ho - san - na Lord! Ho - san - na in the high - est!

Words: Reginald Heber (1783-1826), alt.
Music: *Hosanna*, John Bacchus Dykes (1823-1876)

LM with Refrain

## 487                      Jesus Christ our Lord

1 Come, my Way, my Truth, my Life: such a
2 Come, my Light, my Feast, my Strength: such a
3 Come, my Joy, my Love, my Heart: such a

way as gives us breath; such a truth as ends all
light as shows a feast; such a feast as mends in
joy as none can move; such a love as none can

strife; such a life as kill - eth death.
length; such a strength as makes____ his guest.
part; such a heart as joys____ in love.

Words: George Herbert (1593-1633)
Music: *The Call*, Ralph Vaughan Williams (1872-1958)

77. 77

## 488                      Jesus Christ our Lord

1 Be thou my vi - sion, O Lord of my heart;
2 Be thou my wis - dom, and thou my true word;
3 High King of hea - ven, when vic - tory is won,

all else be nought to me, save that thou art—
I ev - er with thee and thou with me, Lord;
may I reach hea - ven's joys, bright hea - ven's Sun!

thou my best thought,__ by day or by night,
thou my great Fa - ther; thine own may I be;
Heart of my heart,__ what - ev - er be - fall,

| wak - ing | or | sleep - ing, | thy | pres - ence | my | light. |
| thou | in | my | dwell - ing, | and | I | one | with | thee. |
| still | be | my | vi - sion, | O | Ru - ler | of | all. |

Words: Irish, ca. 700; versified Mary Elizabeth Byrne (1880-1931);
    tr. Eleanor H. Hull (1860-1935), alt.
Music: *Slane*, Irish ballad melody; adapt. *The Church Hymnary*, 1927

10 10. 9 10

## Jesus Christ our Lord

**489**

1 The great Cre - a - tor of the worlds, the sov - ereign God of heaven,
2 He sent no an - gel of his host to bear this might - y word,
3 He sent him not in wrath and power, but grace and peace to bring;
4 He sent him down as send - ing God; in flesh to us he came;
5 He came as Sa - vior to his own, the way of love he trod;

1 his ho - ly and im - mor - tal truth to all on earth hath given.
2 but him through whom the worlds were made, the ev - er - last - ing Lord.
3 in kind - ness, as a king might send his son, him - self a king.
4 as one with us he dwelt with us, and bore a hu - man name.
5 he came to win us by good will, for force is not of God.

6 Not to oppress, but summon all
     their truest life to find,
  in love God sent his Son to save,
     not to condemn mankind.

Words: *Epistle to Diognetus*, ca. 150; tr. F. Bland Tucker (1895-1984), rev.
Music: *Tallis' Ordinal*, Thomas Tallis (1505?-1585)

CM

1 I want to walk as a child of the light.
2 I want to see the bright-ness of God.
3 I'm look-ing for the com-ing of Christ.

I want to fol - low Je - sus.
I want to look at Je - sus.
I want to be with Je - sus.

God set the stars to give light to the world. The
Clear sun of right-eous-ness, shine on my path, and
When we have run with pa-tience the race, we

star of my life is Je - sus.
show me the way to the Fa - ther.
shall know the joy of Je - sus.

In him there is no dark-ness at all. The night and the day are both a-like. The Lamb is the light of the ci-ty of God. Shine in my heart, Lord Je - sus.

Words: Kathleen Thomerson (b. 1934)
Music: *Houston*, Kathleen Thomerson (b. 1934)

Irr. with Refrain

## 491

1 Where is this stu - pen-dous stran-ger? Pro - phets, shep-herds, kings, ad - vise.
2 O Most Might - y! O Most Ho - ly! Far be - yond the ser-aph's thought:
3 O the mag - ni - tude of meek-ness! Worth from worth im - mor - tal sprung;
4 God all - boun-teous, all - cre - a - tive, whom no ills from good dis - suade,

Lead me to my Mas - ter's man - ger, show me where my Sa - vior lies.
art thou then so weak and low - ly as un-heed - ed pro - phets taught?
O the strength of in - fant weak-ness, if e - ter - nal is so young!
is in - car - nate, and a na - tive of the ve - ry world he made.

Words: Christopher Smart (1722-1771), alt.
Music: *Kit Smart*, Alec Wyton (b. 1921)

87. 87

## 492

Jesus Christ our Lord

1 Sing, ye faith - ful, sing with glad - ness, wake your no - blest,
2 Sing how he came forth from hea - ven, bowed him-self to
3 So, he tast - ed death for mor - tals, he, of hu - man -
4 Now on high, yet ev - er with us, from his Fa - ther's

sweet - est strain, with the prais - es of your Sa - vior
Beth - le-hem's cave, stooped to wear the ser - vant's ves - ture,
kind the head, sin - less one, a - mong the sin - ful,
throne the Son rules and guides the world he ran - somed,

let his house re - sound a - gain; him let all your
bore the pain, the cross, the grave, passed with - in the
Prince of life, a - mong the dead; thus he wrought the
till the ap-point - ed work be done, till he see, re -

mu - sic hon - or, and your songs ex - alt his reign.
gates of dark - ness, thence his ban - ished ones to save.
full re - demp - tion, and the cap - tor cap - tive led.
newed and per - fect, all things gath - ered in - to one.

Words: John Ellerton (1826-1893), alt.
Music: *Finnian*, Christopher Dearnley (b. 1930)

87. 87. 87

## Jesus Christ our Lord 493

1 O for a thou - sand tongues to sing my dear Re - deem - er's praise,
2 My gra - cious Mas - ter and my God, as - sist me to pro - claim
3 Je - sus! the Name that charms our fears and bids our sor - rows cease;
4 He speaks; and, lis - tening to his voice, new life the dead re - ceive,
5 Hear him, ye deaf; ye voice - less ones, your loos-ened tongues em - ploy;

1 the glo - ries of my God and King, the tri - umphs of his grace!
2 and spread through all the earth a - broad the hon - ors of thy Name.
3 'tis mu - sic in the sin -ner's ears, 'tis life and health and peace.
4 the mourn-ful bro - ken hearts re - joice, the hum - ble poor be - lieve.
5 ye blind, be - hold, your Sa - vior comes; and leap, ye lame, for joy!

6 Glory to God and praise and love
be now and ever given
by saints below and saints above,
the Church in earth and heaven.

Words: Charles Wesley (1707-1788), alt.
Music: *Azmon*, Carl Gotthilf Gläser (1784-1829); adapt. and arr. Lowell Mason (1792-1872)

CM

Descant

5 Crown him the Lord of heaven, en - throned a - bove;

1 Crown him with man - y crowns, the Lamb up - on his throne; Hark!
2 Crown him the Son of God be - fore the worlds be - gan, and
3 Crown him the Lord of life, who tri - umphed o'er the grave, and
4 Crown him of lords the Lord, who o - ver all doth reign, who
5 Crown him the Lord of heaven, en-throned in worlds a - bove; crown

crown him to whom is given, the won - drous name of Love.

1 how the heaven - ly an - them drowns all mu - sic but its own; a -
2 ye, who tread where he hath trod, crown him the Son of man; who
3 rose vic - to - rious in the strife for those he came to save; his
4 once on earth, the in - car - nate Word, for ran - somed sin - ners slain, now
5 him the King, to whom is given, the won-drous name of Love. Crown

Crown him with man-y crowns, as thrones be-fore him

1 wake, my soul, and sing of him who died for thee, and
2 ev - ery grief hath known that wrings the hu - man breast, and
3 glo - ries now we sing who died, and rose on high, who
4 lives in realms of light, where saints with an - gels sing their
5 him with man - y crowns, as thrones be - fore him fall, crown

fall, crown him, ye kings, for he is King of all.

1 hail him as thy match - less King through all e - ter - ni - ty.
2 takes and bears them for his own, that all in him may rest.
3 died, e - ter - nal life to bring, and lives that death may die.
4 songs be - fore him day and night, their God, Re-deem - er, King.
5 him, ye kings, with man - y crowns, for he is King of all.

Words: Matthew Bridges (1800-1894)
Music: *Diademata*, George Job Elvey (1816-1893); desc. Richard Proulx (b. 1937)

SMD

1 Hail, thou once de - spis - ed Je - sus! Hail, thou Gal - i -
2 Pas - chal Lamb, by God ap - point - ed, all our sins on
3 Je - sus, hail! en - throned in glo - ry, there for ev - er
4 Wor - ship, hon - or, power, and bless - ing thou art wor - thy

le - an King! Thou didst suf - fer to re - lease us;
thee were laid: by al - might - y love a - noint - ed,
to a - bide; all the heaven - ly hosts a - dore thee,
to re - ceive; high - est prais - es, with - out ceas - ing,

thou didst free sal - va - tion bring. Hail, thou u - ni - ver - sal
thou hast full a - tone - ment made. All thy peo - ple are for -
seat - ed at thy Fa - ther's side. There for sin - ners thou art
right it is for us to give. Help, ye bright an - gel - ic

Sa - vior, bear - er of our sin and shame! By thy mer - it
giv - en through the vir - tue of thy blood: o - pened is the
plead - ing: there thou dost our place pre - pare; ev - er for us
spi - rits, all your no - blest an - thems raise; help to sing our

we find fa - vor: life is giv - en through thy Name.
gate of hea - ven, re - con - ciled are we with God.
in - ter - ced - ing, till in glo - ry we ap - pear.
Sa - vior's mer - its, help to chant Em - man - uel's praise!

Words: John Bakewell (1721-1819) and Martin Madan (1726-1790), alt.
Music: *In Babilone*, melody from *Oude en Nieuwe Hollantse Boerenlities en Contradanseu*, 1710

87. 87. D

1 How bright ap - pears the Morn-ing Star, with mer - cy beam -
2 Though cir - cled by the hosts on high, he deigned to cast
3 Re - joice, ye heavens; thou earth, re - ply; with praise, ye sin -

ing from a - far; the host of heaven re - joic - es;
a pit - ying eye up - on his help - less crea - ture;
ners, fill the sky, for this his In - car - na - tion.

O right - eous Branch, O Jes - se's Rod! Thou Son of Man
the whole cre - a - tion's Head and Lord, by high-est ser -
In - car - nate God, put forth thy power, ride on, ride on,

and Son of God! We, too, will lift our voic - es:
a - phim a - dored, as-sumed our ve - ry na - ture;
great Con-quer - or, till all know thy sal - va - tion.

Je - sus, Je - sus! Ho - ly, ho - ly, yet most low - ly,
Je - sus, grant us, through thy mer - it, to in - her - it
A - men, a - men! Al - le - lu - ia, al - le - lu - ia!

draw thou near us; great Em - man - uel, come and hear us.
thy sal - va - tion; hear, O hear our sup - pli - ca - tion.
Praise be giv - en ev - er - more, by earth and hea - ven.

Words: William Mercer (1811-1873), after Philipp Nicolai (1556-1608)
Music: *Wie schön leuchtet*, melody att. Philipp Nicolai (1556-1608)

Irr.

# 497

Jesus Christ our Lord

Je - sus, Je - sus! Ho - ly ho - ly, yet most low - ly,
Je - sus, grant us, through thy mer - it, to in - her - it
A - men, a - men! Al - le - lu - ia, al - le - lu - ia!

draw thou near us; great Em - man - uel, come and hear us.
thy sal - va - tion; hear, O hear our sup - pli - ca - tion.
Praise be giv - en ev - er - more, by earth and hea - ven.

Words: William Mercer (1811-1873), after Philipp Nicolai (1556-1608)
Music: *Wie schön leuchtet*, melody att. Philipp Nicolai, (1556-1608);
    arr. and harm. Johann Sebastian Bach (1685-1750)

Irr.

1 Be - neath the cross of Je - sus I fain would take my stand,
2 Up - on the cross of Je - sus mine eyes at times can see
3 I take, O cross, thy sha - dow for my a - bid - ing place;

the sha - dow of a might - y rock with - in a wea - ry land,
the ve - ry dy - ing form of one who suf - fered there for me;
I ask no o - ther sun - shine than the sun - shine of his face;

a home with - in the wil - der - ness, a rest up - on the way,
and from my smit - ten heart with tears two won - ders I con - fess:
con - tent to let my pride go by, to know no gain nor loss,

from the burn - ing of the noon - tide heat and the bur - den of the day.
the __ won - ders of re - deem - ing love and __ my un - wor - thi - ness.
my __ sin - ful self my on - ly sham my __ glo - ry all the cross.

Words: Elizabeth Cecilia Clephane (1830-1869), alt.
Music: *St. Christopher*, Frederick Charles Maker (1844-1927)

76. 86. 86. 86

# Jesus Christ our Lord

## 499

*Unison or harmony*

Lord God, you now have set your ser-vant free to go in peace as prom-ised in your word; my eyes have seen the Sa-vior, Christ the Lord, pre-pared by you for all the world to see, to shine on na-tions trapped in dark-est night, the glo-ry of your peo - ple, and their light.

Words: Rae E. Whitney (b. 1927); para. of *The Song of Simeon*
Music: *Song 1*, melody and bass Orlando Gibbons (1583-1625);
    harm. Ralph Vaughan Williams (1872-1958)

10 10. 10 10. 10 10

# 500

1 Cre - a - tor Spi - rit, by whose aid the world's foun -
2 O Source of un - cre - at - ed light, the Fa - ther's
3 Plen - teous of grace, come from on high, rich in thy

da - tions first were laid, come, vis - it ev - ery hum - ble
prom - ised Par - a - clete, thrice ho - ly Fount, thrice ho - ly
seven - fold en - er - gy; make us e - ter - nal truth re -

mind; come, pour thy joys on hu - man - kind; from sin and
Fire, our hearts with heaven - ly love in - spire; come, and thy
ceive, and prac - tice all that we be - lieve; give us thy -

sor - row set us free, and make thy tem - ples wor - thy thee.
sa - cred unc - tion bring to sanc - ti - fy us while we sing.
self, that we may see the Fa - ther and the Son by thee.

Words: John Dryden (1631-1700); tr. of *Veni Creator Spiritus*
Music: *Surrey*, melody Henry Carey (1690?-1743)

88. 88. 88

# The Holy Spirit

1 O Ho - ly Spi - rit, by whose breath life
2 You are the seek - er's sure re - source, of
3 In you God's en - er - gy is shown, to
4 Flood our dull sens - es with your light; in
5 From in - ner strife grant us re - lease; turn

1 ris - es vi - brant out of death; come to cre -
2 burn - ing love the liv - ing source, pro - tec - tor
3 us your var - ied gifts make known. Teach us to
4 mu - tual love our hearts u - nite. Your power the
5 na - tions to the ways of peace. To ful - ler

1 ate, re - new, in - spire; come, kin - dle in our hearts your fire.
2 in the midst of strife, the giv - er and the Lord of life.
3 speak, teach us to hear; yours is the tongue and yours the ear.
4 whole cre - a - tion fills; con - firm our weak, un - cer - tain wills.
5 life your peo - ple bring that as one bo - dy we may sing:

6 Praise to the Father, Christ, his Word,
and to the Spirit: God the Lord,
to whom all honor, glory be
both now and for eternity.

Words: Att. Rabanus Maurus (776-856); tr. John Webster Grant (b. 1919), alt.; para. of *Veni Creator Spiritus*
Music: *Komm, Gott Schöpfer*, melody from *Eyn Enchiridion*, 1524; harm. *The Lutheran Hymnal*, 1941                    LM

## 502

The Holy Spirit

1 O Ho - ly Spi - rit, by whose breath, life ris - es
2 You are the seek - er's sure re - source, of burn - ing
3 In you God's en - er - gy is shown, to us your
4 Flood our dull sens - es with your light; in mu - tual
5 From in - ner strife grant us re - lease; turn na - tions
6 Praise to the Fa - ther, Christ, his Word, and to the

1 vi - brant out of death; come to cre - ate,
2 love the liv - ing source, pro - tec - tor in
3 var - ied gifts make known. Teach us to speak,
4 love our hearts u - nite. Your power the whole
5 to the ways of peace. To ful - ler life
6 Spi - rit: God the Lord, to whom all ho

1 re - new, in - spire; come, kin - dle in our hearts your fire.
2 the midst of strife, the giv - er and the Lord of life.
3 teach us to hear; yours is the tongue and yours the ear.
4 cre - a - tion fills; con - firm our weak, un - cer - tain wills.
5 your peo - ple bring that as one bo - dy we may sing:
6 nor, glo - ry be both now and for e - ter - ni - ty.

Words: Att. Rabanus Maurus (776-856); tr. John Webster Grant (b. 1919), alt.;
para. of *Veni Creator Spiritus*
Music: *Veni Creator Spiritus*, plainsong, Mode 8

LM

## 503

The Holy Spirit

*Cantor*

1 Come, Ho - ly Ghost, our souls in - spire,
2 Thou the a - noint - ing Spi - rit art,
3 Thy bless - ed unc - tion from a - bove

*All*

and light - en with ce - les - tial fire.
who dost thy seven - fold gifts im - part.
is com - fort, life, and fire of love.

Words: Latin, 9th cent.; tr. John Cosin (1594-1672); para. of *Veni Creator Spiritus*.
Music: *Come Holy Ghost*, John Henry Hopkins Jr. (1820-1891); **adapt. and harm.** David Hurd (b. 1950)

88

1. Come, Ho - ly    Ghost, our    souls in - spire,    and light - en
3. Thy bless - ed    unc - tion    from a - bove    is com - fort,
5. A - noint and    cheer our    soil - ed    face    with the a -

with ce - les - tial    fire.  2. Thou the    a - noint - ing
life, and    fire    of    love.  4. En - a - ble    with per -
bun - dance    of    thy    grace.  6. Keep far    our    foes,    give

Spi - rit art,    who    dost    thy    seven - fold gifts im - part.
pet - ual light    the    dull - ness of    our blind-ed sight.
peace at home:    where    thou    art    guide,    no ill can come.

7. Teach us    to    know the    Fa - ther,    Son,    and thee, of

both, to    be    but    One,  8. that through the    a - ges

all a - long,    this    may be    our end - less song:

9. praise to    thy    e - ter - nal    mer - it,

Fa - ther,    Son,    and Ho - ly    Spi - rit.

Words: Latin, 9th cent.; tr. John Cosin (1594-1672); para. of *Veni Creator Spiritus*.
Music: *Veni Creator Spiritus*, plainsong, Mode 8

LM

# The Holy Spirit

Words: Johann Niedling (1602-1668); tr. John Caspar Mattes (1876-1948), alt.
Music: *O heiliger Geist*, melody from *Geistliche Kirchengesang*, 1623;
harm. Johann Sebastian Bach (1685-1750); arr. Alastair Cassels-Brown (b. 1927)

10 8. 88. 10

# 506

1 Praise the Spi - rit in cre - a - tion, breath of God, life's
2 Praise the Spi - rit, close com - pan - ion of our in - most
3 Praise the Spi - rit, who en - light - ened priests and pro - phets
4 Tell of how the a - scend - ed Je - sus armed a peo - ple
5 Pray we then, O Lord the Spi - rit, on our lives de -
6 Praise, O praise the Ho - ly Spi - rit, praise the Fa - ther,

1 or - i - gin: Spi - rit, mov - ing on the wat - ers
2 thoughts and ways; who, in show - ing us God's won - ders,
3 with the word; his the truth be - hind the wis - doms
4 for his own; how a hun - dred men and wo - men
5 scend in might; let your flame break out with - in us,
6 praise the Word, Source, and Truth, and In - spi - ra - tion,

1 quick - ening worlds to life with - in, source of breath to
2 is him - self the power to gaze; and God's will, to
3 which as yet know not our Lord; by whose love and
4 turned the known world up - side down, to its dark and
5 fire our hearts and clear our sight, till, white - hot in
6 Trin - i - ty in deep ac - cord: through your voice which

1 all things breath - ing, life in whom all lives be - gin.
2 those who lis - ten, by a still small voice con - veys.
3 power, in Je - sus God him - self was seen and heard.
4 fur - thest cor - ners by the wind of hea - ven blown.
5 your pos - ses - sion, we, too, set the world a - light.
6 speaks with - in us we, your crea - tures, call you Lord.

Words: Michael Hewlett (b. 1916), alt.
Music: *Finnian*, Christopher Dearnley (b. 1930)

87. 87. 87

1 Praise the Spi-rit in cre - a -tion, breath of God, life's or - i-
2 Praise the Spi - rit, close com - pan - ion of our in - most thoughts and
3 Praise the Spi - rit, who en - light-ened priests and pro - phets with the
4 Tell of how the a-scend-ed Je - sus armed a peo - ple for his
5 Pray we then, O Lord the Spi - rit, on our lives de - scend in
6 Praise, O praise the Ho - ly Spi - rit, praise the Fa - ther, praise the

1 gin: Spi - rit, mov - ing on the wat - ers quick-ening
2 ways; who, in show - ing us God's won - ders, is him -
3 word; his the truth be - hind the wis - doms which as
4 own; how a hun - dred men and wo - men turned the
5 might; let your flame break out with - in us, fire our
6 Word, Source, and Truth, and In - spi - ra - tion, Trin - i -

1 worlds to life with - in, source of breath to all things
2 self the power to gaze; and God's will, to those who
3 yet know not our Lord; by whose love and power, in
4 known world up - side down, to its dark and fur - thest
5 hearts and clear our sight, till, white - hot in your pos -
6 ty in deep ac - cord: through your voice which speaks with -

*Interlude/Conclusion*

1 breath - ing, life in whom all lives be - gin.
2 lis - ten, by a still small voice con - veys.
3 Je - sus God him - self was seen and heard.
4 cor - ners by the wind of hea - ven blown.
5 ses - sion, we, too, set the world a - light.
6 in us we, your crea - tures, call you Lord.

Words: Michael Hewlett (b. 1916), alt.
Music: *Julion*, David Hurd (b. 1950)

87. 87. 87

1 Breathe on me, Breath of God, fill me with life a - new,
2 Breathe on me, Breath of God, un - til my heart is pure,
3 Breathe on me, Breath of God, till I am whol - ly thine,
4 Breathe on me, Breath of God, so shall I nev - er die;

that I may love what thou dost love, and do what thou wouldst do.
un - til with thee I will one will, to do or to en - dure.
till all this earth - ly part of me glows with thy fire di - vine.
but live with thee the per - fect life of thine e - ter - ni - ty.

Words: Edwin Hatch (1835-1889), alt.
Music: *Nova Vita*, Lister R. Peace (1885-1969)

SM

1 Spi - rit di - vine, at - tend our prayers, and make this house thy home;
2 Come as the light; to us re - veal our emp - ti - ness and woe,
3 Come as the fire, and purge our hearts like sac - ri - fi - cial flame;
4 Come as the dove, and spread thy wings, the wings of peace - ful love;
5 Spi - rit di - vine, at - tend our prayers; make a lost world thy home;

1 de-scend with all thy gra-cious powers, O come, great Spi - rit, come!
2 and lead us in those paths of life where-on the right - eous go.
3 let our whole soul an of - fering be to our Re - deem - er's Name.
4 and let thy Church on earth be - come blest as the Church a - bove.
5 de-scend with all thy gra-cious powers; O come, great Spi - rit, come!

Words: Andrew Reed (1787-1862)
Music: *Nun danket all und bringet Ehr*, melody att. Johann Cruger (1598-1662)          CM

## The Holy Spirit                                                              510

1 Come, Ho - ly Spi - rit, heaven - ly Dove, with all thy quick-ening powers;
2 See how we tri - fle here be - low, fond of these earth - ly toys:
3 In vain we tune our for - mal songs, in vain we strive to rise:
4 Come, Ho - ly Spi - rit, heaven - ly Dove, with all thy quick-ening powers;

kin - dle a flame of sa - cred love in these cold hearts of ours.
our souls, how heav - i - ly they go, to reach e - ter - nal joys.
ho - san - nas lan - guish on our tongues, and our de - vo - tion dies.
come, shed a - broad a Sa-vior's love, and that shall kin - dle ours.

Words: Isaac Watts (1674-1748), alt.
Music: *Saint Agnes*, John Bacchus Dykes (1823-1876)          CM

**511**

The Holy Spirit

1 Ho - ly Spi - rit, ev - er liv - ing as the Church's
2 Ho - ly Spi - rit, ev - er work-ing through the Church's

ve - ry life; Ho - ly Spi - rit, ev - er striv-ing
min - is - try; quick-ening, strength-ening and ab - solv-ing,

through her in a cease-less strife; Ho - ly Spi - rit, ev - er
set - ting cap - tive sin - ners free; Ho - ly Spi - rit, ev - er

form-ing in the Church the mind of Christ; thee we praise with
bind-ing age to age, and soul to soul, in a fel - low -

end - less wor-ship    for    thy    fruits and   gifts   un - priced.
ship    un - end-ing    thee    we    wor - ship   and    ex - tol.

Words: Timothy Rees (1874-1939), alt.
Music: *Abbot's Leigh*, Cyril Vincent Taylor (b. 1907)

87. 87. D

## The Holy Spirit

**512**

1 Come, Gra - cious  Spi - rit,  heaven - ly  Dove,  with light and
2 The  light of  truth  to  us  dis - play,  and make us
3 Lead  us  to  Christ,  the  liv - ing  way,  nor let us
4 Lead  us  to  heaven,  that  we  may  share  full - ness of

com - fort  from  a - bove;  be  thou our  guard - ian,
know  and  choose  thy  way;  plant ho - ly  fear  in
from  his  pre - cepts  stray;  lead  us  to  ho - li -
joy  for  ev - er  there;  lead  us  to  God,  our

thou  our  guide  o'er ev - ery thought and  step  pre - side.
ev - ery  heart,  that we from  thee  may  ne'er  de - part.
ness,  the  road  that we must  take  to  dwell  with  God.
fin - al  rest,  to  be with  him  for  ev - er  blest.

Words: Simon Browne (1680-1732), alt.
Music: *Mendon*, melody from *Methodist Harmonist*, 1821; adapt. and harm. Lowell Mason (1792-1872)

LM

1 Like the mur - mur of the dove's song, like the
2 To the mem - bers of Christ's Bo - dy, to the
3 With the heal - ing of di - vi - sion, with the

chal - lenge of her flight, like the vig - or of the
branch - es of the Vine, to the Church in faith as -
cease - less voice of prayer, with the power to love and

wind's rush, like the new flame's ea - ger
sem - bled, to her midst as gift and
wit - ness, with the peace be - yond com -

might: come,____ Ho - ly Spi - rit, come.
sign: come,____ Ho - ly Spi - rit, come.
pare: come,____ Ho - ly Spi - rit, come.

*Phrase 1 of each stanza may be sung by one group, with a contrasted group singing phrase 2, and all joining for the final phrase.*

Words: Carl P. Daw, Jr. (b. 1944)
Music: *Bridegroom*, Peter Cutts (b. 1937)

87. 87. 6

1 To thee, O Com - fort - er di - vine,
2 To thee, whose faith - ful love had place
3 To thee, whose faith - ful power doth heal,
4 To thee, by Je - sus Christ sent down,

| for | all | thy | grace | and | power | be | - | nign, |
| in | God's | great | cov | - e - | nant | of | | grace, |
| en - | light - | en, | sanc | - ti - | fy, | and | | seal, |
| of | all | his | gifts | the | sum | and | | crown, |

| sing | we | al | - le - | lu - ia! | al - le - lu | - | ia! |
| sing | we | al | - le - | lu - ia! | al - le - lu | - | ia! |
| sing | we | al | - le - | lu - ia! | al - le - lu | - | ia! |
| sing | we | al | - le - | lu - ia! | al - le - lu | - | ia! |

Words: Frances Ridley Havergal (1836-1879)
Music: *St. Bartholomew's*, David McKinley Williams (1887-1978)

88. 10

## The Holy Spirit                                                    515

1 Ho - ly Ghost, dis - pel our sad - ness; pierce the clouds of
2 Au - thor of the new cre - a - tion, come with unc - tion

na - ture's night; come, thou source of joy and glad - ness,
and with power. Make our hearts thy ha - bi - ta - tion;

breathe thy life, and spread thy light. From the height which
with thy grace our spi - rits shower. Hear, oh, hear our

knows no mea - sure, as a gra - cious shower de - scend,
sup - pli - ca - tion, bless - ed Spi - rit, God of peace!

bring-ing down the rich - est trea - sure we can wish, or God can send.
Rest up - on this con - gre - ga - tion, with the full - ness of thy grace.

Words  Paul Gerhardt (1607-1676); tr. John Christian Jacobi (1670-1750), alt.
Music: *Geneva*, George Henry Day (1883-1966)

87. 87. D

# 516

1 Come down, O Love di - vine, seek thou this soul of mine,
and vis - it it with thine own ar - dor glow - ing;
O Com-fort - er, draw near, with - in my heart ap - pear,
and kin - dle it, thy ho - ly flame be - stow - ing.

2 O let it free - ly burn, till earth - ly pas - sions turn
to dust and ash - es in its heat con - sum - ing;
and let thy glo - rious light shine ev - er on my sight,
and clothe me round, the while my path il - lum - ing.

3 And so the yearn - ing strong, with which the soul will long,
shall far out - pass the power of hu - man tell - ing;
for none can guess its grace, till Love cre - ate a place
where - in the Ho - ly Spi - rit makes a dwell - ing.

Words: Bianco da Siena (d. 1434?); tr. Richard Frederick Littledale (1833-1890), alt.
Music: *Down Ampney*, Ralph Vaughan Williams (1872-1958)

66. 11. D

1 How love-ly is thy dwell-ing-place, O Lord of hosts, to me! My thirst-y soul de - sires and longs with - in thy courts to be; my ve - ry heart and flesh cry out, O liv-ing God, for thee.

2 Be - side thine al - tars, gra - cious Lord, the swal-lows find a nest; how hap-py they who dwell with thee and praise thee with - out rest, and hap-py they whose hearts are set up - on the pil - grim's quest.

3 They who go through the des - ert vale will find it filled with springs, and they shall climb from height to height till Zi - on's tem - ple rings with praise to thee, in glo - ry throned, Lord God, great King of kings.

4 One day with - in thy courts ex - cels a thou-sand spent a - way; how hap-py they who keep thy laws nor from thy pre - cepts stray, for thou shalt sure - ly bless all those who live the words they pray.

Words: Para. of Psalm 84; sts. 1-2, *The Psalms of David in Meeter*, 1650; sts. 3-4, Carl P. Daw, Jr. (b. 1944)
Music: *Brother James' Air*, J. L. Macbeth Bain (1840?-1925)
86. 86. 86

**518** The Church

in thy glo - ry ev - er - more with thee to reign.

help for ev - er, and her con - fi - dence a - lone.
Three a - dor - ing in glad hymns e - ter - nal - ly.
ben - e - dic - tion shed with - in its walls al - way.
in thy glo - ry ev - er - more with thee to reign.

Words: Latin, ca. 7th cent.; tr. *Hymns Ancient and Modern*, 1861, after John Mason Neale (1818-1866), alt.
Music: *Westminster Abbey*, Henry Purcell (1659-1695), adapt.; desc. James Gillespie (b. 1929)          87. 87. 87

## The Church

# 519

1 Bless - ed ci - ty, heaven - ly Sa - lem, vi - sion dear of
2 from ce - les - tial realms de - scend - ing, brid - al glo - ry
3 Bright thy gates of pearl are shin - ing; they are o - pen
4 Man - y a blow and bit - ing sculp - ture pol - ished well those
5 Laud and hon - or to the Fa - ther, laud and hon - or

1 peace and love, who of liv - ing stones art build - ed
2 round thee shed, meet for him whose love es - poused thee,
3 ev - er - more; and by vir - tue of his mer - its
4 stones e - lect, in their pla - ces now com - pact - ed
5 to the Son, laud and hon - or to the Spi - rit,

1 in the height of heaven a - bove, and, with an - gel
2 to thy Lord shalt thou be led; all thy streets and
3 thith - er faith - ful souls do soar, who, for Christ's dear
4 by the heaven - ly Ar - chi - tect, who there - with hath
5 ev - er Three, and ev - er One, con - sub - stan - tial,

1 hosts en - cir - cled, as a bride dost earth - ward move;
2 all thy bul - warks of pure gold are fa - shion - ed.
3 Name, in this world pain and tri - bu - la - tion bore.
4 willed for ev - er that his pal - ace should be decked.
5 co - e - ter - nal, while un - end - ing a - ges run.

Words: Latin, ca. 7th cent.; tr. *Hymns Ancient and Modern*, 1861, after John Mason Neale (1818-1866), alt.
Music: *Urbs beata Jerusalem*, plainsong, Mode 2, Nevers MS., 13th cent.          87. 87. 87

# 520

1 Bless - ed ci - ty, heaven - ly Sa - lem, vi - sion dear of peace and love,
2 from ce - les - tial realms de - scend-ing, brid - al glo - ry round thee shed,
3 Bright thy gates of pearl are shin - ing; they are o - pen ev - er - more;
4 Man - y a blow and bit - ing sculp-ture pol - ished well those stones e - lect,
5 Laud and hon - or to the Fa - ther, laud and hon - or to the Son,

1 who of liv - ing stones art build - ed in the height of heaven a - bove,
2 meet for him whose love es - poused thee, to thy Lord shalt thou be led;
3 and by vir - tue of his mer - its thith - er faith - ful souls do soar,
4 in their pla - ces now com - pact - ed by the heaven-ly Ar - chi - tect,
5 laud and hon - or to the Spi - rit, ev - er Three, and ev - er One,

1 and, with an - gel hosts en - cir - cled, as a bride dost earth-ward move;
2 all thy streets and all thy bul-warks of pure gold are fa - shion - ed.
3 who, for Christ's dear Name, in this world pain and tri - bu - la - tion bore.
4 who there-with hath willed for ev - er that his pal - ace should be decked.
5 con - sub - stan - tial, co - e - ter - nal, while un - end - ing a - ges run.

Words: Latin, ca. 7th cent.; tr. *Hymns Ancient and Modern*, 1861, after John Mason Neale (1818-1866), alt.
Music: *Oriel*, Caspar Ett (1788-1847)

87. 87. 87

# The Church

521

*Descant*

4 O Judge di - vine of hu - man strife! O

1 Put forth, O God, thy Spi - rit's might and
2 Let works of dark - ness dis - ap - pear be -
3 Let what a - pos - tles learned of thee be
4 O Judge di - vine of hu - man strife! O

Van - quish - er of pain! To know thee is e -

bid thy Church in - crease, in breadth and length, in
fore thy con - quering light; let ha - tred and tor -
ours from age to age; their stead - fast faith our
Van - quish - er of pain! To know thee is e -

ter - nal life, to serve thee, to reign.

depth and height, her u - ni - ty and peace.
ment - ing fear pass with the pass - ing night.
u - ni - ty, their peace our her - it - age.
ter - nal life, to serve thee is to reign.

Words: Howard Chandler Robbins (1876-1952)
Music: *Chelsea Square*, Howard Chandler Robbins (1876-1952);
  harm. Ray Francis Brown (1897-1964); desc. Lois Fyfe (b. 1927)

CM

*Descant*

4 Blest in-hab-it - ants of Zi - on, washed in the Re -

1 Glo - rious things of thee are spo - ken, Zi - on, ci - ty
2 See! the streams of liv - ing wa - ters, spring - ing from e -
3 Round each ha - bi - ta - tion hov - ering, see the cloud and
4 Blest in-hab-it - ants of Zi - on, washed in the Re -

deem - er's blood! Whom their souls re -

of our God; he whose word can - not be
ter - nal love, well sup - ply thy sons and
fire ap - pear for a glo - ry and a
deem - er's blood! Je - sus, whom their souls re -

ly on, makes them kings and priests to God.

bro - ken formed thee for his own a - bode;
daugh - ters and all fear of want re - move.
cov - ering, show - ing that the Lord is near.
ly on, makes them kings and priests to God.

'Tis his love his peo-ple raise o-ver

on the Rock of A - ges found- ed, what can shake thy
Who can faint, when such a riv - er ev - er will their
Thus de - riv - ing from their ban - ner, light by night, and
'Tis his love his peo - ple rais - es o - ver self to

self to reign: and as priests, his

sure re - pose? With sal - va - tion's walls sur -
thirst as - suage? Grace which, like the Lord, the
shade by day, safe they feed up - on the
reign as kings: and as priests, his sol - emn

sol - emn prais - es each an of - fering brings.

round - ed, thou may'st smile at all thy foes.
giv - er, nev - er fails from age to age.
man - na which he gives them when they pray.
prais - es each for a thank - of - fering brings.

Words: John Newton (1725-1807), alt.
Music: *Austria*, Franz Joseph Haydn (1732-1809); desc. Michael E. Young (b. 1939)

87. 87. D

# 523

## The Church

1 Glo - rious things of thee are spo - ken, Zi - on, ci - ty
2 See! the streams of liv - ing wa - ters, spring - ing from e -
3 Round each ha - bi - ta - tion hov-ering, see the cloud and
4 Blest in - hab - it - ants of Zi - on, washed in the Re -

of our God; he whose word can - not be bro - ken
ter - nal love, well sup - ply thy sons and daugh-ters
fire ap - pear for a glo - ry and a cov - ering,
deem - er's blood! Je - sus, whom their souls re - ly on,

formed thee for his own a - bode; on the Rock of A - ges
and all fear of want re - move. Who can faint, when such a
show - ing that the Lord is near. Thus de - riv - ing from their
makes them kings and priests to God. 'Tis his love his peo - ple

found - ed, what can shake thy sure re - pose? With sal -
riv - er ev - er will their thirst as - suage? Grace which,
ban - ner, light by night, and shade by day, safe they
rais - es o - ver self to reign as kings: and as

va - tion's walls sur - round-ed, thou may'st smile at all thy foes.
like the Lord, the giv - er, nev - er fails from age to age.
feed up - on the man - na which he give them when they pray.
priests, his sol - emn prais - es each for a thank - of - fering brings.

Words: John Newton (1725-1807), alt.
Music: *Abbot's Leigh*, Cyril Vincent Taylor (b. 1907)

87. 87. D

## The Church

### 524

1 I love thy king - dom, Lord, the house of thine a - bode, the
2 For her my tears shall fall; for her my prayers a - scend; to
3 Be - yond my high - est joy I prize her heaven - ly ways, her
4 Je - sus, thou friend di - vine, our Sa - vior and our King, thy
5 Sure as thy truth shall last, to Zi - on shall be given the

1 Church our blest Re - deem - er saved with his own pre - cious blood.
2 her my cares and toils be given, till toils and cares shall end.
3 sweet com - mun - ion, so - lemn vows, her hymns of love and praise.
4 hand from ev - ery snare and foe shall great de - liv - erance bring.
5 bright - est glo - ries earth can yield, and bright-er bliss of heaven.

Words: Timothy Dwight (1725-1817)
Music: *St. Thomas (Williams)*, melody Aaron Williams (1731-1776); harm. Lowell Mason (1792-1872)

SM

# 525

The Church

1 The Church's one foun - da - tion is Je - sus Christ her Lord;
2 E - lect from ev - ery na - tion, yet one o'er all the earth,
3 Though with a scorn - ful won - der men see her sore op - pressed,
4 Mid toil and tri - bu - la - tion, and tu - mult of her war
5 Yet she on earth hath un - ion with God, the Three in One,

1 she is his new cre - a - tion by wa - ter and the word:
2 her char - ter of sal - va - tion, one Lord, one faith, one birth;
3 by schi - sms rent a - sun - der, by her - e - sies dis - tressed;
4 she waits the con - sum - ma - tion of peace for ev - er - more;
5 and mys - tic sweet com - mun - ion with those whose rest is won.

1 from heaven he came and sought her to be his ho - ly bride;
2 one ho - ly Name she bless - es, par - takes one ho - ly food,
3 yet saints their watch are keep - ing, their cry goes up, "How long?"
4 till with the vi - sion glo - rious her long - ing eyes are blessed,
5 O hap - py ones and ho - ly! Lord, give us grace that we

1 with his own blood he bought her, and for her life he died.
2 and to one hope she press - es, with ev - ery grace en - dued.
3 and soon the night of weep - ing shall be the morn of song.
4 and the great Church vic - to - rious shall be the Church at rest.
5 like them, the meek and low - ly, on high may dwell with thee.

Words: Samuel John Stone (1839-1900)
Music: *Aurelia*, Samuel Sebastian Wesley (1810-1876)

76. 76. D

## The Church  526

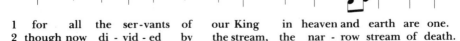

1 Let saints on earth in con - cert sing with those whose work is done;
2 One fam - i - ly we dwell in him, one Church, a - bove, be - neath,
3 One ar - my of the liv - ing God, to his com - mand we bow;
4 E'en now by faith we join our hands with those that went be - fore,
5 Je - sus, be thou our con - stant Guide; then, when the word is given,

1 for all the ser - vants of our King in heaven and earth are one.
2 though now di - vid - ed by the stream, the nar - row stream of death.
3 part of the host have crossed the flood, and part are cross - ing now.
4 and greet the ev - er - liv - ing bands on the e - ter - nal shore.
5 bid Jor - dan's nar - row stream di - vide, and bring us safe to heaven.

Words: Charles Wesley (1707-1788), alt.
Music: *Dundee*, melody from *The CL Psalmes of David*, 1615; harm. Thomas Ravenscroft (1592?-1635?), alt.

CM

527 The Church

1 Sing - ing songs of ex - pec - ta - tion, on - ward
2 One the light of God's own pres - ence, o'er his
3 One the strain the lips of thou - sands lift as

goes the pil - grim band, through the night of
ran - somed peo - ple shed, chas - ing far the
from the heart of one; one the con - flict,

doubt and sor - row, march - ing to the prom - ised land.
gloom and ter - ror, bright - ening all the path we tread:
one the per - il, one the march in God be - gun:

Clear be - fore us through the dark - ness gleams and
one the ob - ject of our jour - ney, one the
one the glad - ness of re - joic - ing on the

burns the guid - ing light: trust - ing God we
faith which nev - er tires, one the ear - nest
far e - ter - nal shore, where the one al -

march to - geth - er step - ping fear - less through the night.
look - ing for - ward, one the hope our God in - spires.
might - y Fa - ther reigns in love for ev - er - more.

Words: Bernard Severin Ingemann (1789-1862); tr. Sabine Baring-Gould (1834-1924), alt.
Music: *Ton-y-Botel*, Thomas John Williams (1869-1944)

87. 87. D

# The Church's Mission

1 Lord, you give the great com - mis - sion: "Heal the sick and
2 Lord, you call us to your serv - ice: "In my name bap -
3 Lord, you make the com - mon ho - ly: "This my bo - dy,
4 Lord, you show us love's true mea - sure: "Fa - ther, what they
5 Lord, you bless with words as - sur - ing: "I am with you

1 preach the word." Lest the Church ne - glect its mis - sion
2 tize and teach." That the world may trust your prom - ise,
3 this my blood." Let your priests, for earth's true glo - ry,
4 do, for - give." Yet we hoard as pri - vate trea - sure
5 to the end." Faith and hope and love re - stor - ing,

1 and the Gos - pel go un - heard, help us wit - ness to your
2 life a - bun - dant meant for each, give us all new fer - vor,
3 dai - ly lift life hea - ven - ward, ask - ing that the world a -
4 all that you so free - ly give. May your care and mer - cy
5 may we serve as you in - tend, and, a - mid the cares that

*Refrain*

1 pur - pose with re - newed in - teg - ri - ty;
2 draw us clos - er in com - mu - ni - ty;
3 round us share your chil - dren's lib - er - ty; with the
4 lead us to a just so - ci - e - ty;
5 claim us, hold in mind e - ter - ni - ty;

Spi - rit's gifts em - power us for the work of min - is - try.

Words: Jeffery Rowthorn (b. 1934)
Music: *Rowthorn*, Alec Wyton (b. 1921)

87. 87. 87 with Refrain

*Unison or harmony*

1 In Christ there is no East or West, in
2 Join hands, dis - ci - ples of the faith, what -
3 In Christ now meet both East and West, in

him no South or North, but one great fel - low -
e'er your race may be! Who serves my Fa - ther
him meet South and North, all Christ - ly souls are

ship of love through - out the whole wide earth.
as his child is sure - ly kin to me.
one in him, through - out the whole wide earth.

Words: John Oxenham (1852-1941), alt.
Music: *McKee,* Afro-American spiritual; adapt. and harm. Harry T. Burleigh (1866-1949)          CM

1 Spread, O spread, thou might - y word, spread the king - dom of the Lord,
2 word of how the Fa - ther's will made the world, and keeps it, still;
3 word of how the Sa - vior's love earth's sore bur - den doth re - move;
4 word of how the Spi - rit came bring - ing peace in Je - sus' name;
5 Word of life, most pure and strong, word for which the na - tions long,

| | | | | | | | | | | |
|---|---|---|---|---|---|---|---|---|---|---|
| 1 | that | to earth's re - | mot - est | bound | all | may heed the | | joy - ful | sound; |
| 2 | how | his on - ly | Son he | gave, | earth | from sin and | | death to | save; |
| 3 | how | for - ev - er, | in its | need, | through | his death the | | world is | freed; |
| 4 | how | his nev - er - | fail - ing | love | guides | us on to | | heaven a - | bove. |
| 5 | spread | a - broad, un - | til from | night | all | the world a - | | wakes to | light. |

Words: Jonathan Friedrich Bahnmaier (1774-1841); tr. Arthur William Farlander (1898-1952)
and Charles Winfred Douglas (1867-1944), alt. St. 4, F. Bland Tucker (1895-1984)
Music: *Gott sei Dank*, melody from *Geistreiches Gesangbuch*, 1704;
adapt. and harm. William Henry Havergal (1793-1870)

77. 77

## The Church's Mission

# 531

| | | | | | | | | | |
|---|---|---|---|---|---|---|---|---|---|
| 1 | O | Spi - | rit | of | the | liv - ing | God, | in |
| 2 | Give | tongues | of | fire | and | hearts of | love, | to |
| 3 | Be | dark - ness, | at | thy | com - ing, | light; con - | |
| 4 | Con - vert | the | na - tions! | far | and | nigh | the | |

| | | | | | | | | |
|---|---|---|---|---|---|---|---|---|
| all | thy | plen - i - | tude of | grace, | wher - e'er the | foot | of |
| preach the | rec - on - | cil - ing | word; | give power and | unc - tion | |
| fu - sion, | or - der | in thy | path; | souls with - out | strength in - | |
| tri - umphs | of the | cross re - | cord; | the Name of | Je - sus | |

| | | | | | | | | |
|---|---|---|---|---|---|---|---|---|
| man | hath trod, | de - scend on | our | a - pos - tate | race. | |
| from | a - bove, | when - e'er the | joy - ful | sound is | heard. | |
| spire | with might, | bid mer - cy | tri - umph | o - ver | wrath. | |
| glo - ri - fy, | till | ev - ery | peo - ple | call him | Lord. | |

Words: James Montgomery (1771-1854), alt.
Music: *Melcombe*, Samuel Webbe (1740-1816)

LM

1 How  won-drous and  great  thy  works, God  of  praise!
2 To  na-tions of  earth  thy  light shall be  shown;

How  just, King  of  saints,  and  true  are  thy  ways!
their  wor-ship and  vows  shall  come  to  thy  throne:

O  who shall  not  fear thee, and  hon-or  thy  Name?
thy  truth and  thy  judg-ments shall  spread all  a - broad,

Thou  on-ly  art  ho-ly, thou  on-ly  su-preme.
till  earth's ev-ery  peo-ple con-fess thee  their  God.

Words: Henry Ustick Onderdonk (1759-1858), alt.; para. *The Song of the Redeemed*
Music: *Old 104th*, melody from *The Whole Booke of Psalmes*, 1621; har. *Hymnal 1982*

10 10. 11 11

1 How won-drous and great thy works, God of praise!
2 To na-tions of earth thy light shall be shown;

How just, King of saints, and true are thy ways!
their wor-ship and vows shall come to thy throne:

O who shall not fear thee, and hon-or thy Name?
thy truth and thy judg-ments shall spread all a - broad,

Thou on - ly art ho - ly, thou on - ly su - preme.
till earth's ev - ery peo - ple con - fess thee their God.

Words: Henry Ustick Onderdonk (1759-1858), alt.; para. *The Song of the Redeemed*
Music: *Lyons*, att. Johann Michael Haydn (1737-1806)

10 10. 11 11

1        God    is ____ work-ing his   pur - pose     out   as ____
2 From   ut - most ___ east  to ____   ut - most     west,  wher -
3        March  we ____ forth in the   strength of    God, with  the
4        All    we  can do  is ___     noth - ing     worth un -

*May be sung in canon*

1        God    is ____ work-ing   his
2 From   ut - most ___ east  to ____
3        March  we ____ forth in   the
4        All    we  can do  is ____

year __ suc - ceeds __ to    year: _____ God is __ work-ing his
ev - er  foot __ hath        trod,          by the mouth of __ man - y ____
ban - ner of  Christ __ un - furled,        that the light of the glo-rious __
less __ God bless - es the   deed;          vain-ly we hope for the

pur - pose out     as ____   year __ suc-ceeds __ to    year; _____
ut - most west,    wher - ev - er - foot __ hath trod,       by the
strength of God,   with the ban - ner of Christ __ un - furled,       that the
noth - ing worth   un - less __ God bless-es the deed; _____

pur - pose __ out, and the time  is   draw-ing ____ near; _____
mes - sen - gers goes __ forth the   voice of ____ God; _____
gos - pel of truth may __ shine through-out the ____ world: _____
har - vest - tide till ____ God gives life  to the  seed; yet

God    is ____ work-ing his pur - pose __ out, and the time is   draw-ing __
mouth of ____ man - y ____  mes - sen - gers goes __ forth the voice of ____
light of the glo-rious ____ gos - pel of truth may __ shine through-out the __
vain - ly we hope for the har - vest - tide till ____ God gives life to the

near - er and near - er draws the time, the time that shall sure - ly
give ear to me, ye con - ti - nents, ye isles, give ____ ear to
fight we the fight with sorrow and sin to set their ____ cap - tives
near - er and near - er draws the time, the time that shall sure - ly

near; ____ near - er and near - er draws the time, the time that shall
God; ____ give ear to me, ye con - ti - nents, ye isles, give ____
world: ____ fight we the fight with sorrow and sin to set their ____
seed; yet near - er and near - er draws the time, the time that shall

be, when the earth shall be filled with the glo - ry of God as the
me, that the earth may be filled with the glo - ry of God as the
free, that the earth may be filled with the glo - ry of God as the
be, when the earth shall be filled with the glo - ry of God as the

sure - ly be, when the earth shall be filled with the glo - ry of
ear to me, that the earth may be filled with the glo - ry of
cap - tives free, that the earth may be filled with the glo - ry of
sure - ly be, when the earth shall be filled with the glo - ry of

[1-3]  |Final Ending

wa - ters cov - er the sea.
wa - ters cov - er the sea.
wa - ters cov - er the sea.
wa - ters cov - er the (sea.) sea. ____

God as the wa - ters cov - er the sea.
God as the wa - ters cov - er the sea.
God as the wa - ters cov - er the sea.
God as the wa - ters (cov - er the sea.) cov - er the sea. ____

Words: Arthur Campbell Ainger (1841-1919), alt.
Music: *Purpose*, Martin Fallas Shaw (1875-1958)

Irr.

1 Ye ser-vants of God, your Mas-ter pro-claim,
2 God rul-eth on high, al-might-y to save;
3 Sal-va-tion to God who sits on the throne!
4 Then let us a-dore, and give him his right:

and pub-lish a-broad his won-der-ful Name;
and still he is nigh: his pres-ence we have.
Let all cry a-loud, and hon-or the Son.
All glo-ry and power, all wis-dom and might,

the Name all-vic-to-rious of Je-sus ex-tol:
The great con-gre-ga-tion his tri-umph shall sing,
The prais-es of Je-sus the an-gels pro-claim,
and hon-or and bless-ing, with an-gels a-bove,

his king-dom is glo-rious; he rules o-ver all.
as-crib-ing sal-va-tion to Je-sus our King.
fall down on their fa-ces, and wor-ship the Lamb.
and thanks nev-er-ceas-ing and in-fi-nite love.

Words: Charles Wesley (1707-1788), alt.
Music: *Paderborn*, melody from *Catolisch-Paderbornisches Gesang-buch*, 1765;
    harm. Sydney Hugo Nicholson (1875-1947)

10 10. 11 11

# The Church's Mission

536

"Torah ora" is Hebrew for, "The Law is our Light."

Words: Willard F. Jabusch (b. 1930), alt.
Music: *Torah Song [Yisrael V'oraita]*, Hasidic melody; arr. Richard Proulx, (b. 1937)

98. 95 with Refrain

1 Christ for the world we sing! The world to
2 Christ for the world we sing! The world to
3 Christ for the world we sing! The world to
4 Christ for the world we sing! The world to

Christ we bring with lov - ing zeal; the poor, and
Christ we bring with fer - vent prayer; the way - ward
Christ we bring with one ac - cord; with us the
Christ we bring with joy - ful song; the new - born

them that mourn, the faint and o - ver - borne,
and the lost, by rest - less pas - sions tossed,
work to share, with us re - proach to dare,
souls, whose days, re - claimed from er - ror's ways,

sin - sick and sor - row-worn, whom Christ doth heal.
re - deemed at count - less cost from dark de - spair.
with us the cross to bear, for Christ our Lord.
in - spired with hope and praise, to Christ be - long.

Words: Samuel Wolcott (1813-1886)
Music: *Moscow*, melody Felice de Giardini (1716-1796); harm. *The New Hymnal*, 1916,
    based on *Hymns Ancient and Modern*, 1875, and Lowell Mason (1792-1872)

664. 6664

1 God of mer - cy, God of grace, show the bright - ness of thy
2 Let thy peo - ple praise thee, Lord; be by all that live a -

face. Shine up - on us, Sa - vior, shine, fill thy
dored. Let the na - tions shout and sing glo - ry

Church with light di - vine, and thy sav - ing health ex -
to their Sa - vior King; let all be, be - low, a -

tend un - to earth's re - mot - est end.
bove, one in joy, and light, and love.

Words: Henry Francis Lyte (1793-1847), alt.
Music: *Lucerna Laudoniae*, David Evans (1874-1948)

77. 77. 77

1 O Zi - on, haste, thy mis - sion high ful - fill - ing,
2 Pro - claim to ev - ery peo - ple, tongue, and na - tion
3 Send her - alds forth to bear the mes - sage glo - rious;
4 He comes a - gain! O Zi - on, ere thou meet him,

to tell to all the world that God is Light;
that God, in whom they live and move, is Love;
give of thy wealth to speed them on their way;
make known to ev - ery heart his sav - ing grace;

that he who made all na - tions is not will - ing
tell how he stooped to save his lost cre - a - tion,
pour out thy soul for them in prayer vic - to - rious
let none whom he hath ran - somed fail to greet him,

one soul should fail to know his love and might.
and died on earth that all might live a - bove.
till God shall bring his king - dom's joy - ful day.
through thy ne - glect, un - fit to see his face.

Pub - lish glad ti - dings: ti - dings of peace,

ti - dings of Je - sus, re - demp-tion and re - lease.

Words: Mary Ann Thomson (1834-1923), alt.
Music: *Tidings*, James Walch (1837-1901)

11 10. 11 10 with Refrain

1 A - wake, thou Spi - rit of the watch - men
2 O Lord, now let thy fire en - kin - dle
3 Send forth, O Lord, thy strong E - van - gel

who nev - er held their peace by day or night,
our hearts, that ev - ery - where its flame may go,
by man - y mes - sen - gers, all hearts to win;

con - tend - ing from the walls of Zi - on
and spread the glo - ry of re - demp - tion
make haste to help us in our weak - ness;

a - gainst the foe, con - fid - ing in thy might.
till all the world thy sav - ing grace shall know.
break down the realm of Sa - tan, death, and sin:

Through-out the world their cry is ring - ing still,
O har - vest Lord, look down on us and view
the cir - cle of the earth shall then pro - claim

and bring - ing peo - ples to thy ho - ly will.
how white the fields; the la - bor - ers, how few!
thy king - dom, and the glo - ry of thy Name.

Words: Karl Heinrich von Bogatzky (1690-1774); tr. Arthur William Farlander (1898-1952)
and Charles Winfred Douglas (1867-1944)
Music: *Dir, dir, Jehovah,* melody from *Hamburger Musikalisches handbuch,* 1690

9 10. 9 10. 10 10

1 Come, la - bor on. Who dares stand i - dle
2 Come, la - bor on. The en - e - my is
3 Come, la - bor on. A - way with gloom - y
4 Come, la - bor on. Claim the high call - ing
5 Come, la - bor on. No time for rest, till

1 on the har - vest plain, while all a - round us
2 watch - ing night and day, to sow the tares, to
3 doubts and faith - less fear! No arm so weak but
4 an - gels can - not share— to young and old the
5 glows the west - ern sky, till the long sha - dows

1 waves the gold - en grain? And to each ser - vant
2 snatch the seed a - way; while we in sleep our
3 may do ser - vice here: by feeb - lest a - gents
4 Gos - pel glad - ness bear: re - deem the time; its
5 o'er our path - way lie, and a glad sound comes

1 does the Mas - ter say, "Go work to - day."
2 du - ty have for - got, he slum - bered___ not.
3 may our God ful - fill his right - eous___ will.
4 hours too swift - ly fly. The night draws___ nigh.
5 with the set - ting sun,___ "Ser - vants, well done."

Words: Jane Laurie Borthwick (1813-1897), alt.
Music: *Ora Labora*, Thomas Tertius Noble (1867-1953)                    4. 10 10. 10 4

1 Christ is the world's true Light, its Cap-tain of sal - va - tion,
2 In Christ all rac - es meet, their an - cient feuds for - get - ting,
3 One Lord, in one great Name u - nite us all who own thee;

the Day - star clear and bright of ev - ery race and na - - tion;
the whole round world com - plete, from sun-rise to its set - ting:
cast out our pride and shame that hin-der to en - throne thee;

new life, new hope a - wakes, for all who own his sway:
when Christ is throned as Lord all shall for - sake their fear,
the world has wait - ed long, has tra - vailed long in pain;

free - dom her bond - age breaks, and night is turned to day.
to plough-share beat the sword, to prun - ing - hook the spear.
to heal its an - cient wrong, come, Prince of Peace, and reign.

Words George Wallace Briggs (1875-1959), alt.
Music: *St. Joan*, Percy E. B. Coller (b. 1895)

67. 67. 66. 66

Words: Philip Doddridge (1702-1751); based on *The Third Song of Isaiah*
Music: *Eastview*, J. V. Lee (1892-1959)

66. 66 88

# 544

The Church's Mission

Words: Isaac Watts (1674-1748), alt.
Music: *Duke Street*, John Hatton (d. 1793)

LM

1 Lo! what a cloud of wit - ness - es en -
2 Let us, with zeal like theirs in - spired, strive
3 Be - hold a Wit - ness no - bler still, who
4 He, for the joy be - fore him set, and
5 Thith - er, for - get - ting things be - hind, press

1 com - pass us a - round! They, once like us with
2 in the Chris - tian race; and, freed from ev - ery
3 trod af - flic - tion's path: Je - sus, the au - thor,
4 moved by pit - ying love, en - dured the cross, de -
5 we to God's right hand; there, with the Sa - vior

1 suf - fering tried, are now with glo - ry crowned.
2 weight of sin, their ho - ly foot - steps trace.
3 fi - nish - er, re - ward - er of our faith.
4 spised the shame, and now he reigns a - bove.
5 and his saints, tri - um - phant - ly to stand.

Words: *Translations and Paraphrases*, 1745, alt.; para. of Hebrews 12:1-3
Music: *St. Fulbert*, Henry John Gauntlett (1805-1876)
CM

1 A - wake, my soul, stretch ev - ery nerve, and press with vi - gor
2 A cloud of wit - ness - es a - round hold thee in full sur -
3 'Tis God's all - an - i - mat - ing voice that calls thee from on
4 Then wake, my soul, stretch ev - ery nerve, and press with vi - gor

on; a heaven - ly race de - mands thy zeal, and
vey; for - get the steps al - read - y trod, and
high; 'tis his own hand pre - sents the prize to
on; a heaven - ly race de - mands thy zeal, and

an im - mor - tal crown, and an im - mor - tal crown.
on - ward urge thy way, and on - ward urge thy way.
thine as - pir - ing eye, to thine as - pir - ing eye.
an im - mor - tal crown, and an im - mor - tal crown.

Words: Philip Doddridge (1702-1751)
Music: *Siroë*, George Frideric Handel (1685-1759); adapt. *Melodia Sacra*, 1815      86. 866

1 A - wake, O sleep - er, rise from death, and Christ shall
2 To us on earth he came to bring from sin and
3 There is one Bo - dy and one hope, one Spi - rit
4 Then walk in love as Christ has loved, who died that
5 For us Christ lived, for us he died and con - quered

1 give you light, so learn his love— its length and
2 fear re - lease, to give the Spi - rit's u - ni -
3 and one call, one Lord, one Faith, and one Bap -
4 he might save; with kind and gen - tle hearts for -
5 in the strife. A - wake, a - rise, go forth in

| 1 | breadth, | its | full - ness, | depth, | and | | height. |
| 2 | ty, | the | ve - ry | bond | of | | peace. |
| 3 | tism, | one | Fa - ther | of | us | | all. |
| 4 | give | as | God in | Christ | for - | | gave. |
| 5 | faith, | and | Christ shall | give | you | | life. |

Words: F. Bland Tucker (1895-1984)
Music: *Marsh Chapel*, Max Miller (b. 1927)

CM

## Christian Vocation and Pilgrimage

# 548

| 1 | Sol - diers | of | Christ, | a - rise, | and | put | your |
| 2 | strong | in the | Lord | of | hosts, and | in | his |
| 3 | Stand | then in | his | great | might, with | all | his |
| 4 | From | strength to | strength | go | on, wres - tle, | and |  |
| 5 | That, | hav - ing | all | things | done, and | all | your |

| 1 | ar - mor | on, | strong | in the | strength | which |
| 2 | might - y | power: | who | in the | strength | of |
| 3 | strength | en - dued, | and | take, to | arm | you |
| 4 | fight, | and | pray: tread | all the | powers | of |
| 5 | con - flicts | past, | ye | may o'er - come, | through |

| 1 | God sup - | plies through | his | e - ter - nal | Son; |
| 2 | Je - sus | trusts is | more | than con - quer - | or. |
| 3 | for the | fight, the | pan - o - | ply of | God. |
| 4 | dark - ness | down, and | win the | well - fought | day. |
| 5 | Christ a - | lone, and | stand com - | plete at | last. |

Words: Charles Wesley (1707-1788)
Music: *Silver Street*, Isaac Smith (1734?-1805)

SM

1 Je - sus calls us; o'er the tu - mult of our
2 as, of old, Saint An - drew heard it by the
3 Je - sus calls us from the wor - ship of the
4 In our joys and in our sor - rows, days of
5 Je - sus calls us! By thy mer - cies, Sa - vior,

1 life's wild, rest - less sea, day by day his clear voice
2 Gal - i - le - an lake, turned from home and toil and
3 vain world's gold - en store; from each i - dol that would
4 toil and hours of ease, still he calls, in cares and
5 may we hear thy call, give our hearts to thine o -

1 sound - eth, say - ing, "Chris - tian, fol - low me;" say - ing
2 kin - dred, leav - ing all for his dear sake. leav - ing
3 keep us, say - ing, "Chris - tian, love me more." say - ing
4 plea - sures, "Chris-tian, love me more than these." "Chris-tian,
5 be - dience, serve and love thee best of all. serve and

1-4     Final Ending

1 "Chris - tian, fol - low me;"
2 all for his dear sake.
3 "Chris - tian, love me more."
4 love me more than these."
5 love thee best of (all.) all.

Words: Cecil Frances Alexander (1818-1895), alt.
Music: *St. Andrew,* David Hurd (b. 1950)

87. 877

# Christian Vocation and Pilgrimage

1 Je - sus calls us; o'er the tu - mult of our life's wild, rest - less sea, day by day his clear voice sound - eth, say - ing, "Chris - tian, fol - low me;"

2 as, of old, Saint An - drew heard it by the Gal - i - le - an lake, turned from home and toil and kin - dred, leav - ing all for his dear sake.

3 Je - sus calls us from the wor - ship of the vain world's gold - en store; from each i - dol that would keep us, say - ing, "Chris - tian, love me more."

4 In our joys and in our sor - rows, days of toil and hours of ease, still he calls, in cares and plea - sures, "Chris - tian, love me more than these."

5 Je - sus calls us! By thy mer - cies, Sa - vior, may we hear thy call, give our hearts to thine o - be - dience, serve and love thee best of all.

Words: Cecil Frances Alexander (1818-1895), alt.
Music: *Restoration*, melody from *The Southern Harmony*, 1835; harm. *Hymnal 1982*,
after *The Southern Harmony*, 1835

87. 87

1 Rise up, ye saints of God! Have done with less - er things, give
2 Rise up, ye saints of God! His king - dom tar - ries long: Lord,
3 Lift high the cross of Christ! Tread where his feet have trod; and

heart and soul and mind and strength to serve the King of kings.
bring the day of truth and love and end the night of wrong.
quick-ened by the Spi - rit's power, rise up, ye saints of God!

Words: William Pierson Merrill (1867-1954), alt.
Music: *Festal Song*, William H. Walter (1825-1893)                                      SM

1 Fight the good fight with all thy might, Christ is thy
2 Run the straight race through God's good grace, lift up thine
*3 Cast care a - side, lean on thy Guide; his bound - less
*4 Faint not nor fear, his arms are near; he chan - geth

strength and Christ thy right; lay hold on life, and
eyes and seek his face; life with its way be -
mer - cy will pro - vide; trust, and thy trust - ing
not, and thou art dear; on - ly be - lieve, and

it shall be thy joy and crown e - ter - nal - ly.
fore us lies, Christ is the path and Christ the prize.
soul shall prove Christ is its life and Christ its love.
thou shalt see that Christ is all in all to thee.

Words: John Samuel Bewley Monsell (1811-1875), alt
Music: *Pentecost*, William Boyd (1847-1928)

LM

## Christian Vocation and Pilgrimage

# 553

1 Fight the good fight with all thy might, Christ is thy
2 Run the straight race through God's good grace, lift up thine
*3 Cast care a - side, lean on thy Guide; his bound - less
*4 Faint not nor fear, his arms are near; he chan - geth

strength and Christ thy right; lay hold on life, and it shall be thy
eyes and seek his face; life with its way be - fore us lies, ____
mer - cy will pro - vide; trust, and thy trust - ing soul shall prove ____
not, and thou art dear; on - ly be - lieve, and thou shalt see that

joy ____ and crown e - ter - nal - ly.
Christ is the path and Christ the prize.
Christ is its life and Christ its love.
Christ ____ is all in all to thee.

Words: John Samuel Bewley Monsell (1811-1875), alt.
Music: *Rushford*, Henry G. Ley (1887-1962)

LM

'Tis the gift to be sim - ple, 'tis the gift to be free,

'tis the gift to come down where we ought to be,

and when we find our - selves in the place just right,

'twill be in the val - ley of love and de - light.

When true sim - plic - i - ty is gained to

bow and to bend we shan't be a - shamed, to turn, turn, will

be our de - light till by turn - ing, turn - ing we come round right.

Words: Shaker song, 18th cent.
Music: *Simple Gifts*, Shaker melody

Irr. with Refrain

1 Lead on, O King e - ter - nal, the day of march has come;
hence - forth in fields of con - quest thy tents shall be our home:
through days of prep - a - ra - tion thy grace has made us strong,
and now, O King e - ter - nal, we lift our bat - tle song.

2 Lead on, O King e - ter - nal, till sin's fierce war shall cease,
and ho - li - ness shall whis - per the sweet a - men of peace;
for not with swords loud clash - ing, nor roll of stir - ring drums,
but deeds of love and mer - cy, the heaven - ly king - dom comes.

3 Lead on, O King e - ter - nal: we fol - low, not with fears;
for glad - ness breaks like morn - ing wher - e'er thy face ap - pears.
Thy cross is lift - ed o'er us; we jour - ney in its light:
the crown a - waits the con - quest; lead on, O God of might!

Words: Ernest Warburton Shurtleff (1862-1917)
Music: *Lancashire*, Henry Thomas Smart (1813-1879)

76. 76 D

1 Re - joice, ye pure in heart! Re - joice, give thanks, and sing! Your
2 With all the an - gel choirs, with all the saints of earth, pour
3 Your clear ho - san - nas raise, and al - le - lu - ias loud; while
4 Yes, on through life's long path, still chant-ing as ye go, from
5 Still lift your stand-ard high, still march in firm ar - ray, as

1 glo - rious ban - ner wave on high, the cross of Christ your King.
2 out the strains of joy and bliss, true rap - ture, no - blest mirth.
3 an - swering ech - oes up - ward float, like wreaths of in - cense cloud.
4 youth to age, by night and day, in glad - ness and in woe.
5 war - riors through the dark - ness toil, till dawns the gold - en day.

*Refrain*

Re - joice, re - joice, re - joice, give thanks, and sing.

re - joice, re - joice,

*6 At last the march shall end;
    the wearied ones shall rest;
    the pilgrims find their Father's house,
    Jerusalem the blest.

      *Refrain*

*7 Then on, ye pure in heart!
    Rejoice, give thanks, and sing!
    Your glorious banner wave on high
    the cross of Christ your King.

      *Refrain*

Words: Edward Hayes Plumptre (1821-1891)
Music: *Marion*, Arthur Henry Messiter (1834-1916)

SM with Refrain

# Christian Vocation and Pilgrimage

1 Re - joice, ye pure in heart! Re - joice, give thanks, and
2 With all the an - gel choirs, with all the saints of
3 Your clear ho - san - nas raise, and al - le - lu - ias
4 Yes, on through life's long path, still chant-ing as ye
5 Still lift your stand - ard high, still march in firm ar -
*6 At last the march shall end; the wea - ried ones shall
*7 Then on, ye pure in heart! Re - joice, give thanks, and

1 sing! Your glo - rious ban - ner wave on high, the
2 earth, pour out the strains of joy and bliss, true
3 loud; while an - swering ech - oes up - ward float, like
4 go, from youth to age, by night and day, in
5 ray, as war - riors through the dark - ness toil, till
6 rest; the pil - grims find their Fa - ther's house, Je -
7 sing! Your glo - rious ban - ner wave on high, the

*Refrain*

1 cross of Christ your King.
2 rap - ture, no - blest mirth.
3 wreaths of in - cense cloud.
4 glad - ness and in woe. Ho - san - na, ho -
5 dawns the gold - en day.
6 ru - sa - lem the blest.
7 cross of Christ your King.

san - na! Re - joice, give thanks, and sing.

Words: Edward Hayes Plumptre (1821-1891)
Music: *Vineyard Haven*, Richard Wayne Dirksen (b. 1921)

SM with Refrain

1 Faith of our fa - thers! liv - ing still in spite of dun - geon,
2 Faith of our fa - thers! faith and prayer shall win all na - tions
3 Faith of our fa - thers! we will love both friend and foe in

fire, and sword: O how our hearts beat high with joy,
un - to thee; and through the truth that comes from God,
all our strife: and preach thee, too, as love knows how,

*Refrain*

when-e'er we hear that glo - rious word:
man - kind shall then in - deed be free.    Faith of our fa - thers,
by kind - ly deeds and vir - tuous life.

ho - ly faith! We will be true to thee till death.

Words: Frederick William Faber (1814-1863), alt.
Music: *St. Catherine*, Henri Frédéric Hemy (1818-1888); adapt. and arr. James G. Walton (1821-1905)          88. 88. 88

1 Lead us, heaven-ly Fa - ther, lead us o'er the world's tem -
2 Sa - vior, breathe for - give - ness o'er us; all our weak - ness
3 Spi - rit of our God, de - scend-ing, fill our hearts with

pes - tuous sea; guard us, guide us, keep us, feed us,
thou dost know; thou didst tread this earth be - fore us;
heaven - ly joy; love with ev - ery pas - sion blend-ing

for we have no help but thee, yet pos - ses - sing
thou didst feel its keen - est woe; yet un - fear - ing,
plea - sure that can nev - er cloy; thus pro - vid - ed,

ev - ery bless - ing, if our God our Fa - ther be.
per - se - ver - ing, to thy pas - sion thou didst go.
par - doned, guid - ed, noth - ing can our peace des - troy.

Words: James Edmeston (1791-1867), alt.
Music: *Dulce carmen*, melody from *An Essay on the Church Plain Chant*, 1782;
    adapt. *Collection of Motetts or Antiphons*, ca. 1840; harm. William Henry Monk (1823-1889)     87. 87. 87

*Antiphon*

Re-mem-ber your ser-vants, Lord, when you come in your kingly pow - er.

1. Bless-ed are the poor in spi - rit; for theirs is the kingdom of hea - ven.

2. Bless - ed are those who mourn; for they shall be com - fort - ed.

3. Bless - ed are the meek; for they shall in - her - it the earth.

4. Bless - ed are those who hunger and thirst af - ter right - eous-ness;

for they shall be sat - is - fied. 5. Bless - ed are the mer - ci - ful;

for they shall ob - tain mer - cy. 6. Bless - ed are the pure in heart;

for they shall see God. 7. Bless - ed are the peace - ma - kers;

for they shall be called the chil - dren of God.

8. Bless - ed are those who are perse - cut - ed for right-eous-ness' sake;

for theirs is the kingdom of hea - - ven.

9. Bless - ed are you when the world re - viles you and per - se - cutes you;

and utters all manner of evil against you false - ly for my sake:

Re - joice and be ex - ceed - ing glad; for great is your reward in hea - ven.

*Antiphon*

Re - mem - ber your ser - vants, Lord, when you come in your kingly pow - er.

*The second bass part is optional.*

Words: Russian Orthodox liturgy; Matthew 5:3-12
Music: *Beatitudes*, Russian Orthodox hymn; arr. Richard Proulx (b. 1937)

Irr. with Refrain

1 Stand up, stand up, for Je - sus, ye sold - iers of the cross;
2 Stand up, stand up, for Je - sus; the trum - pet call o - bey;
3 Stand up, stand up, for Je - sus; stand in his strength a - lone;
4 Stand up, stand up, for Je - sus: the strife will not be long:

lift high his roy - al ban - ner, it must not suf - fer loss:
forth to the might - y con - flict in this his glo - rious day:
the arm of flesh will fail you, ye dare not trust your own:
this day, the noise of bat - tle; the next, the vic - tor's song.

from vic - tory un - to vic - tory his ar - my shall he lead,
ye that are his now serve him a - gainst un - num - bered foes;
put on the Gos - pel ar - mor, and watch - ing un - to prayer,
To val - iant hearts tri - um - phant, a crown of life shall be;

till ev - ery foe is van - quished and Christ is Lord in - deed.
let cour - age rise with dan - ger, and strength to strength op - pose.
when du - ty calls, or dan - ger, be nev - er want - ing there.
they with the King of glo - ry shall reign e - ter - nal - ly.

Words: George Duffield, Jr. (1818-1888), alt.
Music: *Morning Light*, George James Webb (1803-1887)

76. 76. D

1 On - ward, Chris - tian sol - diers, march - ing as to war,
*2 At the sign of tri - umph Sa - tan's host doth flee;
*3 Like a might - y ar - my moves the Church of God;
4 Crowns and thrones may per - ish, king - doms rise and wane,
5 On - ward, then, ye peo - ple, join our hap - py throng;

1 with the cross of Je - sus go - ing on be - fore!
2 on, then, Chris - tian sol - diers, on to vic - to - ry!
3 Chris - tians, we are tread - ing where the saints have trod;
4 but the Church of Je - sus con - stant will re - main;
5 blend with ours your voic - es in the tri - umph song:

1 Christ, the roy - al Mas - ter, leads a - gainst the foe;
2 Hell's foun - da - tions quiv - er at the shout of praise;
3 we are not di - vid - ed, all one bo - dy we,
4 gates of hell can nev - er 'gainst that Church pre - vail;
5 glo - ry, laud, and hon - or, un - to Christ the King;

1 for - ward in - to bat - tle, see, his ban - ners go.
2 Chris - tians, lift your voic - es, loud your an - thems raise.
3 one in hope and doc - trine, one in char - i - ty.
4 we have Christ's own prom - ise, and that can - not fail.
5 this through count - less a - ges we with an - gels sing.

*Refrain*

On - ward, Chris - tian sol - diers, march - ing as to war,

with the cross of Je - sus go - ing on be - fore!

Words: Sabine Baring-Gould (1834-1924), alt.
Music: *St. Gertrude*, Arthur Seymour Sullivan (1842-1900)

65. 65. D with Refrain

1 Go for-ward, Chris-tian sol - dier, be - neath his ban - ner true:
2 Go for-ward, Chris-tian sol - dier, fear not the se - cret foe;
3 Go for-ward, Chris-tian sol - dier, nor dream of peace-ful rest,
4 Go for-ward, Chris-tian sol - dier, fear not the gath - ering night:

the Lord him-self, thy Lead - er, shall all thy foes sub - due.
far more o'er thee are watch - ing than hu - man eyes can know:
till Sa - tan's host is van - quished and heaven is all pos - sessed;
the Lord has been thy shel - ter; the Lord will be thy light.

His love for - tells thy tri - als; he knows thine hour - ly need;
trust on - ly Christ, thy Cap - tain; cease not to watch and pray;
till Christ him - self shall call thee to lay thine ar - mor by,
When morn his face re - veal - eth thy dan - gers all are past:

he can with bread of hea - ven thy faint - ing spi - rit feed.
heed not the treach-erous voic - es that lure thy soul a - stray.
and wear in end - less glo - ry the crown of vic - to - ry.
O pray that faith and vir - tue may keep thee to the last!

Words: Laurence Tuttiett (1825-1895)
Music: *Lancashire*, Henry Thomas Smart (1813-1879)

76. 76. D

# Christian Vocation and Pilgrimage

**564**

1 He who would val - iant be 'gainst all dis - as - ter,
2 Who so be - set him round with dis - mal sto - ries,
3 Since, Lord, thou dost de - fend us with thy Spi - rit,

let him in con - stan - cy fol - low the Mas - ter.
do but them - selves con-found, his strength the more is.
we know we at the end shall life in - her - it.

There's no dis - cour - age-ment shall make him once re - lent
No foes shall stay his might, though he with gi - ants fight;
Then fan - cies flee a - way; I'll fear not what men say,

his first a - vowed in - tent to be a pil - grim.
he will make good his right to be a pil - grim.
I'll la - bor night and day to be a pil - grim.

Words: Percy Dearmer (1867-1936), after John Bunyan (1628-1688)
Music: *St. Dunstan's*, Charles Winfred Douglas (1867-1944)

65. 65. 6665

1 He who would val - iant be 'gainst all dis - as - ter,____
2 Who so be - set him round with dis - mal sto - ries,____
3 Since, Lord, thou dost de - fend us with thy Spi - rit,____

let him in con - stan - cy fol - low the Mas - ter.____
do but them-selves con - found, his strength the more is.____
we know we at the end shall life in - her - it.____

There's no dis - cour - age - ment shall make him once re - lent
No foes shall stay his might, though he with gi - ants fight;
Then fan - cies flee a - way; I'll fear not what men say,

his first a - vowed in - tent to be a pil - grim.
he will make good his right to be a pil - grim.
I'll la - bor night and day to be a pil - grim.

Words: Percy Dearmer (1868-1936), after John Bunyan (1628-1688)
Music: *Monk's Gate*, Sussex folk melody; adapt and arr. Ralph Vaughan Williams (1872-1958)          11 11. 12 11

1 From thee all skill and sci-ence flow, all pi-ty, care, and love,
all calm and cour-age, faith and hope: O pour them from a - bove!
Im - part them, Lord, to each and all, as each and all shall need,
to rise, like in - cense, each to thee, in no - ble thought and deed.

2 And has-ten, Lord, that per-fect day when pain and death shall cease,
and thy just rule shall fill the earth with health and light and peace;
when ev - er - blue the sky shall gleam, and ev - er-green the sod,
and our rude work de - face no more the hand - i - work of God.

Words: Charles Kingsley (1819-1875), alt.
Music: *The Church's Desolation*, traditional melody; harm. J. T. White (19th cent.);
adapt. C. H. Cayce (19th-20th cent.)

CMD

1 Thine arm, O Lord, in days of old was strong to
2 And lo! thy touch brought life and health, gave hear - ing,
3 Be thou our great de - liv - erer still, thou Lord of

heal and save; it tri - umphed o'er dis - ease and death,
strength, and sight; and youth re - newed and fren - zy calmed
life and death; re - store and quick - en, soothe and bless,

o'er dark - ness and the grave. To thee they went, the
owned thee, the Lord of light: and now, O Lord, be
with thine al - might - y breath: to hands that work and

| blind, | the | deaf, | the | pal | - | sied, | and | the | lame, | the | lep | - | er |
| near | to | bless, | al - | might - | | y | as | of | yore, | in | crowd | - | ed |
| eyes | that | see, | give | wis - | | dom's heaven - ly | | lore, | that | whole | and | | |

| set | a - | part | and | shunned, the | | sick | with | fe | - | vered frame. |
| street, | by | rest - | less | couch, | as | by | Gen | - | nes - | aret's shore. |
| sick, | and | weak | and | strong, | may | praise | thee | ev | - | er - more. |

Words: Edward Hayes Plumptre (1821-1891), alt.
Music: *St. Matthew*, from *Supplement to the New Version of Psalms by Dr. Brady and Mr. Tate*, 1708          CMD

1 Fa - ther all lov - ing, who rul - est in ma - jes - ty,
2 Bless - ed Lord Je - sus, who cam - est in pov - er - ty,
3 Come, Ho - ly Spi - rit, cre - ate in us ho - li - ness,
4 Ho - li - est Trin - i - ty, per - fect in u - ni - ty,

judg - ment is thine, and con - demn - eth our pride;
shar - ing a sta - ble with beasts at thy birth,
lift up our lives to thy stand - ard of right;
bind in thy love ev - ery na - tion and race;

stir up our lead - ers and peo - ples to pen - i - tence,
stir us to work for thy jus - tice and char - i - ty,
stir ev - ery will to new ven - tures of faith - ful - ness,
may we a - dore thee for time and e - ter - ni - ty,

sor - row for sins that for ven - geance have cried.
tru - ly to care for the poor of the earth.
flood the whole Church with thy glo - ri - ous light.
Fa - ther, Re - deem - er, and Spi - rit of grace.

Words: Patrick Robert Norman Appleford (b. 1925), alt.
Music: *Was lebet*, melody from *Choral-Buch vor Johann Heinrich Reinhardt*, 1754;
    harm. Ralph Vaughan Williams (1872-1958)
                                                                  12 10. 12 10

# Christian Responsibility

569

1 God the Om - ni - po - tent! King, who or - dain - est
2 God the All - mer - ci - ful! earth hath for - sak - en
3 God, the All - right - eous One! earth hath de - fied thee;
4 God the All - prov - i - dent! earth by thy chas - tening

thun - der thy clar - ion, the light - ning thy sword;
thy ways all ho - ly, and slight - ed thy word;
yet to e - ter - ni - ty stand - eth thy word,
yet shall to free - dom and truth be re - stored;

show forth thy pi - ty on high where thou reign - est:
bid not thy wrath in its ter - rors a - wak - en:
false - hood and wrong shall not tar - ry be - side thee:
through the thick dark - ness thy king - dom is haste - ning:

give to us peace in our time, O Lord.
give to us peace in our time, O Lord.
give to us peace in our time, O Lord.
thou wilt give peace in thy time, O Lord.

Words: Sts. 1-2, Henry Fothergill Chorley (1808-1872), alt.; sts. 3-4, John Ellerton (1826-1893), alt.
Music: *Russia*, Alexis Lvov (1799-1870)

11 10. 11 9

1 All who love and serve your ci - ty, all who
2 in your day of loss and sor - row, in your
3 In your day of wealth and plen - ty, wast - ed
4 For all days are days of judg - ment, and the
5 Ris - en Lord! shall yet the ci - ty be the

1 bear its dai - ly stress, all who cry for peace and
2 day of help - less strife, hon - or, peace, and love re -
3 work and wast - ed play, call to mind the word of
4 Lord is wait - ing still, draw - ing near a world that
5 ci - ty of de - spair? Come to - day, our Judge, our

1 jus - tice, all who curse and all who bless,
2 treat - ing, seek the Lord, who is your life.
3 Je - sus, "I must work while it is day."
4 spurns him, of - fering peace from Cal - vary's hill.
5 Glo - ry; be its name, "The Lord is there!"

Words: Erik Routley (1917-1982), rev.
Music: *Birabus*, Peter Cutts (b. 1937)

87. 87

1 All who love and serve your ci - ty, all who
2 in your day of loss and sor - row, in your
3 In your day of wealth and plen - ty, wast - ed
4 For all days are days of judg-ment, and the
5 Ris - en Lord! shall yet the ci - ty be the

| | | | | | | | |
|---|---|---|---|---|---|---|---|
| 1 bear | its | dai - ly | stress, | all | who | cry | for |
| 2 day | of | help - less | strife, | hon - | or, | peace, | and |
| 3 work | and | wast - ed | play, | call | to | mind | the |
| 4 Lord | is | wait - ing | still, | draw - | ing | near | a |
| 5 ci - | ty | of de - | spair? | Come | to - | day, | our |

| | | | | | | | |
|---|---|---|---|---|---|---|---|
| 1 peace and | jus - tice, | all | who | curse | and | all | who | bless, |
| 2 love re - | treat - ing, | seek | the | Lord, | who | is | your | life. |
| 3 word of | Je - sus, | "I | must | work | while | it | is | day." |
| 4 world that | spurns him, | of - | fering | peace | from | Cal - | vary's | hill. |
| 5 Judge, our | Glo - ry; | be | its | name, | "The | Lord | is | there!" |

Words: Erik Routley (1917-1982), rev.
Music: *Charlestown*, melody from *The Southern Harmony*, 1835

87. 87

## Christian Responsibility

# 572

| | | | | | | | |
|---|---|---|---|---|---|---|---|
| 1 Wea - ry | of | all | trum - pet - ing, | wea - ry | of | all | kill - ing, |
| 2 Cap - tain | Christ, O | low - ly Lord, | Ser - vant King, your | dy - ing |
| 3 To the | tri - umph | of your cross | sum - mon all the | liv - ing; |

| | | | | |
|---|---|---|---|---|
| wea - ry | of | all | songs that sing | prom - ise, non - ful - fill - ing, |
| bade us | sheathe the | fool - ish sword, | bade us cease de - ny - ing. |
| sum - mon | us | to | love by loss, | gain - ing all by giv - ing, |

| | | | |
|---|---|---|---|
| we would raise, | O Christ, one song; | we_____ would join | in sing - ing |
| Trum - pet with | your Spi - rit's breath | through_____ each height and hol - low; |
| suf - fering all, | that we may see | tri - umph | in sur - ren - der; |

| | | | |
|---|---|---|---|
| that great | mu - sic pure and strong, where- | with heaven is | ring - ing. |
| in - to | your self - giv - ing death, | call us all to | fol - low. |
| leav - ing | all, that we may be | part - ners in | your splen - dor. |

Words: Martin H. Franzmann (1907-1976), alt.
Music: *Distler*, Hugo Distler (1908-1942)

76. 76. D

1 Fa - ther e - ter - nal, Ru - ler of cre - a - tion,
2 Rac - es and peo - ples, lo, we stand di - vid - ed,
3 En - vious of heart, blind - eyed, with tongues con - found - ed,
4 Lust of pos - ses - sion work - eth des - o - la - tions;
5 How shall we love thee, ho - ly hid - den Be - ing,

1 Spi - rit of life, which moved ere form was made,
2 and, shar - ing not our griefs, no joy can share;
3 na - tion by na - tion still goes un - for - given,
4 there is no meek - ness in the powers of earth;
5 if we love not the world which thou hast made?

1 through the thick dark - ness cov - ering ev - ery na - tion,
2 by wars and tu - mults love is mocked, de - rid - ed;
3 in wrath and fear, by jea - lous - ies sur - round - ed,
4 led by no star, the ru - lers of the na - tions
5 Bind us in thine own love for bet - ter see - ing

1 light to our blind - ness, O be thou our aid:
2 his sav - ing cross no na - tion yet will bear:
3 build - ing proud towers which shall not reach to heaven:
4 still fail to bring us to the bliss - ful birth:
5 thy Word made flesh, and in a man - ger laid:

*Refrain*

thy king - dom come, O Lord, thy will be done.

Words: Laurence Housman (1865-1959), alt.
Music: *Langham*, Geoffrey Turton Shaw (1879-1943)　　　　　11 10. 11 10. 10

1 Be - fore thy throne, O God, we kneel: give us a con - science
2 Search out our hearts and make us true; help us to give to
3 For sins of heed - less word and deed, for pride am - bi - tious
4 Let the fierce fires which burn and try, our in - most spi - rits

quick to feel, a rea - dy mind to un - der - stand the
all their due. From love of plea - sure, lust of gold, from
to suc - ceed, for craft - y trade and sub - tle snare to
pu - ri - fy: con - sume the ill; purge out the shame; O

mean - ing of thy chas - tening hand; what - e'er the pain and
sins which make the heart grow cold, wean us and train us
catch the sim - ple un - a - ware, for lives be - reft of
God, be with us in the flame; a new - born peo - ple

shame may be, bring us, O Fa - ther, near - er thee.
with thy rod; teach us to know our faults, O God.
pur - pose high, for - give, for - give, O Lord, we cry.
may we rise, more pure, more true, more no - bly wise.

Words: William Boyd Carpenter (1841-1918), alt.
Music: *St. Petersburg*, Dimitri S. Bortniansky (1751-1825)

88. 88. 88

# 575

Christian Responsibility

1 Be - fore thy throne, O God, we kneel: give us a con-science
2 Search out our hearts and make us true; help us to give to
3 For sins of heed - less word and deed, for pride am - bi - tious
4 Let the fierce fires which burn and try, our in - most spi - rits

quick to feel, a rea - dy mind to un - der - stand
all their due. From love of plea - sure, lust of gold,
to suc - ceed, for craft - y trade and sub - tle snare
pu - ri - fy: con - sume the ill; purge out the shame;

the mean - ing of thy chas - tening hand; what - e'er the pain and
from sins which make the heart grow cold, wean us and train us
to catch the sim - ple un - a - ware, for lives be - reft of
O God, be with us in the flame; a new - born peo - ple

shame may be, bring us, O Fa - ther, near - er thee.
with thy rod; teach us to know our faults, O God.
pur - pose high, for - give, for - give, O Lord, we cry.
may we rise, more pure, more true, more no - bly wise.

Words: William Boyd Carpenter (1841-1918), alt.
Music: *Vater unser im Himmelreich*, melody from *Geistliche lieder auffs new gebessert und gemehrt*, 1539;
adapt. Martin Luther (1483-1546); harm. Hans Leo Hassler (1564-1612)

88. 88. 88

*Descant (after stanzas 2 and 3)*

God is love, God is love,

*Refrain*

God is love, and where true love is

God him - self is there. there.

*1-3* *Final Ending*

God him - self is there. there.

1 Here in Christ we gath - er, love of Christ our call - ing.
2 When we Chris - tians gath - er, mem - bers of one Bo - dy,
3 Grant us love's ful - fill - ment, joy with all the bless - ed,

Christ, our love, is with us, glad - ness be his greet - ing.
let there be in us no dis - cord but one spi - rit.
when we see your face, O Sa - vior, in its glo - ry.

Let us fear and love him, ho - ly God e - ter - nal.
Ban - ished now be an - ger, strife and ev - ery quar - rel.
Shine on us, O pur - est Light of all cre - a - tion,

*Repeat Refrain*

Lov - ing him, let each love Christ in one an - oth - er.
Christ, our God, be al - ways pres - ent here a - mong us.
be our bliss while end - less a - ges sing your prais - es.

Words: Latin; tr. James Quinn (b. 1919), alt.
Music: *Mandatum*, Richard Proulx (b. 1937)

12. 12. 12. 12 with Refrain

*Refrain*

God is love, and where true love is God him-self is there.

1 Here in Christ we gath - er, love of Christ our call - ing.
2 When we Chris-tians gath - er, mem-bers of one Bo - dy,
3 Grant us love's ful - fill - ment, joy with all the bless - ed,

Christ, our love, is with us, glad-ness be his greet - ing.
let there be in us no dis-cord but one spi - rit.
when we see your face, O Sa - vior, in its glo - ry.

Let us fear and love him, ho - ly God e - ter - nal.
Ban-ished now be an - ger, strife and ev - ery quar - rel.
Shine on us, O pur - est Light of all cre - a - tion,

Lov - ing him, let each love Christ in one an - oth - er.
Christ, our God, be al - ways pres - ent here a - mong us.
be our bliss while end - less a - ges sing your prais - es.

*Repeat Refrain*

Words: Latin; tr. James Quinn (b. 1919), alt.
Music: *Ubi caritas (Murray)*, A. Gregory Murray (b. 1905)

12. 12. 12. 12 with Refrain

## Christian Responsibility

578

*Unison or harmony*

1 O God of love, O King of peace, make wars through-
2 Re - mem - ber, Lord, thy works of old, the won - ders
3 Whom shall we trust but thee, O Lord? Where rest but

out the world to cease; the wrath of na - tions now re -
that thy peo - ple told; re - mem - ber not our sin's dark
on thy faith - ful word? None ev - er called on thee in

strain, give peace, O God, give peace a - gain!
stain, give peace, O God, give peace a - gain!
vain, give peace, O God, give peace a - gain!

Words: Henry Williams Baker (1821-1877), alt.
Music: *Eltham*, melody Nathaniel Gawthorn (18th cent.); harm. Samuel Sebastian Wesley (1810-1876)

LM

# 579

Christian Responsibility

1 Al - might - y Fa - ther, strong to save, whose arm hath bound the
2 O Christ, the Lord of hill and plain o'er which our traf - fic
3 O Spi - rit, whom the Fa - ther sent to spread a - broad the
4 O Trin - i - ty of love and power, our peo - ple shield in

rest - less wave, who bidd'st the might - y o - cean deep its
runs a - main by moun - tain pass or val - ley low; wher -
firm - a - ment; O Wind of hea - ven, by thy might save
dan - ger's hour; from rock and tem - pest, fire and foe, pro -

own ap - point - ed li - mits keep: O hear us when we
ev - er, Lord, thy peo - ple go, pro - tect them by thy
all who dare the ea - gle's flight, and keep them by thy
tect them where - so - e'er they go; thus ev - er - more shall

cry to thee for those in per - il on the sea.
guard - ing hand from ev - ery per - il on the land.
watch - ful care from ev - ery per - il in the air.
rise to thee glad praise from space, air, land, and sea.

Words: Sts. 1 and 4, William Whiting (1825-1878), alt.; sts. 2-3, Robert Nelson Spencer
(1877-1961), alt.
Music: *Melita*, John Bacchus Dykes (1823-1876)

88. 88. 88

# Christian Responsibility

580

*Unison*

1 God, who stretched the span-gled hea - vens in - fi - nite in
\*2 Proud-ly rise our mod - ern ci - ties, state - ly build-ings,
3 We have ven - tured worlds un - dreamed of since the child-hood
4 As each far ho - ri - zon beck - ons, may it chal - lenge

time and place, flung the suns in burn - ing ra - diance
row on row; yet their win - dows, blank, un - feel - ing,
of our race; known the ec - sta - sy of wing - ing
us a - new, chil - dren of cre - a - tive pur - pose,

through the si - lent fields of space: we, your chil - dren
stare on can - yoned streets be - low, where the lone - ly
through un - trav - eled realms of space; probed the se - crets
serv - ing o - thers, hon - oring you. May our dreams prove

in your like - ness, share in - ven - tive powers with you;
drift un - no - ticed in the ci - ty's ebb and flow,
of the at - om, yield - ing un - im - ag - ined power,
rich with prom - ise, each en - deav - or well be - gun:

Great Cre - a - tor, still cre - at - ing,
lost to pur - pose and to mean - ing,
fac - ing us with life's de - struc - tion
Great Cre - a - tor, give us guid - ance

show us what we yet may do.
scarce - ly car - ing where they go.
or our most tri - um - phant hour.
till our goals and yours are one.

Words: Catherine Cameron (b. 1927), alt.
Music: *Holy Manna*, from *The Southern Harmony*, 1835

*Harmony (the melody is in the tenor)*

1 God, who stretched the span - gled hea - vens in - fi - nite in
*2 Proud-ly rise our mod - ern ci - ties, state - ly build-ings,
3 We have ven - tured worlds un - dreamed of since the child-hood
4 As each far ho - ri - zon beck - ons, may it chal - lenge

time and place, flung the suns in burn - ing ra - diance
row on row; yet their win - dows, blank, un - feel - ing,
of our race; known the ec - sta - sy of wing - ing
us a - new, chil - dren of cre - a - tive pur - pose,

through the si - lent fields of space: we, your chil - dren
stare on can - yoned streets be - low, where the lone - ly
through un - trav - eled realms of space; probed the se - crets
serv - ing o - thers, hon - oring you. May our dreams prove

in      your    like - ness,    share   in - ven - tive    powers   with   you;
drift   un  -   no - ticed   in    the    ci - ty's    ebb    and    flow,
of      the    at - om,    yield - ing   un - im  -  ag - ined   power,
rich    with   prom - ise,   each   en - deav - or    well   be  -  gun:

Great   Cre  -  a  -  tor,    still   cre  -  at  -  ing,
lost    to     pur - pose    and    to    mean  -  ing,
fac  -  ing    us     with   life's   de  -  struc - tion
Great   Cre  -  a  -  tor,    give    us    guid  -  ance

show    us     what    we    yet    may    do.
scarce - ly    car  -  ing   where   they   go.
or      our    most    tri  -  um  -  phant   hour.
till    our    goals   and    yours   are    one.

Words: Catherine Cameron (b. 1927), alt.
Music: *Holy Manna*, from *The Southern Harmony*, 1835

87. 87. D

## 581

Christian Responsibility

1 Where char - i - ty and love pre - vail there God is ev - er found;
2 With grate-ful joy and ho - ly fear his char - i - ty we learn;
3 For-give we now each o - ther's faults as we our faults con - fess;
4 Let strife a-mong us be un - known, let all con - ten - tion cease;
5 Let us re-call that in our midst dwells God's be - got - ten Son;

1 brought here to-geth-er by Christ's love by love are we thus bound.
2 let us with heart and mind and strength now love him in re - turn.
3 and let us love each o - ther well in Chris-tian ho - li - ness.
4 be his the glo - ry that we seek, be ours his ho - ly peace.
5 as mem-bers of his Bo - dy joined we are in him made one.

6 Love can exclude no race or creed
if honored be God's Name;
our common life embraces all
whose Father is the same.

Words: Latin; tr. J. Clifford Evers (b. 1916)
Music: *Cheshire*, melody and bass from *The Whole Booke of Psalmes*, 1592, alt.;
    harm. *Hymns III*, 1979

LM

## 582

Christian Responsibility

1 O ho - ly ci - ty, seen of John, where Christ, the Lamb, doth reign,
2 O shame to us who rest con-tent while lust and greed for gain
3 Give us, O God, the strength to build the ci - ty that hath stood
4 Al - rea - dy in the mind of God that ci - ty ris - eth fair:

with - in whose four-square walls shall come no night, nor need, nor pain,
in street and shop and ten - e - ment wring gold from hu - man pain,
too long a dream, whose laws are love, whose crown is ser - vant - hood,
lo, how its splen-dor chal - leng - es the souls that great - ly dare—

and where the tears are wiped from eyes that shall not weep a - gain!
and bit - ter lips in blind de - spair cry, "Christ hath died in vain!"
and where the sun that shin - eth is God's grace for hu - man good.
yea, bids us seize the whole of life and build its glo - ry there.

Words: Walter Russell Bowie (1882-1969), alt.
Music: *Sancta Civitas*, Herbert Howells (1892-1983)

86. 86. 86

## Christian Responsibility

**583**

1 O ho - ly ci - ty, seen of John, where Christ, the Lamb, doth reign,
2 O shame to us who rest con - tent while lust and greed for gain
3 Give us, O God, the strength to build the ci - ty that hath stood
4 Al - rea - dy in the mind of God that ci - ty ris - eth fair:

with - in whose four-square walls shall come no night, nor need, nor pain,
in street and shop and ten - e - ment wring gold from hu - man pain,
too long a dream, whose laws are love, whose crown is ser - vant - hood,
lo, how its splen - dor chal - leng - es the souls that great - ly dare—

and where the tears are wiped from eyes that shall not weep a - gain!
and bit - ter lips in blind de - spair cry, "Christ hath died in vain!"
and where the sun that shin - eth is God's grace for hu - man good.
yea, bids us seize the whole of life and built its glo - ry there.

Words: Walter Russell Bowie (1882-1969), alt.
Music: *Morning Song*, melody att. Elkanah Kelsay Dare (1782-1826)

86. 86. 86

1 God, you have given us power to sound depths hith-er-to un-known,
2 Great are your gifts; yet great-er far this gift, O God, be-stow:
3 Let wis-dom's god-ly fear dis-pel the fears that hate im-part;
4 So for your glo-ry and our good may we your gifts em-ploy,

to probe earth's hid-den mys-ter-ies, and make their might our own.
that as to know-ledge we at-tain we may in wis-dom grow.
give un-der-stand-ing to the mind, and with new mind, new heart.
lest, mad-dened by the lust of power, we shall our-selves des-troy.

Words: George Wallace Briggs (1875-1959), alt.
Music: *Culross*, melody from *The Psalmes of David in Prose and Meeter*, 1635          CM

1 Morn-ing glo-ry, star-lit sky, soar-ing
2 O-pen are the gifts of God, gifts of
3 Love that gives, gives ev-er more, gives with
4 Drained is love in mak-ing full, bound in
5 There-fore he who shows us God help-less
6 Here is God: no mon-arch he, throned in

1 mu-sic, schol-ar's truth, flight of swal-lows,
2 love to mind and sense; hid-den is love's
3 zeal, with ea-ger hands, spares not, keeps not,
4 set-ting o-thers free, poor in mak-ing
5 hangs up-on the tree; and the nails and
6 eas-y state to reign; here is God, whose

1 au - tumn leaves, mem-ory's trea - sure, grace of youth:
2 a - go - ny, love's en - deav - or, love's ex - pense.
3 all out - pours, ven - tures all, its all ex - pends.
4 man - y rich, weak in giv - ing power to be.
5 crown of thorns tell of what God's love must be.
6 arms of love ach - ing, spent, the world sus - tain.

Words: W. H. Vanstone (b. 1923)
Music: *Bingham*, Dorothy Howell Sheets (b. 1915)

77. 77

## Christian Responsibility

586

1 Je - sus, thou di - vine Com-pan - ion, by thy low - ly
2 Where the man - y toil to - geth - er, there art thou a -
3 Ev - ery task, how - ev - er sim - ple, sets the soul that

hu - man birth thou hast come to join the work - ers,
mong thine own; where the sol - i - tar - y la - bor,
does it free; ev - ery deed of hu - man kind - ness

bur - den - bear - ers of the earth. Thou, the car - pen - ter of
thou art there with them a - lone; thou, the peace that pass - eth
done in love is done to thee. Je - sus, thou di - vine Com -

Naz - areth, toil - ing for thy dai - ly food, by thy pa - tience
know - ledge, dwell - est in the dai - ly strife; thou, the Bread of
pan - ion, help us all to work our best; bless us in our

and thy cour - age, thou hast taught us toil is good.
heaven, art bro - ken in the sac - ra - ment of life.
dai - ly la - bor, lead us to our Sab - bath rest.

Words: Henry Van Dyke (1852-1933), alt.
Music: *Pleading Savior*, melody from *The Christian Lyre*, 1830

87. 87. D

587

Christian Responsibility

1 Our Fa - ther, by whose Name all fa - ther-hood is known,
2 O Christ, thy - self a child with - in an earth - ly home,
3 O Spi - rit, who dost bind our hearts in u - ni - ty,

who dost in love pro - claim each fam - i - ly thine own,
with heart still un - de - filed, thou didst to man-hood come;
who teach - est us to find the love from self set free,

bless thou all par - ents, guard - ing well, with con-stant love as
our chil-dren bless, in ev - ery place, that they may all be -
in all our hearts such love in - crease, that ev - ery home, by

sen - ti - nel, the homes in which thy peo - ple dwell.
hold thy face, and know-ing thee may grow in grace.
this re - lease, may be the dwell-ing place of peace.

Words: F. Bland Tucker (1895-1984)
Music: *Rhosymedre*, John Edwards (1806-1885)

66. 66. 888

```
1 Al-might-y    God,    your word is
2 Let not  our  self - ish-ness and
3 Let not  the  world's de - ceit-ful
```

```
cast like seed up-on the   ground,   now let the  dew   of heaven de-
hate this ho-ly seed re - move,    but give it   root  in  ev-ery
cares the ris-ing plant des-troy,  but let it   yield a  hun-dred-
```

**1-2**      *Final Ending*

```
scend  and right-eous fruits a - bound.
heart  to bring forth fruits of   love.
fold   the fruits of peace and (joy.)       joy._____
```

Words: John Cawood (1775-1852), alt.
Music: *Call Street*, Roy Henry Johnson (b. 1933)

CM

```
1 Al - might-y  God,   your  word is cast like   seed up-on  the   ground,
2 Let  not our self - ish - ness and hate this  ho-ly seed re - move,
3 Let  not the world's de - ceit-ful cares the  ris-ing plant de - stroy,
```

```
now  let the dew of  heaven de-scend and  right-eous fruits a - bound.
but  give it root in  ev - ery heart to  bring forth fruits of   love.
but  let it yield a   hun-dred-fold the  fruits of peace and   joy.
```

Words: John Cawood (1775-1852), alt.
Music: *Walden*, Jane Manton Marshall (b. 1924)

CM

1 O Je - sus Christ, may grate - ful hymns be ris - ing,___
2 Grant us new cour - age, sac - ri - fi - cial, hum - ble,___
3 Show us your Spi - rit, brood-ing o'er each ci - ty,___

in ev - ery ci - ty for your love and care;___
strong in your strength to ven - ture and to dare;___
as you once wept a - bove Je - ru - sa - lem,___

in - spire our wor - ship, grant the glad sur - pris - ing___
to lift the fall - en, guide the feet that stum - ble,___
seek - ing to gath - er all in love and pi - ty,___

that your blest Spi - rit rous - es ev - ery - where.
seek out the lone - ly and God's mer - cy share.
and heal - ing those who touch your gar - ment's hem.

Words: Bradford Gray Webster (b. 1898), alt.
Music: *Charterhouse*, David Evans (1874-1948)

11 10. 11 10

1 O God of earth and al - tar, bow down and hear our cry,
2 From all that ter - ror teach - es, from lies of tongue and pen,
3 Tie in a liv - ing teth - er the prince and priest and thrall,

our earth - ly ru - lers fal - ter, our peo - ple drift and die;
from all the eas - y speech - es that com-fort cru - el men,
bind all our lives to - geth - er, smite us and save us all;

the walls of gold en - tomb us, the swords of scorn di - vide,
from sale and prof - a - na - tion of hon - or, and the sword,
in ire and ex - ul - ta - tion a - flame with faith, and free,

take not thy thun - der from us, but take a - way our pride.
from sleep and from dam - na - tion, de - liv - er us, good Lord!
lift up a liv - ing na - tion, a sin - gle sword to thee.

Words: Gilbert Keith Chesterton (1874-1936)
Music: *King's Lynn*, English melody; adapt. Ralph Vaughan Williams (1872-1958)

76. 76. D

## Christian Responsibility

592

1 Teach me, my God and King, in all things thee to see, and
2 All may of thee par - take; noth - ing can be so mean, which
3 A ser - vant with this clause makes drudg - er - y di - vine: who
4 This is the fa - mous stone that turn - eth all to gold; for

what I do in an - y - thing, to do it as for thee.
with this tinc - ture, "for thy sake," will not grow bright and clean.
sweeps a room, as for thy laws, makes that and the ac - tion fine.
that which God doth touch and own can - not for less be told.

Words: George Herbert (1593-1633)
Music: *Carlisle*, Charles Lockhart (1745-1815)

SM

1 Lord, make us ser - vants of your peace: where there is
2 Where all is doubt, may we sow faith; where all is
3 Je - sus, our Lord, may we not seek to be con -
4 May we not look for love's re - turn, but seek to
5 Dy - ing, we live, and are re - born through death's dark

1 hate, may we sow love; where there is hurt, may we for -
2 gloom, may we sow hope; where all is night, may we sow
3 soled, but to con - sole, nor look to un - der - stand - ing
4 love un - self - ish - ly, for in our giv - ing we re -
5 night to end - less day: Lord, make us ser - vants of your

1 give; where there is strife, may we make one.
2 light; where all is tears, may we sow joy.
3 hearts, but look for hearts to un - der - stand.
4 ceive, and in for - giv - ing are for - given.
5 peace, to wake at last in hea - ven's light.

Words: James Quinn (b. 1919), based on prayer att. Francis of Assisi (1182-1226)
Music: *Dickinson College*, Lee Hastings Bristol, Jr. (1923-1979)

LM

# Christian Responsibility

594

1 God of grace and God of glo - ry, on thy peo - ple pour thy power;
2 Lo! the hosts of e - vil round us scorn thy Christ, as - sail his ways!
3 Cure thy chil - dren's war - ring mad - ness, bend our pride to thy con - trol;
4 Save us from weak res - ig - na - tion to the e - vils we de - plore;

crown thine an - cient Church - 's sto - ry; bring her bud to glo - rious flower.
From the fears that long have bound us free our hearts to faith and praise:
shame our wan - ton, self - ish glad - ness, rich in things and poor in soul.
let the gift of thy sal - va - tion be our glo - ry ev - er - more.

Grant us wis - dom, grant us cour - age, for the fac - ing of this
grant us wis - dom, grant us cour - age for the liv - ing of these
Grant us wis - dom, grant us cour - age, lest we miss thy king-dom's
Grant us wis - dom, grant us cour - age, serv - ing thee whom we a -

hour, for the fac - ing of this hour.
days, for the liv - ing of these days.
goal, lest we miss thy king-dom's goal.
dore, serv - ing thee whom we a - dore.

Words: Harry Emerson Fosdick (1878-1969), alt.
Music: *Cwm Rhondda*, John Hughes (1873-1932)

87. 87. 877

1 God of grace and God of glo - ry, on thy peo - ple
2 Lo! the hosts of e - vil round us scorn thy Christ, as
3 Cure thy chil - dren's war - ring mad - ness, bend our pride to
4 Save us from weak res - ig - na - tion to the e - vils

pour thy power; crown thine an - cient Church - 's sto - ry;
sail his ways! From the fears that long have bound us
thy con - trol; shame our wan - ton, self - ish glad - ness,
we de - plore; let the gift of thy sal - va - tion

bring her bud to glo - rious flower. Grant us wis - dom,
free our hearts to faith and praise: grant us wis - dom,
rich in things and poor in soul. Grant us wis - dom,
be our glo - ry ev - er - more. Grant us wis - dom,

grant us cour - age, for the fac - ing of this hour.
grant us cour - age for the liv - ing of these days.
grant us cour - age, lest we miss thy king - dom's goal.
grant us cour - age, serv - ing thee whom we a - dore.

Words: Harry Emerson Fosdick (1878-1969), alt.
Music: *Mannheim*, melody from *Vierstimmiges Choralbuch*, 1847; harm. Lowell Mason (1792-1872)      87. 87. 87

1 Judge e - ter - nal, throned in splen - dor, Lord of lords and
2 Still the wea - ry folk are pin - ing for the hour that
3 Crown, O God, thine own en - deav - or; cleave our dark - ness

King of kings, with thy liv - ing fire of judg - ment
brings re - lease, and the ci - ty's crowd - ed clang - or
with thy sword; feed all those who do not know thee

purge this land of bit - ter things; sol - ace all its
cries a - loud for sin to cease; and the home - steads
with the rich - ness of thy word; cleanse the bo - dy

wide do - min - ion with the heal - ing of thy wings.
and the wood-lands plead in si - lence for their peace.
of this na - tion through the glo - ry of the Lord.

Words: Henry Scott Holland (1847-1918), alt.
Music: *Komm, o komm, du Geist des Lebens*, melody from *Neu-vermehrtes und zu Ubung Christl.*
  *Gottseligkeit eingerichtetes Meiningisches Gesangbuch*, 1693

87. 87. 87

# Christian Responsibility

*Introduction*

1 O day of peace that dim - ly shines through all our
2 Then shall the wolf dwell with the lamb, nor shall the

hopes and prayers and dreams, guide us to jus - tice, truth, and
fierce de - vour the small; as beasts and cat - tle calm - ly

love, de - liv - ered from our self - ish schemes. May swords of
graze, a lit - tle child shall lead them all. Then en - e -

hate fall from our hands, our hearts from en - vy find re -
mies shall learn to love, all crea - tures find their true ac -

lease, till by God's grace our war - ring world shall see Christ's
cord; the hope of peace shall be ful - filled, for all the

*Interlude*

prom - ised reign of peace.
earth shall know the (Lord.)

*Final Ending*

Lord.____

Words: Carl P. Daw, Jr. (b. 1944)
Music: *Jerusalem*, Charles Hubert Hastings Parry (1848-1918)

LMD

# Christian Responsibility

**598**

1 Lord Christ, when first thou cam'st to earth, up - on a cross they
2 O awe - ful Love, which found no room in life where sin de -
3 New ad - vent of the love of Christ, shall we a - gain re -
4 O wound - ed hands of Je - sus, build in us thy new cre -

bound thee, and mocked thy sav - ing king - ship then
nied thee, and, doomed to death, must bring to doom
fuse thee, till in the night of hate and war
a - tion; our pride is dust, our vaunt is stilled,

by thorns with which they crowned thee: and still our wrongs
the powers which cru - ci - fied thee, till not a stone
we per - ish as we lose thee? From old un - faith
we wait thy rev - e - la - tion: O love that tri -

may weave thee now new thorns to pierce that
was left on stone, and all those na - tions'
our souls re - lease to seek the king - dom
umphs o - ver loss, we bring our hearts be -

stead - y brow, and robe of sor - row round thee.
pride, o'er-thrown, went down to dust be - side thee!
of thy peace, by which a - lone we choose thee.
fore thy cross, to fi - nish thy sal - va - tion.

Words: Walter Russell Bowie (1882-1969), alt.
Music: *Mit Freuden zart*, melody from "Une pastourelle gentille," 1529; adapt. *Pseaumes cinquante de David*, 1547, and *Kirchengeseng darinnen die Heubtartickel des Christlichen Glaubens gefasset*, 1566

87. 87. 887

*Introduction*

1 Lift ev-ery voice and sing till earth and hea-ven ring, ring with the
2 Ston-y the road we trod, bit-ter the chas-tening rod, felt in the
3 God of our wea-ry years, God of our si-lent tears, thou who hast

har - mon - ies of lib - er - ty. Let our re-joic-ing rise
days when hope un - born had died; yet, with a stead-y beat,
brought us thus far on the way; thou who hast by thy might

high as the lis - tening skies; let it re - sound loud as the
have not our wea - ry feet come to the place for which our
led us in - to the light; keep us for ev - er in the

roll - ing sea. Sing a song full of the faith that the dark past has
par - ents sighed? We have come o - ver a way that with tears has been
path, we pray. Lest our feet stray from the pla - ces, our God, where we

taught us; sing a song full of the hope that the pres-ent has
wa - tered; we have come, tread-ing our path through the blood of the
met thee; lest, our hearts drunk with the wine of the world, we for -

brought us; fac - ing the ris - ing sun of our new
slaugh - tered, out from the gloom - y past, till now we
get thee; sha-dowed be - neath thy hand may we for

day be - gun, let us march on, till vic - to - ry is won.
stand at last where the white gleam of our bright star is cast.
ev - er stand, true to our God, true to our na - tive land.

Words: James Weldon Johnson (1871-1938)
Music: *Lift Every Voice*, J. Rosamond Johnson (1873-1954)

66 10. 66 10. 14. 66 10

1  O day of God, draw nigh in beau-ty and in power, come
2  Bring to our trou-bled minds, un - cer-tain and a - fraid, the
3  Bring jus-tice to our land, that all may dwell se - cure, and
4  Bring to our world of strife thy sov-ereign word of peace, that
5  O day of God, draw nigh as at cre - a - tion's birth, let

1  with thy time-less jud-ment now to match our pres-ent hour.
2  qui-et of a stead-fast faith, calm of a call o-beyed.
3  fine-ly build for days to come foun-da-tions that en-dure.
4  war may haunt the earth no more and des-o-la-tion cease.
5  there be light a-gain, and set thy judg-ments in the earth.

Words: Robert Balgarnie Young Scott (b. 1899)
Music: *Bellwoods*, James Hopkirk (1908-1972)

SM

1  O day of God, draw nigh in beau-ty and in power, come
2  Bring to our trou-bled minds, un - cer-tain and a - fraid, the
3  Bring jus-tice to our land, that all may dwell se - cure, and
4  Bring to our world of strife thy sov-ereign word of peace, that
5  O day of God, draw nigh as at cre - a - tion's birth, let

1 with thy time-less judg-ment now to match our pres-ent hour.
2 qui-et of a stead-fast faith, calm of a call o-beyed.
3 fine-ly build for days to come foun-da-tions that en-dure.
4 war may haunt the earth no more and des-o-la-tion cease.
5 there be light a - gain, and set thy judg-ments in the earth.

Words: Robert Balgarnie Young Scott (b. 1899)
Music: *St. Michael*, Louis Bourgeois (1510?-1561?); harm. William Henry Monk (1823-1889)

SM

## Christian Responsibility

**602**

*Chorus*

Je - su, Je - su, fill us with your love, show

us how to serve the neigh-bors we have from you.

1 Kneels at the feet of his friends, si - lent-ly wash-es their
2 Neigh-bors are rich___ and poor, neigh-bors are black___ and
3 These are the ones we should serve, these are the ones we should
4 Lov - ing puts us on our knees, serv - ing as though we were

*Repeat Chorus*

feet, Mas - ter who acts as a slave to them.
white, neigh-bors are near - by and far a - way.
love. All___ are neigh-bors to us and you.
slaves; this is the way we should live with you.

Words: Ghanaian; tr. Thomas Stevenson Colvin (b. 1925), alt.
Music: *Chereponi [Jesu, Jesu]*, Ghanaian folk song; adapt. Thomas Stevenson Colvin (b. 1925)

Irr.

1 When Christ was lift - ed from the earth, his
2 Still east and west his love ex - tends and
3 Where gen - er - a - tion, class, or race di -
4 Thus free - ly loved, though ful - ly known, may

arms stretched out a - bove through ev - ery cul - ture,
al - ways, near or far, he calls and claims us
vide us to our shame, he sees not la - bels
I in Christ be free to wel - come and ac -

ev - ery birth, to draw an an - swering love.
as his friends and loves us as we are.
but a face, a per - son, and a name.
cept his own as Christ ac - cept - ed me.

Words: Brian A. Wren (b. 1936)
Music: *St. Botolph*, Gordon Slater (1896-1979)           CM

604              Christian Responsibility

1 When Christ was lift - ed from the earth, his arms stretched out a -
2 Still east and west his love ex - tends and al - ways, near or
3 Where gen - er - a - tion, class, or race di - vide us to our
4 Thus free - ly loved, though ful - ly known, may I in Christ be

bove    through    ev - ery    cul - ture,    ev - ery    birth,    to
far,    he    calls    and claims    us    as    his    friends    and
shame,    he    sees    not la - bels    but    a    face,    a
free    to    wel - come and    ac - cept    his    own    as

*Optional interlude between stanzas*    *Final Ending*

draw    an    an - swering    love.      (love.)
loves    us    as    we    are.      (are.)
per - son,    and    a    name.      (name.)
Christ    ac - cept - ed    (me.)      me.

Words: Brian A. Wren (b. 1936)
Music: *San Rocco*, Derek Williams (b. 1945)

CM

## Christian Responsibility

# 605

1 What does the Lord re - quire for praise and of - fer - ing?
2 Rul - ers of earth, give ear! Should you not jus - tice show?
3 Still down the a - ges ring the pro - phet's stern com-mands.
4 How shall my soul ful - fill God's law so hard and high?

What sac - ri - fice de - sire, or trib - ute bid you bring?
Will God your plead - ing hear, while crime and cru - el - ty grow?
To mer - chant, work - er, king he brings God's high de - mands.
Let Christ en - due our will with grace to for - ti - fy.

*1-3*

Do just - ly; love mer - cy; walk hum - bly with your God.
Do just - ly; love mer - cy; walk hum - bly with your God.
Do just - ly; love mer - cy; walk hum - bly with your God.
Then just - ly, in mer - cy we'll (hum - bly walk with God.)

*Final Ending*

hum - bly walk with God.

Words: Albert F. Bayly (b. 1901), alt.
Music: *Sharpthorne*, Erik Routley (1917-1982)

66. 66. 33. 6

# 606

Christian Responsibility

*Antiphon*

Where true char - i - ty and love dwell, God him-self is there.

1 Since the love of Christ has joined us in one bo - dy,
2 As we are all of one bo - dy, when we gath - er
3 Now we pray that with the bless - ed you grant us grace

let us all re - joice and be glad now and al - ways.
let no dis - cord or en - mi - ty break our one - ness.
to see your ex - alt - ed glo - ry, O Christ our God,

And as we hear and love our Lord, the liv - ing God,
May all our pet - ty jeal - ous - ies and ha - tred cease
our bound-less source of joy and truth, of peace and love,

so let us in sin-cer - i - ty love all peo - ple. [Ant.]
that Christ the Lord may be with us through all our days. [Ant.]
for ev - er and for ev - er - more, world with - out end. [Ant.]

Words: Latin; tr. Joyce MacDonald Glover (b. 1923)
Music: *Ubi caritas*, plainsong, Mode 6

12. 12. 12. 12 with Refrain

# Christian Responsibility

## 607

1 O God of ev-ery na - tion, of ev-ery race and land,
2 From search for wealth and pow - er and scorn of truth and right,
3 Lord, strength-en all who la - bor that we may find re - lease
4 Keep bright in us the vi - sion of days when war shall cease,

re - deem the whole cre - a - tion with your al-might-y hand;
from trust in bombs that show - er de-struc-tion through the night,
from fear of rat-tling sa - ber, from dread of war's in - crease;
when ha-tred and di-vi - sion give way to love and peace,

where hate and fear di - vide us and bit - ter threats are hurled,
from pride of race and na - tion and blind - ness to your way,
when hope and cour - age fal - ter, your still small voice be heard;
till dawns the morn-ing glo - rious when truth and jus - tice reign

in love and mer - cy guide us and heal our strife - torn world.
de - liv - er ev - ery na - tion, e - ter - nal God, we pray!
with faith that none can al - ter, your ser - vants un - der - gird.
and Christ shall rule vic - to - rious o'er all the world's do - main.

Words: William Watkins Reid, Jr. (b. 1923), alt.
Music: *Llangloffan*, melody from *Hymnau a Thonau er Gwasanaeth yr Eglwys yng Nghymru*, 1865;
harm. *The English Hymnal*, 1906

76. 76. D

1 E - ter - nal Fa - ther, strong to save, whose arm hath bound the
2 O Christ, whose voice the wa - ters heard and hushed their ra - ging
3 Most Ho - ly Spi - rit, who didst brood up - on the cha - os
4 O Trin - i - ty of love and power, thy chil - dren shield in

rest - less wave, who bidd'st the might - y o - cean deep its
at thy word, who walk - edst on the foam - ing deep, and
dark and rude, and bid its an - gry tu - mult cease, and
dan - ger's hour; from rock and tem - pest, fire and foe, pro -

own ap - point - ed lim - its keep: O hear us when we
calm a - mid its rage didst sleep: O hear us when we
give, for wild con - fu - sion, peace: O hear us when we
tect them where - so - e'er they go; thus ev - er - more shall

cry to thee for those in per - il on the sea.
cry to thee for those in per - il on the sea.
cry to thee for those in per - il on the sea.
rise to thee glad hymns of praise from land and sea.

Words: William Whiting (1825-1878), alt.
Music: *Melita*, John Bacchus Dykes (1823-1876)

88. 88. 88

1 Where cross the crowd - ed ways of life, where sound the
2 In haunts of wretch - ed - ness and need, on sha - dowed
3 The cup of wa - ter given for thee still holds the
4 O Mas - ter, from the moun - tain side, make haste to
5 till all the world shall learn thy love, and fol - low

1 cries of race and clan, a - bove the noise of
2 thresh - olds dark with fears, from paths where hide the
3 fresh - ness of thy grace; yet long these mul - ti -
4 heal these hearts of pain; a - mong these rest - less
5 where thy feet have trod; till glo - rious from thy

1 self - ish strife, we hear thy voice, O Son of Man.
2 lures of greed, we catch the vi - sion of thy tears.
3 tudes to see the true com - pas - sion of thy face.
4 throngs a - bide, O tread the ci - ty's streets a - gain;
5 heaven a - bove, shall come the ci - ty of our God.

Words: Frank Mason North (1850-1935), alt.
Music: *Gardiner*, from *Sacred Melodies*, 1815; arr. William Gardiner (1770-1853)

LM

to      your    pur - pose    ev - ery  gift    that   you  im  -  part.
Spi -  rit     kin - dles     still  to  save    and   make us    whole.
tire - less    striv - ing,   your   a - bun - dant  life  to    share.
Lord,  in      free - dom     may your mer  -  cy   know and    live.

Words: Albert F. Bayly (b. 1901), alt.
Music: *Blaenhafren*, Welsh melody

87. 87. D

## Christian Responsibility

# 611

|  | Leader | | | All | | |
|---|---|---|---|---|---|---|
| 1 | Christ | the | work - er, | Christ | the | work - er, | born | in |
| 2 | Bless - ed | man - child, | bless - ed | man - child, | born | of |
| 3 | Skill - ful | crafts - man, | skill - ful | crafts - man, | bless - ed |
| 4 | Yoke | ma - ker, | yoke | ma - ker, | fa - shioned |
| 5 | All | who | la - bor, | all | who | la - bor, | lis - ten |
| 6 | Hea - vy | la - den, | hea - vy | la - den, | glad - ly |
| 7 | Christ | the | work - er, | Christ | the | work - er, | Love | a - |

| 1 | Beth - le - hem, | born to work and | die for ev - ery | one. |
| 2 | Naz - a - reth, | grew in wis - dom | as he grew in | skill. |
| 3 | car - pen - ter, | prais-ing God by | la - bor at his | bench. |
| 4 | by his hands, | eas - y yokes that | made the la - bor | less. |
| 5 | to his call, | he will make that | hea - vy bur - den | light. |
| 6 | come to him, | he will ease your | load and give you | rest. |
| 7 | live for us, | teach us how to | do all work for | God. |

*The leader may begin successive stanzas here.

Words: Ghanaian work song; tr. Thomas Stevenson Colvin (b. 1925), alt.
Music: *African Work Song*, African work song; adapt. Thomas Stevenson Colvin (b. 1925)
Words, Music: Copyright © 1969 by Hope Publishing Company. International Copyright Secured. All Rights Reserved.
Used by Permission.

444. 9

1 Gra-cious Spi - rit, Ho - ly Ghost, taught by thee we cov - et most,
2 Love is kind, and suf - fers long, love is meek, and thinks no wrong,
3 Pro - phe - cy will fade a - way, melt - ing in the light of day;
4 Faith and hope and love we see, join - ing hand in hand, a - gree,

of thy gifts at Pen - te - cost, ho - ly heaven-ly, love.
love than death it - self more strong; there - fore, give us love.
love will ev - er with us stay; there - fore, give us love.
but the great-est of the three, and the best, is love.

Words: Christopher Wordsworth (1807-1885)
Music: *Troen*, Daniel Moe (b. 1926)

777. 5

1 Thy king - dom come, O God! Thy rule, O Christ be - gin!
2 Where is thy reign of peace, and pu - ri - ty, and love?
3 When comes the prom-ised time that war shall be no more,
4 We pray thee, Lord, a - rise, and come in thy great might;
5 Wher - ev - er near or far thick dark-ness brood-eth yet:

1 Break with thine i - ron rod the tyr - an - nies of sin!
2 When shall all ha - tred cease, as in the realms a - bove?
3 op - pres-sion, lust, and crime shall flee thy face be - fore?
4 re - vive our long-ing eyes, which lan - guish for thy sight.
5 a - rise, O Morn-ing Star, a - rise, and nev - er set!

Words: Lewis Hensley (1824-1905), alt.
Music: *St. Cecilia*, Leighton George Hayne (1836-1883)

66. 66

## The Kingdom of God

# 614

1 Christ is the King! O friends up - raise an - thems of
2 O Chris-tian wo - men, Chris-tian men, all the world
3 Let Love's un - con - quer - a - ble might your scat - tered

joy and ho - ly praise for his brave saints of an - cient days,
o - ver, seek a - gain the Way dis - ci - ples fol - lowed then.
com - pa - nies u - nite in ser - vice to the Lord of light:

who with a faith for ev - er new fol - lowed the King, and
Christ through all a - ges is the same: place the same hope in
so shall God's will on earth be done, new lamps be lit, new

round him drew thou - sands of ser - vants brave and true.
this great Name, with the same faith his word pro - claim.
tasks be - gun, and the whole Church at last be one.

Words: George Kennedy Allen Bell (1883-1958)
Music: *Christus Rex*, David McKinley Williams (1887-1978)

888. 888

1 "Thy king-dom come!" on bend-ed knee the pass-ing a-ges pray;
2 But the slow watch-es of the night not less to God be-long;
3 And lo, al-rea-dy on the hills the flags of dawn ap-pear;
4 the day to whose clear shin-ing light all wrong shall stand re-vealed,
5 when know-ledge, hand in hand with peace, shall walk the earth a-broad;

1 and faith-ful souls have yearned to see on earth that king-dom's day.
2 and for the ev-er-last-ing right the si-lent stars are strong.
3 gird up your loins, ye pro-phet souls, pro-claim the day is near:
4 when jus-tice shall be throned in might, and ev-ery hurt be healed;
5 the day of per-fect right-eous-ness, the prom-ised day of God.

Words: Frederick Lucian Hosmer (1840-1929)
Music: *St. Flavian*, melody from *Day's Psalter*, 1562; adapt. and harm. Richard Redhead (1820-1901)    CM

616                                    The Kingdom of God

1 Hail to the Lord's A-noint-ed, great Da-vid's great-er Son!
2 He comes with suc-cor speed-y to those who suf-fer wrong,
3 He shall come down like show-ers up-on the fruit-ful earth,
4 Kings shall bow down be-fore him, and gold and in-cense bring;
5 O'er ev-ery foe vic-to-rious, he on his throne shall rest;

1 Hail, in the time ap - point - ed, his reign on earth be - gun!
2 to help the poor and need - y, and bid the weak be strong;
3 and love, joy, hope, like flow - ers, spring in his path to birth:
4 all na - tions shall a - dore him, his praise all peo - ple sing;
5 from age to age more glo - rious, all bless - ing and all blest:

1 He comes to break op - pres - sion, to set the cap - tive free;
2 to give them songs for sigh - ing, their dark - ness turn to light,
3 be - fore him on the moun - tains shall peace, the her - ald, go;
4 to him shall prayer un - ceas - ing and dai - ly vows a - scend;
5 the tide of time shall nev - er his cov - e - nant re - move;

1 to take a - way trans - gres - sion, and rule in eq - ui - ty.
2 whose souls, con-demned and dy - ing, were pre - cious in his sight.
3 and right - eous - ness in foun - tains from hill to val - ley flow.
4 his king - dom still in - creas - ing, a king - dom with - out end.
5 his Name shall stand for ev - er, his change - less Name of Love.

Words: James Montgomery (1771-1854); para. of Psalm 72
Music: *Es flog ein kleins Waldvögelein*, German folk song; adapt. and harm.
A *Student's Hymnal*, 1923, after Henry Walford Davies (1869-1941)

76. 76. D

# 617

The Kingdom of God

*Unison or harmony*

1 E - ter - nal Ru - ler of the cease - less round
2 We would be one in ha - tred of all wrong,
3 Oh, clothe us with thy heaven - ly ar - mor, Lord,

of cir - cling plan - ets sing - ing on their way,
one in the love of all things sweet and fair,
thy trust - y shield, thy sword of love di - vine;

guide of the na - - tions from the night pro - found
one with the joy that break - eth in - to song,
our in - spi - ra - - tion be thy con - stant word,

in - to the glo - ry of the per - fect day;
one with the grief that trem - bleth in - to prayer;
we ask no vic - to - ries that are not thine;

rule   in   our   hearts, that   we   may   ev - er   be
one   in   the   power that   makes thy   chil - dren free
give   or   with - hold,   let   pain   or   plea - sure be;

guid - ed   and   strength-ened and   up - held  by   thee.
to   fol - low   truth,   and   thus   to   fol - low thee.
e - nough to   know   that   we   are   serv - ing thee.

Words: John White Chadwick (1840-1904), alt.
Music: *Song 1*, melody and bass Orlando Gibbons (1583-1625);
      harm. Ralph Vaughan Williams (1872-1958), rev.

10 10. 10 10. 10 10

Unison

1 Ye watch-ers and ye ho - ly ones, bright ser - aphs, cher - u -
2 O high - er than the cher - u - bim, more glo - rious than the
3 Re - spond, ye souls in end - less rest, ye pa - tri - archs and
4 O friends, in glad-ness let us sing, su - per - nal an - thems

Harmony                                                Unison

bim, and thrones, raise the glad strain, Al - le - lu - ia! Cry
ser - a - phim, lead their prais - es, Al - le - lu - ia! Thou
pro-phets blest, Al - le - lu - ia, al - le - lu - ia! Ye
ech - o - ing, Al - le - lu - ia, al - le - lu - ia! To

out, do - min-ions, prince-doms, powers, vir - tues, arch - an - gels, an - gels'
bear - er of the e - ter - nal Word, most gra-cious, mag - ni - fy the
ho - ly twelve, ye mar-tyrs strong, all saints tri - um - pha raise the
God the Fa - ther, God the Son, and God the Spi - rit, Three in

Harmony

choirs, Al - le - lu - ia, al - le - lu - ia, al - le -
Lord, Al - le - lu - ia, al - le - lu - ia, al - le -
song, Al - le - lu - ia, al - le - lu - ia, al - le -
One, Al - le - lu - ia, al - le - lu - ia, al - le -

| | | | | | | |
|---|---|---|---|---|---|---|
| lu - ia, | al - le - lu - ia, | al - le - lu - - ia! |
| lu - ia, | al - le - lu - ia, | al - le - lu - - ia! |
| lu - ia, | al - le - lu - ia, | al - le - lu - - ia! |
| lu - ia, | al - le - lu - ia, | al - le - lu - - ia! |

Words: John Athelstan Laurie Riley (1858-1945)
Music: *Lasst uns erfreuen*, melody from *Auserlesene Catholische Geistliche Kirchengeseng*, 1623; adapt. and harm. Ralph Vaughan Williams (1872-1958)

88. 44. 88 with Refrain

## The Church Triumphant    **619**

1 Sing al - le - lu - ia forth in du - teous praise,
2 Ye powers who stand be - fore thee e - ter - nal Light,
3 Then let the ho - ly ci - ty raise the strain,
4 Ye who have fought and joined the star - ry throng,
5 Your songs of tri - umph shall for ev - er ring,
6 Such song is rest and food and deep de - light
7 Al - might - y Christ, to thee our voic - es sing

1 ye ci - ti - zens of heaven, O sweet - ly raise
2 let all your choirs re - ech - o to the height
3 and with glad songs re - sound - ing wake a - gain
4 ye vic - tors, now take up the e - ter - nal song,
5 the hymns which tell the hon - or of your King,
6 to saints for - giv - en; let them all u - nite
7 glo - ry for ev - er - more; to thee we bring

1 an end - less al - le - lu - ia.
2 an end - less al - le - lu - ia.
3 an end - less al - le - lu - ia.
4 an end - less al - le - lu - ia.
5 an end - less al - le - lu - ia.
6 in end - less al - le - lu - ia.
7 an end - less al - le - lu - ia.

Words: Latin, 5th-8th cent.; ver. *Hymnal 1940*
Music: *Martins*, Percy Carter Buck (1871-1947)

10 10. 7

1 Je - ru - sa - lem, my hap - py home, when
2 Thy saints are crowned with glo - ry great; they
3 There Da - vid stands with harp in hand as
4 Our La - dy sings Mag - ni - fi - cat with
5 Je - ru - sa - lem, Je - ru - sa - lem, God

1 shall I come to thee? When shall my sor - rows
2 see God face to face; they tri - umph still, they
3 mas - ter of the choir: ten thou - sand times would
4 tune sur - pass - ing sweet, and bless - ed mar - tyrs'
5 grant that I may see thine end - less joy, and

1 have an end? Thy joys when shall I see?
2 still re - joice in that most hap - py place.
3 one be blest who might this mu - sic hear.
4 har - mo - ny doth ring in ev - ery street.
5 of the same par - ta - ker ev - er be!

Words: F. B. P. (ca. 16th cent.), alt.
Music: *Land of Rest*, American folk hymn; adapt. and harm. Annabel Morris Buchanan (1889-1983)    CM

# The Church Triumphant

621

1 Light's a-bode, ce - les-tial Sa-lem, vi - sion whence true peace doth spring,
2 There for ev - er and for ev - er al - le - lu - ia is out-poured;
3 There no cloud nor pass-ing va - por dims the bright-ness of the air;
*4 O how glo-rious and re-splen-dent, fra - gile bo - dy, shalt thou be,
5 Now with glad-ness, now with cour-age, bear the bur-den on thee laid,

1 bright-er than the heart can fan - cy, man-sion of the high - est King;
2 for un - end-ing, for un - bro - ken is the feast-day of the Lord;
3 end-less noon-day, glo - rious noon-day, from the Sun of suns is there;
4 when en-dued with heaven-ly beau-ty, full of health, and strong, and free,
5 that here-af-ter these thy la - bors may with end-less gifts be paid,

1 O how glo - rious are the prais-es which of thee the pro-phets sing!
2 all is pure and all is ho - ly that with-in thy walls is stored.
3 there no night brings rest from la - bor, for un-known are toil and care.
4 full of vi - gor, full of plea-sure that shall last e - ter - nal - ly!
5 and in ev - er - last-ing glo - ry thou with bright-ness be ar - rayed.

Words: Latin, 15th cent.; tr. John Mason Neale (1818-1866), alt.
Music: *Rhuddlan*, Welsh melody

87. 87. 87

1 Light's a - bode, ce - les - tial Sa - lem, vi-sion whence true peace doth spring,
2 There for ev - er and for ev - er al - le - lu - ia is out-poured;
3 There no cloud nor pass - ing va - por dims the bright-ness of the air;
*4 O how glo - rious and re-splend-ent, frag - ile bo - dy, shalt thou be,
5 Now with glad - ness, now with cour-age, bear the bur - den on thee laid,

1 bright-er than the heart can fan - cy, man-sion of the high-est King;
2 for un - end - ing, for un - bro - ken is the feast - day of the Lord;
3 end - less noon-day, glo - rious noon-day, from the Sun of suns is there;
4 when en - dued with heaven-ly beau - ty, full of health, and strong, and free,
5 that here - af - ter these thy la - bors may with end - less gifts be paid,

1 O how glo - rious are the prais - es which of thee the pro - phets sing!
2 all is pure and all is ho - ly that with - in thy walls is stored.
3 there no night brings rest from la - bor, for un - known are toil and care.
4 full of vi - gor, full of plea - sure that shall last e - ter - nal - ly!
5 and in ev - er - last - ing glo - ry thou with bright-ness be ar - rayed.

Words: Latin, 15th cent.; tr. John Mason Neale (1818-1866), alt.
Music: *Urbs beata Jerusalem*, plainsong, Mode 2; Nevers Ms., 13th cent.; ver. Schola Antiqua, 1983      87. 87. 87
Music: Melody rhythmic version © 1984, Schola Antiqua Inc. Used by permission.

1 O what their joy and their glo - ry must be,
2 Tru - ly, "Je - ru - sa - lem" name we that shore,
3 There, where no trou - bles dis - trac - tion can bring,
4 Now, in the mean - while, with hearts raised on high,
5 Low be - fore him with our prais - es we fall,

1 those end-less Sab - baths the bless - ed ones see;
2 ci - ty of peace that brings joy ev - er - more;
3 we the sweet an - thems of Zi - on shall sing;
4 we for that coun - try must yearn and must sigh,
5 of whom, and in whom, and through whom are all;

1 crown for the val - iant, to wea - ry ones rest:
2 wish and ful - fill - ment are not sev - ered there,
3 while for thy grace, Lord, their voic - es of praise
4 seek - ing Je - ru - sa - lem, dear na - tive land,
5 of whom, the Fa - ther; and in whom, the Son;

1 God shall be all, and in all ev - er blest.
2 nor do things prayed for come short of the prayer.
3 thy bless - ed peo - ple e - ter - nal - ly raise.
4 through our long ex - ile on Bab - y - lon's strand.
5 through whom, the Spi - rit, with them ev - er One.

Words: Peter Abelard (1079-1142); tr. John Mason Neale (1818-1866), alt.
Music: *O quanta qualia*, melody from *Antiphoner*, 1681;
  harm. John Bacchus Dykes (1823-1876)

10 10. 10 10

624

The Church Triumphant

1 Je - ru - sa - lem the gold - en, with milk and hon - ey blest,
2 They stand, those halls of Zi - on, all ju - bi - lant with song,
3 There is the throne of Da - vid; and there, from care re - leased,
4 Oh, sweet and bless - ed coun - try, the home of God's e - lect!

be - neath thy con - tem - pla - tion sink heart and voice op - pressed:
and bright with man - y an an - gel, and all the mar - tyr throng:
the shout of them that tri - umph, the song of them that feast;
Oh, sweet and bless - ed coun - try that ea - ger hearts ex - pect!

I know not, oh, I know not, what joys a - wait us there;
the Prince is ev - er in them, the day - light is se - rene;
and they who with their Lead - er have con - quered in the fight,
Je - sus, in mer - cy bring us to that dear land of rest,

what ra - dian - cy of glo - ry, what bliss be - yond com - pare!
the pas - tures of the bless - ed are decked in glo - rious sheen.
for ev - er and for ev - er are clad in robes of white.
who art, with God the Fa - ther, and Spi - rit, ev - er blest.

Words: Bernard of Cluny (12th cent.); tr. John Mason Neale (1818-1866), alt.
  St. 4, *Hymns Ancient and Modern*, 1861
Music: *Ewing*, Alexander Ewing (1830-1895)

76. 76. D

**Descant**

4 My soul, bear thou thy part, tri - umph in God a - bove: and

1 Ye ho - ly an - gels bright, who wait at God's right hand,    or
2 Ye bless - ed souls at rest, who ran this earth-ly race    and
3 Ye saints, who toil be - low, a - dore your heaven-ly King,    and
4 My soul, bear thou thy part, tri - umph in God a - bove:    and

with a well - tuned heart sing thou the songs of love! Let all thy

through the realms of light fly at your Lord's com - mand, as - sist our
now, from sin re - leased, be - hold the Sa - vior's face, God's prais - es
on - ward as ye go some joy - ful an - them sing; take what he
with a well-tuned heart sing thou the songs of love! Let all thy

days till life shall end, what - e'er he send, be filled with praise.

song, for else the theme too high doth seem for mor - tal tongue.
sound, as in his sight with sweet de - light ye do a - bound.
gives and praise him still, through good or ill, who ev - er lives!
days till life shall end, what - e'er he send, be filled with praise.

Words: Richard Baxter (1615-1691); rev. John Hampden Gurney (1802-1862)
Music: *Darwall's 148th*, melody and bass John Darwall (1731-1789);
      harm. William Henry Monk (1823-1889), alt.; desc. Sydney Hugo Nicholson (1875-1947)     66. 66. 44. 44

1 Lord, be thy word my rule; in it may I re - joice;
2 thy prom - is - es my hope; thy prov - i - dence my guard;

thy glo - ry be my aim, thy ho - ly will my choice;
thine arm my strong sup - port; thy - self my great re - ward.

Words: Christopher Wordsworth (1807-1885)
Music: *Quam dilecta*, Henry Lascelles Jenner (1820-1898)

66. 66

*Unison or harmony*

1 Lamp of our feet, where - by we trace    our path when wont to stray;
2 bread of our souls, where - on we feed,    true man - na from on high;
3 pil - lar of fire, through watch - es dark,    and ra - diant cloud by day;
4 word of the ev - er - liv - ing God,    will of his glo - rious Son;
5 Lord, grant us all a - right to learn    the wis - dom it im - parts;

1 stream from the fount of heaven-ly grace, brook by the trav-eler's way;
2 our guide and chart, where-in we read of realms be-yond the sky;
3 when waves would whelm our toss-ing bark, our an-chor and our stay;
4 with-out thee how could earth be trod, or heaven it-self be won?
5 and to its heaven-ly teach-ing turn, with sim-ple, child-like hearts.

Words: Bernard Barton (1784-1849)
Music: *Nun danket all und bringet Ehr,* melody att. Johann Cruger (1598-1662), alt.

CM

## Holy Scripture 628

1 Help us, O Lord, to learn the truths your word im-parts: to
2 Help us, O Lord, to live the faith which we pro-claim, that
3 Help us, O Lord, to teach the beau-ty of your ways, that

stu-dy, that your laws may be in-scribed up-on our hearts.
all our thoughts and words and deeds may glo-ri-fy your Name.
yearn-ing souls may find the Christ and live a life of praise.

Words: William Watkins Reid, Jr. (b. 1923), alt.
Music: *St. Ethelwald,* William Henry Monk (1823-1889)

SM

*Introduction*

1 We lim-it not the truth of God to our poor reach of mind, to no-tions of our day and place, crude, par-tial, and con-fined; no, let a new and bet-ter hope with-in our hearts be stirred; the Lord has yet more light and truth to break forth from his word.

2 Who dares to bind to one's own sense the or-a-cles of heaven, for all the na-tions, tongues, and climes and all the a-ges given? That u-ni-verse, how much un-known! The o-cean un-ex-plored! the Lord has yet more light and truth to break forth from his word.

3 O Fa-ther, Son, and Spi-rit, send us in-crease from a-bove; en-large, ex-pand all liv-ing souls to com-pre-hend your love; and make us all go on to know with no-bler powers con-ferred— the Lord has yet more light and truth to break forth from his word.

*Interlude/Conclusion*

Words: George Rawson (1807-1889), alt.
Music: *Halifax*, George Frideric Handel (1685-1759); adapt. and arr. David Hurd (b. 1950)       CMD

# Holy Scripture

630

1 Thanks to God whose Word was spo-ken in the deed that
2 Thanks to God whose Word In-car-nate heights and depths of
*3 Thanks to God whose word was writ-ten in the Bi - ble's
*4 Thanks to God whose word is pub-lished in the tongues of
5 Thanks to God whose Word is an-swered by the Spi - rit's

1 made the earth. His the voice that called a na - tion;
2 life did share. Deeds and words and death and ris - ing,
3 sa - cred page, rec - ord of the rev - e - la - tion
4 ev - ery race. See its glo - ry un - di - mi - nished
5 voice with - in. Here we drink of joy un - mea - sured,

1 his the fires that tried her worth. God has spo - ken:
2 grace in hu - man form de - clare. God has spo - ken:
3 show - ing God to ev - ery age. God has spo - ken:
4 by the change of time or place. God has spo - ken:
5 life re - deemed from death and sin. God is speak - ing:

1 praise God_____ for his o - pen word.
2 praise God_____ for his o - pen word.
3 praise God_____ for his o - pen word.
4 praise God_____ for his o - pen word.
5 praise God_____ for his o - pen word.

Words: R. T. Brooks (b. 1918), alt.
Music: *Wylde Green*, Peter Cutts (b. 1937)

87. 87 with Refrain

1 Book of books, our peo-ple's strength, states-man's, teach-er's, he-ro's
2 Thank we those who toiled in thought, man-y di-verse scrolls com-
3 Praise we God, who hath in-spired those whose wis-dom still di-

trea - sure, bring - ing free - dom, spread - ing truth,
plet - ing, po - ets, pro - phets, schol - ars, saints,
rects us; praise him for the Word made flesh,

shed-ding light that none can mea - sure: wis-dom comes to
each a word from God re - peat - ing; till they came, who
for the Spi - rit which pro - tects us. Light of know-ledge,

those who know thee, all the best we have we owe thee.
told the sto - ry of the Word, and showed his glo - ry.
ev - er burn-ing, shed on us thy death-less learn - ing.

Words: Percy Dearmer (1867-1936)
Music: *Liebster Jesu*, melody Johann Rudolph Ahle (1625-1673); alt. *Das grosse Cantional oder Kirchen-Gesangbuch*, 1687; harm. George Herbert Palmer (1846-1926)

78. 78. 88

1 O Christ, the Word Incarnate, O Wisdom from on high,
O Truth, unchanged, unchanging, O Light of our dark sky;
we praise thee for the radiance that from the scripture's page,
a lantern to our footsteps, shines on from age to age.

2 The Church from our dear Master received the word divine,
and still that light is lifted o'er all the earth to shine.
It is the chart and compass that o'er life's surging sea,
mid mists and rocks and quicksands, still guides, O Christ, to thee.

3 O make thy Church, dear Savior, a lamp of purest gold,
to bear before the nations thy true light as of old;
O teach thy wandering pilgrims by this their path to trace,
till, clouds and darkness ended, they see thee face to face.

Words: William Walsham How (1823-1897), alt.
Music: *Munich*, melody from *Neu-vermehrtes und zu Übung Christl. Gottseligkeit eingerichtetes Meiningisches Gesangbuch*, 1693; adapt. and harm. Felix Mendelssohn (1809-1847)

76. 76. D

# 633

1 Word of God, come down on earth, liv-ing rain from
2 Word e-ter-nal, throned on high, Word that brought to
3 Word that caused blind eyes to see, speak and heal our
4 Word that speaks your Fa-ther's love, one with him be-

heaven de-scend-ing; touch our hearts and bring to birth
life cre-a-tion, Word that came from heaven to die,
mor-tal blind-ness; deaf we are: our heal-er be;
yond all tell-ing, Word that sends us from a-bove

faith and hope and love un-end-ing. Word al-might-y,
cru-ci-fied for our sal-va-tion, sav-ing Word, the
loose our tongues to tell your kind-ness. Be our Word in
God the Spi-rit, with us dwell-ing, Word of truth, to

we re-vere you; Word made flesh, we long to hear you.
world re-stor-ing, speak to us, your love out-pour-ing.
pi-ty spo-ken; heal the world, by our sin brok-en.
all truth lead us, Word of life, with one Bread feed us.

Words: James Quinn (b. 1919)
Music: *Mt. St. Alban NCA*, Richard Wayne Dirksen (b. 1921)

78. 78. 88

# Holy Scripture

Words: Miles Coverdale (1487-1568)
Music: *Ich ruf zu dir*, melody from *Geistliche Lieder*, 1533;
   harm. *Thuringer Evangelisches Gesangbuch*, 1928

Irr.

## 635

The Christian Life

*Unison or harmony*

1 If thou but trust in God to guide thee, and hope in him through all thy ways, he'll give thee strength what-e'er be-tide thee, and bear thee through the e-vil days. Who trusts in God's un-chang-ing love builds on a rock that nought can move.

2 Sing, pray, and keep his ways un-swerv-ing; so do thine own part faith-ful-ly, and trust his word, though un-de-serv-ing; thou yet shalt find it true for thee; God nev-er yet for-sook in need the soul that trust-ed him in-deed.

Words: Georg Neumark (1621-1681); tr. Catherine Winkworth (1827-1878), alt.
Music: *Wer nur den lieben Gott*, Georg Neumark (1621-1681)

98. 98. 88

1 How firm a foun-da-tion, ye saints of the Lord,
2 "Fear not, I am with thee; O be not dis-mayed!
3 "When through the deep wa-ters I call thee to go,
4 "When through fier-y tri-als thy path-way shall lie,
5 "The soul that to Je-sus hath fled for re-pose,

1 is laid for your faith in his ex-cel-lent word!
2 For I am thy God, and will still give thee aid;
3 the riv-ers of woe shall not thee o-ver-flow;
4 my grace, all suf-fi-cient, shall be thy sup-ply;
5 I will not, I will not de-sert to its foes;

1 What more can he say than to you he hath said,
2 I'll strength-en thee, help thee, and cause thee to stand,
3 for I will be with thee, thy trou-bles to bless,
4 the flame shall not hurt thee; I on-ly de-sign
5 that soul, though all hell shall en-deav-or to shake,

1 to you that for ref-uge to Je-sus have fled?
2 up-held by my right-eous, om-nip-o-tent hand.
3 and sanc-ti-fy to thee thy deep-est dis-tress.
4 thy dross to con-sume, and thy gold to re-fine.
5 I'll nev-er, no, nev-er, no, nev-er for-sake."

*Optional Interlude*

**Words:** K. in John Rippon's *Selection*, 1787, alt.
**Music:** *Foundation*, melody from *The Sacred Harp*, 1844

11 11. 11 11

*Descant*

5 "The soul that to Je - sus hath fled for re - pose,

1 How firm a foun - da - tion, ye saints of the Lord,
2 "Fear not, I am with thee; O be not dis - mayed!
3 "When through the deep wa - ters I call thee to go,
4 "When through fier - y tri - als thy path - way shall lie,
5 "The soul that to Je - sus hath fled for re - pose,

5 I will not, I will not de - sert to its foes;

1 is laid for your faith in his ex - cel - lent word!
2 For I am thy God, and will still give thee aid;
3 the riv - ers of woe shall not thee o - ver - flow;
4 my grace, all suf - fi - cient, shall be thy sup - ply;
5 I will not, I will not de - sert to its foes;

5     soul _____ to   shake,   no,

1 What   more   can   he   say   than   to   you   he   hath   said,
2 I'll   strength - en   thee,   help   thee, and   cause thee   to   stand,
3 for   I   will   be   with   thee,   thy   trou - bles   to   bless,
4 the   flame   shall   not   hurt   thee;   I   on - ly   de - sign
5 that   soul,   though   all   hell   shall   en - deav - or   to   shake,

5   I'll   nev - er,   no,   nev - er,   no,   nev - er   for - sake."

1 to   you   that   for   ref - uge   to   Je - sus   have   fled?
2 up - held   by   my   right - eous, om - nip - o - tent   hand.
3 and   sanc - ti - fy   to   thee   thy   deep - est   dis - tress.
4 thy   dross   to   con - sume,   and   thy   gold   to   re - fine.
5 I'll   nev - er,   no,   nev - er,   no,   ne - ver   for - sake."

Words: K. in John Rippon's *Selection*, 1787, alt.
Music: *Lyons*, att. Johann Michael Haydn (1737-1806); desc. Lois Fyfe (b. 1927)

11 11. 11 11

# 638

1 Come, O thou Trav - el - er un - known, whom
2 I need not tell thee who I am, my
3 Yield to me now, for I am weak but
4 'Tis Love, 'tis Love! Thou diedst for me! I

still I hold, but can - not see; my com - pa -
mis - er - y or sin de - clare; thy - self hast
con - fi - dent in self - de - spair; speak to my
hear thy whis - per in my heart: the morn - ing

ny be - fore is gone, and I am left a -
called me by my name, look on thy hands, and
heart, in bless - ings speak, be con - quered by my
breaks, the sha - dows flee. Pure U - ni - ver - sal

lone with thee. With thee all night I mean to
read it there. But who, I ask thee, who art
in - stant prayer. Speak, or thou nev - er hence shalt
Love thou art; thy mer - cies nev - er shall re -

stay, and wres - tle till the break of day.
thou? Tell me thy name, and tell me now.
move, and tell me, if thy name is Love.
move, thy na - ture and thy name is Love.

Words: Charles Wesley (1707-1788), alt.
Music: *Vernon*, traditional melody

88. 88. 88

# The Christian Life

1 Come, O thou Trav - el - er un -
2 I need not tell thee who I
3 Yield to me now, for I am
4 'Tis Love, 'tis Love! Thou diedst for

known, whom still I hold, but can - not see; my com - pa -
am, my mis - er - y or sin de - clare; thy - self hast
weak but con - fi - dent in self - de - spair; speak to my
me! I hear thy whis - per in my heart: the morn - ing

ny be - fore is gone, and I am left a - lone with thee.
called me by my name, look on thy hands, and read it there.
heart, in bless-ings speak, be con-quered by my in - stant prayer.
breaks, the sha - dows flee. Pure U - ni - ver - sal Love thou art;

With thee all night I mean to stay, and wres - tle till the
But who, I ask thee, who are thou? Tell me thy name, and
Speak, or thou nev - er hence shalt move, and tell me, if thy
thy mer - cies nev - er shall re - move, thy na - ture and thy

**1-3**                                    **Final Ending**

break of day. _____
tell me now. _____
name is Love. _____
name is (Love.)            Love. _____

Words: Charles Wesley (1707-1788), alt.
Music: *Woodbury*, Eric Routley (1917-1982)

88. 88. 88

1 Watch-man, tell us of the night, what its signs of prom-ise are. Trav - eler, o'er yon moun-tain's height, see that glo - ry— beam - ing star. Watch-man, does its beau - teous ray aught of joy or hope fore - tell? Trav -eler, yes; it

2 Watch-man, tell us of the night; high - er yet that star a - scends. Trav - eler, bless - ed - ness and light, peace and truth its course por - tends. Watch-man, will its beams a - lone gild the spot that gave them birth? Trav -eler, a - ges

3 Watch-man, tell us of the night, for the morn-ing seems to dawn. Trav - eler, dark-ness takes its flight, doubt and ter - ror are with - drawn. Watch-man, let thy wan - derings cease; hie thee to thy qui - et home. Trav -eler, lo! the

brings the day, prom - ised day of Is - ra - el.
are its own; see, it bursts o'er all the earth.
Prince of Peace, lo! the Son of God is come!

*Two groups may sing antiphonally, alternating by sentences.*

Words: John Bowring (1792-1872)
Music: *Aberystwyth*, Joseph Parry (1841-1903)

77. 77. D

## The Christian Life

# 641

1 Lord Je - sus, think on me, and purge a - way my sin;
2 Lord Je - sus, think on me, with care and woe op - pressed;
3 Lord Je - sus, think on me, nor let me go a - stray;
4 Lord Je - sus, think on me, that, when the flood is passed,

from harm - ful pas-sions set me free, and make me pure with - in.
let me thy lov-ing ser - vant be, and taste thy prom-ised rest.
through dark - ness and per-plex - i - ty point thou the heaven-ly way.
I may the e-ter - nal bright- ness see, and share thy joy at last.

Words: Synesius of Cyrene (375?-414?); tr. Allen William Chatfield (1808-1896), alt.
Music: *Southwell*, from *Daman's Psalter*, 1579; adapt. *Hymnal 1982*

SM

1 Je - sus, the ve - ry thought of thee with sweet - ness fills the breast;
2 No voice can sing, no heart can frame, nor can the mem - ory find,
3 O hope of ev - ery con - trite heart, O joy of all the meek,
4 But what to those who find? Ah, this nor tongue nor pen can show;
5 Je - sus, our on - ly joy be thou, as thou our prize wilt be;

1 but sweet - er far thy face to see, and in thy pres - ence rest.
2 a sweet - er sound than Je - sus' Name, the Sa - vior of man-kind.
3 to those who fall, how kind thou art: how good to those who seek!
4 the love of Je - sus, what it is, none but who love him know.
5 in thee be all our glo - ry now, and through e - ter - ni - ty.

Words: Latin, 12th cent.; st. 5, Latin, 15th cent.; tr. Edward Caswall (1814-1878), alt.
Music: *Windsor*, melody William Damon (1540?-1591?); harm. Thomas Este (1540?-1608?)     CM

*Unison or harmony*

1 My God, how won - der - ful thou art, thy ma - jes - ty how bright,
2 How dread are thine e - ter - nal years, O ev - er - last - ing Lord,
3 How won - der - ful, how beau - ti - ful, the sight of thee must be,
4 O how I fear thee, liv - ing God, with deep - est, ten-derest fears,
5 Yet I may love thee too, O Lord, al - might - y as thou art,

1 how beau-ti-ful thy mer-cy seat, in depths of burn-ing light!
2 by pros-trate spi-rits day and night in-ces-sant-ly a-dored!
3 thine end-less wis-dom, bound-less power, and awe-ful pu-ri-ty!
4 and wor-ship thee with trem-bling hope and pen-i-ten-tial tears!
5 for thou hast stooped to ask of me the love of my poor heart.

Words: Frederick William Faber (1814-1863)
Music: *Windsor*, melody William Damon (1540?-1591?), alt.; harm. *Booke of Musicke*, 1591          CM

## The Christian Life

# 644

1 How sweet the Name of Je-sus sounds in a be-liev-er's ear!
2 It makes the wound-ed spi-rit whole, and calms the trou-bled breast;
3 Dear Name, the rock on which I build, my shield and hid-ing-place,
4 O Je-sus! Shep-herd, Guard-ian, Friend, O Pro-phet, Priest, and King,
*5 Weak is the ef-fort of my heart, and cold my warm-est thought;

1 It soothes our sor-rows, heals our wounds, and drives a-way our fear.
2 'tis man-na to the hun-gry soul, and to the wear-y, rest.
3 my nev-er-fail-ing trea-su-ry, filled with bound-less stores of grace!
4 my Lord, my Life, my Way, my End, ac-cept the praise I bring.
5 but when I see thee as thou art, I'll praise thee as I ought.

Words: John Newton (1725-1807), alt.
Music: *St. Peter*, Alexander Robert Reinagle (1799-1877)          CM

## 645

The Christian Life

1 The King of love my shep-herd is, whose good-ness
2 Where streams of liv - ing wa - ter flow, my ran - somed
*3 Per - verse and fool - ish oft I strayed, but yet in
*4 In death's dark vale I fear no ill with thee, dear
5 Thou spread'st a ta - ble in my sight; thy unc - tion
6 And so through all the length of days thy good-ness

1 fail - eth nev - er; I noth - ing lack if
2 soul he lead - eth, and where the ver - dant
3 love he sought me, and on his shoul - der
4 Lord, be - side me; thy rod and staff my
5 grace be - stow - eth; and oh, what trans - port
6 fail - eth nev - er: Good Shep - herd, may I

1 I am his, and he is mine for ev - er.
2 pas - tures grow, with food ce - les - tial feed - eth.
3 gent - ly laid, and home, re - joic - ing, brought me.
4 com - fort still, thy cross be - fore to guide me.
5 of de - light from thy pure chal - ice flow - eth!
6 sing thy praise with - in thy house for ev - er.

Words: Henry Williams Baker (1821-1877); para. of Psalm 23
Music: *St. Columba*, Irish melody

87. 87

## 646

The Christian Life

*Descant*

6 And so through all the length of days thy

1 The King of love my shep - herd is, whose
2 Where streams of liv - ing wa - ter flow, my
*3 Per - verse and fool - ish oft I strayed, but
*4 In death's dark vale I fear no ill with
5 Thou spread'st a ta - ble in my sight; thy

6 good - ness fail - eth nev - er: Good Shep-herd, may I

1 good - ness fail - eth nev - er; I noth - ing lack if
2 ran - somed soul he lead - eth, and where the ver - dant
3 yet in love he sought me, and on his shoul-der
4 thee, dear Lord, be - side me; thy rod and staff my
5 unc - tion grace be - stow - eth; and oh, what trans-port

6 sing thy praise with - in thy house for ev - er.

1 I am his, and he is mine for ev - er.
2 pas - tures grow, with food ce - les - tial feed - eth.
3 gent - ly laid, and home, re - joic - ing, brought me.
4 com - fort still, thy cross be - fore to guide me.
5 of de - light from thy pure chal - ice flow - eth!

6 And so through all the length of days
thy goodness faileth never:
Good shepherd, may I sing thy praise
within thy house for ever.

Words: Henry Williams Baker (1821-1877); para. of Psalm 23
Music: *Dominus regit me*, John Bacchus Dykes (1823-1876); desc. David Willcocks (b. 1919)

87. 87

# The Christian Life

1 I know not where the road will lead I fol-low day by day,
or where it ends: I on-ly know I walk the King's high-way.
I know not if the way is long, and no one else can say;
but rough or smooth, up hill or down, I walk the King's high-way.

2 And some I love have reached the end, but some with me may stay,
their faith and hope still guid-ing me: I walk the King's high-way.
The way is truth, the way is love, for light and strength I pray,
and through the years of life, to God I walk the King's high-way.

3 The count-less hosts lead on be-fore, I must not fear nor stray;
with them, the pil-grims of the faith, I walk the King's high-way.
Through light and dark the road leads on till dawns the end-less day,
when I shall know why in this life I walk the King's high-way.

Words: Evelyn Atwater Cummins (1891-1971)
Music: *Laramie*, Arnold George Henry Bode (1866-1952)

CMD

# The Christian Life

1 When Is - rael was in E - gypt's land, let my peo - ple go;
2 The Lord told Mo - ses what to do, let my peo - ple go;
3 They jour-neyed on at his com - mand, let my peo - ple go;
4 Oh, let us all from bond-age flee, let my peo - ple go;

op - pressed so hard they___ could not stand, let my peo - ple go.
to lead the chil-dren of Is - rael through, let my peo - ple go.
and came at length to___ Ca - naan's land, let my peo - ple go.
and let us all in___ Christ be free, let my peo - ple go.

*Refrain*

Go down, Mo - ses, way down in E - gypt's land;

tell old Pha - roah to let my peo - ple go.

Words: Afro-American spiritual
Music: *Go Down, Moses*, Afro-American spiritual; arr. Horace Clarence Boyer (b. 1935)

85. 85 with Refrain

1 O Je - sus, joy of lov - ing hearts, the fount of
2 We taste in you our liv - ing bread, and long to
3 For you our rest - less spi - rits yearn wher - e'er our
4 O Je - sus, ev - er with us stay; make all our

life and our true light, we seek the peace your love im -
feast up - on you still; we drink of you, the foun - tain -
chang - ing lot is cast; glad, when your pres - ence we dis -
mo - ments calm and bright; oh, chase the night of sin a -

parts, and stand re - joic - ing in your sight.
head, our thirst - ing souls to quench and fill.
cern, blest, when our faith can hold you fast.
way, shed o'er the world your ho - ly light.

Words: Att. Bernard of Clairvaux (1091-1153); tr. and para. Ray Palmer (1808-1887), alt.
Music: *Dickinson College*, Lee Hastings Bristol, Jr. (1923-1979)                    LM

1 O Je - sus, joy of lov - ing hearts, the fount of life and
2 We taste in you our liv - ing bread, and long to feast up -
3 For you our rest - less spi - rits yearn wher - e'er our chang - ing
4 O Je - sus, ev - er with us stay; make all our mo - ments

our true light, we seek the peace your love im - parts,
on you still; we drink of you, the foun - tain - head,
lot is cast; glad, when your pres - ence we dis - cern,
calm and bright; oh, chase the night of sin a - way,

and stand re - joic - ing in your sight.
our thirst - ing souls to quench and fill.
blest, when our faith can hold you fast.
shed o'er the world your ho - ly light.

Words: Att. Bernard of Clairvaux (1091-1153); tr. and para. Ray Palmer (1808-1887), alt.
Music: *Jesu dulcis memoria*, plainsong, Mode 2

LM

## The Christian Life

# 651

1 This is my Fa - ther's world, and to my lis - tening ears
2 This is our Fa - ther's world, oh, let us not for - get

all na - ture sings and round me rings the mu - sic of the spheres.
that though the wrong is great and strong, God is our Fa - ther yet.

This is my Fa - ther's world: I rest me in the thought of
He trusts us with his world, to keep it clean and fair, all

rocks and trees, of skies and seas, his hand the won - ders wrought.
earth and trees, all skies and seas, all crea - tures eve - ry - where.

Words: St. 1, Maltbie D. Babcock (1858-1901); st. 2, Mary Babcock Crawford (b. 1909)
Music: *Mercer Street*, Malcolm Williamson (b. 1931)

SMD

# 652

The Christian Life

1 Dear Lord and Fa-ther of man-kind, for - give our fool-ish
2 In sim - ple trust like theirs who heard, be - side the Syr - ian
3 O Sab - bath rest by Gal - i - lee! O calm of hills a -
4 Drop thy still dews of qui - et - ness, till all our striv - ings
5 Breathe through the heats of our de - sire thy cool - ness and thy

1 ways! Re - clothe us in our right - ful mind, in
2 sea, the gra - cious call - ing of the Lord, let
3 bove, where Je - sus knelt to share with thee the
4 cease; take from our souls the strain and stress, and
5 balm; let sense be dumb, let flesh re - tire; speak

1 pur - er lives thy ser - vice find, in deep - er rev - erence, praise.
2 us, like them, with - out a word, rise up and fol - low thee.
3 si - lence of e - ter - ni - ty in - ter - pret - ed by love!
4 let our or - dered lives con - fess the beau - ty of thy peace.
5 through the earth-quake, wind, and fire, O still, small voice of calm.

Words: John Greenleaf Whittier (1807-1892), alt.
Music: *Rest*, Frederick Charles Maker (1844-1927)

86. 886

1 Dear Lord and Fa - ther of man-kind, for-
2 In sim - ple trust like theirs who heard, be-
3 O Sab - bath rest by Gal - i - lee! O
4 Drop thy still dews of qui - et - ness, till
5 Breathe through the heats of our de - sire thy

1 give our fool - ish ways! Re - clothe us in our
2 side the Syr - ian sea, the gra - cious call - ing
3 calm of hills a - bove, where Je - sus knelt to
4 all our striv - ings cease; take from our souls the
5 cool - ness and thy balm; let sense be dumb, let

1 right - ful mind, in pur - er lives thy ser - vice find, in
2 of the Lord, let us, like them, with - out a word, rise
3 share with thee the si - lence of e - ter - ni - ty in-
4 strain and stress, and let our or - dered lives con - fess the
5 flesh re - tire; speak through the earth-quake, wind, and fire, O

1 deep - er rev - erence, praise, in deep - er rev - erence, praise.
2 up and fol - low thee, rise up and fol - low thee.
3 ter - pret - ed by love! in - ter - pret - ed by love!
4 beau - ty of thy peace, the beau - ty of thy peace.
5 still, small voice of calm, O still, small voice of calm.

Words: John Greenleaf Whittier (1807-1892), alt.
Music: *Repton*, Charles Hubert Hastings Parry (1848-1918), alt.

86. 886

Day by day, dear Lord, of thee three things I pray:
to see thee more clear - ly, love thee more dear - ly,
fol - low thee more near - ly, day by day.

Words: Att. Richard of Chichester (1197-1253)
Music: *Sumner*, Arthur Henry Biggs (1906-1954)

Irr.

1 O Je - sus, I have prom - ised to serve thee to the end:
2 O let me hear thee speak - ing in ac - cents clear and still,
3 O Je - sus, thou hast prom - ised to all who fol - low thee,

be thou for ev - er near me, my Mas - ter and my friend;
a - bove the storms of pas - sion, the mur - murs of self - will;
that where thou art in glo - ry there shall thy ser - vant be;

I shall not fear the bat - tle, if thou art by my side,
O speak to re-as - sure me, to has-ten or con - trol;
and, Je - sus I have prom - ised to serve thee to the end;

nor wan - der from the path - way, if thou wilt be my guide.
O speak, and make me lis - ten, thou guard-ian of my soul.
O give me grace to fol - low, my Mas - ter and my friend.

Words: John Ernest Bode (1816-1874), alt.
Music: *Nyland*, Finnish folk melody; adapt. David Evans (1874-1948)

76. 76. D

## The Christian Life

# 656

1 Blest are the pure in heart, for they shall see our God; the
2 The Lord, who left the heavens our life and peace to bring, to
3 he to the low - ly soul will still him-self im - part and
4 Lord, we thy pres-ence seek; may ours this bless-ing be; give

se - cret of the Lord is theirs, their soul is Christ's a - bode.
dwell in low - li - ness with us, our pat - tern and our King;
for his dwell-ing and his throne will choose the pure in heart.
us a pure and low - ly heart, a tem - ple fit for thee.

Words: Sts. 1 and 3, John Keble (1792-1866), alt.; sts. 2 and 4, William John Hall (1793-1861), alt.
Music: *Franconia*, melody Johann Balthasar König (1691-1758):
adapt. and harm. William Henry Havergal (1793-1870)

SM

# 657

1 Love di - vine, all loves ex - cell - ing, joy of heaven, to
2 Come, al - might - y to de - liv - er, let us all thy
3 Fi - nish then thy new cre - a - tion; pure and spot - less

earth come down, fix in us thy hum - ble dwell - ing, all thy
life re - ceive; sud - den - ly re - turn, and nev - er, nev - er -
let us be; let us see thy great sal - va - tion per - fect -

faith - ful mer - cies crown. Je - sus, thou art all com - pas - sion,
more thy tem - ples leave. Thee we would be al - way bless - ing,
ly re - stored in thee: changed from glo - ry in - to glo - ry,

pure, un - bound - ed love thou art; vis - it us with
serve thee as thy hosts a - bove, pray, and praise thee
till in heaven we take our place, till we cast our

thy sal - va - tion, en - ter ev - ery trem-bling heart.
with - out ceas - ing, glo - ry in thy per - fect love.
crowns be - fore thee, lost in won - der, love, and praise.

Words: Charles Wesley (1707-1788)
Music: *Hyfrydol,* Rowland Hugh Prichard (1811-1887)

87. 87. D

## The Christian Life

**658**

1 As longs the deer for cool - ing streams in
2 For thee, my God, the liv - ing God, my
3 Why rest - less, why cast down, my soul? Hope
4 To Fa - ther, Son, and Ho - ly Ghost, the

parched and bar - ren ways, so longs my soul, O
thirst - y soul doth pine: O when shall I be -
still, and thou shalt sing the praise of him who
God whom we a - dore, be glo - ry, as it

God, for thee and thy re - fresh - ing grace.
hold thy face, thou Ma - jes - ty di - vine?
is thy God, thy health's e - ter - nal spring.
was, is now, and shall be ev - er - more.

Words: *New Version of the Psalms of David,* 1696, alt.; para. of Psalm 42:1-7
Music: *Martyrdom,* melody and bass Hugh Wilson (1764-1824); adapt. and harm. Robert Smith (1780-1829)    CM

1 O Mas-ter, let me walk with thee     in low-ly
2 (Help me the slow of heart to) move     by some clear,
3 (Teach me thy pa-tience; still with) thee     in clos-er,
4 (in hope that sends a shin-ing) ray     far down the

paths of ser-vice free;     tell me thy se-cret; help me
win-ning word of love;     teach me the way-ward feet to
dear-er com-pa-ny,     in work that keeps faith sweet and
fu-ture's broad-ening way,     in peace that on-ly thou canst

bear     the strain of toil, the fret of
stay,     and guide them in the home-ward
strong,     in trust that tri-umphs o-ver
give,     with thee, O Mas-ter, let me

**1-3**             *Final Ending*

care.     2 Help me the slow of heart to
way.     3 Teach me thy pa-tience; still with
wrong,     4 in hope that sends a shin-ing
live.

Words: Washington Gladden (1836-1918)
Music: *de Tar*, Calvin Hampton (1938-1984)           LM

1 O Mas-ter let me walk with thee     in low-ly
2 Help me the slow of heart to move     by some clear,
3 Teach me thy pa-tience; still with thee     in clos-er,
4 in hope that sends a shin-ing ray     far down the

paths of ser - vice free; tell me thy se - cret;
win - ning word of love; teach me the way - ward
dear - er com - pa - ny, in work that keeps faith
fu - ture's broad - ening way, in peace that on - ly

help me bear the strain of toil, the fret of care.
feet to stay, and guide them in the home - ward way.
sweet and strong, in trust that tri - umphs o - ver wrong,
thou canst give, with thee, O Mas - ter, let me live.

Words: Washington Gladden (1836-1918)
Music: *Maryton,* Henry Percy Smith (1825-1898)

LM

## The Christian Life

# 661

1 They cast their nets in Gal - i - lee just
2 Con - tent - ed, peace - ful fish - er - men, be -
3 Young John who trimmed the flap - ping sail, home -
4 The peace of God, it is no peace, but

off the hills of brown; such hap - py,
fore they ev - er knew the peace of
less, in Pat - mos died. Pe - ter, who
strife closed in the sod. Yet let us

sim - ple fish - er - folk, be - fore the Lord came down.
God that filled their hearts brim - ful, and broke them too.
hauled the teem - ing net, head - down was cru - ci - fied.
pray for but one thing— the mar - vel ous peace of God.

Words: William Alexander Percy (1885-1942), alt.
Music: *Georgetown,* David McKinley Williams (1887-1978)

CM

1 A - bide with me: fast falls the e - ven - tide;
2 I need thy pres - ence ev - ery pass - ing hour;
3 I fear no foe, with thee at hand to bless;
4 Hold thou thy cross be - fore my clos - ing eyes;

the dark - ness deep - ens; Lord, with me a - bide:
what but thy grace can foil the tempt-er's power?
ills have no weight, and tears no bit - ter - ness.
shine through the gloom, and point me to the skies;

when o - ther help - ers fail and com-forts flee,
Who, like thy - self, my guide and stay can be?
Where is death's sting? where, grave, thy vic - to - ry?
heaven's morn - ing breaks, and earth's vain sha - dows flee;

help of the help - less, O a - bide with me.
Through cloud and sun - shine, Lord, a - bide with me.
I tri - umph still, if thou a - bide with me.
in life, in death, O Lord, a - bide with me.

Words: Henry Francis Lyte (1793-1847)
Music: *Eventide*, William Henry Monk (1823-1889)

10 10. 10 10

# The Christian Life

663

1 The Lord my God my shep - herd is; how
2 To whole - ness he re - stores my soul and
3 Yea, e - ven when I must pass through the
4 Thou hast in grace my ta - ble spread se -
5 Then sure - ly I can trust thy love for

1 could I want or need? In pas - tures green, by
2 doth in mer - cy bless, and helps me take for
3 val - ley of death's shade, I will not fear, for
4 cure in all a - larms, and filled my cup, and
5 all the days to come, that I may tell thy

1 streams se - rene, he safe - ly doth me lead.
2 his Name's sake the paths of right - eous - ness.
3 thou art here, to com - fort and to aid.
4 borne me up in ev - er - last - ing arms.
5 praise, and dwell for ev - er in thy home.

Words: F. Bland Tucker (1895-1984); para. of Psalm 23
Music: *Crimond*, melody Jesse Seymour Irvine (1836-1887); harm. *Hymnal 1982*

CM

1 My Shepherd will supply my need, Jehovah is his Name; in pastures fresh he makes me feed beside the living stream. He brings my wandering spirit back when I forsake his ways, and leads me, for his mercy's sake, in paths of truth and grace.

2 When I walk through the shades of death, thy presence is my stay; one word of thy supporting breath drives all my fears away. Thy hand, in sight of all my foes, doth still my table spread; my cup with blessings overflows, thy oil anoints my head.

3 The sure provisions of my God attend me all my days; oh, may thy house be mine abode and all my work be praise. There would I find a settled rest, while others go and come; no more a stranger or a guest, but like a child at home.

Words: Isaac Watts (1674-1748); para. of Psalm 23
Music: *Resignation*, American folk melody

CMD

1 All my hope on God is found - ed; he doth still my
2 Mor - tal pride and earth - ly glo - ry, sword and crown be -
3 God's great good - ness e'er en - dur - eth, deep his wis - dom
*4 Dai - ly doth the al - might - y Giv - er boun - teous gifts on
5 Still from earth to God e - ter - nal sac - ri - fice of

1 trust re - new, me through change and chance he
2 tray our trust; though with care and toil we
3 pass - ing thought: splen - dor, light, and life at -
4 us be - stow; his de - sire our soul de -
5 praise be done, high a - bove all prais - es

1 guid - eth, on - ly good and on - ly true. God un -
2 build them, tower and tem - ple fall to dust. But God's
3 tend him, beau - ty spring - eth out of nought. Ev - er -
4 light - eth, plea - sure leads us where we go. Love doth
5 prais - ing for the gift of Christ, his son. Christ doth

1 known, he a - lone calls my heart to be his own.
2 power, hour by hour, is my tem - ple and my tower.
3 more from his store new - born worlds rise and a - dore.
4 stand at his hand; joy doth wait on his com - mand.
5 call one and all: ye who fol - low shall not fall.

Words: Robert Seymour Bridges (1844-1930), alt., after Joachim Neander (1650-1680)
Music: *Michael*, Herbert Howells (1892-1983)

87. 87. 337

1 Out      of  the  depths  I       call,    to    God  I  send  my        cry;    Lord,
2 My       soul  with  pa - tience   waits    for   thee, the  liv - ing    Lord,   my
3 My       long-ing  eyes  look      out      for   thy  en - liv - ening   ray,    more
4 Let      Is - rael  trust  in      God;     no    bounds his mer - cy     knows;  the

hear  my  sup - pli - cat - ing  voice  and  gra - cious - ly  re - ply.
hopes  are  on   thy  prom - ise  built,  thy  nev - er - fail - ing  word.
du - ly  than  the  morn - ing  watch  to  spy   the  dawn - ing  day.
plen - teous source and  spring from whence re - demp-tion  ev - er  flows.

Words: *A Supplement to the New Version of the Psalms of David*, 1698, alt.; para. of Psalm 130
Music: *St. Bride*, Samuel Howard (1710-1782)                                    SM

1 Some - times  a   light sur - pris - es  the  Chris-tian while he   sings;
2 In       ho - ly  con-tem - pla - tion  we  sweet - ly then pur - sue
3 It        can bring with it  noth - ing but  he   will bear us   through:
4 Though  vine nor fig tree  nei - ther their  wont - ed fruit should bear,

it       is   the Lord who  ris - es  with  heal - ing  in   his   wings:
the      theme of God's sal - va - tion, and  find  it  ev - er  new;
who      gives the lil - ies  cloth - ing will  clothe his peo - ple,  too:
though   all   the fields should  with - er, nor  flocks nor herds be  there;

when  com-forts are   de -  clin - ing, he   grants the soul  a -   gain
set    free from pres-ent   sor -  row, we  cheer-ful-ly can   say,
be - neath the spread-ing   hea -  vens no   crea-ture but is   fed;
yet,   God the same  a -  bid - ing, his   praise shall tune my   voice;

a   sea-son of   clear   shin - ing, to   cheer it af - ter   rain.
let   the un-known to -  mor - row bring  with it what it   may.
and  he who feeds the   rav - ens will  give his chil-dren  bread.
for,  while in him  con -  fid - ing, I   can-not but  re - joice.

Words: William Cowper (1731-1800)
Music: *Light*, melody from *The Christian Lyre*, 1830

76. 76. D

## The Christian Life

# 668

1 I   to the  hills  will   lift  mine eyes; from whence shall come  my   aid?
2 He  will not  let   thy   foot be moved, his  own  he   safe - ly   keeps;
3 Thy faith-ful  guard-ian  is   the Lord, thy  shelt - er   and   thy shade;
4 From e - vil  he  shall   keep thee safe and  shall thy strength re - store

My  help is  from the   Lord a - bove who heaven and   earth hath made.
with watch-ful and un -  tir - ing eye  he  slum - bers   not,  nor sleeps.
nor  sun by  day, nor   moon by night, need make thy   soul a - fraid.
and  guard thy  go - ing   out and in, both  now  and   ev - er - more.

Words: *The Psalms of David in Meeter*, 1650, alt.; st. 4, F. Bland Tucker (1895-1984); para. of Psalm 121
Music: *Burford*, from *A Book of Psalmody*, 1718

CM

1 Com - mit thou all that grieves thee and fills thy heart with
2 O trust the Lord then whol - ly, if thou wouldst be se -
3 Thy last - ing truth and mer - cy, O Fa - ther, see a -
4 Hope on, then, bro - ken spi - rit; hope on, be not a -

care to him whose faith - ful mer - cy the
cure; his work must thou con - sid - er for
right the needs of all thy chil - dren, their
fraid: fear not the griefs that plague thee and

skies a - bove de - clare, who gives the winds their
thy work to en - dure. What prof - it doth it
an - guish or de - light: what lov - ing wis - dom
keep thy heart dis - mayed: thy God, in his great

cours - es, who points the clouds their way; 'tis
bring thee to pine in grief and care? God
choos - eth, re - deem - ing might will do, and
mer - cy, will save thee, hold thee fast, and

he will guide thy foot - steps and be thy staff and stay.
ev - er sends his bless - ing in an - swer to thy prayer.
bring to sure ful - fill - ment thy coun - sel good and true.
in his own time grant thee the sun of joy at last.

Words: Paul Gerhardt (1607-1676); tr. Arthur William Farlander (1898-1952)
and Charles Winfred Douglas (1867-1944), alt.
Music: *Herzlich tut mich verlangen [Passion Chorale]*, Hans Leo Hassler (1564-1612);
adapt. and harm. Johann Sebastian Bach (1685-1750)

76. 76. D

## The Christian Life

# 670

*Unison or harmony*

1 Lord, for ev - er at thy side let my place and por - tion be,
2 When I come be - fore thy Word, qui - et my anx - i - e - ty;
3 What thy Spi - rit doth re - veal, that may I in faith re - ceive;
4 Is - rael, now and ev - er-more in the Lord Al - might - y trust;

strip me of the robe of pride, clothe me with hu - mil - i - ty.
teach me thou a - lone art Lord, let my heart find rest in thee.
though my doubts I sore - ly feel, thy sure prom-ise I be - lieve.
him, in all his ways, a - dore, wise, and won - der - ful, and just.

Words: Sts. 1 and 4, James Montgomery (1771-1854), alt.; sts. 2-3, Charles P. Price (b. 1920)
Music: *Song 13*, melody and bass Orlando Gibbons (1583-1625); harm. *Songs of Praise*, 1931, alt.

77. 77

1  A - maz - ing  grace!  how  sweet  the  sound,  that
2  'Twas  grace  that  taught  my  heart  to  fear,  and
3  The  Lord  has  prom - ised  good  to  me,  his
4  Through  man - y  dan - gers,  toils,  and  snares,  I
*5 When  we've  been  there  ten  thou - sand  years,  bright

1  saved  a  wretch  like  me!  I  once  was  lost  but
2  grace  my  fears  re - lieved;  how  pre - cious  did  that
3  word  my  hope  se - cures;  he  will  my  shield  and
4  have  al - rea - dy  come;  'tis  grace  that  brought  me
5  shin - ing  as  the  sun,  we've  no  less  days  to

1  now  am  found,  was  blind  but  now  I  see.
2  grace  ap - pear  the  hour  I  first  be - lieved!
3  por - tion  be  as  long  as  life  en - dures.
4  safe  thus  far,  and  grace  will  lead  me  home.
5  sing  God's  praise  than  when  we'd  first  be - gun.

*The melody may be sung in canon at distances of either two or three beats.*

Words: John Newton (1725-1807), alt.; st. 5, John Rees (19th cent.)
Music: *New Britain*, from *Virginia Harmony*, 1831; adapt. att. Edwin Othello Excell (1851-1921);
    harm. Austin Cole Lovelace (b. 1919)

CM

# The Christian Life

672

1 O ve - ry God of ve - ry God, and
2 Our hopes are weak, our fears are strong, thick
3 And e - ven now, though dull and gray, the
4 O guide us till our path is done, and
5 We wait in faith, and turn our face to

1 ve - ry Light of Light, whose feet this earth's dark
2 dark - ness blinds our eyes; cold is the night; thy
3 east is bright - ening fast, and kin - dling to the
4 we have reached the shore where thou, our ev - er -
5 where the day - light springs, till thou shalt come our

1 val - ley trod that so it might be bright:
2 peo - ple long that thou, their Sun, wouldst rise.
3 per - fect day that nev - er shall be past.
4 last - ing Sun, art shin - ing ev - er - more!
5 gloom to chase, with heal - ing in thy wings.

Words: John Mason Neale (1818-1866)
Music: *Bangor*, from *A Compleat Melody or Harmony of Zion*, 1734

CM

# 673

The Christian Life

1 The first one ev - er, oh, ev - er to know of the
2 The first one ev - er, oh, ev - er to know of Me -
3 The first ones ev - er, oh, ev - er to know of the

birth ___ of Je - sus, was the Maid ___ Ma - ry, was ___
si - ah, Je - sus, when he said, "I am he," was the Sa -
ris - ing of Je - sus, his ___ glo - ry to be, were ___

Ma - ry the Maid ___ of Gal - i - lee, and
mar - i - tan wo - man who drew from the well, and
Ma - ry, Jo - an - na, and Mag - da - lene, and

bless - ed is she, is she who be - lieves. Oh,
bless - ed is she, is she who per - ceives. Oh,
bless - ed are they are they ___ who see. Oh,

bless - ed is she who be - lieves in the Lord, oh,
bless - ed is she who per - ceives ___ the Lord, oh,
bless - ed are they ___ who see ___ the Lord, oh,

bless - ed is she who be - lieves. ___ She was ___
bless - ed is she who per - ceives. ___ 'Twas the Sa -
bless - ed are they ___ who see. ___ They were ___

Ma - ry the Maid___ of Gal - i - lee, and
mar - i - tan wo - man who drew from the well, and
Ma - ry, Jo - an - na, and Mag - da - lene, and

bless - ed is she, is she who be - lieves.
bless - ed is she, is she who per - ceives.
bless - ed are they, are they ___ who see.

Words: Linda Wilberger Egan (b. 1946), alt.
Music: *Ballad*, Linda Wilberger Egan (b. 1946)

Irr.

## The Christian Life

# 674

1 "For - give our sins as we for - give" you
2 How can your par - don reach and bless the
3 In blaz - ing light your cross re - veals the
4 Lord, cleanse the depths with - in our souls, and

taught us, Lord, to pray; but you a - lone can
un - for - giv - ing heart that broods on wrongs and
truth we dim - ly knew, how small the debts men
bid re - sent - ment cease; then, rec - on - ciled to

grant us grace to live the words we say.
will not let old bit - ter - ness de - part?
owe to us, how great our debt to you.
God and man, our lives will spread your peace.

Words: Rosamond E. Herklots (b. 1905)
Music: *Detroit*, from *Supplement to Kentucky Harmony*, 1820

CM

1 Take up your cross, the Sa - vior said, if
2 Take up your cross, let not its weight fill
3 Take up your cross, heed not the shame, and
4 Take up your cross, then, in his strength, and
5 Take up your cross, and fol - low Christ, nor

1 you would my dis - ci - ple be; take up your cross with
2 your weak spi - rit with a - larm; his strength shall bear your
3 let your fool - ish heart be still; the Lord for you ac -
4 calm - ly ev - ery dan - ger brave: it guides you to a -
5 think till death to lay it down; for on - ly those who

1 will - ing heart, and hum - bly fol - low af - ter me.
2 spi - rit up, and brace your heart, and nerve your arm.
3 cept - ed death up - on a cross, on Cal - vary's hill.
4 bun - dant life and leads to vic - tory o'er the grave.
5 bear the cross may hope to wear the glo - rious crown.

Words: Charles William Everest (1814-1877), alt.
Music: *Bourbon*, melody att. Freeman Lewis (1780-1859)                    LM

*Refrain*

There is a balm in Gil - e - ad, to make the wound - ed

whole, there is a balm in Gil - e - ad, to

heal the sin - sick soul.                          soul.

1 Some - times I feel dis - cour - aged, and __
2 If you can - not preach like Pe - ter, if you

think my work's in vain, but __ then the Ho - ly
can - not pray like Paul, you can tell the love of

*Repeat Refrain*

Spi - rit re - vives my soul a - gain.
Je - sus, and say, "He died for all."

Words: Afro-American spiritual
Music: *Balm in Gilead*, Afro-American spiritual

Irr. with Refrain

## The Christian Life

677

*Unison or harmony*

1 God moves in a mys - te - rious way    his won - ders to per - form:
2 Deep in un - fath - om - a - ble mines,    with nev - er - fail - ing skill,
3 Ye fear - ful saints, fresh cour - age take;    the clouds ye so much dread
4 Judge not the Lord by fee - ble sense,    but trust him for his grace;
5 His pur - pos - es will ri - pen fast,    un - fold - ing ev - ery hour:

1 he plants his foot - steps in the sea,    and rides up - on the storm.
2 he trea - sures up his bright de - signs,    and works his sov - ereign will.
3 are big with mer - cy, and shall break    in bless - ings on your head.
4 be - hind a frown - ing prov - i - dence    he hides a smil - ing face.
5 the bud may have a bit - ter taste,    but sweet will be the flower.

6 Blind unbelief is sure to err,    God is his own interpreter,
   and scan his work in vain;    and he will make it plain.

Words: William Cowper (1731-1800)
Music: *London New*, melody from *The Psalmes of David in Prose and Meeter*, 1635, alt.;
    harm. John Playford (1623-1686)

CM

1 Sure - ly    it    is    God_____    who    saves    me;
2 Make    his    deeds____    known    to    the    peo - ples;

trust - ing    him,    I    shall    not    fear.    For    the    Lord    de - fends    and
tell    out    his    ex - alt - ed    Name.    Praise    the    Lord,    who    has    done

shields    me    and    his    sav - ing    help    is    near.    So    re - joice    as
great    things;    all    his    works    his    might    pro - claim.    Zi - on,    lift    your

you    draw    wa - ter    from    sal - va - tion's    liv - ing    spring;    in    the
voice    in    sing - ing;    for    with    you    has    come    to    dwell,    in    your

day    of    your    de - liv - erance    thank    the    Lord,    his    mer - cies    sing.
ve - ry    midst,    the    great    and    Ho - ly    One    of    Is - ra - el.

Words: Carl P. Daw, Jr. (b. 1944); para. of *The First Song of Isaiah*
Music: *College of Preachers*, Arthur Rhea (b. 1919)

87. 87. D

1 Sure - ly    it    is    God__    who    saves    me;    trust - ing    him,    I    shall    not
2 Make    his    deeds__    known    to    the    peo - ples;    tell    out    his    ex - alt - ed

fear.    For    the    Lord    de - fends    and    shields    me    and    his    sav - ing
Name.    Praise    the    Lord,    who    has    done    great    things;    all    his    works    his

help is near. So re - joice as you draw wa - ter from sal -
might pro - claim. Zi - on, lift your voice in sing - ing; for with

va - tion's liv - ing spring; in the day of your de -
you has come to dwell, in your ve - ry midst, the

liv - erance thank the Lord, his mer - cies sing.
great and Ho - ly One of Is - ra - el.

Words: Carl P. Daw, Jr. (b. 1944); para. of *The First Song of Isaiah*
Music: *Thomas Merton*, Ray W. Urwin (b. 1950)

87. 87. D

## The Christian Life

### 680

1  O    God, our help in    a - ges past,    our  hope for years to   come,
2  un - der the sha - dow    of  thy throne thy   saints have dwelt se - cure;
3  Be - fore the hills in    or - der stood, or   earth re - ceived her   frame,
4  A    thou - sand a - ges   in  thy sight are   like  an  eve - ning  gone;
5  Time, like an ev - er - roll - ing stream, bears  all  our years a - way;

1  our  shel - ter from the   storm - y   blast, and   our e - ter - nal   home:
2  suf - fi - cient is thine   arm  a - lone, and   our de - fense is   sure.
3  from ev - er - last - ing   thou art   God, to   end - less years the   same.
4  short as  the watch that   ends the   night be - fore the ris - ing   sun.
5  they  fly, for - got - ten,  as  a   dream dies   at  the  o - pen - ing  day.

6  O God, our help in ages past,        be thou our guide while life shall last,
   our hope for years to come,          and our eternal home.

Words: Isaac Watts (1674-1748), alt.; para. of Psalm 90:1-5
Music: *St. Anne*, melody att. William Croft (1678-1727), alt.; harm. William Henry Monk (1823-1889)

CM

Unison or harmony

1 Our God, to whom we turn when wea-ry with il-lu-sion,
*2 Thou art thy-self the truth; though we who seek to find thee
*3 All beau-ty speaks of thee: the moun-tains and the riv-ers,
*4 Where good-ness comes to light we glimpse thy plan un-fold-ing;
5 Thou hid-den fount of love, of peace, and truth, and beau-ty,

1 whose stars se-rene-ly burn a-bove this earth's con-fu-sion,
2 have tried, with thoughts un-couth, in fee-ble words to bind thee,
3 the line of lift-ed sea, where spread-ing moon-light quiv-ers,
4 where jus-tice wins its fight thou art the King-dom mold-ing;
5 in-spire us from a-bove with joy and strength for du-ty.

1 thine is the might-y plan, the stead-fast or-der sure
2 it is be-cause thou art we're driv-en to the quest;
3 the hymns thy peo-ple raise, the psalms and an-thems strong,
4 the blood of friend as sign of love for com-rade spilt,
5 May thy fresh light a-rise with-in each cloud-ed heart,

1 in which the world be - gan, en - dures, and shall en - dure.
2 till truth from false-hood part, our hearts can find no rest.
3 hint at the glo - rious praise of thy e - ter - nal song.
4 re - flects the vast de - sign by which thy house is built.
5 and give us o - pen eyes to see thee as thou art.

Words: Edward Grubb (1854-1939), alt.
Music: *O Gott, du frommer Gott*, melody from *Neu ordentlich Gesangbuch*, 1646;
harm. Johann Sebastian Bach (1685-1750), alt.

67. 67. 66. 66

## The Christian Life

682

1 I love thee, Lord, but not be - cause I hope for heaven there - by,
2 but for that thou didst all the world up - on the cross em - brace;
3 and griefs and tor - ments num-ber - less, and sweat of a - gon - y;
4 Then why, most lov - ing Je - sus Christ, should I not love thee well,
5 not with the hope of gain-ing aught, not seek-ing a re - ward;

1 nor yet for fear that lov - ing not I might for ev - er die;
2 for us didst bear the nails and spear, and man - i - fold dis - grace,
3 e'en death it - self; and all for one who was thine en - e - my.
4 not for the sake of win-ning heaven, nor an - y fear of hell;
5 but as thy - self hast lov - ed me, O ev - er lov-ing Lord!

6 E'en so I love thee, and will love,
   and in thy praise will sing,
   solely because thou art my God
   and my eternal King.

Words: Spanish, 17th cent.; tr. Edward Caswall (1814-1878); adapt. Percy Dearmer (1867-1936), alt.
Music: *St. Fulbert*, Henry John Gauntlett (1805-1876)

CM

1 O for a clos-er walk with God, a calm and heaven-ly frame,
2 Where is the bless-ed-ness I knew when first I saw the Lord?
3 Re - turn, O ho - ly Dove, re - turn, sweet mes-sen - ger of rest;
4 The dear-est i - dol I have known, what-e'er that i - dol be,
5 So shall my walk be close with God, calm and se - rene my frame;

1 a light to shine up - on the road that leads me to the Lamb!
2 Where is the soul - re - fresh-ing view of Je - sus and his word?
3 I hate the sins that made thee mourn, and drove thee from my breast.
4 help me to tear it from thy throne, and wor - ship on - ly thee.
5 so pur - er light shall mark the road that leads me to the Lamb.

Words: William Cowper (1731-1800), alt.
Music: *Beatitudo*, John Bacchus Dykes (1823-1876)

CM

1 O for a clos-er walk with God, a calm and heaven-ly frame,
2 Where is the bless-ed-ness I knew when first I saw the Lord?
3 Re - turn, O ho - ly Dove, re - turn, sweet mes-sen - ger of rest;
4 The dear-est i - dol I have known, what - e'er that i - dol be,
5 So shall my walk be close with God, calm and se - rene my frame;

1 a light to shine up-on the road that leads me to the Lamb!
2 Where is the soul - re - fresh -ing view of Je - sus and his word?
3 I hate the sins that made thee mourn, and drove thee from my breast.
4 help me to tear it from thy throne, and wor - ship on - ly thee.
5 so pur - er light shall mark the road that leads me to the lamb.

Words: William Cowper (1731-1800), alt.
Music: *Caithness*, from *The Psalmes of David in Prose and Meeter*, 1635; harm. *The English Hymnal*, 1906    CM

## The Christian Life                                                 685

1 Rock of a - ges, cleft for me, let me hide my-self in thee;
2 Should my tears for ev - er flow, should my zeal no lan - guor know,
3 While I draw this fleet-ing breath, when mine eye - lids close in death,

let the wa - ter and the blood from thy wound - ed side that flowed,
all for sin could not a - tone: thou must save, and thou a - lone;
when I rise to worlds un - known and be - hold thee on thy throne,

be of sin the dou - ble cure, cleanse me from its guilt and power.
in my hand no price I bring, sim - ply to thy cross I cling.
Rock of a - ges, cleft for me, let me hide my-self in thee.

Words: Augustus Montague Toplady (1740-1778), alt.
Music: *Toplady*, Thomas Hastings (1784-1872)

77. 77. 77

1 Come, thou fount of ev - ery bless - ing, tune my
2 Here I find my great - est trea - sure; hith - er,
3 Oh, to grace how great a debt - or dai - ly

heart to sing thy grace! Streams of mer - cy nev - er
by thy help, I've come; and I hope, by thy good
I'm con - strained to be! Let thy good - ness, like a

ceas - ing, call for songs of loud - est praise.
plea - sure, safe - ly to ar - rive at home.
fet - ter, bind my wan - dering heart to thee:

Teach me some me - lo - dious son - net, sung by
Je - sus sought me when a stran - ger wan - dering
prone to wan - der, Lord, I feel it, prone to

flam - ing tongues a - bove. Praise the mount! Oh, fix me
from the fold of God; he, to res - cue me from
leave the God I love; here's my heart, oh, take and

on it, mount of God's un - chang - ing love.
dan - ger, in - ter - posed his pre - cious blood.
seal it, seal it for thy courts a - bove.

Words: Robert Robinson (1735-1790), alt.
Music: *Nettleton*, melody from *A Repository of Sacred Music, Part II*, 1813

87. 87. D

# The Christian Life

1 A might-y for-tress is our God, a bul-wark
2 Did we in our own strength con-fide, our striv-ing
3 And though this world, with dev - ils filled, should threat-en
4 That word a - bove all earth - ly powers, no thanks to

nev - er fail - ing; our help-er he a - mid the flood
would be los - ing; were not the right man on our side,
to un - do us; we will not fear, for God hath willed
them, a - bid - eth; the Spi - rit and the gifts are ours

of mor-tal ills pre - vail - ing: for still our an - cient foe
the man of God's own choos - ing: dost ask who that may be?
his truth to tri - umph through us; the prince of dark-ness grim,
through him who with us sid - eth: let goods and kin - dred go,

doth seek to work us woe; his craft and power are great,
Christ Je - sus, it is he; Lord Sa - ba - oth his Name,
we trem - ble not for him; his rage we can en - dure,
this mor - tal life al - so; the bo - dy they may kill:

and, armed with cru - el hate, on earth is not his e - qual.
from age to age the same, and he must win the bat - tle.
for lo! his doom is sure, one lit - tle word shall fell him.
God's truth a - bid - eth still, his king-dom is for ev - er.

Words: Martin Luther (1483-1546); tr. Frederic Henry Hedge (1805-1890); based on Psalm 46
Music: *Ein feste Burg*, Martin Luther (1483-1546)

87. 87. 66. 66. 7

and, armed with cru-el hate, on earth is not his e-qual.
from age to age the same, and he must win the bat-tle.
for lo! his doom is sure, one lit-tle word shall fell him.
God's truth a-bid-eth still, his king-dom is for ev-er.

Words: Martin Luther (1483-1546); tr. Frederick Henry Hedge (1805-1890); based on Psalm 46
Music: *Ein feste Burg,* melody Martin Luther (1483-1546);
  harm. Johann Sebastian Bach (1685-1750)

87. 87. 66. 66. 7

## The Christian Life

**689**

1 I sought the Lord, and af-ter-ward I knew he
2 Thou didst reach forth thy hand and mine en-fold; I
3 I find, I walk, I love, but oh, the whole of

moved my soul to seek him, seek-ing me; it was not
walked and sank not on the storm-vexed sea; 'twas not so
love is but my an-swer, Lord, to thee; for thou wert

I that found, O Sa-vior true; no, I was found of thee.
much that I on thee took hold, as thou, dear Lord, on me.
long be-fore-hand with my soul, al-ways thou lov-edst me.

Words: Anon., *Pilgrim Hymnal,* 1904
Music: *Faith,* J. Harold Moyer (b. 1927)

10. 10. 10. 6

1 Guide me, O thou great Je - ho - vah, pil - grim through this
2 O - pen now the crys - tal foun - tain, whence the heal - ing
3 When I tread the verge of Jor - dan, bid my anx - ious

bar - ren land; I am weak, but thou art might - y;
stream doth flow; let the fire and cloud - y pil - lar
fears sub - side; death of death, and hell's de - struc - tion,

hold me with thy power - ful hand; bread of hea - ven,
lead me all my jour - ney through; strong de - liv - erer,
land me safe on Ca - naan's side; songs of prais - es,

bread of hea - ven, feed me now and ev - er -
strong de - liv - erer, be thou still my strength and
songs of prais - es, I will ev - er give to

more, feed me now and ev - er - more.
shield, be thou still my strength and shield.
thee, I will ev - er give to thee.

Words: William Williams (1717-1791); tr. Peter Williams (1722-1796), alt.
Music: *Cwm Rhondda*, John Hughes (1873-1932)

87. 87. 877

## The Christian Life

## 691

1 My faith looks up to thee, thou Lamb of Cal - va - ry,
2 May thy rich grace im-part strength to my faint - ing heart,
3 While life's dark maze I tread, and griefs a - round me spread,

Sa - vior di - vine! Now hear me while I pray, take all my
my zeal in - spire; as thou hast died for me, O may my
be thou my guide; bid dark-ness turn to day; wipe sor-row's

guilt a - way; O let me from this day be whol - ly thine.
love to thee pure, warm, and change-less be, a liv - ing fire.
tears a - way, nor let me ev - er stray from thee a - side.

Words: Ray Palmer (1808-1887)
Music: *Olivet*, Lowell Mason (1792-1872)

664. 6664

1 I heard the voice of Je-sus say, "Come un - to me and rest;
2 I heard the voice of Je-sus say, "Be - hold, I free - ly give
3 I heard the voice of Je-sus say, "I am this dark world's light;

and in your wea - ri - ness lay down your head up - on my breast."
the liv-ing wa - ter; thirst - y one, stoop down and drink, and live."
look un - to me, your morn shall rise, and all your day be bright."

I came to Je - sus as I was, so wea - ry, worn, and sad;
I came to Je - sus, and I drank of that life - giv - ing stream;
I looked to Je - sus, and I found in him my Star, my Sun;

I found in him a rest - ing place, and he has made me glad.
my thirst was quenched, my soul re - vived, and now I live in him.
and in that light of life I'll walk till pil-grim days are done.

*The bracketed notes are to be treated as triplet groups.

Words: Horatius Bonar (1808-1889), alt.
Music: *The Third Tune,* Thomas Tallis (1505?-1585); ed. John Wilson (b. 1905)      CMD

1 Just as I am, without one plea, but that thy
2 Just as I am, though tossed about with man - y a
*3 Just as I am, poor, wretch - ed, blind; sight, rich - es,
4 Just as I am: thou wilt re - ceive; wilt wel - come,
5 Just as I am, thy love un - known has bro - ken

1 blood was shed for me, and that thou bidd'st me
2 con - flict, man - y a doubt; fight - ings and fears with -
3 heal - ing of the mind, yea, all I need, in
4 par - don, cleanse, re - lieve, be - cause thy prom - ise
5 ev - ery bar - rier down; now to be thine, yea,

1 come to thee, O Lamb of God, I come, I come.
2 in, with - out, O Lamb of God, I come, I come.
3 thee to find, O Lamb of God, I come, I come.
4 I be - lieve, O Lamb of God, I come, I come.
5 thine a - lone, O Lamb of God, I come, I come.

6 Just as I am, of thy great love
   the breadth, length, depth, and height to prove,
   here for a season, then above:
   O Lamb of God, I come, I come.

Words: Charlotte Elliott (1789-1871)
Music: *Woodworth*, William Batchelder Bradbury (1816-1868)

LM

# The Christian Life

God be in my head, and in my un-der-stand-ing;

God be in mine eyes, and in my look-ing;

God be in my mouth, and in my speak-ing;

God be in my heart, and in my think-ing;

God be at mine end, and at my de-part-ing.

Words: *Sarum Primer*, 1514
Music: *Lytlington*, Sydney Hugo Nicholson (1875-1947)

Irr.

# The Christian Life

695

1 By gra-cious powers so won-der-ful-ly shel - tered,
and con-fi - dent - ly wait-ing come what may,
we know that God is with us night and morn - ing,
and nev - er fails to greet us each new day.

2 Yet is this heart by its old foe tor-ment - ed,
still e - vil days bring bur-dens hard to bear;
O give our fright-ened souls the sure sal - va - tion,
for which, O Lord, you taught us to pre - pare.

3 And when this cup you give is filled to brim - ming
with bit-ter suf - fering, hard to un - der - stand,
we take it thank-ful - ly and with-out trem - bling,
out of so good and so be - loved a hand.

4 Yet when a - gain in this same world you give us
the joy we had, the bright-ness of your Sun,
we shall re - mem - ber all the days we lived through,
and our whole life shall then be yours a - lone.

Words: F. Pratt Green (b. 1903), after Dietrich Bonhoeffer (1906-1945)
Music: *Intercessor*, Charles Hubert Hastings Parry (1848-1918)

11 10. 11 10

1 By gra - cious powers so won - der - ful - ly
2 Yet is this heart by its old foe tor -
3 And when this cup you give is filled to
4 Yet when a - gain in this same world you

shel - tered, and con - - - fi - dent - ly wait - ing come what
ment - ed, still e - - - vil days bring bur - dens hard to
brim - ming with bit - - - ter suf - fering, hard to un - der -
give us the joy___ we had, the bright-ness of your

may, we know that God is with us night and
bear; O give our fright - ened souls the sure sal -
stand, we take it thank - ful - ly and with - out
Sun, we shall re - mem - ber all the days we

morn - ing, and nev - er fails to greet us each new day.
va - tion, for which,___ O Lord, you taught us to pre - pare.
trem - bling, out of___ so good and so be - loved a hand.
lived through, and our___ whole life shall then be yours a - lone.

Words: F. Pratt Green (b. 1903), after Dietrich Bonhoeffer (1906-1945)
Music: *Le Cénacle*, Joseph Gelineau (b. 1920)

11 10. 11 10

1 My God, ac - cept my heart this day, and make it al - ways thine,
2 Be - fore the cross of him who died, be - hold, I pros-trate fall;
3 A - noint me with thy heaven-ly grace, and seal me for thine own,
4 Let ev - ery thought and work and word, to thee be ev - er given;

that I from thee no more may stray, no more from thee de - cline.
let ev - ery sin be cru - ci - fied, and Christ be all in all.
that I may see thy glo - rious face, and wor - ship near thy throne.
then life shall be thy ser - vice, Lord, and death the gate of heaven.

Words: Matthew Bridges (1800-1894), alt.
Music: *Song 67*, from *Llyfr y Psalmau*, 1621; adapt. Orlando Gibbons (1583-1625), alt.;
    harm. Mary Monica Waterhouse Bridges (1863-1949); alt. Charles Winfred Douglas (1867-1944)
    CM

## The Christian Life

# 698

1 E - ter - nal Spi - rit of the liv - ing Christ,
2 Come, pray in me the prayer I need this day;
3 Come with the vi - sion and the strength I need

I know not how to ask or what to say;
help me to see your pur - pose and your will—
to serve my God, and all hu - man - i - ty;

I on - ly know my need, as deep as life,
where I have failed, what I have done a - miss;
ful - fill - ment of my life in love out - poured—

and on - ly you can teach me how to pray.
held in for - giv - ing love, let me be still.
my life in you, O Christ, your love in me.

Words: Frank von Christierson (b. 1900), rev.
Music: *Flentge*, Carl Flentge Schalk (b. 1929)

10 10. 10 10

1 Je - sus, Lov - er of my soul, let me to thy bos - om
2 O - ther ref - uge have I none, hangs my help - less soul on
3 Plen - teous grace with thee is found, grace to cleanse from ev - ery

fly, while the near - er wa - ters roll, while the tem - pest
thee; leave, ah! leave me not a - lone, still sup - port and
sin; let the heal - ing streams a - bound, make and keep me

still is high: hide me, O my Sa - vior, hide,
com - fort me! All my trust on thee is stayed;
pure with - in. Thou of life the foun - tain art,

till the storm of life be past; safe in - to the
all my help from thee I bring; cov - er my de -
free - ly let me take of thee: spring thou up with -

ha - ven guide, O re - ceive my soul at last.
fense-less head, with the sha - dow of thy wing.
in my heart, rise to all e - ter - ni - ty.

Words: Charles Wesley (1707-1788), alt.
Music: *Aberystwyth*, Joseph Parry (1841-1903)

77. 77. D

## The Christian Life

### 700

1 O love that casts out fear, O love that casts out sin,
2 True sun - light of the soul, sur - round us as we go;
3 Great love of God, come in! Well - spring of heaven - ly peace;
4 Love of the liv - ing God, of Fa - ther and of Son;

tar - ry no more with - out, but come and dwell with - in.
so shall our way be safe, our feet no stray - ing know.
thou Liv - ing Wa - ter, come! Spring up, and nev - er cease.
love of the Ho - ly Ghost, fill thou each need - y one.

Words: Horatius Bonar (1808-1889)
Music: *Moseley*, Henry Thomas Smart (1813-1879)

66. 66

1 Je - sus, all my glad - ness, my re - pose in sad - ness,
2 Hence with earth - ly trea - sure: thou art all my plea - sure,
3 Flee, dark clouds that low - er, for my joy be - stow - er,

Je-sus, heaven to me; ah, my heart long pain - eth, ah, my spi - rit
Je-sus, my de - sire! Hence, for pomps I care not, e'en as though they
Je-sus, en - ters in! Joy from tri - bu - la - tion, hope from des - o -

strain-eth, long-eth af - ter thee! Thine I am, O ho - ly Lamb;
were not rank and for-tune's hire. Want and gloom, cross, death and tomb;
la - tion, they who love God win. Be it blame or scorn or shame,

on - ly where thou art is plea - sure, thee a - lone I trea - sure.
nought that I may suf - fer ev - er shall from Je - sus sev - er.
thou art with me in earth's sad - ness, Je - sus, all my glad - ness.

Words: Johann Franck (1618-1677); tr. Arthur Wellesley Wotherspoon (1853-1936), alt.
Music: *Jesu, meine Freude*, Johann Cruger (1598-1662), alt.

665. 665. 786

# The Christian Life

*Unison or harmony*

```
1 Lord,      thou hast searched me   and    dost   know   wher -
2 My         words from thee  I      can - not     hide;  I
3 Where      can  I   go   a - part   from   thee,  or
4 If         I    the wings of   morn - ing   take,  and
5 If         deep - est dark - ness  cov - er    me,    the
```

```
1 e'er  I   rest, wher - e'er   I       go;  thou   know - est all
2 feel  thy power on   ev - ery       side; oh,    won - drous know -
3 whith - er from they  pres - ence   flee? In     heaven?  It    is
4 far   a - way my    dwell - ing     make, the    hand  that  lead -
5 dark - ness hid - eth not     from   thee;  to     thee both night
```

```
1 that  I  have planned, and   all   my  ways  are  in    thy    hand.
2 ledge, aw - ful  might, un - fath - omed depth, un - mea - sured  height!
3 thy dwell-ing  fair;  in   death's a - bode? Lo, thou   art    there.
4 eth  me  is   thine, and   my  sup - port thy power  di -   vine.
5 and  day  are  bright, the   dark - ness shin - eth  as    the    light.
```

Words: *The Psalter Hymnal,* 1927; para. of Psalm 139:1-11
Music: *Tender Thought,* from *Kentucky Harmony,* 1816

LM

# 703

*Unison or harmony*

1 Lead us, O Fa - ther, in the paths of peace;
2 Lead us, O Fa - ther, in the paths of right;
3 Lead us, O Fa - ther, to thy heaven - ly rest,

With - out thy guid - ing hand we go a - stray,
blind - ly we stum - ble when we walk a - lone,
how - ev - er rough and steep the path may be;

and doubts ap - pall, and sor - rows still in - crease;
in - volved in sha - dows of a dark - some night;
through joy or sor - row, as thou deem - est best,

lead us through Christ, the true and liv - ing Way.
on - ly with thee we jour - ney safe - ly on.
un - til our lives are per - fect - ed in thee.

Words: William Henry Burleigh (1812-1871), alt.
Music: *Song 22*, melody and bass Orlando Gibbons (1583-1625)

10 10. 10 10

# The Christian Life

1 O thou who cam - est from a - bove the fire ce -
2 There let it for thy glo - ry burn with ev - er
3 Je - sus, con - firm my heart's de - sire to work, and
*4 Still let me prove thy per - fect will, my acts of

les - tial to im - part, kin - dle a flame of
bright, un - dy - ing blaze, and trem - bling to its
speak, and think for thee; still let me guard the
faith and love re - peat, till death thy end - less

sa - cred love up - on the al - tar of my heart.
source re - turn in hum - ble prayer and fer - vent praise.
ho - ly fire and still stir up the gift in me.
mer - cies seal, and make the sac - ri - fice com - plete.

Words: Charles Wesley (1707-1788), alt.
Music: *Hereford*, Samuel Sebastian Wesley (1810-1876)

LM

*Unison or harmony*

1 As those of old their first fruits brought of vine-yard, flock, and
*2 A world in need now sum-mons us to la-bor, love, and
3 With grat-i-tude and hum-ble trust we bring our best to

field to God, the giv-er of all good, the
give; to make our life an of-fer-ing to
thee to serve thy cause and share thy love with

source of boun-teous yield; so we to-day our
God that all may live; the Church of Christ is
all hu-man-i-ty. O thou who gav-est

first fruits bring, the wealth of this good land, of
call-ing us to make the dream come true: a
us thy-self in Je-sus Christ thy Son, help

farm and mar - ket, shop and home, of mind, and heart, and hand.
world re-deemed by Christ-like love; all life in Christ made new.
us to give our - selves each day un - til life's work is done.

Words: Frank von Christierson (b. 1900), alt.
Music: *Forest Green*, English melody; adapt. and harm. Ralph Vaughan Williams (1872-1958)

CMD

## The Christian Life

### 706

1 In your mer - cy, Lord, you called me, taught my
2 Lord, I did not free - ly choose you till by
3 Now my heart sets none a - bove you, for your

sin - filled heart and mind, else this world had
grace you set me free; else for my heart would
grace a - lone I thirst, know - ing well, that

still en - thralled me, and to glo - ry kept me blind.
still re - fuse you had your love not cho - sen me.
if I love you, you, O Lord, have loved me first.

Words: Josiah Conder (1789-1855); alt. Charles P. Price (b. 1920)
Music: *Halton Holgate*, William Boyce (1711-1779)

87. 87

707

Words: Frances Ridley Havergal (1836-1879), alt.
Music: *Hollingside*, John Bacchus Dykes (1823-1876)

77. 77. D

# The Christian Life

**708**

1 Sa - vior, like a shep-herd lead us; much we need thy
2 Ear - ly let us seek thy fa - vor, ear - ly let us

ten - der care; in thy plea - sant pas - tures feed us;
learn thy will; do thou, Lord, our on - ly Sa - vior,

for our use thy folds pre - pare. Bless - ed Je - sus!
with thy love our bos - oms fill. Bless - ed Je - sus!

Bless - ed Je - sus! Thou hast bought us, thine we are.
Bless - ed Je - sus! Thou hast loved us: love us still.

Words: *Hymns for the Young*, ca. 1830, alt.
Music: *Sicilian Mariners*, Sicilian melody, from *The European Magazine and London Review*, 1792          87. 87. 87

Unison

1 O God of Beth- el, by whose hand thy peo - ple still are fed;
2 Our vows, our prayers, we now pre - sent be - fore thy throne of grace:
3 Through each per-plex- ing path of life our wan-dering foot-steps guide;
4 O spread thy shel-tering wings a - round, till all our wan-derings cease,
5 Such bless-ings from thy gra - cious hand our hum - ble prayers im - plore;

1 who through this earth - ly pil - grim - age hast all thine Is - rael led:
2 O God of Is - rael, be the God of this suc - ceed-ing race.
3 give us each day our dai - ly bread, and rai - ment fit pro - vide.
4 and at our Fa - ther's loved a - bode our souls ar - rive in peace!
5 and thou shalt be our cov - enant God and por - tion ev - er - more.

Words: Philip Doddridge (1702-1751), alt.
Music: *Dundee*, melody from *The CL Psalmes of David*, 1615;
fauxbourdon *The Psalmes of David in Prose and Meeter*, 1635                    CM

Harmony (the melody is in the tenor)

1 O God of Beth - el, by whose hand thy peo - ple still are fed;
2 Our vows, our prayers, we now pre - sent be - fore thy throne of grace:
3 Through each per-plex - ing path of life our wan-dering foot- steps guide;
4 O spread thy shel-tering wings a - round, till all our wan-derings cease,
5 Such bless-ings from thy gra - cious hand our hum - ble prayers im - plore;

1 who through this earth-ly pil-grim-age   hast all thine Is-rael led:
2 O God of Is-rael, be the God   of this suc-cee-ing race.
3 give us each day our dai-ly bread,   and rai-ment fit pro-vide.
4 and at our Fa-ther's loved a-bode   our souls ar-riv in peace.
5 and thou shalt be our cov-enant God   and por-tion ev-er-more.

Words: Philip Doddridge (1702-1751), alt.
Music: *Dundee*, melody from *The CL Psalmes of David*, 1615;
       fauxbourdon *The Psalmes of David in Prose and Meeter*, 1635

CM

## Rounds and Canons

# 710

Make a joy-ful noise un-to the
Singt dem Herr-en! Sing-et ihm und

Lord,__ O__ sing the hon-or of his ho-ly
ju-bi-lier-et al-le samt in die-ser Mor-gen-

Name,__ give____ him glo-ry ev-er-more.
stun-de, kommt__ her-bei und dank-et ihm!

Words: German; adapt. Ann M. Gilman (b. 1932) and Lawrence Gilman (b. 1930)
Music: *Singt dem Herren*, Michael Praetorius (1571-1621)

Irr.

1 Seek ye____ first the king - dom of God
2 Ask, and it shall be giv - en un - to you,

and its right - eous - ness, and all these things shall be
seek, and ye shall find, knock, and the door shall be

add - ed un - to you; Al - le - lu, al - le - lu - ia!
o - pened un - to you; Al - le - lu, al - le - lu - ia!

*Refrain*

Al - le - lu - ia, al - le -

lu - ia, al - le - lu - ia!

Al - le - lu, al - le - lu - ia!

Words: St. 1, Matthew 6:33; adapt. Karen Lafferty (20th cent.). St. 2, Matthew 7:7.
    Stanza 2 is not part of the hymn as originally written.
Music: *Seek Ye First*, Karen Lafferty (20th cent.)

13. 11. 7 with Alleluias

Do - na no - bis pa - cem, pa-cem. Do - na no - bis

pa - cem. Do - na no - bis pa - cem.

Do - na no - bis pa - cem. Do - na

no - bis pa - cem. Do - na no - bis pa - cem.

Words: Traditional Latin
Music: *Dona nobis pacem*, traditional canon

Irr.

Christ is a - ris - - en. Al - le - lu - ia,
Christ ist er - stan - den. Al - le - lu - ia,

al - le - lu - ia! Al - le - lu - ia, al - le - lu - ia!___
al - le - lu - ia! Al - le - lu - ia, al - le - lù - ia!___

___ Christ is a - ris - en.___ Christ is a - ris - en.
___ Christ ist er - stan - den.___ Christ ist er - stan - den.

Words: German, ca. 1529, adapt.
Music: *Christ is arisen*, Richard Rudolf Klein (b. 1921); based on the chorale *Christ ist erstanden*

Irr.

Sha - lom, my__ friends, sha - lom, my__ friends, sha -
Sha - lom cha - ve - rim, sha - lom cha - ve - rim, sha -

lom, sha - lom. Sha - lom, my__ friends, sha -
lom, sha - lom. Sha - lom cha - ve - rim, sha -

lom,      my___ friends. Sha - lom,     sha - lom.
lom     cha - ve - rim.    Sha - lom,     sha - lom.

Words: Israeli round
Music: *Shalom chaverim*, Hebrew melody

Irr.

## Rounds and Canons

**715**

When Je - sus wept, the fall - ing tear in

mer - cy flowed be - yond all bound; when Je - sus groaned, a

trem - bling fear seized all the guilt - y world a - round.

Words: *The New England Psalm Singer*, 1770
Music: *When Jesus Wept*, William Billings (1746-1800)

LM

1 God bless our na - tive land; firm may she
2 For her our prayers shall rise to God, a -

ev - er stand through storm and night: when the wild
bove the skies; on him we wait; thou who art

tem - pests rave, ru - ler of wind and wave,
ev - er nigh, guard - ing with watch - ful eye,

do thou our coun - try save by thy great might.
to thee a - loud we cry, God save the state!

Words: Siegfried August Mahlmann (1771-1826); tr. Charles Timothy Brooks (1813-1883) and
John Sullivan Dwight (1812-1893), alt.
Music: *America*, from *Thesaurus Musicus*, 1745

664. 6664

Words: Samuel Francis Smith (1808-1895)
Music: *America*, from *Thesaurus Musicus*, 1745

664. 6664

# 718

**718** — National Songs

1 God of our fa - thers, whose al - might - y
2 Thy love di - vine hath led us in the
3 From war's a - larms, from dead - ly pes - ti -
4 Re - fresh thy peo - ple on their toil - some

hand leads forth in beau - ty all the star - ry band
past, in this free land by thee our lot is cast;
lence, be thy strong arm our ev - er sure de - fense;
way, lead us from night to nev - er - end - ing day;

of shin - ing worlds in splen - dor through the skies,
be thou our ru - ler, guard - ian, guide, and stay,
thy true re - li - gion in our hearts in - crease,
fill all our lives with love and grace di - vine,

our grate - ful songs be - fore thy throne a - rise.
thy word our law, thy paths our cho - sen way.
thy boun - teous good - ness nour - ish us in peace.
and glo - ry, laud, and praise be ev - er thine.

Words: Daniel Crane Roberts (1841-1907)
Music: *National Hymn*, George William Warren (1828-1902)

10 10. 10 10

# National Songs

**719**

1 O beau-ti-ful for spa-cious skies, for am-ber waves of grain,
2 O beau-ti-ful for he-roes proved in lib-er-at-ing strife,
3 O beau-ti-ful for pa-triot dream that sees be-yond the years

for pur-ple moun-tain ma-jes-ties a-bove the fruit-ed plain!
who more than self their coun-try loved, and mer-cy more than life!
thine al-a-bas-ter ci-ties gleam, un-dimmed by hu-man tears!

A-mer-i-ca! A-mer-i-ca! God shed his grace on thee,
A-mer-i-ca! A-mer-i-ca! God mend thine ev-ery flaw,
A-mer-i-ca! A-mer-i-ca! God shed his grace on thee,

and crown thy good with bro-ther-hood from sea to shin-ing sea.
con-firm thy soul in self-con-trol, thy lib-er-ty in law.
and crown thy good with bro-ther-hood from sea to shin-ing sea.

Words: Katherine Lee Bates (1859-1929), alt.
Music: *Materna*, Samuel Augustus Ward (1848-1903)

CMD

Words: Francis Scott Key (1779-1843)
Music: *National Anthem*, source unknown, ca. 18th cent.

Irr.

# Indexes

# Copyright Acknowledgments for Service Music

The following texts are copyrighted by The Church Pension Fund:

S-1, S-3, S-8, S-21, S-22, S-23, S-24, S-25, S-26, S-28, S-30, S-31, S-32, S-33, S-51, S-52, S-53, S-54, S-55, S-56, S-57, S-58, S-60, S-62, S-64, S-65, S-66, S-68, S-69, S-70, S-73, S-74, S-75, S-80, S-82, S-92, S-102, S-103, S-106, S-110, S-112, S-115, S-118, S-119, S-120, S-129, S-142, S-159, S-163, S-173, S-174, S-177, S-185, S-203, S-205, S-210, S-217, S-222, S-223, S-228, S-231, S-235, S-250, S-253, S-265, S-263, S-272, S-287

The following melodies are copyrighted by The Church Pension Fund:

S-46, S-90, S-113, S-157, S-201, S-208, S-237

Individual copyright acknowledgments are as follows:

S-2    Melody © 1985, Bruce E. Ford.
S-11    Melody © 1985, Bruce E. Ford.
S-16    Melody © 1985, Bruce E. Ford.
S-27    Melody © by Estate of Victor Judson Schramm.
S-29    © 1971 by Mason Martens.
S-34    Melody © 1985, Bruce E. Ford.
S-35    © 1971, Walton Music Corporation. Used by permission.
S-41    Melody © 1985, Bruce E. Ford.
S-42    Used by permission of Peter Hurford.
S-45    By permission of Oxford University Press.
S-50    © 1982, David Hurd.
S-59    Melody © 1985, Bruce E. Ford.
S-61    Copyright © 1984, Theodore Presser Co. Used by permission of the publisher.
S-63    © 1971 by Mason Martens.
S-67    © 1927 by Wallace Goodrich, Secretary for the Joint Commission on Church Music.
S-71    © 1971 by Mason Martens.
S-72    © 1971 by Mason Martens.
S-76    © 1971 by Mason Martens.
S-77    Copyright © 1979, G.I.A. Publications, Inc.
S-78    © 1971 by Mason Martens.
S-79    Copyright © 1979, G.I.A. Publications, Inc.
S-81    Copyright © 1979, G.I.A. Publications, Inc.
S-83    Copyright © 1979, G.I.A. Publications, Inc.
S-84    Copyright © 1979, G.I.A. Publications, Inc.
S-85    Rhythmic reconstruction © 1983, Schola Antiqua Inc. Used by permission.
S-86    Copyright © 1981, G.I.A. Publications, Inc.
S-87    © 1978, Jackson Hill.
S-88    From: *Music For The Lord's Supper* © 1984, Theodore Presser Company. Used by permission.
S-89    © 1976, James McGregor.
S-91    By permission of Oxford University Press.
S-93    © 1937 by the H.W. Gray Co., a division of Belwin-Mills Pub. Corp. Copyright renewed. Used with permission. All Rights Reserved.
S-94    © 1984 by Mason Martens.
S-95    Copyright © 1985, G.I.A. Publications, Inc.
S-96    Copyright © 1985, G.I.A. Publications, Inc.
S-97    © by E.C. Schirmer Music Company, Boston, Mass. Reprinted by permission.
S-98    © Oxford University Press 1976.
S-99    Melody © 1985, Bruce E. Ford.
S-100    Copyright © 1981, G.I.A. Publications, Inc.
S-101    By permission of Oxford University Press.
S-104    ©1984 by Mason Martens.
S-105    Copyright © 1975, G.I.A. Publications, Inc.
S-107    © 1985, Bruce E. Ford.
S-108    © 1982, David Hurd.
S-109    © 1971 by Mason Martens.
S-111    © 1971 by Mason Martens.
S-114    By permission of Oxford University Press.
S-116    Melody copyright © 1915, by Charles Winfred Douglas.
S-117    © 1976, James McGregor.
S-121    © 1983, James McGregor.
S-122    © 1983 by Mason Martens.
S-123    © 1985, Howard E. Galley, Jr.
S-124    Copyright © 1981, G.I.A. Publications, Inc.
S-126    © by E.C. Schirmer Music Company, Boston, Mass. Reprinted by permission.
S-127    Copyright © Inter-Lutheran Commission on Worship. Used by permission of Augsburg Publishing House.
S-128    By permission of Oxford University Press.
S-125    Copyright © 1971, 1977, G.I.A. Publications, Inc.
S-130    Adaptation copyright © 1985, G.I.A. Publications, Inc.
S-131    © 1985 by Aureole Editions, Dallas, Texas.
S-132    © 1985, Bruce E. Ford.
S-133    © 1971 by Mason Martens.
S-134    Copyright © 1985, G.I.A. Publications, Inc.
S-135    © 1974, Jackson Hill.
S-136    © 1971 by Mason Martens.
S-137    © 1983 by Mason Martens.
S-138    Copyright © 1984, Theodore Presser Co. Used by permission of the publisher.
S-139    © 1983 by Mason Martens.

S-140    Copyright © 1985, G.I.A. Publications, Inc.
S-141    © 1984, Theodore Presser Company. Used by permission.
S-143    © 1983 by Mason Martens.
S-144    © 1983 by Mason Martens.
S-145    © 1983 by Mason Martens.
S-146    © 1984, Theodore Presser Company. Used by permission.
S-147    © 1984, Theodore Presser Company. Used by permission.
S-148    © 1971 by Mason Martens.
S-149    From: *Music For The Lord's Supper* © 1984, Theodore Presser Company. Used by permission.
S-150    Copyright © 1979, 1982, G.I.A. Publications, Inc.
S-151    Copyright © 1979, G.I.A. Publications, Inc.
S-152    © 1971 by Mason Martens.
S-153    © 1971 by Mason Martens.
S-154    Copyright © 1981, G.I.A. Publications, Inc.
S-155    © 1985 by Aureole Editions, Dallas, Texas.
S-156    © 1985 by Aureole Editions, Dallas, Texas.
S-158    By permission of Oxford University Press.
S-160    © 1984 by Mason Martens.
S-161    Copyright © 1981, G.I.A. Publications, Inc.
S-162    © by E.C. Schirmer Music Company, Boston, Mass. Reprinted by permission.
S-164    Adaptation copyright © 1985, G.I.A. Publications, Inc.
S-165    By permission of Oxford University Press.
S-166    © 1985 by Aureole Editions, Dallas, Texas.
S-168    © 1971 by Mason Martens.
S-169    © 1984, by Ray W. Urwin.
S-170    © 1983 by Mason Martens.
S-167    © 1971 by Mason Martens.
S-171    © 1971 by Mason Martens.
S-172    © 1971 by Mason Martens.
S-176    Copyright © 1979, G.I.A. Publications, Inc.
S-180    © 1985, Bruce E. Ford.
S-188    By permission of Oxford University Press.
S-189    © 1985, Benjamin Hutto.
S-190    Melody © 1985, Bruce E. Ford.
S-194    By permission of Richard Lloyd.
S-196    Antiphon © 1985, Bruce E. Ford.
S-202    By permission of Oxford University Press.
S-208    Antiphon melody © 1985, Bruce E. Ford.
S-213    Melody © 1985, Bruce E. Ford.
S-216    © 1970, David Hurd.
S-214    From *The Oxford American Psalter* by Ray F. Brown. Copyright © 1949 by Ray F. Brown, renewed by 1976 by Stuart Brown. Reprinted by permission.
S-220    © Ned Rorem. Used by permission of Ned Rorem and Boosey and Hawkes.
S-227    © 1976, J. Marcus Ritchie.
S-236    © 1985, Oxford Universtiy Press.
S-237    Adaptation © 1985, Bruce E. Ford.
S-240    © Ned Rorem. Used by permission of Ned Rorem and Boosey and Hawkes.
S-242    Melody © 1985, Bruce E. Ford.
S-245    © 1985, Benjamin Hutto.
S-247    Copyright © 1978 Celebration. P.O. Box 309, Aliquippa, PA 15001, USA. All rights reserved. Used by permission.
S-248    Melody © 1985, Bruce E. Ford.
S-254    Melody © 1985, Bruce E. Ford.
S-259    © 1985, The Estate of Charles B. Fisk.
S-260    © 1984, Ronald Arnatt.
S-261    Melody © 1985, Bruce E. Ford.
S-266    © 1984, M. Pambrum.
S-267    Melody © 1985, Bruce E. Ford.
S-272    © by D. W. Steel.
S-273    © 1971 by Mason Martens.
S-277    Copyright © 1981, G.I.A. Publications, Inc.
S-274    Rhythmic reconstruction © 1983, Schola Antiqua Inc. Used by permission.
S-278    By permission of Oxford University Press.
S-279    © 1985 by Aureole Editions, Dallas, Texas.
S-281    Copyright © by E.C. Schirmer Music Company, Boston, Mass. Reprinted by permission.
S-282    Melody © 1985, Bruce E. Ford.
S-285    © 1985, Benjamin Hutto.
S-288    © 1971 by Mason Martens.

# Copyright Acknowledgments for Hymns

The following texts are copyrighted by The Church Pension Fund:
16(Sts.1-3), 17(1-3), 18, 19(1-2), 20(1-2), 25, 26, 38(1-4), 39(1-4), 40(1-4), 41(1-4), 44(1-3), 45(1-3), 48(4), 56, 60, 63, 64, 81(3), 91, 121, 139, 152, 153, 159, 162, 164, 165, 166, 173(1,4), 176(3), 177(3), 193, 220, 221, 231, 232, 233, 234, 261, 262, 282, 283, 302, 303, 314(1-3), 319, 320, 329, 330, 331, 353, 356, 364(6-8), 366, 375, 390, 421, 428, 443, 475(1,2,4), 478, 489, 499, 530, 540, 579(2,3), 619, 647, 663, 668(4), 669.

The following musical settings are copyrighted by The Church Pension Fund:
9, 37, 107, 153, 157, 163, 185, 187, 312, 316, 403, 454, 514, 515, 532, 542, 564, 614, 647, 654, 661.

The following harmonizations and accompaniments are copyrighted by The Church Pension Fund:
8, 149, 172, 203, 359, 364, 366, 404, 505, 697.

Individual copyright acknowledgments are as follows:

1 Words: By permission of Oxford University Press.
2 Words: By permission of Oxford University Press. Music: Melody rhythmic version © 1984, Schola Antiqua Inc. Used by permission.
3 Words: Sts.2-4 Copyright © 1972, Peter J. Scagnelli. From *Catholic Liturgy Book*. Used by permission.
4 Words: Sts.2-4 Copyright © 1972, Peter J. Scagnelli. From *Catholic Liturgy Book*. Used by permission.
6 Music: Copyright by Edward B. Marks Music Company, New York, NY. International Copyright Secured. ALL RIGHTS RESERVED. Used by permission.
8 Words: By permission of David Higham Associates Limited, London.
9 Words: By permission of Hodder and Stoughton Limited.
12 Words: © 1982, Charles P. Price.
13 Words: © 1982, Charles P. Price.
14 Words: St.3 © 1982, Charles P. Price.
15 Words: St.3 © 1982, James Waring McCrady.
16 Words: St.4 © 1982, Anne LeCroy.
17 Words: St.4 © 1982, Anne LeCroy. Music: By permission of Oxford University Press.
19 Words: St.3 © 1982, James Waring McCrady.
20 Words: St.3 © 1982, James Waring McCrady.
21 Words: St.3 © 1982, James Waring McCrady.
22 Words: St.3 © 1982, James Waring McCrady.
23 Words: © 1982, Charles P. Price.
27 Words: © 1982, Anne LeCroy.
28 Words: © 1982, Anne LeCroy.
31 Words: © 1982, Anne LeCroy. Music: Reprinted from the *New Catholic Hymnal* by permission of the publishers, Faber Music Ltd., London.
32 Words: © 1982, Anne LeCroy. Music: Melody rhythmic version © 1984, Schola Antiqua Inc. Used by permission.
33 Words: © 1982, Anne LeCroy.
34 Words: © 1982, Anne LeCroy. Music: © 1984, Richard W. Dirksen.
35 Words: © 1982, Anne LeCroy. Music: Copyright © 1985, G.I.A. Publications, Inc.
38 Words: St.5 © 1982, Anne LeCroy.
39 Words: St.5 © 1982, Anne LeCroy. Music: By permission of Oxford University Press.
40 Words: St.5 © 1982, Charles P. Price.
41 Words: St.5 © 1982, Charles P. Price. Music: Copyright © 1985, G.I.A. Publications, Inc.
44 Words: St.4 © 1982, James Waring McCrady.
45 Words: St.4 © 1972, James Waring McCrady.
48 Words: St.3 © 1982, Charles P. Price.
49 Music: Copyright © 1977 by Hinshaw Music, Inc. Used by permission.
51 Words: By permission of John E. Bowers. Music: © 1984, Richard W. Dirksen.
52 Music: Copyright © 1936 Ascherberg, Hopwood and Crew Limited, Chappell Music Limited London. Reproduced by permission.
54 Words: Sts.3-4 © 1982, James Waring McCrady.
55 Words: © 1982, Charles P. Price.
59 Music: Descant used by permission of Cambridge University Press.
61 Words: © 1982, Carl P. Daw, Jr.
62 Words: © 1982, Carl P. Daw, Jr.
65 Words: © 1982, Charles P. Price.
69 Words: © 1971, Carol C. Stone.
70 Words: By permission of Margaret Waters. Music: © 1983, Robert J. Powell.
74 Words: Copyright © 1974 by Hope Publishing Company, Carol Stream, IL 60188. All Rights Reserved. Used by Permission. Music: Harmonization © 1984, Ronald Arnatt.
75 Music: © 1938, H. Hugh Bancroft.
78 Music: By permission of Oxford University Press.

80 Words: Translation copyright © 1978, LUTHERAN BOOK OF WORSHIP. Used by permission of Augsburg Publishing House.
84 Music: By permission of Oxford University Press.
85 Words: Copyright © 1978, Lutheran Book of Worship. Used by permission.
86 Words: Copyright © 1978, Lutheran Book of Worship. Used by permission. Music: By permission of Oxford University Press.
88 Music: By permission of Oxford University Press.
92 Words: Copyright by G. Schirmer, Inc. Reprinted by permission. Music: Used by arrangement with G. Schirmer, Inc.
94 Music: Descant by permission of Novello and Company Limited.
95 Music: Copyright © 1985, Theodore Presser Co. Used by permission of the publisher.
96 Words: By permission of Fleming H. Revell Company.
98 Words: From The Oxford Book of Carols © 1964, Oxford University Press. Music: By permission of Oxford University Press.
99 Music: Arrangement © 1984, Horace Clarence Boyer.
102 Words: St.3 © 1982, James Waring McCrady. Music: Copyright © 1957, Novello and Company Limited. Used by permission.
103 Words: Copyright © 1964, G.I.A. Publications, Inc.
104 Words: Copyright © 1961 by Richard Wilbur. Reprinted from his volume, *Advice to a Prophet and other Poems* by permission of Harcourt Brace Jovanovich, Inc. Music: Copyright © 1984, G.I.A. Publications, Inc.
105 Words: By permission of Fleming H. Revell Company.
109 Music: Alternative setting with descant by permission of Oxford University Press.
113 Words, Music: Copyright © 1954, University of New Mexico Press. Used by permission.
114 Words: English text by J. E. Middleton. Used by permission of The Frederick Harris Music Co., Limited. Music: Setting Copyright © 1978, LUTHERAN BOOK OF WORSHIP. Used by permission of Augsburg Publishing House.
116 Music: By permission of Oxford University Press.
120 Words: From *English Praise*. By permission of Oxford University Press. Music: By permission of Oxford University Press.
123 Music: Melody rhythmic version © 1984, Schola Antiqua Inc. Used by permission.
125 Music: Music Copyright © 1964 by Abingdon Press. Used by permission.
127 Music: Harmonization by permission of K. D. Smith.
129 Words: Copyright © 1977 by Hope Publishing Company, Carol Stream, IL 60188. All Rights Reserved. Used by Permission. Music: Copyright © 1985 by Hope Publishing Company, Carol Stream, IL 60188. All Rights Reserved. Used by Permission.
130 Words, Music: Copyright © 1977 by Hope Publishing Company, Carol Stream, IL 60188. All Rights Reserved. Used by Permission.
131 Words: Reprinted from *The Hymn Book of the Anglican Church of Canada and the United Church of Canada*. Used by permission.
132 Words: Reprinted from *The Hymn Book of the Anglican Church of Canada and the United Church of Canada*. Used by permission.
133 Music: © 1982, Cary Ratcliff.
137 Music: Descant by permission of Royal School of Church Music.
143 Words: By permission of Oxford University Press.
144 Words: © 1982, Anne LeCroy. Music: By permission of Oxford University Press.
145 Words: From *The Oxford Book of Carols* © 1964, Oxford University Press. Music: By permission of Oxford University Press.

# Authors, Translators, and Sources

Bridges, Robert Seymour (1844–1930)  5, 36, 46, 158, 168, 169, 427, 665
Briggs, George Wallace (1875–1959)  289, 305, 306, 542, 584
Bright, William (1824–1901)  242, 281, 337
Brokering, Herbert F. (b. 1926)  412
Brooks, Charles Timothy (1813–1883)  716
Brooks, Phillips (1835–1893)  78, 79
Brooks, R. T. (b. 1918)  630
Browne, Simon (1680–1732)  512
Brownlie, John (1859–1925)  73, 313
Bunyan, John (1628–1688)  564, 565
Burleigh, William Henry (1812–1871)  703
Byrne, Mary Elizabeth (1880–1931)  488
Byrom, John (1692–1763)  106

Cain, Thomas H. (b. 1931)  149
Caird, George B. (1917–1984)  422
Cameron, Catherine (b. 1927)  580
Campbell, Jane Montgomery (1817–1878)  291
Campbell, Robert (1814–1868)  174, 223, 224, 244
Carpenter, William Boyd (1841–1918)  574, 575
Casanate, Hieronimo (d. 1700)  261, 262
Caswall, Edward (1814–1878)  257, 310, 311, 479, 642, 682
Cawood, John (1775–1852)  588, 589
Chadwick, James (1813–1882)  96
Chadwick, John White (1840–1904)  617
Chandler, John (1806–1876)  3, 4, 29, 30, 76, 124
Charles, Elizabeth Rundle (1828–1896)  97, 190, 217, 218
Chatfield, Allen William (1808–1896)  641
Chesterton, Gilbert Keith (1874–1936)  591
Chorley, Henry Fothergill (1808–1872)  569
Christian Hymnbook, 1865  116
Claudius, Matthias (1740–1815)  291
Clausnitzer, Tobias (1619–1684)  440
Clement of Alexandria (170?–220?)  163, 478
Clephane, Elizabeth Cecilia (1830–1869)  498
Coffin, Charles (1676–1749)  3, 4, 29, 30, 76, 124
Coffin, Henry Sloane (1877–1954)  475
Coles, Vincent Stucky Stratton (1845–1929)  268, 269
Colvin, Thomas Stevenson (b. 1925)  602, 611
Conder, Josiah (1789–1855)  323, 706
Cosin, John (1594–1672)  503, 504
Cosnett, Elizabeth (b. 1936)  476
Coventry carol, 15th cent.  247
Coverdale, Miles (1487–1568)  634
Cowper, William (1731–1800)  667, 677, 683, 684
Cox, Frances Elizabeth (1812–1897)  194, 195, 286, 408
Crawford, Mary Babcock (b. 1909)  651
Crossman, Samuel (1624–1683)  458

Crum, John Macleod Campbell (1872–1958)  204
Cummins, Evelyn Atwater (1891–1971)  647

Daw, Carl P., Jr. (b. 1944)  18, 61, 62, 266, 358, 359, 513, 517, 597, 678, 679
Dearmer, Percy (1867–1936)  1, 2, 98, 145, 211, 312, 564, 565, 631, 682
Decius, Nikolaus (1490?–1541)  421
de Santeüil, Jean Baptiste (1630–1697)  257
Dix, William Chatterton (1837–1898)  115, 119, 460, 461
Doan, Gilbert E. (b. 1930)  85, 86
Doane, George Washington (1799–1859)  457
Doane, William Croswell (1832–1913)  363
Doddridge, Philip (1702–1751)  71, 72, 284, 321, 543, 546, 709
Donne, John (1573–1631)  140, 141, 322
Douglas, Charles Winfred (1867–1944)  76, 173, 375, 530, 540, 669
Drake, Carol Christopher (b. 1933)  69
Draper, William H. (1855–1933)  400
Dryden, John (1631–1700)  500
Dudley-Smith, Timothy (b. 1926)  431, 437, 438
Duffield, George, Jr. (1818–1888)  561
Dwight, John Sullivan (1812–1893)  716
Dwight, Timothy (1725–1817)  524

Eastern Orthodox Memorial Service  355
Eddis, Edward W. (1825–1905)  37
Edmeston, James (1791–1867)  559
Egan, Linda Wilberger (b. 1943)  673
Ellerton, John (1826–1893)  24, 77, 179, 255, 259, 280, 345, 492, 569
Elliott, Charlotte (1789–1871)  693
English carol, 18th cent.  109
English carol, ca. 18th cent.  453
English Hymnal, The, 1906  175, 216, 225
English Praise, 1975  347
Ephrem of Edessa (4th cent.)  443
Epistle to Diognetus, ca. 150  489
Evans, Mark (b. 1916)  295
Everest, Charles William (1814–1877)  675
Evers, J. Clifford (b. 1916)  581
Exodus 15:1–2  425

Faber, Frederick William (1814–1863)  469, 470, 558, 643
Farjeon, Eleanor (1881–1965)  8
Farlander, Arthur William (1898–1952)  375, 530, 540, 669
Fawcett, John (1739/40–1817)  344
F. B. P. (ca. 16th cent.)  620
Feith, Rhijnvis (1753–1824)  484, 485
Findlater, Sarah B. (1823–1907)  68
First Song of Isaiah, The  678, 679
Fishel, Donald (b. 1950)  178
Fortunatus, Venantius Honorius (540?–600?)  161, 162, 165, 166, 175, 179, 216, 225

# Composers, Arrangers, and Sources for Service Music

# Composers, Arrangers, and Sources for Hymns

Howells, Herbert (1892–1983)   582, 665
Hughes, John (1873–1932)   594, 690
Hullah, John Pyke (19th cent.)   447, 483
*Hundert Arien,* 1694   187, 269
Hunterian MS., 15th cent.   266
Hurd, David (b. 1950)   35, 41, 104, 268, 322, 395, 459, 463, 503, 507, 549, 629
*Hymnal 1940*   299
*Hymnal 1982*   173, 203, 364, 532, 550, 641, 663
*Hymnau a Thonau er Gwasanaeth yr Eglwys yng Nghymru,* 1865   68, 607
*Hymns Ancient and Modern,* 1875   20, 137, 353, 365, 371, 372, 401, 537
*Hymns Ancient and Modern,* 1916   228
*Hymns Ancient and Modern,* 1922   94
*Hymns Ancient and Modern, Revised,* 1950   72, 207, 284
*Hymns and Sacred Poems,* 1749   428
*Hymns for Church and School,* 1964   414
*Hymns III,* 1979   581

Ireland, John (1879–1962)   458
Irish ballad   482, 488
Irish melody   69, 370, 645
Irvine, Jesse Seymour (1836–1887)   663
Isaac, Heinrich (1450?–1517)   46, 309

Jackson, Francis (b. 1917)   424
Jacob, Gordon (b. 1895)   517
Jenner, Henry Lascelles (1820–1898)   626
Johnson, David N. (b. 1922)   373, 412
Johnson, J. Rosamond (1873–1954)   599
Johnson, Robert Sherlaw (b. 1932)   189
Johnson, Roy Henry (b. 1933)   588
Jones, W. Thomas (b. 1956)   49
Jones, William (1726–1800)   73

*Katholisches Gesangbuch,* 1686   366
*Katholisches Gesangbuch,* 1863   210
*Kentucky Harmony,* 1816   243, 702
Kievan chant   355
King, Charles John (1859–1934)   426
*Kirchengeseng darinnen die Heubtartickel des Christlichen Glaubens gefasset,* 1566   408, 598
Kirkpatrick, William James (1838–1921)   101
Klein, Richard Rudolf (b. 1921)   713
*Klosterneuburger Hymnar,* 1336   22
Knapp, William (1698–1768)   20, 137, 353
Kocher, Conrad (1786–1872)   119, 269, 288, 366
König, Johann Balthasar (1691–1758)   244, 334, 656
Kremser, Eduard (1838–1914)   433

Lafferty, Karen (20th cent.)   711
Lang, Craig Sellar (1891–1971)   72, 94, 290, 326, 368, 390, 410
*Laudi Spirituali,* 14th cent.   239
Layriz, Friedrich (1808–1859)   338
Lee, J. V. (1892–1959)   543

*Les cent cinquante Pseaumes de David,* 1564   252, 308
Lewis, Freeman (1780–1859)   147, 276, 675
Ley, Henry G. (1887–1962)   52, 553
*Little Book of Christmas Carols,* ca. 1850   105
*Llyfr Tonau Cynnulleidfaol,* 1859   299
*Llyfr y Psalmau,* 1621   697
*Lochamer Gesangbuch,* 1450?   281, 471
Lockhart, Charles (1745–1815)   138, 592
Loh, I-to (b. 1936)   340
Löhner, Johann (1645–1705)   244, 334
Lovelace, Austin Cole (b. 1919)   671
Luther, Martin (1483–1546)   151, 575, 687, 688
*Lutheran Hymnal, The,* 1941   501
Lvov, Alexis (1799–1870)   358, 569
*Lyra Davidica,* 1708   207

*Mailander Hymnen,* 15th cent.   40, 217, 263
*Maintzisch Gesangbuch,* 1661   159
Maker, Frederick Charles (1844–1927)   498, 652
Mallory, Charles (b. 1950)   178
Mann, Arthur Henry (1850–1929)   102
Marshall, Jane Manton (b. 1924)   242, 466, 589
Mason, Lowell (1792–1872)   100, 182, 365, 371, 411, 419, 436, 493, 512, 524, 537, 595, 691
Medieval French carol   204
*Medieval [German or] Bohemian Carol Melody,* 1544   200, 237
Mehrtens, Frederik August (b. 1922)   274
*Melodia Sacra,* 1815   546
Mendelssohn, Felix (1809–1847)   87, 255, 281, 397, 471, 632
Messiter, Arthur Henry (1834–1916)   556
*Methodist Harmonist,* 1821   419, 512
Miller, Edward (1731–1807)   321, 474
Miller, Max (b. 1927)   547
*Miltenberger Processionale,* 15th cent.   319
Milton, John, Sr. (1563?–1647)   462
Mims, George (b. 1938)   178
Moe, Daniel (b. 1926)   612
Moissac MS., 12th cent.   123, 273
Monk, William Henry (1823–1889)   59, 76, 119, 150, 154, 181, 208, 210, 286, 288, 337, 391, 397, 447, 483, 559, 601, 625, 628, 662, 680
Moyer, J. Harold (b. 1927)   689
*Münster Gesangbuch,* 1677   384
Murray, A. Gregory (b. 1905)   202, 233, 577
*Musicalishes Hand-Buch,* 1690   76, 391

Native American melody   385
Neander, Joachim (1650–1680)   180
Near, Gerald (b. 1942)   37, 454
*Nederlandtsch Gedenckclank,* 1626   433
Neswick, Bruce (b. 1956)   442
*Neu ordentlich Gesangbuch,* 1646   681

Smart, Henry Thomas (1813–1879)   93, 368, 555, 563, 700
Smith, Alfred Morton (1879–1971)   306, 406
Smith, Henry Percy (1825–1898)   660
Smith, Isaac (1734?–1805)   548
Smith, K. D. (b. 1928)   127
Smith, Robert (1780–1829)   658
Sohren, Peter (1630?–1692?)   375
*Songs and Games of American Children, 1884–1911*   468
*Songs of Praise*, 1925   249, 331, 437
*Songs of Praise*, 1931   670
Source Unknown   77, 131
Source Unknown, ca. 18th cent.   720
*Southern Harmony, The*, 1835   118, 213, 238, 439, 550, 571, 580
Sowerby, Leo (1895–1968)   125, 305
St. Gall MS., 10th cent.   155, 165
Stainer, John (1840–1901)   109, 160
Stanford, Charles Villiers (1852–1924)   84, 296, 370, 420, 477
*Strassburger Kirchenamt*, 1525   429
*Student's Hymnal, A*, 1923   616
Suitor, M. Lee (b. 1942)   229, 256
Sullivan, Arthur Seymour (1842–1900)   90, 179, 191, 199, 245, 562
*Supplement to Kentucky Harmony*, 1820   674
*Supplement to the New Version of Psalms by Dr. Brady and Mr. Tate*, 1708   567
Sussex melody   478, 565
*Swenska Psalmboken, Then*, 1697   65
Swenson, Warren (b. 1937)   318

Tallis, Thomas (1505?–1585)   25, 43, 170, 260, 489, 692
Taylor, Cyril Vincent (b. 1907)   129, 195, 379, 511, 523
Terry, Richard Runciman (1865–1938)   270, 446
Teschner, Melchior (1584–1635)   74, 154
Thatcher, Reginald Sparshatt (1888–1957)   39, 394
Theoretikerquellen MS., 12th cent.   271
*Thesaurus Musicus*, 1745   716, 717
Thomerson, Kathleen (b. 1934)   490
*Thuringer Evangelisches Gesangbuch*, 1928   634
Toolan, Suzanne (b. 1927)   335
Traditional canon   712
Traditional melody   566, 638
*Trente quatre pseaumes de David*, 1551   472
Trier MS., 15th cent.   124, 193
Trinity College MS., 15th cent.   218, 449
Turle, James (1802–1882)   20, 137, 353

"Une pastourelle gentille," 1529   408, 598
Urwin, Ray W. (b. 1950)   679

Vaughan Williams, Ralph (1872–1958)   12, 78, 116, 175, 216, 225, 231, 259, 272, 287, 293, 315, 370, 398, 400, 435, 478, 480, 487, 499, 516, 565, 568, 591, 617, 618, 705

Verona MS., 11th cent.   27
Verona MS., 12th cent.   19, 146
*Vesperale*, 1746   360
*Vierstimmiges Choralbuch*, 1847   595
*Virginia Harmony*, 1831   671
Vulpius, Melchior (1560?–1616)   205, 295, 356

Wade, John Francis (1711–1786)   58, 83
Wainwright, John (1723–1768)   106
Walch, James (1837–1901)   539
Walker, David Charles (b. 1938)   294, 382
Walter, William H. (1825–1893)   551
Walton, James G. (1821–1905)   558
Ward, Samuel Augustus (1848–1903)   719
Warren, George William (1828–1902)   718
Watson, Sidney (b. 1903)   317
Webb, George James (1803–1887)   561
Webbe, Samuel (1740–1816)   72, 212, 228, 321, 531
Weisse, Michael (d. 1534)   53
Welsh hymn   423
Welsh melody   610, 621
Werner, Eric (b. 1901)   393
Wesley, Charles (1757–1834)   476
Wesley, Samuel Sebastian (1810–1876)   386, 422, 434, 461, 525, 578, 704
Westbrook, Francis B. (1903–1975)   300
Wetzel, Richard (b. 1935)   464
White, David Ashley (b. 1944)   327
White, J. T. (19th cent.)   566
Whitlock, Percy William (1903–1946)   241
*Whole Booke of Psalmes, The*, 1570   259
*Whole Booke of Psalmes, The*, 1592   94, 581
*Whole Booke of Psalmes, The*, 1621   71, 462, 532
Wigbert [Wipo of Burgundy] (d. 1050?)   183
Wilkes, John Bernard (1785–1869)   389
Willan, Healey (1880–1968)   109
Willcocks, David (b. 1919)   646
Williams, Aaron (1731–1776)   411, 524
Williams, David McKinley (1887–1978)   312, 316, 514, 614, 661
Williams, Derek (b. 1945)   253, 604
Williams, Robert (1781–1821)   214
Williams, Thomas John (1869–1944)   381, 527
Williamson, Malcolm (b. 1931)   6, 651
Willis, Richard Storrs (1819–1900)   89
Wilson, Hugh (1764–1824)   658
Wilson, John (b. 1905)   170, 414, 481, 692
Winn, Cyril (1884–1973)   210
Wood, Charles (1866–1926)   192
Woodward, George Ratcliffe (1848–1934)   48
Worcester MS., 13th cent.   5, 38, 233, 236, 261, 283, 361
Wyton, Alec (b. 1921)   8, 230, 363, 369, 491, 528

Yin-Lan, Su (20th cent.)   342
Young, Michael E. (b. 1939)   450, 522

*Zisterzienser Hymnar*, 14th cent.   136, 166, 220, 223, 329, 330
Zundel, John (1815–1882)   470

# Index of Tune Names

# Index of First Lines

Lo! what a cloud of witnesses   545
Look there! the Christ, our Brother, comes
   196, 197
Lord, be thy word my rule   626
Lord Christ, when first thou cam'st to
   earth   598
Lord, dismiss us with thy blessing   344
Lord, enthroned in heavenly splendor   307
Lord, for ever at thy side   670
Lord God, you now have set your servant
   free   499
Lord Jesus, Sun of Righteousness   144
Lord Jesus, think on me   641
Lord, make us servants of your peace   593
Lord of all being, throned afar   419
Lord of all hopefulness, Lord of all joy   482
Lord, thou hast searched me and dost
   know   702
Lord, we have come at your own invitation   348
Lord, who throughout these forty days   142
Lord, whose love through humble service   610
Lord, you give the great commission   528
Love came down at Christmas   84
Love divine, all loves excelling   657
Love's redeeming work is done   188, 189
Lully, lullay, thou little tiny child   247

Make a joyful noise unto the Lord
   (Singt dem Herren!)   710
Many and great, O God, are thy works   385
Master of eager youth, see:
   Jesus, our mighty Lord
May choirs of angels lead you   356
May the grace of Christ our Savior   351
Morning glory, starlit sky   585
Morning has broken   8
Most High, omnipotent, good Lord   406, 407
Most Holy God, the Lord of heaven   31, 32
My country, 'tis of thee   717
My faith looks up to thee   691
My God, accept my heart this day   697
My God, how wonderful thou art   643
My God, I love thee; not because, see:
   I love thee, Lord, but not because
My God, thy table now is spread   321
My Shepherd will supply my need   664
My song is love unknown   458

Nature with open volume stands   434
New every morning is the love   10
New songs of celebration render   413
Not far beyond the sea, nor high   422
Not here for high and holy things   9
Nova, nova   266
Now greet the swiftly changing year   250
Now Holy Spirit, ever One   19, 20
Now let us all right merry be, see:
   From heaven above to earth I come
Now let us all with one accord   146, 147
Now let us sing our praise to God   16, 17

Now, my tongue, the mystery telling
   329, 330, 331
Now quit your care   145
Now thank we all our God   396, 397
Now that the daylight fills the sky   3, 4
Now the day is over   42
Now the green blade riseth from the buried
   grain   204
Now the silence   333
Now yield we thanks and praise   108

O all ye works of God, now come   428
O beautiful for spacious skies   719
O bless the Lord, my soul!   411
O blest Creator of the light, see:
   O blest Creator, source of light
O blest Creator, source of light   27, 28
O Bread of life, for sinners broken   342
O brightness of the immortal Father's face   37
O Christ, the Word Incarnate   632
O Christ, you are both light and day   40, 41
O come, all ye faithful   83
O come, O come, Emmanuel   56
O day of God, draw nigh   600, 601
O day of peace that dimly shines   597
O day of radiant gladness   48
O day of rest and gladness, see:
   O day of radiant gladness
O Food to pilgrims given   308, 309
O Food of men wayfaring, see:
   O Food to pilgrims given
O for a closer walk with God   683, 684
O for a thousand tongues to sing   493
O gladsome Light, O grace   36
O God, creation's secret force   14, 15
O God of Bethel, by whose hand   709
O God of earth and altar   591
O God of every nation   607
O God of love, O King of peace   578
O God of love, to thee we bow   350
O God of truth, O Lord of might   21, 22
O God, our help in ages past   680
O god, to those who here profess   352
O God, unseen yet ever near   332
O God, we praise thee, and confess   364
O God, whom neither time nor space   251
O gracious Light, Lord Jesus Christ   25, 26
O heavenly Word, eternal Light   63, 64
O holy city, seen of John   582, 583
O Holy Spirit, by whose breath   501, 502
O Jesus Christ, may grateful hymns be
   rising   590
O Jesus, crowned with all renown   292
O Jesus, I have promised   655
O Jesus, joy of loving hearts   649, 650
O Light of Light, Love given birth   133, 134
O little town of Bethlehem   78, 79
O Lord Most High, eternal King   220, 221
O love, how deep, how broad, how high
   448, 449